MORE OUTRAGEOUS THAN
"HORRIBLE BOSSES"

The
Tormentor

Jacques Meyer

BASED ON A TRUE STORY

THE TORMENTOR

iUniverse books may be ordered through booksellers or by contacting:

iUniverse
1663 Liberty Drive
Bloomington, IN 47403
www.iuniverse.com
1-800-Authors (1-800-288-4677)

Because of the dynamic nature of the Internet, any web addresses or links contained in this book may have changed since publication and may no longer be valid. The views expressed in this work are solely those of the author and do not necessarily reflect the views of the publisher, and the publisher hereby disclaims any responsibility for them.

Any people depicted in stock imagery provided by Thinkstock are models, and such images are being used for illustrative purposes only. Certain stock imagery © Thinkstock.

ISBN: 978-1-5320-0034-8 (sc)
ISBN: 978-1-5320-0035-5 (e)

Library of Congress Control Number: 2016910402

Print information available on the last page.

iUniverse rev. date: 09/12/2017

Foreword

IN HIS MOST recent book, *The Tormentor*, author Jacques A. Meyer weaves a fascinating tapestry of characters. In the fashion of classic stories of human overcoming, Pierre Choucart is a dedicated, hard-working, intelligent, and resourceful man. He, of course, being focused on doing good becomes easy prey for his paranoid and narcissistic employer, the classically evil Arthur Valois Dourville de Montrissart.

Meyer's story is about the powerful and the powerless; superiors and their subordinates; the controllers and those they would control. The scenarios he describes are all too common between bosses and their direct reports. Unfortunately, the disparity of power between business owners and those who work for them are accentuated by the disparity of resources available to them.

It's the tale of the haves versus the have nots. More specifically, it's about the liberties the haves can take with the have-nots. Apparently there are only two recourses the have nots have available to them (1) Don't stand for the treatment they receive at the hands of the haves (i.e. resign and go to work for another have somewhere else) as Meyer's character, Robert Leansing, did or (2) become a have themselves, thereby deflating and power the haves have over them.

Readers, especially those, who must work to survive, will no doubt find much of themselves manifest in the character of Pierre Choucart. Others will not be hampered one way or the other as Meyer's character, Melanie, doesn't seem to be. Hopefully, if a reader is consciously aware of how similar he or she is with the most disagreeable Arthur, the reader will seek immediate help from a competent executive coach or psychotherapist.

Author John Hoover Ph.D

How to Work for an Idiot:
Survive and Thrive Without Killing Your Boss.

Another nonfiction book by Jacques A. Meyer

TERRE MON AMIE

A Journey Around The World On A Low Budget

"Terre Mon Amie takes us from the ubiquitus poverty, overcrowding and street violence of Calcutta to the limitless plains and crisp climate of Australia 'the last frontier', from a jubilant arrival in Europe at the Port of Le Havre to a Jeep ride through machine-gun fire on a jungle road in Cambodia. The universal expression of human love in different cultures establishes the theme throughout Terre Mon Amie."

—Vantage Press

"A charming travel-adventure book with vivid descriptions of exciting places and delightful impressions of people the author met on his way."

—The New York Times

"Jacques trust the readers of his book will find inside into the character and deep feelings of the author whose main intention is to give the world a message of love and peace among all human being, wherever they are."

—World-Wide News Bureau

To Grace...for being there

Chapter 1

MONSIEUR ARTHUR VALOIS Dourville de Montrissart, the owner of the French Restaurant *Le Cerisier* (The Cherry Tree) located in Sherman Oaks, California was a short burly man, only five feet in height with rubber lifts in his shoes to draw himself tall. He had a round face with fat smooth cheeks and thick bull neck, deep lines on his forehead with enormous hairy ears the size of New Zealand mussel-shells. His nose 'the charm of painters' was quite peculiar, prominent but still harmonious, a distinguishing trait from one generation to another; parted lips and penetrating almost unblinking eyes with sometimes a dangerous gleam. His head was crowned with carefully styled silky white hair with a little thatch that stood-up like the cockatiel's feather and the size of his fat belly was considerably increased by the shortness of his arms and legs.

Arthur's voice with such a melodious French accent has become harsh and staccato yet people loved it. This along with unfaltering manners can be the secret of his brilliance, of his ingenuity in business as he elevated himself to the pinnacle of power with the family fortune.

Born in Labège par Castanet near Toulouse, France Arthur who claimed his ancestral line was of the old feudal aristocracy was ironically without any chivalry or true nobility.

1

Here was one of his pet sayings: "I'm the head of the noblest branch of the family." In reality Arthur was living in dishonor to the very name he so proudly carried. Instead of showing courage, sobriety and strength he developed a reputation for being frivolous, cowardly and irresolute. Although he became a perverted predator always skulking behind corners his general appearance was jovial. Among customers with that engulfing smile he appeared to be charismatic and just a *bon vivant*. If one didn't know Arthur well he seemed to be the most honest person in the world with a curious façade of gentility.

Arthur with his perpetual chatter on all subjects was a great entertainer and fabulist. He also had gathered about himself a group of loyal followers. Just like 'The Little Corporal' with the gift of gab he was equally a redundant orator with good industry experience. Recurrently his moral and social failings were allayed by his expertness as a great restaurateur. Pushing his way by his talents as a salesman, this man could sell snow to Eskimos. And in order to please some of his regular wealthy patrons Arthur would bow in front of their wives with polished, pleasing sentences the way an Englishman would have bowed to his queen. Arthur seriously believed with grandiloquence to be proficient but he willfully would entrap a friend into a disastrous speculation or bad deed. When people disallowed his views he would growl like a lion, but Arthur would praise any man that would praise him as compliments would carry him to seventh heaven.

Yet, it didn't take long for his faithfull employees to realize that their employer was just a paper tiger with a mother complex who faints at the sight of blood. He was just a faux cultivated intellect. With that insipid pretence that his life was fine, he secretly objected to other people's happiness because in reality he had lost his own. With his dull insensibility to all that is charming Arthur actually hates happy people just as eunuchs hate successful lovers. Drinking was as necessary to him as daily bread as he was often in a woeful state of drunkenness-of tipsy confusion. If one didn't know anything about his grossly primate behavior this man could probably have succeeded in any field anywhere- as a public servant in D.C., as a preacher and for sure as an actor or comedian.

To express a Navy saying the owner of the restaurant in addition was 'an old saltwater sea dog.' He once sailed the big oceans with a mandolin in his bag fluttering like a bewildered bee on a flower from Europe to Africa and all of South America. Those experiences on the high seas aboard *Les Lignes de la Marine Marchande*-French Lines made him a skilled diplomat sneaky like a fox.

Later on when Arthur had shaken off the salt of the sea for work on *terra firma* he continued fearing everyone at first sight. By trying to swallow up contentment of so many people one will soon realize that the pugnacious Arthur as a basket of pestilent corruption even more elusive than a serpent occupied a far lower place than the offspring of a Neanderthal. In short he was a fool-a vicious fool as well for a man that can betray friendship also violate honor. And just like in Swift's *Gulliver's Travels*, would anyone doubt after reading this book that such a person like Arthur had really existed?

Le Cerisier restaurant represented a typical inn you would discover in the rich valley land with deep virgin forests and giddy precipices of *The Massif Central* or in Provence amidst French formal gardens and gay arabesques overlooking the Mediterranean. With beams across the ceiling, the establishment was vastly decorated with shining brass ornaments and striking paintings hanging on the walls that were paneled in fake red bricks with shelves of books all around. A long-case polished grandfather clock stood like a security guard near an authentic Austrian marble-table desk. Very old tapestries depicting rural figures of men and women from the sixteenth century were drooping on display in the conveniently designed private room where ten people could comfortably sit. The entire dining room was well furnished in such exquisite taste. The booths upholstered with Venetian velvet enhanced warm intimacy as every table was decorated with a bouquet of fresh cut flowers enlivened next to a lighted candle. Stained-glass windows representing a few harvest scenes were imbedded on either side of *Le Cerisier's* front entrance. Outside, in the street one can observe a plant under each one. A little further, almost at the edge of the sidewalk, there was a curious tree with its branches intermingled in a strange embrace.

As soon as the sun was low above the western hills, when the twilight was covering the San Fernando Valley under its umbrella the restaurant would open its doors. It was on such time that Arthur in spite of a hip surgery would leap in the air like a grasshopper to lightheartedly lead the customers to their reserved tables. With the habit of embracing everyone to make them feel at home he would congratulate women on their great looks before ruling the place like Louis XIV, *le roi soleil* ruled Versailles. With such manners some of our patrons would meet Arthur with a vivacity that could only flatter him…

I am Pierre Choucart, a Belgian from Woluwé Saint Lambert, a Brussels suburb. Balding, but endowed with shining skin and clear eyes I still present the impression of youthfulness. With the years passing by a little stoop has come to the shoulders. My late parents by no means wealthy nonetheless enjoyed a contented life in that corner of the large metropolis.

Prior to the arrival at *Le Cerisier*, I have known Arthur Valois Dourville de Montrissart long ago when we both managed one of the establishments from the restaurant's chain *La Fricassée* which locations were in Los Angeles' finest spots. I was le directeur de salle at *La Fricassée Rotisserie* on Wilshire Boulevard in Beverly Hills. Arthur oversaw *La Fricassée Grillade* on the Sunset Strip. Because of his unique culinary experience Arthur had thoroughly won my esteem and admiration. Taken generally at that time he was of mild disposition, honest and very polite.

As the unsteady economy dictated it, the chain went out of business. Furthermore the owner of the chain Mr. Henri Wizain drank himself to death and his wife was left a widow. But the enthusiasm for taking over the chain had been buried with her husband's demise…

Suddenly the unemployed Arthur eagerly decided in partnership with a wealthy actor to open a new place: *La Mousson*, a hideout for Hollywood celebrities and suitably situated on Vine Street. Soon, Arthur's life and my life had diverged. Fortunately for me, my childhood dream, my *château en Espagne* of travelling the world came to fruition.

To break the monotony of a regular life I took to foreign travel like an eagle takes to air, filled with a zeal for discoveries. As a spendthrift with a small backpack and a great amount of *joie de vivre* I boarded a southbound bus that would carry me to the first stage of an extended trip. This represented a journey that would lead me to the far reaches of the earth traveling by buses, trains, boats, camels, on foot enduring fatigue, submitting myself to privation and exalting in pleasure. Frequently I slept on park benches *à la belle étoile*, in religious temples even in pauper's cemeteries. From the Panama Canal Zone after that long bus ride through Mexico and all of Central America I embarked on a Spanish cargo ship headed for Europe and from 'terra firma' on to the Middle East and Central Asia.

The pervasive spirituality in India among the poor and hungry, determined not to change their ways enlivened my penchant for writing. I came alive with a pen in my hand, *la plume de ma tante* as I immersed myself into literature. At this point my life was more accurately described as vagabondish but with the mind of an observer, getting more involved in creative writings, working off and on as a free-lance. What I first become aware about India was how happily even merrily people could live on such little cost. Afterward I discovered the mighty Ganges winding its way into the vermin ditch at Varanasi where scarcity too bitter to describe is as naked as babies are; where sickness seems to be a companion of famine. This was so different from the comforting world I always knew. Wearing just a loincloth I bathed and prayed in the sacred water.

Subsequent to cavorting with the locals and appreciating being the recipient of their hospitality *la grande aventure* took me for that Kodak moment in front of the Taj Mahal and further on to Southeast Asia presenting myself as a *journaliste de passage* and soldier of fortune in war-torn Cambodia. Finally, in Australia kicking up the dust in so immense a land 'Down Under' I passed by the gleaming hill-slopes and the bushes along the road that stretched away towards the rising sun. I was left with fifteen dollars in my pocket. Being fatigued with travelling I came off the road. At first, to find employment was a hard task. Fortunately a belt-operator quit in desert Kalgoorlie's gold mine and I landed the job...

A year passed by. Escaping the humdrum of daily routine at the mine with a side-trip to Papua-New Guinea, Japan and

Korea I finally boarded a Greek ship in Sydney, bounded for Acapulco via New Zealand and Fiji.

Upon my return to California after trekking the globe I was thrilled to see the saga from my day to day journal published into a book.

Still in that adventurous spirit, vibrant with daring experiences, I drifted for awhile in San Francisco, feeling as free as a homeless gypsy. Trudging barefoot in the city by the bay, cloaked with a blanket over my shoulders I was there for a culture of love, listening in a concert hall foyer to a 'Siddhartha by the river' *exposé*.

Thereafter as fate would have it I accepted Arthur's offer to work with him at *Le Cerisier*, his brand new place in Sherman Oaks. For long he had conceived the idea of having his very own establishment.

At *Le Cerisier* restaurant I was christened 'the dummy.' Arthur bestowed me with this title as he decided one day to boost his present unstable personality by creating mental turmoil. As I scrutinized his face I knew at once that he wasn't the same. I rapidly discerned what sort of a man he really was. It looked as if my employer took a vow to be extremely disagreeable to me. He set himself on a pedestal of infamy and his plan was to instigate tension, implying the severe wounding of one's pride. I would have never before suspected the evil traits lurking in the character of Arthur.

As I recalled, when we both worked at the *Fricassée's* chain restaurant Arthur seemed quite cheerful. I had liked him eagerly with such a warm fervor as he displayed such a courteous attitude. Now a strange subdued expression showed upon his countenance. He also became even quite vulgar. He would look at me with a curious dream-like fixity. In his face a crushing impression flaunted as for the possibility to make life of his subservient underlings miserable. In order *de se faire valoir*-to be worth I became his *bête noire*. In the illustration from Herman Melville's *Billy Budd*, regarding the mean Master-at-Arms Claggart, one can discover an analogy with my employer's character. My employer *"...was the mania of an evil nature, not engendered by vicious training or corrupting books or licentious living but born with him and innate, in short 'a depravity according to nature.'"*

Arthur never acknowledged to any of our customers that prior to becoming my boss, at one time in the past we both held the same management position. During that earlier period I navigated my way from busboy to waiter and night host.

Now, because of the owner's shamed mentality I was bestowed a new name. If Caligula made his horse a consul of the empire Arthur baptized me with another epithet: the village idiot, subject to constant mockery. And just like in the military my employer was now expecting from me to 'high hats' him. Becoming totally nonsocial, along with vexations and humiliations my tormentor-boss indignantly enjoyed picking on me a little more every day with any new rotten things, making me the butt for his satire. Thinking about our friendship from the past I was bitterly disappointed with his new attitude. Just as in Sigmund Freud's theories Arthur became a great killjoy, discovering hatred at the root of love, malice of the heart of tenderness and guilt in generosity. He turned into a *Thanatos*, thus carrying an aggressive instinct. There is still in my mind that vivid image of Arthur laughing at me like I was his marionette giggling for a deranged puppeteer; a marionette pulled by unskilled fingers that dislocated me! So often I felt that instead of blood, acid run in his veins as he would give me that gawk reminding me of the cold intentness of a curator. That man was impelled to cast me down at any opportunity. Still, because of my experiences in India I decided to do the best I could at work. Under the circumstances I was peacefully waiting for the outcome.

As I arrived at the restaurant on this cold month of January, the day grew darker and the air was rather chill. Shortly, the dull sky was sending down herald drops of rain when the stagnant air changed into a fitful breeze. Arthur would greet me with those three French words: *Bonjour la bête-* good morning beast!

Whenever a customer graciously offered me a glass of wine, the boss with his throat thick over the aftertaste of too much bourbon would arrive at the table in a strange trot like a clumsy horse. And in an abrupt savageness, snatching the glass from my hand with the sure instinct of an animal going to its prey he would shout in a high pitched howling laugh with a sort of peremptory flash in his eye:

"Don't give it to that ass. He is a nincompoop with the brain of a fly, too stupid to appreciate good wine! Give him a Ripple, he won't taste the difference," and he would add: "You know what else? For being so gullible, Pierre believes that Taco Bell is a telephone company and that the Easter bunny lays hard-boiled eggs!" This would indulge a barrel of laughs amidst our patrons. Casting a still surreptitious glance, Arthur said further in a different tone of voice: "One day I picked up Pierre in the street. He was wild, barefoot and wearing a dirty shirt on his back. He smelled so bad, but I taught him good manners and showed him how to be handsomely dressed. Now he's all shining clean with well-fitted clothes. He still has to learn everything but now he has become 'an obedient, quite submissive soldier.'" At that precise moment I asked myself the question: "Have I been living in a dream or was this for real?" Afterward Arthur began to entertain even more hostile feelings, making my life unendurable.

At one time I came to the table where he sat with customers. As I asked if everything was fine, the boss poured himself another beer and simply blew suds at me meaning "just go away idiot." Still on another occasion when a satisfied patron complimented me for my work, Valois Dourville de Montrissart bestowed me with another one of his volley of profanities. With some kind of narcissism my gauleiter would compare this faithful employee as being just 'dead wood, part of the furniture and just lifeless!'

His insults along with the smacking of my ears and cheeks came upon me with such cruelty. He even used a word extremely disgusting, so odious my pen couldn't write it down. This was his way of amusing himself. All in all, from that day on my joy in life had been shattered for I felt I was so utterly worthless, as worthless as the bottom of somebody's shoe! Being so unjustly calumniated those silly jokes fostered with vulgarity and obscenity were going on and on like a broken record. Arthur did not let an exceptionally quiet moment go by without inflicting one of his lowly tricks.

Next day I walked into *Le Cerisier* in a joyful frame of mind as I still recalled an event at the Ralph's supermarket in Santa Monica that morning: the long line of people at the cash-register had been as slow as a turtle walk. Just in front of me a blond, long-legged lady, the domineering type was holding everyone up… for a ten dollar food coupon that had been expired.

"Well, it's not my fault. I owned two houses; one in Brentwood the other in Palm Desert" she said, bouncing her expensive stylish handbag, smelling of her Nina Ricci fragrance. With some inkling of arrogant enjoyment she added: "At first I didn't remember in which of those two residences I had left the coupon." Four times, the woman mentioned again the fact that she owned those two houses.

Fluffing up her hair like an actress she said it in a tone of voice and with pharaonic gesture as if NBC was about ready to take her picture for the six o'clock evening news.

Now, she started a general commotion and concern as no one in the queue wanted to listen to anyone else's problems at such a time of day. While refitting her glasses and dumping her purse on the counter, the lady finally related the entire story to the store-manager who, as a warm gesture had decided to honor the expired voucher. When it was time for me to have my Ralphs card screened, something flashed through my brain. I suggested to the employee in charge to verify if my card was still up-to-date because for quite some time I didn't remember in which one of my 'three houses' I had left it. The roar of laughter and comments around the line of customers went uninterrupted:

"Touché, young man!"

"That's the spirit!"

"Maybe you left your card in your Lamborghini…ah…ah…ah?"

An aged woman holding to her cane even offered me a candy…

Later, in the kitchen at *Le Cerisier* I was busy opening a can of *foie gras* for chef Picharon when my employer arrived. His hair was disheveled and his shirt unbuttoned as if he'd just got out of bed. Standing near the glass-refrigerator he started to devour a wheel of Brie on a piece of French bread. Afterward popping some baby-shrimps into his mouth, Arthur on the spur of the moment, sensing that I was in a particularly good mood decided to create another deception. He turned around, facing me. Afterward, he sucked his lips and, with pure malice and evil he smashed a raw egg on my forehead. In the most damned barbaric manner, with a careless mockery on his face Arthur laughed his head off. It was a horrible laughter, as unnatural and ghastly as a laugh in hell. That man so coldly cruel, so wickedly despotic was possessed by some sort of a demon. Spitting crumbs from his food, he scratched his stomach and conveyed indistinctly: "I'm dreadfully sorry Pierrot; I really thought this was a hard-boiled egg. I meant you no harm whatever!"

I really seemed to be upon the verge of comprehension that Arthur would do such a silly thing. Quite satisfied, I noticed that he had secretly chuckled over the wound he had inflicted in my mind. The broken egg had created huge splotches that had soaked through my shirt and apron. Still horrified at what Arthur had done, before I cleaned myself and the apron, my colleague handed me an extra white shirt that he always kept in his locker.

This was one of Arthur's kicks in life: finding a perverted sense of gratification by performing a stupid prank simply because my happiness infuriated him. At other times my employer still using me as the butt of some unrefined practical joke would enjoy snapping a squelchy wet towel at my legs and buttocks as I hopped around like a cat while he continued the whipping. That man, that barbaric and cowardly creature had fallen lower than a cow's droppings and became as sensitive as a public bathroom! I constantly had to use up that energy and sensibility which was dwelling in me in order not to quit my job. Oh yes, I was irritated. But like Gandhi I managed to contained myself. To some degree, I even felt compassion for my employer. The regulars who dined at *Le Cerisier* found his tasteless jokes amusing because after all they came to have a good time and enjoy a fine meal. The boss, on the other hand was charmed to receive the tribute of their laughter.

Arthur resented that I socialized with customers. The egotistical little man constantly reminded me to avoid talking to them as he ungraciously kicked me in the derriere the way you would kick a donkey. If I continued talking, my employer, with his lower lip wobbling would come down on me like a ton of bricks to strike again, yet much harder with the sound of a wild beast, his face twisted like that of a gargoyle's scowl, before telling the people that I was better to keep my mouth shut; that I was unhinged mentally, acting like a fool and an imbecile. He then pulled me back by the skin of the neck like a rabbit. Again I felt that intolerable encroachment of despair. This was another hour of torment when Arthur tried once more to dump his deep imprint on me. The owner would perambulate, bubbling over with his own importance, his only *raison d'être*, flattering his vanity and cracking other insolent dry jokes for the people at their table. At this point I started to realize once more how much of a vulgar person he was, like a poisonous fungi that grow beneath human society; no less than an insect that one can crush on a fingernail. That man, full of ironic pride had been misleading me into a deceitful friendship.

At another time, with his ears standing up as if about to bark, this boss of mine would openly insult me by claiming that I pissed on the bathroom floor rather than in the urinal. That affront; that humiliation which was being imposed on me came after other employees and customers visited the privy. On so many instances Arthur acted like a matador. With a sword that he kept sticking at me till I bled he tried to make me enfeebled a little more each and every day. He would hammer me obstinately until I became a malleable metal. My employer never fully realized how deeply I suffered by the monstrosity and personal insults created by those words he so indolently lashed at me.

With time I managed to keep the harm inside as not to give him that extra enjoyment he was seeking. I kept on sharing my thoughts between my actual position as a waiter and the great things I had done while circling the globe. What I learned during my travels is the simple fact that you must delight in the suffering as well as in the pleasure.

Frequently the stressful Arthur acted like a zombie, wandering with no direction in life because he didn't know what he was living for. Infrequently, a few, very few concerned customers who were continually offended upon noticing the owner of the restaurant's obnoxious attitude toward me wondered aloud why he treated me that way and why he hired me at the first place. Never to be caught off guard by such an observation, Arthur brooding on his malevolent thoughts would reply with boastfulness in his imbecile sneer: "HERE WE DON'T DISCRIMINATE, WE HIRE THE HANDICAPPED."

As the clients focused in my direction I began to feel more uncomfortable than ever. It was as if I had been stabbed in the back by a man possessed by demons and I stood there in intense mental agony! For sure I did not feel I merited so much antagonism; so much hostility! Arthur had really been successful on his devilish mission.

Oftentimes following such a statement and somewhat worn out with the bullying, I wanted to know all the thoughts that passed through his head. Just like the Russian writer Anton Chekhov's temperament, readers will find more and more bewilderment with the mind of yours truly: "...*a gentle, suffering soul*" and *a wise observer with a wistful smile and an aching heart*". I already knew that some might even classified me as simply being an irresponsible victim while others might conclude that I was a watcher of characters with unique moving experiences...

* * * *

Melanie, Arthur's daughter was a woman of steel. Her strong personality effervesced in intellectual activity with good oratorical skills that she inherited from her father. Along with expensive tastes and a greedy thirst for luxury 'the little princess' donned herself with a well-furnished wardrobe. There was in her that *je ne sais quoi*, certain boundless appetite. Being a spoiled child, money was the motivation for nearly everything as she contracted an almost pathological compulsion to sue everybody as the opportunity presented itself.

Her mouth ravishingly curved, revealing a gleam of the loveliness of her teeth was slightly full and well etched, and her artfully rumpled hair was streaked with blond. She had the Madonna-like eyes with penciled, almost invisible eyebrows. I watched her grow up since she was a gawky, wide-eyed sixteen, a healthy athletic child with cheek like an apple. At the same time she was really the contrast to her mother who was the most feminine of women.

At eighteen with her beautiful hair framing her face with a smile on her lips she was still having some marked reluctance to attend balls and other festivities unless accompanied by her father. And as bizarre as it may seem, Melanie probably bored with her easy lifestyle as a child heeded the spiritual calling to join a religious order to live a life of contemplation.

However she quickly realized that the convent was a living grave. The oath of obedience, poverty, chastity and the rituals of walking with a veil over her face with eyes fixed on the ground took little hold upon her mind. Prior to taking her final vows, ready to be forever the bride of Christ, that piously-minded girl had doubted the truth of her faith. For awhile on certain days she still venerated 'the sacred heart.' She would remain in meditation for at least an hour in a local church. But

I could never think that her belief was more than skin-deep for with time even that she carried a rosary in her pocket as a tool of her piety she became notoriously godless.

She had been a spoiled child and now later in life she turned into an even more spoiled lady. The physical attribute she inherited from her mother become more and more apparent: big hips, exploding breasts and skin as fine as silk. Now that she possessed all the charming outlines of the woman, she became the reigning queen of *Le Cerisier,* a Victorian Dowager. Not just bossy, but the bossiest person in the restaurant beside her father. She was a tower of strength, blossoming like a beautiful wildflower nevertheless with eyes full of malice. Frequently her laugh was garrulous. She still carried the childish vice of finger biting and the strange habit of standing like a boy, legs far apart with her head thrown back. The pain she suffered from lumbago did not deter her from being a fine golf player. Furthermore she was still the best pastry chef in town.

Melanie kept busy at home by tending a flower garden in a small corner of the backyard when listening to her favorite music. Her social life was hobnobbing with society women. She liked partying in ritzy Bel Air estates wearing great feminine attire with seductively scented perfume. On other occasions, alike George Sand's eccentric conduct Melanie would dress like a man *"…a suggestion which she was only too glad to adopt. Clad in a loose blouse, or in coat and trousers she felt stronger, felt as though she was acquiring a degree of virility…"* Such demeanor, she thought would give her some stature in the eyes of her several Malibu girlfriends.

During the day Melanie worked as a secretary for a law-firm in Mission-Hills. Prior to her job with the attorneys her dad had opened a small coffee and pastry shop near the Malibu Colony. It was called *The Malibu-Paris Place.* Because of Melanie's expertise in cooking wonderful cheesecakes, she had been gratified to supply the business with them and be intrusted with its management.

However some of her Malibu's friends had connived at her desertion of her duties and responsabilities. With the beach nearby, the lure of the waves and the warm California sun shining almost all year round Mademoiselle Melanie thought of just one thing: to feel the warmth into every part of her body and to get a glorious tan while sniffing out the scents of the faint breeze, along with the same friends. On other occasions she would enjoy an afternoon at Zuma's nudist camp. Most of the time, affixed on the shop's window one could read the sign: Closed-will return at 5 PM.

A steady customer from *Le Cerisier* had reported the situation at *The Malibu-Paris Place* to Arthur. Upon hearing this, my employer was angry at his daughter and quite disappointed. He decided to dump the place for good: *Adieu la boutique.*

Chapter 2

MY FELLOW COUNTRYMAN Leon Nicolas Van Meerstellen was my colleague in the dining room. Given that his name reveals a Flemish background, Leon was a typical French speaking Carolingien, inhabitant from Charleroi, Belgium. Tall with finely chiseled features he had dark-brown hair and thick dark-brown beard he wears to cover an ebbing chin. He had been thin-skinned child. Because of the exceptional length of his legs and long arms hanging down people used to call him: *Leon l'asperge-* the asparagus, and Pipi Longstocking, tall as a publicity pole. With his small head at the end of an extended neck some of our lady customers would refer to him as 'the giraffe.' He also had a physical need for a rather violent eau de cologne. Sometimes as he spoke I was able to detect bronchial rattles and he repeatedly sneezed. He regularly cleaned his soul with a diet of prune juice before meditating straight on the toilet, his place for peace and serenity.

As a former Stanford University student and a member of the fraternity 'Gamma Phi Beta' Leon had a great reservoir of knowledge; a real walking encyclopedia, and at once he became Arthur's *protègè*. On the campus bowl luncheonette from Stanford which accounted from that state's superiority over so many other institutions my colleague would carry on a long discourse with his student-friends about astral plane, empyrean transcendental philosophy, Plato's Timaeus, Critias, or differential calculus. At about the same time, each afternoon at the restaurant while twiddling contentedly at his beard Van Meerstellen would announce in a strong resounding voice the arrival of the boss: "Here comes *Le Petit Napoléon*, the mighty potentate like a king in his castle." On many occasions he mockingly pictured Arthur as a trumpeted warrior with blue and red plumage nodding over his high-crested helmet in a suit of armor waving his saber and blowing his horn. In reality Leon was obviously aware that Arthur was *un cabot;* a ham actor no less than a scary Lilliputian.

My fellow worker cherished two hobbies which one can say clashed with each other. He was getting all riled up by the vroom...vroom, by the metal crashing of racecars and at the same time he relaxes with soothing classical music. He was an avid collector for sports paraphernalia and had a sharp ear for Shubert and Mozart. NASCAR being his first love Leon collected automobile race events on videos since 1986 and sold them worldwide through the miracle of e-bay.

On a hot summer afternoon, upon his invitation I accompanied him to his quite dilapidated apartment. With a pen in hand before he cleared a space on the table he first took a spoonful of his cough syrup. As he leaned forward, he proceeded to pinned down on a map of Europe and Africa on which he was tracing, meandering his fingers, pointing the route of the motor-cars rally Paris-Dakar and checking the *caravanserai*.

With a Socratic method of acquiring a sponge soaking knowledge his curiosity knew no bounds. A man of high academic education Van Meerstellen was an oenophile as well; a great connoisseur of wines and beers, especially Belgian beers. This again made Arthur very pleased. Leon's voice expressed such confidence and submission that he advanced insensibly in the good graces of the boss. Because of his talent as time passed Arthur carried the highest opinion of him. At all times the boss graciously praised Leon as a skillful, extremely reliable employee. Mephistopheles himself would have been charmed by it.

If a refined customer would request a particular wine for his meat or fish Leon was ceaselessly at hand to choose a good vintage bottle. If one disagreed with him, he was chivalrous enough to compromise (something Arthur was unable to do.) On the other hand Leon always showed an extreme gallantry to Arthur whom he admired devotedly. However, Leon always resented impolite customers. On one occasion, as he kept busy removing the wire from a Cordon Rouge champagne bottle, a client whistled at him for service. Turning around as he popped the cork that almost hit the wall he answered back in a dignified attitude:

"Sir, I am a waiter, not a dog!" On another occasion Leon gave this good lesson of humility over pride: a customer grabbed my co-worker by the edge of his apron asking about the delay of the duck *à l'orange* he ordered awhile ago. Five minutes later the same client stood up telling Leon:

"Maybe you don't know who I am? I'm a California State Senator, Chairman of State Energy and Natural Resources Committee. In your language you will call it: *Le Corps legislatif*!"

"Maybe you don't know who I am." Leon retorted, "I'm the server who is in charge of your duck *à l'orange*." On another day a client left a pile of little change on the plate. As he left, Leon took the pile of change and threw it in the middle of Ventura Boulevard, saying: "with all respect Sir, you need your 'chicken scratch' more than I do!'"

With his intellect Leon could have carved a brilliant career for himself with a flashy job in public accounting but he overlooked the opportunities for riches and fame. However his divorce from his wife Wendy, after so many disagreements that had darkened their love, that matrimonial disaster had finally created such a great wretchedness on him. From that day on he started to skip classes to finally quit Stanford and started to drink heavily. He so much indulged in drinking that it affected his walk. Lost, just like a sailor adrift without any 'mariner's compass' Leon no longer found any pleasure in this world and he decided to live a life of recluse, considering himself a psychological disaster. Leon had sacrificing such an opportunity for a great position to his grief at being forsaken by a cruel, unfeeling woman. Once he announced: "What do money; what do success matter if I haven't Wendy with me to share in them?" The lady's warm body given to him in love had been as a yacht in which he had floated contentedly.

But one day, after so many disputes Leon saw his wife's hand resting at the edge of the sofa. He rushed to take it but she withdrew it gently with sad, resolute dignity. On that instant Leon knew without any doubt that by this simple gesture as she now stepped away from him they were separated forever when their marriage was going to the dogs. But as soon Leon discovered marks of her infidelity, his excessive jealousy became troublesome. My friend had tried to renew that old intimacy with his wife but it was in vain. As written in *Virginibus Puerisque: "Marriage is not a bed of roses but a field of battle."*

Their divorce made Arthur's heart rejoice since he had always hated Wendy deeply. The boss had always anticipated a rapprochement between his own daughter and Leon; a rapproachement that so far never materialized...

And, all of a sudden Van Meerstellen found himself with a broken heart and a crushed ambition. Thereafter the desperate

Leon would come to work with straw in his hair as if he had slept in a stable. Glazed by the encounter with the past he began drinking more and more heavily.

Strangely enough, as an atheist also neo-Darwinian and true iconoclast my colleague appeared to have embraced monasticism; the supreme abnegation. What's more Leon expressed his admiration for the Bauls of India-A religious sect where the devotees prayed all their lives for the ultimate joy: that is the day they would die as they surely would attain great serenity. Leon was dragging his life like the ball and chains of a condemn man; more like a balloon which has lost its moorings as his thoughts were running in all directions.

His now ex-wife, the domineering and demanding Wendy as described by Arthur, in spite of her nose that quite too prominently reminded me of the Tower of London and with slightly droopy breasts was still a surpassingly graceful woman with a face that can launch a thousand ships.

During those early days of their relationship there wasn't a drop of blood in Leon's veins that didn't throb for her. He always sought his former spouse with the most expensive flowers. She was the center of her own universe. With her unbound and floating hair, the color of autumn leaf Wendy was not just beautiful. She as well appeared to be an innocent virgin with a noble mouth, but malicious eyes quite overwhelmingly good to glance at. The down-to-earth lady, a major in psychology with her long, almost perfect legs and neat little feet who had been the delight of Leon's life was a cosmetologist by profession. To use Steinbeck's analogy in *Travels with Charley,* she was "…a prettyish blond girl trying her best to live up to the pictures in the magazines. A girl of products, home permanents, shampoos, rinses, skin conditioners…Her only company was found in the shiny pages of *Charm* and *Glamour*."

Wendy at all times exquisitely well dressed was conscious of her appeal, and her eyes were sparkling gleefully. However, aside from charm and glamour it looked as if money was the one way to her heart. She thought for awhile that Leon was well off; that he was to conduct her to bouncing prosperity. But she kept on living in a world of dreams. Her foremost concern had been to parade the smart shops or sharing lunches with friends at *Jeffrey's*, a lavish, outstanding beach restaurant in Malibu. But my friend left his wife without provision. An enthusiast on all subjects of interest, Wendy was of great intellectual radiance equal to that of Jezebel and Catherine de Médicis. Although she had become as cold as an iceberg, unable to make an adequate response to her husband's display of affection, Leon still cared for her so much. He was determined never to give any other woman an opportunity of expunging the happy recollection. He would never again go down on one knee telling a lady that he loves her. Later on, I noticed some women, all good-looking and seductive with a sympathetic leaning toward him. But Leon stood there, silent, thinking that they all were trying to impose on him a miserable servitude fate; that they were striving to corrupt him for their own ends, leading to an immoral life.

At one point in his life (even as an agnostic), Van Meerstellen was convinced that his marriage had been arranged in heaven. He still recalled her bridal veil that fluttered harmoniously in the wind. He had been intoxicated with fever and amazement. In spite of frigidity from her part, there had been infidelity too. Leon suspected her of having been in love with a physician and with her hairdresser who was not only dressing her hair!

Once, Wendy who was rather sharply dressed with a Ralph Lauren outfits, all decked with brilliant ornaments, looking like a store-window mannequin came to the restaurant escorted by a Hollywood celebrity. Appearing tranquil and fresh with a sort of feline smirk she was beaming with joy as her smile illuminated her lips. With that wistful naughty charm, she had grown talkative. Leon kept on gawking witheringly, wide-eyed at his former spouse with an expression of disbelief dawning in his eyes as if he chanced upon her for the first time. He was exceptionally struck by the expression of melancholy on her face. How good looking she was, with such an angelic face. Never has Wendy looked more beautiful. For Leon it was like 'a century of torment.' As he realized that her beauty was still dazzling; that she had an agreeable and rapturous smile a cold chill swept through him. Van Meerstellen didn't stop looking at her new friend, thinking of him as the villain who seduced his ex-wife. This kindled Leon's desire for her with even more intensity. Van Meerstellen, inflamed with jealousy was disappointed in love as he realized that she was happy without him.

Soon, being a *célibataire*- a bachelor Leon lived alone. But as a good speaker he was too gregarious to immure himself like a complete hermit. He lived in solitude; not as a penitent or a saint but as someone who had missed the mark. At the restaurant, recurrently like in a lady's boudoir the toilet was Leon's refuge where in trance-like passivity he segregated from a restless world. Sinking into reverie he stayed in the bathroom long enough to make us think he had to go. On one occasion Arthur would find him asleep right 'on the pot', doggedly rooted to his seat as he started snoring. Leon would sit on a chair outside, lost in thoughts or performing Gregorian chant before the arrival of the first customers.

Van Meerstellen became a rather unobtrusive man, secluding himself in his now depressed and grimmest apartment that resembles a prison, away from society; from social events. On numerous occasions while conversing with one of our steady customer, in an emotionally drained and lifeless bitterly lamenting voice I heard him say:

"I am a bastard and a complete failure." Later on, he articulated to me in a whisper: "I feel like I'm pinned down in a foul cesspool no less than an antechamber to death. Now I'm ready to sleep 'the big sleep.'"

I was surprised by so much bitterness in his tone of voice and how his unhappy heart was torturing him. Leon never knew his real unsympathetic father who was never able to cope with him and ungratefully abandoned him as a child.

For Van Meerstellen, the surest way to be uplifted was to participate at a funeral and hear burial eulogies with the majesty of a hymn, as a non- involved observer. One never can get Leon to go anywhere, except the cemetery. He loved those black corteges, delighting himself in the smell of decay strangely confounded with the scent of flowers. Even for a complete stranger Leon would find compassion. Every so often, in an incoherent mumbling, inarticulate despair, more like a sober humanist he would grieve over the grave of the death of a lovely young girl or boy cut off in the flower of their youth. I personally hate funerals but he loved them. Leon became fascinated by memorial orations. As he started to read about Peter the Great, he was thrilled by a passage related to Mary Hamilton who threw her illegitimate child in a well, and consequently was beheaded: *"The beheading was a notable affair, with Mary Hamilton dressed handsomely in her finest silks. When her head rolled in the street, the Csar picked it up, kissed it twice and delivered a funeral oration. Then he kissed it again and threw it back into the gutter."*

What's more, compelled by force of habit my friend was a caffeine junkie carrying his own special elaborately patterned mug quite mechanically. Sometimes forgetting that the coffee was too hot, gulping at the still well nigh and scalding beverage he was recurrently driven back by the heat, blinking and gulping again. Within a few hours with his grip tightened on his mug Leon would drink an entire pot of premium Costa Rican freshly roasted coffee-the best in town. And after another swallow of coffee he thought that the adrenaline rush could stimulate his brains.

Leon's view of the world has become more and more cynical as he grew older and as a result he hated conformity. Because of his black beard a few customers at the restaurant would refer to him as Bin Laden…

Chef Jean-Luc Picharon and his direct assistant Jesus Betancourt were *les pilliers d'acier* for kitchen preparations. The pantry chef Gustavo Santillas, an expert in his field was related to the dishwasher Bernardo Echeviran.

Bernardo with his quite young, almost boyish face with the first signs of a light beard showed two front teeth missing. He was skinny, weak-looking, somewhat frail in appearance with wrists as slim as spaghetti and trousers a shade too large for him, but very courageous and he laughted at everything just like children do. He also always wore a light blue turtleneck sweater.

All of the workers, with the exception of chef Picharon carried a submissive attitude toward Arthur. Reverently, with great courtesy they would address the owner of the restaurant as *patron*-the boss. They always saluted him respectfully as though they felt him to be a superior being. Jesus Betancourt learned all his expertise from Arthur and Jean-Luc.

Gustavo Santillas on the other hand was incumbent. His creative mind would design the most unusual very tasty hors d'oeuvres. However besides his extraordinary skills he would constantly come out of the bathroom with unwashed hands, thus disregarding Arthur's warnings over that simple hygiene practice. It was so unhealthy. Arthur literally forced him to wear plastic gloves or he would be loosing his job.

Santillas was tall, slightly obese and his swarthy complexion showed a full mouth. Occasionally he would express some strained grimaces as his nerves brittled from sleeplessness. He had two steady jobs; one at *Le Cerisier,* the other one in a Mission Hills Cantina. But, before we opened the doors of the restaurant fatigue took over him. Next he would lay down on a booth in the dining room, his hat tilted over his eyes. Before long he started snoring so hard that the walls would shake like a sixteen-wheeler passing by. At twenty-six years old, still beardless Gustavo was completely without bristly appendage, anywhere on his body except for a full head of hair that was confined by a light net. There was a rabbit paw suspended from a gold chain spanning his shirt.

Nondescript as you watch him you can discover a synthesis of a multifarious indigenous source. Being from Puebla in the south part of Mexico, his Mayan blooded line predominated. He had an ancient face that crinkled in a smile but with a certain ascetic hardness.

The pantry chef enjoyed his beer. Every day he arrived at the restaurant, a cap on with a slanted visor almost down on his nose and his fly half unbuttoned (as he relished with great dignity and deference for the demands of nature to urinate gushingly in the back alley over a rhododendron bush.) Afterward he would hide his six pack of *Corona* in the refrigerator.

On occasions Santillas would become dysfunctional, showing a broody pestering mood to anyone that disagreed with his culinary expertise. Yet, I had the feeling that he was displeased with himself without really knowing why. However he was so proud to admit that he had been conceived in the back seat of an old Cadillac Eldorado, giving him that feeling of greatness!

* * * *

In the week that followed the 'egg incident' all was quiet at work. It was a fall day such as we sometimes have in the City of Angels, cold and wet with a heavy fog that was lying over the city.

And suddeny in the dead of night I was awakened by a telephone call from the Calabasas Police Department. Arthur Valois Dourville de Montrissart was on the line, hysterical and emotional too. I sensed his uneasiness and fear as he stuttered like a little boy left out in the cold. My employer related to me that he had been arrested for suspicion of driving under the influence (DUI) and was handcuffed. He admitted to having only one drink; that he almost hit a Greyhound bus and barely passed the sobriety test. Even that the sergeant on duty at the police station let him off with a warning, he ordered Arthur to leave his car at the station and requested him that somebody should come and pick him up since he was drowsing. While still on the phone, as he was desperate and gasping for breath Arthur begged in a salvo of coughing:

"Please petit Pierre can you come and get me at the station?"

Noblesse oblige, I agreed to pick him up. As I cruised past the residential area of Calabasas, there was nothing but blackness with the wind whistling. Nothing appeared to be alive except for the monotonously barking of stray dogs. And in the distance I observed a hint of light. The new white painted police station was quite isolated.

Inside the building I located a scared and nervous Arthur all shacking-up in a corner of a deafeningly quiet room. As he caught sight of me, the little fat-bellied Buddha with his rimmed eye glasses on the end of his nose leaped in the air and stood-up like a meerkat from the African savanna. With bemused amazement he felt a surge of adrenaline and his face still gray as ashes abruptly irradiated with tremendous joy. About the same time a tall African-American female police officer with a belly of a whale castigated him in a thundered voice to remind in his corner silently while the sergeant finished his paperwork. Shivering all over as a little mouse this scared little man politely squeaked in a low voice: "Yes madam." And, just like a fallen soldier his convulsive shadow leaped and fell upon the wall as a sissy. My employer was now yelping and writhing like a dreamy dog. The sight of Arthur almost on his knees was so pitiful I was wrought up with tears in my eyes. As I looked at him, I felt a lump in my throat. For the first time I discerned how deeply frightened my employer was. What has become of that tiger, all-powerful 'mighty king', that shrewd human being obstinate as a mule that made my life so difficult; a boss who treated me like the retarded Charley Gordon "playing with Algernon, his white pet mouse?" An employer that regarded me as little more than a piece of furniture and who was now humiliated by a lady cop and under my mercy? Surely, the tiger had been tamed!

At the timid birth of another day as I drove him home, Arthur's old cocky self surfaced once again and he smiled more blandly than ever. Now that he was out of danger from 'the enemy' he boasted:

"Pierre, did you notice the way that fat, black policewoman talked to me?" And in an even strong authoritative voice he announced: "NEXT TIME I WILL SHUT HER TRAP!" Having quickly forgotten his brush with the law Arthur, again in that good mood began to sing a very romantic song. He had learned its English version aboard a ship from the merchant marine, when on its way down to the Panama Canal:

Volare, oh, oh, cantare oh, ho, ho, ho.
Let's fly way up to the clouds
Away from the maddening crowds…

All that happened just as I have written it. It was irritating to peep at my employer's radiant unscrupulous eagerness. I had never so clearly perceived his strange character, his weakness and puerile petulance.

After that event, everything was going on greased wheels as matters went on pretty smoothly for several days. Again, the boss donned his feigned amiability and cheerfulness toward us, his trustworthy employees. Being in that spirit he even decided to buy a little French red hair female poodle for his wife Angeline who was now suffering the early signs of diabetes. The pooch's name was Pompadour; a name related to Louis XV's mistress at the Court of Versailles.

* * * *

Chef Jean-Luc Picharon a skinny short man with brown eyes and blond hair was a fair and best-mannered person. However he could become very rude under stress. Repeatedly he and Arthur exchanged horrified glances.

Once, Picharon was tackling the boss. He drove his head into his opponent's stomach and this became a hand to hand fight. They were slashing at each other's throats, pulling each other's hair or seizing wrists over some specific food preparations or they would pace nervously across the kitchen yelling and hitting the knuckles of one hand against the palm of the other hand to decide on recent dishes from *La Nouvelle Cuisine*. Occasionally, a surge of conflict with whirling arguments erupted between them, and it lasted for days. At one time when my employer was on his knees fixing the wire from behind the glass-refrigerator, Picharon pounced forward and with his powerful hands seized Arthur's ankles. The chef began to drag him about the kitchen as the boss' pants stretched out. Arthur quickly changed position and stuck his fingers all over Picharon's face. Next they tore at each other's clothes and punched each other noses. At that juncture, Jean-Luc ducked and kicked out the owner of the restaurant in wild fury. He caught his arm and twisted it. He was twisting the arm until I thought he would break it. Therefore, they rolled off on the floor, arms and legs thrashed around. Arthur trolled his head, lifting it from the ground and kicked at Picharon with his knees and hit him several times in the belly. But the chef struck him a violent blow on the right side before punching him in the face. Arthur struggled frantically under the rain of blows. He kept getting up and getting knocked down once again. Jean-Luc straightened his body on the ground, pressing with his knee on his chest while he tried to pinion his arms. And now, as Picharon's weight dragged on Arthur's chest the owner of the restaurant, flat on his back looked like a doggy with all four paws waving appealingly in the air. The sound of thumping and struggling went on for some time. But, subsequent to a few karate-type blows, Arthur couldn't stand up to the strength of the blusters as he appeared to have given up all thought of brawled resistance. An unearthly cry came out of his throat: "Arch! Arch! Arach! And, freeing himself the boss slipped back to the dining room, totally disheveled.

At the same moment, just as he passed the door that separated the kitchen from the dining area, Picharon yelled at him: "Arthur, you lack the first qualification of being a chef since you can barely cook French fries! In the past you were just a military *cuistot*; a kitchen worker, nothing else. And because of your objectionable odor, you should be working with pigs!"

This event had reminded me so much when as a child my parents took me to the circus. In a way it recaptured the memories of my early childhood. My favored part among all other performances was precisely related with a scene when one of the clowns was trying to pull another buffoon by the leg, but he only succeeded to draw out his pants. I would laugh and wave my arms in such a delightful frenzy…

However, with a sort of beatific smile Arthur with a bruise developing on his forehead, his legs and back aching from the struggle went off brushing the dust from his clothes. His comment to me, in a sad dragging voice was always the same: "We didn't exactly quarrel; we just had a difference of opinion!" And on other similar events Arthur would utter: "Pierre, for sure you cannot make an omelet without breaking eggs!"

I have to remind my readers that only *le Chef de Cuisine* dared to confront the owner of the restaurant in such irrational way. Arthur knew that Jean-Luc was one if not the best chef in town and for sure he didn't want to lose 'his gold mine!'

In order to enhance the appetite of our clientèle, chef Picharon would browned onions sauté with *herbes de Provence* in a sliver of butter the way they do it in the old country. The scent would permeate, hissing through the whole dining room. From the open door of the restaurant came the most tantalizing and appetizing smells. Jean-Luc knew everything there was to know about fine French cuisine. However, at dinnertime the chef cultivated a bad habit toward his co-workers. Unconsciously he would tell us in a malicious chuckle: "CATTLE, YOUR FOOD IS READY!"

But he was skillful, quick and decisive enough to change a plan in the very act of execution whenever an emergency occurred, such as a late cancellation of a special order for a group of twelve. Next, that cancellation order would artfully be re-written on the black board for our regular customers and proficiently introduced as *le plat du jour*. In those rare circumstances when a late cancellation occurred, a beaming Arthur would be in heaven. The deposit from the party, who had abrogated their order, was non-refundable.

The restaurant owner really owes his titre de noblesse Valois Dourville de Montrissart (old noblesse from time immemorial, with a line unbroken as far as the Crusaders, the arrogant Arthur would proclaimed), from his all-knowing and all-caring wife.

Angeline, from illustrious birth and ample wealth was *une femme du monde*-a lady of rank alltogether from France, Germany and Russia. Still, a remarkably fine-looking human being, burning with love, she was a model lady with great acuteness of observation, abundant of experience and of high moral. Angeline was fond of the high society, yet she loved the poor, the homeless and *les affligés*. She was married to Arthur in a small convent on the outskirt of the city of Narbonne. And just like in *The Sound of Music*, all the nuns were present for the entire ceremony as they sang 'The Hymn to Angels.' The bishop himself proceeded in the sacrament of marriage and the blessings. I can dwell so much on the life and labors of this great and good woman. Angeline's relatives were large landowners, not only in Toulouse but in the fertile area of Lille as well.

Occasionally Arthur tried to portray himself as *Le Grand Bourgeois*, but in reality, even with the family riches, he was from the lower divide of society. Long ago, prior to the wedding ceremony, a personal sympathy along with a certain compatibility of fortune had brought them together. At that time, strangely enough they seemed to be destined to each other.

Once, that good woman uttered that as a child Arthur had lived in the absence of affection from his father; only his mother loved him. She added that in his youth, her future husband had repeatedly skipped school. He would slip away into the woods, listening to the birds calling their mates or practicing on his mandolin. Angeline on the other hand was a dame from *La Grande Epoque* with a real aristocratic figure and aristocratic culture who never used any makeup. She was recognized as a weighty figure of European diplomacy by so many high-ranking persons and men of letters from the *Académie Française*. Her circle of friends had been only the learned, the distinguished and the philanthropists.

Later on in California, her popularity and good nature did not wane away with old age, while Arthur on the other hand dragged the family's name in the mud with his constant low-class attitude. Well versed in six languages Angeline was never shy to express her feelings. Her kind face revealed thin lips curved in a candid and friendly smile, and her eyes sparkled as bright as precious stones. She had vivid passions and keen feelings. She loved sport, more specifically exciting and somewhat violent sport, and never missed the Man's Heavyweight Wrestling Championship. Mrs. Valois Dourville de Montrissart constantly pulled her hair back in a braid. Everyone at the restaurant loved her so much and I believe to this day that Angeline always strongly supported her husband and that she was the reason for the tremendous success of *Le Cerisier*. She always kept a good track of the business as well as household expenses.

Toward her daughter Melanie she neglected no opportunity of inculcating precepts of sound morality. Confidentially, Angeline muttered to me-something I already knew: that Arthur was good to those who were good to him. Still he could be vicious as the Devil, the demon of hatred, showing persistent hostility with people who contradict him...

Eddy Roy Freedman was a mannerist human being. For him, being vice-president at *Le Cerisier* was not simply a job, it was a position. A position granted to him by his longtime friend Arthur. In his advanced age, Eddy with a complexion as smooth as a child was still elegant with a mass of elaborately curled blond hair and dreamy eyes that hid behind his gold-rimmed glasses. His nose was full and somewhat red from so many years of hard liquor (apple martini was still his favored drink.) He had gaunt tapering fingers-the fingers of a pianist. Freedman had equally an unusual gift of observation. Eddy's keen-eyed, vigilant never missed anything. At all times, aside from 'his little black book' he constantly took mental notes about people's remarks and behavior. He had several hobbies, and as an amateur genealogist he kept on looking to trace the family tree of important and influential people.

Sometimes in life, when you don't know someone's character, you are on your guard. In the beginning I had had doubts about Eddy for I found him an alarming figure at first. His manners seemed unusually restrained and enigmatic before I realized how mistaken one's earliest perception of Freedman was. When one knew him better, one discovered under his deceptive appearance so much warm humanity. My suspicions had really been groundless: Eddy rapidly showed the bourgeois standard of admiration with genteel manners in addition to an acute sense of humor. He rapidly became my ally and favored friend.

From a very early age, Freedman displayed a marked disposition for the profession of private investigator prior to becoming a policeman. As a former highway patrolman back in Lincoln, Nebraska he became a well-esteemed gentleman without stain or blemish with quickness of intellect, precise and methodical. By nature of education he was a wise, well-bred man with a certain degree of contentment, and for him the essential part in a conversation was to be tacit. Being a tight-lipped person he was slow of speech and of a slow tongue, and at all times he let Arthur do all the talking. Eddy never spoke except when literary conversation compelled him to break silence as he had been brought up never to exercise his own judgment. Being socially introverted, he was a man that never tried to appear intellectual, but whatever he said seemed obvious and natural. And, if occasionally he appeared to be very witty and somewhat deaf, he would pretend not to be by reading the movement of people's lips. Eddy was one of those good natured people with a big heart who seemed to be just passing stealthily through life. Freedman's life was like a fine ship's course without any deviations or accidents. Long ago, at his school of self-defense and martial arts, Eddy was regarded as an extremist, as others were won to esteem by his methodical but quiet thinking. Eddy never gambles as he was averse to all games of chance. And he constantly found women mysterious and so full of contradictions. Just like Sophocles in *Ajax,* Eddy announced that: *"Silence gives the proper grace to women."* In the presence of a beautiful lady he would tell me discretely that she was too pretty to be good, but he would add: "So many women can be quite appealing, each in their own way and without any provocation."

Freedman was always quite concerned with his well-being. Extremely neat about his person, he kept on washing his hands and cleaning his teeth almost every hour, on the hour. As a former Vietnam War Navy Fighter, though he was the perfect picture of health, and still suspicious of all sorts of medical treatments, he would go for a thorough physical examination at the Veterans Hospital every three months or so. Eddy had a vast knowledge on all subjects that he gained mostly through reading and perception. He used to shut himself up, being an omnivorous reader in public libraries. At one time he enjoyed the works of great authors such as Voltaire, Thoreau, Proust, Twain (especially him), and now he reads almost nothing else but USA Today. However, I was amazed by the alertness of his mind. Also, there wasn't anything Freedman could turn his hand to, always ready for some little things that need to be fixed. He was a crafty, artful man and a real Jack-of-all-trades. Even in his old age, he appeared to have lost none of his skill.

Eddy, as an intimate friend of the Valois Dourville de Montrissart's family literally build-up *Le Cerisier* from the ground up. He patched up, roofed, painted and fixed the poorly lighted building adding his talents as an iconographer to create beautiful mural paintings. Freedman chose the new windows, the door and all the best fittings as he gave infinite care to every detail. He really couldn't be satisfied until he secured something. He might do anything if he tried hard enough. And frequently Eddy took long walks in the morning. Recurrently he got out of bed at dawn when the sun had not yet painted the east. On other time, with some kind of an infantile gaiety, with a sudden startling energy he would quickened his pace to a run to the very depth of his lungs, hearing only his own breathing. With unceasing dynamism and subsequent exhaustion over jogging a mile or two, Eddy sometimes came back to the house with upbraiding breathlessness and a slight weakness in the legs. With that intense level of exhaustion he seemed to walk with some form of arthritis.

As Arthur's constant devoted friend and silent partner, in sharp contrast, there was so much difference from one to another in nature and spirits. As opposed to Arthur, Freedman had yet to learn the easy tossing of compliments. The pure-minded Eddy was always ready to devote himself blindly to the broadening of the bosse's views. He was sticking to him like a leech, ready to cut his right hand for him. Freedman akin to a lovesick servant, *son valet-de-chambre* would look up at him adoringly. Afterward he would roll on his back for Arthur; grovel with his legs in the air like a puppy that feels the warmth toward his master, and to observe the owner of the restaurant laugh, he was making jokes and played tricks, thus becoming no less than a paragon of docility.

Although Arthur and Eddy considered each other to be best of friends in the world but they were entirely made of different clay. Freedman had a grave, deep-toned voice sounding in strange contrast to Arthur's. Still, in the tradition of Sherlock Holmes and Dr. Watson, the Valois-Freedman team was inseparable. They talk to each other a lot, sometimes in whispers when they decided to carry on secret conversations. On bright hot days, Arthur and Eddy would drive to the beach, drowsing in the sun. And with a great show of cheerfulness, they would splash water in each other's faces like little kids. Eddy knew Arthur's thoughts for he always stood, gazing silently in awe at his actions. In that strange alliance, though that quarrels were often breaking out between them, they completely understood each other. Even that Eddy was an unambitious person they shared the same activities together like two peas in a pod. Wherever you saw Arthur, you'd likely see Eddy. Arthur's liaison with Eddy, without being proclaimed was suspitious. But so was the case with many French restaurant owners and their associates. Some of them believed that those kinds of relationships would complement their prestige. But for Arthur's wife (since Eddy lived under the same roof), this conduct was inexplicable and she suffered intensely of humiliations.

As an ex-draconian abiding law enforcement agent with a still procrustean approach, Eddy knew exactly what the code of honor command. When he arrived at *Le Cerisier,* nothing would escape his eagle eye that didn't even bat. His imagination was linked to great analytical power and insight. Being overburdened with principle Freedman would leave no smaller detail incomplete. He seemed capable of an inexhaustible immobility as he mentally catalogued the guests. Eddy would glimpse at a face in the restaurant and never forget it. And with the same method of looking at things as lieutenant Colombo, wearing the identical gabardine trench coat he would seriously deviate from routine work and emphasize on 'little things' with great accuracy. He left no stone unturned to achieve perfection. And, since Eddy left the police department in Lincoln, the destiny of his life was to live and to care for his mentor.

Robert Leansing III gladly volunteered his services at the restaurant on busy weekends. Marked by acne scars, his face showed an openhearted smile and an aquiline nose. With a small tight mouth he was borderline obese, somewhat weak in appearance, and he wore a peruke that was veering at a slope toward his right ear. His hands were sprinkled with liver spots. Being the embodiment of politeness and punctuality Bob had tact, intelligence and dignity and he was a 'fresh breeze' at *Le Cerisier.* He had an exuberant personality and charm that goes with genuine good nature. He was scrupulously clean about his person, and at all times impeccably dressed, *comme il faut* in a well-pressed matching black Armani suit, a shirt with a yellow and brown cravat secured with a silver pin and patent leather meticulously shined shoes. He seemed to know so well how to choose a fine tailor. And, since he had a tendency to perspire a lot, he always carried a small bottle of *eau de Cologne*. However his features as well as his clothes had a clerical cut, and occasionally he would affect an austere and puritanical air. Abysmally timid of girls he looked the very picture of a sensitive man. He had been a gay priest (actually defrocked) with a doctor of Divinity Degree, a DD in a gay church in Vermont. With his parishioners his *sensus fidelium* or liberty of conscience of others had been quite important to him. At all times he found great satisfaction with his continual preaching. Robert once revealed to me with the sublimity of his language: "Ambition is just selfish vanity. What is the good of a university education if it is not to be used for the glory of God?"

Although he was at all times with his nose in self-helped books, a twist of expression showed that trouble or remorse still fretted him. There were exaggerated feelings of guilt like he had weathered several stormy years. Looking at his eyes, one can observe an occasional shadow that never wholly disappeared as if a kind of self-suppression had left its mark. Earlier, in his youth he had made up his mind on the deeper questions of existence. Robert, well grounded in the Holy Scriptures has always been outspoken in proselytizing his faith with Ciceronian rhetorical principles, for he started nurturing his own views with little of the dogmatical kind. He would add, "Always remember this from Ecclesiastes: All is vanity, vanity and more vanity'" I was so fascinated by his wit and eloquence that I kept on hunging upon his lips with rapture. Musically gifted and excellent organ player, he was an obsessive reader as well who spoke quietly and contemptuously.

Leansing, a hyper sensitive person with ravishing manners, innocuous with a slightly defective hearing always tried fiercely, with great ingenuity to think of deeds to perform in a way to enhance his friendship in the eyes of his co-workers. There was in him a grace of a kindly nature with intellectual strength and such an imprinted gentleness in his heart. More than once, ladies took a liking of the priest and they even had tried to seduce him. Leansing had countless other virtues. As a former clergyman he did much good among the poor for he had been involved in Youngsters Rehabilitation Program, some charitable institutions and occupational counseling.

However, Robert had a serious physical weakness. With his poor range of audibility (Ménière syndrome), his proboscis didn't help either.

In the dining room, after wearing his stiff starched apron, in the presence of customers with his belly rumbling, he would belch like an MK 48, and almost blew the roof off the restaurant without any control of himself. Robert never showed the slightest realization of that grievous impediment.

On a particular evening, with such an outburst he broke wind at the table where Arthur was entertaining several business people over a bottle of *Veuve Cliquot*. The owner, quite embarrassed by the situation looked down at the carpet bemused and he retorted: "Bob, I can hear your creaking new shoes again!" There was a sudden wild excitement and an uncontrollable restlessness, and this would indulge lots of laughs amidst the men as the former priest poured more of that fine Champagne in their crystal flutes. Even that most of our clients were well-brought-up people, they loved pranks.

* * * *

At an early age, because of poor health I was delayed in my studies. Afterward, my parents sent me to a special school situated above the gorgeous Lake Geneva in Chamby near

Montreux, Switzerland. I stayed there for a full year. But in order to boost his earlier statement that he didn't discriminate Arthur who was buzzing like a fly in his malicious fancy regarding my infantile weakness would declare:

"Pierre is not really dangerous; he's just a happy idiot. He can understand anything. Pierrot had been very wild in his youth, a real problem child totally screwed-up: the dumbest of the dumb! At nine years old, sitting on a wooden horse, he thought he was Alexander the Great. He began to steal furtive glances at little girls and kept on beating them, clanging them with a rubber sword. Pierre was hated by all the mothers. Boys from his neighborhood pissed on his clothes and that made his own mother hysterical." Boisterous gusts of laughter would radiate from all tables at the restaurant. This would encourage the boss to continue maligning the story of my gender: "Next, my little friend here quite unbalanced became meaner and meaner, a real pest who constantly argued with his teacher and doing arm-pit farts in the classroom. At one time he ate suppositories, thinking they were candies-a real treat. Through *L'Oeuvre Nationale de l'Enfance,* a Belgian charity organization, Pierre who had flunked his exams before being kicked out from school was sent by a 'shrink' to a lunatic institutional care child institute in a remote area of Switzerland. Over there, he had been under the supervision of the Belgian baron Anatole Bompain who donated his estate to the children's fund."

Upon hearing this, as Arthur, laughing deep in his belly went wandering off to consort with other customers, I stammered as a dreamer would when awakened to factual reality. I tried to say something, but no words would come out and I hardly knew what to do. Prompted by what devilish inspiration I did not know, this man had blackened my character, had humiliated me and even slandered me. This was his way of finding relief for bitterness long repressed. I went outside. The atmosphere was stagnant and humid. Except for the moon in the sky, the entire neighborhood appeared to be in darkness. I felt lonely and the loneliness was intensified by the bark of a dog.

Back in the establishment, as I silently noticed Arthur's enjoyment of making a laughingstock out of me, I started thinking. And swiftly, deep inside I began to smile for I was privy to the fact that he was just covering up for his own insecurity and inadequacy, whatever they might be. As for the clients, most of Arthur's stories were far out of their customary orbit of interest. There were constant narratives of interminable length from the owner of the restaurant, but it could not make head or tail of what he was saying. However, with some kind of loving reverence, customers would listen to his bla...bla...bla... and, like good lawyers those same clients bestowed him polite attention.

Chapter 3

FREQUENTLY ARTHUR WAS practicing the cunning use of corruption. Here is a perfect example: On a busy evening a customer requested from Robert Leansing a bottle of wine, on the sweet side and not too cold. My colleague came back from the bar and opened a Gewürztraminer.

"Not sweet enough" retorted the old gentleman as he tasted the wine by rolling his tongue and gaping vacantly at the ceiling. "Let me check for something else" replied Leansing as he walked away toward the wine-refrigerator. However Arthur who was entertaining other patrons became aware of the situation with the displeased client. He followed Robert in his steps. Customers had hardly noticed my employer's reaction. Knowing full well as for the waiter's intention to get another bottle of wine, the little boss with a stare whose haughtiness froze charged as loose cannon as soon he saw Robert in the act of replacing the wine. Growling like an approaching storm Arthur quipped:

"Idiot, are you working for or against the house? Why don't you go back to your church! That's where you belong because you are a nuisance, absolutely incompetent and really not fit at all to be in this business?" Casting Leansing a devastating glance, in an almost insane violence he caught his arm and twisted it brutally before kicking him in the belly and on his leg. The blow was so strong that Robert almost felt to the ground. And Arthur uttered: "What you want me to do with that open-bottle of wine hey...! Tell me dumbbell?" At the top of his voice, with an expression of inquiry on his face, the boss, trying to cut Robert's self-esteem to pieces continued, "I ask you Most Reverend what are you doing with my profit here? Can you take it into your stupid head that a dollar saved is a dollar earned? I'm really fed up with calf's brain imbeciles such as you!"

Following more awful cursing Arthur grabbed the bottle from Leansing's hand and walked to the kitchen. Adding a spoonful of sugar into the wine he went on shaking the bottle and its contents. In a clever and cheating gimmick with some kind of fastidious but fake polished dignity the great liar went back to the customer's table. With a flush of triumph on his face he became so excited that a little saliva dripped down from his mouth as he spoke: "Sir, I am really sorry about the wine. Occasionally it can be corky or 'passed away' in flavor. I just opened another bottle of Gewürztraminer. I tasted it; it is sweet and at the perfect temperature. You'll definitely like it.'" After the client tinged the wine he proclaimed:

"It's perfect. Arthur, you are a good and honest person and I really appreciate your kindness. I knew I could always count on your excellent expertise and it is such an honor to have you as a friend. Now can you please join me for a glass of that excellent wine?"

Staring at the boss with bewildered eyes, Robert with his heart sinking down to the depth and still suffering from that blow below the ribs was shooked with righteous indignation as he shuddered from head to toe. Arthur had wounded his pride and disquieted his honor. Wiping the sweat from his drained and pale face my friend stood there in an almost religious silence, puzzled and outraged by such a disgruntled employer that was empty of all feelings. Holding on to a suppression of a nervous rage, in a gesture of subservience and with a convulsive smile that twitched his lips he vouchsafed not a single word since he could not think of anything to say.

However deep inside I already knew that Robert was still holding back an angry reply as never before had I seen him in such an intense state of repressed agitation. Wriggling humiliation had seriously tormented him. And later he conveyed to me:

"As God is my witness I'll murder him one of these day; I will stab his old carcase with a kitchen knife because I hate the bastard and I cannot endure his presence any longer!" Afterward Leansing uttered that famous sentence from Stendhal in The Charterhouse of Parma: *"It is better to kill the devil than to let the devil kill you."* On the other hand within Arthur's lies and inherent instability of character this had been Honoré de Balzac's *La Comédie Humaine* in full strength. My employer so much loved flattery, the little tap on the shoulder. *"My idea of an agreeable person is a person who agrees with me."*-Disraeli.

When patrons at the restaurant would tell him that he was lucky enough to have a quite successful restaurant, Arthur would reply: "Oh yes I'm one of the best-known restaurateurs in Southern California! It was never my intention to become a fat cat. Luck has nothing to do with it, and I'm not a gambler either." And with deep pride like Napoleon when he was on the apex of his power and triumph Arthur would proclaim that he was born with the emblem of greatness; owing to guts that regular people don't have.

Later on Robert Leansing, a good judge of character continued to plunge into dreadful despair. He became equally the recipient of the idiotic, tasteless demeanor of Monsieur

Arthur Valois Dourville de Montrissart who was using some sort of 'primal scream' annoying technique against him. At one time Leansing lost his coolness. Next, the former gay priest held me by the arm:

"Watch me Pierre; I'm going to beat the hell out of him." After he eyed the boss with his hands put together in a praying motion he drew a deep breath and quipped with a sort of grandiloquence and *sang froid* but with deadly politeness: "If you will pardon me sir, for all your intelligence you seem to have acquired little wisdom and as for a Christian that you claim to be you show a very non-Christian attitude. It seemed to me that you have lost touch with the world. So be careful that you don't commit unpardonable sins. You should repent for the wrongs you have done already. I'm praying not for my sake but for yours and I hope heaven would show mercy on your soul." Surprisingly the boss kept quiet; very quiet scared for that former clergyman reminded him he had a soul.

On another evening Arthur sat alone on a booth picking his nose. Subsequently to munching a tuna sandwich he started whining. At that moment, Leansing whispered to me: "Talk of the devil and you discover his meanest-looking horns. What's he hanging around here for?"

Nevertheless on one busy Saturday Robert was unable to take any more degradation from our employer's unerring instinct for manipulation. I knew very well it was coming. I knew it would happen as soon as Arthur had punched him on the stomach and leg over that bottle of wine. Leansng' spirit had been deeply agitated and he had reach a point at which he had felt he no longer could bear Arthur's depraved opinion 'puffed up by the tongues of flatterers' and dancing on the edge of such madness. Robert became really tired of the boss' domineering disposition to always go his own way while disregarding that of others. And looking at me, he started talking voluptuously: "I've shown a trusting naïveté with Arthur but I'm fed up with him. I won't be made a fool any longer!" Robert had wondered more than once whether he should or shouldn't stay at *Le Cerisier*.

But on that warm day, right in the middle of the service my friend with a restrained graceful impulsiveness simply untied his burgundy apron. He threw it at the owner's face and quickly moved his hands sideways in the same manner you would brush off a fruit fly from your shirt. Bearing in mind that Leansing was slow to anger, the anger came like firecracker. It seemed that all the disdain and contempt that had been festering in his heart for so long had abruptly boiled to the surface. The former priest was feeling himself driven like a cloud of fire coming down from heaven. With all the passion of an emotion too long bottled, all his worries safely immured in deepness came rushing to the forefront of his head and with unparalleled courage he told Arthur what was on his mind. Robert, with the eloquence of his irreproachable morality was now gazing at my employer with such intensity. From the depths of his lungs, after snapping his fingers those were his ultimate words before he directed himself to the kitchen back door leading to the parking lot:

"Arthur, you're a wretched scoundrel, a monster of depravity and a real apostle of corruption. You are a drunk and a lunatic who never showed any decency. And now this place is turning like a cesspool of immorality. You're a coward and a fraud as well. With your tyrannical and vulgar conduct of a satanic reveler nobody could long retain his reason working in such an environment. I even started doubting my own identity!" Shaking his head in exasperation Robert drew a deep breath, and in an almost calm voice with faintly quivering lips he went on to chastise Arthur: "Because of your haughty and grotesque attitude, *Le Cerisier* has become an idiotic, mad circus; a *Grand Guignol!* And I can tell you right now that I don't trust you, never has and never will. I would much rather go and work in a coffee shop than to stay here for another day! And one last thing; God forgive me but you can kiss my arse!" Arthur didn't move. He remained in that sentinel posture with an expressionless countenance. He hated Robert's speech given so nonchalantly in front of the entire *Le Cerisier* team. The boss was in one of the abstract silent moods common to him when he was deeply upset. Curiously, at that precise moment my own misery seemed to have eased a great deal.

As Bob left the stage at *Le Cerisier* as his conscience dictated it I gave him credit for his honorable behavior; for his standpoint of human goodness will remain. This honest human being with notable merit had shown himself to be warm-hearted. He was not only a fine human being, but a friend as well. He had been highly esteemed and respected; the ablest and bravest employee we ever had…

We no longer heard from Robert. To this day I still cheer one of his maxims: "When I feel low I always try to get contentment."

Leansing's abrupt departure had an unusual effect on Arthur. On Monday we found him in a very quiet, subdued mood and standing there like a tailor's dummy. The boss was exceptionally calm, sober but haggard; quite different from last Saturday. He showed uncharacteristic courtesy and a genuine smile. Arthur had become amiable and charming as never before. A cloud of stillness and a sense of serenity had descended upon the entire restaurant as a heavy load had been taken off my mind. There was a ray of hope, a sigh of relief in the air. I was so pleased to catch the boss in a good mood. My employer, now breathlessly silent, started to gaze benevolently at the carpet before pacing back and forth the entire length of the building.

With several years of experience at his side I was able to read his thoughts and looked right through him. I firmly believed that Arthur's new attitude greatly helped to ease his conscience. But again I asked myself the question: Is Arthur making just a pretense of being sociable? In the back of my mind I had still the strange feeling that he was apparently drawing back in order to leap better- just like a man that caresses a rabbit before he breaks its neck. I already knew that he was a man capable of the most villainies, lurking around and taking pleasure by routinely intimidated his friends, family and faithful employees. With ungovernable fits of temper and supercilious sarcasm full of stormy passion he sometimes would rise for his own evil ends. But, contrary to all expectations Arthur's changed attitude was attuned to a gentlemanly unruffled stand. Smiling with good humor my employer seemed more well-mannered now and he teased me less. I even had the feeling that he laughed with me and not at me. Arthur appeared to be inclined to atone for his many misdeeds by an actual kindness of behavior.

First my colleagues and I little trusted a change so sudden, the reason for which we could not comprehend and we were all wondering whether he was shifting his approach for good or trying to show remorse for the way he had treated Robert? For awhile Arthur peacefully stood by the front door, again, contemplating the carpet-floor pensively, arms crossed on his chest in his best and most tranquil temper. After another stretch of awkward silence Arthur passed on to matters where I would be even more at peace. He kept looking at me in a reflective sort of way. He even patted my shoulder as he was paying me a compliment, and his voice grew gentle. Later on I watched with skepticism how he excitedly bragged to the customers about my world travels and eventually had a book published about such exhilarating experiences.

To our surprise, feeling slightly embarrassed as one does when one changes his mind over a good deed, the owner of the restaurant put in an appearance of goodwill and cooperation and decided to work with us. Wearing an apron over his suit Arthur looked at us with the belief of a father trying to satisfy his children and he became a bundle of energy. He was laborious and passionate as he let himself be overworked like a bee in the hive with a superabundance of vitality, cleaning tables and taking orders, burning his candle at both ends. From an alcoholic he became a workaholic, panting and perspiring all over with the work. And, in a burst of creative energy my employer personally decided to prepare his own recipe of cherries jubilee at a customer's table. At the end of the day he was more dead than alive.

But in a way the turmoil that had been going on in my mind before Leansing's departure was nonteless present: "*Was I going to put up with this man and stick to him more like a fly to honey or quit like my confrère Robert did?* I was still really tired of Arthur's bitter laughs and sneers that made people shake their heads; a sneer at anything which could be called good! The entire Christmas holiday I pondered over that question and thought of nothing else. As I went back to work I finally decided to try 'the patience of Job' and resolved to be the bigger person. Holding my head high I would follow the straight and narrow path of Gandhi, as he spoke to his people regarding the atrocities perpetuated by the British soldiers: "Accept the beatings and love them deeply." I would prove to Arthur that long-suffering nature would not necessarily rebel or rise up in storm. And, in a fleeting moment my mind drifted back in time to a few old memories…

The year was 1958, mid December. In the encroaching morning light, in a wild gust of wind and rain spitting in my face at the *Citadelle de Diest* I enlisted with the Belgian paratroopers. In the same manner as the French Foreign Legion and the "Semper Fidelis" U.S. Marines we were known as one of the toughest unit in the world. Prior to the flight to the ex-Belgian Congo (now the Democratic Republic of Congo), Captain Jean-François Delperdange, the son of the famed archaeologist colonel Jacques Delperdange stopped me in the middle of the courtyard as I leisurely squandered after having fed our two wild boar mascots.

The high cheek-boned and blazing baby blue eyed captain with clipped military mustache who wore an impeccably cut and tight-fitting uniform was gifted with good looks. He was a striking and commanding figure, extremely handsome. I felt struck with the dignity of his appearance. Just like his father- a *bourgeois élite*, aside from nobility and wealth he had a strong desire as in the time of Louis XV for military honor. This aristocratic dandy captain was surnamed 'the iron man', sardonic and ruthless.

Unexpectedly without hesitation the officer smacked me very hard on the face to which I responded hastily with a salute. Captain Delperdange had been quick and erect in his movement. Sounding a little bit embarrassed he stroked his mustache and gave it a twist. The captain remained standing before me for a few seconds. Next, resuming an air of importance after saluting back at a group of military men walking by, he inquired in that soldierly spirit:

"Choucart, I have been an officer for so long and have met generations of *bleus* (new recruits). Most of them have hated me but you are the exception. I hit you and you gave me the impression that it didn't bother you; you even smiled. Why is that?" I simply replied that I knew it was his duty to turn us into real men and that I was aware it was part of the training in order to boost our moral and endurance and to be ready to confront straining torture if we had to. For a moment the officer, wiping the perspiration which had dripped down his face lost his military bearing.

From that day on no matter what problem would come up I believed I could handle it. With a sort of sublime ecstasy I radiated like a magnetic field, ready for any adversity or prosperity in life. I had a belief in fate that ran deep. I also recalled those powerful and wise words from our major-chaplain: "Even that you are now tough para-commandos please never harden your hearts!" Enlivened with a fine spirit I started to inscribe in my daily journal remembering what Fr. William McNamara said as he was defining high creativity in some difficult moments: *"When you live in tension that is the best possible atmosphere for high creativity. That's where the void is and that's where God is-in between. We need a two-eyed view. Otherwise there will be no charge, no electricity, there will be no joy."*

Marcel Proust with his set of seven novels *Remembrance of Things Past* was very influential in my life as a young student. Even that, during his difficult time in life, as he cloistered himself for thirteen years in his soundproofed (with cork) apartment, Proust found real joy in high creativity.

Yet I didn't know that with the slow parade of seasons I would be dealing with much more unpredictable and severe human behavior. Now my life was spinning out of control. I became Arthur's *cheval de bataille* and the most unfortunate ill-treated employee. I got the feeling that my employer took a vow to be disagreeable to me.

The week after, a special exhibition showed up at the Convention Center in Los Angeles. It was the Soviet Union Expo. Everything Russian was on display; from the gigantic bronze statue of Vladimir Ilyich Lenin depicting the cultural patterns of the 1917 revolution to the *Sputnik,* urban modernization and…propaganda.

At *Le Cerisier* among customers this particular event was a great subject of conversation. Arthur was with me in the kitchen as I entreated him about the exposition I visited earlier at its opening ceremony. However, during our exceptional little chat we didn't pay any attention to Chef Picharon who was feverishly waiting for me to pick up a hot plate of food standing on the warm shelf to be served to one of our patrons. With sweat showing under his armpits, smoke blew out of the chef's nose. As a kettle was gently simmering above the gas-flame, to our astonishment Picharon unexpectedly dropped his pants; turned around and tapped his hairy butt saying:

"Au nom de Dieu here is your Soviet Expo! I want this dish to go out immediately, pronto!" Arthur with an expression of utter despair and in order to please Picharon added his own comment: "Hey dumbbell what you waiting for?"

* * * *

Occasionally Arthur requested from me a special favor but always in a disagreeable fashion:

"Pierre, I still have seven filets de sole in the refrigerator. I'm going to eat one of them *belle meunière* style. However by tomorrow or the day after they won't be fresh any longer, and I would have to throw away the remaining six" and he concluded: "If you don't sell those fishes tonight you pay for it and I am serious!" Knowing he was about to lose his investment the stony hearted employer was blowing steam and wanted me to pay for his mistake of over-purchasing those filets. Throughout the years the trickster never admitted a mistake. He always pointed the blame to his employees including members of his own family that helped *Le Cerisier* land a top spot in the Los Angeles Best Restaurant Guide.

It was an exceptionally quiet evening. As I flicked a glance at my wristwatch, eight o'clock rolled around and I didn't sell a single filet de sole. After that from time to time while pacing back and forth in the dining room I continued casting a furtive look at the grandfather's clock that stood there like a sentinel.

At exactly closing time for the kitchen as the bells of Our Lady of Grace's church clanged in the darkness, striking nine Heaven must have heard my silent prayer throughout the evening and a miracle happened. I heard the squeaky front door swing open and six Japanese businessmen bowing to the earth with their backs stooped marched in. *Thank you God* I thought they looked like angels with their white faces and smiley eyes. The angels were starved and wanted to enjoy a good dinner before heading to Los Angeles Airport for their Trans-Pacific flight back to Osaka. They stayed at the nearby Princess Hotel and had walked out from a black limo parked in front of *Le Cerisier.*

During my prolonged saga round the globe I worked for awhile in a private school at the Chiba Prefecture in Japan as an English-conversation teacher (and now all my students from the Bissan Nahouchi Chemical Factory speak good English with a strong French accent.) As I had learned the rudiments of the Japanese language I thus introduced myself to our tardy customers:

"Dōmo arigatō gozaimasu.Watakushi wa Pierre-zuu dezu."

The vernacular was a little rusty yet my attention was caught and I received a warm acclaim including another solemn low bow. One of them even shook my hand. Surprisingly all of my Oriental clients requested a Budweiser as a start. Working in partnership, I conferred to Leon: 'Six Buds!' As they drank their beer, they were exchanging written notes and looking at some files. As they were gabbling in that foreign tongue, the most talkative one that appeared to be the Chief Executive Officer entreated me regarding our extended menu:

"What best salad in kitchen?" I replied:

"Mushroom salad, specialty of the house." The man showed six fingers and I wrote down "6 MS." As for the main course he shouted in the prettiest broken English and French I ever heard:

"What's *hitotsu*, number one for *plat du jour?*" This time with an anticipated smile I announced "*Filets de sole* excellent fish: number one!"

"*Pierre-San, dozo*: six number one O.K."

Later on, my friendly Japanese customers who really enjoyed their meals kept on looking at their watches. It was time to board their limo for the airport. In a simple dignified manner they rose from their seats and again, after more bows; the sweetest bows I ever seen they retired.

Bearing in mind that I sold the remaining fishes I went to meet Arthur, feeling a ray of happiness and expecting at least a 'thank you.' But the boss never gave me any token of sympathy for what I did. Again he was in a cruel, bestial disposition. He looked like one of those dangerous dogs waiting to jump at someone. And just as he had been touched with senile dementia, with slumbering sadism in his eyes, that ungrateful man demoniacally hit me hard with his pocketbook. Afterward he seized me violently by the collar. Arthur held me by the neck like a cat and tweaked my ears a bit. Furthermore he spat at my hair, rubbed his hands in it saying:

"Pierre here is your reward; this is the best shampoo money can buy!"

With a demon stirring inside him my agent provocateur, that miserable reptile of a lower order has now become a psychopath and sometimes I thought his brain had ceased to function! It would have been the same if Arthur had stabbed me in the heart as the pulses in my temples were beating like sledgehammers. Again, I was deeply humiliated and angry. That utterly uncivilized person, that self-hatred pygmy hopelessly vulgar was as empty of human sentiments as the emptiness of the galaxy's edge. A jungle animal could have behaved better than him! He was a man who had no more feelings than a butcher in front of a piece of meat about to be cut. Only by hate Arthur was able to disarray himself from love. Every so often I tried to forget those stupidities but the little boss would come back day after day showing more callous bearings.

At that juncture as I took out my handkerchief to wipe a spot on my forehead I recalled the words of the great Kosinski in *The Painted Bird*, and I found this correlation: *"I was treated no less than an abused dog...when I failed to answer a question he would hit me...I quivered and sweated with fear as the blows rained one after another...he tormented me ceaselessly in his seemingly unmotivated fits of rage and on other occasions he was beating me harder than usual... my shoulders were becoming numb...it was a strange, dull, penetrating pain and each day he invented new ways of persecuting me as the world seemed to close over my head like a massive stone vault."* There was scarcely an evening in which Arthur showed a bad attitude. As for this faithful employee each day would represent a new challenge in life. Yielding gracefully to my employer, with no particular skills I really had no other place to go. I learned to be calm whenever the storm hit and fearless under menaces and frowns. I experienced upside-downs yet I developed a mind that made constant corrections. The good part is that I could immerse myself contently in the daily routine to please my customers as I unraveled good relationship with them. A few even regarded me as their personal friend like the famed

actor Kelsey Grammar playing the hilarious shrink doctor on
the number one TV show. Kelsey always greeted me warmly
with that French touch accent:

"*Bonjour Pierrrrre;* today I will have that crrrrrrispy duck
à l'orange."

On a particular evening another one of those friends, an
old client who was a man of simple and delightful character
whispered wholeheartedly in my ear that I shouldn't let myself
get so damned uncomfortable or be laughed at by a selfish
and unscrupulous employer; that there are many places where
folks would treat me right. The old man that was speaking
with the prudence which age and experience confer added
that I didn't merit that kind of hostility; that Arthur was
more of a fool than even he thought he was. He concluded
that my employer had never shown me any gratitude for what
I have done for him. All he did was to talk about himself.
Afterwards, putting down his knife and fork and with his hand
resting on my shoulder, he conveyed: "Pierre, you have good
blood. In the legal profession one meets all kinds of people
but none as so special as you. You're likable and easy going,
quiet and observant. However you're too modest as to your
own intelligence. You have such a contagious cheerfulness as
you always reach for moral beauty. I really believe you should
be in charge here. So many people hate their jobs, but even
with that kind of a boss around you you seemed to enjoy your
work" and he continued:

"I know you are more than just a waiter; you are a
psychologist and I feel good talking to you. Back in the Old
Continent you must have been trained so differently to be
able to work for such a man as Arthur? You should not go to
waste under the whims of an imbecile employer. I know that
aside of being tormented by a creep you breathed your own
interesting life. You have been eating the dust for so long. On

the other hand you already lived a glorious life by travelling the world with a small backpack. I have to confess that besides my enviable executive position at the bank I have a restless wish to discover all the continents like you did."

After such a sincere and warm revelation, this CEO customer with much sensitive feelings reassured me by adding that without that buffoon Arthur, that ill-mannered churlish clown of a boss going around tables with his stupid demeanor and BS tales, *Le Cerisier* would be the best dining place in Southern California.

* * * *

Mistaken identification can happen in the most unusual places. Tonight, after I took care of 'a party of two' Arthur appeared very concerned:

"Pierre we have a problem. The customer from table seven left without paying his bill. I know him well; and after eating he usually ended up at *The Red Arrow* bar from across the street. I want you to go to *The Red Arrow* and ask for that client to come and take care of his check at *Le Cerisier.*" and he went on: "You won't have any difficulty finding him: remember: tall, white hair, always wearing a brown suit, a cream shirt and light brown tie."

I dashed to the well-illuminated place and was there in no time. A bull's head that looked rather ferocious stood above the main entrance of the Red Arrow Bar. I experienced no difficulty in locating the customer. There he was, sitting at the bar; white hair, brown suit, cream shirt, light brown tie, and... quite drunk. As he continued sipping at his dry martini I noticed that his eyes seemed to be without depth after so much alcohol consumption. I waved at the barman and we started a swift conversation in a corner of the room.

With the unfortunate embarrassment of the situation and in order to avert suspicion I was mistaken I requested the worker behind the bar to talk to our drunkard. Showing gestures of impatience he narrowed his eyes on the man and in a low tone of voice he immediately summoned the lone customer to follow me to *Le Cerisier* and settle his account.

"Okay...hic... I'm coming!" We crossed Ventura Boulevard at a turtle's pace. I almost had to drag him to the other side as he kept showing the finger to drivers who didn't even slow down their cars. They just zoomed on by with horns blaring steadily. There were no other pedestrians than us to brave that crazy gridlock. Suddenly a red light caused brakes screeching in all directions. And as the light changed I had to wave frantically to get the traffic to slow down. I managed to get the man safely to *Le Cerisier*. Had he crossed the boulevard by himself under the influence of hard liquor he could have been knocked down by a passing car without even seeing it.

At the restaurant, Arthur first thought of nothing whatsoever as he kept on staring intensely at that person. For my employer this seemed to be like an apparition. After he recovered his senses, a few seconds of silence prevailed and a worried gaze surfaced on Arthur's brow. His eyes grew distressed and it appeared that he was almost seized by an apoplectic stroke. I noticed that he was in no fit mood for merriment. With a frightful contraction that distorted the corners of his mouth the boss leaped over at me like a wild animal to his prey. Dropping his voice to a low whisper, on a verge of an outbreak of hysteria he retorted:

"*Imbécile, ce n'est pas lui-* I don't know what came over you but it's not him!" And with a trifle of hesitation I said: "Well... uh... according to the description, I thought..."

"You thought wrong stupid Brussels' sprout head!"

The intoxicated client didn't even pay attention to our little chatter. His mouth hung open as he struggled to open his wallet, revealing an amalgam of credit cards as he was mumbling in a slurred speech: "Where is my check? I…hic… want to take care of it right away…hic"

Gazing at Arthur's strange smile I knew the thought had already flashed across his mind to have the man pay for that bill. So with the ill-fated embarrassment of the situation I took the initiative of telling the unfortunate gentleman that a mistake had been made; that he never set foot in this place before. The chef, who couldn't resist taking a peek at what was going on decided to provide the man with a bowl of hot onion soup to sober him. Afterwards our stranger lodged the wallet in his trousers' back pocket and took a nap on a booth in the private room before departing.

At closing time a tall white-haired man in a brown suit, cream shirt and light brown tie walked in and appeared clearheaded. Even that his face was more high-boned this was *déjà vu* all over. Was he the twin brother of the man I had fetched earlier at *The Red Arrow?* Now with a kind of embarrassment he started to apologize: "Arthur I'm so sorry. I just remember that I forget to pay my bill earlier. Please can you get me a Virgin Mary? Oh, and for you, let me guess…a bourbon and Coke? Just add it on my tab."

* * * *

Today is another day and Arthur found another way to wound my self-respect once more. Unfortunately I went to work wearing a pair of pants with a slight tear that was hardly visible. It wasn't intentional on my part. It happened just as I was getting out of my automobile. With a blast of cold wind in the face as summer drew to an end all of a sudden I realized that my left pocket got caught on the inside door handle causing this to occur. It wasn't a big deal for my apron would have concealed it and I would have fixed the damage first thing in the morning. Arthur's ever roving eyes immediately noticed that rend. Drawing his eyebrows together with a wink and slight pinching of the lips this insecure and neurotic man got hold of the damaged pocket and with a sort of malevolent spirit ripped it totally. With my 'Fruit of the Loom' underwear in view to everyone in the kitchen he continued to rip and rip my pants until they dropped down on the floor like a filthy shapeless rag. After that Arthur uttered a scornful laugh and started pirouetting on his septuagenarian heels leaping up and down over what was left of my garment. Next he threw a very mean look at me and started spitting and cursing; cursing at me with words I don't intend to repeat. As his face became distorted into an expression of hatred, he struck-up a bad song that was originally created by students at *La Sorbonne* Campus:

> *"Ah la salope, va laver ton cul malpropre,*
> *Car il n'est pas propre tirelire,*
> *Car il n'est pas propre tirela…"*

(Ah you dirty woman go and wash your behind because you're so unclean, tirelire, because you're so unclean, tirela…) As I lingered there crushed and stupid I could not stop myself from pondering on the question, "Was this for real or was I dreaming?"

Subsequent to that crude exhibition my employer thrusting his fingers up his nose ordered me to get a new pair of pants at once adding that nobody, but nobody is going to work in his four star restaurant with damaged slacks. That cold, rude man with so much disenchantment with life kept on torturing my mind bitterly. Putting on a pair of jogging shorts that I fortunately always kept in my locker I drove to the C&R, a local men's store located on Sepulveda Boulevard. It was closing time but the manager let me in and I purchased a pair of brand new pants- the perfect fit.

Back at *Le Cerisier* after I had been hurt in the heart to unavoidable extremes more than I had imagined, Arthur who had settled comfortably in a booth in the dining room looked at me with his elbow on his knee and his chin in his hand. Raising his head and searching in my eyes for a sign of sympathy he announced in a savage enjoyment:

"Petit Pierre now you are so clean, neat and handsome, I'm really proud of you!" I noticed upon his face a peculiar expression of ecstasy. The entire episode was so ugly; simply a mean and devilish deed. This had been the worst kind of degradation so far. Everything had been so base and vile and Arthur had conducted himself no less than a mad dog.

Chapter 4

DURING EVENING TIME after Melanie was done with her work at the law firm she would casually drop by the restaurant for a lively time. In order to entertain some loyal customers and personal friends she would spin stories with utter imagination that would ridicule me. Aside from that chronic back pain from disc herniation, her mental attitude had a translucent clearness. I truly believe that she inherited this trait from Arthur. I had a feeling that from father to daughter a family's moral degeneration had persisted. She walked just like Arthur, taking short hasty steps. Being the dominant character of the household, next to her dad, Melanie swiftly conned in her mind the more dazzling passages of her quaintness. She would talk about specific events or trivial things, carrying a charming but cruel finesse to amuse the patrons with the dream of fancy. With increasing gravity, she first laughed at herself over a few throat-clearing raps. Her laugh was rather hard and mocking. And, with her body erect in the posture of an Egyptian princess, she said: "The police stopped Pierre for driving in an erratic manner after he jounced over a pothole. He had been weaving all over the road, non stop for a mile or so. But they let him go without giving him a ticket because they would have to carry a load of paperwork, a 50/51 as they call it. The 50/51 is reserved only for retarded people." Melanie's fictional story would elicit amusement from our regular clients; however I personally found the joke in bad taste. I felt as if she was twisting a knife in my belly. Just like her father, with *le diable au corps*, the devil inside she knew that those kinds of quips were really out of place, but she continued. Melanie was sharp like *un cheval de prise* and soon with excitement leaping inside her, and energetic eloquence 'the pretty little thing' was shuffling her cards again before she continued with increasing vehemence to pour more oil on the fire. As her body righted itself and with her hand that slightly trembled with pleasure the young lady with a raised chin would start on a new bout of oratory. Her annoyance persisted and she recalled another incident. 'Arthur's princess' received a similar reaction as she narrated with a theatrical voice a tale about me when I was invited to a wedding in Santa Barbara:

"On the return trip to Los Angeles, being light-headed with too much champagne Pierre was zigzagging on the freeway. A patrolman stopped him and directed him to the side of the road:

"Officer I can explain everything," he said. The man in uniform definitely noticed Pierre's strange behavior, he then asked for his driver's licence and proof of insurance. After a moment, in a quiet voice he announced: "Mr. Choucart, past the hill straight ahead on your right there is an IHOP restaurant," and he added: "This time I will save you a ticket. But please after you rest for awhile since you look a bit under the weather have a cup of coffee and be careful when you are back behind the wheel." Next, while tasting the sweetness of her triumph Melanie continued in a screech of mirth: "Again Pierre got no fine, just a sympathetic tap on the shoulder from a compassionate cop." The same customers in the dining room would experience such a great source of enjoyment that a few began to hiccup. After telling her stories with such ardor there were endless encores.

Before long Mademoiselle Melanie, with so much amusement in her eyes came up with a different story that would make the bemused clients fall off their chair. They were guffawing; some with tears of joy trickling down their cheeks as she resumed:

"After work, on a busy Friday night Pierre went home to his apartment on Vineland Boulevard in North-Hollywood and parked his old beat-up Buick in the carport. He stopped the engine and fell asleep like 'a babe in arms' right on that spot with the car's headlights still on. An hour later he woke up startled and pushed on the brake-pedal to the floor believing he was on the road about to hit a wall!" As Melanie was displaying her pleasure, *en veux-tu, en voilà,* without end, an old lady chuckled and got her soup coming out of her nose as she burst in a strange and comical convulse. The clients in the entire dining room lay down their knives and forks and kept on laughing from ear to ear unretrainedly till the ceiling shook.

To this point it looked as if it never once entered Melanie's delicate head that she was making an odd fish out of me. Now, for *le coup de grâce*: "Finally what can you expected from this booby who decided during vacation time to swim in the ocean off the coast of Chile during the harsh Antarctic winter? Pierre had no idea what the water temperature was; yet he swam in the midst of penguins! (Big laughs again.) On that glacial day as women were covering themselves with furs he came out from his swim purple-blue, kicking his feet against the rocks because of that burning sensation when the freezing went deep!"

Well I have to assert that the story was quite accurate. Once ashore the cold that had frozen my cheeks was so intense that my head was throbbing with pain. For some time I was beating my hands together to warmed them.

Rather than losing my composure I joined the crowd in the dining room that experienced such a source of good humor. As a Frenchman with carefully styled graying hair grabbed my arm, he commented: *"Ah Pierre, tu es vraiment unique…!*

Next to my encounter with the Magellanic penguins so rigorously described by Melanie I continued on that same vacation year to unwind in South America. Subsequent from climbing the rocky path of the Cordillera of Andes I went on by bus to the sun-drenched tropical *Foz de Iguazu* (Iguasu Falls) in Brazil. From far away one can hear the roar of the shimmering waterfall and its raging torrent as toucans and other water birds abound everywhere. I was on my way to meet my Christian missionary daughter and son-in-law stationed in Ciudad Del Este, Paraguay. Afterward, I meandered through lush rainforests, some already badly defoliated, and smoked a water pipe of *yerba mate*. Away from the waterfall among cluster of trees, the strong fragrance of woods filled the air. With so many lotus, faint whispers of hidden trickles of running water were to be seen everywhere among colonies of other unusual rare plants.

This time along with newfound friends in their Cherokee 4x4, on a winding road that resembled more of a trail, going north toward the Paraguayan border we stopped for lunch in a clearing. Stones were left there from a previous fire and lizards were sunbathing without any fear. The jungle was sighing, crying out, and in no time we were amused by a pack of little black Howler monkeys chattering, when suddenly one of them, the tallest set out to throw his excrements at the others. With their faces full of 'poop' and their nasty gustatory sensation flies were grazing, together with other insect sibilance. Next with a quizzical look the black monkeys wiped their mouths with the back of their hairy hands, and as they nodded at each other they developed a ferocious temper. Flashing their teeth they expressed their displeasure by growling threateningly. The grossly comical episode brought a smile on my face as I remembered the mean boss at the restaurant throwing mud at his dedicated employees. Certainly, one would be able to identify Arthur with the tall black Howler monkey!

While in the South American continent, during the same vacation I took the pleasant habit along with my daughter and son-in-law to drink my morning *yerba mate*-herb tea. That powerful rainforest drink really boosted physical energy as it likewise helps stimulate focus and clarity for its high amount of amino acids and antioxidants. That bitter, but very healthy beverage made from South American Atlantic rainforest leaves: *Ilex Paraguariensis* with its rejuvenated effects is revered from Argentina to Paraguay, to Bolivia and Brazil by rainforest people as 'the drink of the gods.' This is the kind of tea you slowly sip from a *popote*-a sort of a pipe with a strainer at the end...

Back in California I was extremely pleased to discover a company who with their co-founding partner sustainably harvested organic yerba mate. So I bought some and hid it inside a drawer in the dining room.

At *Le Cerisier* restaurant when for the very first time Arthur saw me sipping the juice from this tropical herb, he falsely accused me of drinking a powerful drug just for the pleasure of him to entertain and make our customers laugh once more. Even that my health had improved with those herbs my employer continued to harass me stipulating that I had become completely 'loco', with all sorts of crazy things running in my head and that I was almost ready for the hospice. Melanie accentuated her father's lies by suggesting that from being a total nut I was not even be trusted to go to the bathroom alone.

However on a warm afternoon day that engulfed the entire San Fernando Valley I arrived at *Le Cerisier* earlier than usual. After I opened the door, classical music flooded in the air. The red curtains from the private room were drawn and I heard a conversation. No one even had heard the sound of my latch-key. I stopped as I drew closed. Arthur and his assistant Eddy Freedman just finished sipping their *yerba mate*. Apparently Arthur had found my reserve of those herbs that I always left inside a drawer on the marble topped-desk and along with Eddy they had secretly tried the 'drink of the gods' concoction.

Now the boss staring at me with astonishment articulated: "Imbecile, you're not supposed to be here at this time of day!" A while later from a side corner of the main dining room Eddy confided to me that twice he took an infusion of the rainforest herb tea adding he never felt better; that he no longer had indigestion problems and that the stiffness in his neck was gone. He concluded by declaring: "Pierre, forget about those silly attacks from Tutur: altogether he has changed his mind too and he enjoy the yerba mate for his gout."

* * * *

With his advanced age Arthur had spells of absent-mindedness characterized as: Transient Global Amnesia or lost of memory that can last a few minutes or several hours. He would either forget or confuse identities of people. His recollection of recent events and situations, name of places and persons has been eluding him. There was always in Arthur's mind a puzzling multitude of faces to most of which he could not put a name. With his problematic memory he would stare at a customer sitting at a corner table and whispering in my ear he would say:

"Pierre, watch over there, do you recognize Mr.…What's-his-name again I couldn't place him?"

Yesterday an unfamiliar customer came in the restaurant and Arthur's attention was momentarily distracted by this new arrival. He stopped in the middle of the dining room and kept on looking with the utmost curiosity into the client's eyes. The boss had a harsh expression as if he tried to remember something. First he was furious with himself for his lack of memory. Afterward with eagerness utterly unmistakable Arthur scanned him sternly once again. My employer kept on staring at the visitor, looking at him inquiringly like one who searches for some lost piece to a puzzle. And, dropping his voice confidentially, after another stretch of silence he uttered in my ear: "I remember now: I have seen him twice before." The man had not shaved for a fortnight. With his bony nose, strikingly narrow forehead, dark eyebrows and bitter-sweet smiling lips Arthur believed he was an old customer that he would least expect to meet again for he had settled in New York long ago. He seemed so delighted to see that client whom he appeared to know so well. He had been one of the smartest persons he had ever met. Focusing at me once more Arthur articulated:

"Yes, I know him by sight as well as I know my own father. His name is Craig." A few moments later, surprisingly my employer advanced closer toward him with his hands outstretched. He then bestowed the customer a bear hug and kissed him on both cheeks: "Craig, I've thought so much of you lately. I've been longing to see you again. It has been awhile since your last visit at *Le Cerisier* and I really miss you. You haven't changed at all except for that wig you're wearing; it's almost undetectable! Tell me: what brings you in town?"

Through the veil of confusion as he appeared short sighted with an embarrassing sour and discontented face, the blond-bearded man with prominent eyeballs veined with blood appearing haggard stood more erect. He stared at Arthur in total bewilderment. First he was baffled how to respond. Walking a few steps backward, a pace like a crab with an absent-minded shake of the head he conveyed:

"Sir, this isn't Craig. My name is Joshua Nierumberger. This is the first time I set foot in here and just between us: this is my real hair! Now let me ask you a question: who the hell are you?" After introducing himself; without another word Arthur's tongue glued to the roof of his palate. For a few seconds he stood there, his mouth hunging open like a braying donkey. Being much confused, he frowned and blushed as he maintained a deadly silence. Chewing his lip with that near-martyred expression the boss fluttered away like a bird with a broken wing. Turning on his heel he stalked out the door for awhile.

On another occasion my employer congratulated a 'so-called' British actor. He was bald with a heavy mustache and bushy whiskers encroached over his cheeks very much British soldiery-Major Thompson-style:

"Sir," said Arthur "your face is not unknown to me. I remember you from the screen as you played the role of a general during the occupation of India. If I recalled correctly it was in the movie *The Four Feathers*."

The gentleman had such a great laugh by telling Arthur in a thick Italian accent that he was just a Sicilian from Chicago on a visit in California. Later he was to meet his brother Giovanni in El Monte. Once more, quite embarrassed and appearing as stupid as a baby on its potty, Arthur with his lips quivering faintly and a face that had stiffened into lockjaw fled with his tail between his legs as he stammered out incoherent words.

Some time ago as he bent down to stretch his socks I noticed that my employer was wearing a purple sock on one foot and a blue Navy sock on the other. Oh well, they almost matched!

Being so chronically disorganized, Eddy acting more like his confessor kindly reminded Arthur that it was time for him to consult an eye doctor or a specialist of the mind who could analyze his brain. For that observation Eddy was rewarded with a slap on the face from his dear friend. Freedman first darted out for his hand but the boss was too quick for him.

Arthur would spend time hunting tirelessly for his reading glasses (actually resting on his forehead) or a set of keys (lying in his pocket.) At one time the boss kept on foraging inside his attaché-case not knowing what he was looking for. This reminded me of a Corsican joke: "From sunrise to sundown that old farmer from Ajaccio kept on searching for Pipino, his brown horse to finally realize that he sat on Pipino at all times and never left him!" My employer was really an uncontestable champion in regard to those many *faux pas*. Frequently he had such a confusing mind that even the Devil couldn't make head or tail of it! As he walked from the kitchen to the dining room he frequently no longer knew what he had come for. Drinking had equally blunted his powers of awareness and sometimes I wonder how he remembered that his head is on his shoulders. As he erected his neck it seemed that he had lost the head that belongs on it?

* * * *

In the biography of *Madame de Staël*, a brilliant authority expressed himself this way: "...*it is generally felt that women are better educated than men, outside of the great professions. And why not, since they have more leisure for literary pursuits than men."*

Occasionally Lady Olborough a well-known British science-fiction author born with the components for mastery with her pulse-quickening novel would come for dinner at *Le Cerisier* wearing that now familiar flowery dress and white hat topped with a pink feather. On the very confines of middle age, not embittered by solitude she was still pretty in a certain sentimental way graceful too with still elegant hands and her great pride of bearing that always enchanted me. Though a slight slackness of her throat one can only see that once upon a time she had been utterly beautiful. She preferred to sit by herself in a small booth far away from the front door.

This evening she was back, wearing a smart London gown. As I was about to recite the special menu, Lady Olborough with an absolute stillness of her head and features reached for my hand. With much nobleness and a face still luminous, she spoke: "Pierre, last time I was here I heard about the book that you wrote. Leon provided me with such a lengthy description about your saga around the world that I went to Barnes and Noble and got myself a copy of your work. I carry it in my purse and later I would love you to autograph it." Noticing we were having a hearty *tête-à-tête*, Arthur slowly inched his way toward us and before long he was within hearing distance from us. Lady Olborough looked at me straight in the eye with intensity and self-assurance that comes with age. After giving me a great open smile she proclaimed with candor:

"Your book possesses that certain blend of literary genius which reminds me of Hemmingway's perception that 'good writers are also a little bit crazy!'" and she continued, "Pierre, after I read your book I realized that you are a little bit crazy!'" We both chuckled at the silly description. Although the word 'crazy' connotes a kind of mental dysfunction; being categorized with one of Mr. Hemmingway's 'good writers' (even that the story needed more fleshing out in some areas) was more than laudatory.

Lady Olborough's unsolicited comment has blotted out all of Arthur's disparaging outbursts about me. Whatever spurious and shuffling titles he has bestowed upon me did not matter any longer for I have been unofficially awarded a fundamental compensation and a trophy for life ...*Thanks Mr. Hemmingway for your unconventional wisdom.*

During all those years spent at *Le Cerisier* I met numerous actors/actresses, singers, comedians, late night show talk hosts. I always gratified them with a copy of my previous book. When I received 'the backing' of my employer he usually would add little comments just for the fun of it; the same kinds of stupid remarks that were directed at the writer Gogol when he was ridiculed in *les salons de la litterature* by other, already well-known Russian authors.

* * * *

The business turned out to be lucrative and so, at the first breath of summer weather Arthur' with the backing of two silent partners opened another place in Solvang, the Danish capital of the U.S. The new restaurant, *La Bagatelle* that was sandwiched between a bakery shop and a still empty store became quite popular especially with the prosperous farmers from the Santa Ynez Valley. The vast and fabulous wealth of this region is incredible. Here in a symphony of beauty and scents of the flowers one can experience all the richness of the generous deep topsoil of the earth with huge live oaks willows, sycamores, azaleas and wild berry vines. The sculptured mountains rose in sharp outline as the sparrows skittered among the raucous cry of crows and blue jay's squawks. There were hermit-birds that ever fly alone; bright chanticleer, bees and other sibilant insects humming amongst the flowers, all in full chorus. Within such an extraordinary sight, with the pale disc of the early sun, you can hear the tiresome chirping of crickets rasping near the green alfalfa on Cachuma Lake with pleasant tinkling sounds and enjoy the neighing of the curious horses that stood there, sleek and shining. The languid perfume of the summer fruits, the hay and the flowers seemed to make bees and butterflies drowsy. Cattle and sheep obsequiously followed the shadow of the first large tree at hand.

A brochure described that: "The city of Solvang founded in 1911 by Scandinavian immigrants is a well-grounded place where tourists can buy fine artifacts. The body structure of the Wulff windmill soaring above town represents the place where people would meet and decide on their plan for the rest of the day."

La Bagatelle was located on Main Street neighboring the Hans Christian Andersen Park. At first glance the restaurant clean as a whistle looked like a monastic-type building with a picturesque surrounding of a large field sloping away. And right in front, on each side of the entrance path, in the same manner as a typical French tavern the building commanded a garden full of a variety of vegetables.

Customers would arrive at the restaurant with their automobile, in all kinds of shackly cars or on old-fashioned horse-drawn vehicles warmly decorated with scenes reminiscent of *La Belle Epoque*. Still others would take a *calèche*, a little two-wheeled much lighter local horse-carriage that jolted down narrower streets and driven by an old man dressed in colorful antique costume.

At one time, during a parade of historic vehicles, Arthur along with his wife, Melanie and Eddy Freedman decided to join the long motorcade in a '30 model T. Ford; the same T. Ford that he had stored in Eddy's garage for years. The entire electrical system of the car along with the tires had to be replaced at exhorbitant costs.

The restaurant with its newly shingled roof was larger than *Le Cerisier*. Arthur Valois Dourville de Montrissart actually bought the building, giving him *carte blanche* to transform the establishment nicely as he extended it with a covered patio. The sunlight would filter through the top of the partly sheltered roof of the addition. Metal-framed windows protected by Venetian shutters were outstanding. The richly colored mosaics stood all around. And soon the place was 'Spic and Span', thoroughly clean.

Remembering, that years ago I used to play guitar at *La Fricassée Rotisserie,* the owner begged me to entertain his clientele on Sundays at *La Bagatelle*. I would work with the expectation of tips and a fine meal on the house. Eddy Freedman, Arthur's business partner in this particular venture would supervise the brunch.

On my first day as an entertainer, wearing a blue scarf around the neck and a large cowboy hat I was introduced as 'the Belgian Johnny Cash!' I arrived at the restaurant a little earlier and while a young waitress was arranging bouquets of flowers in small glass vases I started rehearsal. On the horizon the sunset glow was dying and small clouds stretched across the red sky. For a moment in the ensuing silence I struck a sequence of notes. Next I began to sing for the clients. However my *répertoire* was limited with songs from European French singers such as Edith Piaf, Charles Aznavour and Maurice Chevalier. None of those wealthy ranch owners (some of them with Old Testament looking faces) understood a word of French, but surprisingly it seemed that they loved my list;

some eyes even became misted with tears as I made a little pocket money.

Nevertheless after several weeks of my musical stint at *La Bagatelle* a serious dilemma aroused. The customers showed appreciation by tipping me, but the saddest thing of all was that they mistakenly took out part of the gratuity from the plate left on the table, that was intended for the waitresses at the first place. Thinking that I was sharing in their tips, these hardworking girls showed resentment. Each time upon my arrival at the restaurant when a few of them were breaking the neck of another bottle of Sonoma wine, I sensed their unease by their frigid, contemptuous gaze as a flush started crawling up my cheeks. Consequently my determination to quit this gig was an easy choice...

Since the entire Valois Dourville de Montrissart family spent most of their Sundays up at *La Bagatelle* they became upset upon learning of my decision. The owner grew more cynical than ever. Repeatedly, upon his arrival at *Le Cerisier,* Arthur was as grumpy as a preacher 'who hated going to church' and his bad temper had a serious effect on some customers who would advise him to take it easy and be more amiable. In the dining room, when the telephone rang more than twice, Arthur would roar while glancing at me, his face turning red. And in a wild outbreak of anger he would articulate: "Isn't there an imbecile in this place capable to pick up that damn phone?"

* * * *

One evening Mr. Lars Borgunden, a faithful customer and a man of letters with great refinement arrived at the restaurant for a fine dinner. He had excellent taste and showed extensive knowledge for art in all its forms.

JACQUES MEYER

Lars wore a patch, since a splinter had injured the cornea of his right eye leaving him partly sightless.

As he started to eat, Mr. Borgunden called our attention to the fact that his filet mignon was tough and overcooked. In this situation, any conscientious restaurateur would try to be apologetic. He would offer the guest to replace the dish or to let him choose something else from the extended menu. Instead what Arthur did was to violate a universal business code of ethics who stipulate that: THE CUSTOMER IS ALWAYS RIGHT.

The boss rushed to the table carrying a flashlight and a steak knife. Cutting the meat in half he directed the beam of light toward the center of the object of complaint. His audacity went further and shamelessly berated Mr. Borgunden with a rather arrogant and even offensive tone of voice:

"This is a tender cut and it is not overcooked, look for yourself: there is some red in there!" Being a perfect gentleman with exceedingly good manners Mr. Borgunden sat quietly for a moment and motioned with a raised hand for me to clear his table. When I started to pick up the plate with the still untouched filet mignon embedded with a segment of fat, Lars gently tapped my shoulder and whispered in a leisurely calmness:

"Pierre I have always considered you and Leon as my good friends at *Le Cerisier* but that clown of a boss is the most boring person I ever listened to. Please convey to him that he saw me for the last time." That said we realized that the restaurant had lost a prized client forever. Unfortunately Leon and I had 'one less amigo!'

The pedantic Arthur never held back and kept imposing his 'fabricated rules.' Ridiculous and nonsensical ideas were constantly crowding his mind. And now from out of the blue he decreed that having a cup of coffee before enjoying a gourmet dinner, just like sweets would dampen the taste of fine food. Therefore he officially declared it an in-house regulation by telling us: "Do not serve to our clients any sort of coffee, latte, cappuccino or espresso before the meal." That stupid decree fell like a bolt upon our patrons and some of them became extremely unhappy with it.

Now almost everyone knows it does not pay to ignore the business code of ethics, and again the restaurant lost several steady customers. For those same customers this represented an infringement of their rights to choose whatever they wanted from the extensive menu.

On a busy Friday night a couple fall victim to Caesar's decree when a gentleman requested to have a cup of coffee before the main course. Without any option to satisfy his request the man inquired to talk to the owner. Although the client explained to Arthur that he was tired after a long day's work and that he was really anticipating a cup of hot coffee, the stubborn 'Caesar' still refused to honor the demand. And pointing his thumb toward the front door Arthur abruptly suggested for them to go first at the Seven-Eleven store. Upon hearing this, the couple suddenly decided to leave the premises. Afterward, calling for his coat and hat, the man shouted:

"We will never set foot here again!"

"I certainly hope so" was the little despot's reply. At the front door the equally furious wife flipped a finger at the boss: "This is for you little fool; you're such a weirdo!"

That was just a prelude to Arthur's troubles. He was completely clueless as to the identity of that client who was none other than Mr. Roushe, a famed radio-talk host and a gossip columnist. The following Monday morning Roushe took advantage of his having a radio show on KGIVT station to knock over the reputation of *Le Cerisier* and Arthur became the talk of the town. My employer didn't realize how powerful the media was and that in a public place you should be careful about what you say at all times.

Possessing a great gift of gab, Roushe lambasted my employer and ultimately referred to him as 'Adolph, the little Austrian corporal.' Minutes later, the restaurant was literally bombarded with such a bad publicity that in the evening people were calling upon Arthur for his shameful behavior. Before long, the callers wore him down and he decided not to pick up the phone and retreated in the kitchen. I was involuntarily assigned to answer the incessant stream of ringing. My ears could not believe what people were saying. This came as strong as the devastating power of an explosion:

"Fucking idiot!"

"You fruitcake!"

"Good-for-nothing trash!"

"Go back to France, jerk!"

With the exception of Melanie who kowtowed to daddy's instructions, Leon and I decided to ignore that foolish edict and started serving coffee at the customer's whim.

* * * *

To point out about Arthur's character I realized how much I liked that sad drunkard; that irascible old man for whom I even developed certain tenderness and who ultimately put me up with those constant humiliations.

Because of the virtue of obedience I had learned with the military time and time again there were no seeds of rebellion in my heart. Occasionally I found him fumbling in the dark and I seldom pity him. I already knew how Arthur was prone to violence in tense situations but today my employer's action was shocking, even unthinkable.

I arrived at the restaurant a little earlier than usual and I noticed that Arthur looked discontented; he seemed to be tormented by gloomy thoughts. He was unshaven, utterly unlike himself, looking very old and steaming like a furnace in a sort of insane irritability. Arthur proceeded in a bestial manner like a drunken and hostile savage the way a medieval man would when promoting the science of demonology and abruptly sank into a serious crisis. Without any announcement he came toward me and in an abominable fit of temper, with the swing of his arm the boss in a crouching brutal way hit me on the head with a large long-handed wooden spoon. So violent it sounded like whiplashes in the air until it rolled into echoes.

For a few seconds, twisting around in pain with my knees that tottered I was unable to perceive anything, except black dots. This really knocked the breath out of me. As the spoon bounced off my skin broke and there was a humming in my ears as well. A small trickle of blood oozed from the wound and cascaded toward the forehead in the direction of my left eye. Half-stunned by the blow, a sharp pain gripped me and I began to sweat. Caught in a clutch of agony and shaking from head to foot I felt everything whirled around me. As the humming in my ears increased I first rocked back on my heels and stood there, bewildered. The blow had been hard; the pounding became so intense that I had to close my eyes to repress my tears. In an excruciating agony I thought first I had a fractured skull and I knew without any doubt I would have a purple bruise in no time. Through the blur of my eyesight as I came back to myself I first understood nothing about what had happened and I felt that my senses were leaving me.

Arthur had been drinking again and in his alcoholic delusional insanity he stamped his foot angrily. Jerking his body savagely from side to side he became loud and excited with motion and started to growl threateningly just like a dog. With incoherent mumbled sounds of shattered words he gave me to understand that the night before at closing time I had left the refrigerator's sliding door open. It could have been me or someone else but this certainly didn't justify that blow on the head. I had been so unjustly hurt. For that inhuman treatment I had a growing sense of desperation with the feeling that suddenly my patience wasn't enough to endure his strange conduct. At that moment I was surprised at myself for not hitting him back.

I glanced at Arthur's face and a strange tremor shot through me. And for the first time I was now wondering why God doesn't sweep sick people like him off the surface of the earth. My eyes followed his retreating steps toward the dining room, and along with the pain I was tormented by a sensation of stupor. As I strolled near the kitchen public-phone unnerved I kept my handkerchief that I pull out from my pocket and held it to the bleeding gash to dab the blood away. In a misery such as I had never felt before my rotten to the core 'Gestapo employer', more than probably thought I was going to call upon the authorities.

With a frightened expression, almost like an attack of senile madness he decided to humiliate me even more. After chewing his lower lip in a burst of false emotion, the spectacular showman yelled like a naughty child with some agony on his face:

"Wait! I can fix this. Just stay in the kitchen; I don't want any bloodstains on my carpet in the dining room." Thereafter he grabbed our first aid kit hidden inside the marble furniture near the front door. He came back and proceeded to bath the injury with peroxide before covering it with a gauge pad. With a friendly tap on the shoulder as I fought to ignore the pain my strange employer adamantly explained in a low reassuring voice: "You see Pierrot now you're a new man again. I really never meant for you to get hurt." And, after nervously twisting his fingers things went from bad to worse. He simply announced in a weak smile:

"If a customer inquired about that bandage on your head just tell him that you fell down from your mountain bike in the Santa Monica Mountains!" With that slumbering sadism in his eyes he walked along pretending that nothing outrageous had happened. Under that barbarous approach I asked myself the question of what can have induced him to behave that way with such harshness inhumanity? Yet I have to recognize that when I did not detect evil the moment it appeared was a lack of wisdom from my part.

Nonetheless in the back of my mind only one thought seethed: *"Good men are rotting in jail while this irresponsible tyrant, more of an apparent monster with all his invective and sarcasm was free as a bird in the wild. And how can I continue to resist this tyranny?"* At that precise moment I very much wanted to hear a professional opinion of a competent physician, expert in psychiatry."

Eddy arrived at *Le Cerisier* awhile later and expressed his surprise on viewing the bandage on my head. After pulling myself together I explained to him all about that latest event. As he watched me with affectionate concern, his broad face brightened with astonishment and became wreathed in some sort of a smile. And suddenly he propounded in a half whisper that in the impulse of the moment I seriously forget that blow incident and keep it out of my mind. Freedman unraveled to me that Arthur was tormented with serious problems concerning the restaurant in Solvang. The same morning he quarreled and almost got into a fistfight with Arthur.

Up north at *La Bagatelle* establishment, an unsettled dispute had occurred between my employer and the owner of a bakery shop next door over their joint parking spaces. The sturdy barrel-chested Danish baker claimed that too many spaces were taken for the restaurant while his own customers had to park in the street away from his place of trade. The local authorities took this matter into consideration. In the wake of a diligent analysis of the facts, a rational ground became propitious toward the baker. In his wild imagination Arthur openly implied that there had been discrimination; that a plot by the Scandinavian business people from Solvang was in process, trying to suffocate him. (A French restaurant in a so-called Danish city was just unthinkable.)

However I found out that the members of the City Council were good, honest and courteous people and their maxim was: "The sun can rose for everyone, French as well as American and Scandinavian without any prejudice whatsoever." The major problem that made Arthur so irritable was the fact that *La Bagatelle* has been tottering on the ragged border and had fallen apart like a spider web under the razor's edge. Now the boss was unable to keep his head above water much longer. This was the very first time I learned anything about what had been going on in that northern California city's fine dining place. There was no longer a sufficient supply of raw materials since the boss received no more credit from the suppliers, especially from the butcher and the fish handler who were really fed-up for not being paid on time. After several weeks in the same restaurant the personnel didn't receive any paycheck. Plots were even hatched against the owner. Previously most of Arthur's cash money for the place had been expended in a variety of particulars such as Utrecht brown velvet booths, fine tables and tableclothes and a great amount of *argenterie*.

My employer had been ill equipped to cope with the stealing that was going on among employees. There had been some sort of mutiny and ransacking; more like a drunken battle between workers. The maintenance of the restaurant had been completely neglected. Last time Arthur was there, the heavy wooden gate had been left open all the time; an air of desolation and of long neglect was now hanging about the place. As with sailors busy cleaning the Titanic before the vessel hit an iceberg, the few honest employees remaining in *La Bagatelle* continued polishing silverware. This reminded me of a man with pneumonia who had been given intensive care, so he could die in good health…!

I firmly recognized the desperation of Arthur's position at the Solvang place of business but after that blow with the wooden spoon I was wondering again if whether or not I would keep on working at *Le Cerisier*?

Weekend nights were usually spent at my friend's flat in the Marina. Just as I arrived near the house I found myself in one of those dense seashore fogs. Since the car-port went into restoration I parked the Buick not too far from the beach and started walking toward the old, still handsome white stone bridge. In the salt-laden mist I could hear the whisper of the ocean; it was a dull, prolonged sound that never ceased. The fog had descended over the marina. This was one of those gray-looking, uninviting smothers that roll in off the sea. On the left bank of the canal, with the soft murmur of the current there were attractive enclosures full of flowers, the same enclosures that joined the channel leading to the ocean. The other bank was almost entirely lost in dimness. Afterward I sunk deep in an abyss of thought. As that terrible look of Arthur returned in my mind in full force I went into a deep quarrel with myself. Afterward a stream of questions flooded my mind: *"Are you composed? Can you continue to bear the vexations of life without bitterness and without despair?"* I felt frightened and inclined to look behind me over a beating of wings until I ducked into a 'Seven-Eleven' for a cup of coffee. The air was chilly and my hands and feet already grew colder as I sensed myself elbowed in the fog. The darkness had made the fog jam-packed. The mist in which the channel occasionally swathed its banks had spread at first all over the area. And as I listened to the sound of the sea and the smooth hissing purr of the waves I thought that I must calm myself and think things over again. Several of my friends and relatives, well informed about Arthur's character were begging me to seek another job. At that juncture I thought about peace; peace in my heart. Mr. Jack Kornfield, Ph.D. in clinical psychology wrote a book entitled: The Art of Forgiveness, Lovingkindness, and Peace. And I remember perfectly well his illustration concerning peace: *"If you put a spoonful of salt in a cup of water, it tastes very salty. If you put a spoonful of salt in a lake of fresh water, the taste is still pure and clear. Peace comes when our hearts are open like the sky, vast as the ocean."* The reflection of my face revealed itself in the window, and looking at the prematurely aged Indian man working silently with a much younger woman, neither pretty nor ugly I made the final decision:

"People make choices every day and in my case a choice was created: I am not going to quit. I'm quite capable of preserving a proper air of dignity. At *Le Cerisier* I underwent great struggles. I felt that my self-respect had been trampling under Arthur'foot. There were humiliations after humiliations. But in my trials I stood in good health with warm blood circulating in my veins. I have health and strength enough for anything and the customers like me. The purest metal comes of the most ardent furnace; the most brilliant lightning comes of the darkest clouds." Yet, the anxiety was not immediately lifted.

I arrived on Fiji Way a little after midnight and found Helena wearing her white nightgown and soft-soled slippers. She had almost fallen asleep with her African Gray parrot perched on her right shoulder as *The Tonight Show* was still on. Stirring her tisane with a spoon she seemed quite staggered upon discerning the large bandage on my forehead. I tried to concoct a story that I slipped on the kitchen floor in trying to grab a *marmite* -cooking pot from the shelf and I added: "It was just an unfortunate mishap!"

After a short silence I thought that somehow she fell for my tale. It rapidly dawned on me that for Helena, lying is a mortal sin. With her love and kindness I realized that we were two wings of one mind. And when I thought of her intently she would be compelled to think of me. She first sank upon the sofa, abruptly sat up inflexible. With her arms folded and glancing at me with that look I knew so well she immediately made me realize that she didn't believe my explanation. I never have been able to hide anything from her. It was as clear as daylight, and a flush came to my cheeks as I suddenly felt like a bad boy in the principal's office:

"An unfortunate mishap heh?" a silence. And with her large eyes staring at me with brow furrowed like those of a wild animal she articulated:

"I am pretty sure Arthur did this to you, right?" At this point, unable to give her a straight answer she continued as her indignation mounted high: "Why for Chrissakes are you putting up with all this? Around the world you went, you wrote a book about that saga, you ran Marathons. You even reminded me more than once that with your paratroop unit you had thrown yourself so many times head first out of the plane, like a diver from a springboard into a swimming pool! And now you keep on working in disgrace in that *Kommandatur* of a restaurant for a bossy and grumpy little man! With that wound you need to seek out a doctor with no delay!" Without hesitation she rushed to the phone.

"What are you doing Helena?"

"I'm calling the police for that boss of yours must be quartered in a cage. Arthur should be in jail behind barred windows. That man already endangered your life. It's good that you seemed to have intercepted in time the fatal blow from that near-assassin. But who knows, tomorrow Arthur can kill you!" With my neck muscles tightening like the Hulk and palms sweating, I begged her not to take any action adding with sudden apprehension that I am able to deal with this matter.

Placing down the handset, she swallowed an extra strength Tylenol before cleaning and bandaging the gush properly. Afterward she eased herself down on the arm of the sofa. Her eyes showed that she was hurt; really hurt, and for seconds her spirits lost their wings. With her hands clasped on her lap and her voice becoming much harder, she mumbled: "Sometimes I wonder if instead of a brain you don't have mashed potato in your head. Well do as you wish but remember: I am not even going to buy flowers for your funeral!" Fixing at me with a stony glare she put her arms round my shoulders and continued in an aggrieved voice:

"Arthur might be the worse person on the planet but I must agree with one thing he stated correctly: you're a dummy."

Recurrently, my lady friend railed at me for my struggles and ignorance as I felt so stupid and confused. But on the other hand Helena always corrected me with vivid passions and with keen feelings and piety.

The news of the 'wooden spoon' incident had spread around like wildfire. Eddy recounted that event to *le chef de cuisine* that in turn relayed it to his assistants.

Unexpectedly Arthur arrived in the kitchen as one could foresee a frightening expression on Bernardo Echeviran's face. The dishwasher had just broken three dishes; now he was overtaken by fear. At the same time, as the boss approached him and retorted blusteringly, Bernardo got so scared that he instinctively shut his eyes and waved his arms over his head as if warding off blows from a wooden spoon…

Following this event I tried to cultivate temperance as it tends to procure that coolness and clearness of the mind along with constant vigilance. I always kept in mind that God is the fountain of wisdom, and I generally solicit His assistance for acquiring it.

* * * *

I can recall that during 'the good days'of business in Solvang, in spite of a full house at *La Bagatelle,* there had been an excess of a few pounds of shrimps which Arthur covered with ice and loaded onto his red Nissan truck which did not retain an air conditioning system. He resolved to drive from Solvang to the other restaurant in Sherman Oaks, a distance of well over one hundred miles away. With the hot California sun the ice commenced to melt and as Arthur approached the outskirts of Los Angeles most of that fine seafood was no longer a delicacy. That same evening, after the boss washed those crustaceans with pure baking soda soaked in warm water they were served to our customers on top of a fresh bouquet of Boston lettuce (the only fresh item) and gratified with cocktail sauce.

The next day *Le Cerisier* was stormed by a barrage of phone calls from those same customers who complained that they had experienced rashes including gastrointestinal inflammation, septicemia and violent flux! Others got burning taste in their mouthswith flashes before their eyes and ringing in their heads. Considering that a week earlier a client swallowed a bad oyster, this latest event didn't help Arthur in reassuring his clientele. His promotion of 'fresh from the ocean seafood' appeared to be unfounded; it looked more like a huge lie...

The bruise from the wooden spoon over my head was still there but it looked much better and my thoughts went to Leon. Lately, Van Meerstellen has been exhibiting an obsessive and compulsive behavior as his thoughts appeared to be a thousand miles away. He kept on walking about the streets absent-mindedly as if against his own will. Just like Jack Nicholson's role in *As Good As It Gets*, day-in, day-out, upon his return home, Leon, in some sort of a mechanical habit walked forward the shortest way on the same side of the street, along the façades of stores with the steady pace of an experienced hiker. However there was a slight bias in his gait that inclined him somewhat to the right. After he had proceeded with sagging shoulders to walk the length of four blocks he set off counting the remaining steps in order to reach the signal-lights just as they turned green.

Returning night after night to the wretchedness of his little hideaway, where he immured himself like a hermit among battered old furniture around, he would first rest on the sofa-bed. And, after scrubbing his face and hands Leon would open the counter of kitchen utensils, picked out the very same kitchen-knife with a serrated edge he was using day after day. He would cut a slice of salami, a slice of cucumber and a piece of pumpernickel bread for his midnight snack. The dull diet of salami and cucumber never tired him. Van Meerstellen would stay awake till the early uncivilized morning hours, packaging some of his videos for local and overseas collectors. He would usually hit the *paillasse* no sooner than 4:00 A.M. lying down, still fully clothed. As he got up by midday he had no feeling of fatigue. On other times Leon would 'fade away' into the night just to feel the calm and serenity.

Chapter 5

A T *LE CERISIER,* the days flew by each like the one before and we encountered another quiet evening. Outside the wisps of ribbed clouds were lower and before long they turned into mist.

My employer was sitting next to Mr. John Beck, an astute and tough attorney who also happened to be a friend and general adviser. Mr. Beck could not help but comment on the lack of business: "Arthur, you have an empty restaurant here" said Mr. Beck, "what's going on? I don't understand. Maybe your menu is overpriced. I'm sure this situation makes it difficult for you to make ends meet?"

Repeatedly people would ask Arthur why he carried such an expensive menu. The restaurant owner never fails to answer with the same monotonous story that I have heard many times before. With a quick-wit and a vivacious tone of voice he started to narrate his life story. And it was always a well-prepared, emotional speech:

"Decades ago, upon my arrival in California, as a manager of a famed restaurant at the Sunset Strip I worked like a conscientious and laborious artist who left no small detail unattended. All my energy and my strength were concentrated in preparing those menus with all the pride and joy of my soul." Thoroughly imbued with that 'so called' reputation of integrity he continued, "I never willfully entrapped my customers by boosting the price of any dish nor was I ever gossiped about by knowingly cutting items from the *table d'hôte* or set menu." After gulping down his glass of half bourbon and half Coke Arthur with a face reddened like a drunken sailor and puffed as those cranes in the marshland would go on:

"Was I ever rewarded for my honesty, for my sweet religion of the heart? No sir!" Further on Arthur explained that he became the victim of female fickleness, the evil trait lurking in the character of a woman. The sequel of the following narrative with the encounter of the past will show precisely the reason for Arthur's sudden change of attitude:

"On a busy Saturday night, almost at closing time a lady dressed like *une dame de la Haute Sociètè*-a lady at the very apex of society came in the restaurant and requested to have a set menu arranged for a party of thirty people. She insisted that the dinner should omit nothing."

"Let's see what you can offer me?" she said.

"Well, we'll start with an aperitif." replied Arthur.

"The potage du jour."

"A fresh garden salad- your choice of dressing."

"The main course: filet mignon or fish, including three fresh vegetables."

"Coffee and dessert."

A few seconds dragged by. Showing a happy smile, the lady retorted:

"Great! And what would be the cost per person?"

"I already figured-it out: along with tips and taxes: $10.95."

Much to Arthur's surprise the lady's reaction was of total confusion and disappointment which finally dissolved into a shaky laughter: "You know what Monsieur; I'm shocked! I cannot commit myself to this. How in the world can you possibly prepare a fine dinner like you mentioned for such a low and ridiculous price? It's simply unrealistic and unacceptable! Well…just forget it!'" The lady's face creased into channels of disgusts and she made no further reply.

According to my employer, he had never been subjected to such disgrace and never had been so deeply offended. This incident was written in his book of destiny for that woman's refusal of that set menu was like Divine Providence for which opened Arthur's eyes on how to do business with the upper echelons of society in the wealthy enclaves of Los Angeles.

My boss did not wait a single day but immediately raised the prices on the menu. Strange as it may seem Arthur honestly felt convinced that these wealthy Americans from Beverly Hills or Bel Air did not mind paying exhorbitant dollars on French cuisine. Not wanting to appear too greedy the boss requested me to bring an *Elixir d'Anvers,* a premium after-dinner drink to Mr. Beck…on the house.

* * * *

One of the few kind gestures Arthur has done for me through all these years was to instruct the Chef to prepare a high carbohydrate meal the day before every 26.2 mile Los Angeles Marathon. Every first Sunday of March, I would run the world-famous Los Angeles Marathon, just behind the Boston Marathon. On that day my employer sincerely made a conscious effort to please me. It is at times like this that a good side of him emerges. And, with a bit of trepidation, I LIKED THE MAN…

Monday night, the day after the Marathon, I returned to work at the restaurant triumphantly but still limping slightly because of sore muscles. Jesus Betancourt cheerfully welcomed me as though I was an Olympic athlete. I guess he still wonders to this day how a bald eagle of my age is able to withstand that level of endurance for that 26.2 mile run?

Feeling a sense of pride in my accomplishment my boss made me wear the medallion that was awarded me at the finish line. With an authoritative gesture, like a general who pin a decoration on a soldier's shirt uniform he was holding the medallion attached to a ribbon around my neck. After stroking my hair with an adorable gesture, the pride in Arthur's radiant face was unmistakable as he delightfully escorted me in the dining room. He really felt the excitement creeping through him. And soon he paraded 'the athlete' at every table. I felt as if a bell had been fastened on me and that the boss was pulling me like an ox while pinching my arm. In such poignant intensity as he kissed me sweetly on the forehead he acted as my mentor. It was a pleasure of observing my employer suddenly so kind. I was able to discover in his eyes a brief glimpse of unexpected joy. For a moment I was really surprised and delighted to feel that I had won such a high opinion from Arthur. It was comical to see that he was paying me such unexpected warm compliments. It was also difficult to grasp all the hands from clients that were extended to me in congratulation.

But in order to shift attention to himself, thus creating a noisy whoop of giggle among customers he would add his own silly comment: "Although Pierre looks like an idiot he still run like a horse, almost as fast as Forrest Gump can!" Customers and friends were constantly curious with questions about the Marathon that I felt the urge to write an essay about the event. I made a composition that was later published in a newspaper including a Spanish translation printed in *El Aviso* magazine. Here are a few excerpts of the article exclusively presented under the by-title: The Legacy Marathon Runner: "…Having completed all the Marathons in the City of Angels

since its inception in 1986 that follow the Olympic games
of 1984, on February 2000, I became a Los Angeles Legacy
Marathon Runner. The mayor himself awarded me a special
commendation. Amidst over twenty thousand athletes who
run that race every year, only three hundred and sixty-six
people in the world receive that award…After finishing the
26.2 mile run, as I painfully limped in the direction of the exit-
fenced corridor, my ultimate joy was that simple bouquet of
red roses presented to me by my islander sweetheart. Most of
the time, enlivened by the fine weather she graciously awaits
the arrival of her Belgian champion… The very unique aspect
of that sport event is that anyone who run a Marathon to the
finish line is a winner, regardless of time."

Marathon day was not always blessed by the famous
California sunny weather. Rain or shine, the show must go
on as in the old Hollywood tradition. On the first Marathon
of the new millennium it rained cats and dogs. Yet the deluge
did not dampen my spirit as well as of my fellow Legacy
Runners. The storm came with unbridled ferocity and almost
immediately Hollywood Boulevard became a sluggish, stygian
river. In order to get a little support from the by-standers I was
wearing a shirt where people could read the sign BELGIUM
embroidered in the front mesh. At the 22nd mile mark, I
sprinted and past a few dreadfully bored athletes who were
appallingly foaming at the mouth. As I was approaching the
finish line I heard the noisy fanfares and merry trumpeter.
Surprisingly I was cheered by an enthusiastic crowd; more like
a parade of warm expressions and faces.

Unexpectedly, aside from a sea of welcoming Angelinos
screaming "Go Belgium, go!" I heard others expressing
themselves in French "*Allez la Belgique, vas-y!*" A few customers
from the restaurant recognized me too: "*Run, Le Cerisier, run
Pierre!*" And on that day I really found myself the object of

JACQUES MEYER

interest. At the finish-line a city councilman wearing a long raincoat and yellow hat awarded me with the medallion. Rubing my knees with a lotion he commented happily, "I thought that Belgium exported only good chocolate; so far I notice that good legs are on the list too."

Every year at Marathon time I always ask myself the question: *"Why torture myself to achieve a goal with no tangible reward or significance other than what I assigned to it."* I found the answer on a stop-over in Luzon in the Philippine Islands. A young author by the name of Francis J. Kong- *One Day at a Time* explained under his by-title: *Learning from Marathoners:* "Because only you know what it means, only you are able to make yourself do it. When you do, then you know there isn't anything you can't do. No amount of hype, no cheering section; no personal glory, no place in the annals of history can carry you all those miles. You have to do it yourself."

On a few occasions, during the 26.2 mile road that started at the Colliseum, as bizarre as it may seem I ran several miles without any effort, feeling no contact whatsoever with the hard cement. It was as though within the endurance's limit I suddenly became weightless. Through a meander of streets, boulevards and avenues, my sense of orientation sometimes vanished. Afterward I simply followed the other runners not knowing where I was. Less than four hours or so to my surprise, among a cheering crowd I was back at the Coliseum after having circling most of the City of Angels with my eyes half closed most of the time.

* * * *

I've always considered Arthur a businessman with good industry experience having the know how to please the customers with his fancies. Throughout the many years he has built an elite clientele. However his attitude has changed most drastically. Being the owner of *Le Cerisier,* a well known four star restaurant Arthur decided to align himself with the cooking expertise of Monsieur Ernest Pointide. My employer was actually attracted to him like a magnetic force.

Monsieur Pointide was the classy French culinary master known the world over, not only for his food preparation but for his tact and etiquette, also his code of decorum and gallantry vis-à-vis his clients as well. He would personally take care of his patron's hats and coats while he kissed the perfumed hands of Parisian ladies, prior to inquiring if the meal had been to their liking?

On one circumstance a group of five Texans arrived on a limo for dinner at Monsieur Pointide's secluded establishment in Aix-en-Provence in the south of France. *Le Soleil du Midi* restaurant was actually set in the countryside with French windows that opened to a garden of organic vegetables surrounding a solitary olive tree.

One of Ernest Pointide famed maxim was: "A meal without wine is like a day without sunshine." However, half way to the main course, as a *modus operandi,* the same customers ordered a bottle of Chambole Musigny 1967 "ON ICE!" Because of the hot and humid weather outside, the Texans thought they could refresh themselves that way.

In France a red wine on ice, especially a 1967 Chambole Musigny is a serious crime. In utter astonishment the great restaurateur stood there in mortal agony for a fraction of a second before mopping his brow with a white handkerchief. In a cold sweat that ran down his spine Monsieur Pointide kept looking at his customers in dismay and was lost for words. And since politeness is an essential part of French conversation and manners; without emotional strains and in a mannerly way, after a little while the owner of *Le Soleil du Midi* brought back their coats and hats at the table. Eventually he advised the

American clients that it would be his pleasure to escort them to the door and that their dinner was entirely on the house, no charges whatsoever. This unique example of extraordinary courtesy was the reason for *Le Soleil du Midi* to be the top restaurant indicated in *Le Guide Michelin* throughout Europe.

Like a recording devise Arthur was telling our clients the same story over and over again. And now he was ready, willing and able to imitate Ernest Pointide, the French culinary giant.

On a rather quiet evening, six people showed up at *Le Cerisier;* two men and four ladies. They just dropped by for drinks and small appetizers. As I was writing down their orders, Arthur overheard about the trivial items they were about to choose from our extended menu. Without any warning he rushed to their table. Assuming an air of even greater importance than usual he behaved with some sort of arrogance. And, addressing the customers the boss told them haughtily:

"I'm sorry but you must order a main course or you will be charged a set-up fee of twelve dollars and fifty cents per person." and he continued:

"This is a four star restaurant; not a coffee-shop!" *First of all, we were not in France and there were only two other people in the entire dining room. Voicing out my unsolicited idea, I suggested my employer to compromise. Yet he refused and stood there stubborn as a mule.* Quite embarrassed, one of the ladies stood up:

"Let's get out of here!" As Arthur was holding the front door open, another woman looked at him straight in the eyes with her nose almost touching his. And with an expression of moral indignation she conveyed: "Impudent little man you think you're mighty smart don't you? You're just an idiot and a plain male chauvinist pig!"

* * * *

Again, Arthur in his distorted imagination and for the lack of his own hilarious experiences would narrate to our customers at *Le Cerisier* my amusing life encounters:

"One Friday night as Pierre arrived at his condo in North Hollywood he was greeted by two plain-clothes policemen in *gabardines* and hats. They flashed their badges and Pierre recognized they were from homicide. Choucart was warned to be extremely quiet as the investigators were assessing what was now a crime scene. A dead man was lying in a pool of blood on the cement right in front of his apartment, and the police was waiting for the coroner to conduct the post-mortem examination.

Later on, a neighbor explained to Pierre that the tenant from flat 152 had murdered the manager of the building over a rent-fee dispute. He was shot point-blank and at close range. It seemed to be no more than an apparent violent and obvious psycho-case. The killer abruptly had left the premises in his old Chevrolet station wagon. It had been determined that the renter in question was a mentally ill, potentially violent man. A bulletin alert had already been issued to find the vehicle and its occupant. The police had set up roadblocks on all main arteries. The day had been extremely hot, and in the evening the temperature was still over eighty-five degrees." and Arthur went on: "With the door of his living-quarter half open Pierre installed a stand-up fan and with his TV on he had also a full view of the body. The two undercover cops went back to their un-marked LAPD car for more instructions on the car-phone from the forensic expert and subsequently picked-up the yellow tape used to cordon off the crime scene. And for a brief moment before the crime investigation went under way nobody no longer paid too much attention to that man laying there. Suddenly my little friend here on the course of his observation decided accordingly to gently switch his

old, crumbling Salvation Army boots for the brand new pair
of shining brown Bellagio shoes the corpse was still wearing.
And guess what? The fitting was perfect!"

With Arthur's anecdote laughs burst in the entire room.
At this phase of my writings one can easily recognize the wild,
horrendous verve of that little man who would invent the most
peculiar, idiosyncratic narrative for the simple plaisir of his
faithfull clients from that fine dining place!

Chapter 6

I N OBSERVING A European tradition, every year as summer turned into fall the owner would close *Le Cerisier* for the entire mellow month of September, as California would shed its tropical exuberance as well. This hibernation allowed us to take that well deserved vacation. During all those few late summer days through the peaceful sequence of weeks I have been lucky enough to discover far away and exotic lands.

China which recently opened its doors to international tourism was one of my ultimate experiences. With a small backpack and little pocket money I already cheerfully made several experimental trips to that great land, and being especially astonished by the grandeur of the mythical Shangri-La that isTibet. Once again I became a bewildered seeker, contemplating on Mao's doctrines; *The Communist Manifesto* from Marx and Engels, analyzing simple human behavior. I achieved this by randomly moving through overcrowded trains that kept on puffing with short, heavy blasts for three or four days, climbing mountains, trestle rivers and narrow passages. Hurtling through immense grasslands I was able to observe farming on a large scale performed mainly on platforms carved out of the hillside, from Canton to Chengdu and Shanghai to Xian.

Shortly the vacation would be over and like an apiary where bees kept the apple tree productive we find ourselves again reunited at *Le Cerisier* and resume the humdrum of life. Our encounters from place to place were propitious for a new fruitful season. Feeling rejuvenated, we excitedly shared last summer's escapades among us and with our customers.

As in the previous years Melanie's destination has invariably been France to rendezvous with her ninety-year old grandmother for a sailing trip to Athens, Lisbon or Istanbul.

Leon Van Meerstellen flew to Belgium. And later on he went to France to visit *Les Châteaux de la Loire*.

Eddy Freedman on the other hand preferred the simmering climate of Palm Springs in the comfort of his time-sharing unit for he had no doubt that there was no better place than this. And I believe he loved this particular area more than anything else in the the whole wide world.

Mr. and Mrs. Valois Dourville de Montrissart enjoyed their vacation in another region of the Seychelles Islands in a place called Praslin. Story has it that Arthur met *Monsieur Louis*, whom the islanders recognized to be a descendant of the Royal French Family. This was truly a riveting and unprecedented subject of conversation.

As Arthur related this anecdote to our diners, it was a joy to witness his frenzy. In a quite embellished speech he would recount that after King Louis XVI's execution, his son escaped and sailed to that Indian Ocean paradise. That same offspring, a cultured man in his early fifties had blue eyes, nose slightly curving at the edge and carefully groomed graying, hair which has been all authenticated by local historians. Nowadays, that illustrious descendant was peacefully awaiting those curious and very inquisitive tourists to the island.

Arthur, with a flush of enthusiasm would further add that in the Seychelles Islands, sharks are extremely friendly "You can even pet them" he boasted. The stoutly little man, in his rhapsody of nonsense finished up his amusing tale by bragging that as a matter of fact in that part of the world, the hairy double-shaped coconut really reminded you of a "woman's behind!" Arthur felt like he was a candle that attracted moths that hovered round its flame. And so night after night in the restaurant there would regularly be a bunch of customers willing to show interest with his gibberish. On the other hand, Leon and I enjoyed watching the boss make a fool of himself with his stupid chatter in front of brilliant and intelligent clients. But as soon as he turned his back around, his audience snickered at him much to our approval and amusement. In his struggle to be funny, he continued using his employees as the butt of his gags. He always masquerade his evil intentions on me as jokes and felt like a successful entertainer after having elicited a laugh or two not realizing that in fact he was the big joke. Much as we human beings need air to breathe, Arthur needed flattery to survive. And like a fox in the wilderness he was just as sneaky and crafty in order to thrive.

* * * *

Arthur was a little tired after having strolled off all night, up and down, from block to block through a labyrinth of deserted streets in search for Pompadour, his French poodle that inadvertently escaped through the back door of his house. At this late hour, the streets which ordinarily throbbed with life had been bleak and empty. With a long tired face and a day's growth of beard, the boss had heavy-lidded eyes and the disarray of his hair made him look sleepy. Trudging with a feeble and unsteady gait he tripped several times and became stiff in the joints. He had searched almost the entire neighborhood to no avail. The doggy seemed to have liquefied into thin air. Feeling like he was about to come down with the sniffles he finally decided to give up the search but not before making a side trip to the First Nazarene Church where he found little Pompadour playing with a Siamese cat on the front steps.

Just like his wife Arthur was madly enamored of Pompadour. My employer, with his shirt blotched with sweat was worn out with exhaustion; the last stage of exhaustion so strong that you could read sleeplessness round the eyes. He was still in pain, looking grumpy as he lay down on a booth in the private room. Arthur was so tired with hardly any strength left that he staggered about like a drunken man. In order to find his little dog, he didn't leave a stone unturned.

Eddy started rubbing Arthur's back and legs. For muscle pain this always soothed him, and after awhile my employer was dozing. Later on Arthur became well awake and felt no more fatigue. Eddy had restored him to his feet in no time.

Back in the main dining room, with the habit of brushing his nose with two fingers my employer requested some attention from our patrons in the middle of their ambrosia for an important announcement. On a sound of trumpet he heralded:

"This morning Pierre got a ticket for slow driving with his car on the fast lane on the 405. Yet he thought he travelled faster than the speed of light. (Soft chuckles emanated from his audience.) and he continued, "Not only that but he was also driving dangerously. Prior to be stopped by the police, all other drivers became extremely upset. A few of them passed him while pointing the finger in the air. This dummy thought these were greeting signs from those warm and respectable people, and he responded tirelessly by waving at them with his left hand, not realizing that he had just made a lot of enemies." This time a barrel of laughter followed. Arthur with his eyes blinking stealthily continued: "and that's not all. When the sheriff requested for his driver's license this jackass didn't realize that forty-two miles an hour on the far-left lane of a 65 mile limit freeway was not permissible. With a little tapping of his hand on the law-enforcer's uniform, Pierre admitted that he didn't understand; that his foot on his two-cylinder '66 mini-Subaru had been on the gas-pedal right to the floor all the time!" and Arthur went on: "After the officer told Pierre that on this kind of speed he was endangering everyone's lives as a collision between cars loomed, he asked him to recite the alphabet to find out if he wasn't inebriated. Pierre stated it correctly…in the French language. At this point, the sheriff who didn't comprehend a thing was pissed. Totally exhausted he simply requested my little friend here to sign the ticket (for extremely low speed on the freeway) before going on to his routine business."

As on previous occasions our respectable clientele was bathing in utter pleasure. Arthur repeated the same story to different customers, but oftentimes the narrative varied on some particular points. The boss always tried to embellish and beef-up his tale thus making it sound more hilarious.

* * * *

Le Cerisier decided to introduce on the bill of fare a most unusual delicacy. Always wanting to be an innovative restaurateur Arthur offered lion meat on the *menu du jour* for our exclusive customers.

As bizarre as it seems the owner of the restaurant found a middleman in San Francisco who specialized in a variety of tropical wild animals such as crocodile, giraffe and lion. Numerous loyal customers dared to try the lion meat by curiosity or just for the fun of it and to brag to their friends that the feverish blood of the 'king of the jungle' flowed in their veins. I was obligated to taste a piece of lion cutlet too in order to better explain the experience to the clients. The flavor reminded me of a fine combination of pork and veal and it was not at all gammy.

Chef Picharon skillfully served the delicacy on a bed of spinach, topped with archduke- mushrooms sauce. As for the rabbit cooked in dark beer with prunes and mustard spread on a slice of white bread, Arthur decided to cancel that dish. One of our best customers, a lady from The Malibu Colony started to cry as we mentioned it. She had a pet-rabbit named Alexandria who was running free in her large estate.

During one of Arthur's visits to the Yucca Valley he met an old acquaintance that provided him information that would be useful to the restaurant business. The lady had known of an ostrich farm in Tehachapi.

Lately, 'long neck' ostrich meat had been getting a lot of publicity on TV and had been praised as being not only fine meat, free of fat and cholesterol as well. Several health associations had highly recommended its nutritional advantages. As the idea had presented itself to him, my employer didn't hesitate to add ostrich on the menu.

Upon watching a covey of those gorgeous and gigantic birds running up and down in that clean environment, clear of rocks and of bushes, the boss purchased several filets of ostrich meat. Rolling the dice, Arthur used one of his favored aphorisms: "I will give it a shot." And to further his culinary ambition Arthur decided to prepare the ostrich with pepper sauce.

The man in charge of raising those unique species had gratified my employer with an ostrich egg and a cluster of a distinctive ostrich feathers too, complimentary of the house. During the same week as we explained to our clients this new item on the menu, my employer decided that the restaurant be dressed up in 'an ostrich theme.' Not only there were pictures of ostriches in the wilderness all over the place Arthur dressed himself like one of them. He first blackened face then he put up four ostrich plumes strapped around his head with the addition of one more plume attached on his behind. Holding his round belly with both hand he started to flutter from table to table without any shame. As he tried very hard without any success to move with the agility of an acrobat, he launched a sudden spring and pitched headlong down before ducking under one of them, imitating ostriches concealing their heads in the sand. I already knew this grand scheme had taken up every moment of his time. But some of our patrons didn't quite understand. They became confused because Arthur's apparent short legs and bulbous, swollen belly that hung down like a sack as an overfed beast showed nothing at all that reminded them of the gracious looks of the toed flightless bird. There was no other way to describe this event as his behavior had not been amusing. For a fact it had been hopelessly childish and grotesque. The addition of filet of ostrich on the menu appeared to have resuscitated the restaurant's business that had slowed down during that particular time of year. The chef had prepared that fine meat so well, and our customers simply loved it. Precisely, during that same period, along with other international culinary experts, The Heart Association of America had correspondingly suggested to consume the fat-free and cholesterol-free ostrich. This was equally the result of a great amount of continuous advertising announcements in newspapers and on TV.

* * * *

On that last summer's day of '82, extraordinary things happened gradually at *Le Cerisier*. As impressive as it seems chance had it that on this bright, warm Monday Mr. Newt Gingrish the Speaker of the House of Representatives had dinner with us.

The middle-aged, white-haired, round face and still good looking politician was accompanied by two Congressmen and a young lady with alligator stilettos shoes. She kept on taking notes during the men's lengthy conversation. She was actually Mr. Gingrish's personal secretary. At dessert-time, the skinny "fashion-girl" secretary was still writing when Mr. Gingrish requested Arthur to join in at the table.

"You must be the Manager, I presume?"

"Mr. Gingrish I am the owner and chef of *Le Cerisier* and my name is Arthur Valois Dourville de Montrissart, at your service sir."

"I like this place. It has such a rich, warm décor and the food… Oh, the food is out of this world; such a real ambrosia! I've never tasted anything like this before. It's simply divine. My friend, for sure you can cook!" And after a hesitation, the Speaker of The House continued: "Uh-huh…by any chance, can you prepare food on a grand scale for me; I mean…huh… for the boys on the Hill, you know? I am talking here about a special dinner for well over a hundred guests in D.C.

As Arthur stood there dumbfounded, with an offer THOUSANDS OF RESTAURATEURS WOULD DIE FOR, Mr. Gingrish was quick to respond: "Arthur…uh, you don't have to give me any answer right now; think it over. The moment I get back in Washington I will send you a FAX containing all the details and thereafter, you make a decision."

Along with Arthur and Leon we directed our V.I.P guests back to their chauffeured black limo parked in front of the establishment.

Staring at the ceiling with his elevated spirit and that new impulse of enthusiasm, a joyful Arthur was beaming. He had a smile as wide as Ventura Boulevard and this time it was a smile of genuine pleasure. There was a glow of heightening fervor surprise and gratification on his face as his dream of the future was unfolding. His fate has assured him a position in the industry. He was so pleased with Mr. Gingrish that for the time being any other thoughts had escaped his mind. Since becoming the owner of this fine four star restaurant the boss had never been more convinced of anything in his life. Something as unexpected as this had never happened to him before. Losing his brooding melancholy Arthur became full of eager plans for the improvement of *Le Cerisier*. And once more with a warm voice my employer uttered:

"I can't believe this! That man, that good Mr. Gingrish must be a personal friend of the President of the United States?" And with enhanced forbearance as he was pulling a gusty sigh of satisfaction he could scarcely contain his feelings of triumph. He felt again crushed under a weight of happiness. This did stir him to a new drive of eagerness as a forceful exaltation continued to overwhelm him when he added: "Surely with all the publicity involved the exposure would be priceless. This is going to bolster the business at Le Cerisier too. And tomorrow, God be willing I would be the star in the Restaurant-Hotel Association magazine! Now I'm certain that a much more brilliant destiny awaited me."

I was also beside myself with frenzy. Currently Arthur was dreaming only about future plans and future success and about outdistancing his challengers in the culinary art; but now he would outshine them all. I had the feeling that from that moment on the realization of his ambitious dreams were assured as he now would achieve all he wanted in life. This was like music of a heavenly harp; like the arch of a brilliant rainbow.

Unexpectedly after a pleased silence and still lost in the depths of reverie Arthur looked with intensity into my eyes with a kind of ineffable paternity. Next, he took my hand in his own tiny hand and pressed it with cheerfulness. I could not help meeting his glance radiantly as his mood was euphoric. With a howl of delighted excitement he slapped my back with such enthusiasm and did something that in the world I would never have expected of him: Being transfigured he hugged me so hard I thought my ribs would crack. I felt as if I was being squeezed to death. And surprisingly he kindly muzzled his own face into my shoulder before running his hand through my hair with real warmth. That man; a man that dictated so much of my life, looking as charming as the clouds of dawn, now embraced me triumphantly on the cheeks and on top of the head (a gesture he would commonly repeats in moments of exceptional bliss.) I was so amazed and secretly pleased by those very unusual signs of uncontrollable affection. His sudden change in attitude for life irradiated me into forgetting my past sorrows. In that instant, Arthur explained to me that he almost died in infancy for he was born 'a blue baby.' and he added: "The doctor shook me first before slapping me very hard on the rear. I survived mainly on account of God. He came to my rescue and I'm sure He had this particular project in mind for me!" Afterward the boss requested me to join him in a prayer of thanksgiving in front of the Madonna and child painting on the wall for from this day on he did believe in miracles. Kneeling down upon one knee with the reverential devotion of a clergyman at the altar Arthur kept looking down at the carpet in that very humble stance, and I heard him mumbling part of a prayer in French: "… *Mère de Dieu, priez pour nous pauvres pêcheurs.*" For quite some time I sat there on a booth openmouthed. His attitude had been as a ray of sunshine in my life; as fine a day as the sun could boast for suddenly the wolf became a lamb. That evening we parted mutually charmed.

Next day Arthur wore a brand new suit with the addition of his father's gold wristwatch. For the following days there had been a great deal of talk about the events connected to that coming catering in our nation's capital. Customers caught the infection of my employer's enthusiasm as his high spirits manifested itself in his face; on his general *contenance*. Everyone complimented Arthur for that ultimate opportunity to prepare dinner on a grand scale for all those lawmakers. Some clients even had noticed the warmth in his manners. Now his expression was marked by serenity; his politeness definitely a royal grace reminiscent of the king of France. Arthur's new assignment in DC will be faithfully carried out. At this point, everything seemed to be drifting precisely in the right direction, and Arthur appeared to be in the best humor with everything he was doing. Swiftly, in a mood of emotional exaltation his legs gave way and he sat down to save himself from falling. It was just a slight attack of faintness resulting from such eagerness. After that exhilarating experience he recovered his equilibrium in no time. That day Arthur had given me grounds for hope in a matter which meant so much to me.

As I started the Buick and drove on Ventura Boulevard in the direction of North Hollywood, a certain feeling of euphoria came to me. I started smiling stealthily as I passed through the sleeping neighborhood of Sherman Oaks for I felt like being born again...

However, the excitement had been quite short lived.

Less than a week later when I did the opening for the restaurant on that day, as I kept looking at the owner's face it appeared to me that his eagerness all of a sudden had been faded away just like a day without sunshine whenever heavy clouds emerged in the sky. That vibrant new happiness wasn't there any longer. Suddenly, his face was older and weary. A quizzical frown was puckering his forehead. Arthur, with a grim flicker of a smile looked completely lost. I noticed that his thoughts were somewhere else as he leaned down on the desk frozen-eyed. Gazing at me silently he looked like he was paralyzed by anguish and a bitter taste came in his mouth. With yet a sour expression in his eyes he continued to watch me as a lost dog looks into the faces of people on a street. Unexpectedly he mumbled in a none-too-pleased grave and somber tone of voice:

"Pierre I am very sorry about the D.C. dinner; I just can't do it!" With a modicum of *sang-froid* I decided to try to lift up his spirit:

"Arthur you never give a damn about anything I say but for Heaven's sake why can't you do it? This could be the most dazzling success of your life! Over a few minutes of pained reflection my employer, after filling his glass of Stella Artois let the foam sink a little until it stood still. He took a swallow and gave me that certain stare over the rim of the glass. Indulged in a wry smile he continued: "Pierre, I have calculated the risks. You have to realize that for such an operation I would be forced to close the place for awhile; consequently I might lose many of the steady customers at *Le Cerisier*. I'm an old man now and this operation would be too tiring for me. In addition, chef Picharon's wife doesn't want her husband to leave town…well, let's just forget it. Let everything be just as it was before; this was just a distraction!"

After he got cold feet he left me to pursue other issues since he could think of nothing else to say or do. At that instance I felt sorry for Arthur. I could feel the tears coming, and I fought hard to hold them back. I was drunk with sorrow. It wasn't easy for me to get over my keen disappointment and to forget about the entire matter.

For awhile I could not sense anything as though I had no more feeling left in me at all. Later on I tried to think of something cheerful but it was all in vain. Aside from those silly excuses I kept asking myself the question as why Arthur so disliked in consigning himself? This wasn't some kind of a joke. The Speaker of the House was a man of integrity, of good social standing who later on even became a presidential candidate. As I remember, all about him bore the impression of a very acute observer and thinker. Arthur simply had refused an honest, very rewarding proposition from the highest level in the U.S. capital. He had turned his good luck into an undue meanness of fortune. Arthur could have been the center of interest. He could have been the subject of conversations among the best chefs of the world and second to no other restaurateur anywhere on the American continent. My employer had missed the accomplishment of a great destiny. His whole bright future had just disappeared right before my eyes. He had a brief moment of glory with an offer that had been handed to him on a silver platter. But Arthur was that kind of a man with a talent for paring away at an idea, peeling it down like iceberg lettuce until there was nothing left. He was a little man but this D.C. venture could have made him the biggest man of the day. He frittered away his energies on inconsequential side-issues. Arthur had been just jogging along in a slothful, ambitionless sort of way, getting nowhere and having overlooked such a unique opportunity. To make an analogy with Churchill's speech in the House of Commons, this would have been my employer's 'finest hour!' Again, in every sense of the word, Arthur had been an unfortunate man to pass through life, missing a great prospect.

But later on as I studied his face, the owner of the restaurant shed bitter tears over his disappointed hopes of glory. This had been the result of his startling noncommittal temper. It was a disgrace, but I knew that there were conflicting feelings crowded in his heart as he felt puzzled and tormented. However, to set his mind at rest he reiterated to me that as the owner of a successful four star restaurant his position after so long an absence would have been threatened; that he would have lost his fine, his most wealthy customers. Now at his old age all that was left in his life was to leave the restaurant business like a tired actor get off the stage with some kind of dignity and to die comfortably in his bed. That's all there was. *Arthur, you have been dissatisfied all your life; now you drowned the boat to that exclusive transaction of a lifetime. Having always prospered by proceeding in one direction you were unable to persuade yourself to change. This is quite unforgivable that you didn't show any guts for that unique achievement in Washington that could have carried you on a pedestal of culinary success. The whole thing had been disheartening.*

* * * *

Years ago Arthur was the recipient of a special culinary award presented to him by the charismatic five-term African-American mayor of Los Angeles: The Honorable Mr. Tom Bradley. The Los Angeles International Airport had been named after that man's captivating spirit. Arthur really appreciated that gesture and had proudly hung that priceless award on the dining room's wall. While the restaurant had its stake of African-American applicants, Leon articulated what everyone already suspected all along: Arthur had never hired an African-American to work for him. As a matter of courtesy he would dismiss those same applicants with a phone call, even that a position was open. In reality, Arthur gave preference not just to Caucasians, but to French speaking Caucasians or eventually Latino as kitchen-workers.

Out of curiosity about this, Leon and I decided to cross-examine him as for the reason for that apparent partiality. Arthur's answer was direct and well prepared. With a radiant, glowing and most contented face he rationalized:

"I have nothing against those likeable people. As a matter of fact I love them deeply. I know they are bright, fine workers, very athletic and always well dressed; the best well dressed people in the world." and he concluded:

"But just remember: This is a four star French restaurant; for sure I don't want our little abode to turn into *La case de l'oncle Tom*-Uncle Tom's Cabin!"

* * * *

Arthur decided to increase the work force by hiring a young man by the name of Stavros Papandrea. Even that as a child he had been asthmatic and underdeveloped, the young Stavros was now an attractive human being with regular features who looked like an angel in those old paintings. He was tactful, happy, radiant and irresistibly attaching but without the advantages of an education. He was also incapable of taking any initiative of his own.

His father, a Greek dairyman did not believe in giving his children good schooling. Debarred from the comfort and peace of mind with his relatives, Stavros ran away from home at ffteen. Since that time, he had encountered problems which had taught him much that his brothers and sisters didn't know; but he was still young and hungry for life. Later on he experienced several trades that included working as a busboy for Sofitel Hotel chain in Houston. He was happy to finally settle down in Los Angeles.

Earlier he had caught a glimpse of Hollywood, but to live there was a little too expensive for his purse. So, in order to shape his life to match his salary, Stavros found a charming apartment in Panorama City for around seven hundred dollars a month (in sharing with two friends.) As for his English, he always imitated those who were speaking correctly, but he still was swallowing the ends of his words. Afterward he took an advance course in order to polish up his grammar.

Papandrea, with his round face and fresh complexion was no more than eighteen years old. Short, very slim and quite effeminate, with the eager kindness of a child he had buttocks that looked more like those of a Spanish Flamingo dancer. His face was totally hairless, smooth and shining as a woman's, except for bad teeth, several of them gone. Arthur, after examining the youngster from head to foot just kept on admiring him, admiring his shimmering beauty. He would comb his ebony black hair, buttoned his shirt over his delicate shoulders or tied-up his apron. At one time, the owner of the restaurant even took Stavros in his arms and pressed him hard to his chest since he took a real fancy to that boy. Everyone at the restaurant thought that the boss was entertaining a prince. And, in moments like this, Arthur's heart was jubilant.

As a new *comis* or busboy working at *Le Cerisier,* Stavros had a curious pet-hobby. Prior to getting for himself a good second-hand bicycle, I drove him home on several occasions. On the first time I accepted his invitation to stay awhile for coffee. Upon entering the house I was taken aback at the sight of a python curled on top of the chandelier hanging on the center of the living room. This was really an eerie, rather embarrassing situation, considering it was already a good size snake.

Stavros Papandrea was a good worker, very reliable. He did all sort of menial tasks for Arthur, and not at all related to his job as a busboy in the dining room. The poor young man was working his fingers to the bone, 'burning the midnight oil.' At one time, since our dishwasher was sick at home, my employer forced Papandrea to jump inside the trash-bin with a brush and a bottle of Awsome cleaner with bleach in order for him to wash-away that terrible smell of left over pieces of fish that were rotting. The stench was really alarming for our neighbors, especially Mr. Matt Brend, the next-door hairdresser. Some of his lady-customers already had refused to get out of their cars as the result of that appalling odor.

This is when Stavros, sweating, and with dirt all over his body had categorically refused to complete the job, saying: "*Patron* I'm sorry but I'm not a slave; just call the sanitation or Public Health Department because that's it for me!"

Well, for once Arthur must have realized that he went too far by exploiting that young, innocent man for he vouchsafed no reply.

Although less than six months Stavros left *Le Cerisier*. He had found a new job as steward on a luxurious Greek passenger ship from the *Chandris Line*. Prior to his departure for the high-seas my little friend had inquired if I would be willing to take his python along with the cage. However my African Grey parrot, while flurried his wings didn't agree with the proposal; I had to refuse that generous offer. I believe that that friendly serpent ended up living in his new condo… in the Los Angeles Zoo!

Chapter 7

ANOTHER DAY AND new festivities: July the fourteenth is not just an ordinary sporadic time for our Francophile clientele because it is Bastille Day. The restaurant celebrates this historic event to the hilt.

Within France and as *vox populi*, among French people from all parts of the earth this day is the reminiscence of the overthrow of the French noblesse by the French populace. Although Arthur, ironically was a monarchist to the bone it was in fact that along with the philosophy of Locke, Voltaire, Montesquieu and Rousseau that on a particular hot and humid morning on July 14, 1789 an angry crowd created a radically different social and economic structure of the government. It was mostly Voltaire's ideas that produced the moral climate in which the French Revolution took place. In that same way of thinking, Voltaire seduced the intellectuals and Rousseau touched the hearts. The menacing rise of the *bourgeoisie*, like a rising flood, engulfed the entire nobility. The social inferiority was no longer *à l'ordre du jour*. The public opinion became the great power of the moment, so well supported by all that is honorable and just. With frenzy eyes the revolutionists took authoritative control. At that time prior to the revolution, the poets no longer bowed their heads before insolent, foppish nobles who were trying to impress their superiority upon men of letters. Witticisms were coined and the satires and lampoons of the day composed. Soon showing at once incredulous ferocity, those same revolutionists ejected all those princes, dukes, counts, barons and chevaliers from the buildings over those high-carved windows, down to the granite cobblestones on the market place. The masses, scattered like a covey of pigeons were literally devouring *la noblesse*. Around the Bastille the stench of dead corpses was pervasive. People were singing about the insurgency with full force:

Ah, ça ira, ça ira, ça ira
Les aristocrates on les aura

(Everything is going to be fine; we will get all the aristocrats.)

The revolution had robbed hundreds of thousands of people of their lives. However, for the poor laborers this day became a day of freedom and was celebrated all over the land. Earlier, the privileged classes, kings, nobles, and priests were the first to offer excuses for those much-abused advantages which they enjoyed. They never doubted but that they would retain them, but feigned indifference to them...

Tonight, Place de la Concorde would be as jubilant as our Americans' Fourth of July with fireworks and concerts. People would dance and drink wine on the Place and streets everywhere all over Paris to celebrate the national rejoicing. Here are the thoughts of Victor Hugo in *Les Misérables* regarding the French Revolution: *"The French Revolution had its reasons. Its wrath will be pardoned by the future; its result is a better world. From its most terrible blows comes a caress for the human race."*

The festivities of that exact same day over two hundred years ago that repeated itself all over French speaking lands will be masterfully recreated by yours truly with the assistance of my two esteemed colleagues, Leon Van Meerstellen and

Melanie. We transformed *Le Cerisier* into a parliament of lavish decorations of blue, white, red banners and multi colored paper garlands and all sorts of blazons. The surprising prop for the occasion was a *papier maché* guillotine seated at the center of the dining room which dreadfully greeted each arriving Francophile. The famed Rouget de Lisle's composition of *La Marseillaise* was playing in the background. As in the previous years every customer wore the red Capetian hat, symbol of the Hugh Capet dynasty and of the revolution. Hoisting a fake *sabre* in his right hand Arthur played a little game of anointing an unsuspecting King and Queen who were to be the sacrificial lambs at the fake guillotine. Naturally, this brought amusement to the guests but a faint embarrassment to the appointed ones who thought they had won a free dinner…

On one Bastille Day celebration Arthur as usual had already too much champagne that included a gallon of Belgian ale that he had engulfed earlier.

Not surprisingly, he unashamedly volunteered to drive a customer's brand new Rolls Royce Corniche Convertible for a joy ride. The car belonged to a wealthy stockbroker. Since he had too much to drink himself the distracted Mr. Sagey willingly handed the carkeys to the boss.

As he started the engine Arthur had the gear on without stepping on the brake pedal. The automobile shot out from the curb. With a deafening sound the right side of that luxury car smashed against a truck parked right in front of it. In spite of a churning pain in the stomach, Arthur was in shock thinking about the consequences of his arrogant deed. The stockbroker, equally full of arrogance assured him not to worry- nothing that his premium insurance policy can't cover. If there were not so many people watching, I'm sure that our calm millionaire couldn't wait to have his hands on Arthur's neck.

As the night was progressing, the drunken guests grew livelier. Now the inebriated revelers were in the mood for dancing. And so, out of rearranging the tables and chairs against the walls, a dance floor emerged. With great enthusiasm, we regaled our clients until the early morning hours with *ball musette* and Edith Piaf songs. Several clients, relatively reserved during the rest of the year leaped on the dance floor and became immersed in the music. I tossed up and down with the betrothed of a famed British high-energy nuclear physicist. Abruptly, in a surprise move Rabinadrah Singh Patel, an Indian heart surgeon clutched me by the arm and with his head held high, while tapping his foot to the music he retorted:

"Pierrot, my wife is so happy; please invite her for another waltz." The dance was in full swing; the music at its height. It became louder and louder as we moved together harmoniously. We kept on waltzing wildly round that little space in the dining room. The joyful Indian lady that left a stab of perfume in the air held her head up. She danced divinely and gracefully 'as a kite in the sky', flushing with delight while the doctor kept on gazing with pleasure at the scene. I swayed with the memories from my teenage years in Belgium. Anticipating a slow polka as in a cotillion we started exchanging partners as we continued dancing merrily to the music. There were brushing of skirts, elbows and bumping of shoulders. In the entire dining room there was a savage intoxication to which everyone anxiously clung. The dancing, the drinking kept on and on, and by midnight the hilarity had increased. The customers did not want it ever to end.

During this exciting time, in spite of the boisterous merrymaking, I realized that Arthur was missing; he was nowhere to be seen around. We all started looking for him; however he did not put in any appearance. We searched the kitchen, the bathroom, even the attic. He remained invisible. It was as though the earth had swallowed him up and he had simply vanished into another and unknown seclusion.

Suddenly everybody made a rush to the front door. Knowing his habits like the palm of my hand, Arthur would surely be found outside, extending his social duties amidst our cigar-smoking patrons, blowing clouds of smoke into the air. Needing respite for my dancing legs, and anticipating the break of dawn, I decided to go outside too, with the feeling that 'God knows what' an unexpected incident had occurred. There was a little commotion of slow moving automobiles that started to double-park in front of the restaurant. I heard a loud cacophony of a great crowd, like a battalion as a storm of people also came out of their cars. The scent of cigar wafted down the awnings, still no Arthur in sight. I had an almost instinctive feeling of what the fuss was all about. Carving my way, I walked toward a gathering of other onlookers appearing like a cloud of flies settling upon a wound. They huddled on the sidewalk, laughing and talking incessantly. To my surprise, a patron holding me by the arm announced:

"Pierre, come and look at this; this happens once in a lifetime." I rapidly found out that the disturbance in the street had been occasioned by the frantic behavior of Arthur. In the midst of that brouhaha, I craned my neck to see through the frenziesd crowd and suddenly my gaze was glued. There he was: *le petit Napoleon* in his underwear, drunk as can be, puffing on his cigar and appearing to take a plunge from the rooftop, yodeling like the king of the jungle. The drivers on the boulevard along with our patrons from the restaurant, possibly inebriated themselves applauded as they would a trapezist. But what held them the most was the expression on Arthur's face. After mouths held their breath, the same crowd being quite agitated articulated a cheer: "Jump! Jump! Jump!"

Amidst the chaos and excitement, they incessantly jeered with total fun at the free entertainment.

Monsieur Arthur Valois Dourville de Montrissart, the self proclaimed mannered aristocrat was still standing on the rooftop wearing almost nothing. He looked like an overgrown baby twisting on his fat, grotesque and hairy belly-a dead weight of plumpness, gyrating with the rhythm of a samba from the loud speakers beneath. With the most extravagant contortions, he kept beating the air wildly. Cupping his hands around his mouth, he made strained grimaces at the audience who appeared to be having a great time.

Eddy, Leon, Melanie and a few customers suddenly blended with the sidewalk crowd not wanting to miss a good laugh at the transpiring circus. Behaving like a squealing pig, he was grunting and snuffing. From that slanting roof 'the aristocrat' was roaring in a cavernous, sullen voice. Earlier, he thought he was Tarzan. Now, acting as a rooster he started yapping at the top of his lungs: "cock-a-doodle-doo, cock-a-doodle-do!" Imitating the sound of a trumpet, Arthur tooted a shrill grunting noise, and started to sing the French national anthem:

> *"Joyeux enfants de la patrie,*
> *le jour de gloire est arrivé…"*

Someone in the crowd, a customer who also was totally drunk had been wandering in the kitchen area, picked up a tomato and aimed it at Arthur. It hit him on the face, making him lose his balance. Eventually he crash landed on the rooftop slope. The boss fell on his back like a heavy sack of potatoes. Luckily my employer was able to grab a cable from *Le Cerisier'* neon sign, that stopped his sliding. This had provoked much laughter among the bystanders.

A thrumming chopper rattling in the darkness passed over and, dipping its nose it illuminated the entire building. Shortly, taking altitude it was gone over tree-tops. At this point, Melanie who first could not make head or tail of what was happening was almost in a state of hysteria. As she tried desperately to pave her way through the crowd, she kept on saying:

"Watch please, coming through; watch please, coming through!" As she realized what the culprit was, with a hard look on her face, and hair disheveled, she had a different tone of voice than I had yet heard her used. Wagging her head, she nodded in the quicksand of her own despair as she was crying at the top of her voice:

"Papa, what in God's name you doing? Have you lost your senses? Why are you making such a horse's ass of yourself? Come down from there at once! You are a dishonor; a shame to the family and to the dignity of the family's title!" More than once, Arthur unearthed a nasty scandal, *seulement* this had been one of the worse.

The festivities, the customer's gaiety, the popping of corks that began at the timely hour of 9.00 PM were kept up late, well past midnight.

In the early morning hours when the last customer had left the premises, we moved back tables and booths to their original position. Everything reminded us that our clients had really enjoyed themselves.

Now, the evening which had built itself up for hours in fevered fancy was over. After the sound of music has long come to an end, the restaurant became quiet and dark. There was humdrum calm in the street too as a sudden emptiness seemed to flow now from the front door. After all, this had been a day of great excitement.

* * * *

Arthur, just like a dictator regarded us, his employees as subjects and would tell us what to do even after working hours, with or without our approval. I remember the incident with the Miranprotter twin sisters. They came to visit us at *Le Cerisier* at least once a week.

The Miranprotters were middle-aged ladies with auburn tresses, keenly cut lips, always religiously decked-out in black, wearing a yellow hat. A gold medallion engraved with the picture of Prince Albert of England was suspended on a chain around their necks. Yet, with the character of being eccentric, they were extremely prudish Englishwomen, sometimes crabby like nuns. They knew Arthur quite well for the boss had done catering for them at the time he owned *La Mousson* which was located in the heart of Hollywood.

The Miranprotter's drank so much wine and aperitifs that they could never finish their dinner. On one of those nights, as they still sat on their booth, I wrapped their leftover food that they simply forgot on the table when they walked out.

Less than thirty minutes later, one of the sisters called Arthur informing him that she will come back right away to pick-up their leftover. They actually resided less than four miles away from *Le Cerisier*.

"Don't bother dear," Arthur replied, "It's almost closing time: I'm sending you Pierre to your residence with your food. I know where you live." The boss began scribbling the address on a pad, and feeling like 'a meal-on-wheels' volunteer, I drove to the Miranprotter's residence. Even that the sisters lived in the opposite direction from my place I didn't mind rendering a service for such nice ladies. However, this wasn't just a request from Arthur. In like manner as with an army recruit, this was an order and I had to obey. I drove from the restaurant directly to the sister's house.

The French door of that sumptuous mansion opened electronically. I climbed a few stairs. Upon reaching the last steps leading to the vestibule, I found myself facing a beautiful Mynah, a black bird with a yellow beak imprisoned inside a large antique cage. Mynahs are known to be even better talkers than regular parrots. The sight was reminiscent of the way the twin sisters dressed. I was really impressed by its shinning feathers and harmonious yellow beak that I couldn't resist to start a conversation:

"Twit, twit, what a charming bird you are!" The Mynah stared at me for a few seconds and, with a shrilled voice that resounded in the entire surrounding he twitted back: "GET THE FUCK OUT OF HERE, YOU BASTARD!" The tone of that ugly vernacular was sharp and sardonic. I did not know whether to laugh or to swear back at him. As I shacked my head and shrugged my shoulders with evident embarrassment both sisters came out of the living room as fast as they could. With a flash of dignity, trying to be graceful, they stood there in their nightgowns and white stockings as they warned that silly bird to behave, and they added:

"Pierre, we are so sorry. We bought our little sweetheart Gaspard from our last trip to Europe. He is really from good blood, but it looks like he went to the wrong school or he stayed too long among bad birds during his quarantine. We definitively have to teach him good manners…"

As I drove home, I could still feel myself laughing.

* * * *

The deep cruelty that Arthur propagated had no boundaries. I already knew how weak and malleable I was in his hands, but sometimes as he crawled out from under a little rock the profound hatred he created was unbearable. At the restaurant, after the weekend, I had a conversation with Chef Jean-Luc Picharon. It was about a lady I was supposed to meet at the Santa Monica Mall for an evening of dancing, but she never showed up. I found out later that she was involved in a car accident and had been unable to reach me by phone. Meanwhile, Arthur who was eavesdropping from behind the thin wall of the private room appeared unexpetedly. Jabbering and guffawing with joy in bemused amazement, he cackled victoriously on a musical tone:

"Tralala, lala, lala, I knew it! Who wants to go out with an old bald eagle dumb-dumb?" As a dark chill crossed my heart Jean-Luc and I were not surprised that this insensitive buffoon celebrated my disappointment at what could have been a lovely weekend with a dance partner. In my defense, Jean-Luc jabbered back:

"Arthur, we know you are hopelessly void of real passion and that you cannot seem to bear pleasure. You can't dance either; you don't know no more how to dance than a rabbit does; you have two left feet, ha...ha...ha!"

While not showing it candidly Arthur kept on envying contented people. Now, regarding happiness, the French author André Gide who was awarded the Nobel Price for literature mentioned in *The Immoralist* that *"Envying another man's happiness is madness: you wouldn't know what to do with it if you had it. Happines isn't something that comes ready-made, to order."*

* * * *

A few days later, Melanie who was a real expert in all sort of variety of cheesecakes purposely dropped by at *Le Cerisier* to meet clients who happened to be her good friends from work at the law firm. They were all enjoying her dessert creations.

Esther, an attractive lady-attorney with strong-willed temperament was some kind of a genius for legal erudition and cross-examination. Being close to the Valois Dourville de Montrissart's family, she started to praise Melanie:

"You should be well compensated for such talent!" Melanie in frustration blurted out what has been bothering her for sometime. She confessed that she has not gotten a cent from her father, the restaurant owner who pocketed all the profit from the the sale of the pastries!

Such trivial injustice infuriated the lawyer in Esther. She immediately ordered the telephone at their table and dialed Arthur at home. Abruptly, she was easily transformed as a defendant's attorney about to deliver a convincing closing statement as in a courtroom:

"It's shameful that the poor Melanie is never appreciated for all her ingenious hard work. That poor girl makes the best cheesecakes this town has to offer. However, you as head of the Valois Dourville de Montrissart household, and her own father better show monetary reward!"

Just as the ticking of a grandfather's clock, Arthur, under that so-called 'law-firm atmosphere and polished presentation' felt his arteries beating so fast. Nobody, but nobody ever talked to him this way. As I listened at Esther's tirade, my mind acknowledged the boss at the other end of the line, steaming with anger at his daughter's betrayal of privileged matters, reserved for family members only. After Arthur slammed down the handset in the cradle, I could almost visualize him with sweating face hidden beneath a wooden mask and convulsed with rage, thinking that her daughter had been acting like an impertinent little brat.

Le petit Napoleon was already formulating a confrontation plan in his head. Now the boss really believed it was necessary for him to go and punish 'such ingratitude' from his own daughter.

The next evening, feeling like a victorious *emperador*, my employer quietly trudged to the nearby Ralph's Market. Now, for a reason of which I could not comprehend, with intolerable unconcern he bought some éclairs, mini apple tarts, Black Forest cherry tarts and a few other sweets that he later displayed on a marble comprehend. Instantaneously, Arthur carried out his retaliation by ordering Melanie to "cease and desist" from creating anymore desserts for the restaurant. And, talking to himself: *"I'll break that brat's neck; that hothead is always brewing up something!"*

In no time, Melanie came around and uncovered the result of her father's devious deed. After she lowered the corners of her lips she burst out crying. She started sobbing so loudly that Picharon and I helped her to soothe down in the private room. It seemed as if her heart had plunged over a precipice. Her weak body had lost its balance and with her legs trembling she felt a sudden frailty in her arms too. I held out my hand to Melanie who threw her arms around my neck, and convulsively wept. She hid her face in both hands as she continued to weep bitterly. I felt tears in my own eyes too. Arthur, feeling no compassion for his daughter, went on with his macabre harassment:

"Next time, I will tear your ears off, you little devil!" Melanie's heart was now beating fast and her palms were sweating. With her head still clasped in her hands, she continued to cry in agony, realizing her father's overwhelming sense of betrayal. Following this dramatic event, the chef expressed sympathy for her: "I can't believe your father did this to you!" I felt bad for Melanie as well. The whole scene was not only a disgrace; it was almost inhuman.

* * * *

Growing up in the plain fields of Nebraska, Eddy Freedman had spent his boyhood raising horses with his father who had been as dexterous on horseback as a Cossak. Although the well-groomed young man ceaselessly tried to please his father in any ways possible, he had developed a strong distrust of horses. He rode a horse for awhile in his youth. But when a man hasn't been riding for a long time you can't really make ones believe that he has ever ridden one. Eddy never thought of the horse as a companion to humans. Now, with those bitter years behind him he decided it was time for a second chance at getting re-acquainted and get on a horse once more. And so, on this Labor Day weekend, the entire Valois Dourville de Montrissart's family, along with Eddy and I jaunted to Rosarita, Mexico, a place renowned for horseback riding. In that pristine, quiet environment with trees clustered to the water's edge and with a very low hum of traffic, one can play cowboy for almost an entire day alongside the ocean on the long stretch of beach for just about twenty dollars. All of us indulged on the fantasy, except for Arthur. Not too long ago, the boss had a traumatizing experience with an almost similar equine in nearby Griffith Park. Strolling along, not too far from the zoo he chanced upon kids' pony rides, merry-go-rounds, seesaws and other games. The liveliness of the sight stirred the child in Arthur. Being short in height, he thought that he could pass as one of the kids in line to straddle a pony. The perplexed gamekeeper admonished him plainly that with his jiggling stomach he was much too heavy to mount that poor, skinny animal.

No sooner than snapping out of that childhood trance, Arthur swore that no ponies, donkeys, mules, horses, zebras or emus would ever have the pleasure of squiring a Valois Dourville de Montrissart again.

While in Rosarita we took long walks alongside the beach. Arthur's legs being unusually short make it hard for him to keep pace with us.

Eddy was thus introduced to Blacky. True to its name, Blacky was a stunning and shining black horse. Being a weather-beaten animal, Blacky was slow-witted and he had large eyes that were still glowing with fire. At first Blacky didn't seem to like Eddy or anyone else for that fact. He seemed quite unmanageable and showed Eddy that all he desired was to be left alone.

Speaking with a strong Spanish accent, *l'écuyer*-horse-handler with 'Old Testament Eyes', was wearing a long coat with a grey hat. With a whip folded up in his hand he instructed Eddy that he should not hesitate to kick the animal to assert who the master is! He added that strangely enough, occasionally Blacky can be as clever a jumper as a tiger. First, swinging the saddle over him, the horse-handler let Blacky exercise round and round in front of the stable. The animal reared two or three times in succession. With his head held high, nostrils flared and ears twitching he was sniffing, neighing, prancing and kicking impatiently. Reining him, *l'écuyer* let the quadruped choose his pace for awhile. However he was not moving much faster than an old lady on her way to church, and I gathered more strongly that still no great affection flowed between Eddy and the horse.

Nevertheless, my friend who stood by the horse's shoulder waited to be in some sort of harmony with Blacky. Next he hoisted himself. At the same moment, being almost *en croupe*, his trousers too large for him were slipping down; he had to pull them up. As he tried hard to hold his feelings, the still tensed Eddy patted the horse's back. Holding the saddle tight he finally remained tethered. Freedman was so unprepared for this adventure that the motion of his arms was like the flapping of a falcon's wings. Afterwards, he handed the animal a piece of sugar, telling him: "good boy, just remember that I'm your friend." Surprisingly, Eddy started to pray a simple prayer to Saint James, the patron of horse-riders.

Blacky extended his nostrils to him and sniffed his hand first. Freedman had a faint smile on his face as he was thumping the side of the horse with his heels. The animal was now clopping along with his rider, casting a dark shadow on the sand. More than once, Eddy slumped down over the saddle like a lump of heavy lead. Arthur's companion managed with a great deal of trouble to force Blacky into a mere gallop before it shot forward like an arrow. It first seemed to be a happy ride, and Eddy was having the time of his life. Surprisingly the furious horse started to poop like the pour of Niagara Falls. We all started to laugh. Eddy got a little more confident as he whipped Blacky to a brisker pace. Soon, the horse seemed to devour the beach before him. In the motion, sharp sweat of the animal was visible. After a few hundred feet or so of a steady run, Freedman drew rein and pulled hard on the strap trying to halt him, but the poor animal stopped abruptly on its course in front of a large seal that decided to take a nap on the warm beach. The seal had really terrified the horse and rider alike. Eddy was ejected from the saddle and ended-up with deadly force on the hard sand. My friend now scarcely shaken had bruises all over his body, but luckily enough no broken bones, only a quite painful "Charley's horse."

However, as he was grinding his teeth against the suffering, still making convulsive movements, the weight of disappointment on his face was more serious. After he had been canopied under a palm-tree, a Mexican lady with dark hair and sun burned skin, actually the *écuyer*'s wife sponged

Eddy's face and head and handed him a bottle of Corona with a shot of Tequila, adding: "Amigo, this is good medicine for pain!" The bruises were quite painful, but after a few moments or so of misery the invalid was on his feet again. Ultimately Eddy started to mumble:

"That damn horse! ... That's it, no more horseback-riding for me either!"

* * * *

In Los Angeles, the 405 stood for one of the busiest freeway in the U.S. With the bumper to bumper traffic in the procession of cars, I have decided to give my battered aged Buick three days off per week. I purchased a Metro Bus monthly pass. During the relaxing atmosphere of the bus-ride, I had the pleasure of time to read; even work on my manuscript.

Anyone that is commuting that way can recollect unpredictable events. I readily noticed that among so many people riding on city buses, there were many 'Chiefs' yet few 'Indians.' Here are some of the conversations I overheard:

"My stocks really rocketed to the moon. I'm definitely going to buy that estate in Bel Air."

"I'm now the new CEO of *Lolita Fruit Pie, Inc...*"

"Yesterday I've been promoted General Manager of *Cookado Chicken.*"

On another late afternoon as the sun was still shining down everywhere over Southern California, I experienced the summit of burlesque; no less than a real Vaudeville. It looked like a scene straight out of Molière's. This great man of French comedy himself could not have prescribed a better medicine for hilarity: I boarded a Metro-Bus to the North-Hollywood station. On the second stop, a young good-looking lady with a gleaming face, long black hair and a firm mouth stepped inside the vehicle. She was fashionably dressed in a well-tailored coat and shirt, holding a bible in one hand, an umbrella in the other. With utter graciousness she said:

"Driver, I don't have any money, but I'm a friend of Jesus and I hate the devil. Can you please give me a free ride?" The chauffeur, a skinny bearded middle-aged African-American man was quick to respond: "Madam, the fare is a dollar and fifty cents, and you better pay!"

"Well...I love Jesus... but you know what driver? You look like Jesus. I can tell that you hate the devil too." The lady didn't let go. She stood on the platform at the edges of the stairs in front of the open door.

"OK Madam, please sit down and be quiet." the man added. The woman with her newfound happiness, filling the bus with some heavy perfume kept staring at the passengers:

"I know that you all love the Lord because you look like the lilies of the fields. We are all privileged to be here today; this is the holy of holies." and she continued: "Let me tell you: the driver is Jesus and this is a safe bus 'cause' we are under the protection of God, the supernatural power. "Amen." said I. At that point the lady strolled in my direction. In a gentle way she said: "Give me a high five, Jesus."

At the next bus-stop more people embarked in the vehicle. As the lady regaining her tongue, she continued her diatribe: "Driver, look around, more friends of Jesus are on board. I know for sure, they are enemies of the devil." By this time, the conductor's face flushed with anger. With a little irascibility he warned the lady that if she didn't shut-up, he would be forced to throw her out of the bus or call the sheriff!

Apologetically, brushing her feelings aside, she replied:

"I'm really sorry Jesus; I know I've been talking too much." And surprisingly, after the stop at Universal City, she held out a hand to the driver and departed, a smile on her face. This had been such a fine performance and everyone on that bus applauded. I could not but think of Christ talking to his disciples after he went up the mountain: *Blessed are the poor in spirit, for theirs is the kingdom of heaven...*

At the restaurant, curiously enough, Arthur looked like a different person. He greeted me with an unusual show of cheerfulness. A smile beamed upon his lips as I heaved a sigh of relief. Tonight he didn't slap me in the face or kicked me in the derrière. No harassment in any forms whatsoever; it was a miracle. Who knows, maybe I have been blessed in that bus after all?

Chapter 8

San Diego, California 10.00 AM

S UNDAY, IN THE early morning hours I got a call from Arthur. Somehow, I had a hunch what it was all about:

"Pierre, get ready. I'm coming with Eddy to pick you up. We are going to the culinary trade-fair in San Diego," and he added: "This trip will give you an opportunity to get well acquainted with French and California-Sonoma wines. I want you to become an expert like Leon." For that particular occasion, Arthur and Eddy wore tailor-made suits. They were well dressed in their best looks, and both carried on their attaché cases.

We reached the Port City at ten o'clock sharp at precisely the right time when the fair opened its doors to the public. The air was full of the aroma of roasting beef, hamburgers, hot dogs; you name it. I had the feeling that a dense crowd had been bivouacking in the nearby park, for this was quite a special event. There were well over one hundred stands exhibiting fine wines, Champagnes and food products from all over the world. Arthur kept busy writing on new recipes from *La Nouvelle Cuisine*.

Later on we directed ourselves to the wine tasting area. For this occurrence, my employer was unable to moderate himself. His tongue was rolling, *en veux-tu, en voilà* on all sorts of excellent vintage wines from France to California and from Chile to Australia as well.

More than once, throughout my writings I pointed out Arthur's non-compromising attitude toward some of our customers. In his illogical thinking, the pot-bellied owner of *Le Cerisier* restaurant who constantly ingratiated himself with reviewers from gourmet magazines was still gambling with the dignity of his customers. Whenever Arthur succeeded in convincing an unhappy patron that nothing was wrong with the food, and consequently he or she better eat it, he would feel good in his skin. Back in the kitchen, with a sort of a triumphant jig, he would tell the chef: "I know how to handle people!" However, without any foresight, just like in the case of the unashamed betrayal of Mr. Lars Borgunden and his overcooked filet mignon, Arthur maneuvered in such a way that he would wind up losing good and respectable clients. I have witnessed at *Le Cerisier* a few quiet Americans unwilling to make a fuss over a particular dish, who simply decided *à contre-coeur*, with a heavy heart, to finish their meal! Unfortunately for us, this was their ultimate meal in our little abode.

Now, according to Chef Picharon who was familiar with most of the great chefs in metropolitan Los Angeles, Arthur on the other hand had a bad reputation of being an extremely difficult customer himself. In order to be recognized as a master in the culinary field, twice a week my employer, along with his wife and Eddy would dine in other four or three star restaurants. After presenting his credentials and lending out his gold colored business card, Arthur being an enemy of conformity would sneak in the kitchen to observe the chef building up a béarnaise sauce. And, without any shame he would even request to taste *le potage du jour*.

Following that extraordinary visit at the culinary trade-fair, we decided on a lunch at *La Tourelle d'Argent,* one of San Diego finest restaurants. Rattling his orders from the extended menu, Arthur was acting like a grand seigneur. He ordered three *lapins aux pruneaux*-rabbits cooked with prunes in a lyonnaise sauce, along with a series of hot appetizers. Almost immediately, as the first small dishes were served, Arthur called upon the manager who arrived at the table, looking as rigid as a starched shirt. Amazingly my employer, totally unconstrained, and with a commanding eye, announced:

"Monsieur, those appetizers are ice-cold, and my friend Eddy found some hair on the hot, white asparagus. Can you take them back at once? And please don't have them reheated; we want fresh new dishes!" With a certain agitation *le maître d'hôtel* was compelled to yield to his demand. Every customer at *La Tourelle d'Argent* looked up at us questioningly as Arthur expressed himself in a quizzical smile: "In this business it pays to speak up!"

I stood there, embarrassed as Eddy shouldered his friend. Tapping Arthur's hand, he whistled to his ear "Well done Tutur, you played it smart." Arthur's little feet were kicking my leg from under the table to reassure me he did the right thing; that it was a sound and reasonable complaint. As I directed myself toward the bathrooms I heard employees in nearby kitchen hoarsely growling like the voice of thunder. Chefs and cooks, in general hate complaints. In view of this late episode I have nothing else to add. One can really envision that 'two faced' man.

* * * *

On a crisp, cold evening of an autumn-blooming colchicum, with the steady falling of leaves, as the day turned into a dark, dolefulness night, with people standing out in the Arctic air, I looked forward to Thanksgiving.

Arthur was still a nervous man, easily depressed, and once more I took a personal interest in his state of mind.

In his well-researched, entertaining and greatly inspiring book: How to Work for an Idiot: Survive And Thrive Without Killing Your Boss, Dr. John Hoover explained it clearly: "Idiot bosses are the mutant hiccups of organizational evolution with cockroach-like immunity to calamities that wipe out truly talented and creative people. Although idiots are barnacles on the ship of executive survival, they can nonetheless serve valuable functions as long as they are not in charge. The bad news is they usually are in charge. The good news is, talented and dedicated people can rise above the situation and thrive in spite of their idiot bosses."

Arthur, in his continuous yelling and utter quavering, associated with bad temper could have been related to nervousness and mental or emotional disturbances. This employer in my belief experienced psychotic depression and a form of paranoid schizophrenia. His general demeanor however was within the normal limits, but on the other hand his interactions with people were quite distinctive. On one occasion a customer revealed to him: "Behind that great smile, you are an aggressive person with an unusual degree of activity that made you justifiably conceited." For me, the problem with that idiot boss was the fact that as Dr. Hoover explained it so clearly: *"He is in charge; he was the one who wrote the payroll and handed us our paychecks. Fools in position of power are everywhere."*

In talking about 'surface calm' Arthur displayed similar syndrome. He might have major problems, but for his entourage he would show a shinning face. He might appear to have great self-confidence, but inside there is thunder. A friend once told me: "When you hide your feelings, it's like covering cow-dung with a nice bouquet of roses." However, in my particular case, the relationship with that fool became productive, even with increased hostility. I promptly realized that Arthur was using his own anxiety as a weapon for aggression. He manufactured deceptive tricks with that affinity for evil. Estranged from reality, the boss was living a life of fantasy and imagination. The military training, the moral discipline that the Belgian Para-Commando unit had instilled in me has over the years built-up a great emotional strength. With time, Arthur Valois Dourville de Montrissart's own approach to life forged in me increased tolerance and patience. But, on many instances, in this murky world it is wise to acknowledge the idiot within us. I recognized that more than one occasion I could walk in the streets carrying that huge sign bearing the words 'Idiot of the month' written on it in block letters.

The very bright Leon Van Meerstellen, the Stanford University student could be a potential boob too. At one time he carried a filet of sole to a wrong table. Just at that moment, as he explained the blunder to chef Picharon who started fuming with anger, Leon immediately took the blame for himself: "Please chef, despise me as much as you care, I know that I'm a worthless moron; an imbecile who makes blunders all the time- *Mea culpa, mea maxima culpa*. Now you can beat the hell out of me for I deserve it!"

It was unbelievable that with Leon's conceited manners, Arthur nevertheless admitted blame.

The following day my friend Leon had a thrilling glance in his eyes. I thought I was dreaming; but to our surprise, like a slimy eel, making castanets of his thumb and forefinger and with a slouched sombrero on his head, he indulged in a great sketchy fandango for us, with the same agility as Fred Astaire. Nodding his head with delight in the prospect, Leon took great pleasure in that Andalusia dance-step with the graceful motion of his bouncing long legs, spinning one foot high in the air. But the highlight of the performance came about when he sang a tune with such attractive charm. His voice was beautiful, so dignified with grace and eagerness. With that spark of enthusiasm he was like an infant that just awakend after a glorious dream. All of us hailed him with jubilation, with a thumbs-up for approval. I even tapped out the rhythm with my hand. Though before, he seldom revealed such an extraordinary mood, bewilderment would be a weak word to describe the enjoyment. Leon distinguished himself as he continued dancing with extraordinary gaiety just like he was in an ecstatic state. Suddenly he went off balance, spun and started again. As he twisted his body sideways like a matador he was whistling another song with his lips curling in amusement. We all experienced considerable bliss from the sight. As we were clapping our hands and beating our feet on the ground, the hilarity became quite contagious; the mirth rang louder and louder.

Late last night on the Internet, through e-bay Leon managed to sell an old, very unique car-race video to a British collector for two hundred and fifty dollars!

But Leon's temporary cheerfulness was that of complete cynicism since later on he conveyed to me that "anything will do to pass the time 'till my slow death.'" However, with regard to his dancing, a correlation definitively existed with a closest member of his family. At one time, a dear cousin of his had been a champion of Mazurka.

* * * *

The egotistic child in Arthur always carried a strong desire to be approved, needed and highly respected. He had no doubt in his mind that his made-up stories forcing the imagination to extremes with his affiliations among celebrities or people in power would satisfy his insecurity and feed his ego. As Abdel Simpson simply put it: *"Never tell a lie when you can bullshit your way through."* Not once before had Arthur given such proof of the scope of his eccentric thoughts; of his collection of absurdities. Everytime he would add more embellishments or invented new details. It was important for Arthur to practice the routine of lying. How many times have I heard my employer say that he had inherited rights to seat among delegates in the French Congress as he recounted with great exultation these outstanding quips!:

"In my younger years, I played tennis with a Danish prince!" *He and his friends were probably snooping from outside the palace gates while the prince kept busy in a serious tennis match.*

"The Shah of Iran was a friend of mine. He came to *Le Cerisier* to taste the Crystal Roederer, the finest Champagne in the world!" *He was referring to a local client who was a look-alike of the Shah and who in fact played bit roles in Hollywood as a Middle-Easterner.*

"My uncle was the commander in chief of the *Gendarmerie"*- the equivalent of the Highway Patrol in the U.S. Angeline, Arthur's wife divulged to me later on that *that uncle was actually a police sergeant in a small community.* Those kinds of stories would only get repeated and exaggerated. Here is another one of his quite amusing shaggy dog tales, as he thought that he had gained much knowledge of the properties of nature's herbs and roots: "In Labège par Castanet, my village near Toulouse, I discovered a very special herb, believing it was a real cure for cancer. Upon hearing this, a Chinese delegation specializing in natural sciences came to greet me, and decided to check this out for themselves. They traveled from afar to inspect the quest of the mysterious roots and herbs," and Arthur continued: "After cutting samples from that vegetation from the field right under my feet, they adjudged that an herbalist would analyze it for free in a laboratory in Beijing. The delegation returned to China, bringing with them what could be a potential cure for cancer. They took the patent and used my discovery to save their own people." *And now the Chinese will forever be cancer-free!*

Those kinds of Arthur's imagined tales *sans queue ni cerise*-without any good sense were replayed over and over at every table, whose listeners became more annoyed than amused. However, some people fell driven to the limits of his imagination. A few patrons would show such vivacity that could only flatter Arthur, while behind his back other customers shooked their heads as those fantasies of his mind went into one ear and out of the other. Arthur's lack of formal education in any academic matter was shrouded by an overdeveloped skill in weaving a story, thus made it sound more dramatic. What's more he never perceived those 'make-believe' narratives as lying!

Being a Marathon runner, addicted to the rapture of running, part of my training routine was to sprint on the hard sands of Santa Monica Beach or in Zuma with a passion for nature which impelled me to take a daily dip in the ocean, among the splash of waves. I have always shared James F. Fixx, author of The Complete Book of Running, uplifting philosophy: *"My life has been much more exciting, much more fun as a result of running. The first bird in the spring, cardinals singing in the snow, the perfume of early morning- I would have missed those things and many others. Life is so much richer as a result of running..."*

On one occasion, on a brilliant day from an alcove along the coast highway, after watching people on the beach pattering on their naked feet, I meditated. The air was sweet with the scent of flowers. The scenery was appealing as in a postcard. As the sea washed the rocks from below distant shrouded mountains, with the sound of waves breaking on the shore, I almost lulled into sleep. In that pristine environment I dashed for a six-mile run before jumping into the water. While swimming, something slimy wiggled and brushed my leg; maybe a striped bass or a sort of lichen waving in the gentle currents.

I decided to impart that lighthearted experience with Melanie and Angeline, unaware that the proprietor of the restaurant was still eavesdropping while watching Chef Picharon preparing *la sauce Hollandaise*. I went to the dining room, as I was ready to take the first order from "a party of five". At that precise moment a renowned car dealer sitting along with the guests clutched my arm asserting with amused interest and utter amazement:

"Pierre, did you really swim in shark-infested water as one of them with his fin surfacing and circling above the ocean did impinge you on the leg?" Certainly, those sheltered waters were free of sharks. As the story was spreading around like brush fire in Agoura I was quick to humbly admit it was not a shark that brushed me, only an unknown sea creature or marine plant such as plankton! All this went on and on. Arthur didn't even realize that with so much of false pretentiousness he had lost a great deal of support and understanding from our patrons.

After the boss revealed to the customers about his far-away past, he really had nothing else to talk about. Given that his weekends were usually dull, he would put more spin on my experiences. Just like in sensational novels where writers would use their wild imagination, Arthur would amuse our clientele by embellishing my real stories with fanciful details.

On another occasion my employer didn't stop talking; he was still in his element. With a childlike glow in his eyes and a touch of triumph in his voice he pursued his most exuberant chatter, saying:

"A few days ago, my fearless Pierrot here decided again to swim in the Pacific at midnight. After a mile away of tireless efforts from shore, heavy fog landed on the water like the London Pea Soup and Pierre was lost; completely lost in that colossal, hostile ocean. Next he swam, swam and swam for hours. As the fog finally had lifted itself, Pierre discerned a light in the distance and, with an expression of triumph he saw the coastline of Avalon...on Catalina Island, some thirty miles away!"

Well, I was far away from Catalina Island. In reality I had been swimming in circles. Those lights came from the illuminated Sumitomo Bank in Santa Monica squatting against the night sky!

Arthur had the ability to dramatize his stories the way Orson Welles did in his 1938 radio series in which he startled most of Americans with his daring report of a Martian invasion of the earth.

If my employer had not succeeded as a restaurant owner, surely he would have made it as a stand-up comic at the exclusive Whiskey à Gogo on the Sunset Strip in Hollywood. On the other hand several customers were so exhausted to listen to Arthur's pointless chatters that they were happy to go. As for the charistmatic relationship between my employer and some of our patrons, I usually recalled Shakespeare when he wrote: "I had rather have a fool to make me merry than experience to make me sad."

* * * *

I got the news that Mr. Kevin Planery, one of our good customers got sick and died from lung disease. Kevin was a very active man who never missed a day working out on the treadmill. At thirty-nine years old he had been such an enthusiast of sport activities, and blessed financially. Over the years it still surprised me to observe young athletic people leaving us as they die in the peak of their youth. However, in the case of Mr. Plamery, Arthur showed real compassion. He invited Mrs. Plamery and her two children for a dinner on the house.

Likewise, on other occasions my employer would express concern: for those many years of being in the restaurant business, one thing continually disturbed me, especially in the U.S. For such a multitude of people in the world that are suffering from hunger and malnutrition, so many Americans, upon dining would leave untouched quantities of food on their plates; food that is going straight to the trash-can and this is dreadful. Among the many places I came across, especially in Asia and Africa, entire families would be satisfied with a bowl of rice, a little manioc or a slice of chapatti-flat bread. Some have not even that wretched pittance. However, at *Le Cerisier* I noticed that the domineering Arthur, that 'horrible boss' was equally shocked by leftover resting on several of our client's plates. My employer became so offended that the comedian part of him was resurfacing in a very concerned fashion. Arthur would approach a table, announcing in an uplifted spirit:

"Mr. Glenfield, so far I can visualize that you never even touch your vegetables. If you refuse to eat them, there would be no dessert for you whatsoever; and I 'm dead serious!"

Surprisingly, patrons like Mr. Glenfield would respond positively and would clean their dishes thoroughly. This reminded me about the unbelievable amount of food that went down the trash-can in Versailles under the kings of France (they ate nine to twelve courses on every meals.) Ambassador Caraccioli coined this facetious aphorism: "In France nine-tenths of the population die of hunger and one-tenth of indigestion."

I always ate everything on my plate for when travelling the world, I occasionally went to bed without any food. Again, among so many iniquities, for Arthur this was one more noble quality that remained unswerving.

When some of our patrons are unable to make up their mind over a particular dish from our extended menu, the owner of *Le Cerisier* restaurant would concoct something that can please his or her palate. The Blanchard couple for instance, steady customers who pay us a visit at least once a week, never even checked at the menu. They would call upon the boss to make the appropriate decision over the entire dinner, from beginning to end, including a wine selection from our extended wine list.

Chapter 9

FOR AWHILE, THE rain that impinged upon the earth roared on the small trees, as the blinding sheets of lightning shattered the air. In North-Hollywood, with a wind coming in from Canada it was damp and cold-a perfect day for a funeral. In that nebulous, mackerel sky I could smell the fragrance of the hills and of wild azaleas.

This evening at the restaurant I watched the heavenly mare's-tail. The wind was wailing at the windows. Soon, the sky became pierced again by white, glaring bolts, as a roll of thunder came from the horizon. It seemed an invisible power had fettered the wind. Even the top of the solitary tree in front of the establishment shook as if struck by a missile. This was the most frightful thunderstorm I had ever seen. Now it became a swirling mass of dark clouds and, so suddenly the dysfunctional rain teemed, and started pouring down in sheets as though the heavens had been opened. The droplets grew larger. They rattled savagely against the front windows of *Le Cerisier* as city-lights were gleaming on the wet asphalt. The wind that sounded angry swept howling on the plants too. It commenced raining even harder than before and rained all night in torrent. Before long Ventura Boulevard became a gray, murky river with debris of trees washed away like matches. The Los Angeles River kept on rising till it was over its banks.

At one point, it flooded the boulevard and all the neighboring streets. Within the black, yellow water I saw a small tree-trunk floating right in front of the restaurant. A little later a crazy young man in a wet suit decided this was the perfect time for kayaking!

In such a kind of weather, as the last draws of daylight faded away, Arthur definitively preferred to stay at home. He would curl himself in front of the fireplace, jolting a snifter of Courvoisier in one hand, puffing at his dappled expensive Cuban cigar in the other, building up a steady cloud of smoke into the air, (at home or in the street, his cigar was an integral part of his face) as he listened to the downpour and blustering wind outside.

During all those years working in the same establishment, Leon and I have refined a very trusting relationship with our clientele. Numerous patrons had the impression that we were the real owners of *Le Cerisier* since Arthur was so busy with the place up north. Along with the chef we created our own code of ethics in order to please everyone. Nobody was ever unhappy with our work, and we made lots of new, steady friends. If a client became dissatisfied with a particular dish we would replace it immediately with something else to his or her choice.

* * * *

Occasionally on Mondays, providing that there were no reservations in the reservation book before 2:00 PM Arthur would contact us all by phone to inform his faithful employees that the restaurant wasn't open for business. In my case, as a sport enthusiast, running through the canyons or in the unpolluted air on the hard sand beach every day of the week, I would carry a beeper (that was quite *vieux jeu*-old fashion since there were no cell phones at that tme.) Here was our arrangement: If the beeper started beeping at half-past one, I would take off for the day.

On a particular ebb tide Monday when the waters turned landward again in their ceaseless coming and going, since my employer didn't call, I went straight to the restaurant presuming I would be on duty. After last night's thunderstorm, the sun shone out all the more brilliantly and the air was balmy and clear.

Upon my arrival in Sherman Oaks, an apologetic notice was plastered on the front door of the establishment indicating that we were close on this day for inventory. This was Arthur's usual perversion of truth directed to the attention of our eventual 'walk-in customers.' On other occasions my employer's lie was related to a water leak in the kitchen. With this note on the door, I realized that Arthur simply forget to call me, for we were not open. And there I was, feeling like a fish out of the water, fifteen miles away from Northhollywood after a bumper to bumper ride, crouched in line of screeching traffic and mad honkings from the 405 to the 101 freeways.

Patting my head awkwardly and filled with gloomy thoughts, I sat huddled up in a corner of the parking lot, pensive. Grumbling in frustration and despondent for quite some time, I was wondering what I was going to do with myself for the rest of the day that stretched ahead of me endlessly. Since it was already late in the afternoon I was unable to fashion new plans *pour passer le temps*- to kill time, I proceeded to stroll aimlessly doing window-shopping on Ventura Boulevard and looking at some gargoyles on a local church.

In a faint sunshine, as the afternoon slowly ripened I walked to nearby Balboa Park and commenced throwing stones that ricocheted in the lake that flows without foam or ripples. There was a small gust of wind that barely corrugated the surface of the water before it stood calm, still as glass. Occasionally there would be a flash as a good size fish would jump above the surface of the lake, before splashing down like a missile. This is when I decided to play hide-and-seek with a squirrel that had been scampering at a tree-trunk. As a kid, in my neighborhood I always hid so well that no one could ever find me. Afterward, watching a swan flap its wings I took a little nap on a park bench. Soon after, I began scratching my sides and elbows.

And, to my surprise I discovered that someone either forgot or intentionally set down a small book next to me. The title: *All I Really Need To Know I learned In Kindergarten* by Robert Fulghum. Shuffling a few pages, the introduction showed clearly why Mr. Fulghum called it "His storyteller's license." I believed this was a blessed day after all. The author specified that this license allowed him permission to use his imagination in rearranging his experience to improve a story so long as it serves some notion of truth. Here is Mr. Fulghum storyteller's creed:

> *"I believe that imagination is stronger than knowledge."*
> *"That myth is more potent than history."*
> *"That dreams are more powerful than facts."*
> *"That hopes always triumphs over experience."*
> *"That laughter is the only cure for grief."*
> *"And I believe that love is stronger than death."*

As I kept on listening to the whisper of the trees, I meditated for awhile on those beautiful and powerful words…

My thoughts were interrupted by a well-dressed gentleman gliding swiftly towards me. At that juncture he kindly handed me a sealed box that looked very much like a food-to-go container. The friendly stranger who had a pale thin face and fair hair decided to shake my hand. Before leaving, he spoke cheerfully:

"Sir, I wish you bon appétit, hope you'll enjoy it." I opened the box and to my surprise I discovered a note inside, more like an apologetic annotation with a deep religious insight: "God loves you. Please come and meet us- First Presbyterian Church." Underneath that spiritual message I discovered half a roasted chicken with boiled potato, broccoli, a chocolate pudding dessert, a small container of fresh orange juice and plastic utensils. Having missed my 5:00 o'clock dinner at the restaurant and being ravenously hungry, the timing had been perfect. Before eating, indulging my insatiable appetite I prayed, thanking God for that angel He had sent me. Since nobody was around, being quite content I started to hum and break into that little song from my youth:

"Mon petit ventre rejouis-toi, tout ce que je mange,
tout ce que je mange. Mon petit ventre rejouis-toi,
tout ce que je mange, c'est pour toi."

(My little belly, please rejoice, everything I eat, everything I eat. My little belly, please rejoice, everything I eat is just for you.)

On another bench, a lady unfastened her blouse to let her newborn suckling. The rays of the setting sun were as gold as her golden hair. When the baby had taken its fill, she turned her head in my direction and smiled such a pure smile. That day the beauty of nature; the warm approach from that angel that fed me had been a blessing indeed.

As the late-afternoon advanced, with the ducklings darting about on the surface of the lake, in the sublime serenity, looking at the autumn colors of leaves in the dying summer, I rejoiced. The rustling of withered leaves made strange noises;

they crackled under my foot as they were carpeting most of the paths of Balboa Park. There was still a kind of winter sun in the air, quite agreeable, warm without scorching. It was a receding sun shining down on the lake, glancing upon the ceaseless water.

Now the sun had long set and one could still observe a reddish gleam, like an afterglow in the western sky. The moon still manifested itself lean and pale like a dying woman. A mellow light appeared to embrace the surrounding trees. I stood there until the copper band of light around the lake snapped out. After I listened to the twitter of the birds, enjoying the scent of nature, I left Balboa Park in excellent spirit with a smile on my face. The traffic had abated as working people had already rushed home. I was now speeding on an almost empty freeway, back to North-Hollywood.

That night I slept soundly till next morning.

* * * *

A few stars were beginning to glisten in the sky, and minutes before the opening of the restaurant I heard a strong knock on the front door as if someone wanted to tear it down. It was Mr. Cluttens, Arthur's neighbor who got back from a shopping spree in Sherman Oaks Galleria. He was holding his bulldog on a leash. The short plump round shouldered meat-and-potato man stooped and frowning with a full head of hair was grotesque and quite grumpy, really nothing pleasant about him. With that ugly sack of flesh hanging under his chin that was threatening to run down on his shirt he had a face frequent in those whose sight has decayed by stages. Except for his cold, ruthless rat's eyes always watery that would not meet the gaze, and compressed lips he was a mirror image of his pet. His well-trim, white mustache looked like a worn-out brush. Altogether Mr. Cluttens who appeared old before his time had an unsmiling face twitching with anxiety and uncountrollable trembling only a mother could love.

Arthur came to meet him at the door and a serious discussion followed:

"I need very much to speak to you!" And, with his mouth that started foaming with spittle he continued, "Your beast pooped on my lawn again!"

"Sir, I'm very sorry about this," replied Arthur. "However I want to let you know that my Pompadour is not a beast; a beast is something dirty. My dog on the other hand is really valuable. She has a pedigree and was handed to me by my cousin Count Raoul Valois Dourville de Montrissart from Bordeaux, France, owner of two estates in the Gascogne province. I sincerely believe that Pompadour is lovelier and much smarter than your brainless, ugly and vicious bulldog!"

This was only but one of the many arguments those 'happy neighbors' exchanged during the course of time. That wrangling relationship started years ago, when Arthur claimed that Mr. Cluttens erected a new fence that stood three inches right inside the Valois Dourville de Montrissart's property...

On that same day it was announced that Mr. Howard Olstrum the very popular wealthy car dealer from Vosto Ford in Topanga, and a good customer at the restaurant passed away from pancreatic cancer. He was barely fifty-eight years old, such an elegant man with fine abilities; clever and well-informed on all subjects. It seemed that he never grew old, since there was forever springtime in his heart. With the most caressing look and a sexy moodiness of style he had been a gentleman in his clothes, in his manners. Even that he had been exceedingly well off he was an enchanting human being, untroubled and vigorous, framing a round face and still quite handsome with the finest saturation of intelligence. He had lived a life far from languid old age. Howard always knew exactly what he thought should be done next for his salespersons. And at all times, with humorous fierceness he was ready for a little fun. In short, Mr. Olstrum was a much-respected figure in the community. This great car dealership owner had been quick and active in carrying his plans of business into execution weeks after weeks for so many years. Even that his life had been a great success, the pursuit of money had always been an insufficient purpose in his life. Riches had been of less interest to him than to most people. He always lived with the desire to do good deeds for good's sake.

Ironically Howard met his death in the stress of action. It was as if the peculiar richness of his youth had itself marked its limit. During the last week of his life he had suffered intensely from that incurable illness, but never lost his zest for life.

Prior to breathing his last I had a chance to visit Mr. Olstrum at the Woodland Hills Hospital. Although experiencing pain, he had asked me to hold his hand. And, as though in a confession, Howard already so weak and pale, who appeared to me like John the Baptist opened his heart to me. Still quite as handsome as ever, I will always remember his tender, wise words as long as I live:

"Petit Pierre, it is well-known that Arthur treats you badly and I hated him for his arrogance and stiff-necked attitude. God alone knows how far we are in the grip of our bodies. Yet, now that I'm dying I started to comprehend how much I really love the people I despised most." and Mr. Olstrum continued, "Pierrot, you went to India. In your book, I remember you quoted Gandhi's maxim in regard to his people's brutality in the hands of the British: 'Accept the beatings and love them deeply!' My dear friend, stay humble, that's your nature. Throughout the seasons continue to forgive and forget Arthur's irrational behavior. And who knows, some day something as a good seed may spring up in his heart. You may even write another book and tell the entire world that love always prevails over malice.'" In another thought Howard explained to me that he had been a very successful man, but 'many so-called successful people barely live a few decades because of financial stress and a lavish life of ephemeral pleasures.' Surprisingly he read to me a passage from *The Prophet* by Kahlil Gibran: *"Brief were my days among you, and briefer still the words I have spoken. But should my voice fade in your ears, and my love vanish in your memory, then I will come again, and with a richer heart and lips more yielding to the spirit, will I speak. Yes I shall return with the tide, and though death may hide me and the greater silence enfolded me, yet again will I seek your understanding... Know therefore that from the greater silence, I shall return..."*

In Arthur's presence Eddy wasn't much of a talker. He arrived at the restaurant in pain. He had cut his left foot on a rusty piece of metal. However, since he had waited too long to seek emergency care, blood poisoning had set in. Finally, after he went to Saint Benedict Hospital, he started walking with his foot wrapped in a bandage and was standing on a crutch. Yet, the untimely death of Mr. Howard Olstrum touched him deeply too. My friend who was so good in concealing all emotions, burst into tears. Freedman had bought his first automobile from Vosto Ford. With a curious mixture of feelings, Eddy got all soft hearted. Surprisingly, besides his grief I had the feeling that on that day he opened the recesses of his mind. In a sympathetic manner, he revealed to me in ample details of an agreement he and Arthur have forged together in the event of their demise: If one of them died, the surviving partner would inherit almost all of the real estate properties; and Eddy went on: "As Arthur's best friend for over thirty years, if I'm the first one to crawl six feet under 'in my box' within the deep earth, my four bedroom house in Gaviota which is overlooking the Pacific will be his. If on the other hand Arthur checks out first to his last resting place, I will inherit *La Bagatelle* restaurant in Solvang and a piece of land he purchased near the Klamath Falls in Oregon. Eddy further underlined that both their wishes were incorporated in their joint will.

Upon trusting me with such confidential information I felt I had a special place in Eddy's life. However he told me to keep this secret communication for myself just as if I had spilt it into the confessional.

I already knew that Melanie was the one who kept on looking at the family wealth closely, and it didn't take long with her uncanny resourcefulness to learn of her father's dubious plan between himself and Eddy. With shadows under her eyes, she became furious and wasted no time in confronting him in the presence of the entire restaurant crew. Melanie told him to his face:

"Dad, for Chrissakes Eddy is not even a member of the family. Because of him I would be left with a bleak heritage. How could you do this to me, your own flesh and blood and only child, while he's just a parasite no more than a vermin in our lives? Just remember, if I'm determined enough to kill Eddy, nothing would stop me!"

Since it was Arthur who really oversaw the entire family's finances, from that day on it was crystal clear that great animosity existed between father and daughter. I also gathered that no great affection either flowed between Eddy and Melanie as well, as the gulf that lay between them was wider now that it had ever been.

* * * *

JACQUES MEYER

On a few occurrences, when I became responsible for a blunder Arthur, with that extraordinary flair for business would rescue me from desperate situations. He would achieve his goal by picking on me in a most unconventional way and I have to recognize his amazing, but strange skills for diplomacy.

Once, I accidentally, so gauchely dropped a glass of water on a customer's lap. After I handed the gentleman several napkins, I stood there, horrified, asking the client for forgiveness. My employer having witnessed my awkwardness arrived at the table with a kitchen towel under his arm. As he helped our unfortunate patron dry-up, he conveyed:

"Pierre, don't you realize that Mr. Jacob Lieberman already took a shower this morning? Mr. Lieberman doesn't have to take a shower every hour, on the hour heh?" and for the grand finale, in a curious refining way: "Of course, just between us, Pierrot doesn't know the meaning of a shower. He's not right in his head. Before he was taken away to the cuckoo's nest prior to his arrival at *Le Cerisier,* he washed himself in the Los Angeles River and he smelled like a monkey!" Laughs followed in the entire dining room as everyone became flabbergasted by Arthur's unusual cool. Mr. Lieberman, a fairly well-off real estate broker not wanting to be 'a wet blanket' for that incident joined everyone in the hilarious outcome. Soon, every vestige of embarrassment was gone. The Jacob Lieberman's party left the restaurant contented, and to my surprise, a lavish tip lay on the table next to an empty bottle of *Chassagne Montrachet.* Upon a quick change of heart Mr. Lieberman had gratified me handsomely.

Amid frequent, thoughtful endeavors to remember, I must emphasize the fact that Arthur, in the midst of some of his bad behaviors, his insults and his struggles, had a good side. Next from saving us in compromising situations (just like the one I just mentioned), our employer insisted that our clients at the restaurant were supposed to reward us with a reasonable gratuity of no less than fifteen percent-tip of the amount of the check. For the tight-fisted, stingy ones, this would have been their last meal at *Le Cerisier*, since this particular attitude angered Arthur. His wrath would fall upon their heads rather than to us, his faithful subordinate servers. He would walk to their table and politely address those patrons in a lower tone of voice, not to embarrass them too openly:

"Was there something wrong, something unsuitable with the service...? If not, please give my boys what they honestly deserved. Their fifteen percent-tip, your ultimate token of appreciation is part of their living." With this show of compassion and kindness, once more I LIKED THE MAN.

* * * *

Earlier at *Le Cerisier*, on a gray day compounded of mist and drizzle, Wendy, Leon's ex-wife came in and handed Arthur a book for her ex-husband. This was all about Krishna Consciousness. Wendy's luxuriant hair was reflecting in the light every tone of gold and brown. Her expression was as decently limpid as clean water, and she started chattering along in her harmonious voice. She had decided, in deep, quiet intimacy to join the Krishna Organization after she had lost her job and some of her overseas investments with Finington Corporation stocks she inherited from her father. The peace of mind and the best of health she got from those vegetarian devotees prompted her to inform Leon about the goodness of life by forgetting bad experiences such as a marriage that had turned sour. She added that she was unable to find spiritual freedom in this modern, materialistic world; but now all her old wants and desires had vanished from her heart. At present, she looked more receptive, intelligent, graceful and chaste as a vestal, also extremely beautiful in personal appearance. She had become a lady-in feeling and nature, with a taste for art, music and high culture. It seemed at this point that because of strong religious influence, she had reached that period in her life that happen to every woman when amorous affairs are no longer lurking around the next corner.

Leon wasn't at the restaurant; it was his day off. Being busy replacing napkins in the breadbaskets for customers, I was eavesdropping. Unexpetedly, Wendy in a meditative manner poking her swift elongated nose as a pointer showed to Arthur some interesting passages from the Hindu Bible.

After Leon's ex-wife departed, Arthur leafed through the pages of that impressive book that she handed to him and he discovered a line affirming that humans lived past lives. As usual, he had that bourbon smell on him just as he shouted at me:

"Pierre, this is amazing! That statement from that Holy Book is right. A few days ago I was aroused from my deep sleep, while still mentally within another civilization long ago past, with the universe in space and history in time." With his arm stretched out Arthur went on: "I always thought in the back of my mind that, centuries ago I was a general of an immense army. The site was near a large river with palm trees and white houses with flat roofs on its banks." Afterwards, looking up at the ceiling, he added: "Was it Egypt? Frequently, in my dreams, I remember noticing next to me a man who was wearing a long white robe with a gold necklace. His hat was decorated with a sort of a gold snake. Was he the Pharaoh? And was I really an Egyptian general?"

When I revealed to him that Leon was equally right in his assertion that the boss reminded him of Napoleon Bonaparte, Arthur had a smile on his face. With a condescending pat on my shoulder he declared: "Pierre, although you're a nitwit, I have to recognize that you're a good observer. Yes, Leon is quite right; being very much of a French patriot, I loved the empire. As a matter of fact just look at me, my weight, my height are similar to the ones of that great emperor. I was Bonaparte. There is absolutely no doubt about it!" Later on, in that same line of thinking Arthur started telling our clients that some people might have lived for thousands of years and have known Alexander the Great.

Leon was pleased to have received that book from Wendy but he wasn't that much into religion. However, a few weeks later he expressed his pleasure after he read one particular passage relating to the subject of 'cravings' and the discipline for the characteristic cessation from all kinds of material desires and enjoyment of which sex was the chief element.

Chapter 10

THURSDAY BROUGHT AN atmosphere of alarm in the air. An inspection by the Health Department revealed that the restaurant had been in violation of a major health code. Six roaches had been discovered on the side of the small service table sitting in the private room, along with the scurrying of mice on a wood-panel inside a booth. In addition, in the refrigerator next to a pile of German sausages lying there for Angeline's lunch the inspector kept on sniffling pointedly at the smell of fish that was covered by almost no ice at all; consequently not at the right temperature. The argument from my employer that a slight weakness with the refrigerator's compressor pump had occurred was not the inspector's problem; that it really mattered little to him. What had to be re-equipped had to be re-equipped; it was as simple as that! The inspector's eyes continued to travel over the kitchen.

Last but not least, a leak was found in one of the sink as greasy water flowed below from every joint on to the floor. The entire kitchen was really in a shocking state. I knew that it was bound to happen sooner or later. All this made our employer furious, in addition to realizing that we had to surrender the place for the two busiest days of the week- Friday and Saturday. Arthur was no longer himself; the worried frown on his brow had deepened as he waited with curiosity for what the inspector might say. And there was no waiting: "Sir, from this moment on, the place is now officially closed for business. The entire establishment has to be fumigated. Furthermore, all the fish has to be replaced before the reopening."

Prior to the inspector's report, my scheming employer hinted that I pull a sort of influence on Mr. Kim who obviously was of Korean descent. I had to spread my charms around by telling him in a theatrical performance that I had a Korean girlfriend; that I visited Korea on several occasions, including a side-trip to Palmunjung's joint security area to the north. Arthur would remind me of the maxim: *"In order to catch a fly you have to use a little honey!"* My boss was as obsequious to the inspector as he was arrogant to his employees.

Mr. Kim was a tall, slim man with a sallow countenance, reserved, cold but with polite manners. He had high cheekbones, full-lipped mouth, eyebrows as black as a raven's, a lofty, intelligent forehead and hair that was sprinkled with gray and parted in the center to cover a bald spot. He was a gentleman with good, general education, *entre deux âges;* sixty year old, more or less. His gray flannel suit was a mixture of old and modern style. One of his legs was shorter than the other, and he limped as he walked. Even that he had developed a stoop he was a 'well preserved human being, with a face that had none of those wrinkles. Without being handsome, the man had an easy-going expression, and he was *toute oreille* as I addressed him. Although we chatted with some enthusiasm, Mr. Kim did not seem swayed, as he did not tolerate infractions. His integrity as a county health employee was unshakable; his morals still remained uncorrupted. He had been nominated inspector after he had climbed the ladder of respectability, and I was unable to blind his clear-headed mind, the unbending strength of his personality. The somewhat severe expression in his eyes made equally the meaning of his words more evident. Mr. Kim appeared to be a man of authority; a man of different caliber accustomed to give orders and have them obeyed without question. He was very strict about those rules.

Thereafter, the county employee unbuttoned his vest complacently with deference, and grabbed a pen and papers. Arthur already knew that Mr. Kim was like a conscientious bee going from pedicel to pedicel. A largesse- gift of money made for bribe, commonly known as 'palm greasing' was of course out of question. Now, with the place that had to be closed for at least two days, our highly regarded "A" rating sign became a "B" sign. This represented such a bad publicity for our four star, well-known abode.

"Inspector," Arthur had squeaked imploringly, while holding the reservation book in his hand, sniffling ill-temperedly in the bristles of his nose, "we have a full house for the busiest days of the week." With a sad voice, his eyes fixed on Mr. Kim in supplication Arthur went on, "how can I afford to close *Le Cerisier?*" Now the conversation became as serious as if they had entered a church. With a glance of puzzled scrutiny and the objectivity of a lawyer Mr. Kim restricted himself by saying:

"Please Mr. Valois Dourville (he couldn't pronounce the rest of Arthur's last name), don't gape at me like that. You sound as if I was your enemy, but I'm not. Hold your horses and be quiet now. Just acknowledge the reasonableness of my position and the rightness of my duty! I'm only here to uphold the law and I'm abiding by the department regulations that are to enforce the general rules of hygiene." Flashing his badge, with a ringing pride in his voice, his jaws settling in a rhythmic movement, Mr. Kim went on to say, "Let me give you an objective picture of the situation: my job is related to inspections. I've had twenty-five years of it; it's just routine procedure. In an honorary custodial way, I represent Mr. Flowching, the head of The Health Department. Mr. Flowching expects my report to be on his desk tomorrow morning. That's all there is to it and it is as simple as that! I know how to transact my business!"

For our employer, those powerful words appeared to fling off the last vestige of restraint. He could contest the point with Mr. Kim no further. In a low tone of voice Arthur simply reiterated after him the same words: "That's all there is to it…" Even that he was deeply pissed, the owner of the restaurant knew that arguing was totally useless. He just stood there, a frozen expression on the face. Eddy, standing next to Arthur nodded, definitely agreeing with the inspector's testimony. He accepted the event with as good a grace as possible. Previous to the arrival of the Health Department officer, Eddy had warned our employer about roaches in the dining room and also regarding the lack of cleanliness in the kitchen area. Nothing was ever done. "Don't worry about this" had been the little despot's response!

The inspector strode across the dining room and stooped to the threshold of the doorway. Glancing across the establishment for a last time, Mr. Kim could retain the restaurant owner any longer. He flashed Arthur a customary, friendly but gushing smile, and after solemnly bowing his head gallantly in the most, good natured, respectful manner possible, he aforementioned:

"A pleasant journey to you sir, you will hear more of me sometimes, not before long. So, try to correct all that has to be corrected."

Having said about all he could say, the Health Department Officer left the premises of *Le Cerisier*. When the inspector had reached the sidewalk, Arthur had less than a kind word to say about him. Now tension had reached a breaking point as anger really choked the boss. He turned out to be totally unmanageable. The all powerful Arthur had collided with the iron arm of Mr. Kim, and had been unable to do a thing about it. He kept on brooding on the thought that he would be losing ever so many of his exceptionally good weekend clientele. Once more I became my employer's *bête noire*. In the depths of his eyes, with rage that contorted his mouth, the boss glared at me like a bull in the arena ready to charge. He imparted everyone to have this place in order ASAP. As we frantically pitched the fumigation cans, I was promptly addressed with a stinging slap across the face. Arthur, grunting his head, with sweat running down his body barked at me like a dog. In a stream of insults, he declared:

"Idiot, when you talked to Mr. Kim you didn't try hard enough to please him. I believe it's your fault that we have lost our good 'A' rating sign!" In reality, Arthur was grumbling at his inefficiency in not having checked up everything prior to the arrival of the health inspector.

* * * *

In light of this abeyance and unscheduled holiday, I decided to board the midnight Greyhound bus to Mesa, Arizona to connect with my old friends.

In the twilight of the morning from my seat, with my head against the window the desert that spread its immensity before me was already parched and burning under the ardent sun. Earlier the bus passed through the golden cliff of the High Sierras. I watched the ageless cacti in the blazing desert sucked from all its moist by the starving luminary that appeared like a fire-red ball just above the horizon in the east. There was such great scenery in that limitless sky. It was a good feeling to be here in the Arizona countryside and not being cooped up in the city. Rapidly I felt physically and socially at ease among these new surroundings. Several hours had passed and the sun was still high in the heaven.

Mesa with its smoldering red sky was full of the smell of hay in that shimmering dry heat. The celestial body streaming down on the squeaking earth burned straight down the center of the frying concrete. This was a hot, stock-still day that glared down upon the city until it was as bleached and polished as a marble stone. There was something depressing about the loneliness, the desolation of the region. But when the torrid silence settled down, no one can look for long at the desert and remained impassive to its slight quiescence. Shortly I was standing in front of a shingle roof house, gleaming among the trees. This was a cheerful and comfortable place in a sleepy little town with so much open space. Over there, the air was different-such a kind of air you never get in Los Angeles.

Steve Decarpantel, a tall well-built man with a moustache and smiling little eyes like *Hercule Poirot*, but much taller than the Belgian inspector, was my companion-in-arms with the paratroopers stationed in the Democratic Republic of Congo. We hugged each other with great warmth.

Inside the house I noticed that the living room was furnished in a particular style of elegance. Tasteful ornament such as African ebony statues and rare carvings in ivory stood on a marble table. As we sat down in those comfortable *Utrecht* green velvet chairs, Steve carefully put down on the desk the book he had been reading (the same I already read twice-*The Rise and Fall of the Third Reich.*)

His wife Geneviève, a broad-shouldered woman was serving us a very cold *Stella Artois*. As she prepared *les carbonnades Flamandes*-beef stew cooked in dark beer with prunes, a typic Belgian dish from the Flemish part of the country, Steve and

I spend on hours on end recalling of our operational jump at N'djili airport in Kinshasa with submachine riffles slung over our shoulders. This was the place where we had lost our captain Joss-Antoine Vandenbrecht killed in the hands of Bantu rebels. At that time, as we were touching down on the tarmac on that stifling day bereft of sunshine, much to our astonishment, Russian Aeroflot planes and Mig-Jets were taxiing in. We further recalled how the situation was getting worse. Lawlessness and drunkenness was everywhere as citizens were firing gunshots in the air.

During those wheels of war, words fail to describe the horror we had witnessed in the streets of the Congolese capital, on the eve of the independence from colonial rule. People stormed the city, spreading death and destruction everywhere. In that infernal struggle within so many tribes, like dragons that vomit fire, there were no longer men fighting, but demons holding machetes, for demons attacked as ghosts resisted.

At the close of the Congo war, Steve joined a group of mercenaries working for the separatist state of Katanga under the leadership of President Moïse Tshombe who fought against Congolese nationalism. Until the eleventh hour, Tshombe, prior to his famous speech *"Je m'incline devant l'ONU"* (I will accept the international rule of law), had full control of the gold mines of l'Union Minière du Haut Katanga, with the blessings of the Belgian government. Consequently the Katangese President provided each and every one of those mercenaries 'head of state' salary. Steve left Africa a happy and very wealthy man. Now, that former 'free-fall' parachutist instructor is a stay-home retiree. Aside from his old Nuremberg clock, he still kept up his prior interests in old kind of curiosity. As a professional stamps and cigar-bands collector he would engage in those hobbies, as passionately as ever.

For a last time, after another *café-filtre*, prior to hit the sack, I filled up my lungs with that non-smoggy desert air. On the west, in the late afternoon, the sun appeared to be like a gigantic flame burning the sky...

In the morning, as I awake before the return-trip to California the bright sun had risen too. That short trip to the Grand Canyon State was a refreshing experience. Over there, my mind had been free to think about so many other things and it had heightened my spirit for some time. Those two days in Mesa had been a real enjoyment of uninterrupted leisure. The vastnesses of Arizona cured my soul by lessening my grief over Arthur's bad attitude.

Prior to leaving the desert city and the blazing heat, Steve wanted to know what my new manuscript was all about. I explained to my friend that it is a story of the powerful and the powerless. Again, I was using the illustration of Jean de Lafontaine regarding the yarn where all the animals were dying from pestilence. I fathomed plainly that I frequently felt like the poor, defenseless donkey that received all the blame for eating a little grass on the other side of the fence from a monastery property while the lion, tiger and other ferocious animals, the real killers got away with less than a little slap on the shoulder. This was the terrible trial, from which the weak come forth disgraceful, as the puissant exalted. On the other hand, Victor Hugo expressed his thoughts that the powerless with "their dignity trampled underfoot, living in bitterness and desperation" can get their reward. Here is an excerpt from a famed French writer and philosopher: *"They are noble and mysterious triumphs which no eye sees, no renowned rewards, and no flourish of trumpets salutes. Life, misfortune, isolation, abandonment and battlefields which have their heroes- obscure heroes who are at times greater than illustrious heroes. Firm and exceptional natures are thus created: misery, which is nearly always a stepmother is at times a mother, want brings forth the power of soul and mind: distress is the nurse of pride, and misfortune is an excellent milk for the magnanimous."*

* * * *

On this Mother's Day; a day bathed in a special radiance Arthur looked pretty stiff, gloomy and crushed. He arrived at the restaurant suffering from hemorrhoids. Eddy Freedman, as a former medical orderly in the Navy, during the Korean War, followed him with a large pillow under his arm, as his friend experienced intensive pain, especially from the left side. The boss, feeling an agonizing distress that took his breath away was struggling as if he would go into convulsions. He had a dazed look on his face, like he had been walking in his sleep. And suddenly, in an unpleasant sensation he uttered a loud, shrill cry. Still, in the private room, Freedman was nursing his friend with the tenderness of a woman. He showed the care which a mother bestowed upon a child as he started to rub Arthur's lower back with ointment before covered him. In a warm, plausible way, Eddy spoke kindly to his friend, "Tutur, don't you go and strain yourself in the dining room, O.K.?"

Later on, as they sat on the same booth they remained silent. Yet, as Eddy began to try to feed him soup out of a spoon Arthur became obsessed with the fact that his body gave off an offensive odor. My employer had his regular drink but there wasn't any enthusiasm in his eyes. At that moment, Eddy like a guardian angel touched his face to seek if he had some fever. The boss let himself over to that hand. He again thanked Freedman for the attention knowing very well that his good friend would follow him to the ends of the earth. Freedman was able to accept his own sufferings, but not that of Arthur.

In that line of thinking, something unusual happened to Eddy: he never covered his hair, but today he wore a hat that came down over his head, concealing his forehead close to his eyes. Earlier during the day my friend had mistakenly grabbed a bottle of Eastern European fungus lotion thinking it was a shampoo, and most of his hair had been half-burned.

After awhile, Arthur utterly anxious for solitude went on just to greet a few customers in the dining room before deciding with his pillow in hand to get into his Nissan truck, heading home along with Eddy.

* * * *

"Arthur, you are a gentleman, and since every now and then you always exceptionally take good care of me I've decided to help you. I'm now awarding you with a McDonald franchise. And this is at no cost to you."

The year was 1965 at *La Mousson* restaurant located on Vine Street, a stone's throw away from Hollywood Boulevard. The pleasant bald headed man that was talking with such a fertile imagination was none other than Mr. Raymond Kroc also known as Ray Kroc. A pioneer of the fast food restaurant industry, Mr. Kroc was the founder of the immensely, flourishing McDonald franchise. After meeting the brothers Dick and Mac Donald in their drive-in restaurant in San Bernardino, California, the future owner of *The Padres'* baseball team formed a partnership with the brothers. In addition, Ray Kroc, the incredible visionary was granted the use of McDonald's name that included the golden arches symbol. That man; that giant who revolutionized the restaurant business the same way Henry Ford did with the automobile industry was a regular customer at *La Mousson*.

In 1972, my future employer left his partner at that famed Hollywood establishment and opened *Le Cerisier* in Sherman Oaks.

Now, according to Arthur's version of that story my boss had refused that almost unbelievable opportunity of having a McDonald franchise for free during the '60's, telling Mr. Kroc:

"Ray, my friend I really appreciate your immense generosity but I'm not in the fast food business," and Arthur continued, "I was educated in the Lyon's culinary school, the best culinary school in the world; I dedicated my entire life to fine cuisine. Can you imagine me, Arthur Valois Dourville de Montrissart flipping hamburgers?"

My employer probably thought that by accepting that outstanding offer of franchise would have compromised his dignity! Arthur so far had had no vision of the future of the McDonald Empire.

Day in, day out, everywhere it's still the same regretful tune:

"Ah, if I would have started this kind of business twenty years ago I won't have to worry about my retirement." Or, "Why in the world have I sold my house prior to the massive real estate boom?" Those missed opportunities that are now gone with the wind have caused many tongues to wag. In 1985, a McDonald franchise would have cost Arthur two hundred and fifty thousand dollars, and at the turn of the new millennium, those numbers already passed the million dollar mark! Not bad considering that Mr. Kroc started in the business of selling equipment for milk shakes, in addition of paper cups!

Oftentimes Arthur felt so low, thinking over that gold mine he had missed, that he suffered from dreadful depression. On the other hand, after having worked tirelessly for so many years at *Le Cerisier*, exhibiting a degree of loyalty and good service, beyond reproach for his French expertise, I knew my employer quite well. He kept on narrating to our faithful customers the same 'McDonald' tale over and over. It didn't take me long to realize that he needed someone to listen. So, I reassure him by telling him that being the owner of a classy 'four star' French restaurant, and by promoting his recipes from *la nouvelle cuisine*, he had made the right decision after all!

As for the veracity of Arthur's narrative, I must ask the indulgence of my readers, since not knowing what was real or fabricated I couldn't substantiate that scenario! With Arthur, as his imagination kept on taking wind, I had been schooled for the unexpected. I have been careful enough not to omit any facts that could come to my knowledge.

Here is another one of his unbelievable, far-fetched and unpredictable story line that I overheard him telling our clients at *Le Cerisier*. This also happened at Arthur's former restaurant *La Mousson*, back in 1968.

One evening in that famed Hollywood establishment, patrons sensing the urge to gratify their inner needs were perusing the menu that was written on a small blackboard, when my employer's attention suddenly riveted in the direction of the front door. Senator Robert Kennedy wearing a fine, well-tailored gray suit stood waiting at the entrance with three of his guests, one of them being the famed singer Andy Williams. Arthur directed them to their table, adjacent to the fireplace. This occurred at the eve of Mr. Kennedy's famous speech at the Ambassador Hotel where he won the California Democratic Primary. The 'happy campers' were talking about politics; of the outcome at the Democratic Convention in Chicago, leading to the ultimate presidential race.

Arthur didn't want any waiters to even approach those V.I.P. patrons. He alone would take their order, even serve them. However, after several attempts to make them decide on what to choose from the menu they were still undecided. At this point, Arthur became short-tempered and his blood pressure was mounting. The little man came back at the senator's table. Suddenly, in an explosion of words unwilling to wait any longer he articulated:

"Bobby I'm sorry, I really have to take your order as well as of your friends. Tomorrow you'll have all the time in the world to talk in front of all major television and radio network as the entire country would be listening. But right now I'm in charge OK? I want you all to pick-up an item from my extended menu from this blackboard."

After a quick glance on the board, the senator and his friends, showing high marks of restraint decided with some sort of dignity on *le plat du jour* adorned with a fine bottle of Chevrey Chambertain.

At that particular moment, prior to the opening of *Le Cerisier,* I was working part-time at *The Cove*-a German restaurant only a stone's throw away from the Ambassador Hotel. So, next day, following that event at Arthur's fine dinning place, as a fervent admirer of Robert Kennedy I mingled among the crowd that stood on the grounds of that famed structure, to hear the politician's victory speech, and unfortunately witnessed his destiny through the hands of an assassin!

Never in my life did I feel so emotional for a person with political background, but subsequent to that criminal act, like thousands of supporters in California and all over the U.S. I felt tears in my eyes. I loved the man; I loved his views for the future of this great land.

At the same time (according to his story), Arthur got drunk and he didn't touch any food for an entire day. Hopping sadly from one table to another, he lamented, saying: "I have lost a dear friend."

Chapter 11

V AN MEERSTELLEN WAS an agnostic to the bone. Anyone who opened the topic of God or religion with him would be faced into a heated debate. He was greatly appalled by the events of the Crusades and the two World Wars. For him, this had propelled the moral decay of Christianity. The mention of 'holy war' on radio or television was unsettling to him because he reasoned that this was equal to total compliance to evil. All these malevolence in the world carried in his breast the darkness of hell. Though I doubt that Leon even believed in hell, human imperfection, suffering and evil in the world were his significant enigma. He considered annihilation a frightful joy; the submission of the inevitable. Van Meerstellen was most interested in the controversial topic of our discussion of creation versus evolution that was carried on with dissension. After all our opinions had been exhausted he declared to me:

"Pierre, have you ever read Nietzsche? Don't you know that God is dead?" As we were discussing the 'big bang' theory and life on earth, I conveyed to him this excerpt from Albert Einstein's assumption: *"The probability of life originating from accident is comparable to the probability of the unabridged dictionary resulting from an explosion in a print shop."*

And I continued, "God created man and endowed him with a good will. The Intelligent Designer rejoiced in His finished product. He had been pleased by designing it." Leon responded by facing his back to me. Surprisingly, he bends over and tapped his butt. I didn't need any further explanation. I knew I had been talking to a brick wall; this gesture alone suggested ample awareness of his reasoning.

Afterwards, Leon showed his anti-elitism and low achievement motivation regarding spiritual matters as he conducted a conversation with two brothers enjoying their meal at *Le Cerisier*.

Jeffrey and Dennis Contraros were Christian rock musicians. As *Opus Dei* faithful members, they voluntarily submitted to morning flagellation. Following the rhythmical atonement of flagellation, thin trickles of blood would appear all over the upper part of their bodies. They mortified their flesh in every possible way with voluntary humiliation. Bodily torment and severe austerities for the spiritual impulse was a must to strengthen their hope for martyrdom. Being extremists, they prayed with the thought that it would be a blessing if they could be afflicted with painful ulcers in order to purchase eternal benefit; to find safety to the port of salvation. In addition, they prostrated themselves on the ground with their arms extended like a cross for several hours. Furthermore, *Opus Dei* members would expose themselves to the prospect of a thousand deaths every night for the exclusive unparalleled joy to live in the heavenly world, sooner than later. Dennis conveyed that according to General Flavious Josephus quotation from *The Jewish War*, he and his brother followed the spirit of the Essenes who condemned the miseries of life and who were above pain by the generosity of their minds. From the same quotation, Dennis went on, *"In addition, we smile in our very pains and laughed to scorn those who inflicted torments*

*upon us. For us, dying is such a source of ravishment; a bliss in a form
of beatification too."*

However, the brothers, after they drank from the
water of that divine fountain found themselves in extreme
physical weakness. Their piety was mystical, often visionary.
What's more, they learned the art of conversation and of
poetry blended with religious self-discipline. They were both
tremendously knowledgeable regarding bible scriptures as they
devoted their lives for the propagation of their faith. Their
argument with my co-worker made some sense, even for an
uninformed listener. However, as Jeffrey mentioned with the
same ardor as Monsignor Fulton Sheen that it is impossible
to rule without God, Van Meerstellen's face turned red. In a
vibrating voice he argued that the brother had no idea what
he was talking about.

The conversation became strained, even awkward. Like
runaway trains, the discussion took them where they had no
intention to go, but almost immediately it got off its tracks.
There was some sputtering protest from both the Opus Dei
brothers.

Sensing a heated situation about to erupt Arthur took
Leon aside and warned him in a rather unpleasant way that he
didn't want to lose customers over a religious estrangement.
Obediently, without rapture, Leon stopped talking. Still, a
little embarrassed the boss joined the Contraros's at their
table, offering them a bottle of *Clos du Bois* Cabenet Sauvignon.
However, after picking up his nose, Arthur came up with his
own personal opinion:

"I still have the conviction that we may have descended
from the chimpanzees." Jeffrey, after a sip of wine wound
up the conversation summarily by exclaiming, "Whenever
you visit a zoo, as you look at a few intellectual inadequate
macaques, do you greet them as cousins?" Arthur didn't reply;

he simply scowled like a wounded animal. He was quite angry with himself for having blurted out his thoughts that didn't produce the effect he was expecting: merely an approval.

Frequently, the boss exertion to monopolise the conversation embarrassed so many customers who politely kept on listening to his diatribe, to his hodge-podge. A few of them, upon a good excuse would decide on a graceful exit. For my employer, who still believes that we are direct descendants of apes, I found this quote from W.N.P. Barbellion well presented in The Best of Clarence Day (This Simian World) by the estate of Clarence Day: *"How I hate the man who talks about 'brute creation,' with an ugly emphasis on brute... As for me, I am proud of my close kinship with other animals. I take a jealous pride in my Simian ancestry. I like to think that I was once a magnificent hairy fellow living in the trees, and that my frame has come down through geological time via sea jelly and worms and Amphioxus, fish, dinosaurs, and apes. Who would exchange these for the pallid couple in the Garden of Eden?"*

* * * *

Tonight, we had a surprise visit from Bernard C. Bleecken, son of the prominent theologian and preacher *LL Dei Gratia* John Bleecken from the 300 Faith Org. At one time, when I was already employed at *Le Cerisier,* Bernard worked as a part-time busboy. He had been molded by his father who had trained him in the field of religion. But to the surprise of everyone, he eventually became a brilliant Beverly Hills lawyer, ambitious enough to be named law-firm CEO. And with daddy's fortune Bernard established himself as a businessman. He now owns two commercial real estate properties. Being Leon Van Meerstellen's former schoolmate at Stanford he always ended-up being the first of the class with the highest marks. Among his fellow-students, he was a great favorite, so smart, so eloquent that he occasionally played hooky. He had been the star at the basketball team. At Stanford, Bleecken made brilliant speeches as he read voraciously to store vast amounts of information. And his peers endowed him with special honors. On several occasions he had been a guest lecturer on criminology and behavioral science.

Being the best man at Leon's wedding, he was recommended to Arthur. At that time, the business happened to be exceptionally good and Bernard was hired as a busboy. Leon had a feeling of trusting tenderness for his friend. Bernard drove a Continental, his dad's. Almost immediately Arthur had equally conceived an extraordinary liking for Leon's friend.

As an employee at *Le Cerisier,* Bernard already had a considerable belly, a big head, fat arms with a tattoo of a cross on the back of his neck. He then claimed that he was a cosmic lover. It was comical, quite sad too that he would talk about malnutrition, hunger in the world, and people starving in Somalia while he was so well fed, so well taken care of.

He would lift his head and look at the sky, rasping out a sardonic chuckle. I had the vague impression of him standing solemnly against some distant pattern of bright stars. Looking at me, he would touch his protuberant forehead adding in a tone of religious fervor: "Pierre, life is rapture, an ecstasy. Look at the shower of stars, the arrival and departure of the comets, all the beauty of creation. When you stare at the cosmos it's like you experience a spiritual intercourse. You don't need encyclopedia knowledge, there is absolute evidence, a certainty that God exists."

On other nights, lifting his eyes to heaven, as he was again scrutinizing the darkness of the dome he would smoke a joint saying that it creates an extraordinary effect upon the brain. In a state of quietude, with the smelling of a faint whiff of marijuana, Bleecken informed us that with a light intoxication of the mind he kept 'his head clearer' in order to positione himself better for an-out-of-body experience with God, the Master of celestial mechanics and Commander-in-Chief of the universe. After another long drag on the joint, blowing clouds of smoke all over he added that God is a happy God and that he was His instrument. The dull poet concluded that a master plan from the divine Architect had been laid out for him "the future preacher." Dancing under the moon after he cast the final blessing, Bleecken renewed his promise not to have any desire for riches nor the love of worldly things in order not to fall short of his Messianic vocation. To live in honest poverty with the power to lay his hand on the sick, and make them recover would be his calling. He would become an apostolic errand; a servant of the suffering humanity, living on plants, wild honey and water. He would traverse the desert; the jungle and fight ambition for the surest reward in Heaven. At dinnertime Bernard would thank the Lord for our daily bread.

One day, Arthur who praised the busboy, knelt in front of Bernard. With his shoulders bowed and his head lifted, he was anxiously searching his face. He saw before him a man in the ecstacy of a burning, prophetic faith. Holding a brass Crucifix, the boss's eyes lingered with a sort of admiration toward the preacher's son. Now, he urged Bleecken to proceed with the imposing of hands on his forehead. Bernard, expressing himself with missionary zeal, articulated with pontifical gravity:

"With the blessing of heaven and the saints, through the power of the Holy Spirit vested in me, let the light of Christ shine upon you. Please Lord granted Arthur remission for his sins!" His talk was all of beatific visions, as he concluded: "Arthur, keep in mind that by faith men can move mountains. By purging your energy from contamination, I ward off all illnesses from your body as well as faults and shortcomings from your mind. I will now set you on microcosmic orbit. For now on you shall be a ruler among men for God is your resource's supplier!" At this point Arthur surreptitiously crossed himself.

Bleecken reminded me so well of that large toothless lady who picked-me up while hitch-hiking on my way to Canberra, Australia. For a long time, she didn't talk; not a word. But as we arrived at a stop-light on the outskirts of the capital, like a gross ape that gave me the creep she grabbed my wrist with tremendous strength and scornfully retorted with fire in her eyes:

"Do you believe in Jeeeeeesuuuuus?"

"Yes madam." I replied. "I also believe this is where I get off, thank you kindly..."

Bernard was in a feverish gaiety on his own consecrated ground, drunk with the joy of his achievement. At that precise moment, they both fell on their knees and spent some time in prayer. As a finale, Arthur took the hand of the future preacher, and kissed it.

Yawning unrestrainedly Van Meerstellen who was listening to Bleecken and telling Arthur to clean his soul, discreetly laughed in his beard. Turning a cold shoulder, he became pissed with this comical imbecility, the fanatical zeal that animated the followers of any sort of religion or sect. This reinforced his idea that religious scriptures are apocryphal; that it is a science of ignorance; just an ugly farce! Leon didn't really comprehend that anyone can be a worshipper of the unseen...

By the way, Bernard, that purist thinking he had been ordained by God to redeem the country and who was preaching the greatness of renunciation; the release from the pomp, the vanities of this wicked world didn't live up to his word. Several weeks later while still working at the restaurant, Bernard C. Bleecken broke the law of decency and was arrested in Westwood following a homosexual act with a college-student in the luxury Continental. Since that student was under eighteen years old, there was *détournement de mineur*-statutory rape too. This incident, a serious charge of immorality was quite surprising, considering that the man had also a mania for preaching chastity. Bernard had had many sexual encounters with other male partners, but because of daddy's fortune, relationship and plea bargaining, he had been able to escape the real punishment he deserved.

Later on in life, as a lawyer (forgetting his spiritual calling), the city council investigated him for slush funds after a succession of ill-planned adventures in overseas finances. Furthermore he had been indicted for writing checks without provision.

Eventually, Bernard got married to a wealthy widow by the name of Jennifer. Jennifer lived with her late husband (some kind of a Hungarian baron) in Switzerland before moving in a large house near Santa Barbara. Now that the former busboy came back at *Le Cerisier* as a client, Leon proceeded to ask him that simple question: "What about your promise to live in honest poverty?" The former schoolmate simply replied with a curious expression of self confidence: "No comment!"

Rumors would have it that not long ago Bleecken got a stroke following a heavy drug habit. Later, and this had been confirmed to me as being absolutely true: on numerous occasions, as Bernard was still hooked on marijuana, his wife picked on him. Being deeply tormented following a stroke, he killed her with a hatchet that was hanging in the garage next to his tool-boxes, before cutting her in pieces in the bathtub. The poor woman had first bled to death almost instantly. Soon after, a man found Bleecken unconscious on the sidewalk as he retorted weak groans. This had been the most terrible shock for his pastor's father, his family, the entire congregation and TV watchers. There was evidence from a court-appointed psychiatrist that Bernard had been mentally ill and consequently had not been responsible for his actions at the moment he killed his wife as he was heavily on drugs. Hs short life ended in the criminal insane institution of Atascadero. He had died of massive heart attack. . .

* * * *

With so much malice and cruelty in his heart, I believe that guilt and grief had soared in Arthur's brain. Occasionally I observed my employer sitting alone in the private room, staring at the ceiling. He was flooded with conflicting emotions, trying to discover the meaning of life. Being an occasional religious fanatic, providing that difficulty occurred, Arthur was in the opinion that an act of natural pity would seat him in communion with the Almighty.

In the dining room, my employer would kneel in front of a painting of the Madonna and Child until his knees were so stiff that he could scarcely rise. He felt strong enough that a good prayer is an insurance that can help the business to thrive. Repeatedly, Arthur retained that habit of kneeling before the icon for a special favor, sniveling; asking pardon for his transgressions.

At one time, in the dead of winter I witnessed at *Le Cerisier* a young couple. They came to the establishment to celebrate their first wedding anniversary. However everything became dysfunctional. Disharmony filled their little corner of the dining room. Arthur, being informed of the happenings went to the table and his eyes shone with a moist. After holding the couple's hands together, the boss started to pray. This was a deep, powerful prayer for reconciliation. Next, with tears in their eyes, the young couple decided to sit side by side. The husband tenderly kissed his wife and everything went fine. Peace was in the air.

On another occasion, a man came at the door with his children, and pleaded with Arthur: "Sir, I'm a homeless, dying from hunger and so are my two sons." Immediately the owner of the restaurant ordered the pantry-chef to prepare three thick roast beef sandwiches that he handed to them, along with Evian bottle water. I thought for a moment that my employer got into the skin of an honest, of a compassionate man that felt the warmth of love, but not for long. Soon the fuddling Arthur was as scheming as ever again. With his ears red with rage, and steaming like a furnace, he came back at me with a new volley of insults that shows the terrifying depths of his character:

"Pierre, forty-five dollars are missing in the cash register from Saturday night's transactions." And, clearing his rasping throat Arthur concluded, with no evidence that it was me who had made a mistake: "I must have that money returned today or no paycheck for you!"

This is how the little boss welcomed me on this cold Monday. I reminded him that last Saturday the three of us were on the floor, working on the dining room and that we all opened the cash register. Standing on that pedestal of infamy with a mesmeric trance and eyes fixed in a stare, he adjudged me guilty. In his mind, it seemed wholly improbable that someone else was at fault and he scornfully retorted:

"Only an imbecile, a complete slow-witted moron like you would give back too much money in change to a customer!" With that revolting language, that horrid, grotesque statement of flagrant willful gross injustice, that despicable human being became abusive, even more threatening. For so many years, being the depository in charge of the money not a penny was ever missing, and now the boss indignantly implicated me with the loss.

At dinner-time, as I explained to my co-workers that unfair and silly approach from Arthur, I noticed that Leon listened receptively. I already knew that from his early childhood his life was inspired by the fundamental principle of justice. He had moral discipline, dignity and manly self-respect; a real man who did not tolerate infractions. For him, thinking well was the next thing to acting well. It had been his habit to take the lead in all important decisions. In a judicial way he saw it all quite clearly. He laid his rolled-up serviette beside his plate and abruptly interrupted the conversation. With the Wisdom of Solomon, he pointed out in a matter-of-fact tone: "Let's go on with the particulars. Actually I am not perfect, neither is Melanie. It is clear as day that anyone of us could have been at fault since we are all liable to error. Frankly and honestly this is what I suggest since it's best to get things done the right way: Let's divide the amount in three equal parts: fifteen dollars each." This reminded me so well of one of Abraham Lincoln answer to Horace Greenley's attacks in the *New York Tribune:* "I will try to correct errors when shown to be errors; I will adopt new views as fast as they shall appear to be true views."

Surprisingly Melanie went along with the proposal, no objections whatsoever. I was so delighted to have found favor in the eyes of friendly co-workers who had done what was correct. I never doubted Leon's good sense and judgment. I was really thankful to him for being constantly at my side during difficult times. We didn't say a word of our arrangement to the laconic Arthur. I simply counted the money in front of him. Highly intended, the boss laughed an ugly sound. He already had liquor on him, and leaning forward he declared that he knew I would understand. Still, with that strange look of a brute, after he first heaved me with a gentle tap on the shoulder, he concluded in an ironical voice and without any feelings:

"You know Pierre, for that amount I would have knocked your god-damn head off!" *Arthur's wickedness appeared to me in all its ugliness as my mind became a prey to gloomy thoughts. For sure, that man knew how to make me feel miserable for the more diabolical power he had, the more evil he could achieve, and I often felt he had sold himself to the devil!*

* * * *

Another time-consuming year went by and on this Fourth of July holiday *Le Cerisier* restaurant was closed for business.

Tonight, along with Helena and a few of her friends from the Pacific-Island country, we went to Chase Park, alongside the Marina Del Rey channel, leading to the ocean to watch the gigantic fireworks. The day had been very hot and exhausting. With our B.B.Q.'s and San Miguel beer in hand we were ready for the outstanding show. As the crowd swayed forward, close to the end of the channel, the Fourth of July celebration started in total darkness. The explosion, the whizzing of multicolor flashing lights high into the sky was extraordinary. It sounded like huge gun-shots here, there, on every side. With the burst of detonations and the stream of little colorful stars, a murmur of approval came from the large crowd. The 'ooohhh' and the 'aaahhh' from the throng were relentless. Those reflected lights were glaring on a large area of the channel like so many diamonds. Next, we heard from the background several other sounds of nationalistic music with boisterous laughter that emanated from sailboats and gorgeous luxury shining yachts.

Arthur, his family and good old Eddy decided to observe a similar glimmering show on the other side of the hills, on Balboa Park in the San Fernando Valley.

On that exceptional day, when high spirits were out of control, with the shower of sparkling stars that continued to soar over each other with all the colors of the rainbow, and claps of thunder, I was fortunate enough to meet French people from Aix-en-Provence on an extended vacation in California. Right in the middle of the festivities they started to sing *La Marseillaise*, reminiscent of the marquis de Lafayette's contribution in the creation of this great land: The United States of America. With their angelic voices I felt very touched, even emotional as hundreds of other viewers sang 'The Star Spangled Banner.' There was a group of men and women still in their old service uniforms; some from the Navy, the Army and of the Marines. Next was *la grande finale* that looked more like a warship using most of its arsenal under vast umbrellas of even more dwindling colorful lights created by multifarious explosions.

On our way to a Venice Beach disco to continue the celebration Helena was *rayonnante de joie*, quite joyful. She said that next to New York's Fourth of July celebrations this had been the best show ever. And on that certain night, I felt so grateful that I received *e pluribus unum* the privilege of being adopted by the U.S. such a great country with unparalleled prosperity.

Chapter 12

IT HAS INVARIABLY been the policy of the owner for employees not to take any food or drinks outside the restaurant's premises; this was sternly forbidden. We were only allowed to eat and drink a beer or a glass of wine inside the establishment. But After his nasty divorce Leon Van Meerstellen felt a lingering feeling of unhappiness and depression. His marriage was perfect on paper but incomplete in communication; his wife had been an absolute big spender. And before long, he started to drink heavily.

On a particular time, beyond the darkness of the day Leon sneaked out of the kitchen back door which led to the parking-lot where his Camaro was stationed. He decided to conceal two bottles of wine and a *paté* in his car's trunk. Simultaneously there was the sound of a motor vehicle searching its way into a parking space. But Leon didn't hear the hooting of the engine shunting in the alley. At that precise timing, with a screeching sound on the almost hard-packed gravel that had left a low wake of dust Arthur arrived. He floored the breaks of his red Nissan truck with that fretful odor of gasoline behind. He abruptly swerved to the right where Leon's automobile was parked. At this moment the noise of the gravel made my collegue raise his head. The boss diverting his eyes to the open trunk was so stunned that he kept the engine idling for a few seconds before turning off the ignition. Bobbing his head out of the car's window, ill tempered the restaurateur watched with discomfiture and morbid thought the evidence of the theft. Arthur could not have been more astonished if a bolt of lightning had struck in the midst. He came out of his vehicle with some sort of paralyzed attitude.

Our employer already suspected Leon of pilfering, but without any proof. My co-worker realizing that he was actually caught 'a thief in the act', more like a little boy surprised with his hands in the cookie-jar, was petrified. Moreover, losing his composure, after snatching a private, brief chat, Arthur fired Leon on the spot, without any further comment.

Van Meerstellen stood there for awhile. Afterward he let his hands fumbling clumsily alongside his black pants, then left. Leon could not forgive himself. By this act he had betrayed his future and his dreams for a good, decent and honest life as he had been caught in comitting a disloyal sham to his employer.

However, I always suspected that the firing of my colleague was not entirely related to the stealing. This had been utterly created as a diversion. As I mentioned earlier, the fact had been the constant disapproval of my employer about Leon's marriage to his wife Wendy. For many years, the Valois Dourville de Montrissart and Van Meerstellen lived as next door neighbors in Calabasas. From kindergarten to high school Leon and Melanie grew together. It appeared so natural for Melanie's parents to experience a warm encounter between those teenagers. Arthur always wanted his daughter to love Leon. He had never understood Leon's passion for his wife Wendy. By choosing another spouse, Van Meerstellen had created in the owner's mind an atmosphere of heart-burning indignation.

That evil ardor of hate, of jealousy that had taken seed in Arthur's life was stronger than ever. At the eve of the marriage between Leon and Wendy the boss told my friend and colleague: "I think you are making a serious mistake; one you will intensely regret!"

After Leon's departure, subsequent to excellent reviews *Le Cerisier* garnered from television and newspapers, Arthur was forced to hire two new waiters. He found them at a boardwalk café on the Malibu shore, sipping their mimosa drink with colorful little umbrellas planted on a slice of orange.

Horst Bourget and Paul Larivière were both from Vevey, Switzerland, a picturesque little town surrounded with high peak mountains and rolling hills in a pleasant landscape. In their country, amidst different ethnic groups of people, they both became purist of the French language, always picky to find the perfect locution.

As a Swiss citizen, Horst especially spoke that gracious tongue like a poet. With that vivid sensory diction, he articulated his words perfectly as fast as a Parisian, even as fast as a Polish can drink his beer. At one time, as a well-bred young man, he had climbed the social ladder by being a member of the Marcel Proust Society. And, with such elegance he was able to master the arts in language art. Moreover, I had the strong feeling that Horst still lived in the Seventeenth-Century Society in France as he had some definite knowledge as to the matter in which *la haute noblesse* survived. Once he recalled to me those quatrains from Monsieur Voltaire: *"Politeness is to the mind what beauty is to the face. It is the sweet image of a good heart, and it is this goodness which we cherish."*

Prior to their arrival in the U.S. Horst and Paul drove their caravan Renault Camper from France to Spain, seeking the warmth of the sun amidst the myriad villages nearby the Mediterranean coastline. Horst who always walked elegantly had been born of healthy well-to-do parents. He was a full-blooded bourgeois with an aristocratic face. Relishing his distinguished birth with a dreamer of myths of ancient times he walked with a pedantic air and conceited manners. Yet, there was something enjoyable about his sneering air of condescension. Except for his highly respected father who was still living on his estates, the family ramifications at one time fully known in the entire vicinity was now quite extinct. Short, with curly dark hair and high forehead he had bright eyes and a sharp mind. Still, his mouth was somewhat too small with the thinnest kind of lips in the world delicately lined for a man's. Before meals Horst always drank tea. And in the Russian manner he would put a small lump of sugar in his mouth and sip the tea through it.

Paul, on the other hand was quite the opposite. He was far to be a man of elegant upbringing from a good family, and he didn't feel at ease in the bourgeois- aristocratic society. His blond hair had a deeper glint of gold while his eyes were a starting blue in the bronze of his face as he was always oblivious of the day's heat. Tall and healthy-looking, he reflected the typical image of a California surfer, always carrying a bottle of sun-oil lotion. But for cosmetic reason, Paul got a surgical liposuction. Horst, on the other hand would turn lobster-red under the sun.

Aside from being a macho-man with exaggerated physical mannerisms, next to his friend, Paul was at some time more of a mixture of doll and puppy. Oftentimes he would act like a most temperamental lunatic, not knowing how the season was advancing or the day had lengthened. He was unable to face existence without drugs. At once, I saw in Paul's face the very signs of schizophrenia. For quite some time with a history of violence Paul had been involved in a drug rehabilitation program. His English was poor; his sentences very clumsy, often nearly incomprehensible. They bore not the slightest resemblance to the Anglo-Saxon language. Paul talked in his own particular idiom; in his own vernacular. He seemed desirous to speak but he only spoke in short, abrupt phrases by using imperfect sounds, practically indecipherable. With his babbling, he was not always understood, but he had managed to accumulate a store of clever-sounding words. After awhile he started telling funny stories, but they were always vulgar. Occasionally, with his purple stockings he had some kind of feminine evasiveness as he would do a tapster dance right on the kitchen floor.

Towards women, my new colleague seemed to act discourteously. Every day, in the bathroom, in front of the mirror Paul kept on scanning his face to a few seconds scrutiny looking searchingly at his image.

Over a serious argument with Horst (they had frequent quarrels and said revolting and venomous things to each other, even using a language that would have been an affront to a prostitute on the boulevard), as all the blood in their veins rushed to their faces. By calling each other 'bitch', they appeared to harmonize perfectly in the midst of a sudden unlikeness to each other. In extreme case they would work together without exchanging a single word. Paul who wore a golden cross around his neck also followed a strict Chinese diet of macrobiotics prepared mostly with grains and beans. However, he had a serious case of ptyalism. Every time he spoke, if you were close enough from his mouth, particles of saliva would get into your face. Because of a weak chest, his voice was unfitted for singing the "Happy Birthday Song" addressed to our clients. Paul couldn't carry a tune if he had it in a sack. Sometimes he would be sick for unknown reasons and strangely enough when he had fever he would bleed himself, using that old-time recipe medicine. Unlike his friend, Paul had no definite aim or concern about his future.

Both were attired in the *dernier cri* fashion. They wore soberly, austere Panama hats and dark-brown Bruno Magli leather boots with that strong effluvium of shoe polish. Their pants were cut very tight in the crotch with an army belt with buckle on their bellies, and colorful garish Bermuda shirts loosed in the wind. Their gold bracelets glittered in the light. Furthermore, they lived as a couple. Even that there was something girlish about them as for the way they moved around, they were good looking, obliging, and altogether they had good manners. They were perhaps a little snobbish especially when they drunk their coffee from a coffee-cup, their pinkies up in the air with much gentility, but never been unkind. They drove an old, light green Jaguar with leather-seats, and were quite proud of it. That was the kind of car I had not been able to take my eyes off. Horst always made a point of supervising Paul by checking on his health, on his happiness. And by the way both of them never missed the Gay Pride Parade. On that occasion, Paul walked freely in his underwear!

From the very beginning, I noticed a good chemistry between them and Arthur who behaved very differently in their presence.

In the same manner as with Archie Bunker in "All in the family", Paul reminded us that at one time on Zuma Beach he provided mouth-to-mouth resuscitation to a transvestite, which for him was a great and wonderful experience!

Their first preoccupation upon their hiring was to lodge a down payment on a house with a swimming pool, around the corner from *Le Cerisier*. During their eighteen years of living together, as a pleasant habit, to save time and money they would seek residence near their working place. They received a low-interest loan from a bank in West Hollywood.

The proximity of their household from *Le Cerisier* made them more punctual than a time-devise. Before long, we would become very good friends. Frequently, Bourget and Larivière would invite me in their dwelling for a beer over *une omelette aux champignons*, as we watched the late news on NBC. At all times their house was scrupulously clean. In spite of their way of living, we shared a mutual respect with the understanding that there would never be any sexual approach between them and myself. A quite rapidly pleasant, warm camaraderie had developed between us as I took a real delight in their companionship. Later, we bathed in the swimming pool and rode our bicycles together. In addition, we enjoyed gardening by planting special herbs for new food recipes.

During one of those activities Horst informed me that at one time Paul was engaged to a nice lady. However she decided to marry someone else. And he added, "He suffered for more than a year until we met." As the woman had left him, Paul decided to be free of so many of the female idiosyncrasies and he decided to become Horst's lover.

For an unknown reason (except maybe by simple jealousy), our employer was resentful of their friendship with me. One evening, after the closing of the restaurant I decided again to spend time at my new friends' house. Sitting in front of the fireplace where a cheerful fire was blazing, next to the woven bamboo bar we were sipping our margarita quietly in the way a pigeon swallows clear water. Soon, a whiff of tobacco smoke struck my nostrils: Horst and Paul were savoring their Turkish cigarettes, sending a stream of smoke toward the ceiling. The smoke had really lingered in the atmosphere. Being heavy smokers the ashtray was almost always full of cigarette butts. After they flung away their crushed cigarettes, Horst read to me excerpts of *House Of Incest* from Anaïs Nin: *"Loving without knowingness- moving without effort, in the soft current of water and desire, breathing in an ecstasy of dissolution…The lamentations of flutes, the double chant of wind through our slender bones, the cracking of our bones distantly remembered when on beds of down the worship we inspired turned to dust."* As Paul started to re-build the fire until one heard the crackling again, the stillness of the night was interrupted by the sudden arrival of Arthur.

Standing on the empty street from the other side of the freshly painted white picket fence, he was sniffling at it like a terrier at a rathole. And showing off his crushed vulcanized face like that of a bulldog, he was screaming my name on top of his lungs. The boss, thinking that Paul and Horst had monopolized so much time on me, simply felt envious. Now he was urging me to go home; that I had nothing to do in that house! Arthur's voice rose up piercingly until he remembered it was nighttime.

Horst, the one who ultimately did all the talking came out in white silk, striped *robe de chambre*- dressing-gown. In addition, he was wearing pink bobby socks and sabots that he bought in Holland. His face was smothered with white powder, a towel wrapped around his head.

Horst did not hide his discomfort. Once more, in rising excitement he answered back, *deux ex machina* that I was able to decide for myself to stay or not to stay; that I was not under any employer's supervision after working hours. And in a magnanimous spirit he added:

"Pierre is not a poodle that you can keep on a leash! Please don't tell him how to manage his life!" Paul, with yet another cigarette he held in the corner of his month watched the whole scene with amusement. As the smoke lingered around us all Arthur kept on beating the fence with his fists. He was shuddering as he held onto the fence's latch with both hands, almost snatching new pickets that had just been installed by trying to get to the front door. Again he was yelling with hysteria. With his bull neck craning and his face turning red, the shouting was growing louder and louder. His speech was hammering back and forth as if he was the only living creature in the neighborhood. With the exception of a few dogs growling and barking, the three of us remained silent while staring with disdain at our own boss who was morphing into a madman.

Realizing that his boisterous act was ignored Arthur hung about the fence for awhile and crawled to the driver's seat of his truck like a furtive little animal before heading home. I also had the feeling that the owner of the restaurant was quite resentful of my friends who were able to buy a respectable property in Sherman Oaks,that included a swimming pool.

Over one more nightcap with the couple, prior to a demi-tasse of espresso I came to understand that Paul was an alcohol addict which explained his dysfunctional behavior at work. His favored drink was Cinzano dry vermouth and Bombay gin on ice with the addition of a zest of lemon. Without the boss's knowledge he would imbibe at least two, sometimes three full glasses of that liquor in one evening. We did not mind his jabbering until he found his way to the dining room to entertain our customers some of whom felt quite uncomfortable. Still others found his antic amusing...

* * * *

October arrived with drizzle and depression. It was a month of frequent ups and downs. At that juncture came Halloween; *laissez le bon temps rouler*-let the good time rolling, and we all agreed to wear familiar period costumes.

The owner donned a red-rabbit outfit and was leading his daughter by the hand. She masqueraded herself as a head nurse holding a gigantic syringe in her hand as Eddy impersonated

Count Dracula with fake blood drawn at the edges of his mouth. He also wore a black Napoleon's hat.

I was Louis XVI, king of France wearing an ermined cape and mantle lined with miniver with Horst as Marie-Antoinette.

Horst, just like the late queen had a heraldic coronet that sparkled on his hair. His own guiding taste had given character to the theatrical game. That extraordinary white garment had been a replica; the almost exact copy of the one that famed queen wore from a sketch in a portrait. With a contented face Horst graciously smiled and bowed at the crowd.

Paul, holding up elegantly on his long trailing dress, carrying a tulip in his right hand enjoyed being the queen's first maid. With a sort of comical humility, Paul dancing the minuet appeared more like a waiting-woman to her ladyship. Along with the scent of heavy perfume that hung about him, he wore a wig quite too wacky, a dab of powder on it with bracelets and high-heeled shoes attributed more to the gay Louis XIII. Both Horst and Paul had their faces powdered.

As we paraded ourselves around, customers were laughing en masse. Horst kept on crossing the dining room in graceful minuet steps and started to sing that madrigal, medieval poem that was all about a new hat:

"Mon chapeau à trois cornes; trois cornes à mon chapeau…
S'il n'y avait pas trois cornes, ce ne serait pas mon chapeau."

A customer seemed to be like a grand mogul with a turban, still another reminded me of Robin Hood in green hunter outfit.

The highlight of the frivolity happened when the drunken Arthur inadvertently (or intentionally?) tripped on the fringe of Paul's chambermaid dress, showing his Victoria's Secret pink underwear.

Later on, I was admiring the elegant silhouette of a young woman and my eyes involuntary continued to drift in her direction. As I continued watching the swing of her body, Paul (who regarded feminine beauty with apathy), standing in the middle of the dining room was smitten over a gorgeous macho male customer by the way he moved his shoulders. Talking to himself, Paul started twaddling. The cortege of whimsical fashion reveled on late into the night. Afterward we joined our customers at their tables and enjoyed with them a flute of fine champagne like if we were one great family. All of a sudden, Arthur with all that bubbling liquor going to his head decided to make an announcement:

"Ladies and gentlemen, may I please have your attention. Paul is going to tell you the story of his gay rooster." Later on, the customers answered with a roaring jeer of laughter. It was a hilarious joke, but quite unclean too as I refrained to mention it. Paul really lacked the faculty of knowing how far he can go with a particular gag. Most of our patrons kept on guffawing, a few with tears in their eyes. But from a side table, a lady with arched eyebrows crossed herself. Under the vigilant eye of her pastor-husband she soon expressed her real dissatisfaction upon hearing such a nasty quip. The couple didn't care for those witticisms and they regarded all these as a hindrance to their enjoyment. The lady informed Arthur that this so-called banter was misplaced and of very poor taste; that this fine restaurant was turning into another *La Cage aux Folles*-The Bird Cage. And now they were waiting for *l'addition*, ready to leave 'this awful niche of sinners in that cesspool of immorality.' Customers from the table next to theirs seemed to be struggling to repress a laugh...

* * * *

Here is another pet story still fresh in my mind. A few months ago, Arthur became quite interested over an ad in a local equine newspaper: in a farm near Tucson, Arizona, an Australian couple was raising Arabian horses, people would commonly regard as miniature horses that looked like short-legged Moldavian ponies. They are actually smaller than Great Danes or Saint Bernards. Arthur showed his wife a lovable picture of the small *equus caballus* as his interest in acquiring such a pet grew obsessive. Although Angeline found the animal attractive, she kept gazing at her husband with suspicious eye. Knowing him so well for so long on this good earth, she was evidently displeased with the prospect of Arthur's trip to the Grand Canyon State to purchase a miniature horse. She had not insofar been able to overcome a feeling of fear, when later on she did spy on Arthur and Eddy taking measurement of the pickup truck's long bed, already covered with a fiberglass dome. With a brilliant logic and sensitiveness, Angeline nevertheless was still overpowered with her husband's stubborn decision. Slouching in her chair she simply waited for the outcome. In the very early morning hours on Saturday, as the sky was still dark, the mildly hysterical Angeline, scowling was observing Arthur and Eddy as they embarked with Pompadour on the Nissan truck that jolted forward for the long journey to Arizona…

It looked as if Arthur was extremely pleased with the deal. He purchased a black and white miniature horse that fit perfectly in the back of his vehicle. The boss christened him Oreo as in Oreo Cookie. Oreo was so little that Pompadour, the French poodle almost reached its height. Arthur and Eddy came back from the desert-state the next Sunday, late at night. They both got out of the truck and let Oreo descend from the flat bed at the same time. The horsy was restless and he kicked Eddy in the butt. In the semi-darkness, a neighbor, rather large red-faced woman that happened to walk her golden retriever became curious. With signs of confusion in her face, she politely inquired as to what kind of a hound dog with such funny, heavy legs was and why it stood there trembling and waiting? At that precise moment, Arthur was trying to decide whether or not he should tell anything about Oreo. But, by fear of gossip and not to alarm anybody he was quick to respond: "This is an *Enouchi dog* born in Siberia!" That fantastic lie given with such an inflamed imagination eluded the lady who simply left the premises and went home. Upon hearing the truck chugging, Angeline stood up. Something blurry moved in front of the house. Mrs. Valois Dourville de Montrissart who had not been very well that day was barely awake and restless. Washing her face quickly, she rubbed her eyes and put on her glasses. After positioning herself near the window, she leaned out gazing at Arthur and Eddy. As her suspicious were soon reawakened, she realized what the culprit was- her husband and his friend just had pulled Oreo, his head hanging down under the branches in the garden leading toward the garage. First she cast furtive glances at them from time to time, as lines of concern were ploughed upon her forehead. Now, with the window wide open, her hands remained motionless on her lap. She stood there, petrified with astonishment, upset by gloomy thoughts. Ultimately she started talking in an alarming voice: "I can't believe what I see. So you did it after all? Arthur you really get on my nerves like the devil...!" As Arthur experienced an extraordinary joy for having that little horse, Angeline was in profound agony. (Later on she conveyed to me that once Arthur got a thing in his head, you can hardly stop him. She added that if he didn't complicate his life so needlessly he would die of ennui...!) The next morning, the mailman was quick to announce to Arthur that some horse poop lay right in front of the house. Angeline, who so far didn't want to talk to her husband any longer, noticed that their garage had now become a stable. Oreo kept on butting the garage-door with her head. Providing that you live in a small community it's really hard to hide any kind of news. While Arthur was bedding Oreo on good fresh straw, the culprit came into light; it exploded like a firecracker among all the people around: "There is a horse in the Valois Dourville de Montrissart household! This ain't any dog; the smell of a sweating horse is in the air. And, from another French-speaking family: *"Il y a de la merde et encore de la merde partout!*-We saw horse-shit all around Arthur's residence! We certainly don't want any farm-house in this neighborhood!" A formal complaint was filed at city hall. The judgment from the commissioner was that my employer didn't reside in a ranch estate. Consequently, the horsy had to go. And, in no time, Oreo got a new owner: a wealthy gentleman farmer from the Santa Ynez Valley.

At *Le Cerisier* Arthur became somewhat sardonic whenever he spoke of anything connected with Oreo the miniature horse. Being still mad at the people in his neighborhood he kept on pacing the floor, sapping his teeth with a sudden spasm of rage. For several days the boss was 'under the weather' trying to forget it all and felt as sick as any human can be. Recurrently, on his way to Solvang the image of Oreo came into Arthur's mind as he kept gazing unwarily on horses running happily in the meadows, alongside a solitary pony.

Chapter 13

NOVEMBER TURNED INTO December. As the days shortened and the weather worsened, I had found the long evenings at *Le Cerisier* monotonous and few clients showed up. In observing 'old continent' tradition the restaurant was closed for business during the Christmas holidays.

Every year on Christmas Day Mr. and Mrs. Picard, loyal customers of *Le Cerisier* hosted a sumptuous dinner party for their close friends and relatives at their impressive mansion situated on Mandeville Canyon in Pacific Palisades. The area actually boasts of celebrities and friends of the Reagan family. The ever gracious, friendly hosts Glen and Alicia Picard extended us the invitation to partake in their delightful brunch.

Everyone would spend Christmas with somebody, except Leon. Glen had invited him as well, yet he kindly refused the offer for he preferred so much to stay alone during holidays as he was still busy with his overseas packaging business. He always gave plausible pretext for refusing any sort of invitation. Leon even declined a request by his landlady to join her party downstairs in the house. Leon always felt like a stranger to all such gatherings. For not being disturbed by those people that banded together cheerfully, my friend, in order to ward off his anxiety kept on listening to his favored music of Vivaldi and of Beethoven's adagio of Moonlight Sonata…

On that damp and misty day, Sunset Boulevard and Hollywood Boulevard were full of strangers who had come in from all parts of the country on account of the day. Along with Helena we drove the winding Mandeville Canyon road curtained with foliage fringed with tall eucalyptus trees to the abode located *à mi-chemin* from the top of the hill. The parterre of mille-fleur surrounding the house was exquisite. With a light rain I heard the hollow sound of the water pattering on the leaves.

In front of the Picard's residence, on each side of the balustrade on the terrace stood two stone lions which have been staring at the trees for several decades now. The mansion proper; that squatted in full view loomed huge against the sky with a certain air of dignity. It was one of those old-fashioned buildings in which many generations lived their lives together on that same location. The garden was large, delightfully tended, with a constellation of flowers, rare plants, trees and vines that were running along a wall. There was as much roughness and grandeur as in a virgin forest. From a bronze nymph, a thin rill of water was gushing out into a small fishpond. The rain was creeping into the mud as nature rustled with moist. But rapidly the glowing iridescence of a rainbow enchanted our eyes. In addition there was a well that was no longer pumping.

Before entering the gray stone building you have to move beneath a rippling shawl of leaves, as white violets ran wild in the pathways. There is such a dichotomy between life in the heart of the city and country, but here as the scent of the new-cut grass was still in the air it looked as if we were divorced from reality.

Glen Picard, a well respected member in the community was an attractive gentleman with a goatee, thick black hair and a long cut on his jaw caused in a boating accident. But, strangely enough his bill-hook nose and bold eye suggested arrogance. Glen waited for us at the entrance and directed Helena with her car to a small space in the parking lot. Mr. Picard, an enthusiastic and mannered person still in the freshness and strength of his youth elevated himself to the zenith of power with the family wealth. He became an *armateur*- a ship outfitter, selling and buying boats on several California marinas from Long Beach to San Pedro and Marina Del Rey. Picard was a very successful entrepreneur who was able to lay down his hand *à toutes les pâtes*-on almost anything.

His wife Alicia, equally an Islander found great companionship with Helena. As feathers make fine birds, I had never till now realized the artistic excellence of Alicia's limbs and features. She was a good-looking lady.

For several years Glen's mother suffered from a stroke. She would spend hours sitting with dignity in her wheelchair. Even with her ailment she won't miss her spring cruise to Rio, Hong Kong or South Africa. She was extremely wealthy. Thus her son obtained in life almost anything he wanted; all the goodies as he vainly had striven for them. The rich maman Picard was always fond of those successful giants from French literature. She divulged to me that she went along with the views of Montesquieu in *Pensées Diverses* regarding success: *"I have always observed that to succeed in the world one should seem a fool, but be wise."*

The dining room was spacious and the carpet thick. Marie, the housekeeper already extended the dinner table by adding a leaf in the center. A giant Christmas tree so well decorated with the addition of electric candles stood near the wall. Despite the curtains that tumbled profligately on the floor, the windows outlined themselves. In the banquet hall, next to a pile of Majolica plates, lay a gleaming array of trays full of victuals, including cold cuts, gilded sturgeons and pikes; a real feast to the eye. Afterward, Alicia laid the best silver upon the lace napery that covered the table with china, white cloth napkins along with the candles and silver holders.

As I started to play with the golden retriever, the bell rang. Marie went to open the door. Arthur, his wife Angeline and Eddy just arrived.

Daughter Melanie had decided earlier to join some sheriff's friends at a Trancas Beach party. Looking at his countenance, with his bloated face, bloodshot eyes and red nose I became aware that Arthur had already been drinking at home. He was tipsy not just on beer but of bourbon as well. He had nicked himself twice while shaving in hurry, and this time his springing gait reminded me of a bird. His trousers were sopping with dew after he fell in the heavy grass.

In the back room the television was on, however none of the guests cared to watch the ongoing football game. Soon, even the festal strains of classic music faded away.

Marie, with her hair ruffled like a bird's nest moved around among a clatter of culinary utensils from the dining room to the kitchen. Her cheeks were red with shyness as she rarely saw so many guests reunited.

Arthur kept on drinking heavily until his wife Angeline decided to launch him a warning: "If you keep on drinking, even if I have to take the bus, I would be heading home without you!" However, Eddy who moderated himself fetched Valois Dourville de Montrissart a strong cup of coffee. They both went to the kitchen to help Alicia to prepare *la sauce archiduc* for the victuals. Next, they carved the goose. The juicy slices were cut out of its inside until only the skeleton and a little flesh remained. The savor of sucking pig and goose was under one's nostrils as it impregnated the entire room. The frugal meal included cold viands too. I joined them at the precise moment that Arthur was pouring himself a mug of

Canadian Club bourbon. Looking at me, his excuse was brief and direct:

"I'm extremely thirsty this evening." He rapidly downed the liquor in two extended drafts. After Marie had dimmed the chandeliers, as the feeble rays of dawn had passed through the slots of the blinds we all sat down to enjoy the feast. The food was outstanding! It was complemented with pastries and pies of all shape, with puddings topped with dry fruits. It was such a pleasure to marvel at the faces of the hungry guests. In the middle of the late brunch as the day drew to a close and the long winter evening set in Arthur, in a ravenous appetite and with the gravy trickling from his lips decided to talk about me with vehemence. After another helping of meat, as the well-mannered nobleman opened his mouth that cracked into a kind of a smile he started to speak when a piece of flesh fell out from his mouth onto his plate. With a ringing of pride in his flamboyant voice, after wiping his greasy chin with the back of his hand he informed the audience in a glow of strange enjoyment:

"Years ago, in the early days of November, Pierre feeling the thrill of an explorer, instructed his wife that he was going around the corner to get a carton of milk at the local liquor-store. Guess what? He ran away with little pocket-money, carrying a small backpack containing only two extra underwear, two pair of socks and a toothbrush (this created burst of laughter all around), and he came back home a year later. Independent of what people would say, Pierre went around the world like a real maverick. In Thailand he lived in a Pagoda with gay monks- (again, people were hooting without control.) In Kalgoorlie, Western Australia, right in the middle of the desert the venturesome Pierre worked in a gold mine. Upon his return to that five dollar a day motel a naked aboriginal woman leaped right in his arms from a large tree-top in the middle of the courtyard. After awhile, he let the lady in his room, serenading her with a guitar that he borrowed..." and Arthur went on, "Back to California, Pierre was surprised that his wife handed him divorce papers before the money in a joint savings account did a disappearing act. He didn't understand how a man in his right mind can leave his family to travel the world and come back a year later with a big smile on his lips?" As my employer articulated those words, especially the ones related to the divorce part, old memories came up to my mind.

Even that I wrote a successful book about my odyssey I had neglected my children, my spouse and my thoughts went back for my ex-wife. With my foolishness, in spite of the fact of having abandoned my family for so long, my ex-wife never fully realized the intensity of regret that filled my heart, and for the myriad letters I have sent to her with solemn passion from all corners of the planet; letters that have helped me to build up my travel-book.

"So dear wife, I know that you made me responsible for breaking up the happy home and I'm so sorry about this. But, on the other hand there must be no anger on your part since we were never absent from one another in thoughts, as my sentiments of tender affection were still present. Without adding to the guilt of my inappropriate evasion, when we talk of the past it must be without bitterness. Now that I can open my heart to you once more, I feel sure that as time unfolded, you understand me and approved somewhat of what I have done, even as irresponsible and unthinkable as it appeared to be. I also could have lost my life in so many instances: by poisonous taipan snake-bites in Northern Australia's sugarcane fields; in the hands of Khmere Rouges in Cambodia during the communist take-over; by being almost beaten to death by a crowd of angry religious fanatics outside the sacred mosque in Meshed, Iran, or even by contracting hepatitis 'A' following a prolonged stay at the Ganges river in Varanasi,

India. As strange as it seems it had never entered my mind that I did something wrong when I abandon you and the children for that long, sublime journey around the world. This had been my ultimate dream since childhood. Many days, weeks and months were taken away from you and the children, as I kept on building a manuscript from so many places around the globe. But, that same long journey, my day's adventure had taken a detour from reality; from responsabilities. I acknowledge your great sacrifices, and after all those years I again beg your forgiveness.'"

By the way, once in Katmandu, Nepal a monk wearing a safran robe, with his head shaved, approached me with that familiar Californian accent. He greeted me with that common phrase: "Hey man, are you from L.A.?"

Jeff, originally from a good, influential family, right on the outskirts of Los Angeles went 'around the corner too' in order to get a loaf of bread at the 7-Eleven store, but his wife was still waiting for him after twenty years of absence! Jeff violated his two week visa for Nepal, and got full membership within a Buddhist pagoda in that serene environment, where he managed quietly to smoke his hashish. My friend had been haunted by the fragrance of the Himalayas Mountains, the fresh air, meditation and...drugs.

After that extraordinary, quite embroidered introduction from Arthur I became the culprit of discussion. I was forced to explain the entire odyssey that started on a Greyhound bus heading to the Mexican border and on, with different transportations to the Panama Canal Zone. What impressed them the most was the bus ride through Pakistan via the Khyber-Pass and the treacherous task of crossing Cambodia on a dangerous mission as a free-lance war correspondent for *Télémouche*-educational Belgian TV. (On a stop over in Brussels, a cousin of mine, working for that station handed me the introduction paper as free-lance writer.) This happened to be at a period when the country was almost under total control by the Khmère Rouges?

I arrived in Phnom-Penh as a shriek of rockets continued to fall non-stop throughout the night. After heavy fights in North-Vietnam, the elite Vietcong in combat readiness would cross the border and scatter here and there throughout Cambodia to hide. I joined the 13th Infantry Brigade under the command of General Norodom Chanteremsei (cousin of Prince Norodom Sihanouk.) In the face of sweeping chaos, Phantom Jets were flying uninterruptedly over the border area. From his high-intensity field-radio an officer got voice contact with the pilot of one of the planes. The flyer had requested the coordinate instructions from a map showing a temple-ruin where the enemy took refuge. I helped in the logistics by talking directly in English to the pilot (since my friends on the ground, aside from Cambodian understood only French.) Minutes later, in this 'undeclared involvement in the Cambodian war by the U.S.', the border area was bombarded with napalm. Like an illumination apparatus the entire site was in flames. Subsequently, in my whole life I never experienced so many bear-hugs from the uniformed personnel around me, all the way to general Chanteremei who handed me a cold glass of ice-tea. Four days after I left Cambodia, the border was closed. The Khmère Rouges got full control of the country. This was the very beginning of "The Killing Fields…"

At dessert-time as his face lit up and trembled with pleasure, Arthur took an enormous bite from the slice of his strawberry tart topped with Crème Chantilly. He was munching loudly, emitting strange sounds with mild spell of hiccups while his eyes still grew rapacious. After he cleaned up his plate as if it had been licked by a wild cat he started to speak indistinctly. Clearing his throat, he unexpectedly mentioned to us that he went to the Oxnard Strawberries Festival and recalled that alongside the field stood a little brick-house. This was the place where the special crimson, deep purplish red strawberries were preciously aligned in individual designed containers. From there they would be sent directly to all the crowned heads of Europe. Those delicacies carrying a royal patent were only reserved for kings and queens, with no exception.

An old man with a fastidiously trimmed beard, weak in the chest and sitting near the fireplace, probably tired of hearing of my employer's imaginary bragging and fatuity commentaries was cutting into the conversation. He asked that neat question: "Arthur, please tell us something about your father."

"My father?" Arthur quipped with a new interest. And with a cynical reply the old man added:

"Yes, and I believe you know him very well. Isn't he the emperor of Japan?" At this point, the laughs were uncontrollable. The only one who remained serious was Arthur as he realized he had become a little more than an object of derision. Now, with his body swaying from side to side, the biggest talker in town was silent. Acting like a dethroned king, he was melting like *un bonhomme des neiges*-a snowman. Looking furtively at the window Arthur excused himself and beats a hasty retreat to the bathroom.

Back in the dining room he started humming a little tune to give himself an air of confidence. But, for the rest of the day Arthur became sulky and out of humor since this wasn't his show anymore. At that precise moment my thoughts went to Ervin Seale when he wrote: "... *Inability to get along with other people is the inability to get along with one's own thoughts.*"

* * * *

Occasionally, subsequent to some particular unpleasant event, a writer can become frustrated with the thought that his writings are a waste of time and energy, almost like he was in a vacuum's strain. What I'm about to explain is related to an idiotic as well as quite an unfair situation perpetrated by Arthur. As the pen fell from my hand and refused to write, I tried to pretend that this event didn't happen and simply shut the door on it. Yet I couldn't. I mentioned earlier that repeatedly, clashes erupted in the kitchen between my employer and Chef Picharon. These encounters overshadowed scenes from the 'War of the Roses.' However, Picharon's genius at food preparation was the height of culinary excellence. The Valley Times, Bon Appetite Review, and the Journal of the Heart Association of America have trumpeted good reviews of *Le Cerisier.* The specialties of the house so well presented by Chef Picharon were a treat to the palate. Each meal was like a poem portraying the countryside of the city of Lyon and the highlands of Aix en Provence. The crispy duck with black cherries was a favorite of the clientele who hailed our chef de cuisine from as far as San Diego and San Francisco. Arthur who always whistled all the way to the bank was well aware that this culinary expert was his gold mine. He also knew that Picharon could easily quit or be lured to work for another, even more renowned restaurant *de la nouvelle cuisine* on La Cienega Boulevard, The Sunset Strip or Melrose Avenue.

As the year was coming to a close, when Christmas shopping was still in full swing, Arthur must have decided to allay his fear of losing 'his gold mine.'

And so, on New Year's Eve, as we, the revelers at the restaurant befuddled to the countdown, Arthur affectionately clutched Picharon's arm. He then led him outside to the parking lot and started to sing that famed world renowned song. Since the establishment is always closed for Christmas, the boss thought that the carol was appropriate for that moment:

"Jingle, bells! Jingle, bells
Jingle all the way!
Oh what fun it is to ride
In a one-horse open sleigh!"

Thinking it might be another showdown, Horst, Paul, Melanie and I followed the two gladiators. Under the frightful clouds of that winter's night, with the neon that was flickering in the wind stood a brand new white Volkswagen Rabbit Diesel bedecked with a gigantic red and blue ribbon. Arthur who would have done anything in the world for Picharon was setting him upon a pinnacle of happiness.

We were all dumbfounded as all four of us read the license plate: TOP CHEF. The shining 'Rabbit' automobile appeared to spring out from a magic box and was being presented to appease the kitchen god. Arthur's face was dimpled with smiles when he said:

"Happy New Year Petit Chef, hope you like my humble present." The ever-arrogant employer added with a chuckle: "On the front seat you will find a white, polo-jumper that perfectly matched your new toy."

Feeling confident that all is forgiven, the tormentor sealed the tribute with not one but three kisses on the god's cheeks and forehead. He tightened his embrace to a squeeze. Though he felt confused, yet pleasurably thrilled, Picharon hesitatingly thanked him with a single kiss. And, looking at the sky, he articulated: "Yes Virginia, there is a Santa Claus!" Even that he had quarreled forever so long with chef Picharon, Arthur provided him with the ultimate present someone can ever dream of.

As we stood quietly staring at the phenomenal, exquisite gift, we all wondered what this great spender Santa had in store for his Four Musketeers. By this time the shocking event that had just unfolded before our very eyes, sobered us up. As we were wrapping things up back at the restaurant Melanie could no longer contain her excitement and she asked:

"What have you got for us Daddy?" Oh yes, Arthur had another surprise up his sleeve. He first frowned, rubbed his nose and shook his head as a very faint smile twitched his lips and wriggled uneasily:

"My children, of course I didn't forget you." and, throwing a glance of scrutiny he reckoned: "I really appreciate your work. Throughout the year, you have done so much for me and here is your gift." Taking the contents of one of the boxes adorned with a blue ribbon that was scattered across the kitchen floor, he opened it up and reaching into the bottom of the carton, he handed each of us a Hershey chocolate Santa wrapped in foil. As we were holding the cheap candy in our hands, I felt like a shaft had fallen in our midst as the spirit of the Holidays drained off our wearied working bodies. Horst, the skinnier of the two gay waiters, holding a glass of inexpensive champagne must still be a bit intoxicated for he declaimed in an undertone of peevish displeasure:

"Your highness, we are deeply humbled by your humble gift of a chocolate Santa. You're just a mean stingy creature. Hope you rot in hell!" Thanks Horst, you said it for everybody!

* * * *

On this happy January day, as the sun shone gloomier, I arrived at the restaurant earlier in a relaxed atmosphere in order to prepare the dining room for a very important event. Mr. Gelson, the owner of the Gelson's Food Chain

Supermarkets had arranged a meeting with all his Southern California district store managers.

Around 5.30 PM, half an hour before the opening of *Le Cerisier* I heard a knock at the door. I let the person in, thinking (as it regularly occurred) that it was someone who came in to request the issuance of a gift certificate.

The extremely well dressed gentleman, bald with gray at the temples, breathed respectability. His brown eyes still vibrant with the intensity of a young executive kept looking at me with a warm, refreshing smile. He stretched out his arm and shook my hand:

"I am Mr. Gelson, what's your name son?" After this incredible introduction, the founder and CEO of one of the most prosperous food chain stores in America went on: "Pierre, I've heard that this is one of the top restaurants in Los Angeles. I'm sure you have good wine in your wine cellar?" and he added, "Can you find me something exquisite I can taste right at this moment? You know, one of those bottles with the French Chateau's label on it. And please, don't mind the price." I showed Mr. Gelson a *Chateau La Tour 1967.*

"I'll take it the way it is, no need for decanting." I opened the expensive bottle with extreme precaution to avoid breaking the cork, and let him taste it, "Excellent, it has a fine bouquet." With his eyes riveted on me in a surprising gaze, he all of a sudden laughed good-humoredly uttering:

"My friend, I certainly can't drink this alone. Get yourself a glass."

Afterward, the chain store owner went around the dining room to each table to observe that all the manager's name tags were properly in place.

Mr. Gelson had a noble forehead, slightly bronzed by great outdoor activities such as sailing or simply enjoying nature. With a quick glance at his Rolex, he decided to repose his hand on my shoulder, saying:

"I wish my staff would show a little more promptness. The meeting was scheduled for 6.00 o'clock and it's already 6.05, this is really unpunctual!"

At ten past six, all the managers were present. The culprit for those few minutes delay had been for a parking problem. Adjoining the beauty salon's space in the back of the restaurant, less than ten cars were able to park at *Le Cerisier*. Most of our customers if lucky enough would park their vehicles on Ventura Boulevard.

Everything went fine, especially for the fact that Arthur was busy up north at the other location in Solvang. *Never was any doubt in my mind that if my employer would have been at Le Cerisier that night, he would have taken away from my hand the glass of wine that had been so generously offered to me by Mr. Gelson.* At dessert time the founder of the chain made a great speech. He encouraged his associates for a job well done:

"It is the commitment to our customers that makes us stand apart. Our credibility comes from our personnel at cash-registers and from our inventory people too." Clasping his hands tight together he declared in a warm and sincere voice:

"I'm so proud of you all; you are the reason for our successes." He added that without their efforts Gelson stores wouldn't have reached the height of being la crème de la crème over any other food supermarket in the U.S....

Surprisingly Arthur appeared. He was back from Solvang, and the CEO praised him for the outstanding food. He concluded by proclaiming to all his regional managers: "Monsieur Arthur Valois Dourville de Montrissart is one of the greatest restaurateurs in America; I'm very pleased that he was able to accommodate us in his warm abode." With this quiet compliment Arthur was in heaven. Nothing else could have made him more joyful…

Later on in Marina Del Rey, after I explained to Helena all about the occurrence with Mr. Gelson and his top managers her eyes became as big as saucers. Next she blasted at me:

"You fool, why didn't you asked Mr. Gelson for a position in one of his stores?" And, after she dabbed her nose with powder, so great was the sudden emotion arousing in her that her voice grew shriller at every sentence: "MY GOSH, YOU SHARE SOME EXPENSIVE WINE WITH HIM! Don't you realize that you could have secured yourself a good future, and most importantly you could have quit being Arthur's slave?" She was right, that day I missed a great opportunity.

Chapter 14

THROUGHOUT MY CONSTANT observations, I came to the realization that Arthur was suffering from personality disorder. Being hypersensitive and suspicious of others, this embittered man could be downcast, pessimistic and elated almost at the same time. While one might regard this behavior as objectionable, little could be done to alter his basic personality. His entire life was an 'open book' which was full of antithesis. Valois Dourville's anxiety, uneasiness, sense of doom with the feeling of inadequacy and guilt might be so well hidden, that only a few recognizable signs would surface. One of those symptoms which I already mentioned would be in reference to his eyebrows that arched upward while he still kept that serene face. However, the grumpy Arthur already quite wealthy constantly lived with the expectation of an even brighter, sound retirement.

To consider the empiricist view of Monsieur Hume, we live in a world of cause and effect: *"We have said that all arguments concerning existence are founded on the relation of cause and effect, that our knowledge of that relation is derived entirely from experience, and that all our experimental conclusions proceed upon the supposition that the future will be conformable to the past."* On one occasion, a doctor and client at the restaurant too informed me that Arthur was a very interesting case.

* * * *

Justin and Betty Liestreman were extremely well-off. They enriched themselves beyond their wildest dreams of wealth; unlimited wealth, literally rolling in opulence. They had so much more money than you know what to do with it. The Liestremans had a great deal of commercial buildings in Century City, some tracts of farmland in Oxnard and a lot of cash in the stock market.

They lived in Agoura Hills, in a manor almost as large as a castle, surrounded by impressive bougainvillea. In that subdivision, a security guard stood at attention at the entrance gate. Next to the estate one can discover a team of horses in the barn. A private road graciously boarded by eucalyptus trees reached the mighty residence surrounded by well-maintained, fresh-cut grassland. A yellow Rolls Royce was always parked in front of the main entrance. That one was Mr. Liestreman's. His wife Betty drove a black Mercedes sports convertible- a simple Christmas present. They lived obscurely in the recesses of that colossal house and rarely put their nose out of doors. But on the other hand, I believe that Liestreman was still poor on millions of dollars compared to someone who felt rich on a new pair of shoes. Wealth is something completely relative, often unsatisfying.

Once in awhile, the Liestreman couple would visit *Le Cerisier* and sit on their own reserved corner booth. Being very touchy they very much objected to be kept waiting. If 'their' corner table wasn't ready in time the unhappy, strangely ill assorted hideous looking couple would simply walk out. They live together without any love, passing their days in annoying each other.

Archibald, the only child sprung from that union became a gay man who occasionally joined his parents for dinner, while accompanied by a tall bearded gentleman.

Upon Justin and Betty's arrival at the restaurant with the Rolls, we had to provide for them a parking spot at the back of the building. A lettered sign on the wall read: THE LIESTREMAN'S PARKING.

Justin was a bristling gray bearded man with pallid cheeks as interesting as a Camembert cheese and diabolical eyes that looked like a bird of prey. He was one among so many extremely rich men with still worried eyes. His ghostly face showed a kind of hyena mouth that extended almost from ear to ear with bad teeth as he talked. He was a net of wrinkles with a nose planted on his face like a carrot on a snowman and with liver spots that reminded me of a lizard face, like ancient parchment. He wore a slightly worn suit with strange colored socks. With his inveterate smoker's cough and rheumatic back pains, he also looked like he was already on the brink to the grave, "ready for the box" to use one of Eddy Freedman's favored expression.

As a real estate mogul, Justin's only thoughts had been in grabbing all he could while ruining most of his investors. Being restrained by no scruples he had filled his *coffres* from many other sources, acquiring riches by plundering his partners and friends.

After he had crushed half a cigarette on the parking lot floor the couple made their way to the dining room by the back door through the kitchen. As he walked with a cane topped with an ivory crook Justin looked as if he might have a stroke at any moment. That man who was the unhandsome type from which all liveliness and verve had long since fled really cultivated the art of being miserable for misery's sake.

Betty Liestreman with her rustic provincial air was frightfully thin as a toothpick with pockmarked face, a wart upon her nose and little ferret eyes; the eyes of an old woman dried like prunes. As Mignon Eberhart once said, "She was tight as the paper on the wall." In addition, her hands appeared like bird's claws. And her coat *à la mode du vieux temps* that looked like it had been washed too many times hangs on her hunched shoulders as though it was made for another person; it really appeared to cover a skeleton.

There was a terrible monotony in their lives without any show of joy or affection. I even heard clients uttering: "For people with money they don't seem to have much enjoyment."

The couple's presence nauseated Arthur. He always found some kind of discomfort around them. My employer had disliked them from the first glance. But, even that those grumpy people bored him beyond all possible limits he nevertheless played the skillful game as if they were our best customers. For people like the Liestremans, the boss would even crawl in the dust. The only reason he would let them in, a big smile on his face was for the smell of money. The almighty dollar was always on Arthur's mind, and Justin was the old goose who could still lay golden eggs. This was Arthur's real goal in life: meet as many wealthy people as possible. My employer knew about the Liestreman's great wealth and eventually was invited in their exclusive estate, along with his wife and daughter. Arthur's hypocrisy had no limits. Even that he hated children that came to the restaurant with their parents, the boss would show with great skill a false air of concern for those youngsters.

Occasionally, Arthur would come at the table and plant a friendly kiss on Justin's head, as bald as an egg, to make him feel at home. Mr. Liestreman was easily angered. He would tempest at the slightest absurd trifle. That man wanted everything to be perfect, from his first drink to the main course, the dessert and coffee. He was cross-eyed and I never knew which eye he was watching me with.

On each of their visit at *Le Cerisier*, Justin would without fail forewarn me: "Pierre, remember that our vegetables must be steamed and no broccoli please! As for the filets mignons I request *Chanterelles* mushrooms sauce. And if the meat is not trimmed properly I would throw it right on the floor before I go in the kitchen to smack the chef's face." As Justin lifted his cane toward the ceiling, he added: "And before I butcher him, my cane would come down on his head too!" Once again I already knew that his words threatened stormy weather.

Being their favorite waiter, I pretended to be attentive to Jusin's pre-recorded admonition. This has schooled me to survive finicky customers like him. That man was as humorless as a washing machine. Arthur who had listened to Liestreman's discourse came by and cast a friendly tap on the old man's shoulder. In a way it was strange enough to realize that the unstable Arthur would patiently handle such an emotionally disturbed individual.

On one evening, at the Liestreman's table while they made slushy sounds with the mushroom sauce on their filets mignons a feud erupted and soon a bloody battle ensued. Before long the couple looked like enemy soldiers with their fixed bayonets ready to plunge at each other.

And, so suddenly, after a sour burp with his mouth wide open and with teeth that shown like fangs of a king cobra, Justin smacked his wife and drove his fork into her thigh. With the shock, the hysterical Betty lost a tooth on a piece of French bread. Her screams filled in the dining room which were subdued by her husband's perverted gesture of a friendly kiss on Betty's cheek as tears gushed from her eyes.

In a laudable degree of cruel finesse, Mr. Liestreman plastered the wound and decided to help his charming spouse to finish eating her *éclair au chocolat*! Arthur, being occupied with the many small details that were calling upon him didn't even realize what the screaming was all about.

When dinner was over, Justin was swaying, as he stood upright. With a quick jerk of the head and flecks of foam appearing on his lips, he was signaling to his wife, after another sour burp that it was time to go:

"Come on dear old mummy we're going to the beach!" At the same moment Betty's face had smoothed out in some kind of submissiveness.

As the 'happy' couple left the grounds, the boss was holding Mrs. Liestreman by the arm, leading them to their expensive automobile. With a big smile the boss patronized the Liestremans:

"My friends, it is such a great pleasure to have you to dine with us. Please come back very soon." But, shortly as the couple was out of sight, my employer gritted his teeth and complained: "Those ancient relics are really a bore and they make me so tired. They are a pain in the ass, and I bitterly hate them!" Once again my employer's common politeness and friendship can simply be called smooth hypocrisy. *Surely, Arthur, you cannot be sincere with customers who have been so drastically difficult. I find it irrational because no reasonable restaurant owner would ever again welcome those kinds of people in their establishment.*

Here is a quotation from Ram Das- *Journey of Awakening* that describes Liestreman character so well: "As you look at many people's life, you see that their suffering is in a way gratifying, for they are comfortable in it. They make their lives a living hell but a familiar one."

After the fork incident less than a month later Mr. Liestreman passed away. Although still mourning, Betty came back to the restaurant a little while later, accompanied by a younger lady.

In a calculated charm with a shining face, a new set of teeth and completely rejuvenated with the most expensive cosmetic surgery from a Beverly Hills clinic, wearing a low-cut light black dress, she introduced me to her new lady friend:

"Pierre, this is Michelle, and next Monday we're going for a round the world cruise via the Panama Canal!" Betty had drunk the cup of bitterness for so long and presently she was happier than ever. She no longer was embittered by the annoyance, by the indignation from her late husband. After she had spoken vaguely of her unfortunate, unhappy former marriage, she continued: "Now that I'm so wealthy, I can attract all kinds of people. They approach me like ants over honey. I know certainly that they come to me not for my shining blue eyes!" And in a final note "Justin had left as much to posterity as his dog!"

Over the years, I've met so many customers who seemed dissatisfied with themselves, bored with their relatives and who never finished their dinners. I saw many unhappy creatures with feverish ambitions but completely out of love. Among those people were career politicians, actors, even TV preachers. Every day I noticed the threads of broken families fluttering. Querulous couples, neglected wives from famed movie actors would come to the restaurant tossing remarks openly in bitter tone of voices. Frequently I noticed the natural shyness of the softer sex, facing the sarcastic attitude of male friends.

Besides the late Mr. Justin Liestreman and his drastic conduct there were several different characters that came to visit *Le Cerisier*. Dr. Edward Bleary was one of them. As a brilliant psychiatrist with a scraggy neck and a protruding nose that almost reached his upper lip, Dr. Bleary, a *habitué* used to come for dinner at least twice a month with his wife and three daughters who looked like Carmelite nuns. The daughters had high-pitched voices and they were plump and pert with fat buttocks.

There never was a conversation at the table neither any expressions of joy. Even with his family at his side Dr. Bleary with his suit hanging loosely on his body and dry as an old fig was an unpleasant sort of man. On every occasion, because of him their attitude reminded me of a somber funeral meal. It was as if a sort of a serious tragedy had upset the psychiatrist's life. Curiously, as a professional man, he was always pensive.

Dr. Bleary regularly ordered the bouillabaisse that he never finished eating. Half way through his fish soup, he would fall asleep with his nose down on top of a mussel with a piece of tiger-shrimp hanging from his mouth. Arthur would arrive at the table, gratifying him with a kiss on top of the head. Afterwards the boss ordered me to grab the pot with the bouillabaisse and packed it in a doggie-bag.

Once Eddy came in with a bell, and chiming it at Bleary's ear he whispered: "Edward, it's time to wake up!"

The same Dr. Bleary would return the following day with a young lady; so young, it's as if he'd been dating his own daughter. It was difficult to know what attracted young women to a man of such an advancing age, except for emotional health. But for the occasion Dr. Bleary was well dressed with a nice sport-jacket. We were later hinted that it was one of his psychiatric patients whose physical appearance obviously revealed a great disparity of ages between them. It was no wonder that he requested Arthur for a table in the most secluded part of the dining room.

It puzzled us that this was the same indifferent man from the previous night for he was now full of life and vitality, enjoying his favorite meal with a young consort. As passions ran high, he grew neglectful of all he had sworn by the Hippocratic Oath. With an emotionally sick person under his care, there were kisses and holding of hands, *en veux-tu en voilà*. Dr. Bleary, the very concerned man was uncontrollable. For the physician that client was simply an instrument of enjoyment-an instrument to avail himself of her as a tool for pleasure. He simply forgot the confidential doctor-patient relationship.

Arthur walked over to meet them at their table and the jubilant doctor started talking about the Korean War that reminded him so much of his youth. Wounded severely in combat, he was decorated by general Douglas Mac Arthur. Dr. Bleary even opened his shirt to show a scar above his stomach.

As they stood up before leaving the establishment I noticed the good doctor's fly was wide open! Once more, you cannot judge a book by its cover: Although most of our clients were respectable people in the community the evening happenings at our quaint restaurant were often quite dishonest. I noticed many unhappy couples. Their marriage had been an immitigable error, but wives with great courage would generally show the appearance of absolute compliance. However there were equally other married couples with winkled faces scourged by times of troubles. Those people lived a quiet, monotonous life with nothing to tell to each other except for nonsense talks from morning till night. They still continue to live together in that terrible inferno to avoid divorce and…financial insecurity. Those same human beings no longer were 'husband and wife' but strangers who, through force of circumstance were obliged to live under the same roof. A man I really admire for his wisdom is Bruce Griffin

Henderson with his book *Waiting*. Mr. Henderson made his living waiting on tables for eighteen years. His book is an amalgam of great individual stories presented by waiters and waitresses from restaurants all over the U.S. Here is an exerpt from Robin Shipley at *Granita,* in Malibu, California: "*...Customers in California are very different from the ones in New York. They're very pretentious; it's very much about the scene. But that's this area too. It's all about the way they look. The ladies have the best boobs on the planet. I mean, the money they spend on their chests is unbelievable. I once waited on a plastic surgeon, and he was adding up how much work had been done on the women in the room; it was incredible. It was much more than the whole restaurant cost to build. It's a trip...Now, how this restaurant works, and this is brilliant, is that we have a meeting every night before service starts, where the maître d' comes out with the trades. She goes through each customers, if they are 'somebody', and they usually are, and she tells us what movies they have done, who they have slept with, if they're divorced and what they like on their food...We know more shit than most gossip columnist. You can't seat so-and-so on this table because his ex-wife is coming in with her new lover. Or this person is having an affair so we have to get him out before his wife is coming in at 9:30 and she can't see them. It's so insane. It's a circus, and we're pulling the strings...*"

Among eccentric landowners, professionals or other well-mannered gentlemen there was that famous Hollywood star ZN wearing his fashionable, careless attire, who came in the establishment.

A mega, bearing one of the greatest names in his profession, he wore long black cloaks and was constantly surrounded by gorgeous blond girls; the best-dressed ladies in Los Angeles. But most of them were uneducated and feather-brained like a certain Queen Marie-Antoinette. I noticed that older women with their hair gathered at the nape of their necks were waging unending war on wrinkles for not to look their ages. Even that ZN's hair had gone prematurely grey, that regiment of women continually gathered at his heels everywhere to admire him from head to foot. Aside from his mercurial temper those same ladies were seemingly in pursuit of uncontrolled pleasure with careless gaiety leading to moral decadence. They treated life as an enormous joke, losing in the midst of this enchanted and false existence like theatrical fairyland, the true idea of life in general. That well-known, quite *blazé* actor, that trivial man of pleasure lived only to eat, drink and hunt for good sexual partners, to roll in the sack with them especially nymphomaniacs who like to play erotic games. He had an air of pretend coolness, of elegant solemnity that contrasted with the easy going playfulness of his personality. I noticed something slightly disturbing about his nose that reminded me of a botch cosmetic surgery. All you could hear from him was *cherchez la femme* and *vive la difference!* His motto: "Never put off till tomorrow the excitement you can experience tonight."

ZN did not show any good manners and he had a nasty character too. Even with his female entourage, there was something unpleasant, something severe in his indifferent stare. Before sitting down on the booth, with that cold superior look on his face, he usually patted me on the behind and, feeling sorry he played the game that he mistook me for one of the girls. Like The Great Gatsby ZN, was the kind of man who always paid for everything. He never used any credit cards for his extravagant spending, since his pockets were at all times full of handbills. At once I saw in ZN the wealthy man's indifference, being kind of apathetic for he has never had to be concerned about almost anything. His perfume however was violent and vulgar; I got a waft of it at each movement of his body. It reminded me of naphthalene.

ZN and his suite usually sat on a large booth. All of them were heavy drinkers of hard liquor especially Long Island ice tea prior to their orgy of wine guzzling. Once, during dessert time one of those young women was anywhere to be seen around. She never passed the front door and never used the bathroom. It didn't take us very long to realize what the mystery was: Mademoiselle went underneath the table doing hanky-panky with such a devilish art. Arthur was in heaven because of the great publicity he already anticipated. For the weeks that follow, every newcomer in the establishment knew that ZN had relished a special treatment...down there!

* * * *

This afternoon, when the slanting rays of the sun were as cold as the moon's, we had the unexpected visit of Mr. Emile Citron, a French Canadian with a soft, singing accent who was camouflaging his gray hair with *l'Oreal de Paris,* and carrying the nickname of 'Fuck Nose.'

This particular nickname was given to him after he had been running to the rear of Melanie in the dining room calling her Fuck Nose as he tried to pinch her buttocks too. Mr. Citron would stay there hesitantly as if at attention. He would stretch out his hands rushing toward Arthur's daughter. Under the warm gaze of my employer who watched the entire scene excitedly, Emile usually would scamp after Melanie between tables, conveying in a high-pitch tone voice:

"Come here my little Fuck Nose; my little hot pants! I know precisely what you really want; what you really need to be happy.

Mr. Citron, a man of fortune was far to be the attractive type: short with a fat belly, his head the size of a pumpkin displayed a face undistinguished with wolf-jaw, lipless smile except for a pair of sharp eyes, a small scarcely visible beard and a back like a mule. With small diamonds in his ear lobes, his movements reminded me of a retired security guard. A few weeks later Emile Citron came back to the restaurant with his wife.

She was a tall, skinny woman wearing a flower-dress, with a blank, expressionless face and an ill-meaning smile. Emile was ravenously devouring a filet mignon. After picking his teeth with his fork he twisted on his chair, farted and looked every which way for Melanie. But she wasn't anywhere to be seen. Citron, holding his huge stomach that was jiggling, even visited the kitchen thinking that Arthur's daughter was playing the game of hide-and-seek. But, soon enough he went back to his seat, profoundly disappointed. That evening Melanie was in the Malibu Colony entertaining some of her wealthy friends. Jane, her best companion with her black Bentley, her jewels and dresses was of extreme elegance. With her great boob job from a top doctor in Thailand she became the envy of the entire colony.

Looking at the boss, Monsieur Citron, after coughing heavily shook his head and mumbled in that still singing French-Canadian accent, *"Arthur, mon ami, ce n'est que partie remise."* I'll take a rain check.

Chapter 15

MELANIE' STIFLING HOME life was choking her. She hasn't had a good time at home. It had become an 'unhappy home' and she hasn't got along with her parents. Feeling almost like a stranger in their habitat, she thought it best if she did not live with them and tried the independence which most girls her age are experiencing. She lived with the conviction that in her life a serious crisis was approaching. To stay entangled with the practical affairs in the relatives' household was not a bright idea. Disagreements can erupted which created quarrels. Melanie had also discovered that her father and mother did not love each other any longer. Her father had been rude and cold. In a way he was still the school bully who twisted up the arms of other little boys, and struck them in the stomach too, a well-known character. So mademoiselle Melanie had decided to leave the dispirited family.

In a similar way, Arthur was using the old maxim from Agatha Christie's book, A Daughter's A Daughter: *"Daughters existed to serve their parents- not the other way about."* How bitter was the awakening in that residence, where she felt condemned to the life of a nun! She measured at first glance the depth of the awful abyss into which she had rapidly plunged. Her father,

her mother and Eddy who were residing under the same roof whirled like specters in the mad chaos of her brain.

With the understanding from her father, after she had convince him to agree to that arrangement Melanie was allowed to use the private room of the restaurant as a nightly lodging. Through her ingenuity, with two pillows, some linen and a blanket she brought along from her parent's house she installed a wood panel astride the booths and aligned the cushions together. It was as good as a snug mattress just an almost neat-looking bed. She brought a television set and her own crystal vase with fresh cut flowers in it which made the room half furnished. There was a photograph of herself with some Malibu's friends in a frame and an alarm-clock too. For security she kept a '38' revolver next to her, concealed in a shawl.

Expectedly, Arthur looking at me with a calculating gaze admonished me in his usual tactless self:

"Pierre, I hope you won't be stupid enough to mention this arrangement I made with Melanie to any of our customers. Don't screw this up; I surely don't want them to spread malicious gossips!" and the boss added, "So remember, you saw nothing; you heard nothing! As far as she's concerned, no one is supposed to know where she stays and where she sleeps at night." And, as he would address a child from first grade, he articulated: "Repeat to me what I just told you; I want to be sure that you heard me right!"

Later on, since she appeared a little pale, Melanie informed me that there was nothing wrong with her health, that it was only her father's harshness that made her unhappy. She had undergone such painful experiences in her parent's house. But now the pleasure of independence she began to feel was like 'Seventh Heavens' since Melanie's relatives had any more control over her than if she were a runaway horse.

Nevertheless, one evening after work, Arthur's daughter was not herself. A cloud had settled over her mind as she was glancing vacantly around the refurbished private room. Terror had lurked in the corner of her eye. Sitting with her legs crossed, her body was stricken by tremors and she was feverish. Her hands were cold as the cobblestones in those European marketplaces. For awhile I decided to keep her company.

Dissolving into tears, she mentioned to me almost like in a confession and with compulsive anxiety of hearing the sound of footsteps on the roof late at night. In a wailing voice, with tears cascading down her cheek that made her make-up run Melanie with eyes staring at me like those of a wild animal begged me to stay a little while later in order to investigate this spooky happening. As she talked after drying her eyes with a handkerchief, she was still shaking all over. Her pronounced pallor made her look like a corpse. I really thought she would die of fright. In my opinion I believed that she was fantasizing about the unknown, about the unseen that causes terrors of the night and ghosts of the mind. This was probably some sort of reverie of scenes from her childhood, like a simple phantasmagoria. For a short time we were watching the news on CNN.

On the stroke of twelve as we heard the chimes from a nearby church, something happened. It was no longer a premonition of fear. The restaurant became an insane asylum; like a prison for a monstrous Minotaur, half bull, half man. It was difficult to describe what we heard. It sounded like an aggressive army of anthropoid tailess, crafty apes.

First they were trundling at a mere walking pace, then in a full stampede they started galloping back and forth in the attic. This was a very steady ta-dam, ta-dam, ta-dam pace. Those mysterious night noises intensified a hundredfold by the echoes. Once again this drove Melanie almost insane with fear as she broke into a sweat despite the chill. Terror was upon her face with insurmountable fear and her eyes appeared such as to make the flesh creep.

At that point she cried as the avalanche of gallops intensified even more. She imagined a herd of large bizarre dark creatures with parchment-like faces and horrible cavernous green eyes or even some antediluvian beasts with long limbs, coming out from a dismal dream country. She could say no more but in this kind of Hades I became procrastinate, afraid to turn into a sociopath…

However, in a matter of seconds I realized that the culprit was simply the flight of a swarm of rats with their hideous red eyes scampering around, scurrying up the walls, doing their night exercises. By the heavy pounding, some of them must have had enormous weight, being as large as cats. They came up in groups, probably with ravenous eyes allured by the scent of food coming out from the kitchen. There were at least over fifty to sixty of them racing furiously in some kind of madness. They had bred intensively. Never had there been such a plague of rats and never had I acknowledged so many of those little carnivores in any other eating places in Los Angeles or any other area of the Golden State.

Melanie was seized with such horror that she could not believe first of the reality of what was happening. She was jumpy like a goat as her heart was wheezing in her throat. At this point I thought she would have a stroke in no time. Though, with her voice and her bearing brighten-up she steadily came back to her senses as she became highly conscious of the fantasy she had wrought. There was even a shade of relief in her voice when she realized we weren't dealing with aliens after all. I helped her with her jacket and directed her to her

Toyota parked in front of *Le Cerisier.* Against her will she sped away straight to her parent's house.

Within the next twenty-four hours we literally bombarded the attic with fumigation cans, along with rat poison spread in all nooks and corners. A few rats came out and staggered around like drunken sailors.

Since Arthur was not so convinced of the effects of the fumigation he had the ingenious idea to get Scotty, a red-haired cat he just got from the pound. The boss let Scotty run wild in the restaurant at night (after closing time), in order to chase away some robust rats who might have survived the deadly fumes. Scotty kept busy for several days. Indeed he did a fantastic job. Rapidly no more four-legged marathoners were to be seen around.

Once the decontamination was completed everything went quiet; there no longer were mysterious nocturnal noises. I came back with Melanie to her private quarters and I saw that that turbulent emotion still possessed her but she recuperated in no time as a pleased serenity drifted across her face. She was perceptibly relieved relaxed and cheerful as she again felt the warm safety of the night.

After beating the cushions lying on the booth Melanie was nestling deep among a soft pillow as I covered her feet with a blanket. Melanie was very tired. Earlier she had gone to sleep almost at once on my shoulder. Freeing myself tenderly I propped her head against the pillow. With a voice that looked more like a murmur she bade good night and let her hands droop into her lap. Afterward, loosening her hair in the solitude of the small room, she buried her face deeper into the pillow with her back leaning against the wall. Her breathing grew steady and after awhile she fell into a reverie; into a profound sleep, dreaming of fantastic scenes outside reality. So light was her breathing; so calm was the beating of her heart, it resembled death and she looked like an angel from heaven. The only sound we could hear was that of a cricket beginning his evening song along with the ticking of the clock.

In order for her not to run throughout the kitchen at night to reach the ladies room I bought her a basin commonly called a *piss-pot*.

To conceal her intimate functions she also had installed a larger red curtain in the enclosure of the private room. She always put herself in total darkness by closing the curtain.

For several months the boss' daughter literally lived at *Le Cerisier*, taking a cursory toilet night after night. In the morning, with her eyes still swollen, she would slip on a pink dressing gown, brewed fresh coffee in the kitchen and ate breakfast.

Occasionally Melanie would wake up in the middle of the night by the music of more crickets serenading behind the cupboard. Afterward she would drink a glass of Absolut vodka on the rocks, her favored liquor.

But, on a warm summer-night as she sat on the chamber-pot, eating a sandwich of cooked ham with a slice of pineapple she lost her balance the way an astronaut would in space. As the toilet bucket started moving it swayed upward. She fell with a terrible crash on the floor. She badly twisted her neck and ricked her ankle as well. There was also a muscle in her cheek that was twitching. For some time later on, with that sturdy pain in her neck she was wearing a strut.

The hot urine had splattered all over the private room's hard wood floor with the piece of pineapple floating like a kayak *à la dérive*-lost. Quite discouraged Melanie mopped the floor and scrubbed it with an abundance of water and soap as she tried to sanitize the entire room; but it didn't really expunge the smell of piss entirely.

Next day after being informed by Melanie of the little incident I gently vacuumed the bacon-soda scented powder she had spread on the entire surface-floor and corners of the private room. But the strong odor was still there, overshadowed somewhat by the scented powder, and I mopped it once more. Before long the place appeared scoured and well swept again.

Later on, the chiropracter who was attending Melanie promised that soon she would managed to turn her head normally again.

After this unfortunate event, over a stroke of luck an incredible miracle occurred. Marie-Thérèse, Melanie's grandmother always showed great love for her. Every year they went on a cruise on the Mediterranean and the Atlantic together. Because of that deep and warm loving relationship Marie-Thérèse simply awarded her granddaughter a four-bedroom house on Topanga Canyon Hills. In addition, Granny bought Melanie a brand new Jeep Cherokee from the family's wealth.

On the property the garden alone was huge. And in order to be protected, Melanie secured herself with two dogs, one German shepherd and a black Belgian Tervuren, closely related to a sheepdog that she rescued from the animal shelter. With their presence she found real peace of mind.

* * * *

In the restaurant's dimly lighted private room a soft glow on the cabinet shown, and upon his beribboned mandolin that was old and battered like him, the boss started playing, scraping away on just two strings. Strangely enough, after he first struck a few chords Arthur was in a finest mood. For the very first time I observed in him a kind of tranquility as a light started beaming in his eyes. He was more contented than he had been for long, and it looked like he had regained his composure long time gone. He played on his mandolin with some kind of priestly dignity, mixed with the same joy as a kid on a merry-go-round. As his fingers continued to gently glide over the strings it seemed as if within the pattern of the emotional complexity of his past life the happy recollection has moved to the present.

I had acknowledged his playing before, however I didn't hear it rendered with that unique essence and vitality. My scrutiny gave but one eye and one ear to his unusual stand out. He wasn't a first rate instrumentalist, yet at the top of his lungs he sang with a clear tenor voice, and I doubt whether the Great Caruso himself sang better than he did:

"Chevaliers de la table ronde, gôutons *voir si le vin est bon.*
Gôutons voir, oui, oui, oui, gôutons voir, non, non, non.
Gôutons voir si le vin est bon, lalalala, lala, lalalala."

With that song from a time immemorial among the Knights of the Round Table, tasting wine together something exquisitely refined and lovely surfaced as the gentle melody was revealed to me. Even that Arthur played as a scraping fiddler, the spirited tune brought him back to the days of his youth in Labège par Castanet and the most exciting time of his life as a sailor when everything had been so wonderful. Watching him carry on with so much excitement almost convinced me to believe that there remained an iota of warmth of genuineness within him. This had filled my soul with ravishment and I felt good, very good for a change. Now I realized that the longer I live, the more my experience widens and the less prone I became to judge my employer. Now, at this point in my writings I followed Spinosa's ideas when he said: *"I have made it my earnest concern not to laugh at, nor to deplore nor to detest, but to understand, the actions of human beings."*

The cheerful atmosphere was interrupted by the phone's ring. Expecting the call to be a customer about to make a reservation Arthur was quick to pick up the handset. The jolly child in him, a moment ago suddenly vanished. He was his old self again. His face which had been gentle from affectionate mood, changed to its old expression. And growling at the caller he alleged:

"What, a Yugo?" Almost immediately I realized that the call was meant for me regarding the purchase of a near-new Yugo automobile. Earlier I became interested in the vehicle which was advertised in The Valley Times. A week ago I met the owner of the car. The man informed me that his son had the Yugo's pink slip with him; that I had to wait until his return from Santa Barbara, after which he would contact me at the restaurant. Now, as he covered the mouthpiece, the handset in his hand and without checking with me, Arthur set himself as the decisive brain in this matter, and dismissed the caller:

"I'm sorry sir Pierre just changed his mind; he no longer is interested in this vehicle and that's final!" He abruptly hung up as though he, the mighty potentate was directly, personally involved in that transaction. Sitting there, absolutely dumbfounded I couldn't believe what I have just heard. Realizing how surprised I was the boss was quick to comfort me: "That car is nothing but a trash; you would have ended up with serious problems. Pierre, you have to remember that the Yugo plant located near the Balkans has been bombarded. The company is actually out of business: no parts anywhere around are available!"

Well this time Arthur had been right. Awhile later some friends and relatives explained to me that the boss took a wise decision on my behalf, suggesting that even my old Buick with its minor occasional repairs, that asthmatic wheeze of the engine and sick pistons was a far better vehicle than a Yugo. On that instance, I LIKED THE MAN.

Chapter 16

MELANIE'S DREAM WAS to join the fire department. She never succeeded because of her height. She fell short of the height requirement. However her love for the department never ceased. All of her friends were firefighters, mostly from the Ventura area. She still actively participated in one of their great sporting events called 'muster'. Under a muster performance the firefighters would show to the public how fast they can unroll the water hoses and tie them to a fire hydrant. After that they have to run fast for a certain distance to a building location, let the water flow in the hoses and extinguish an imaginary fire. Several firefighters from stations located in Thousand Oaks to Calabasas, to Pasadena and Hollywood were able to compete. The best team would be awarded with a trophy. There are interstate musters as well. That particular exercise is not just limited to the U.S. International Musters are equally very unique competitions.

On special occasions such as a birthday or a wedding anniversary at a Ventura Station where most of her friends were stationed Melanie never missed the opportunity to bring one of her delicious homemade cheesecakes along. This was so well appreciated by the firefighters and the captain himself that they allowed her to accompany them to compete for a giant international muster in Melbourne, Australia. She had to pay for the trip and lodging, however the food was graciously provided by the Melbourne fire department. With Arthur's blessings showing great enthusiasm for that fantastic trip to the Land Down Under her daughter boarded a Qantas jet, along with the best firefighters from different stations.

Several weeks later back in the City of Angels everybody would hear Melanie's interminable stories, including those wild parties at night when they would drink Foster beer from the barrel with snacks of fish and chips. On every special occasion at *Le Cerisier* some firefighters would gather to have dinner with Arthur's daughter, bethinking about their adventures on the days they were sober enough to remember things. One of the girls reminded her of the event with the wallaby mascot who was using his boxing skill against a French poodle. Oftentimes the poor dog ended up with a bloody nose to the point that the firefighters simply had to separate them.

On New Year's Eve, those jolly fire people came back with a battalion-chief from the San FernandoValley area.

The chief had a marked liking for Melanie. There was an unfamiliar sparkle in his eyes, like the enthusiasm of a young student looking forward to a new Schwin bicycle. He almost immediately fell in love with her. He likewise saw how keenly her sharp eyes were fixed upon him. Love and happiness had suddenly burst upon Arthur's daughter. It was like a man coming from heaven as wonderful as a dream could be. She felt like a woman in paradise dancing to wondrous music. And, since that moment on Yuri had had no thought except for Melanie.

Yuri Boposkovitch with that rather bizarre, far-fetched name was the firefighter commander who exhibited that Russian military discipline in his gait. His father was from a relatively good and wealthy family. He had been an important member of the communist party in the ex-Soviet Union, bearing the title of *Commissar* therefore having more power than the military as he was sending so many promoters of 'the people's rights' to hard labor in a Siberian Gulag. For such a position Yuri's father gave up everything including the easy and comfortable life with his family at a great estate near Sebastopol, on the black sea.

Yuri was named after the famed space-hero Yuri Gagarin. Tall, with brown hair tinged with gray at the temples, his cheeks and forehead hold the healthy glow of an adolescent. He had a contented gleam in that mysterious smile. In any conventional sense he wasn't handsome but with his constant good humor one cannot stop but like him.

With legs crossed and uncrossed Melanie was glancing to the other side of the table, being well aware of the battalion chief's gaze. Her young heart opened spontaneously, diffusing its songs of tenderness. She felt an ardent tingling at the sound of his voice. Nostalgia was in the air. This was a case of love at first sight too and before long they started dating. Aroused with pleasure Arthur's daughter shyly revealed to me that Yuri was a married man with three children; that he carried an almost frozen relationship with his wife. Later on Melanie admitted to me that she was able to fulfill all of his secret desires denied by the spouse.

The battalion chief's visits to her house grew more and more frequent as their intimacy deepened. Whenever Arthur was busy up the coast near Santa Barbara to purchase live lobsters right at the boat or with his corn-fed chickens from a Lompoc farm, his daughter would graciously invite her new found friend and lover at the restaurant for a satisfied dinner on the house. In their little corner of the establishment they were locked in long embraces. And later at night in her house with Yuri in mind she decided to examine herself naked in front of a large mirror asking herself if she was still attractive.

In no time my employer was informed of that relationship. Along with his friend and former Highway Patrol officer Eddy Freedman they were the first ones to be aware of that intimacy. Arthur didn't like the fact that his progeny did some coquettish with a married man; a family man with a wife and three children. For the owner of the restaurant this was a shameless catastrophic scandal. Arthur never doubted himself at finding the right husband for his daughter; an honest man of rank with an estate and true nobility, a man with good reputation and of sound financial situation.

On one occasion my employer noticed the battalion chief's red car parked in front of Melanie's house. The following day Arthur simply reprimanded her. Nevertheless the liaison encounters continued. Her father became more and more infuriated.

On two occasions Melanie saw Arthur's truck passing by. She then requested Boposkovitch to park his vehicle on a parallel street one block away from the residence. Still that contrivance didn't escape Eddy's watchful eyes; a pair of eyes which seemed to be also at the back of his head. And, on an intensely exhilarating spring day, as they were driving along, shadowing Melanie like detectives Eddy as Arthur's most efficient spy swiftly pointed out the red automobile to his friend and mentor. It was hidden three hundred feet away, adjacent from the daughter's household. My employer on the other hand was sharp enough in using his sensitive nose for discovering misbehavior.

Facing Melanie's residence Arthur came down with a cold expression on his face and his eyes were in a deep pool of anger. He walked out of the car with a sort of clumsiness. His irritability lumped heavily at the pit of his stomach. Frothing at the mouth like a dog, as he mopped away his sweat he started to yell at the firefighter commander in a voice heard clear across the street. Arthur, beside himself with rage and eyes aflame with hatred heaped insults upon Yuri. Next, he advanced toward the door as if he was going to tear it down. With fire in his heart I had the feeling that sparks would fly out of his mouth that turned up to an ugly sneer. Knowing his taste for the dramatic he played his role quite well, almost to perfection. With botches of perspiration on his chest the boss was moving as fast as his body was able to when he screamed at the top of his lungs:

"Scoundrel, dirty rascal get out of that house, you mother fucker! I don't care that you are big chief! I spit on you, I will chastise you, *merde de merde de nom d'un chien*-dog shit! I will get your ass, you son of a bitch!"

During the entire scene Eddy had a nasty little smile on his face. Arthur, still fuming like a three-headed dragon was using other outrageous statements that would be improper for me to repeat.

Inside the house Melanie was sitting on the sofa next to her lover, becoming fearfully pale and feeling a cold shiver going down her spine. For a few seconds she remained motionless, almost petrified. Outside the swearing and the goddaming was escalating. Her world seemed rolling down crushing her heart. It looked as if she had been seized with a severe nervous attack mortally stricken in all her dearest beliefs. Arthur didn't succeed to flush Boposkovitch out of the building. However, considering his reputation as a battalion chief, that same night Yuri drowning in moans of agony became irritated beyond endurance and decided to conclude the illicit pursuit. Realizing that the affair had turned into a dark horse indeed he resolved not to have further contact with her.

Now Arthur's daughter knew only too well that her sweetheart was gone forever. That she would live in a state of stagnation as a state of extreme sexual frustration was her future. She started weeping despairingly as she saw all her happiness slipping through her fingers. This had been her first serious love; thanks to her father her first disillusionment with men as well. She no longer would kick up her heels on the ballroom floor and she began to be fretted by loneliness. Since she thought she was not wanted anymore, she was of no use to anyone and nobody would love her.

Before Melanie met Yuri she had on-again, off-again affairs that end up so fast. In high school every young man was after her, into bed, out of bed, like kids after an ice-cream truck. With the exception of one genuine boy-friend that was really like ancient history, Boposkovitch had brought joy to her dull life. In such a short space of time she realized that she had miscalculated her game. She had lived for excitement rather than true happiness. It was a life without thought or scruple, and now she found herself so much defeated. Everything had been too obvious in the eyes of her father, Eddy and everyone else at the restaurant. Arthur explained to her daughter that the SOB had been a bad omen in her life; that nothing can come to any good from such a relationship. He broke the silence by adding:'

"Mel, your love for this man was only a passing feeling, some sort of drifting intimacy which you will rapidly overcome. Good God, just look at the gravity of the affair. He is a married man with three children and before long for sure he would have leave you! I have so much experience in life, you have to believe me. Please Mel don't feel dejected!" and, in a different tone of voice Arthur went on, "Shortly, along with your mother we will visit Niagara Falls. The sooner you make up your mind to my advice the better! I will help you to find a wealthy gentleman; a gentleman who would be good to you with strong financial provision. My darling believe me, this has been written in the book of your destiny!"

Melanie, still undeterred by her father's advice felt bad because of the break-up of the relationship with her lover. I perceived she was enduring pain with deep emotions. I almost had the feeling that she was going to die as flowers die when the weeds choke them. The bitterness of spirit which she carried about turned out to pessimism. Afterward she locked herself in her bedroom and started crying bitterly.

Now Melanie fell into a dark sorrow as work become repulsive to her. She kept on thinking that what once had been could never be again. With sad eyes she became tired and feverish. That incident that occurred because of her father's intervention had fanned the flame that was burning in Melanie's heart; now the torture was more than she could endure. In her eyes, her father was just a 'kill-joy.' Surely, to a certain extent she got what she had sold herself for: an 'almost' attractive man with an excellent position and good retirement benefits, overseas travels, fine dining; the list goes on.

Out of conviction that certain things needed privacy Melanie trembled like a reed and felt the shame but ironically didn't recognize 'the morally wrong' aspect of the situation. From that day on the daughter's enthusiasm had dissipated. She thought that a malignant fate watched and pursued her. Melanie was now heart-broken for everything had fallen apart. She found no enthusiasm either to call on old friends or urge them to stay with her in that spacious house. And for awhile she had no peaceful sleep.

Days succeeded each others and now her stricken heart had found some consolation with her two faithful dogs. For a long period of time Melanie had grown morose; she no longer laughed with her childish laugh. But at the same time she saw no merit in cultivating a sorrow. She would walk with the dogs for hours on end at the Balboa pond to watch ducks swimming and geese waddling up the bank. Her four-legged friends would offer their paws to her with their tails down. Soon, she decided to live at least free from any sort of annoyance in her large house. For sometimes the young lady was content in her loneliness. No longer was she anxious over a lover who would come and visit her. Once in awhile there were relapses of sorrows, but she became strong enough to overcome them. *Well Melanie, as for your grief, whatever its consequences, time would take care over them. In a few months or even weeks everything would be forgotten, just as if your grief had never been. Right now, just look at your surroundings: birds are still singing and the sun is still shining as it has been since the beginning of creation. Remember Mel, we are all 'passing thought' just like a little wind over the ocean. So, don't make yourself miserable over this broken relationship. Just go to the woods and sing a song; you will come back a new person. Find new friends with lively spirits. This is contagious; in no time you will discover your lost happiness resurfacing again. One day you will come across the right man that can be a good husband, along with a good home in due course.*

The awe is that so many women shed only a few tears over their shattered dreams. They fail to recall their disillusionment and get down to the tiresome disheartening daily round of cooking and housework.

However, later on as Melanie forgot about the battalion chief, out of fear and confusion she drifted continually from lover to lover. She had come to look at sex as an agreeable pastime. Now that Yuri was out of the picture, Melanie was in a frustrated search for contentment. She became popular with several single men firefighters. She had spent a night with just about all of them with little, no particular excitement except for a few 'too hairy ones' who after awhile even frighten her. Other men including two police-officers had tried her but she must have treated them with the same indifference for gradually they left and never returned. She also became excited by watching two men giving each other an intimate massage, as other forms of sexy behaviors had developed in her mind. I believe in the notion of Sheila Roberts in her book *Small Change* that Melanie "needs a man like a diabetic needs a Twinkie."

* * * *

There was about Vic Belurian something distinctly foreign. Vic, as an epicurean *bon vivant* was an extremely wealthy Armenian of fine reputation. Even that he looked like a mobster he was a gentleman with good manners, and a steady customer at *Le Cerisier.*

A serious accident in Damascus had let him with an artificial leg. Out of his burning vehicle Vic had found the courage to crawl away. However his right leg had been crushed. Though a little stiff in appearance, he at once enlisted our warmth. In the same manner as Kahlil Gibran, Mr. Belurian *"was born in the shadow of the holy Cedars of Lebanon, but spent the mature years of his life within the shadows of the skyscrapers of New York."*

Vic, in his early fifties was tall; he really towered over Arthur. Slightly obese, he was quite suntanned with a skin that had dried by years spent in the Middle East, and eyes fierce. His black curly hair showed a little alopecia toward the back of his head. He wore one earring on the right earlobe and on his left finger a huge 'fifty thousand dollar' multi-carat flawless diamond ring; a kind of ring you cannot set your eyes off.

The story would have it that at one time, after traveling intensively from Syria to London, Paris or New York, Vic settled to work as a teller in a Nevada bank. By simple deduction he realized one day as he kept looking at his small paycheck that bankers make money by lending money with huge interests in return. Afterward, he went to the risky business of creating a lending company of his own using the combined limit amount of twenty-five credit cards. He experienced many setbacks that almost ruined him but with the assistance of two CEO and a casino-manager Belurian formed a merchant bank, thus he became a nabob. The spiral stairway that let him to financial independence had been first paved with difficulties. And now this mega-buck man represented the epitome of the American success story-an immigrant worth fifty million dollars! With a bright mind and through perseverance this former member from the lower classes had risen to fabulous loftiness. He had climbed to the heights of financial achievement and had created a great wealth for himself in the most unusual way. At one time Belurian conveyed to us that he really didn't have any true feelings for people who have never fallen or stumbled. His vision of life had been childlike until he saw it trampled in someone else's uncouth misrepresentation.

Normally our rich Middle-Eastern client always overflowed with joy and dynamism. Yet today, even with his tremendous fortune as he arrived at the restaurant he wasn't himself anymore. He looked like a different man desperately lonely. His eyes were heavy with no sleep and he seemed to be quite absorbed in his thoughts. He had a serious air of a man who sees disaster staring him in the face. As usual Arthur who thought the world of Vic came and joined him at his private corner table. Upon serving our disabled customer his regular aperitif I noticed that his famed ring was missing. Never would he come at the restaurant without it. This didn't escape Arthur's attention either. Because of Vic's poor hearing the boss talked so loudly in a manner a Swiss Herdsman would through a fourteen feet alpenhorn:

"My friend, what happened to your expensive ring?" Without hesitation, in a weak and fading voice, staring at the boss with an almost lifelessly look, he replied: "Arthur, you are not going to believe this. At first I thought that I forgot the ring at home but rapidly I realized what the culprit was. Before washing my hands in front of the well-lit mirror at the bathroom at Caesar's Palace I removed the ring from my finger and never placed it back on. Somewhere in Las Vegas there is now a happy man wearing an expensive piece of jewelry!" My employer was now holding Belurian's arm.

The businessman went on: "Arthur, I must tell you why I became so disturbed and forgetful; I just lost a lawsuit with the SEC." and, looking ashen and ravaged, he continued:

"It cost me half of my entire portfolio and bank accounts. Against the Security Exchange Commission even my lawyer was unable to help me. The SEC appeared to set on ruining me. I'm now financially bruised. I really felt crushed against a wall. It's like I am drowning into a bottomless sea! This was as you say in French: *Une affaire flambée*."-A business going to the drain!

Certainly Mr. Belurian had been so dramatically wounded financially. He had found himself outflanked and defeated-twenty-five million dollars lost to be precise! For a man who still had more money than he could count, our wealthy customer was now trembling at every rise or fall of his assets. He really thought he was on the verge of total ruin; that earlier enough he would be in the poor house. *Mr. Belurian, you must remember that no wealth can satisfy the greedy desire for more wealth.* And as Plato in *The Republic IV* put it: "Wealth in the parent of luxury and indolence, and poverty of meanness and viciousness, and both of discontent."

This time, the boss acting more like a father comforting a son who has been hurt called upon me to serve Vic with another drink...on the house. The little boss appeared to be filled with pity as he kept thinking for a few comforting words. Mr. Belurian was not only his friend, Arthur had skillfully convinced the businessman to be a silent partner in the Solvang restaurant's venture up north.

* * * *

Bernardo Echeviran, the dishwasher decided to join his younger sister living in Chicago. Before leaving us he informed Arthur that he would wait for his far-away cousin Pedro Gomez to come and replace him.

To celebrate his departure, Bernardo decided over a few beers and hard liquor at a bar in Little Tokyo in Downtown Los Angeles. This is where he later contracted 'the clap' or genital herpes from a beautiful young Oriental woman...

Pedro took a bus from his native Guatemala to the U.S. border. With borrowed money from Bernardo the relative found a 'Coyote.' To be more explicit a Coyote is a term that designated *le passeur*; an expert for driving people illegally across the borderline. This late Saturday the Coyote carried Pedro Gomez dressed in a zoot suit in addition to seven other undocumented immigrants in his El Camino truck, en route to the U.S.

On a deserted road not too far from Tijuana through mud and rocks, wandering the mountain trails they suddenly marveled at the view of the lush valley below: This was California, *à perte de vue*-all the way. Awhile later the Coyote left the pack of the illegal north of camp Pendleton, on the San Onofre State Beach near the nuclear power plant. From there Pedro called his cousin in Los Angeles to come and pick him up.

In order to avoid the second immigration inspection right on the freeway, Bernardo would wait on a side road a few miles away from the control zone. After a long walk Pedro would come out from the woods near a hunter's cabin. Everything went fine, just like a perfect Swiss watch. The cousins after finding each other engulfed themselves in a bear hug.

On the following day Pedro Gomez started to work at *Le Cerisier.*

Besides a skin pigmentation problem he had had infantile paralysis that left him with a crippled leg. And for working on a ranch his hands were callused. But there was another serious handicap probably due to the food he ate in his native country: Each time Pedro paid a visit to the men's room an offensive odor always filled the air. We were forced to deodorize the entire area and ventilate it with a large electric fan. This posed a problem for customers who had to cross the kitchen to reach the bathrooms.

Like many restaurant owners who hired undocumented employees, usually unskilled day labor Arthur always accommodated them with a delight in his eyes. He would call them 'inferior people, stupid, ill-natured in everything' and 'lower-caste workers' usually self-effacing, hopeless and forlorn, ready to be hired at very low wages. The owner was always ready to assign them to every menial task. No insurance or workman's compensation papers were ever needed, only cash money paid under the table. Those same undocumented people in general are not outrageously materialistic, nor perplexed by prosperity. They simply work very hard to achieve their goals in jobs that most Americans would be reluctant to do. For not getting involved directly my employer was smart enough to dispose the money to one of us in the dining room each Saturday. We would hand that money to the illegal after he or she would post their signature in the reservation book. For Arthur, any person being in the U.S. illegally and willing to work at *Le Cerisier* always represented an excellent deal, and…quite a cheap deal too! Instead of paying a dishwasher forty-seven dollars a day requested by union law my boss would come up with almost half that amount. In the case of Pedro who didn't speak one word of English, unable to write or read he simply signed the book with an "X". Quite often those undocumented people were brutes from remote regions of Mexico or Central America.

On a quiet day Arthur carried a long conversation with me in order to hunt for protection against those undocumented souls. In a serious tone of voice he would articulate:

"Pierre, if someone knocks at the door, always requested the name of the person before you let him or her in. If ever a D.H.S person (Department of Homeland Security) or any immigration officer shows up tell the dishwasher and Santillas to hide under a table as fast as thunder. And remember, its A MUST!"

Though Pedro Gomez was a good worker, his one flaw was that he had a big mouth. Along with the pantry chef Gustavo Santillas the conversations went on and on like a 'well greased machine.' At some other time they were silent even moody. Including Leon we all liked Pedro but my colleague resented his lack of knowledge.

Pedro always badly pronounced my name. He was using the word 'pear' for Pierre, and, soon enough he simply forgot it altogether. Afterward he addressed me as *viego*- the old man. Unfortunately at one time an empty cup fell down from my tray and broke in pieces on the hard cement floor. On that occasion, the new dishwasher added an adjective to my name. I became known as *El viego loco*- the old crazy man!

Rapidly Arthur with exhilarated enthusiasm became very fond of Pedro. It was such a pleasure for my employer to find a newcomer good at insulting people. Although Arthur verbally abused me personally he was precisely delighted with those who picked on me at the first place. He informed his daughter on the phone that I was now officially baptized with the new surname of *El Viego Loco*. When a customer would request my assistance, Arthur would simply announce with a shirking mind: *"Viego loco*, come here." Over the years, only the surname *'Viego'* survived. It was short, and in a way, with my hair turning silver sometimes in mild disarray, I didn't complain.

* * * *

Bobby Sherman a famed singer from the '60's was one of Le Cerisier's loyal celebrity customers. He eventually became Arthur's friend. His music was popular at a time that I was just a teenager contemplating on a career path of joining the Belgian Paratroopers; already imagining my first parachute-jump. The singer's jukebox music was the sort that made giggly teen girls all over the world from New York to Rome, London, and Sydney crazy, wild with infatuation.

One evening, as Bobby Sherman was seated in the restaurant with his agent and two other friends I discreetly divulged to him that my lady friend Helena was one of those giggly teen girls from Asia who swooned over his songs. I was just expecting a blunt 'thank you Pierre' from him. But, unexpectedly, with a smile he pitched in:

"Pierre, just give me her phone number; I will surprise her with a call."

I first doubted that a celebrity of his stature was ever sincere in surprising a fan. Nevertheless I wrote down Helena's number on my writing pad and handed him the small sheet of paper, crossing my fingers that it would not land in the trash. That friendly little chat with Bobby Sherman, the American Idol of the '60s escaped into the darkness of oblivion but I mentioned it to my lady-friend anyway.

It was one of those mid-autumn weekends when the sun refused to shine at the Marina that we decided to stay indoors, lounged in front of a lighted fireplace and turned on Mozart's Adagios. A peculiar quality invaded the air. Moisture came, announcing rain. I was almost falling into dreamlike state with Helena's soothing massage just as the shrill of the phone rudely interrupted my nap. Wanting to cut short the ringing sound, Helena rushed like *un cheval au galop* and grabbed the handset.

"Yes, this is she." A short silence…

"Is this some kind of a joke?"

"Yes, Pierre is here." She covers the mouthpiece, and with an astonished face directed a whispered question at me: "Pierre, he says that he's Bobby Sherman and…" I did not let her finish her barrage of questions. I just nodded and felt a sense of pride realizing that a celebrity like Bobby Sherman would truly consign himself to his promise to call upon my sweetheart. After a short conversation with the singer I hang up the receiver and I explained everything to Helena. She started dancing around like a giggly teenage girl once more. She was overwhelmed by the fact that in addition to speaking to her idol, she was invited for a drink at the restaurant. From that day on I was in her good graces, and she eagerly uttered:

"Thanks so much Pierre for having arranged all this. I never imagined it could happen, not even in a million years!" And she continued her dance of happiness only a young girl from the '60s would understand.

But, as ill-luck would have it I blamed my big mouth for mentioning to Melanie that our most revered, celebrity client favored me with a personal phone call to Helena and I accused my pride for flaunting that he invited her for a drink at the restaurant. Melanie did not take kindly to the news and I sensed in her a tinge of selfishness and envy. For like her father she thought of their friends, specially their celebrity friends as possessions, never to be shared. Like real European royalty, this family of pretentious 'royalty'strictly forbade employees to get too close or too familiar with famous customers. The whole idea that Helena would enjoy a few moments of happiness with her idol Bobby Sherman at *Le Cerisier* infuriated Melanie and she was not going to let it happen for as long as she's alive.

Forgetting that we still live in a democratic country and losing all manner of civility she called Helena insisting that the meeting with Bobby would be called off. Melanie was loud-mouthed and vulgar. Nevertheless Helena knew better to respond to such irrationality. Both parties were aware that no court in the United States would forbid such a meeting in a public place of two free and normal adults.

Mindful of my position at *Le Cerisier* and perceptive enough to realize that at this point the owner's daughter was like a dog gone mad Helena took the higher road and pacified the anger boiling inside Melanie: "I want you to be happy. Is there anything I can do for you?" Melanie must have felt a dagger slowly being hammered on her chest for that controversial meeting nonetheless materialized.

My dear friend donned a colorful Hawaiian dress and finally greeted her 'teen idol' with a bouquet of roses while immortalizing the moment, using a Kodak camera. Bobby Sherman reciprocated by proudly presenting her with an autographed copy of his recently released biography.

* * * *

My employer and pantry-chef Gustavo Santillas arrived at the restaurant later than usual. This was Ash Wednesday, a great Catholic observation rite and both Arthur and Santillas appeared with ashes on their foreheads. With glow on their cheeks they seemed to have discovered pious enthusiasm. Presumptuousness was written all over their faces, especially in Arthur's. For such an occasion the modicum of humility and just simple modesty suppose to be *à l'ordre du jour*-the order of the day.

The arrogance reached its climax when the boss proclaimed that by the power of the Holy Ghost he felt that the hand of God had touched his soul. He continued by stating that they were both full of grace and, as *un fait accompli*, those ashes on their foreheads justified every good thing in life; that they represented the culmination of their faith. *Arthur was really trying to put himself in good terms with God… in case He should exist?*

Readers, I'm sure that you already know how a so-called 'good Christian' Arthur was. Now, let me emphasize more about Santillas' integrity in regard to his association with the Holy Roman Catholic Church. Gustavo never forgot to pray before meals. He attends mass on Sundays, receive the Lord's Supper and worship Our Lady of Guadeloupe.

However, on one occasion Santillas got into a serious argument with chef Picharon who decided to prepare us hamburgers on a Friday:

"Chef", he retorted "Don't you realize that for Catholics eating meat on Fridays is a guaranty for a one-way ticket to Hell where souls will rot for eternity? You should know that this represents a mortal sin!"

Along with those commitments within the church I want to explain here about Gustavo's pernicious conduct in life. Santillas had a wife and two children in Puebla, Mexico; another wife with a daughter in Los Angeles, and a pregnant girlfriend in Bakersfield. Just like in 'The Human Comedy' one can comprehend the pointless substance, the vacuity that characterized Gustavo's faith. By eating only fish or eggs on Fridays, and sustaining that dirt on his forehead on Ash Wednesday my good friend assumed that by those simple hypocritical acts he would be saved. And with the blessings from the clergy and of the Holy See in Rome, he could abrogate his cheating conduct, thus participate in the atonement and secured himself a place in Heaven! In that same line of thinking, I heard the case of another so-called 'religious man' just like Santillas, who on a particular Sunday didn't even want to stop his car to help a stranded motorist who was waving from the side of the road. His excuse was that he was afraid to be late to church!

Chapter 17

MONDAY EVENING, ON a piercingly cold winter compounded by a mist and drizzle, Arthur decided to close the restaurant to the general public for just that day. However, Jean-Luc Picharon and his kitchen assistants had been the only ones uninformed of this. For them it looked like an ordinary working day. Everything had been carefully and secretly well prepared.

In the reservation book was an indication of a 'Smith party' (a fake name that was used for a group of ten people) for the back, private-room at precisely six o'clock.

On the occasion of the chef's thirtieth birthday the owner had planned something quite remarkable. The concealed event that followed took Arthur almost two entire weeks to come to fruition. Picharon was well known by most of Los Angeles greatest chefs. He had a reputation to be a culinary expert and a promoter of 'the new French cuisine' highly approved by the Heart Association of America. Arthur took the initiative to contact personally all of those chefs. Six of them were from France, two from Geneva, Switzerland. In addition, at the last minute, my employer recruited a Belgian and a German, both *Chef de Cuisine*. Afterward, Arthur politely requested their presence at *Le Cerisier* for Jean-Luc's birthday. They were invited to go and sit in the private room where wine and hors d'oeuvres would be served. One executive-chef also decided to take his wife along.

Around five o'clock the owner of the restaurant told Picharon and the pantry chef Santillas to prepare a series of hot and cold appetizers for the so-called John Smith's party.

The group arrived in time, ready to partake in the feast, enjoying the food along with drinks. As soon as the food was ready, it was presented on large silver-plates before I displayed them on the center of the table.

Arthur went back in the kitchen and instructed Jean-Luc that someone from the Smith's party wanted to meet him. The guest claimed to be an old acquaintance. The chef washed his hands, donned a clean apron and went directly to the private room. The surprise was perfect. An unflagging sense of delight was in the air. Everyone stood up, and in eerie unison they all sang the usual happy birthday song in its French version. The only woman in the party held a bouquet of white roses, as the singing went on with much enthusiasm:

Bon anniversaire, nos voeux les plus sincères
Que ces quelque fleurs vous apportent le Bonheur...
Que la vie entire vous soit douce et sincère...

The chef never went back behind his stove. With a smile of anticipation, I opened a bottle of Taittinger Champagne to fire-up the celebration.

At seven o'clock sharp a lady secretly arrived from the kitchen back door. She carried a small suitcase that she laid down on the edge of the table. The lady with sensual lips and a very feminine face had a chestnut colored braided hair; deep-blue eyes that were round, also very communicative. Abruptly, she grabbed Picharon by the shoulders and planted a juicy kiss on his lips.

Roxanne was actually a party strip-tease girl hired by Arthur. From her suitcase she handed my employer a special cassette tape. He climbed on the table that was topped with a narrow wood board. After the boss inserted the tape in the cassette-player, the dancer started gyrating as if she stood on a pedestal. The exotic French music filled the air and Roxanne drank a full glass of Chateau Chevalier Cabernet Sauvignon. I opened another bottle of Taittinger along with two more Chateau Chevalier.

With the music cadenza she undressed very slowly removing her clothing piece by piece, dropping each of them on the table in view of the audience, until completely naked, and glistening as a nugget. As Roxanne silhouetted against the light, trying with a twist of her body to imitate the writhing of a cat, one can observe that she was not exactly *la femme fatale*, far to be seductively beautiful. Her body wasn't slender; her flesh had lost some of its firmness. Yet everything was rightly proportionate. Her large rose-nippled breasts, well-sculptured buttocks reminded me of Rembrandt, of Rubens paintings, depicting women with voluptuous bellies, strong legs, strong arms, with abundant faces. Simply put, with lips red like a gash of blood there was still enough there to excite a man in bed.

The cluster of European chefs kept on drinking Champagne and wine like water. They chugged endless amount of mixed drinks with vodka, gin and bourbon to really be 'in the mood.'

With much grace, like Eve in the earthly paradise the naked lady gently walked toward Jean-Luc, acting amorously attracted to him. Her entire body was clunging with tender love. She was now standing over Picharon's head. Driven by desire, with breasts jiggling, her position was very unusual, also quite provocative. With that certain care, Roxanne decided to speak:

"My dear Jean-Luc, I am a skilled woman. Please try me just to amuse yourself." Since there was no response from Picharon (who first had explored her with great intensity), who was now already half asleep, the rumba became somewhat wild. Twisting her undulating body in all directions, she turned around, bend over as everyone focused on the wiggle of her buttocks. This became very embarrassing, especially for the Belgian chef sitting there with his wife at his side. Without any consideration whatsoever two of the inebriated Frenchmen fell under the table. They almost immediately were snoring slumped on the ground, their faces red and sweaty. Before long, other chefs joined in. The drunken Picharon appeared anesthesized as his head rested on the table. Roxanne had much to drink too.

Not forgetting what her role was for that night she hollered for everyone to hear: "Who wants to do it with me?" The drunkenness was heavy and nobody responded. Unexpectedly the strip-teaser looked at me:

"What about you Pierre, *voulez-vous coucher avec moi ce soir*?" Just like in *Lady Chatterley*, Roxanne was seeking sexual satisfaction as the epitome of pleasure.

With all that boisterous bouts of guzzling, Arthur at that moment was in the ionosphere. After the Champagne, several bourbon and Coke he surely needed wine to wash them down, but didn't miss a word of the request from the lady. As he bestirred himself, struggling to his feet he answered back in an amusing irony with a loud voice as for everyone to hear:

"Roxanne! Forget about Pierrot, he has no experience. He is so dumb, he doesn't know a thing!" Only two people laughed, but it was a cavernous laugh, a croaking broken empty laugh; an almost inauspicious quaintness. Soon, unceremoniously the strip-tease woman lost control of herself. Turning around and taking sidelong glances at the boss as if he were some strange animal, she announced: "I think I would be happier with Pierre than with all those human wrecks lying in the booths; under the table. Anyway, Monsieur Arthur, with all respect I believe that you're a liar; that you just try to pick on Pierre to satisfy yourself…"

For too much wine in her head she began to vomit heavily. The whole scene was no longer arousing. At that precise moment, with undescribable sadness in my heart, more offended than ever I maintained silence. I really felt like the recipient of a sexual assault promoted by my uncaring employer. There was such a lack of moral decency. I had the feeling as if a bucket of cold water had dropped on me. *I went to the farthest reaches threaded into this narrative to flaunt that again, I became the point of mire of my employer's gruesome, depraved imagination and very distasteful behavior. A shock was clouding my eyes as Arthur was using the most graphic metaphor for degradation in order to make me feel embarrassed and publicly humiliated.*

* * * *

As the months and the years went by, the dramatic, hilarious story regarding the relationship I carry on with my employer Arthur Valois Dourville de Montrissart bestowed me the explicit opportunity, with some satisfaction to observe to compile ideas as I immersed myself in my writings. However writing in general is hard and consuming work. John Hall Wheelock expressed himself clearly: *"Most writers are in a state of gloom a good deal of the time. They needed perpetual reassurance."*

No other novelist from the past knew this any better than Gustave Flaubert. After six long years, well into the process of finishing his masterpiece *Madame Bovary*, Flaubert revealed to his friends in a Montmartre's café, *"Writing is a dog's life, but the only life worth living."*

Oftentimes whatsoever, as a writer expects 'a curtain call for a smash hit' depression followed, and I'm no exception. Evidently there is the competition, the realization that you're not alone in this field.

Once I went with Leon to Barnes and Noble in Encino. My friend decided to purchase the latest edition of the illustrated book on NASCAR oldest model sport vehicles.

As I started looking at the thousands and thousands of books on shelves everywhere smoke blew out of my nose. I became aware that I was confronting the intelligence of those great writers from the past which so much overshadowed my own. Their minds were much sharp-witted, brighter than my own. What I took to be so difficult would have been so simple to them. Suddenly I became panic-stricken, ready for 'the funny farm' and I started thinking: *"What difference my book will do in that ocean of literature, not even counting those authors with bad taste, showing a dry, pedantic style, totally uninteresting?"* Maybe my new book would be hardly noticed in fact, made fun of.

For almost an entire week I broke off in consternation as I kept on repeating tirelessly those two words, 'what difference... what difference?' With flashes of bitterness, abasement floated my mind. I thought that I shall ever write anything more, not even a single line since I had nothing else to say. At that precise moment, I was ready to be beaten to death rather than trying to write another word. (I also realized how difficult it is to find an audience for my book.) In The Writer's Quotation Book, I found this notes by Felix Dahn, paraphrased by Sir Stanley Unwin: *"To write a book is easy, it requires only pen and ink and the ever-patient paper. To print books is a little more difficult, because genius so often rejoices in illegible handwriting. To read books is more difficult still, because of the tendency to go to sleep. But the most difficult task of all that a mortal man can embark on is to sell a book."*

The conception of miracles often lay in the eye of the beholder. However in my case, a miracle occurred…

On the next brilliant Saturday, walking alongside Mother's Beach in Marina Del Rey I watched a flight of wild geese. The beach, deserted at this early hour was marked with the prints of sandpiper's feet.

Afterward, I thought about Leon when he walked on that boulevard at night, closing his eyes as he started to count the many steps left to reach a signal light a block away from his apartment. I proceeded to do the same, but instead of reckoning a number of steps, I prayed.

Surprisingly, after that short stroll while I opened my eyes again, I landed with my nose against a billboard and craned my neck sideways to read the lettering. The publicity was related to a real estate company. Underneath a picture, my eyes concentrated on a text written by Ami Domini, entitled: *The Starfish Story:*

Thousands of starfish washed ashore.
A little girl began throwing them in the water.
"Don't bother dear," Said the mother,
"It won't make a difference."
The girl stopped for a moment
and looked at the starfish in her hand.
"It will make a difference to this one."

For me, the writings on that billboard were the writings of a Divine hand. With tears in my eyes, I leaped in the air like a madman. At the realization that it takes only one reader at a time, my relief was intense. A kind of comfort came upon me. Anxiety and resentment had gone; suddenly I had a peaceful face. Never have I felt so serene in mind and more at ease with myself. A mystical force 'the finger of God' had written this message. I really believed that it had been there for me to read it.

Back to Helena's residence, my friend shouted: "What's the matter with you? You act like a little kid who just got a candy; more like a school-boy on a holiday!"

Afterward, I took up my pen with a new feeling of enthusiasm, of vibrancy. I even found joy in solitude, as I recalled the words of Voltaire in a letter to Frederick the Great: *"The happiest of all lives is a busy solitude."*

Back at the restaurant, my exhilaration from experiencing that inward harmony seriously annoyed Arthur. In a peremptory gesture the boss responded once more ungraciously by pulling my hair after a smack on the forehead. With that ugly smile at the corner of his eyes, he commanded a shrill laugh. Yet, deep inside I heard that little reassuring voice:

"Go ahead sucker you no longer can bother me!"

Later on, back at Barnes and Noble I became warmly surprised that my publisher had sent two copies of my previous book at the store. I grabbed them from the bookshelf, signing them with a felt pen. I also affixed on both front-covers an *autographed copy* sticker. It was handed to me by the store's manager before I returned them on the shelf for display.

* * **

Today I found out that the wife of the general manager of an affluent TV station among one the most popular in Los Angeles had slit her wrists and bled to death. Rose had been the happiest woman with the most hilarious smile among all customers at *Le Cerisier.* Just a week earlier she held my hand, saying how much she adored my French accent. She always enjoyed experiencing excellent food and outstanding wine in our little, quiet provincial abode. For awhile, thinking about Rose who took her own life I kept pondering: "Why…? Why…?" over and over again.

Chapter 18

PHILOSOPHERS AND RELIGIOUS people in general have wisely publicized that Man is basically good. St. Augustine claimed that "God gave His irrational creature's memory, perception and appetite, but to His rational creatures He added a mind with intelligence and will." What changed man are the circumstances of life. A person can become cruel to avenge earlier schoolyard injustice. At times, I discerned in Arthur's face a dire mask of suffering. I knew that depressing thoughts kept wandering inside his head. He was overtaken by a hopeless anguish. I figured-out that he had lived a hard life so far, for his smile was a sad one.

As the years went by I was able to read the boss like a book. On one of those days he was so distant- so pensive and solitary as if just a tiny part of himself was in the private room. He sat there glaring ahead of him, pondering over God knows what. His mind was like an uproar of conflicting emotions. He looked lost and puzzled with all expression dying away from his face. I asked myself the question: "On the edge of what abyss was he struggling again?"

Quickly, I learned the truth. My employer had been exposed to the bleak blast of misfortune. The bitterness that must have been in his heart had created shame and downcast sorrow. Oftentimes Arthur was haunted by the smell of rotten and horrible childhood memories in the hands of a monster for a father. I realized now that in his old age he felt unloved.

On that same day, Arthur looked pale and unhealthy. He was sitting huddled up as stiff as stone on the booth in that little room. His eyes as if lost in thoughts were fixed morosely at the tapestry on the wall, devoid of all expressions. For the first time I was worry of his silence. He was distant. With his legs spread wide apart, Arthur unbuttoned his jacket, took it off and placed his elbows on the table. Arthur more impenetrable than ever had the same absented face the people waiting at the bus-stop did, or of a man who was not sure that he had found his right home address. Pulling himself out of his reverie he revealed to me in a pattern of emotions the whole weight of his torment: His boyhood had been in chaos. He hasn't had a pleasant time at home with his parents. Aside from his father's beatings, at one time, for awhile he had also been half-neglected by his mother. He had never been surrounded with tender affection. In the culinary institution in Lyon, France he always ended up being punished. Arthur was forced to peel potato for hours because of his failure to concoct a *béarnaise sauce* or for having missed an important ingredient for the *mousse au chocolat*. Being birched on several occasions by such a strict teacher my employer at that early age was treated like a dumb donkey. He soon spiraled into depression.

At one time, the teacher even grabbed Arthur by his hair and made him swab the kitchen floor on his knees for insubordination. In order to reach the far-corners as well as spots behind the refrigerators he was handed a toothbrush. That beast of an educator was cynically using people's sentiments, sinking them into madness the way new recruits were treated by *les anciens* at the French Foreign Legion. What's more Arthur could recall nothing but frustration; nothing but the embittered rivalry in which he was involved with another schoolmate. He had been sadly exposed to the pitiless struggle for his life. Now what was missing in him was the image of love from adolescence. His life had been like a tire with a large bulge, making the ride rather bumpy. Whenever my employer came home with a bad school report, his own half-demented father in a display of power cracked his whip on him in the manner of a caged animal. With the sweep of the arm he looped his whip over Arthur's legs. He even beat him just for sneezing. Arthur had grown oppressed, really frightened by his dad. At night he threw himself on his bed in a fit of despair. In addition, the boss informed me that during a student demonstration in the streets of Lyon, he joined a large group with well over one thousand students who were shouting: *Demolissez les palissades* (Tear down the barriers.) On his way home, Arthur suffered from police brutality. At one time, they were slam-banging him, heaving clubs into his belly, pinching him on the head after a rain of blows as mustard–gas was sprayed on his face. The authorities claimed that he was 'a dangerous agitator' standing next to the leader Jean Belmont. It took two gendarmes to subdue him before he was thrown in jail. In that distressed environment other prisoners assaulted him. When Arthur came back home, limping, with a blow on his right cheek, his father hit him on the left cheek, saying: "This is to remind you how to behave in public!"

The days of his youth had been full of the ironies of disappointment. Arthur had been living under a strain so great that his feelings had ceased to be normal. As an insecure and troubled human being approaching maturity he became extremely frustrated and was seeking revenge. This underpriviledged childhood had seared its imprint on him. Hidden grief gnawed at Arthur. He was convinced that society had frozen him out, denying him the breaks of life as he lived in hell.

But, in the depth of his agony in that final conflict Arthur heard another voice; the voice of reason that would drive away the memories that have haunted him. If the situation for my employer wasn't that good, it has however become better, much better when he joined *La Marine Marchande Française*. With the calling of the high seas the wealth of magnificence of the ocean, the young sailor temporarily escaped the pollution of the world. I had the feeling that he was delivered from the chains of darkness and the laws of restrictions imposed by such a stern father. This was Arthur greatest's moment. So many somber clouds had deepened the gloom of his life. Now he came out of that depression into which his late unhappy fortune had submerged him. From the anguish of hell my future boss unexpetedly felt the joys of heaven finding sublime solitude of life at sea. For Arthur, the ocean was a welcoming sign for his new era of life. To discover with one's own eyes all the continents on the face of the world was far better than reading all sorts of books on travel. That ignoble bondage from home was gone; his sad expression was now marked by serenity.

During those months spent on water from Montevideo, Terra Del Fuego near the Antarctic Pole to Luanda, at the mouth of the Congo River, to the top of the world in Northern Finland to Thule, the northernmost part of the habitable world, Arthur found real peace. He grew passionately fond of those long trips. One could even observe some warmth in the man, and he became a sentimental soul. After so much of long seafaring, he changed into a pleasant voyager, finding genuine tranquility. This had been the happiest period of his life...

However, keeping awakened to unnecessary remorse like stormy intruders on a tranquil sea of life, the disgust with him was resurfacing. Murky memories of childhood came back to him. It looked that by an unbroken chain of events the past invariably linked to the present. At that moment, Arthur shed tears of despair for something that once was but that was no longer there. As a seizure-causing dose that created permanent damage, my employer informed me as he tried to clench his emotions, that he frequently feels worthless just as empty as a dried plum. Now he looked lonelier than a lone tree in the middle of the savanna. Suddenly, he seemed to be struggling in the tortures of hell as the old forgotten terrors of childhood were back in full force. Those terrors never really left him. The deep roots were still alive. At this point, I cannot but think of the great philosopher and dramatist Jean-Paul Sartre. *Nausea* is unquestionably a key novel of the Twentieth Century and a landmark in Existentialist fiction: *"But is it my fault…if I'm not wanted, if the sincerest of my suffering drags and weighs…I find the same desire again, to drive existence out of me, to rid the passing moments of their fat, to twist them, to dry them, purify myself…"*

Looking down at the carpet, trying to adjust himself mentally, Arthur tried to cross-examine me when he asked in a faltering voice:

"Pierre I do very much need to trust somebody. Tell me honestly: do you hate me? Do you think I'm an awful man?" This was so reminiscent of captain Delperdange's attitude in the Belgian Airborne after he slapped me in the face. During difficult time the image of that officer with the paratroopers came flooding back into my mind. With this inquisitive question Arthur was in fact testing me regarding the feelings of all the other employees working under his supervision.

Frequently I had the feeling that I was different from the other waiters because he kept on watching me all the time. I had a strong perceptiveness that he was about to confess all his faults and blunders. With Arthur's curious behavior of a man who won't hire anyone he can't dominate, I often bent, never broke. Whenever the boss put me down I would erect myself very fast, carrying my head as high as ever.

* * * *

Auspiciously, things changed. For several days Arthur was quite excited after some news he read in a magazine of sensations. I noticed upon his face an unusual expression of ecstasy. From the Malaysia Peninsula in the city of Ipoh near Sam Poh Tong on the Selim River lived a Brahmin. Chandragupi Darwaza Prasad, who knew more about the human body than any doctor, resided in an underground cave. Legend would have it that *Le Grand Sage* was able with the imposing of the hands, and the preparation of teas with special herbs from the wilderness to cure all sorts of diseases, including cancer. He was a cure-all for all diseases. In the same magazine the author explained so sudden healings brought about by simply touching the master's robe. Arthur sincerely thought that the guru gifted with some kind of supernatural powers knew of a few palliatives for his gout and Angeline's diabetes. This would give them relief.

I want to remind the readers that at one time in his village near Toulouse my employer supposedly found a miracle herb. However, according to his version in his astonishingly inventive mind, a Chinese delegation came to visit him and decided to cut all that vegetation for its own use. Now, Arthur has discovered that Guru and shaman, that quack doctor that can fix everything; a man with brilliant eyes that can see through you. For my boss this was something that goes against the course of nature, done only by will power. They couldn't possibly miss that great opportunity! Besides the Arthashastra beliefs, the Swami-Yogi followed Buddha's

271

teachings too, asserting that: *"Sorrow and suffering arose from desire. And in order to overcome suffering, man first had to conquer his own desire."*

According to the magazine's article, just like a moth that lives on tears from large animals the thaumaturgist Chandragupi who swallowed insects and drank water from the river as his only source of food and beverage was born with paranormal abilities. Through conscious holistic enlightenment he was able to make his astral body ageless by controlling the five elements: earth, space, air, fire and water.

In preparation for the religious meeting, Arthur bought an embroidered linen robe as his wife decided to wear a blue and pink silk sari. In addition, she would hang a Saint-Christopher medallion around her neck.

Their journey toward the healing site would start in August because on the eight day on the eight month of the year there is that bright star in the sky. This is when the Guru feels his trance spiritualistic ability, as he acknowledge the incarnation of his Supreme God Krishna…

Three weeks later Arthur and Angeline were back, quite bronzed from that paradise-like land but extremely disappointed. In vain they waited in Sam Poh Tong day after day to meet the extraordinary Yogi. Someone informed them that the holy man temporary lost his power because he suffered from bacterial meningitis and a strangulated roughness in the rectum area. A week passed by…

On the last day, as a nice gesture, still feeling sorry that he couldn't help, the Guru offered my employer and his wife to have one of his disciples to accompany them to the airport. The disciple wore a simple white robe.

Following the luggage handlings, as soon as the religious man had left, Arthur ran back to the airport's exit door to give him alms for his courtesy.

Being nowhere to be seen, this was the conversation he carried on with the security officer guarding both exit and entrance doors, as reported by Arthur:

"Which way did our friend go?" I asked.

"Your friend, sir?" was the guard's reply.

"Yes, the man with the white robe who just went out."

"No one has gone out, sir."

"But...you must have seen him!"

"I tell you I have not seen a man with a white robe, nor anyone else. Many people came in, but you are the first ones to exit."

"I tell you I saw him walk to the door!" For a moment the security officer was alarmed. As he briefly shrugged his shoulders, he declared:

"Sir, you're totally mistaken. There was no one."

Did in fact that disciple had utterly vanished into the twilight? Did the entire story make any credibility? After so many lies and extreme profligation of the mind can one still believe in my employer'spurious tales? In more than one instance I've heard Arthur's comment that there are some people on earth who can just disappear in thin air; that can see through walls or knew everything in advance before it happened. The boss would add: "It is a fact that people who were born three or four centuries ago, even now are alive and in good health!" In my employer's mind there were deep thoughts of immortality. Arthur really believed the Guru or his disciples living in that Malaysian cave; their Shangri-La were some of those few exceptional human beings that has surpassed a normal length of time; a time indefinite.

Now, on the subject of immortality here is an excerpt of *Dragons, Gods and Spirits from Chinese mythology* from the writer Tao-Tao Liu Sanders:

"In the Chinese mythology, there is a beautiful story of Chang'o and the Elixir of Immortality founded in the mountain of Kunlun, under the supervision of the Queen Mother of the West. This Elixir of Immortality is made from a magic peach tree, the fruit of which confers everlasting life. This tree flowers once every three thousand years and its fruit only appear every six thousand years."

I trusted that Arthur, in a sort of messianic zeal was still looking for that Elixir of Immortality! So many people in fact believe in life everlasting. Even in the most remote part of antiquity, immortality right here in our own body was considered a serious possibility. On the other hand, since my employer always talked about 'life after death', I found out a quite different answer in Tibetan Buddhism were we can read from Bardo: *"Whatever the condition of the deceased after death might be any hypothetical personal nucleus vanishes right before birth, so there can be no psycho-mental element transmitted from one life to another. The newborn person doesn't remember anything from previous life or trips into the realm of intermediary."*

Chapter 19

MONSIEUR ARTHUR VALOIS Dourville de Montrissart was extremely proud of his bouillabaisse *Marseillaise,* a fine fish soup with mostly seafood such as clams, lobster tails, shrimps, mussels, scallops and other marine bivalve mollusks. Several customers have already proclaimed that it was *la crème de la crème,* the best bouillabaisse miles away throughout the greater Los Angeles.

A USC-University of Southern California's professor who just happened to come back with his wife from an extended trip to Europe certified that Arthur's bouillabaisse tasted better than the ones served to them in Aix en Provence. My employer grabbed the professor by the shoulders. He looked at him, a pleased expression in his eyes before kissing him on both cheeks.

Friday night was not only bouillabaisse day but one of the busiest days of the week as well. I was working with my two colleagues, Horst and Paul. As usual by the time we let the clients in, Paul already had a few drinks. Even with his open good-natured face and exhilarated enthusiasm, some words in his conversation were incoherent, as he was mumbling meaningless sounds.

The bouillabaisse was served in a putter pot. As a word of caution we always advised customers who ordered this delicacy to wear a bib at all times while consuming this heavenly food to avert staining their clothing. When the fish soup was presented at the table we would thoroughly add in *la rouille,* a mixture of saffron, garlic and herbs for extra flavor.

On a large side-booth in a midst of a group of five people, a lady wearing a lovely, expensive flowery dress made of chiffon, simply refused to wear the bib having as an excuse that she was no longer a child.

Paul was the one who would mix *la rouille* in her bouillabaise. With those few drinks he already guzzled down earlier his thoughts were winging back and forth like a Mediterranean fruit fly. Unfortunately, as Paul took the spoon out of that gourmet mixture, a few drops fell on the lady's flower dress. Quite upset she summoned Arthur to come to the table.

With a look brilliant with excitement the boss listened to the complaint. Afterward my employer immediately raised in a quite objective way the question of whether the accident wasn't her fault since she refused to wear the bib in the first place. And with her eyes frozen inside her skin, the lady started screaming:

"Can't you see that this waiter of yours has alcoholic delusional neurosis; just look at him, he can hardly walk straight!"

Arthur's body quivered with animation when he tried to speak to Paul. As my colleague thoughts lost its clarity, he became confused. Unswevering, the boss in a calm voice and human warmth suggested to the woman to go with her dress and meet a dry cleaner person. Afterward bring him the bill for a complete refund. My employer added that it would be his outmost pleasure to take care of this matter rapidly. Everything went fine. Arthur even bestowed the lady with a piece of *la tarte Tatin* on the house.

As the party left, Valois Dourville, in an ebullience of temperament held a serious talk with Paul who was in the kitchen. Arthur admonished him that he would have to clean up his act; that this was the last time he would envision him intoxicated when at work.

Horst who witnessed the reprimand started to cry. With shaky knees, kneeling at the boss's feet in bitter agony he explained to the owner that Paul doesn't have any mature judgment, that he encountered severe mental, emotional strain; that he was resolved against any sort of conversation with him. Paul also suffered from mysophobia, a fear of dirt as he awakened with nightmares scares with throbbing of the heart. Horst added that lately his friend firmly believed that he carried all sort of diseases. This is specifically known as Munchausen Syndrome. He finally concluded: "We live together for twenty-one years; we always sleep in the nude. And lately Paul did the unthinkable: he wears pajamas!"

As I stood there Arthur abruptly took on their side. In a discordant tone of voice he coveyed to me:

"Leave us alone you stupid. Don't you have eyes? Can't you see how depressed your co-worker is? Go back to the dining room now!"

Awhile later as Arthur was busy entertaining customers, I began to observe that both Horst and Paul were collecting all the leftover bouillabaisse. They poured the mixture in a bigger pot. Knowing that they owned a large shaggy dog, a Siamese cat and a multi-colored parrot, I was curious if this was food for their pets?

Surreptitiously, Horst informed me that next Sunday they would have guests from San Francisco. Surely, those people would appreciate a good bouillabaisse. Horrified by the thought of them inviting guests to eat leftover, I uttered an expression of disgust. I reminded them that customers at

Le Cerisier usually used their fingers to grab the mussels and clams that floated in that *pièce de résistance*. Looking at them I argued:

"How in the world could you serve this to your visitors to whom hospitality is extended?" This time, after hitting me with a scarf Paul came to the rescue: "Well, first we will boil the fish soup and let it run to a strainer. It would be as good as fresh made."

Yet the odor was already musty, pungent and disagreeable. I went back in the dining room feeling a little sickness at the pit of my stomach.

Arthur left ahead of us. My co-workers also stole a good amount of extra *rouille* from the refrigerator; *rouille* that they set in another container. In addition, they helped themselves with three French baguettes to complement that nasty soup for their friends.

A day later, at the restaurant, with a blowtorch in hand Paul just finished to 'caramelized' the thin layer of sugar from a *crème brûlée*. Standing next to him, he revealed to me in a discursive way about the wonderful lunch he partook with Horst, his longtime lover at Gelson's super-market. Paul was quick to explain to me with excitement about that exclusive 'walking lunch', which also happened to be a free lunch:

"Pierre, it's quite simple. While wandering around the store we grabbed a piece of Gouda cheese and started to eat it. After that on another round we tasted their delicious Fiorucci Proscuitto ham accompanied with a piece of Pita bread. On our last round we engulfed an entire cluster of sweet Red Glove grapes that we washed down with Ginseng iced tea." With a smile on his face my colleague continued: "As you can realize it Pierrot, the entire course was on Mr. Gelson's hi… hi…hi…"

In addition, Paul became an expert at getting wood for the fireplace from a building under construction and by destroying fences from the neighborhood. And that's not all! Some nights at the restaurant, after Arthur has departed my friends would make their 'shopping-spree' right in the kitchen. Stealing like dogs round a trash can, those professional thieves would carefully fill-up an empty paper bag with butter, eggs, Camembert cheese, Colombian coffee, sugar... you name it!

Patting my back,Horst reminded me of the monkey's maxim: "You don't hear, you don't see, you don't talk." To reassure himself he would add with a giggle: "Pierre, you don't say a word to Arthur and we won't say a thing about that bottle you broke last week. If the boss find out about this, even that it was a cheap wine, surely he would hit you with an iron spoon or crush every bone in your body!"

Up to now we already knew that Arthur's inventory was unavailing; just simply lousy. We constantly had to throw away so many food items due to over-stocking, and my employer never became aware of my co-workers's theft. The boss donned the same lazy attitude with all his mail, all his bills bills that he let accumulate until he got warnings for past due payments.

As for his wines this was another serious matter. In his garage, Arthur carried some fine wines in carboard boxes that had gathered dust for years, resting in variable temperatures. Now, those fine 'fruit of the vine' dating from as far as the late '50's and '60's had definitely turned bad, with an aftertaste of vinegar. Occasionally some of our expert wine connoisseur's clients would send back a 1957 Chateau d'Yquem or a 1968 Pomerolle that was awfully sour and corky. After we emptied those bottles of wine in the kitchen sink we simply tossed them in the trash-can. Here the saying 'he sees the forest, not the trees' is so well appropriate to Arthur, my careless employer.

* * * *

The lady wearing the flower dress that was damaged by the spilled bouillabaisse called my employer. The dry cleaner man, an expert in his profession was unable to remove the spot on the dress because he needed to fathom each and every ingredient that the chef used, not just for the bouillabaisse but for the mixed saffron sauce as well. Arthur became violently emotional as his thoughts were whirling through his head:

"Madame, do you believe for one instant that I, Arthur Valois Dourville de Montrissart will give you the best bouillabaisse formula west of The Rocky Mountains to a little insignificant dry-cleaner? I know not one restaurateur that would allow sharing their ultimate ambrosia. And please lady, excuse me for the expression but you must be out of your mind to even suggest this to me. Nobody; I mean nobody in the whole wide world would steal my recipe. No one will instruct me how to run my business!"

However, the woman challenged Arthur to an actual TV kangaroo court, and we all watch the event on *le petit écran*-the small screen.

The judge (also a client at *Le* Cerisier) understood Valois Dourville de Montrissart's argument rather well. At that instance Arthur was quite sure of winning the case. He even laughed in the judge's face. However the dry cleaner's owner had equally the right to acquire the knowledge of those ingredients or the chiffon material would be ruined.

In conclusion, after some clamors in the courtroom the judge banged his gavel repeatedly. *L'acte d'accusation* was directed against Arthur. It was a runaway victory for the lady: she was awarded a sum of six hundred dollars in order to purchase a new gown. There was such a storm of cheering in the court. As we continued to follow the trial on TV Arthur, with mounting exasperation became vehement to the point of being improper. Being a complete nervous wreck he kept on gawking at the magistrate with piercing eyes addressing him with loud cries of indignation. When my employer continued to yell, the judge warned him to stop or there would be a contempt of court. A brief silence succeeded. With another blow of the gavel on his mahogany desk *le juge* hammered for order. He soon ended the session before retiring in his chamber.

Well, this was a very brief trial but a hard pill for Valois Dourville de Montrissart to swallow, for on that day the judgement had been right and it had nailed his ass!

Chapter 20

HORST'S BROTHER, HIS wife and two children arrived in Los Angeles from a direct flight from Zurich, Switzerland. They would spend a three weeks' vacation in California, staying at Horst and Paul's house in Sherman Oaks.

Jean-Marie Bourget was taller than his brother, over six feet in height, broad across the shoulders with short black hair. With a pleasing smile on his lips, he had a personality that suffused inner vitality and he always rammed his hands deep in his pockets.

His wife Georgette had brown hair, blue eyes and she wore a purple Oscar de la Renta dress. She also showed a kind face. She was very much in love with her husband to the point of being irrationally submissive.

The children, Hans and Debra were quiet, even reserved. I sensed that from the very beginning, the family bestowed a great amount of politeness toward Horst and Paul; maybe too polite.

Later on, Horst told me that Jean-Marie was a brilliant architect, a well-known figure among realtors in Zurich and other Swiss cities. Horst added that he was deeply loved by his brother. However, a slight rebellion was detected in his voice. Jean-Marie never really understood that abysmal relationship his dear sibling carried on with another man. Horst affection for Paul appeared to have something of a motherly nature…

Once, with tears in his eyes Horst explained to me: "Pierrot, I care for Paul, I cook his meals, I iron his clothes. At night I am the one who give him his warm cup of milk before going to bed and I sing a song to him in a low sweet voice. In the morning I dressed him and combed his hair. I love him with so much filial affection. There is nobody like him in the whole world. All he has to do is to come to me for any reasons. Whenever Paul is unhappy I stop eating, and I develop intestinal tract disorders. I wish my brother can comprehend that I am not a sick person, that I have deep feelings too." And just like in court, in a closing statement with his lips puckering a weak smile he would add:

"Yes, I'm a gay man but I still have self-esteem. I'm not that kind of person to be found loitering near public bathrooms like those pervert, creepy men doing lewd acts. I'm not going to die in the gutter either!" I did not speak a single word but merely kept looking into his quiet concerned eyes.

The following Sunday Paul, Horst and the entire Bourget family invited me for dinner in Redondo Beach. *El Cazador* was an appealing, sidewalk restaurant shaded by an awning overlooking some splendid baroque-style fountains. Not too far from here, the cliffs from time immemorial come down to almost meet the ocean.

After dinner we went for a walk on the pier and at the white sands of the near deserted beach. The rolling waves rose up before they broke with great power and a deafening sound.

Back in Sherman Oaks, Horst mentioned that the evening was not going to be complete without a visit at *Scorpion One*, a modern bar in the Sepulveda Hills. Since one has to be at least eighteen years old to get in the bar, the children Hans and Debra had to stay home, watching a recent movie from the Disney Channel.

What I didn't know is that *Scorpion One* was a very sophisticated gay bar. I had no doubt that Horst wanted his brother to accept that it was quite normal for gays and lesbians to get acquainted, to drink, to have fun together.

At the bustling quarter of *Scorpion One,* with a rotating mirrored ball hunging from the wooden ceiling, in the hazy atmosphere we sat on leather chairs next to a solid black mahogany table. The place was flashy, darker and smoky. In addition on each corner of the room strobe multi-colored lights decorate most of the walls.

People were waddling in so many positions. After gulping a couple of Corona beer, Horst initiated a dance with Paul. It was a very rhythmic motion. Jean-Marie and Georgette just remained there without talking.

Being startled by her attractiveness I chanced upon a gorgeous lady with short fashionable hair and exploding breasts seating at the bar, sipping on her Hawaiian Punch and popping some peanuts in her glamorous mouth. She was dressed with much style. Our eyes crossed; she even smiled and bowed, but not for long. Soon a slim mulatto woman came to join her and bestowed the young lady a tender kiss on the lips. With the disco music that was deafening, almost earsplitting sound I simply realized that I had no other choice than to dance with Georgette.

On my way to the bathroom, in that pre-chilled atmosphere of the air-conditioning someone grabbed me by the arm. It was Matt Brend the hairdresser and a neighbor from *Le Cerisier.* He was wearing one of the musk varieties of erotic perfume. Gaping at me with tender eyes he simply said in a most normal tone of voice:

"Darling, so nice to see you here I hope we can have the next dance!"

However we all left before Matt had a chance to reiterate his hop about.

Coincidentally, next day at the restaurant a large party of twelve people arrived; they were all gay men from the giant Brentwood Florist Company. Coming from different directions they parked their luxury cars right in front of *Le Cerisier*. The florists first kissed and hugged each other with little tappings on the back.

In the group was a flushed-face homosexual bishop from a Tarzana gay church. Some of those happy fellows were from California, others from New England or New York. Still another one, dressed like a ballet-dancer was from as far as American Samoa.

Horst and Paul were exceptionally joyful for that encounter as they began joking with them. Paul didn't hesitate for a second as he settled happily on the lap of the flower-shop's accountant and started to play with his gold necklace before unbuttoning his shirt. Furthermore, after a little hugging and kissing, the satisfied customer slipped a twenty dollar bill into Paul's apron pocket. He kissed him again heartily before planting a gardenia on his head. Later on, this friendship appeared to have been cemented by other substantial gifts.

Just as I finished illustrating the special items on the menu, Arthur arrived, sporting a newly cut mane with a close trim at the back of his neck. The drunken comedian just acquired a haircut. With a great smile on his face he first crowned himself with the gay bishop's mitre, (the prelate took his hat along as it had been dry-cleaned at a local shop.)

Now, with his hands folded quietly on his lap, his throat rasped by the bourbon, the little man who earlier had a long talk with Matt Brend in front of his beauty salon, distinguished himself by telling a practical joke aimed at the florists. His erotic attitude and gestures were quite obvious:

"Yesterday Pierre went to a gay bar wearing a champagne silk short-sleeved shirt. He then fell in love with my hairdresser." and uttering his groan of pleasure, my employer went on, "He was holding him tight, cheek to cheek during a fabulous tango. Love was in the air"

The head florist gazed at me with great compassion and with his pinkie in the air begged the gay bishop to give me the blessings. At the same moment I felt sick inside with that awfull lie from my employer. But as a self-conceived actor I decided to play their game. I did a genuflection and let the high-ranking clergyman blissfully impose his hands on my forehead.

* * * *

Readers, in the same line of relationship between employer and employees, CEO and managers, let me explain to you about the following event. The owner and heiress of Van Houten Jaguar Motor Cars in Beverly Hills, Joan Van Houten associated herself with a grave, unromantic and unsympathetic young gigolo. Her personal fortune was next to incredible. Joan's husband passed away a few years ago from prostate cancer. As for Mrs. Van Houte she had been afflicted with Tourette's syndrome since birth. Tourette's syndrome as described in the Merriam Webster Collegiate Dictionary is "a neurological disorder characterized by recurrent involuntary tics, involving body movement."

Twice a month the wealthy lady would show up at *Le Cerisier*. She would be accompanied by Kevin, her playboy friend along with Mr. Kramer, the general manager of the giant, elegant car dealership located in Beverly Hill's finest quarter. In spite of her health dilemma and advancing age, Joan was still a woman with good features.

They would emerge at the restaurant in a white luxurious late model 'Jag.' Arthur's keen sense for the big buck always heightened with the arrival of Mrs. Van Houten's entourage. He wasted no time in personally welcoming the heiress and her guests, escorting them to their reserved table. But the air with which the lady looked at him betokened a certain unconcern at his presence or what would be his opinion of the way she walked or spoke. Joan always hugged me before covering my face with kisses in so many instances. Everytime the threesome went for a night out Mr. Kramer always voluntarily footed the bill while at the same time pretended to show respect for Kevin. This way he will surely be in good standing with Mrs. Van Houten, her employer thereby securing his position as general manager of the car dealership.

Eventually on that sultry August evening they were back at our restaurant to celebrate Mrs. Kramer's birthday. Unaware of his own rudeness Arthur seated himself at our distinguished guests's table, helping himself with a flute of the most expensive Pink Crystal Roederer Champagne; the Champagne of the Tsars.

When it was time for me to explain the menu, like a giggly teenager Joan held onto my hand as though we were jovial lovers but to the dismay of her boyfriend Kevin. To make matters worse for the gigolo Mrs. Van Houten, out of the blue coquetishly said:

"Arthur, you don't mind if I take Pierre home?" As I went on explaining *la carte du jour*, Joan kept on holding my hand tight under the measly stingy look of the boyfriend. At this point I believe if his eyes were an MK 48 I would be dead on the spot. At dessert-time, the continuing flirtation became too embarrassing for a gigolo like Kevin. He suddenly stood up and, after the general manager took care of the bill he demanded that they leave the place at once since he didn't feel too good.

Losing a customer such as Mrs. Van Houten was to Arthur like the Wall Street crash of 1929. Moreover he was green with envy when Joan unabashedly declared her fondness for me in front of the entire restaurant crowd. Once again I, Pierre Choucart the insignificant waiter have stolen the spotlight from the boss, the ego-maniacal Arthur.

I was still savoring that short moment of satisfaction and pleasure with Mrs. Van Houten when suddenly Arthur's right hand landed on my cheek, awakening me from my *rêverie*. Always having the last word in all matters, my employer could not help but continue to chastise me by saying:

"A dummy waiter like you is not supposed to flirt with such 'wealthy' and influential customers.'"

Chapter 21

FOLLOWING THE GAY-BAR occurrence the strange Arthur displayed his wild imagination when he christened me as 'Pierrette' the feminine name for Pierre. The group of the same florists show-up quite regularly. They would sit in the main dining room since they all resented that claustrophobic sensation in the private room.

On another occasion, as they were reunited again, my boss would tiptoe and join them at their table declaring: "*Ma petite Pierrette* is going to explain the menu but I must warn you, please don't interrupt 'her' because 'she' can be a real bitch!'" This would of course create a chain reaction of laughs all around.

Before I even commenced describing to them *le plat du jour*, an older florist with his white hair pulled in the back as a pony tail and wearing diamond earrings requested with delighted excitement to have *"la petite Pierrette"* for dessert. Two lesbians sitting on a nearby booth also expressed with a flurtation glance the desire to partake in that 'exquisite dessert.'

Another enthusiastic laugh followed and Arthur was in heaven. Intense excitement was building-up. It was hard to realize the eagerness, the uproar and all the emotional effervescence throughout the entire dining room. The boisterous florists attracted the attention of everyone around them and in no time everybody was participating in the carnival atmosphere. Now the entire dining room always ready to be amused was overflowing with loud, idiot laughters. In my employer's mind this was a demonstration of good business. What's more, while clients were savoring the ambrosia-like dinner, they were entertained as well with those silly humorous twists. Throughout all those years that I worked with Arthur I became amazed to discover how charismatic he had become with people who didn't really know him well. He also carried a personal interest in the business affairs of some of our wealthier customers belonging to plutocracy, the potentially rich. A skillful talker with a personality beaming with enthusiasm Arthur would forcefully attempt to unravel the value of their fortunes and of their properties located in the most sophisticated areas of the City of Angels. Displaying the sagacity of a fox scenting a flock of quails, my employer was always prepared and ready to be sniffing around those people as he would have done round an attaché-case full of currency. However he was too much inquisitive as he kept asking far too many questions. Arthur's quest of happiness was in striving for money; he was simply covetous and greedy like stinking fetid water. Providing that I opened an expensive bottle of Champagne at the table, my employer (with the best nose in town) knew precisely that he would be invited to join those clients for the libation as the Dom Perignon was crackling in the crystal flutes.

* * * *

"Among wise men, the wisest knows that he know least; among fools, the most foolish thinks he knows most."

—Antonio de Guevara

Except for those occasional magazines of sensation, I knew for a fact that Arthur never endeavored to divert himself with reading good books. But he enjoyed being puffed up by the tongues of flatterers and all of his opinions represented an amalgam of client's views that he meticulously stored up all he could day after day. He would use those scraps and fragments from that borrowed knowledge to boost his seemingly 'I know it all' approach to impress new customers. This was how Arthur picked-up his education. There is one credible word that can fit my employer's character for this matter: epiphyte-a plant that obtains its nourishment from the air and the rain and usually grows on another plant for support, such as Brussels' sprouts. Nevertheless without realizing it, Arthur in a supposed notion of acknowledgement would turn into ridicule. As a matter of fact my employer never extracted anything from such sources such as political or business events indicated in well-informed magazines or newspapers.

Here is a typical example: one day a group of cardiologists from Crossfield Hospital met in the private room for dinner and to discuss their latest findings. Later, at dessert time over coffee Arthur already with a heavy load of Champagne and wine in his throat appeared 'a curtain call for a smash hit' in the delimited space where the business-gathering occurred. He waited for the silence to be at its peak. And, in a serious tone of voice with his proboscis in the air and a flush of pride that rose to his face he decided to speak. As puffed as a pigeon, in front of the panel of renowned experts he trumpeted with the air of a well-informed showman:

"Gentlemen, did you happen to know that just one aspirin a day can prevent heart attack?" In that pathetic theatrical manner the method of address was so unusual that all turned with curiosity toward Arthur. Some of the physicians gawked at each other and for a moment they pondered over this 'outstanding information.' They were murmuring as they grew speechless while others spoke together in whispers. Feigning amazement with such a marvelous discovery they even clapped a little, enough to make Arthur feel good. With smiles all around there was a general assent to this. In a way it was even hilarious but sufficiently to cause one to wag one's head in despondency. Following this statement the boss thought that perhaps with that turgid oratory he had astutely listed himself as an expert in heart diseases. And glancing around he appeared quite satisfied for the way he had handled himself...

Paul who heard the speech too, simply announced: "I can't believe the crackpot said this. What a prick! Why is he making such a horse's ass of himself in front of those heart physicians? With all his stupidities he can make a cow laugh!" A customer on his way to the bathroom who heard that 'revelation' added: 'Arthur is really too foolish for words.'

With his lack of refinement of social skill and with his grotesque buffoonery, my employer was really mind-boggling. He didn't realize that he was a phony and a counterfeiter intellectual and that some new customers had spotted him before he even said one word.

After that 'brilliant and vaudeville routine performance', the restaurant owner with a look of triumph joined other people in the main dining room, boasting like a real hot shot that he just carried an interesting conversation with a group of cardiologists. With eloquence, he went into endless details:

"Those doctors almost treated me as one of their colleagues when they showed me deep appreciation for my ultimate knowlege."

Recalling his *titre de noblesse*, Arthur was well informed about just one subject: the many royal and imperial mistresses known as ladies-in-waiting to the kings of France to Napoleon.

He knew everything about the private lives of Mesdames de Maintenon, Pompadour, du Barry and Récamier. The boss even made a chronicle of the immorality of the kings and emperors of France.

At some other time, Arthur in his discursive subjects among the castles of imagination would swear that in his small village in the south of France, as strange as it may appear he had noticed a chicken with teeth!

When I went to Arizona to meet my friends The Decarpantels, a gigantic rooster with a fine curving tail and a rose-red comb stood in front of a house. He was acting more or less like a security guard. As I was jogging from the hard, sun-baked field to one of the main artery of the city, the rooster hopped and landed on my back, pecked on my head, on my neck, yet never bit me the way a dog would. On the East Dragoon Road, he was known as 'the mean chicken.' For days on end my employer's boring stories went on and on and on. Arthur was also the most terrific liar I ever saw in my life.

I have always known, especially from his wife that at one time in his life my employer was an assistant cook at the Air Force base in the city of Tours, France. But in front of a group of lawyers this became another dazzling story of fabrication. The little man would annunciate with gravitas that he was a first class airman before becoming *un pilote diplômé* who flew the missions as 'a test pilot!' for French *Mirage* planes; that on a prototype near Toulouse he broke the sound barrier that created a sonic boom. The truth was that Arthur never set foot in a military jet…

While the boss was telling all those absurd and unbelievable nonsense stories to our patrons Horst had a brilliant idea: One day as Arthur was sitting with a family at a dining- table, he revealed to them in a glowing and enthusiastic praise that his uncle was France's top architect. Really tired of hearing the boss tell endless yarns about nothing, my co-worker brought two large telephone directories. He dropped them at the table's edge, informing the family in a peremptory manner that those were all of Arthur extravagant tales of past years tangled up in his unrestrained eagerness. An explosion of laughter occurred, not only from the family side but from people sitting at nearby tables as well. Others simply turned their heads away to hide their smiles. The only one who didn't appreciate the joke was Arthur himself who quietly slid out of his seat and secluded himself in a corner of the kitchen, turning on his heel and walking back toward the front door while hyperventilating. Independently from Arthur's constant harassment, I sometimes admire his uncommon audacity in telling our clients such far-fetched narratives.

* * * *

Here is another fantastic event: Major Raoul B. Rattleput was a bizarre human being. Near-sighted, with robust healt he had a jovial temperament, a haughty pride of movement with that real commanding posture and striking feature in his countenance. With some nobility in his attitude, he was loquacious with a kind of musical voice. Rattleput would come to the restaurant alone or with a group of people.

Almost six feet tall, bearing a martial disposition with a fine military haircut, he always wore a strange uniform, a red beret on his shoulders's strap, purple stockings like the bishop and shining boots. He also carried a stick with which he often strikes his leg in the military fashion. Tall and skinny, with his scanty bristling mustache, he appeared to be extremely young to be a major. At times he had vile, obtuse eyes-*les yeux d'un taureau*, the eyes of a bull running wild in the arena.

Arthur's best friend, Eddy Freedman, a former Navy-Veteran from the Vietnam War happened to be at *Le Cerisier* one of those nights when Raoul came for dinner. Looking at the Major's outfit, Eddy was unable to point out from what branch of the Armed Forces Rattleput belonged to. He was gazing intensely at that uncommon uniform carrying all sorts of ribbons, medals, gold barrettes on the shoulders including a badge of honor for 'courage beyond the line of duty.' He wore so many medals, as if he had fought wars on all continents. It took Freedman some time to realize that our major was not only wearing a ROTC military uniform, but also a masquerade garment with the addition of fake insignia. In fact, Rattleput was an officer from the Pindbury School Regiment in the same manner as the writer Santayana, the day he became lieutenant colonel of the Boston School Regiment.

Major Rattleput with his fancy and colorful uniform that he actually invented would speak constantly with the identical fertile imagination as Arthur. With utmost enthusiasm, that proud officer would sit down with an air of expectation and interest as his full, manly voice thrilled on every ear. The officer would chat about his missions in all parts of the world that included his numerous acts of heroism:

"I just got back from the Ukraine," he said "I was assigned over there by the Chief of Staff on a special assignment to form a team of Special Forces." The major added that in Kiev some of the high-ranking officers were corrupt to the core and that their army had been in poor shape. He was there as the ultimate re-organizer!

On another occasion Rattleput flicking his boots with his stick appeared to be in a hurry: "L'addition, please: At precisely 8:00 PM I have to board a Lear Jet at Van Nuys Airport bound to D.C. Tomorrow I have to participate at a CIA meeting with the right hand of the Commander-in-Chief."

My potbellied employer really loved the major to the point of exposing his name and the one of his entire family to ridicule. Once, with a childlike glow in his eyes and full of pride he tried to sound rightly submissive to a major. Harboring a power of conviction he introduced himself to Rattleput, nodding his head solemnly with theatrical heel-clickers:

"I am Count Arthur Valois Dourville de Montrissart, group-captain and Air Force Flight Commander." With the military salute and another clicking of heels the count hawked: "AT YOUR SERVICE, SIR!"

They blended their greetings so elegantly with deeper reverence and humble gratitude that it appeared they had met in a fraternal level. In reality both of them became like brothers as they had developed a great *esprit de corps*. The two men talked and listened to each other. It seemed to Arthur that a delightful collusion radiated between them as between two top expert military men. Acting as former comrades in arms do, they drank together on the sound of trumpets of a military music CD from the tape-player that Arthur bought. They flattererd each other on their sensational and quite unreal exploits.

On another occasion, with luminous faces they both went outside while the door of the restaurant stood wide open. They actually were drilling to John Philip Sousa's martial tune coming out from the powerful speakers, just as if they were in a parade. In their monkish extravagances, they cooed like two lovebirds on a tree. It was such a hilarious scene to observe them beaming triumphantly, rubbing shoulders like great fighting men. Those 'superior officers', almost social equals in military term carried on their idiotic conversations with great passion till late at night. They were guzzling so much hard liquor that at one time from their table I heard the sound of a loud crash: the flight-commander had fallen on his back from his chair like a heavy sack of potato!

At retiring time, after a last shot of brandy in their coffee they would both stand at attention, remaining erect and stiff like soldiers presenting arms before giving each other the military salute. Rattleput, after bowing to the earth had a last announcement for Arthur:

"Commander, I give you my word that I will do all in my power for you to meet The Secretary of Defense!"

On another slow night at the restaurant, major Rattleput confided to me after a long sighing breath that he would be going back to Afghanistan for an undetermined period of time. He added, radiant and with high spirits: "It's not to plant daffodils; this is a highly classified operation. I am going there for the spring maneuvers as an adviser to the Yusefzai, the Wazirs, the Khattak and the Shinwaris, all former Muhajadines Fighters from the Khyber Pass. Those are the same ones that are presently working along with the CIA against hordes of foreign soldiers, mostly mercenaries. But one of the main problems is that the ethnic Tajiks are still dominated by the Pathans. I was also a friend of Commander Ahmad Shah Massoud who just got killed by a suicide bomber," and the major continued:

"As an *aide-de-camp* to a four star general I've to organize an army; an army that is alert. I would be fighting through the sparkle of bayonets, the light of shells and the collision of thunderbolts, hoping to conquer that despotic enemy who is trying to create a spirit of revolt. Over there, those fighters respect me a lot. At all times they praised me for the precision with which they performed their various drills after I had shown them to do it right. Upon my arrival at the refectory a sergeant would order everyone at attention." Cracking his whip once more, the major added, with a sad face, "I will be facing illness and even death. And for the worse, instead of my daily hot shower in the Washington Military Compound, in that far-away place there will only be sponge baths! But the paths of glory always lead to the grave. I already know that for all I have done for this government, on the day I die, if I am lucky enough I will be buried in Arlington National Cemetery. I will get one snapshot, maybe one column in the local newspaper. But there would be no great funerals that this nation granted their heroes. The Military won't even display flags at half-staff, nor have a street named after me!" and Rattleput concluded:

"Pierre I had been quickly promoted from captain to major because of my visions, of my stratagems and for gaining so many military laurels on the battlefield. I have to confess to you that I was born a leader. The Belgian General Caumont, now Chief of Staff of the Belgian armed forces praised me for my bravery in action as well. Sultan Mohamed Uflir even knighted me. I have a strong gift in that line, and I don't intend to remain in my present position as a major for too long. I'm praised by my superiors and honored at the Pentagon. And, confidentially I'm a friend to the under-secretary of defense. With higher aspirations, I have good reasons for knowing it to be my duty to seek the rank of colonel after my next assignment. Ironically, if I don't die in combat with my boots on I know I will sink into the paltry defeat of old age!" As the major kept on talking, I noticed around his neck a Purple Heart decoration hanging on a blue tape, however it was much too freakish- not the Purple Heart at all…

Lately, we heard from a friend of his so-called driver and *majordome* that Rattleput, beside all his extraordinary missions, experienced an attack of rage. He had been taken away to Camarillo Mental Health Hospital for observation. Almost immediately he was classified as being *dementia praecox,* or mental alienation. When the doctor approached the major, he no longer was in possession of his senses. In a feeling of despair, Rattleput kept on babbling a jumble of words: "Yes Your Excellency...Of course Mr. President... Surely, Sultan Ahmed!" The poor man only had imagined himself of being a real army major. Raoul who became emotionally disturbed, even dangerously violent never recovered his reason. The doctors believed he was a hopeless case.

Awhile after, Eddy Freedman whistled to me in a smile, that a room at Camarillo Mental Health Hospital had also been secured for count Arthur Valois Dourville de Montrissart... Air Force group captain and test pilot...?

As the French writer Boileau said *"A fool always finds a bigger fool to admire him."*

With the sudden incarceration of 'Major' Rattleput, within Arthur's mind, a series of strange developments was taking place. And this filled him gradually with fear. Rattleput had been his dear friend. Now he really missed him deeply.

* * * *

Mr. Roland M. Fitzpatrick a well-known architect from the San Pedro harbor was one of Arthur's best friends.

Roland, a middle aged man with smiling soft brown eyes, dreaded double chin with a mole on his neck, an enormous nose which seemed to grow without any roots and loose gray hair had a face that always looked strained. With his foreign-looking appearance, even that his sweet, light voice overwhelmed me there was something strange, something disturbing about him. One look at his face was enough to tell me about his character. Roland was that kind of man that can smile without parting his lips. Still with a Dublin accent when he spoke, his tongue moving over the edges of his teeth, he would show a nervous jerk of his shoulders. Yet, beside a *façade* of some intellectual radiance, wearing a thousand-dollar gray suit, he was an unprincipled, brutal man of ill nature-a born gambler who enjoyed playing rummy.

As I was glancing at him from that certain angle a strange thrill shot through me. All of a sudden his eyes were becoming somber, probing at me objectively. Mr. Fitzpatrick, in his stylish clothes conducted his business with hardness of heart, and as a trivial person he used all the tricks in the book in order to achieve his goals. A very successful man in his profession, Roland was also a real-estate magnate and the owner of the Cross-Craft chain stores that specialized in boat appliances. So brilliant was his enterprise that he opened his own bank in Brentwood.

In the midst of his prosperity, at the very pinnacle of his prominence, Mr. Fitzpatrick decided to buy one of the most luxurious yachts of the entire harbor. He named it *Irish Soul*. An army of helpers worked on that ship for several weeks, adding the most sumptuous items money can draw, from elegant furniture to fourteen carats gold faucets for the bathrooms, oriental carpets, jacuzzi, sauna, you name it. The boat was a curious and small replica of the fabulous Onassis vessel, the *Christina*. Half of Roland's huge fortune went into the purchase of that 'pearl of the sea.'

On one occasion at *Le Cerisier*, my employer joined Mr. Fitzpatrick and his associates for a toast at their table. I never intentionally listen to our clients' conversations. Still as I poured coffee in the coffee-cups of Roland and his guests who came to joined him, I couldn't stop but be aware of a comment from the architect. As he looked around defiantly, with an extinct cigar between his teeth, this was directed to my boss:

"Arthur, in order to attain a righteous end, my method is justifiable. Here is my best advice to succeed in business: "Fuck all of your best friends, especially the wealthy ones."

Several weeks after that meeting at the restaurant, Mr. Roland M. Fitzpatrick sailed down aboard his *Irish Soul* to Ensenada, Mexico. He was to meet his Cross-Craft partner from the south of the border.

As the yacht anchored in the Ensenada marina, the partner with a sharp, savage nose and a scar on his right cheek, commanded Roland that he was taking over the ship. Following this act of piracy, under the protection of bodyguards, the mutineer simply added with some kind of persuasion:

"Roland, there is a late afternoon *Tres Esterella De Oro* public bus going up north to Tijuana and on to the U.S. border-town of San Ysidro. Be on it, as well as your crew!" Furthermore, the partner warned Roland that if he didn't follow those instructions to the letter, an unfortunate accident might occur!

Having no choice, with an inexpressibly bitter smile, Mr. Fitzpatrick boarded the vehicle that would take him back to California.

Later, Roland, being in possession of the yacht's ownership papers, and the assistance of several lawyers looking into that matter, tried everything in order to reclaim the *Irish Soul*. With so much corruption within the local government and the Mexican police, it was just a lost case. Roland was unable to get back his beautiful yacht 'the jewel of his life.'

Depression followed. His sadness was so profound that he lacked interest in his affairs. Bad management forced Mr. Fitzpatrick to go to liquidation, losing the bank as well. All of his assets remaining went into auction...

Much later, Arthur Valois Dourville de Montrissart swindled his two silent partners in the Solvang restaurant's venture. One of them Dr. Fu Long, a hospital owner, was a straw man for a Pacific-Island president, the other one, Vic Belurian, the Armenian businessman. They both took Arthur to court. But, after cross-examination of the facts the judge declared Arthur guilty as charged. Thus my employer lost the lawsuits that were pending upon him. According to Eddy, on that moment it looked as if Arthur had been struck by thunder as he gave the court what appeared to be a low growl like a furious dog in agony. *So far, so good for the advice Arthur got from Mr. Roland M. Fitzpatrick, as he carefully followed the architect's instructions to the letter.*

Chapter 22

OCCASIONALLY, WE WOULD have the entire restaurant reserved for a large private party. This however should not exceed fifty people, because of fire department regulations.

Today the giant pharmaceutical company *Merck* chose *Le Cerisier* for a business lunch meeting in order to promote a new medication for osteoarthritis, a degenerative joint disease. This was a formal party for forty doctors. Since Paul was sick in bed, I would be working with Horst and Melanie. Arthur would assist Chef Picharon in preparing forty-nine main courses including hot and cold appetizers.

An assistant professor from U.C. Berkeley, director of frontotemporal dementia clinic, also an expert in bone and joint diseases, installed a large screen and a projector on a table to display scientific slides to her audience. She was of great physical fitness.

Surprisingly, only thirty-eight physicians showed up. It was a distinctive lunchtime event. However, most of them were gobbling down the special meal hurriedly to return and consult with their afternoon patients.

During the discourse by the lecturer who spoke with eloquence and high-sounding words, Arthur could not contain himself. After he got to the dining room my employer watched the screen with a touch of excitement.

Back in the kitchen he called his wife on the phone. Sounding as an imp, and leaping in the air like a kid, he quietly revealed to her in a very soft and gentle voice that he was charging *Merck* for forty-nine meals as originally agreed upon, but that only thirty-eight physicians were present. Arthur took so much pleasure in being able to 'skin' for this deal that the rogue side of him was quite evident. Standing next to him, and noticing my uneasiness, the greedy little man with a sharp stare, shouted in a quite different tone of voice: "You have nothing else to do than to stand there like an imbecile. I'm sure there are tables to be cleared, so move on stupid!"

Arthur, embittered by sorrows continually poisoned my life. The multitudinous indignities I suffered as he bad-mouthed me and tried to make me feel weak, even dull were so awful that my pen was unable to write them down, and the punishment always oversized the offence.

* * * *

One evening, Melanie and her mother delivered some fresh made cheesecakes for the restaurant. Being a great pastry chef, Melanie would spend several hours in preparing those fine desserts at home. Her kitchen was equipped with a giant *Wolf* stove too, the same size as the one at *Le Cerisier*. Angeline stood beside the car while waiting for her daughter to return.

Swiftly, a stranger grabbed her from the rear and ripped the gold chain draped around her neck. She screamed and stumbled. The man put her down on the ground and knocked her breathless with several kicks, just as Melanie was approaching.

Realizing what was happening outside, I rushed to help Angeline to get up and regain her composure. A part of her neck was slightly flecked with blood. At about the same time, Matt Brend, the hairdresser came out for his 'nth' smoke of the day and witnessed the perpetrator who was trying to escape through the alley. He described the man as tall, as dark-skinned. Without hesitation, Melanie snatched her gun out of her holster and chased the attacker. She was running faster than she would have thought possible. She ran with such determination and agility which I had often seen her displayed. Melanie had a long searching look in the direction of the boulevard, but the man had too good a start. He already gained some distance and simply vanished.

Back at the restaurant, Arthur's daughter, now completely exhausted and wet with perspiration first wiped her face with her handkerchief as she stood there, frowning and lost. Showing a strength that was greater than anyone would have expected she was heard yelling on top of her voice: "I will kill the bastard, I swear it!" *That day, Melanie felt in herself an energy which she did not know she had. She may not have made it as a firefighter, yet I'm sure she would have been a tough policewoman...*

* * * *

Karl Heinrich von Hammersmith was one of many of Angeline's nephews. Angeline was blessed with a large family tree with ramifications throughout all of Europe, including the Russian Federation.

A financial adviser and stockbroker of international reputation, Karl was a man of superior knowledge and wisdom. It was always hard to tell how old he was. Karl Heinrich's office was headquartered in Frankfurt, Germany where he was on the Board of Directors in the banking world, in addition to being a member of Frankfurt's most aristocratic club. Those members bound themselves by their word of honor. And to use his own words, "In Europe, I'm constantly flying 'a rotary-wing aircraft' from one city to another.'"

Being a man of strength, indecision never crossed his face; he was the same today as yesterday. Karl with that fascinating trace of some foreign accent also spoke French, German, Italian and English, better than most natives did. Every year he visited the company's financial institutions located in several U.S. cities, including Los Angeles. And during his stop in California he never missed the opportunity to look up for Angeline, his dear aunt. According to Angeline, Karl had also been involved in various government functions.

Two days earlier, Karl Heinrich von Hammersmith called from London to announce his imminent visit. Upon his arrival at LAX a black stretch limousine with a black uniformed chauffeur whisked him to his aunt's restaurant. The entire Valois Dourville de Montrissart family was ready with excitement to greet their distinguished visitor. Arthur's astute little eyes twinkled as he greeted such an important guest and family relative. They were all waiting at a special table to enjoy a lavish dinner. A bottle of his favored champagne, *the Crystal Roederer* was chilling on ice in a silver bucket.

Karl Heinrich, a short and slightly 'stomach pouch' middle-aged man with a full head of dark hair, bristling mustache Kaiser Wilhem style and carefully manicured hands had a kind face showing a stamp of majesty. Karl, with that certain Germanic gentleness and noble glance in his eye never failed to give me a bear hug. He was handsomely wearing a *Pierre Cardin* dark suit with a carnation in his buttonhole, a black-tie dinner and a gold-watch chain spanning his jacket.

Angeline motioned her nephew to a seat beside her as she was holding his hand. As he walked to his seat, even the clack of his heels was harmonious. Although raised in an affluent family, Karl was a seductive speaker, unpretentious, warm-hearted and equally a keen observer of the human character. Clothed with strength and authority, despite the ups and downs from the stock market or other investments, Karl had been quite successful. An august figure, he was being beamed upon by greatness and lived like a lord. With the talent of being also a singer and an active member of the German *Liederkranz, Herr Concertmeister* Karl and Angeline begin to sing a delightful melody, entitled *Heimweh:*

> *"Wenn so die Glokken hallen,*
> *Geht es mir durch den Sinn,*
> *Dab wir noch Alle wallen*
> *Zur ew'gen Heimat hin…"*

The *Heimweh* song has been translated in several languages throughout the world. It simply suggested that "Love is made of this."

While I served the family a large plate of appetizers along with Crystal champagne, Karl complimented my still youthful countenance.

Aware that he no longer was the center of attention of our distinguished guest, Arthur in his usual cynical self, with his mouth yet filled with food, announced: "Pierre is old, deaf-and-dumb and he smells bad, age for sure has crept up on him. Now he has floppy legs and can no longer go to the bathroom by himself! He's becoming a real ga-ga."

Like a well-mannered diplomat, having attentively listened to the discourse, Karl Heinrich, tapping the tablecloth with his fingernails came to my rescue. With a voice of authority, he refuted Arthur's *wintermärchen-* lie and inept remark. His thoughts were as well sifted as his words, and invariably I had the highest opinion of him. He was breathing out with a strong but polished courtesy. With the gentlest, most lighthearted manner, appearing to come straight out of the Court of St. James' Palace, the nephew with his eyes fixed kindly upon me like the look of one friend to another shouted at Arthur:

"Was ist denn mit dir, shweinhund?" Enunciating his conviction in that quick German sentence, he commented that in fact I looked great for my age. He admonished the immature elf to stop picking on me, and stop acting like a swine. Even Angeline welcomed with open arms Karl's graceful speech.

As my face lit up with a glow of gratitude, I felt vindicated by the thoughtfulness of a dear friend. Some can bring along life and excitement, others like Arthur can drain off joy and energy with constant quick-tempered disposition, running grudge against everybody. All through those years Karl has been sweet and kind to me and I always felt him like a kind and thoughtful elder brother.

Much later, whenever all those happy people were already 'in the wind' as they were sloshing themselves in champagne, in wine over a lavish dinner, Angeline abruptly raised her glass. And in excellent German, she quipped: *"Hoch lebe Karl der Herzog*-Long live Karl the Duke. For me, considering his outstanding personality, it looked as if it was impossible that he could be anything but a duke.

I bustled off to draw the limousine-driver a cup of coffee just before Karl's trip back at the Ritz Carlton Hotel in Marina Del Rey. His last words to us all as he clicked his heels and bowed politely were: *"Auf Wiedersehen."* Looking at me once more, Karl added in that perfect French slightly laced with German accent: *"Au revoir mon ami...et à bientôt,"*

Chapter 23

CHEF JEAN-LUC PICHARON decided that the time was right for him and his family to hunt for a house. With the help of Marc Van Meerstellen, Leon's father, who recently obtained his real estate license, they tallied the entire San Fernando Valley from Chatsworth to Burbank, and the West Los Angeles area too. They finally decided on a property located on a cul-de-sac in Culver-city. It was a spacious four-bedroom home with French windows, including a sprawling garden…and a swimming pool.

However, one serious hurdle had to be resolved: the financial aspect. Picharon lacked the qualification for the bank to issue a loan. Nevertheless, in the back of his mind he visualized the chance, still quite small, yet a chance that someone might be enticing into loaning him enough funds for a down-payment on the house.

Several days later at the restaurant, Arthur in his usual indiscreet talkativeness spoke to one of our clients about the chef's dilemma.

Mr. John H. Ogden, a kind human being with polite manners and eloquence was also a person who would invariably lend a sympathetic ear. A commanding figure with a definitely foreign-looking appearance, still blessed with good looks was recognized as being essentially a generous man who would laugh for laughter's sake. Well-built, with thinning silver hair, his chin was disconcertingly strong for a spindling type of face that showed a wine-colored birthmark below the left side of his mouth. He was also sporting a small, neatly clipped mustache. Mr. Ogden happened to be the president of a Swiss-affiliated financial company. His rapid elevation was the result of his unfailing audacity, his cool judgments, his connections and his ethical self-reliance. In addition, he knew how to use his name and his brilliant reputation for integrity. John and Chef Picharon knew each other quite well. They always chatted about recipes from *la nouvelle cuisine*.

Afterward, Mr. Ogden went quietly in the kitchen at the precise moment that the chef was forcing the can opener into the tin of a can of imported *foie gras aux truffes*. The businessman engaged the chef into a warm conversation after which a deal came into fruition. John wholeheartedly offered Picharon a personal thirty thousand dollars loan for the house, bearing no interest. In addition, his company would take care of all the paperwork, even the closing escrow.

A silence engulfed the entire kitchen as this was such an unexpected surprise. Picharon stood there motionless, absolutely dumbfounded before hugging Mr. Ogden.

Just before John called it a night, he turned to Arthur to let him know that Jean-Luc's predicament has been settled. Wasting no time at all, the little Napoleon charged into the kitchen to capture all the credit for what had just transpired. And, raising a glass of wine to Picharon, he proudly asserted:

"I'm sure you will appreciate what I did for you?" By the month's end, the chef, his wife Julie with their young daughter received the keys for their dream home…

Occasionally in life, one is dealt with too many good cards. Several months after the Picharons moved into their new abode in Culver City, Jean-Luc's father-in-law pulled into Los Angeles from an extended trip in Mexico and Central America. The tall, bald-headed Monsieur Henri Delacroix became wealthy by inheritance. He came to meet his daughter and son-in-law to lay out a proposition:

"Son, I'm not getting younger and I know that Julie is quite homesick for the old country. On the outskirts from the city of Saint-Etienne, south of Lyon there's a restaurant for sale. It's a good size building with a dwelling on the top floor. I intend to buy the property and give it to you and your little family as a present. We will be reunited and as for you being chef-owner, you will no longer be manipulated or bossed around by someone like Arthur."

Picharon's father-in-law had really twisted his arm with that new proposition. How can anyone refuse such a generous gift?

And soon the excited Picharon was showing us pictures of the property Henri brought along, prior to his trip. His new place of business had a large patio in the front surrounded by a parterre of brilliant purple red bougainvillea. The interior was furnished with cozy leather chairs and rosewood tables which reminded me of ads in *Le Guide Bleu* magazine. Everything seemed to have all the ingredients for a successful restaurant venture that Jean-Luc did not have second thoughts in taking on the new challenge.

* * * *

Arthur was the only slave driver in his treatment of Pedro Gomez, our dishwasher. Knowing Pedro's status as an undocumented alien, thus a target for discrimination, Arthur considered him as nobody; just a lowly *plongeur*-dishwasher.

The boss took advantage of the fact that Gomez did not have working papers, therefore providing cheap labor.

Pedro was a busy man by nature, perpetually in motion, but Arthur made him work menial tasks such as clearing weeds in his garden in Calabasas Hills, which were no longer part of his work in the kitchen. I often saw in his face that he had been exploited intensively. Even with his statute as an illegal, Pedro was a role model, a hard working man. He was the kind of man who would not shrink from any kind of work.

Shortly, as the restaurant union representative showed up at *Le Cerisier* in the late afternoon, once more we had to hide Gomez under a table in order to avoid serious sanctions.

However, in reality, he wasn't different from our wealthy real estate clients, for Pedro Gomez who at one time lived in abject poverty was now a rich landowner in Central America.

On many instances I dropped him off to his home. During one of those rides, Pedro wearing a baseball cap emblazed with the Dodger's name on it, and cowboy boots revealed to me that he was working on two jobs, that every three weeks or so, through Western Union most of his money went straight to Guatemala. He continued by declaring that with extra money he got from winning cockfights he already deposited a down payment on a ranch near Chichicastenango and that his brother who carry a fiduciary relationship with him just bought a luxury motor-boat anchored near Panajachel. Being curious about the size of his property, Pedro explained to me that his ranch was quite large. With several cows happily brooding, he also got himself a mini-tractor that he rented to local farmers for about twenty dollars a day. Now he already envisioned that very soon, next to that respectable ranch in his native Guatemala he would be able to buy a 4x4 all terrain Ford truck.

Once, before we left the restaurant, on our way to Van Nuys where Pedro lived, the churlish Arthur always *à l'avant-garde* with his jokes reminded Pedro to check on me occasionally. He added that because of my irrational driving, instead of Van Nuys we might end up in Tijuana!

Near the dishwasher's place, we stopped at a taco stand and Pedro offered me a *pupusa*, a real delicacy from El Salvador. I didn't ask how the *pupusa* was prepared, neither what kind of ingredients was involved in its preparation but it simply melted in your mouth.

On that hot summer night the temperature indicated eighty-five degrees. Several rental signs were on display everywhere. I intently gaped at Pedro and asked him if in that part of town the lodgings were affordable? He replied: *"La renta es $600.00 por mes pero como somos diez personas, cada uno paga solo $60.00, muy barato!"* (The rent is six hundred dollars a month, but since there are ten of us here we paid sixty dollars each; very cheap!") We approached the old-looking ramshackle house with cracks on the façade. It wasn't my intention of spelunking into Pedro's flat, but he door was partially open. In a quick glance in that peripheral vision, I noticed a fan running at full blast. With a sputtering light and moths dancing in circle I heard what appeared to be a polyphonic music with chants of monks in the background. Soon someone switched to another CD, and Mariachi sounds flooded the air. The scent of incense inundated the place. As we get a little closer, I noticed on the wall above the chimney a picture of Our Lady of Guadeloupe that was hanging, next to a lighted votive candle that flickered. In the studio, ten mattresses were aligned flat on the floor. Indeed, ten people lived in that crowded communal apartment, in that pigeonhole like sardines in a can! A few were already sleeping as Pedro genuflected in front of the Madonna. Like Pedro, all of them were little people living in that single room, but in respect of physique they were quite robust with no lack of vigor and still capable of great endurance.

Pedro was unable to read or write! Humbled as he was in the face of ignorance he was doing a kind of job most of Americans won't even think of doing. Without any education and no particular skills, *a fortiori*, Pedro Gomez made it. He also made me understand in paraphrases that money is like manure. Pile it in one place and it stinks but spread it around it fertilizes.

Prior to working illegally in the U.S. and of becoming a ranch owner in Guatemala Pedro had been a communist agitator carrying the communist banner and singing the "International."

Whenever I have a tendency to show preponderance or be at odd vis-à-vis the illiterate, I always reminded myself of one of Einstein greatest insight: "With fame I become more and more stupid…a very common phenomena."

Chapter 24

FOR SOME TIME, after Jean-Luc's departure, Jesus Betancourt took over the kitchen responsibilities until Arthur found another French chef...

In no time, the boss found a new *chef de cuisine*. Raoul Fouchet was from Vincennes, a suburb of Paris. He was a strong man with a large face, heavy eyebrows, and quite ironically with a squeaky effeminate voice. Beside his enormous rear end (when he moved around his belly was also shaking like a bowl of jelly), his hands were equally gigantic, like the hands of woodcutters from those great Canadian forests. This represented quite an unexpected contrast. Before becoming a culinary expert, Raoul Fouchet worked at the morgue in a large HMO chain hospital.

For awhile we bestowed the spooky feeling that our meals were being prepared by a mortician, busy handling cadavers. Oftentimes the chef was gloomy, enjoying predicting calamities or reading the obituary's page from the Los Angeles Times.

Raoul worked at *Le Cerisier* for a year. However, his 'little sin' was that he was a heavy drinker.

In the kitchen Arthur had installed a tap Budweiser beer keg inside a moving refrigerator. At all times Fouchet was filling up his glass of beer to the rim. He was gulping and gulping like a soldier from *La Légion Etrangère* who had spent several days under the hot Upper Sahara desert sun. However, Fouchet started making many mistakes with his cooking, besides becoming extremely lazy.

One day Arthur discovered him in the kitchen flat on his back, lying on the hard floor in a pool of beer. The chef, being under the influence of that alcoholic beverage brewed by slow fermentation omitted to straight off the barrel handle. With torpid limbs, in a drunken stupor he started snoring. This ostensible act was too much for Arthur to digest and Raoul Fouchet was fired. As Raoul left *Le Cerisier*, there was little good to be said about him.

Eventually we ended up with a platoon of chefs who left almost as soon as they came in. One of them was a French-Algerian chef who for awhile lived a vagabond life. He continually wore a needle crochet work white hat and carry prayer beads in his pocket. One of Mohammed specialty was 'Swedish meatballs.' He learned how to cook them in a Stockholm's smorgasbord where he worked for some time. This was not precisely the kind of food to be served in a four star restaurant and he didn't stay too long either. Aside from his lack of experience in French cooking I noticed in him a serious dislike of Arthur without any particular reason.

An American chef who studied French cuisine in the French capital at the *Cordon Bleu* showed up for the position. He didn't befriend Betancourt and on several occasions he raised a fist to Arthur. Still, another chef applied for the job.

Francis Bevert was eccentric, also warm and cooperative with Jesus Betancourt's own preparations. The tall young man showing a mass of curly raven-black hair radiated an intelligent face. Francis was able to cook the most appealing hot appetizers almost by instinct, and he decided to stay at *Le Cerisier.*

A sport fanatic with an athletic figure the new chef joined me every Sunday for a ten mile run around the Sepulveda dam as we confronted the last rays of day. We ran along the path, so fast until we were exhausted. Later, we did several Marathons together, in Los Angeles, Long Beach and at 'The Valley of the Flowers' in Lampoc. But after his divorce he was so desperate to be loved again, to find the right woman.

* * * *

On a quiet Monday evening, working alone in the dining room, I was quite unprepared to what I would learn in the next few hours.

Mr. John H. Ogden, the president of the Swiss financial company who helped Picharon with a loan for his house came to the restaurant with his wife. He first kept on looking at me with a blank stare and retorted in a somber, quite chagrined mood that Jean-Luc Picharon has passed away following a carcinoma of the intestine, a cancer that metastasized. It happened several weeks ago. John was here to share with me this sad bereavement. In spite that Picharon knew about his diagnosis and his fate, he made a last trip to Los Angeles with his family on borrowed time. This was when Jean-Luc contacted Mr. Ogden again. When the former chef bought his California house originally, his daughter was still a baby. Now, upon reaching her tenth birthday he wanted to show how charming their former property looked like. A visit to Disneyland and Universal Studios followed.

Mr. Ogden went on talking, saying that Picharon's days were counted; they had running out fast. Unexpectedly he squeezed my arm and glanced at the kitchen door to assure us that we were alone. After laying a finger on his lip to enjoin secrecy, he conveyed:

"There is something I have to tell you." In an emotional voice, with a lump in his throat he repeated to me word by word the last conversation he carried on with Picharon at a Denny's coffee shop. This had been Jean-Luc's own utterance: "Please tell Pierre that I really liked him; that I would miss him till the very last day." This brought tears to my eyes.

Mr. Ogden concluded that during his meeting with Jean-Luc he noticed that he had found him fearfully enfeebled but he was still able to speak with remarkable calmness. A feeling of sadness came over me still. It was not just grief of having lost a good friend, but also for the reality that he died so young with such a great spirit. He certainly was far to think about death.

As his short life ended up so abruptly, I became concerned with former chef Picharon's character. I also loved him deeply. *During Pichron's ultimate visit to California, I wondered why he didn't show up at the restaurant and refused to see Arthur? Why that great abyss, the strange nihilism that he carried toward his former employer who at one time so gracefully bestowed Jean-Luc a new automobile as a Christmas present?*

Of course, at *Le Cerisier* sooner or later we all experienced that feeling of revulsion, that infringement of our rights that the employer so obviously enjoyed in his selfish motives. What I believed was unforgettable in Picharon's eyes was Arthur's attitude during some special events…

Monsieur Eugene Lombardi, editor-in-chief and CEO of The Golden State Press was a short man with a goitrous neck and a face full of pimples who frequently came at *Le Cerisier*. One day, as he was alone at his favored corner table, Arthur joined him and I followed with a bottle of Crystal Roederer on ice, on the house. I opened the bottle and poured the

Champagne in the flutes. On that instance, the boss moved his chair close to the editor, saying:

"Please Mr. Lombardi, can you write something in The Golden State Press? Something about my first rate cuisine, and of the good spirit I carry around in the dining room to please my customers?" Filled with excitement engendered by his eloquence, Arthur tried to convince the CEO that he, Arthur Valois Dourville de Montrissart was an incomparable chef and restaurateur. And with much more confidence he continued: "Eugene, can you talk about my exploits; about the charm of *Le Cerisier?* In your article, please show the American public the way I prepare exquisite fine meals and that my four star establishment is second to none?" This time, with warmth, the boss decided to re-fill Mr. Lombardi's flute with the fine Champagne.

Concerning that article, the selfish Arthur didn't mention anything about chef Picharon's culinary skills. Throughout the years, Picharon had really been the architect of fine cuisine, not Arthur.

On two other separate occasions, a gentleman from the well-known TV channel KCCY came to the restaurant for a promotional purpose. Prior to the first television interview, Mr. Armand Doll, the head of the program *Restaurant Corner,* from KCCY was also invited for a Champagne-dinner. At dessert time, Arthur and Mr. Doll were toasting their glasses of Pear Cognac while discussing the many details for the TV event.

Several days later, Mr. Armand Doll accompanied by several cameramen was quite busy. Wires, cameras were to be connected in exact angles.

As Arthur was being worked over by the makeup people who were trying not to make him look too old, he prepared his speech.

Almost instantly, my unabashed employer was all set. Without even consulting the late Jean-Luc Picharon, the boss would wear a white chef jacket with a French flag embroidered on it, with his nametag *ARTHUR VALOIS DOURVILLE de MONTRISSART* written on the collar. And soon, he would soar subsequently to his pots, to his pans to cook a particular dish that would be shown on the little screen. In front of the camera Arthur would simply retorted: "This French *pot-au-feu* is one of my great specialties." With this demeanor Arthur, lacking social grace would take all of the credit and honor for the preparation as well as the brilliancy of success of *Le Cerisier,* while the poor chef Picharon sat on a chair in a corner of the kitchen, feeling betrayed. In those cases, pride and selfishness was the answer to Arthur's uncouth cruelty. Again, the unscrupulous boss decided to be the center of interest with no regards whatsoever to Jean-Luc.

After the cooking demonstration in the kitchen, my employer would walk to the dining room flinging his 'chef's hat' on the service marble table.

I was serving wine to our clients sitting on a side booth. One of the cameramen approached in my direction as Arthur, holding my arm, swiftly grabbed the bottle from my hand, uttering:

"Go away, stupid, this is my show. I will make another announcement to KCCY in regard to my fine cuisine and my best wine from my wine list. So *fou-le-camp…* just disappear hey. I can serve the wine myself!"

Once more, in front of the microphone Arthur knowing full well that the press can inform millions of viewers, that the same press can introduce him as the master chef and one, if not the top restaurateur in Southern-California, was duly ready for *la grande finale.* With great accuracy he was prepared to sell himself, his culinary expertise, his management for people everywhere.

Elbowing Mr. Armand Doll, Arthur was now facing the camera up front. With his jaw thrust forward he breathed heavily, and tilting his head, he announced:

"My name is Arthur Valois Dourville de Montrissart, owner and executive-chef at *Le Cerisier*. If you decide to visit my little abode, I would tell you what to eat; you don't even have to look at the menu. I always know precisely what would enhance your palate. I'm the one that would choose a fine bottle of wine with exclusive vintage, perfect for your 'crrrrrissspy' duck à l'orange or your trout almondine." and Arthur went on and on: "Next, from *La Nouvelle Cuisine* I also created the universally well known 'mushrooms salad.' And for my vegetarian customers, they would be delighted with my 'all vegetarian dish.'"

So far, so good for that little man walking on air, who had beckoned for recognition of himself, thus leaving his faithful employees quietly in the dark, for in front of the camera, Arthur had been on the apex of his power, of his glory...

Less than a week later during dinner at the restaurant, my employer set up a television unit on the service table at the precise moment the presentation of *Le Cerisier* outstanding food and wine documentary was going to be shown on KCCY. The boss hastened to turn on the little screen with the volume on high as for everyone in the dining room could watch and hear Arthur Valois Dourville de Montrissart honored as ONE OF THE GREATEST FRENCH CHEF AND RESTAURATEUR IN AMERICA!

Ironically, even with his strange character and a face that revealed the weariness of life Arthur remained an accomplished businessman. The day Chef Jean-Luc Picharon applied for the job of chef de cuisine he was helding an attaché-case. In it he was carrying several diplomas from the best European institutes of cooking that comprised the Cordon Bleu School

321

of Paris, France. In addition several hotel-chains including the Biltmore in Los Angeles and a Monte Carlo casino restaurant rewarded Jean-Luc with the best recommendations in the world.

However Arthur was far to be impressed with *ces feuilles de laurier*, bearing the signatures of CEO, General Managers or Food and Beverages Managers. The boss was determined enough to probe into his actual qualifications. After he inspected him carefully from top to toe, he simply told Picharon to put everything back in his briefcase; that he wanted to have a masterly performance executed at once. Unexpectedly, Arthur had recourse to that old maxim that every French chef is familiar with:

"Montre-moi ce que tu peux faire derrière le piano!"- Show me what you can accomplish behind the piano (the stove.)

In the old country Arthur knew at least one young man who proceeded to buy himself the post of executive chef through bribery and influence. He was just a great fool, unable to even cook a steak, but who eventually became food and beverage manager in a famed Beverly Hills Hotel!

With the most careful attention, Jean-Luc had to prepare a sauce béarnaise, a sauce archduke along with the trimming of meat, including *les Crepes Suzette flambées au Grand Marnier*. To a pleasing Arthur, Chef Jean-Luc Picharon had succeeded. He passed the test accordingly, with flying colors. Arthur was equally superabundant of activity and energy. Occasionally I noticed some warmth in the man. Unexpectedly he would even surprise us with a good deed. He would wake up at four o'clock in the morning and drive to Santa Barbara. At the seashore he would wait for the boats to come back from their night expedition to buy the best looking fresh live Pacific- lobster for a certain Mr. Cransfield who was to have dinner with us at the restaurant that night. Mr. Cransfield had requested that special order a day earlier, mentioning: "In the norms of possibilities."

The boss would also ask the chef to cook an entire vegetarian dish for Mrs. Colruyt, a city councilwoman. Still, on another occasion, during an exceptionally busy day, as the chef was running out of olive oil, Arthur went to the local super-market to get a bottle of extra-virgin olive oil for the preparation of Mr. Bloom's meal. Mr. Bloom, an archaeologist and regular customer at *Le Cerisier* was allergic to butter or any dairy products. Everything had to be cooked in pure olive oil.

* * * *

A fast moving storm was on its way. As the first droplets of rain roared on the small trees in front of the restaurant, the lightning shattered the air with more intensity.

Melanie parked her Jeep Cherokee near the main entrance of the building.

Across from her round massive shoulders, she wore a blue shawl and brought a box filled with homemade *tartelettes aux pommes*-individual little pastries filled with custard cream nestled with sliced apples, sprinkled with Calvados liquor. (She always cooked at home in order not to be in the way with the chef during working hours.)

In the kitchen, Arthur's daughter displayed those fine desserts on a silver tray with the exception of one since there was no more space on the receptacle. I carefully carried the tray of those sweet baked goods to the dining room. Back in the kitchen, Melanie handed me on a small plate the single dessert remaining and said: "Here Pierre."

With that particular expression in her voice, I really understood that it was for me to experience the flavor of that *tartelette,* in order to explain to the customers what it tasted like.

As I walked away I joyfully consumed it. My employer always cherished the opinion that it is a good idea to sample the food before handling it to our patrons. Thereafter Melanie came in the dining room to contemplate her tray of small pastries resting on a marble top desk. Gawking in my direction, with the small empty plate in my hand, as I was still chewing my food with such a pleasure she questioned me regarding that single dessert she wielded to me earlier, which was now missing.

Like in a crime scene, realizing the accessory after the fact, Melanie's face rose out on all sides like a set of toy balloons. And I suddenly became gratified with all her mean blessings under the heavens:

"Pierre, what on earth have you done? You're just a senile imbecile, a deranged silly old man!"

At that precise moment Arthur arrived, tucking his shirt back into his pants. Eddy Roy Freedman was not far behind him. At once Melanie explained the pastry incident to her father.

The owner of the restaurant, after pinching the flared nostrils of his long proboscis stared at me portentously with eyes cold as polar ice. Something dead, something rotten was written on his malignant, totally distorted face. Never shall I forget that gaze with his immobile compressed mouth he darted upon me; that horrendous look with such hostility which swept over me scathingly. At once, he became violent like a prosecuting attorney. In a throaty chuckle, Arthur bursting out in a flood of vituperation, shaking his fists right under my nose accused me of being involved in a criminal act; of being a miserable, stupid thief. His teeth were tight together. His entire face looked like the one of Mephistopheles, and I could swear he was foaming from the corners of his mouth to an ugly sneer.

As I was listening openmouthed, bolted out of the blue Arthur impetuously got a strong hold of my ears the way one would do with a rabbit that had just been weaned. Snapping like a demon he acted like a savage beast. With implacable ruthlessness, he hit me in the sensitive spot with his right knee before banging my head against the wall. With a voice like a crackpot he began to swear to me belligerently, half in French, half in English: "You, sluggish, incompetent scoundrel! Thick skull waiter *de mes couilles*, this pastry that you just eat will cost you seven dollars and fifty cents. I expect you to get me that money tonight or it would be taken out of your paycheck and…with interests!"

As I stood there, I was unable to utter a single word. In spite of everything, a laugh is usually the greatest tonic in the world and that's what I did. I was content with the store of old pleasant remembrances with which my mind was so crowded, as I kept on writing. So often at the restaurant I felt like I lived in a dream. The Russian writer Andreï Makine expressed it so well too, when he said: *"My dream was an anti-dose and the Notes-a refuge."*

Recalling the slap in the face by Captain Jacques Delperdange with the paratroopers, I kept on laughing knowing very well aware that tomorrow Arthur would praise me eloquently in front of the customers regarding another episode of the myriad of adventures I experienced as a globe-trotter. It has always been that way. What I learned during my travels is the simple fact that you must delight in what you are; how to delight in the sufferings as well as in the happiness. And on the first sign of my endeavoring to quit, my employer, like a lost bleating lamb would show a different face. In reality he didn't want me to be away from his influence and sympathy, his likings and aversions. Because of his fear that I would walk out he would be rather amiable by telling me funny jokes or by giving me a *Hoegaarden-bière blanche*-white Belgian beer. Arthur was really a simple soul. After all, I liked him a lot. On such occasions, I thought that I was part of the Valois Dourville de Montrissart's family.

* * * *

For several days Mr. Adoman, the owner of a Van Nuys flower shop was unable to find us fresh cut red roses. He came personally at *Le Cerisier* and granted Arthur three big bunches of carnations for free-complimentary of the house. Unfortunately, on the first evening, after I displayed those new pedicels in the vases not a single customer showed up.

Late at night, as Arthur kept on staring at all those empty tables, he abruptly clenched his fists:

"I knew it! We are under a curse because of those damn carnations. They bring us bad luck!" And, to my ultimate content he simply mumbled: "Pierre, I hate those flowers. Remove them from their vases, you can offer them to your girlfriend! Tomorrow I'll get red roses from another store!" Those carnations alive on bright crimson stems were absolutely gorgeous. They really rejoiced Helena's heart.

* * * *

On this Memorial Day I settled on with Helena to drive to Apple Valley, California and meet my two sons, Phil and Frank, and their friend Rocky. Along came a feathered visitor-Julius Caesar, our African grey parrot. We avoided the heavy traffic by leaving Los Angeles earlier before rush hours.

In Apple Valley the air was particularly fresh and keen, with some kind of a whisper of mid spring in it. Up the hills stood some summer cottages which are mostly vacant during

326

the winter season. Over there all the noises from the large City of Angels sounded so much remote.

Phil, the oldest son works as a cameraman for Hollywood Studios and he's often on location outside of town or state. Between two major productions he generally took his backpack for a one-week short vacation to ski in Switzerland or to meet a girl in Malaga. With a face of a seducer stepped forth from Arabian Nights, he favors Mediterranean-type women.

Next to smaller houses clustering around, Phil bought a comfortable as well as sentimental inconspicuous cul-de-sac four-bedroom home in a semicircular cemented area. It was an almost monastic-looking prime real estate, with extensive grounds surrounding with poinsettia that correspondingly indicated high-ceilinged rooms with lofty walls. A fixer-upper, but it was still one of the best bright, spacious fixer-upper in the entire neighborhood. The land was good, with a landscape of beauty and magnificence. In addition there was a large attic which ran the whole length of the house. The ironwork balcony door with a window watched out on an alley that ran into the main street. With the exception of the turrets and towers, the entire residence, aside from some religious aspect also looked like an English-style *grand seigneur* home. As we walked toward the entrance in a little spray of dust, crickets shrilled all around. Above the porch a small lamp was swaying and creaking.

Eight years ago, the neighborhood had shown no signs of mushrooming into its present opulence. Investors had come in from so many regions. The locality was now aglitter with many kinds of restaurants, from the mom and pop coffee-shops to the proud plush of Black Angus high class dining room. Phil had sunk all his spare cash in this large house.

As for the transformations, with so various improvements of the grounds via the humdrum process of labor that matter was properly attended by Frank, my younger son. There was still scaffolding on the *façade* of the building, in front of the ironwork balconies. Altogether Frank was an electrician, a plasterer, a roofer and a carpenter as well. The rains had gone through the roof of the house which had required entire renewal. He also had to fix the cracks in the chimney. Frank had remodeled the property from the floors, the ceilings and walls as well. He ingeniously had set up a master light switch that flooded the entire house. He had also replaced all drainpipes and the cornices. The iron-gate half of which had rusted off its hinges had to be replenished. Furthermore, he installed French windows with white curtains that softened the light with fine wooden shutters along the verandahs. In addition, Frank set up a French double door leading to the garden, green with vegetation where he created a fish-pound with a few carps in it. One can discover a spring sloshing at the edge of the pound where you can hear the continual trickling amid large rocks and water lilies, next to an old tree with a mixture of rare plants and flowers. At one time the yard that was wilderness is now an enchanted garden with comfortable rattan chairs. The same garden would have delighted the eye of the scenic painter as the ubiquitous fragrance of the flowers was riding down the wind to the entire neighborhood.

All rooms spotlessly clean as in a hospital were sumptuously, most grandly furnished with so many plants; a forest of plants everywhere. Several kinds of lacquer and mahogany had passed through Frank's hands. The entire décor was a real version of the French Empire. Now, the luxury of their house was a regal to the eyes. It was simply the most exquisite residence in the entire area, the jewel of Apple Valley. In the living room, I noticed a clock of stupendous dimensions, among several couches and other wonderful items. No decorator in the world could have done a better job.

Everything had been measured, calculated and estimated. For him, even the installation of wide framed verandas, a fireplace bricked on the bottom was all routine work.

Each and every day Frank continued to embellish the house and garden until perfection. He kept on looking for objects with fashionable motifs that really pleased him, such as a marble bust of Bonaparte.

There was such an abrupt transition from the life in Los Angeles. Here, even that the town grew rapidly, peace and quietness reigned in the air to a reclusive stillness.

I really miss little Louis, Frank's young son and my grandson as well, who stayed with his mother and parents's mother in Albuquerque, New Mexico on an extended vacation.

Since at a very young age, Phil always took a pleasant habit in stuffing a handful of marshmallows into my mouth. As a growing man, he still indulged in that practice. Now, puzzled and finding myself again with a mouthful of these sweet candies, a current of happiness streamed throughout the room.

Furthermore, inside the house stood an old grant piano with an unruffled wood art work on it. A hasty farseeing of the second floor through a spiral stairway reveals several Dutch and American paintings hanging in each room, all depicting scenes of nature.

Frank who made his living by fixing surrounding residences and restoring houses, mostly old houses, got himself two black pit-bulls from a lady that kept on rescuing abandoned animals. He baptized them Tanky and Bouddhy. Tanky in fact was built like a real 'Sherman Tank.' Bouddhy on the other hand would stare at the window in deep meditation. This was the reason for his name Bouddhy: little Buddha. But contrary to the general notion, even with their fierce faces, those two pit-bulls were the sweetest pet in the world (in the case of pit-bulls, it's really up to the owner to train them well with a great amount of love.)

During each visit in Apple Valley, the dogs appeared to remember us. They came to lick our hands and didn't bark. Tanky always gently put his enormous head on Helena's lap. And when I played harmonica he started to sing a long litany: Greeeeew-Greeeeew-Greeeeew...

Frank is equally an accomplished musician. He's not just good with his music, he's too good; some genius. For sure, he didn't inherit it from me (besides playing harmonica and three notes on my old beribboned string-guitar, I know little about music.) Phil's brother was born with it and as a child Jimmy Hendrix was his idol, and still is. From his Flamingo guitar, electric guitar and piano, Frank always performed wonderfully. When I conjured him again and again to locate a good agent with Las Vegas ties, his answer continuously remained strong and unshakable, when he articulated:

"Pop, I'm not seeking the glamour, the applauses or a large purse of money like 'your petit Napoleon' at *Le Cerisier.* I'm doing this for my own satisfaction'" Upon hearing my son's unmaterialistic motive, my thoughts recalled the writer James Joyce's, Portrait of the Artist as a Young Man: *"The artist, like the God of the creation, remains within or behind or beyond or above his handiwork, invisible, refined out of existence, indifferent, paring his fingernails."*

And, in order to celebrate our happy reunion, we all shared a little libation familiarly known as 'Long Island Iced Tea', one of Rocky' specialties.

Rocky Isaac Hodosh with his small weasel eyes and strong jaws, looking like they might be made of concrete was a highly respectable, discreet man; a good humored man by nature who always smiled generously. Still grave in his bearing behind the bar, he was always seeking perfection. After clearing his throat boisterously, Rocky handled the blender with the grace and manner of a typical English butler.

Before he found God, he had been sunk far down into an ocean of doubt and questioning. But now, being of Jewish faith from a deeply religious family, he always prayed openly to his Creator:

> Barush Atah Adonai, Elohei Avraham,
> Elohei Yitzchak, velohei Ya'akov, Elohei
> Sarah, Elohei Rivkah, Elohei Rachel,
> Velohei Leah.

For Hodosh, Jewry was not just a question of faith. It was above all a question of the practice of a way of life among people inured by faith. What's more, with that strong patriotic impulse he was an advocate for earth's ecology and an expert in *biomimetics*-the science of letting plants and animals instructs researchers as well as engineers. Rocky was modest enough never to claim to distinction that he was the nephew of Meir David Hodosh, a well-known assemblyman.

From the large French kitchen, with a stove in a deep niche of bricks and a range of copper, Phil prepared our lunch: pigeons with white currants-a small seedless raisin and *pommes de terre vapeur*. My oldest son was not only an expert in film-production settings known as grip, but equally a real cordon bleu. Thank heavens those pigeons were substantial enough to fully satiate us. After the outstanding meal, all the men sat in the comfortable leather sofa for cognacs and cigarillos. Time was slipping by.

The moon that night was hanging under a loose cloud, as Helena kept on playing with the dogs. Abruptly she lost one shoe. She stumbled into a chair, and down to the recently well-polished wood-floor. Tanky came to her rescue and started licking her face and neck. Julius Caesar the African Grey had a quite harmonious conversation with Tanky and Buddhy who seemed to really love the bird: "Greeeeew... Greeeeew..."

Julius Caesar from inside the cage, following a breathless moment started tip-toeing in their direction. After munching his grain in silent satisfaction, affectionately with his feet wide apart and that puffing of breast feathers he would respond with ear-splitting shrieks: "Twit...Twit...I love you...I love you..." This would have been an interesting scene at the *Opèra Comique*. Aside from talking, Julius Caesar was one of the few birds I knew that can also sing and dance. A peal of laughter followed as we were all smiling from ear to ear...

Gathering together from the bustle of our daily routine, we drank another Courvoisier, when all of a sudden there was commotion coming from the outside. We heard a whimsical singing from the house next door. This happened to be a celebration for a couple of lawyers originally from England, that successfully passed the bar the day before:

> For they are jolly good fellows
> For they are jolly good fellows
> For they are jolly good fellows
> Which nobody can deny.

Subsequent to a moment's repose, the conversation drifted away into other channels. As a few lights beat upon the pane above the window made me aware it started raining, my sons in a vibrant discussion communicated to me they had long wanted to know more regarding my notes that emphasized on the crazy boss at the restaurant. Both of them already read several chapters of my manuscript. As I related to them about Arthur's fantasies of the mind and irrational behavior, they came up with the idea to have my writings turned into a movie-script. And swiftly, Frank after tapping the coffee-table as a signal for silence, with his voice uplifted announced:

"Papa with that tinge of romance, unexpected elements of your story seemed also to blend with such a variety of characters." He added in a still voluble speech: "I chanced to come across the actor which tallied remarkably well with that given in your manuscript, who could play Arthur's role," and my son concluded by conveying:

"I also happen to have been acquainted with the lady that takes good care of the horses from the movie-director and producer Steven Spielberg. Who knows, she might be able to present the eventual script to that giant of a man? " Vouchsafing no reply, I simply laughed.

When the time had come for us to set out on our journey back to the noisy, opaque megalopolis we left that compassionate household in Apple Valley just when the rain had subsided. Outside, there was no trace of any living thing, except for a bird which fluttered over our heads.

While driving on the freeway in the unfathomable stillness of the night, but still in exuberant spirits, back to the frenetic thrashing sound of the enormous city my thoughts went back to Mr. Spielberg. With my heart joyfully beating, and throbbing with excitement, I heard myself saying: "What if?"

Chapter 25

IN MY STUDY of behaviorism, environmental influences in early childhood I was able to create a character trait in a person. Later in life, a growing child can become a difficult human being feeling very frustrated. Furthermore, that same human being can engage in creative cruelty and annoyance.

In the case of Arthur, because of an arduous childhood, he felt powerless for he had little pleasure in life. With feelings of cold indifference my employer became insecure, but sly as a fox. Erich Fromm explained clearly that: *"Man is not genetically aggressive, but acquires a malignant aggression. He then experiences intense disappointment and rage as any narcissistic- exploitative person does when frustrated. That person is no longer himself nor is he in touch with his inner reality…"*

As a child, whenever my father slapped me for bad behavior I had no reasons to doubt my father's love. With a bad note in my *journal de classe* I was liable to make him the instance for a beating. On other occasions, the pounding wasn't the same. Being sensitive, more than once I felt deep anger in my father's mind, but unrelated to my conduct. On that instance, a serious problem made him feel drained and empty. In the course of his brutal gestures or posture, I sensed a neurotic conduct as he engaged himself in creative cruelty.

334

On the other hand, I can recall quite well what my father explained to me regarding those hard times during World War II. As a forced labor prisoner in Germany, he repeatedly rummaged through a garbage can for a piece of bread, as he lived with constant harassment.

In 1913, Alfred Adler in *New Leading Principles for the Practice of Individual-Psychology*, wrote: "The patient's attitudes and anomalies can always be shown as dominated by the relation of the child to his environment, by his erroneous and in the main generalized evaluation (of himself), by his obstinate and deep-rooted feeling of inferiority and by his striving after power." If we observe a man with an angry face, he might simply be frightened because the tie to mother is still present. Emotionally, that man never left childhood. He is under his mother's wings because of his fears, loneliness and dependency that had felt on him like a blanket.

At ninety-two years of age, Arthur's mother came from France to California with the intention to stay here for good. Before her arrival, my employer's facial expression changed drastically. Like a happy child and overgrown schoolboy in his corduroy baggy pants, he would bounce up and down in the air in the dining room, in front of the customers. He would almost scream in an ever-flowing fountain of energy with blood that rose to his face. *"MY MOMMY IS COMING, MY MOMMY IS COMING!"* He became as excited as if he had won the jackpot in Las Vegas! This external stimulation from that seven-decade old man was really like that of a baby suckling the sweet milk from his mother's breast at the time he was not yet ready for solid food. Arthur for a fact was the apple of his mother's eyes. She still pampered him as she took care of all his intends. As an angry, disgruntled Arthur kept scolding and bawling at his employees, I was able to recognize *le petit garçon à sa maman* – the mom's little boy. Now, I still see his mother with her foot on the cradle which she rocked to the tune:

Fais bien dodo mon petit, ta mama est
là pour te surveiller et pour te rassurer.

(Go to sleep, my little one, your mother is there to look over you.)

Melanie on the other hand convinced herself that her father was the greatest man in the world; that she had no reason to doubt his love for her. Father and daughter cherish the non-moralistic conviction that it's fine to show a neurotic behavior as they insult human honesty. Repressed character traits such as omnipotence, submission and indifference represent for them a concept of reality. They were both endowed with an aggressive incite, and seeking constant center-stage driven by their passions for storytelling. Frustrated at the universe, they experienced uninterrupted series of rebellions within themselves. And here the danger of schizophrenia and boredom are real...

On a cold and windy night, I escorted Melanie to her Jeep Cherokee that was stationed in the parking lot at the back of the restaurant. Again she got a case of dysentery and felt ashamed about mentioning it to anyone except me.

Once in her vehicle, before placing the keys in the ignition she lowered the window as her hair was now hanging over her shoulders. She was strangely quiet and her steps had dragged a little. As she was gripping the steering wheel of her car, Melanie was brooding, thinking of nothing, and her eyes had a haunted look. I felt like a guardian angel watching her as I reminded her to be careful because of gang activities in the neighborhood, that they are really dangerous, eccentric transients 'night birds' who look as if they entertain evil thoughts. Lately street fights were a daily occurrence. There had been an increase of graffiti and assaults. Occasionnally you can hear the quick abrupt resonance of a short-barrel machine gun. A day earlier there were sounds of guns that made a brittle crack in the air when two powerful gangs were pointing guns at each other. A teenager had been shot in the upper torso. He had died on the way to Saint Luc Hospital, and an innocent pedestrian had been hit in the leg subsequent to a ricochet. Later, a wanted parolee responsible for the shooting, who had barricaded himself inside a house, had surrendered to the police. Gazing with woebegone eyes, in her evasiveness Melanie paused, nodding:

"I don't mind what happens to me; I don't give a damn. I really look forward to be assaulted. This would be a real blessing because I'm bitter, I'm angry... I was just born unlucky. I really feel like a fly caught on a spider's web," she added further: "Pierre, you may as well drown me or throw me over a precipice, I really don't care. I just want to die; the quicker, the better. Death for me is definitely better than such a life. It would deliver me from all regrets, all desires and all griefs," and she went on: "What I'm enduring now in my mind is a worse punishment than death. I'm living a dull, shameful existence in that cruel world that I have the apprehension of dying an old maid. Now I must make an end of all things!" Melanie was planning to meet her fate in the same manner as Sir Walter Raleigh when he bravely mounted the scaffold, felt the edge of the axe and smilingly remarked: *This is sharp medicine, but a sure physician for all diseases.*

Aside from her mental struggle she commented that something seemed to have struck her in the chest with the addition of back pain and difficulty to breathe. With her voice that had sunk down to a whisper, she boringly cursed the day she was born, that her depression was like cancer; that she can't take it anymore. With the trembling of her hands, more and more perceptible she appeared as a lukewarm person in a state of lethargy, thinking she was an unfulfilled, disreputable person.

That flame of enthusiasm was out; that once welcome beacon no longer shone. Her beauty, her complexion had obliterated to an unhealthy pallor. And, because of her father's annoyance, she lost her appetite too. Even the smell of food was repulsive to her. Melanie wasn't free to meet her friends on Sundays because she still had to join her parents and Eddy for the brunch at *Wong Kwai*, a local Chinese restaurant. For her, it was always a painstaking experience. And with words that came out bitterly, she would tell her father:

"At all times I have to follow you as if you were my chaperon, but I'm very tired of all that chaperonage. I would like to walk where I want, and for sure I don't want an escort. Because of you I would never meet the man of my dreams. You are the cause of all my sufferings. My meaningless life is unbearable. Just look at me now, my butt is so large and my boobs started drooping! How could I really love anybody? Life's a bitch, no one ever bestowed me flowers to fill up my heart. I want love, but I don't know where to find it. Now you make me feel like a second-rate tart and I am treated as if I was in jail or confined in an institution!" and she continued: "Yes I want love, I really want love but I don't know where to find it." She was an affectionate woman who felt frustrated. Melanie's indifference to everything of this world was noticeable.

As a little girl she had been pampered like a princess, over-tender cared, spoiled to her entire content. She had elements of pure gracefulness, but now she grew older and became peevish like sour wine. She was sinking lower and lower; it was so painful to have witnessed her decline. She suffered such downward mood, feeling an undercurrent of loneliness…

Arthur had talent to influence, impress and persuade people. He could play the perfect role of being friendly, kind and considerate, yet some notice his *Jekyll and Hyde* personality. In reality he was a very disconcerted little man, who only showed a front of kindness. On account of this, being the cause of much of her misery Melanie became a thoroughly unbalanced woman no longer hoping for anything.

With a badly broken heart she would escape the despair that was seizing upon her by reading instructions written on canned food labels or peeling eucalyptus trees in the street upon the grassy bank by the roadside. Furthermore, as she sat on the pavement she kept on counting the cracks on the asphalt and started mooning aimlessly along the road, stepping with the purposeless gait of one who has nothing to do nor any destination to reach. Once, she decided to attack a statue in the local park. She felt locked in her little world with that melancholy languor the French called *Ennui*. Little matters started to bother her. She would get up in the middle of the night to weep over such thing as a brassière she neglected to wash earlier. She had dreamed to run away from her family into distant places. Yet she decided otherwise as she rather suffered in her own little corner.

Yet, on the other hand, Melanie should not accept defeat as inevitable. Life should not be a daily torture. The example of the evilness of her father in comparison with the attitude of a kind, caring mother was such a source of disharmony and alienation that created some weird music…

Before she started the engine of her vehicle, an honest smile flitted over her face as her mood suddenly changed. While holding my hand she said:

"Pierre, I would like to find a man, young or old that I can love. It's a precious matter to be bequeathed into a man's life and I would do my best to please such a man. If that love is not given to me in return, it's fine for I can live in a world with no joys for me. I never stood on the threshold of happiness; I was trained for that. All I'm striving for is a little bit of kindness no more, no less."

And, so surprisingly Melanie made up her mind to turn her life around. She decided it was foolish to excruciate herself by remaining in bed. For awhile she did not succeed to put the bitter disappointment out of her mind. But on the next Sunday, feigning illness she didn't accompany her parents to the Chinese restaurant as she used to. She always abided by her parents'wishes, but now she was determined otherwise. Later on, she invented other pretexts not to join her family on Sunday brunches any longer. Instead, she drove to Ventura to meet a sheriff's friend...

Chapter 26

A LL DAY LONG, the sun baked the houses bone-dry. The city was warming up to a boiling point under a sultry sky. Lately we experienced extreme blistering temperatures and a recurrence of outbreaks of fire showed again in the hills. A warm and gentle breeze started to blow. The sprinklers were working at full blast as a faint smell of moisture rose from the lawns.

I was the first one to arrive at *Le Cerisier.* Jesus Betancourt came a little bit later, wearing a sports type of clothes. Right away I became aware of his changing mood. He looked very worried and was scratching his head absentmindedly.

With some kind of finical anxiety over his choice of words, Jesus told me about an offer he received from his two brothers in Houston, Texas; an offer he couldn't refuse. They just opened their third Mexican restaurant in the most sophisticated part of town and they wanted Jesus to become a full partner in the venture. Knowing Betancourt for so many years, ambition surely was not the spur that activated him. I knew him to be a modest man displaying his activities with a great amount of utter consciousness. This represented for him such a great opportunity to be reunited with close family members in a new environment. The object of getting rich was definitely a secondary factor in his decision. I watched my friend with an oddly grave intentness as I knew about his anxiousness to announce to Arthur his new prospect in life. I instructed Jesus not to worry because our employer wasn't the type of man to offer him a bonus to make him change his mind.

Several amusing encounters with Betancourt were still clearly etched in my memory. I can recall a particular trick that he played on me. Being aware of my extremely, uncontrollable repulsive stand as regard to snakes or any other swarming reptiles, the assistant-chef used me as a recipient for a very frightful, practical joke. This really made my temperature shoot up as blood seethe like wildfire in my veins.

Besides his job at the restaurant, Jesus was trimming gardens for people living in the Sherman Oaks Hills. Occasionally he would grab dead rattlesnakes floating in local swimming pools.

One day at *Le Cerisier*, as I was getting dressed for work, I felt something cold and soft inside my right working shoe. It first seemed quite comfortable, almost like a new sole but carrying too much thickness. I took the shoe off my foot, and with outmost terror I withdrew from it an ugly dead rattlesnake by the tail. With obvious distaste that made me jump right out of my stockings, I swayed helplessly and did some sort of pirouette, being absolutely horrified. All my life I always despised snakes so much and, back in Africa I kept avoiding them at all costs. Gasping and wheezing in an effort to recover my breath, I rushed to the kitchen with that horrible thing in my hands, trying to find out where my tormentor was hiding.

Before dropping the reptile in the trash can, I gaped at Betancourt and he burst laughing until tears came in his eyes.

Angeline came in from the back door with four heads of lettuce inside a brown Gelson's paper-bag in one hand, a *Louis Vuiton* handbag in the other. Pompadour, the darling little poodle accompanied her. With a red face, and sweating like a bull in the arena I explained to her my dilemma. Along with the assistant chef, not only did she explode laughing, she also urinated from joy on the kitchen-floor. Angeline continued to piss straight like an elm as Arthur came and joined us. Likewise, Jesus told him about the snake-prank.

My boss first stared at the dead reptile in the trash-can and added, with a piece of raw meat- *steak tartare* he was still ravenously shoveling down into his mouth: "Next time, insert the snake in Pierre's butt!"

For that particular joke from Betancourt, Arthur was using his typical vulgar topic of conversation whose issue I knew only too well. My employer was so wrapped up in himself that he didn't even comprehend the gaiety expressed by his employees. When one come to think of it, what a disagreeable little man he was.

Sometimes I stood there fumbling in the dark, struggling to find out more about his character. In contrast, Arthur was rather compassionate and delivered admirable comments to our elderly customers. This appeared to be heterogeneous as he kept using a vocabulary quite unsuited toward his employees. Frequently Arthur would show us an over-friendly attitude, but it was really with the prospect to launch a virulent new attack later on. He always tried to demoralize and interfere in the freedom of action to the people who kindly served him.

Moreover, just like the former gay priest Robert Leansing I deeply missed Jesus Betancourt and I wished him all the very best in Texas.

* * * *

This weekend, under a blazing, ecstatic blue sky, along with Helena, Eddy and the entire Valois Dourville de Montrissart family, we decided on a visit to the spa-resort of *Glen Ivy* near Corona, Southern California.

After taking the off-ramp from the 15, San Diego Freeway, we strolled on a breezy road to that famed tourist area. In front of a garden beautifully tended with colorful flowers stood several pavilions, including a small abode that was the main office.

Once in the mud-pool, Arthur was the first one to scratch-up the earth and smear his entire face and torso with that so-called miracle mud that supposedly give you back your youth. Before joining him in that red-clay bath, we took great pleasure to watch the boss wallowing in that earth like *un cochon bienheureux*- a happy pig. For quite some time, after throwing more mud on his face, Arthur decided to let it dry in the scorching sun prior to the shower and the pool of cold water.

Back at the restaurant, our employer feeling good in his skin told every customer, just as a thaumaturgist that he had discovered the fountain of youth.

* * * *

As October drew to a close, one can unmask the pale morning sunlight that was bathing the countryside in a cold shimmering sheen.

Earlier during the day as I was jogging on Marina Del Rey's sandy beaches, a few dolphins appeared to greet me and I heard the rasping of crab claws dragging near the ocean. The Pacific was so flat and the visibilityclear to the horizon. Seagulls were dropping down to the water and rose triumphantly. Looking forward in the distance, sea and sky merged harmoniously...

At *Le Cerisier*, we were all shook-up by what happened as the first customers came in. I have kept lingering on the details hovering over them: A little after six o'clock, I was in the kitchen with Paul, as Arthur and Chef Francis Bevert stood behind the table in front of the oven, studying a new recipe.

Unfortunately that evening the kitchen back door wasn't closed. After he swept the parking lot, the dishwasher simply left the kitchen door unlocked. And, unexpectedly a young man, wearing jeans with an open blue raincoat over his shirt came in with a .38 Smith & Wesson revolver pointing at us. He definitely had a look of a foreign appearance. Arthur who happened to be at the sideboard cutting cold beef, turned around in a virtual panic. He then started to run away, pulling his head between his shoulders like a chicken. Out of reach he walked with as much dignity as was compatible with safety and decided pusillanimously to hide like a mouse under the open counter of kitchen utensils, dropping to his belly...

Our little gangster seemed definitively terrified as he began to sweat profoundly. He was holding the gun which he held before him with an unsteady hand, oscillating in all directions. He stood there, faltering the way a swimmer would do when about to make his plunge, not knowing whether to retreat or to go forward. He only whispered four words:

"Give me the money!" Yet, in his eyes I detected dementia and fear. But, by the present turn of events our lives were really threatened.

Paul, who was already satiated under the influence of a glass of hard liquor did something incredible, just plainly stupid.

As the young man's grip on the gun hardened, my colleague let down his apron on the floor and unbuttoned his white shirt. With his bare chest so drastictly exposed, he took two steps forward at a very short range from the barrel of the pistol. Not knowing if it was really loaded Paul cuddled his hand around the butt of the revolver as he tried to snatch the gun from the young man's hand, and almost overpowered him. At this point, my co-worker could have been easily hit in the region of the heart.

In another very surprised move, as fast as lightning Paul clutched a pot of French dressing and threw it at the bandit's face. The young gunman started a flying run down the alley, out to the street absolutely horrified. Paul tried desperately to catch him but it was unavailing. As the bandit turned around towards Ventura Boulevard he was swallowed up in the crowd. By accident, my friend slipped and fell flat on his back on the oily kitchen floor. Horst came out from the dining room. We both still decided to try our luck in locating our assailant but he simply had slipped through our fingers.

As Arthur emerged slowly from his place of concealment he started walking on tiptoes. He was pale in the face and his forehead became moist with sweat. Clearly short of breath and teeth grinding together, that chicken- hearted poltroon had a look of an old man who felt himself deeply injured. With his bushy eyebrows arched strangely upward, thinking we weren't fast enough to catch our bandit he started hollering:

"God damned you, miserable cowards; go back, run after him now!" Arthur didn't even realize he was the fat frightened coward 'a born coward' while the bandit had been in our midst.

Later on, as the boss was sharing a glass of wine in the company of Dr. Rabinadrah Singh Patel and his family, I heard Arthur who was giving his own interpretation of the drama that took place in the kitchen. He talked incessantly and triumphantly as his breath quickened. By the end of the conversation, shaken by a succession of subdued chuckle he concluded: "I did not fear the thief: I stopped him. He ran away like a shamed dog and I don't think he will ever come back…"

Now, my boss being carried away by eloquence and bourbon, with his nostrils obviously evinced beseeched me to come to the table and pull up a chair. After shaking a bunch of keys from his trouser pocket to order attention he commended me by telling Dr. Patel that I was extremely well informed about India that I visited all its nooks and crannies.

Raising his voice to attract more diligence from his guests, Arthur told the Indian cardiologist and his family that in a small village near the Ganges River, locals identified me as a reincarnated prophet. Patting my shoulder, after wiping his reading spectacles with a handkerchief, he continued his most exaggerated story:

"Thousands of people came to meet Pierre as he was wearing a long white robe like Christ. Indians followed him everywhere throughout the vast country. Dead persons were brought to him in order to get his blessings for the new life to come." Arthur assured his listeners that there wasn't any doubt in the mind of those poor inhabitants that I was a real prophet because they all recognized me in a picture from my past life. And soon I became the object of endless curiosity.

Now, for my readers to understand thoroughly what really happened to me in Varanasi, India aside from those stretched inducements; from that craftiness of Arthur's imagination let me share with you an excerpt of the real story I kept in my notebook. I was accompanied with Randall, my American friend and *companion de voyage:*

"During my stay in the 'River City' I experienced one of the most incredible adventures of my life. Prior to our long walk, I had bought a green necklace that I wore, while my only clothing was limited to some fine, white linen tied around my waist and knotted in front with the two ends. Barefoot of course, with a shaved head and a small beard I thought I could really pass for a Hindu. After awhile, a few children next to us

began shouting 'Baba, hey Baba'. Shortly other youngsters and a dozen adults began walking on our heels, repeating these same words 'Baba, hey Baba'. Randall, somewhat confused hid under a porch while the people continued coming. Before long a sizable crowd had gathered, already more than one hundred persons, some of them were even trying to touch my garment. The very old ones remained in their houses and they were waving from the balconies. At one point they brought an old lady in a wheelchair up to me. A little further on, four men carrying a dead person on some kind of a large board almost dropped the body as they rushed to the scene. So far I couldn't yet understand what all the excitement was all about, but for a moment I really felt like some kind of a seer or a disheveled Christ. Waving at the crowd, I stopped and looking at them with great compassion, I smiled. While a few were kneeling down, someone brought me a captivating picture of a young man, who in their beliefs, only a few months before had been a very old person who died near Bangalore under the name of 'Shebaba'. Like a flash in my mind, everything became very clear. The man in the picture with his beard, shaved head, wearing a necklace and the same garment as I, appeared to be my counterpart. At this point, feeling somewhat like an impostor, I realized I had to stop from fooling all those nice people. I decided from a small platform to tell them that I was only a Belgian visitor; that I had nothing to do whatsoever with the reincarnated Shebaba. It took them awhile to recognize this. The most zealous were still at my heels. They had followed me all the way to the houseboat where Randall had fled after hiding.'"

Before I told those people that I wasn't their reincarnated Shebaba, as I smiled at the large gathering, for that first short time I felt a wonderful feeling inside. It was as Evelyn Underhill suggested: "a definite psychological experience, not at all a self-seeking mysticism."

In Chuang Tzu, regarding reincarnation on Taoism, this is what it is indicated: "Birth is not a beginning; death is not an end. There is existence without limitation, there is continuity without a starting point...there is birth, there is death, there is issuing forth, there is entering in. That through which one passes in and out without seeing its form; that is the Portal of God."

* * * *

Last night it had been such a great moment in my life, so great it will forever stay engraved in my mind.

Michael Jackson the world's number one pop-star came to visit our little abode in Sherman Oaks, along with family friends and four bodyguards.

The reservation had been secretly placed a day earlier. It was specified that they would sit in the private room with the lights dimmed to a maximum. A centerpiece flower arrangement had to be placed on the table, and the dinner should be exclusive, the best money can buy.

The family friends arrived at *Le Cerisier* around 6:30 PM. It took another twenty minutes for the four bodyguards to show up. Two of them stood near the front door, the other two at the kitchen back door leading to the parking lot. Awhile later, a black stretched limousine crushed the gravel to a designated parking space.

Michael came out from the limo and made his entrance in the establishment. The Pop Star was dressed in black leather pants, matching black shoes, a black fedora that was lowered as far down as his eyes, which were concealed by dark sunglasses. I observed Michael crossing the kitchen, tiptoeing and quiet as a cat.

At that still early hour only three other customers were eating in the main dining room: a couple and a single, middle-aged man. With the exception of the kitchen employees,

Arthur, Horst and I were the only ones to notice the arrival of the great singer and choreographer.

The very first thing Michael requested was a glass of orange juice, one of his favored beverages. Aside from champagne, wine, beer, hard liquor and Perrier water, with the exception of tomato-juice for Bloody Mary, we didn't carry any other juices on the premises.

I volunteered to go to the local liquor store located at the street corner, on Ventura Boulevard. Not only did I run but, reminiscent of my Marathon days I dashed to get Michael's orange juice. When I told the liquor-store owner that the orange juice was for Michael Jackson, he looked at me as if I just came back from the moon!

Out of the ordinary the chef prepared a special, all vegetarian plate for the singer. Later, during dessert-time I was carrying a little pastry with a lighted candle on it and walked straight to the main dining room. In front of the lone customer, as I begin to sing the French version of the happy birthday song, I behold Michael behind the open partition from the private room. He leaned forward and started to bounce back up and down on the booth, clapping hands on the sound of my voice. Considering the pop star mighty success the world over it was such a pleasure to observe his face lighting up in humble pride, with tremendous joy. As his friends stood smiling tolerantly next to him, I was equally amazed at the sudden show of friendliness from Michael. Never will I forget his voice as he complemented us for that marvelous dinner.

For a long time thereafter, Arthur blasted at customers on every table in the restaurant. Wearing a glove on his right hand to accentuate his own encounter with Michael Jackson, he added: "I, Arthur Valois Dourville de Montrissart have entertained the greatest entertainer of the century!"

Chapter 27

TODAY, ARTHUR SIMPLY fired Horst and Paul. Following Paul's stupid behavior during the attempted robbery the boss was also fed up with client's bitter constant complaints about this employee's drinking problems and offensive impertinence on the job. Lately, aside from breaking at least two, three dishes every day, this colleague of mine regularly in a state of high intoxication acted strangely. He was clowning around like a monkey, telling an endless provision of unclean jokes, and making noises reminding me of a mooing cow or a baaing sheep. When he heard dogs barking in the street, he went outside and barked with them. With his arms stiffly out, Paul would snap his fingers and give a whistle before taking off like a bird ready for a high-altitude flight. He would zoom, gliding across the dining room, and cupping his hands over his mouth like a loudspeaker he would imitate the the commercialized roadrunner: "Broom…broom…beep… beep." When that successful impersonation was over, as he continued to perform like a seal he would loose his footing. After copying an acrobat he had seen at Muscle Beach in Santa Monica he would slide down the wall before ending-up on the floor. This was followed by his obscene arm-pit farts he enjoyed doing in front of everyone.

And, aside from scratching his butt at a table Paul had tried to seduce several male customers while exposing his naked chest. Clear-headed clients were really troubled by his outrageously vulgar and stupid attitude; they felt more bewildered than entertained. Both florists and steady patrons were obviously splitting their sides over this. Strangely enough, when clients would leave the restaurant after a good meal, Paul was the first one to hold the door telling them in a coarse voice:

See you later alligator
After awhile crocodile
Dig me, pig me
See you on the moon baboon.

My employer was deeply disturbed by those eccentricities, this really annoyed him. However this wasn't the only reason for Arthur's decision. Another element made him stood beside himself with concern.

A few customers who sympathize with my two co-workers would join them after work at their house up the street to enjoy a drink and some snacks as I often did.

At one time, Horst offered the guests a glass of a very special Port wine.

A week later, those same clients would come at *Le Cerisier*. After meal they would taste an exclusive Port wine that Arthur brought back from Lisbon, Portugal. As those happy customers would toast that unique, extremely smooth liquor with Arthur, a lady was shaking her head, and in a surprised mood she would concluded:

"This is really exquisite; it tasted exactly like the Port we drank awhile back at Horst and Paul's residence." Looking at Arthur's face as he was venting his indignation at my friends,

I knew almost right away what he would be driving at. In his impulsive mind, my employer's conclusion was unmistakable: those employees stole one of the bottles of his fine Port wine selection. For a man like Arthur, that rumor was simply strong enough to take action. This of course was an unfounded accusation, with pretty thin shred of evidence since the boss never remembered surely how many bottles of Port he had in stock, or how many were sold.

In his wine cellar the boss hardly recalled that little fortune of those rare, extraordinary vintage wines and ports he carried. As a matter of fact his general inventory was not at all adequate. He was hampered with neglect and carelessness. Sometimes, owing to poor storage, we had to get rid of some of those priceless bottles. While Arthur was away from the restaurant, if inadvertently one of us in the kitchen or in the dining room would break a bottle of wine or hard liquor, the broken parts usually would end-up underneath some trashes in the trash-bin. The idea for this seemingly lack of honesty was due to the reason that we were all afraid that the price tag of the bottle indicated in our exclusive wine-list (three times the price from the liquor-store), would be taken out of our payroll checks.

Once after I made the silverware account, I mentioned to Arthur that at least twelve silver soup spoons were missing. And here was his answer as he looked at me suspiciously:

"In the back of my mind I always knew that you were trying to open your own restaurant by stealing all of my stuff here. I want those spoons returned to me at once or you can forget about your next paycheck!"

It was my friend Eddy that came straight to my rescue when he articulated: "Tutur, you must know as well as I do that Pierre would not even pilfer a carrot from you!"

In the case of the Port wine, although Horst and Paul denied it vehemently, Arthur's decision was still unshakable: those waiters had to go!

As the sentence was given, Paul's body unexpectedly started to shake out of its normal lethargy. First his expressionless eyes were resolutely fixed on the front windows of the establishment, his energy flagging. His talking reached a point of incoherence as some kind of rumbling came in his chest.

As soon as Paul came to the realization of what was really going on, a flush came down his face and his eyes started to fill-up with tears.

On the other hand, Horst who had gone vehemently maternal showed great compassion for his lover; he had a different kind of emotion. Still, feeling cheated of the future he realized that he had no choice but to land in terms with the days to come.

Within less than a week following Paul's and Horst's firing, Arthur felt paranoid because earlier Paul made threats of retaliation. My employer lived with the fear that those former employees would take some sort of revenge for having been fired. Arthur's fear that was rising tight in his throat was genuine, and he wanted to extend his feelings with the entire crew. He felt threatened although he didn't know for sure that there was a real threat. However, he thought he had to protect himself from the hand of justice.

On the following quiet Monday morning, our employer assuming for the worst asked us all to accompany him downtown to the headquarter of the Restaurant and Hotel Association Union. What's more, Eddy had cautioned the owner of the restaurant about the danger of blackmail (a prospect I definitely found distasteful.)

Prior to meet the union boss, my employer put on his best appearance. After having clothed himself in a new gray suit, Arthur kept on repeating that he couldn't afford to take any chances. Aside from Arthur, I joined in with Melanie, Eddy, chef Bevert and Gustavo Santillas.

Mr. Gerd M. Weinstard, the union president greeted us with perfect cordiality although it appeared that we interrupted his work. He was holding other functions such as preparing conferences for job opportunities for new members.

Tall, the size of a bank-vault door with a gentle bewildered look and prominent cheekbones, he was also partly bald. In a very old fashioned way his side-whiskers almost joined his mustache, giving us the impression that he was quite hairy. He also wore a carnation on his buttonhole. The CEO sat in his high-backed revolving leather arm-chair, with his hands clenched in the back of his head. He had loosened his tie. His desk was littered with all sorts of papers. We settled ourselves in our own chairs and Arthur unbuttoned his vest as if making a social call.

But it was far to be a cordial meeting. Considering that his name was everything, Arthur started talking to the union boss the way a nobleman would speak to his king: "I venture to approach you Sir, with the humble request that you would look into my case…"

After listening quietly to Arthur's concern about the two former employees, Mr. Weinstard took off his glasses and started to polish them with a small chamois. He adjusted them on his nose, let his arms fall and raised his head as he kept staring at my employer straight in the eyes. His expression was brooding. Leaning back, after removing a toothpick between his lips, the union president's voice rose in a crescendo. Mumbling out of the right hand corner of his mouth, his head started to shake as he talked quite rapidly:

JACQUES MEYER

"Monsieur Valois Dourville de Montrissart, you have kept me so long answering your question. You know that I have a real concern for all union members and their families. But still, in the name of God why are you so anxious to come to meet me here in the first place? I've been doing my best just to comprehend your situation. My only understanding from what you said on the phone is that you are really afraid of those two people? You also specified that you believe a conspiracy from those waiters has been fomented. You seemed to be as positive in your statement as the FBI was during the Watergate affair!" and the Union CEO continued:

"That explanation could not hold water for a moment. Don't you realize that you are *le patron;* that you have the right to hire or fire anybody?"

Among layers of papers covering his desk, Mr. Weinstard started tapping his pen. Raising his eyes to the ceiling, he thumped the table:

"First things first: by any chance did you think that I was your father; that I was going to give you a candy or something? Excuse me for the expression, but I believe I should kick your butt clear out the door."

In a final thought, Mr. Weinstard added: "If there is any development, I mean reprisals of some sort, just call 911."

At this point the owner of the restaurant looked at the union boss in a confused way. He felt like a cat threatened that was hiding with the arching of the back and the dilation of the pupils. First, Arthur felt for a moment as if he would not let himself be so easily dismissed. But finally my employer understood his own strange behavior. He suddenly realized how vulnerable he had been to false alarms. In his book *Feelings,* Dr. Willard Gaylin explained: *"What we anticipate may be false. The anxiety we feel may be triggered by an unreal danger, an echo of a similar but not identical situation from the past whose relevance*

356

no longer operates. And the future we fear may only be our imagination.
It may once again be a product of distortions from our past. We may end
up 'protecting' ourselves against that which will never come... This is a
non specific emotion that is as equally past oriented as future oriented.'"

Reassured by what had been suggested by Mr. Weinstard
regarding the dismissal of the two waiters, Arthur heaved a
sigh of relief. He was now in the seventh heaven. In a low
and rather submissive tone of voice, as one who received an
unexpected lesson in life, my employer showed the union
president hasty gratitude. With an apologetic smile and a slight
giggle he finally realized that that meeting had not been so
alarming after all, that he had experienced a simple paranoid
delusion. The union head had really put Arthur *au pied de la*
lettre-down to the foot of the letter.

When the serious business of the day was over, as we
slipped out noiselessly from the well-decorated office, my
employer paused at the door for a moment. He looked back
at the man behind the desk as his sympathy overpowered
him in an unusual manner. And, uttering a groan of pleasure
he added with much softness as his voice was capable of
expressing: "Thank you again Mr. Weinstard for your good
advice."

Outside, it started to rain and we walked slowly on
the slippery pavement. Our employer, fluttering gaily, in
a magnanimous mood decided to take us all for lunch at
Le Canard Heureux-The Happy Duckling, a nearby French
restaurant for 'his victory celebration.' On a spit over an open
fire, ducks were roasting...

Back home, Angeline was all in tears. Pompadour, the
cute little poodle has died.

* * * *

Several weeks later much to my surprise I chanced upon Horst again at a Van Nuys flea market. As I made my way through a thin crowd of bargain hunters, I overheard a familiar male voice behind me. I could not see the person yet, but I heard him well:

"With that gait, there can be no mistake." I turned around wanting to place a face to that voice. And right in front of me stood Horst. Nothing ever sounded so good before. We hugged each other for he was so happy to see me again. He was dressed in gay regalia, appearing to be a long lost member of *La Cage Aux Folles*. And he went on: "Pierre, long times, no see you man! And, by the way, there is no one else in the world that walks like you. As you ramble in a bent posture you keep looking at all times at the ground as if a treasure was to be found!"

My friend, with his eyes veiled with tears of joy lost no time in keeping me up to speed about his dear lover Paul; how their life together has somehow survived constant hurtful quarrels and bitter dissension.

With his madness for gambling, Horst who supposedly took care of the financial aspect of life ran so far into debt that they were compelled to sell their house. Their credit was gone too.

They had actually sailed to America where they thought they could make their fortune as so many Europeans did. Now they were ready to return to the Old Continent.

A moment later, Horst switched to a more euphoric mood and blazoned their intent to open a souvenir boutique in Nice, France, a city of contrasting scenes and habits. With the help of Horst's aunt and a little pocket money left over, they were expecting to meet in their shop all those actors and directors, *la crème de la crème* during the Cannes Film Festival season on the *Promenade des Anglais,* thus expecting a comfortable income.

Horst and Paul had decided to return to Europe for which they longed passionately, but Horst added that they really love the U.S.

This reminded me so well of a friend I worked with at the Los Angeles Hilton. Albert Vertroocken was a Belgian national too. He lived in California for several years carrying in his mind a constant '*mal du pays*'- homesick for the land of his ancestors. So, on a warm summer day, after emptying his U.S. bank account, he decided to go back to Belgium. With two partners, he opened a restaurant paradoxically called *The American Grill!*

However, once upon my return to the Belgian capital to visit my mother, I experienced an unbelievable event. In downtown Brussels, from a local tram at a stoplight I noticed a brand new red Ford Mustang convertible bearing California license plates. And the man behind the wheel; that *nouveau riche,* wearing a huge, black Texas hat was none other than my good friend Albert Vertroocken. He was playing the role of a wealthy American in his home country. Since Albert had made his fortune in America, he was foremost in displaying his extravagance on the old continent. So far, so good for a man that claimed to be homesick! There is one powerful French word attributed to a person who carry-on such a kind of behavior, it is: *farceur*- a practical joker...

Recalling our joy rides together in their luxurious Jaguar along the Sunset Strip in Hollywood, Horst burst into laughter when I commented to him that we looked like the *Tres Amigos.*

"Whatever happened to that Jag?" I inquired. And Horst began to relate: "A few days after we left *Le Cerisier,* the car started to fall apart; there were so many engine problems, so much costly repairs. But soon, the Jaguar was 'mysteriously stolen.' It was never recovered," and Horst went on,

"For that lemon, we still collected a fat check from the insurance.'"

A crime had been in want of a person to carry it out; so they sub-let an accomplice. Without being discrete about the story that he was unfolding, Horst further went on, telling me the whole truth:

"As for the theft itself, it was a well organized plot: one night after work we met Pedro Gomez, the dishwasher. He was quietly waiting at the bus stop. We carefully explained to Pedro that our car which was parked in front of our residence had its doors unlocked with the key in the ignition switch. That's all that was said. With a smile on his face, Gomez simply said *"Hoy comprend"*-I understand, as the temptation proved irresistible."

However, Horst summed up by telling him that the Jaguar wasn't running in reverse any longer. But our little dishwasher acting like a real pro managed to drive that leather-seat luxury automobile all the way to a dismantling shop in Pacoima. Furthermore, for that well arranged theft, Pedro Gomez made a little extra money for himself, enough to buy another cow for his ranch in Guatemala. My former colleague concluded:

"I remember that we congratulated ourselves on that clever arrangement by shaking hands all around."

After a warm bear hug, I bid *adieu* to my friend Horst. For awhile I saw him wandering away into the crowd, pouring himself down through the metro.

* * * *

Subsequent to the firing of Paul and Horst, with the addition of a deplorable situation following the closing of the restaurant in Solvang, Arthur had to fill the vacancy caused by the departure of those two waiters. Eddy Roy Freedman gave up his managerial position at *La Bagatelle,* thus becoming our new full-time co-worker at *Le Cerisier* in Sherman Oaks.

La Bagatelle had been ransacked and vandalized. Earlier, the chef and his wife made their escape with brass, copper utensils, pots, pans, dishes, all the silverware and an impressive amount of food. Now the place was closed for good. There was a padlock with a chain upon the gate as a fine web adorned with dead flies decorated the front door.

From Solvang, Eddy Freedman brought along Antoine, his little shaggy black coat, with a fluffy tail schipperke. Antoine wasn't just his dog. He was his best buddy and soul-mate as well, always taking great pleasure in licking his master's face. Schipperkes are very useful animals especially raised to guard barges or ferries on lakes and canals.

Antoine who was suffering from rheumatism, for in cold weather he never stopped shivering, was also a one-trick pony. Freedman would make his dog perform volts and pirouettes. Looking wistfully in his master's face, with pointed ears he would start to wag its tail. Eddy would call and whistle after the dog. The animal with his feet much too heavy for his body scampered a few yards, turned round sprang in the air and flipped before hitting the ground again. Panting hard, nose to the lawn Antoine would find something buried from Eddy by darting forth on the scent. After that exhibition he would bark, turning over on his back and lie on the ground, lifting his front paw to Eddy, as if to tell him 'give me a high five' and moved again to crush silently next to a chair. That doggy was quite smart: he sensed whenever his master was sad. His trusty dog would sit at his feet with ears strains back with affection. He would come close enough to lick his hand. From time to time he would lower his disdainful head and wag his tail to solicit a fleeting caress. Only when Antoine saw Arthur approaching that he would spring forward, crouching low.

JACQUES MEYER

This time his ears would prick up, becoming highly excited, uttering an angry, savage yell. The noble dog always seized my employer by the leg or arm as he tried to pull him down to the ground. Still on other times he would lope toward him, standing up, pawing at his jacket. Aside from that diversion, Antoine would usually look as kindly at a stranger as at Eddy. Eddy's love for Antoine was so strong that he memorized an old saying about dogs that was introduced by Georges G. Vest in a speech in the U.S. Senate in1884:

The one absolutely unselfish friend that man can have in his selfish world, the one that never deserts him, the one that ever proves ungrateful or treacherous, is his dog... He will kiss the hand that has no food to offer... When all other friends desert, he remains.

Freedman was good not only for quadrupeds but of winged creatures as well. My friend really hated to drive down to Los Angeles because at a certain point near Ventura he had to steer between long lines of eucalyptus trees. The simple aroma of eucalyptus made him sick for several hours.

After so many years of wear and tear of time, Arthur's arrogance seemed to have rubbed off on Freedman. I already knew about Eddy's accomplishments aboard a Navy-ship during the Korean War. However, he disclosed to me one aspect of his story I was still unaware of:

"Pierre, during a few weeks leave in Japan, I met a Japanese princess. The princess invited me to a candlelight dinner in her villa north of Chiba Prefecture. And guess what? During meal we never used chopsticks. We ate with knife and fork just like in good old USA. Later on, feeling quite at ease over a little sake, I extended my hand and she even allowed me to take hers: love was in the air. Those meetings repeated themselves for several memorable days," and Eddy went on:

"I could have been introduced to the emperor, but it was time for me to return to my ship. On the last day, her highness offered me a basket filled with fresh fruits and sweets. Subsequently due to the battles, the bombardments from North Korea, I went back to America and never saw my princess again." As my friend kept on talking, he promptly turned away and started weeping…

Working with Eddy was such a source of hilarity; a real *pince-sans-rire* that was able to make people laugh as he would keep a poker face. Every time he explained the desserts to our customers, he ended up with the same sentence: "AND NOW FOR THE OLD FOLKS, WE HAVE PRUNE TART!"

* * * *

Marie-Thérèse, Melanie's grandmother already lived in California for several months and on Sunday the granddaughter would give a special party at her house on Topanga Canyon to celebrate Granny's ninety-fourth birthday. For this occasion Melanie contacted many old-timer customers by phone to invite them to participate in the feast. Next, she beseeched me to arrive a little earlier to set up tables and display the food trays before the guests would arrive.

At the front door of Melanie's large four-bedroom house, I was welcomed by a swarm of flies that was buzzing at my face. Melanie had just spread some manure for the rose bushes. The air was dense with musty smell that was irritating. The dew was heavy, just like a gleaming crust on the long grass. A stream of water was trickling over sheathing leaves and poison ivy. Melanie let me in, along with the sibilance of the ominous hum of pesky insects that were still crawling on me.

The flickering of the flames in the fireplace, pirouetting, cast a happy flaring light on the ceiling. I made the entire room cheerful. The fire had taken the chill of the large room. As I listened to the brisk crackling of the wood, pushing whips of smoke to the ceiling, there were throngs of white moths whirling around the lamps. The beige calico curtains were still closed.

By eleven o'clock people were already sitting on the chairs in the patio, facing a large piece of grassland in the background. I already recognized Dr. Rabinadrah Singh Patel with his wife and children, the commercial *attaché* to the consulate of France, Beatrice Van Meerstellen, Leon's mother who invariably stood in good terms with the Valois Dourville de Montrissart's family. She sat next to Angeline.

Less than an hour later, a sizable crowd was busy as bees to taste the succulent appetizers and swizzling fine California wines. Oddly enough, many appeared to have a gluttonous appetite.

Melanie was dressed in an expensive attire of a rare material, a shawl over her shoulders with matching high heeled shoes that made her look taller. Her gold bracelets were clinking with each of her movements. With a rosy and elegantly ebullient face she seemed to enjoy being a talented hostess. Even the little tapping echo of her shoes that resounded sharply at each step on the terrace made her laugh. There were such pleasant sounds as she passed by. Melanie shook out her hair cheerfully. For the moment she no longer appeared to be problematic, as no more sadness filled her heart. Now, in a graceful motion, with her *derrière* moving with suppleness as she kept on walking, a beaming Melanie really lived her happiness, waiting in suspense for what was to come. With one finger barely touching her lips she looked like Alice-in-Wonderland.

At a certain time the grandmother who just arrived with Arthur came out of the house into the garden. Since it was such a great surprise, they previously waited at my employer's house for the right moment to appear. Both mother and son were dressed in white.

The very accomplished woman wore a long gown with a charm attached on the chest, and on her finger the ring given to her by her late husband. It was a ruby, the size and color that recalled the Arabian Nights. As she walked demurely, her neck rose out like a white plumaged swan. A Cashmere shawl was tied up around her shoulders. She had long white silky hair and a shining face without any wrinkles. With elegant figure and dignified manner she was really phenomenal, considering her age. Even then, she always knew what she was talking about. That maternal protectiveness kept revealing in her face, it looked as if she was floating in a celestial light.

With refined manners, Granny was also an expert artist of water-colored paintings. Being familiar with both the European and the American Stock Market she was knowledgeable in everything that was to be known regarding mutual funds transactions or U.S. treasury obligations. As she openned her newspaper she would be absorbed with the ups and downs of stocks that were listed on the financial page.

Arthur who just got a haircut wore a three piece white suit, even his shoes were sparkling white. The mother of the little septuagenarian was holding firmly on her son's arm. He was escorting Marie-Thérèse with a majestic dignity, and in her absolute glory her prestige rose enormously. With the serenity which a perfect old age possesses, Granny was impressive and splendid. All of a sudden the aged Arthur looked young again. A smile came to his lips as his dear mother kept on looking rapturously at her sibling. Everyone was able to observe Arthur, the little spoiled brat, the suckling babe now being under the authority of maternal tenderness.

As the only child, his mother used to sing a song for him at bedtime in a low, sweet voice:

"Dodo, l'enfant do, l'enfant dormira bien vite.
Dodo, l'enfant do, l'enfant dormira bientôt."

Whenever a problem occurred, his mother's hand was there to hold him. Melanie was taken by a genuine emotion and she shed floods of tears. The food, so well prepared was just outstanding. After Marie-Thérèse finished her lunch, her granddaughter moving at a fast but dignified step turned on the 'Happy Birthday' CD that played out from loud speakers. Awhile later, Melanie brought out the giant cake she had baked. There hardly was any room enough to set up ninety-four candles. Instead she had planted four thick, long cylindrical mass of tallow with lighted wicks that Granny extinguished with a single blow.

Soon puffiness came to her cheeks and Arthur helped her to get inside the house. After he stirred up the cinders and add wood to the dimming glow of the fire, with the still warmth in the living room Marie-Thérèse fell asleep.

I was sitting with Beatrice and Angeline when Arthur started to squeeze my arm. With heightening enthusiasm but in a tone of voice that really surprised me, he conveyed:

"Pierre, don't be lazy," and, staring at me with a curious intent, he continued: "There is work to be done. Go and serve some more wine to our guests!" I never realized for a second that for me, this birthday celebration had become a working day. As I mentioned this to him, he simply urged me not to be silly with such non-appropriated remarks. Suddenly, with an irritated look he said in that military tone of voice, like a command: "Go now!" I did as was told. After all, this was a great honor to celebrate the birthday of a kind woman.

Melanie kept on running back and forth, serving coffee and cognac liquors. She herself drank so much that her explosive laugh frightened off the birds. When everyone had left plenty of food was still lying on the service table. All of it went straight into Melanie's giant refrigerator. With eyes half-opened, Arthur joined his mother who just woke up. And in a quiet voice she announced: "Hi baby, give mama a kiss sugar. I think it's time for you to take a rest as well, you have been working so hard for my birthday!"

A few days later, a friend of the *attaché* to the Consul of France who also happened to have participated at the celebration expressed himself clearly as to Arthur's character: "For a so-called 'aristocrat' he is excessively common!"

Chapter 28

OCCASIONALLY, ON A good day, in a burst of warm feeling Arthur would bring us a couple of roast chicken from Ralph's supermarket, with the addition of a good bottle of wine. And for that juncture he would join us to share our meal. During one of those instances, as we were eating Melanie arrived wearing a scarf tied around her head, dressed in a khaki African bush outfit with matching high soft boots. The daughter has just visited the photograph-shop owner and she handed her father a yellow envelope with pictures, then left.

In the middle of his meal the boss silently kept looking at each sharp professional quality color snapshot with deep interest. He would stare and stare again at one of them and won't let it go. It was a photograph of his late dog Pompadour, the reddish French poodle with her ears ornamented with motley ribbon. The loveable pet had died a few weeks ago. In the picture the nostalgia was so evident and Pompadour looked happy. The love toward the little pet had been Arthur's only magnificent obsession. He started licking the picture, remembering the way his four-legged friend licked his cheek with her warm, gentle tongue. My employer had suspected that a neighbor who hated dogs bestowed Pompadour some antifreeze to drink. After swallowing the poison, the little sweetheart had been unable to eat and began to fade away. After a few days of suffering her heart as well as her breathing had stopped almost simultaneously.

Suddenly Arthur dropped his knife and fork on the table. Considering the amount of food that was left on the plate I knew he was all shaken and deeply afflicted. The very last moment of his dog's agony was still in his mind. My employer planted his elbows on the table. Like a child, after pushing his plate forward he buried his face in his napkin. With the heaving of his shoulders, he started weeping. Abruptly, filled with more tender emotion he continued to cry ceaselessly. Sobbing uncontrollably before bursting into a hysterical fit of tears that streamed down his face Arthur reminded us how much sweetness, how much gay spirit Pompadour had brought at the house and all the wonderful days they had spent together. He remembered the carpet the doggy had walked on as Pompadour lay down her paws on his shoulders before she slept on his lap. She would play with Angeline's shoes from the mantelpiece. That sweetheart of a dog became the Valois Dourville de Montrissart's idol; their little princess. The boss was defying common people by dressing Pompadour in the latest fashion for dogs, and he would brush her hair joyfully. Now Arthur had a look of discomfiture as my sympathy was outpouring. I swallowed hard to keep down my feelings too. I became really affected by the emotion of my employer. So, as not to leave him alone in his weeping, I decided to hold his shoulder in great compassion. He became very thoughtful and patted my hand. For the first time his courage failed him entirely. Again, on that moment I felt irresistible pity for Arthur and I LIKED THE MAN!

However he did not cry for long. After having removed all traces of tears, he was again outwardly composed. The light from the chandelier would gleam on his forehead as he was soaring up into a cloud. Now he would humble his heart, blotting out the rest of the world. He played at life because he was unable to live it. Life never managed to teach him anything, except when he was alone with his dog. With his eyebrows arched upward he started to insult human behavior. This reminded me of a story onboard a German submarine U20 during World War 1 on the North Atlantic. After the German crew torpedoed a South American merchant ship, no attempt was ever made to rescue any sailors from the sinking boat. They all drowned like rats with the exception of a smooth-hair black *Dashmund* dog. Upon getting the animal on board the submarine the entire equipage came with tears in their eyes. I believe that there is a curious likeness between Arthur's behavior and that of those German Navy Fighters!

However I can remember some marvelous time I spent with the Valois Dourville de Montrissart's family as Pompadour accompanied us with a steady trot. We were on our way to Santa Barbara.

On the outskirts of Ventura, near a hitching post that looked more like an empty, very quiet area Arthur stopped and parked his new Dodge-van. Pompadour was the first one to get out of the vehicle as she recognized the smell of fresh air. She kept tripping on clumps of grass, rolling over, turning around like a statue on a pivot. In the glory of the sun we heard the murmur of the water over the stones. Sheep were bleating and calves were lowing. The daylight was brilliant in the warm air and I perceived a quick wavering of flapping wings under the bushes. Some hummingbirds also swerved their feathers in flight as the wind rushed against the trees. We were surrounded with a fragrance of the lilacs as we heard the yellow hammer woodpecker in the beech tree pecking madly at the crevasses in the bark. In the distance we could hear the braying of a mule. A weasel would rustle through the foliage.

Then Arthur's heart began to pound, uncontrolled as he so loved little Pompadour. He knelt and spoke to her in a gentle voice. Arthur rolled with the doggy on the grass from the undulating field trying to catch her tail. It was a helter-skelter game. After awhile the happy little dog with his face clasping the turf was breathing deeply, loading his body with the smell of earth. He would lie on its back, paws up in the air as the stirring grass brushed his small body.

And we got near the horses. They were galloping, hoisting their heels up and down kicking at the sky, slowing to a walk as they approached us. A black horse had blue pompons on its ears and bells ringing from a yellow velvet string attached around its lean neck.

Pompadour was really interested in the black horsy. With her tail twitching, the little dog didn't hesitate. After choosing a spot to pee she came forward; jumped at the animal's equine nostrils and started to kiss him. The horse seemed to respond to Pompadour as he actually lowered his head toward the little one without any fear. The spectacle was so amusing and so tender that we kept on watching and watching. At the same time when we finally decided to leave, the black horse tried endlessly to soar over the fence to follow his new found-friend...

Subsequent to the funeral arrangement for his pet Arthur bought Pompadour the best dog-skirt, pink hat and pink socks money can buy. Ceremoniously, with a prayer on his lips the boss dressed his 'second daughter' as he would call her with all the care in the world. Afterward, he drove with Pompadour to the dog-cemetery. The boss marked down the grave with a little marble plaque where it was written: *To our most faithful friend in life*. And again Arthur started praying, rosary-bead in hand. Earlier he had embraced the tiny casket and had wept profusely while bading the pooch farewell.

Later on, from beside the partition of the private room I heard my employer talking to himself: *"Pompadour deserved as much as any human being…surely there is a heaven for little dogs…my love, my sweet sugar. I will see you again…someday!"*

Within a few days after Pompadour's funeral Arthur went back with Eddy to the outskirts of Ventura to meet the black horsy again. Eddy explained to me that Arthur started caressing the horse's head. With emotion, he spoke to the animal telling him that his girlfriend just passed away. At that precise moment I already knew that without Pompadour, the boss anticipated a gloomy future.

Next day, a framed photograph of 'the little princess'was hanging on one of the walls at *Le Cerisier.*

* * * *

Mr. Emmanuel MacShulton was a dignified, handsome businessman. He had protruding lips, a light scar below his left eye and was wearing thick spectacles. Slightly overweight, he always carried that gentle, honest smile on his face. An architect with offices in the US and in three Chinese cities, including Beijing, he lived in a sumptuous residence in Woodland Hills, along with his Chinese wife and five children.

The spouse, Chung-Fong Dai was a graduate in economics from Beijing University. Extremely tall for an oriental, with a trim figure she was also very cute and showed well-bred manners. She maintained a special relationship with high-ranking Chinese officials and, as a government business adviser she traveled to China five or six times a year.

During an evening dinner at *Le Cerisier* with the entire family, Mr. MacShulton had insistently expressed the desire to invite the Valois Dourville de Montrissart household for a special Peking-duck dinner in one of the best Chinese restaurants in Southern California. I stood right there in front of the table holding hot dishes in my hands. Mr. MacShulton apparently aware that I had been eavesdropping touched my left shoulder as I was serving him along with his family and said:

"Pierre, the invitation is also extended to you. Chung-Fong Dai will inform Arthur for the day and the hour of our meeting."

I accepted the invitation for dinner with great anticipation. I would accompany them, not as their favored waiter but as their friend…

Less than three weeks later, the MacShulton family came back at *Le Cerisier*. Emmanuel was dressed in white, including white socks and white granny sport shoes. It looks like he had just come off the tennis court. His wife Chung-Fong Dai raised a soft voice that was distinct and clear, even though I perceived that certain Chinese accent:

"Pierre, we really missed you for that superb Peking Duck Dinner. It was delightful and I'm so sorry you were unable to make it. Arthur told us you were sick in bed over a bad cold! We sincerely hope it was not too serious?"

All of a sudden I was filled with profound discomfort. With that fabricated excuse from Arthur I was unable to take an apologetic stand. I could not rid myself of the notion that my employer had told that unbelievable lie with such an ungrateful attitude. As I found myself shivering, my heart thudded over that subtle mockery from my boss. I tried to say something, anything, yet words halted as abruptly as if I had lost my tongue. *In Arthur's eye I wasn't of high-class breeding, an aristocratic figure like him, or to be more precise, like he thought he was. In his poor cracked brained and freakish mind such an invitation should not apply to a man belonging to the illiterate masses. That man was totally immature.*

* * * *

I still can't believe it! Almost immediately after this unfortunate event Arthur with his arms resting motionless changed his attitude completely. In the same manner as with Robert, the gay priest he became friendly once more and stopped using bad language. It seemed he was being exhilarated by a sense of well-being. As I watched the boss with a wave of compassion a great sense of relief crept in me. But I also asked myself the question: "How sincere and well intentioned was he?" We were still skeptics as for his change of heart. Arthur had been in a state of rebellion with himself and consequently with The Higher Power. Oscar Wilde explained that "The mood of rebellion closes up the channels of the soul, and shuts out the airs of heaven." Aside from his hindrance I still carry in my mind *une pensée profonde*- a deep thought toward Arthur. Every human being is a reflection of God in the mirror of life. This thinking alone, in its well-defined and direct acuteness is worth a thousand words of aphoristic explanations. I already knew that Arthur, as a child was abused. He had experienced sufferings injustice and misfortune. Now it was time to cultivate love.

For me this wasn't *terra incognita*, just a virtual plausibility. During my travels around the world I discovered the very poor, *les affligé*, breathing ill-fated adversity but also generous and good at heart.

* * * *

After so many setbacks with the restaurant up north in Solvang, Arthur decided to close the business for good. That luxurious eating abode had been an unsuccessful venture, simply a disastrous speculation. However, Arthur managed to get out of it, leaving only his faithful partners in it… and to their necks with their investments! A series of lawsuits against Arthur followed. In the final resort, my employer lost. It also ended up to turned dreadful for his credit report.

However, being a man of imagination, not willing to lose any substantial income the boss finally decided to convert his building into an important souvenir shop, using Eddy's name as for the new ownership...

For some time Arthur had not been at ease with the city-council, claiming that the city-council was mostly Scandinavian, and that he (wrongly) thought that 'they' didn't care about French entrepreneurs. I happened to meet one of the outstanding members of the Solvang city-council who openly declared that great opportunities for business in the Danish Capital of the U.S. are open to any one regardless of country, sex or affiliation. One of the members even used that French expression: *Le soleil brille pour tout le monde*-the sun is shining for everyone.

Now, with a 'kiss-ass' attitude Arthur named the new place *The Swedish House of Fine Imports*. He even got a Swedish flag installed graciously on the roof of his souvenir shop. The Gillinger import-export company furnished my employer with all the items needed, from cuckoo clocks, to shirts, hats, vases, statues, utensils, even paintings depicting Swedish landscapes. An old customer from *La Bagatelle*, also a retired firefighter from Buelton was in charge of the place as Arthur supervised the store on weekends. Soon this place became a full-time tourist attraction.

On a warm summer Sunday I drove with Helena to Solvang and we met Arthur Valois Dourville de Montrissart in front of his shop. He was almost fully dressed (for publicity purpose) as a Swedish Naval Officer, with the royal Swedish insignia embroidered on his *kepi*-military hat. Once more the little clown had to perform in his own silly ways. On another occasion the beaming Arthur looking extremely content was riding a donkey in front of the store in the same Swedish Naval Officer uniform. As for the many visitors wandering around, he could hardly have failed to attract their attention. *"Against stupidity, the gods themselves fight in vain."*-Schiller.

Chapter 29

LAX- Tom Bradley International 6: 00 PM

THE SEASONS SUCCEEDED one another. As weeks had paired off until a month passed, the vacation went by. It was already late September; almost October with yellowing leaves to be seen everywhere but a little flush of summer was still in the air.

I just got back from the Republic of Vietnam. From Tansonnhat International Airport in Ho Chi Minh City (formerly Saigon), as the plane rumbled down the runway before rising up in the air, the nineteen hour flight with a stop-over in Osaka, Japan was long and tiring.

When I arrived in LAX I was still in the ambiance of that megalopolis and *la pétarade*- backfire of those hundreds of thousands of mopeds and scooters driven in all directions even on sidewalks. I also had experienced the charming, tranquil bus-trip to Hanoi, alongside the shoreline among opaline rice fields via Dalat, Nha-Trang and Danang.

On that bus-ride up north to the Vietnamese capital, I was accompanied by three Norwegian friends: Björm, Wemke and Hella. The young, tall and blond Björm was a medical student at Oslo University. Wemke and Hella worked as secretaries in Stavanger. We were such a wonderful team; they even encouraged me to come and visit Norway as their special guest. Aside from the social call at the Ho-Chi-Minh mausoleum where the famed leader and president was embalmed, one of my ultimate pleasures in that former Indochina country was that we met so many French speaking people, even in small villages. During a storm at a stopover in Dalat, I sat with them in some kind of a bamboo hut café and drank San Miguel Beer with exclusive Edith Piaf's music in the background...

Upon my return at *Le Cerisier* restaurant, still jet-lagged and with insomnia that were taking their toll, Arthur's strange appearance had been a shock to me. I saw from the expression on his face that something had happened.

My employer was originally planning to go with his wife on an extended six-week vacation to Portugal as tourists. Years ago, in bewilderment he had found himself standing on a promontory overlooking the seaside community of Bahia de Setubal, south of Lisbon. At that time Arthur had a vision with the prospect to settle down for good come retirement time. This had been his long cherished dream. *Ad valorem*, without mental reservation he eventually bought a piece of land there hoping to build a beach retreat as large as a manor where the scenic view reminded him of the Southern California shore. The building would stand on a field high up, including terrace, balconies, and next to it, a stable with several horses. As for the name, it would be called: *Domaine du Soleil Levant* that he got after the Japanese's Rising Sun! In his dream, the material splendor was looming up in the horizon.

After he had laid out the grounds of his new home with a Portuguese friend he eventually realized soon that his grandiose plan was an ill-advised project that never materialized. This had been one of his many castles in the air; just a deceptive dream of his fancy.

Suddenly Arthur gaped at me and he abruptly tumbled into some indescribable depth. Breathing heavily he was humming at the top of his lungs. They had cancelled the trip because Angeline suffered a stroke. Her state of health had long given warning, and now she had been taken urgently to the hospital. Also, assuming that Angeline was given the incorrect dose of Coumadin therapy during one of her previous treatments, it probably had interfered with her injections of insulin for diabetes mellitus. This finding really infuriated Arthur. His wife was now invalid and bed-ridden. She was to remain with constant strict attendance for the rest of her life. Feeling pity for him I promised that I would go and visit his wife first thing in the morning.

The Good Apostle Hospital in Burbank was a tall modern building. I arrived there as I heard the chiming bells of a nearby church. A fountain on the right shaded by a giant tree was overlooking a series of gardens, and a flock of birds was wheeling in the sky.

Finding my way through the corridors, amidst the noxious vapors of the hospital I finally found Angeline's room. She was lying on a reclining bed as Arthur and Melanie were already on her side. The daughter was gently running her fingers through her mother's silver hair. I noticed that Melanie kept unsteady on her feet. She had such a great affection for her mother. Quite often Angeline would take her defense against Arthur. This would frequently happen whenever Melanie tried to get paid for the expenses she did in preparing those fine cheesecakes for the restaurant. The owner had ceaselessly but one answer for his daughter: "Don't ask me for money, I am broke!"

I left Angeline and made a solemn promise that I would come again to visit her hoping that her health would somewhat improve.

* * * *

At *Le Cerisier*, the days were the same as they had ever been. Beside Eddy a new face showed up in the dining room.

Camille Lavalière was *un Pied Noir*- Black Foot, (a name given to Frenchmen born in Algeria,) and a non conformist. He had been an army man, married and divorced several times. Camille, nearsighted, with a gold tooth that glinted in his mouth was not tall: precisely five feet, three inches. Angelically beautiful and effeminate, with a voice as fresh as a young girl he was the most sympathetic person with a thoughtful gentleness. I liked him already on the first encounter.

In his late forties, he showed a strong chin and a slightly balding head. His thin hair was a mere damp mop as a blue peace sign tattoo etched on his nape. Because of so many hypodermics his skin was full of holes. The Atlas Mountains of North Africa were also tattooed on his right arm, and in his shirt pocket I noticed a pack of *Gauloises* French cigarettes. He kept on smoking like a chimney, even under heavy cold.

As a trailer recluse, he stayed near the beach and lived on a boat with the mania of collecting clean, well-oiled guns (he actually sold a "45" to Melanie). He lived his own life, untrammeled by conventions. Camille, a former corporal with the French Foreign Legion was also an expert in land mines. He ran away from home at the age of fifteen.

A year later, after lying about his age by faking the date on his birth certificate he joined the French Foreign Legion through a Paris recruitment center. A few months later his poor mother had died from a heart attack.

Later on, at the close of his five-year term with the Legion in North Africa, Camille went back to France when he harbored a fugitive from justice, previous to becoming himself involved in 'blood diamond' transactions in Africa. Before shooting rebels with machine-guns from helicopters in South America he learned the trade of smuggling with the Colombian drug cartels and was captured by the military that patrolled the coastline. For a year or so Camille got his meals behind bars.

From Colombia, Lavalière went to Rio and worked as a pimp in Copacabana's lowest district. Curiously enough, once a week he would take several of his hookers to Redemption Church for confession.

After some time of mad excitement, wild delight and sensual pleasure Lavalière moved to California.

Among Camille's dearest friends who came to eat at the restaurant was a certain Mr. John Durandou. A British national graduated from Glasgow's University in Scotland, Mr. Durandou with his cavalryman silhouette was also an ex-French Foreign Legionnaire. Both he and Camille had been comrades-in-arms through all the campaigns. They were thoroughly indoctrinated by the military, ready to fight to the death if they had to.

After several years in the desert among other legionnaires from so many different countries there was definitely a communication problem. They resolved this by using lingua-franca: a corrupt form of various languages, consisting mainly of French, Italian and English mixed with Arabic.

John received many wounds in North Africa in the battles against the hordes of Ben Bella. He had a scar on the right temple where a bullet had brushed his head. With a good *esprit de corps,* even that their French accent had some shades of variance, John and Camille were recollecting so many old souvenirs. They were drawling out long stories of the war in the hot sand of the Upper Sahara; of those long and tiring marches, strengthening their muscles in the desert near

Sidi-Bel-Abbès, resting at night in some oasis next to their machine-guns. As showers of stones and bullets were pouring upon them, they both had been heroes, glittering with medals.

Durandou, with that certain strain of gypsy blood owes his French name from his Huguenot's ancestors. Those same ancestors had fled France to avoid persecution. He had a wrinkled face, scourged by time and trouble. John was small, but he had a great soul. Camille explained to me that his friend was timid at heart, especially with women. He was delicate, passionate and chaste but he had also retired from all friendship with women because of a wrong he had suffered. At twenty years of age he had married the daughter of a major who had been killed by the enemy. Not long, following their wedding, his wife had deceived him with a young lieutenant. His wife died from cancer shortly after and he was left lonelier than ever. He thought successively of becoming a monk and of getting drunk. He started blaming himself and became weary and anxious, wondering if he had treated his late-wife unfairly.

Enlisting in the French Foreign Legion had changed his life completely. He had joined his unit in the Atlas region of Algeria with an unshaken but still hopeless devotion.

Both Lavalière and Durandou kept on talking about their military exploits. They had vowed to brave danger and beavearement together while facing up mortar shells. With some kind of *dignity* and composure, Durandou's voice showed a peculiar emphasis when he articulated:

"Camille, do you remember the time when we had to wear pampers during Ben Bella's attacks by sharpshooters so that we won't pee in the bushes and let their dogs find us through the smell of urine?" and he added:

"Once I was punished because in the dead of night, adjoining a hill near a village full of collaborators with the enemy, in complete silence with *baïonnette au canon*, I broke wind!" A ray of sunshine flickered over Camille's face as he also recollected some of those souvenirs that he shared with all of us:

"Yeah, what's more I can recollect when on a particular evening, gloriously drunk in the canteen we were reunited, still haunted by visions of death. I can visualize that incident as though it just happened yesterday. It had been a tough day in that Algerian *djebel* at the skirts of the Sahara. After so many advances and retreats in a narrow gorge with sloping sides at least twenty feet high, the *fellagha* slid down the hills and fell upon us with fixed bayonets. We had to hold the position till the supporting reinforcement moved up. And for a long time we were under direct hit. This was one of our first combat in hostile territory. We fought bravely, but the pressure of the Arabs was irresistible. Earlier, our lieutenant used the same command given by general Israel Putnam to the American soldiers at the battle of Bunker Hill: *'Don't fire until you see the whites of their eyes,'*" and Camille continued: "After we had heroically resisted a prolonged siege we had witnessed rows of bodies lying on the ground. The enemy had been superior; the Arabs even thrust their bayonets into the bodies of dead legionnaires. The corpses just stayed to rotten in the hot sand. There were men with their throats slashed as the walls were spattered with blood and bits of flesh. Subsequent to several blasts stench of burning flesh soaked the air. Skins of soldiers slain in combat had been cut and stretched on the ground or extended along the sides of a building as that of animals.

That day, after a bloody battle we had lost fifteen of our best comrades, and another six in a *blitzkrieg*-explosion, fallen on the field of honor while fighting. A man with his leg cut off was struggling as so many wounded were still screeching. Corpses with severed heads from their bodies were visible all around the marketplace. A little further something was lying there on the hard cement. It was no longer a corpse, just a parapet of flesh, of bones. Against those 'master executioners' we fight so hard that at one time I plunged my own bayonet into the belly of a terrorist, tearing off his intestines. Soon, instead of water the soil was impregnated with blood! The whole thing along with a procession of disfigured, highly mutilated dead bodies turned out to become 'mass insanity' with entrails and limbs to be seen everywhere!"' *This statement from Camille had been a difficult task for my pen to put down on paper, but my own sergeant Matthieu with the Belgian paratroopers' platoon had linked to me similar events. Prior to join our unit within the Belgian Armed Forces, Matthieu had spent five long years with the French Foreign Legion. While in the Congo zone I was correspondingly present when captain Vandenbrecht had been cut in pieces alive with machetes by revolutionaries and ferocious Bantu warriors. There had been no limit of admiration, of enthusiasm for our commander. Prior to the captain's horrible fate, for his birthday we all went to sing La Marseillaise under the balcony of his house as he just had intercourse with an African whore. A few French Legionnaires from the Brazzaville base in the French Congo, on the other side of the Congo River came to join us.*

Lavalière went on and on with his yarn, more excited than ever:

"Jean-Paul, one of the very desperate legionnaire leaning forward on a bench at the canteen, his body covered with scars with his eyes hidden by his hands was crying like a child because he simply came back from the battle alive. At this point Jean-Paul looked around as if to convince himself that he was actually awake and not dreaming. This had been a blow to his pride! Everyday he offered his body for battle and again this time he suffered just minor wounds. Not dying in combat like a hero and a real man was unthinkable. The Ben Bella soldiers had slit the throat of his best friend; he died in a moment." and Camille continued, "It was at that time that the major came and joined us. With such a wave of compassion the officer, after he heard that confession decided to rest his hand on the legionnaire's shoulder, telling him not to worry: Tomorrow the Legion would bring the war to a victorious conclusion and hopefully an Arab bullet would get him right in the region of the heart. Jean-Paul was so pleased with those personal feelings and such comforting words that he kissed the officer on the cheek!" On the other hand, ironically in the face of death some of those soldiers had acquired a swift entitlement to a life more energetic than that of regular people.

This is a perfect example of what I had experienced with the paratroopers: As a nineteen year old, in a C-119 plane over the outskirts of the city of Diest, Belgium I was waiting dreadfully, my whole body tensed for the 'red-on light- stand at the door' signal. I'd never been so frightened, as this was my very first jump from an aircraft. When the 'green-on light, go' command came I thought that I jumped to my death. I plunged, deeper and deeper until the only voice I heard was the voice of oblivion, the horrified envision of nihilism. This was just my last thought as like in a motion-picture my entire life flashed swiftly before my eyes for those never-ending few seconds prior to perceive the dome of the parachute above my head, above the swinging of my body. It was a miracle! I was alive, floating gracefully in the air. As I hit the ground with that smooth rolling on that carpet of fresh grass I felt like I just had conquest the Everest and life had become more precious than ever...

John and Camille suddenly stood up, jolting free from their seat in the private room exalted, and they started to sing the French Foreign Legion ultimate song; one of their favorite drinking songs as well:

Tiens, voilà du boudin, voilà du boudin, voilà du boudin
Pour les alsaciens, les suisses et les lorrains.
Pour les belges y en a plus, ce sont les tireurs au cul.

(Here, there are sausages for the Alsaciens, the Swiss and the Lorrains. For the Belgians there are no more sausages because they always hide their ass.)

Both John and Camille received *La Croix de Guerre*, 'War Cross' from general Salan.

After his five-year military service was over, following a short stay at the *Hôtel des Invalides*- hospital for invalid soldiers in Paris, John Durandou had divided his time equally between the French capital and Rome. Furthermore, he worked for an American Food Mission for starving children in Ethiopia before taking on the job of concierge at the Ritz-Carlton in Cannes. Later on, John came to Los Angeles to meet his long time 'buddy' from the Legion.

As for Camille, altogether I had the feeling that his life had been a combination of the rough and of the smooth. At the same time he was also profused in his expenses. Camille was always picky as to what manner of fabric his clothes were made of. In his baggy corduroy trousers money was continually jingling from his pocket. He nearly always was in a hurry for some kind of business transaction. He was never happy unless he was buying something; anything. He had that real Midas touch as he enjoyed tossing his currency about like a maniac. At one time he dropped a twenty dollar bill on the bar counter for a patterned-Gauguin Tahitian shirt I was wearing. Lavalière was definitely in the habit of spending more than he ought. Furthermore, he liked to associate himself with wealthy people and used to living of women. Camille was smart with some sort of uncultivated refinement, as he showed irrational behavior. He constantly let his nails grow to a certain length yet he also kept on breaking them.

Being an advocate of fresh juices, he would come to the restaurant with a small container of orange juice that he had squeezed with a reamer. He kept drinking it at dinnertime as we were enjoying a Coke or a glass of cheap red wine. As long as Arthur wasn't around he would forget that healthy beverage by adding a shot of vodka, thus making a perfect screwdriver.

Lavalière, with his talent for flattery had as a *modus vivendi* only three purposes in life, reminiscent of words I already heard in a song: *cigarettes, whiskey et petites pépés*-young girls. He liked tasting forbidden pleasures. Camille was all flames and raptures for women. He would woo one lady while keeping an eye on another lady. At one time he bragged with eloquence about his sexual conquests when he articulated:

"In my village near Toulon I have 'taken on' all of the virgins!'" As his sexual hunger was mounting like madness he added that south of the border he made love in the river with a local girl and both almost drowned in the strong current. In reality he had stormy experiences with persons from the opposite sex. Aside from love, in his mind he had experienced intercourse with every woman in his angle of vision. Camille was conscientious and kind-hearted. Furthermore he was the type of man who was convinced that in life one should always seek for the very best. The clothing that touched his body had to be the best; all the food brought to his table had to be the best. He claimed to have been in love with the daughter of Nicaragua's Defense Minister; had dinner at the minister's residence and that he used Molotov cocktails against rebels in a Managua suburb.

Camille was attracted to strange beauty, to forbidden fruit and for him the age factor was never a problem. Sinning without shame he frequently had vulgar, cheap sort of affairs in disreputable hotels involving nightclubs or *filles de joie*-brothel women in hotpants. Weak and unhappy women also appealed to him since he was able to manipulate them. Occasionally temptations were more than he could bear. At all times Camille needed a woman for intercourse. On a rainy night, beyond the bound of decency, quite ready for what his erotic fancy might dictate he went down on an old lady on the backseat of a new black Mercedes parked right in front of *Le Cerisier.* Camille firmly believed that women of old age indulged in 'such romances' as well. However, in spite of his indecent behavior we became good friends. One evening, as we were all eating he made an announcement that made my heart rejoice in a sympathetic manner:

"Pierre appeared to be a dummy. He acted like a dummy and always let people run over him! He continually lowered himself in the eyes of others, feigning to be less than he is. However as *un fait accompli,* he's far to be such a simpleton as one think he is. In his own way he's very smart indeed, probably more intelligent than all of us. He's just playing the clumsy fool. But look here for Christ's sake: in Belgium this man joined the Para-Commando, his country's toughest military unit and fought in the Congo. He's such a great traveler. He has visited all the continents. He associated himself with the Cambodian army as a soldier of fortune during the war against the Khmère Rouges," and Camille went on: "Pierre often retreats into his own shell but on the other hand he can also run like a gazelle. He received the Los Angeles Legacy Marathon Runner Award from the mayor. In comparison Arthur is simply a midget full of hot air, just a-nobody!"

Following his statement our mutual respect began to grow. With each day we discovered each other's strength.

However Lavaliere's little sin- *son péché mignon* aside from sex was related to his sweet tooth. For his small body, his appetite was unseemly great as his jaws were always busy. He was a champion eater and drinker. Soon after a considerable meal he was hungry again for all sorts of desserts such as *petit fours*, *Napoleon's tarts* and *éclairs au chocolat*. Being so voracious, the business of filling his tummy with those delicacies was another of his major preoccupations. Camille would wait that the last customer had left the restaurant to move unerringly from a corner of the dining room toward the dessert-tray on the service's marble-table and start gorging himself. With his craving he would proceed on for a second helping and I always thought that he would burst. It seemed that Camille was suffering from perpetual hunger pangs.

One evening, Arthur found him stuffing his mouth with cheesecakes left on the marble's table. Judging that it was a too expensive hobby, the boss looking at him though with a cold, intend stare reprimanded him:

"This is the last time you do this. If I catch you again, out you go!"

Several weeks later something had occurred in the most unexpected way. As we almost finished with our dinner in the private room, prior to the arrival of the first customers, Camille in the midst of the clatter of forks and spoons started a lengthy conversation. Still furious with the owner's censurable attitude regarding the tray of pastries he openly declared after taking his last spoonful of soup with a slice of buttered bread in his hand that Arthur was a hypocrite and a very antisocial person!

Unfortunately our employer with his snake-head peeking out very cautiously was listening on the other side of the partition wall that separated the private room from the main dining room.

As he often did, Arthur trod on winged feet from the front door. Before that through the shadowy darkness of the room, in a calculated plan and in order to silence his pace he would remove his shoes, flunging them aside. Inconspicuously sinuous as a nasty serpent, uttering no sounds from that heavy carpet that his little feet hardly brushed he would tip-toe for every stride. Taking a hundred precautions and shifting the full weight of his body on each leg, he would balance himself a little as to steady his aim and went forward like those ancient animals crawling so slowly that fungus grew beneath their feet. While he was timing his footsteps, this was a treacherous ambush just to eavedrop our little chat. For a few seconds he was not breathing and not making the least noise as he continued his way slowly and unobstrusively.

Rapidly, as he took notice of Camille's comments Arthur rose, revealing himself from his concealment unsuspectingly the way a cat that lets the mouse run for awhile and hedge on it's pray. Drawing himself up with his forehead dilated Arthur, livid and moaning in sheer rage appeared as a thoroughbred horse. Fuming and puffing fiercely like a locomotive blowing off steam. With beads of perspiration on his upper lip, his face now turning red appeared as if it would explode. His look was as sharp as a razor.

Camille with his eyes popping out of his head glanced at him, as he was coming out of the blue. A chill came up his spine, head quivered as he almost choked on a piece of bread. My friend, pale and trembling, in an expression of hysterical, powerless uproar was not just surprised; he was petrified as well, feeling completely crushed.

With a revolted pride and indignation Arthur's anger was now to the verge of madness. He banged his fist at the edge of the table as his head started to wobble. At this point I had the feeling that he could have slain Lavalière with his own hand. Bursting with that metallic ring in his voice he took out his handkerchief, wiped his face and breathing shockingly he declared:

"I could not help but overhear what you just said, you dirty loafer, vagabond *Pied Noir!* This is what you're talking behind my back heh? So, that's what I am heh: a hypocrite and an antisocial?"

While hammering the table again he went on: "If you want, you can go home right now. You Goddamn no-good son-of-a-bitch, I will have your tongue torn out from your mouth you rascal! Surely I don't need you anymore. I hope I may never look upon your face again!"

Camille's former confidential conversation came to an abrupt end. That awful situation held my friend fixed in its stare. He couldn't budge his eyes one way or another. On that instant he could not summon up a single word. There was that strained look upon Arthur's face with eyes that made my friend's flesh creep as a bright red flush spread over his cheeks. Without allowing my co- worker to speak the boss went on:

"I am tired of a *'dummkopf'*, of a bad, imbecile and incompetent waiter like you who knows nothing about restaurant business anyway. Before long, I will see you in your grave, you scamp!"

Round the table heads were lifting. We looked at one another in real amazement. A kind of stupor seemed to come on all of us as we became extremely uncomfortable with the entire scene. A lengthy silence had settled between us. It was no longer a cheerful table. While we recognized the face of that sneaky and demoniac employer a feeling of awe, of weirdness crept in the air as we kept on staring at him in stunned stillness.

Camille posed down one hand and suspended his spoon in mid air with the other. Feeling like a cornered goose, he began to sweat heavily. I watched the entire scene absolutely flabbergasted. From that moment on, Arthur not only hated him more than anybody in the world; he simply didn't recognize Camille's existence any longer.

Next day, the boss munching on a lump of Black Forest ham was so upset upon seeing Lavaliere slicing French bread in the kitchen. Arthur watched my co-worker with an air that had become quite threatening. Abruptly, as the last straw the boss growled out menacingly. And suddenly Arthur hurled an open plastic jar of mustard in Camille Lavalière's direction. At that very instant my friend put himself in a posture of defense. He bent down rapidly, docked as the container of mustard flew past his ear, struck and splashed at the wall. If the chef didn't hold Arthur's arm he would have hit Camille on the chin forcefully. In a loud voice, with his mouth still half-full with his ham sandwich my employer shook a fist under Camille's nose and conveyed:

"DAMN YOU. IF I HAD A GUN I'LL SHOOT YOU RIGHT NOW. I CAN'T BEAR THE SIGHT OF YOU. WHY DON'T YOU GET THE HELL OUT OF MY RESTAURANT?"

Because of fear of reprisal the boss never fired Camille. Still he continued to make his life miserable as he hated my friend more and more each day. Following the event with the jar of mustard every day whenever Arthur met Camille he would declare while tossing his head angrily: "Why are you still here stupid?" However soon enough, Camille experienced the last gasp of nervous and physical exhaustion.

In as short a time as a week this colleague, this friend of mine feeling lifeless and empty, with intense unhappiness simply quit his job at *Le Cerisier*. For so much harassment he left in the same path as Robert Leansing, the former gay priest. This was bound to happen sooner or later. As I looked at Camille straight in the eyes there was that ultimate question I was dying to ask him:

"Why in the world didn't you retaliate after Arthur threw that jar of mustard at you? As a veteran French Foreign Legion combatant you could have struck him with one blow in his fat belly and he would be lying straight on the kitchen floor!" Anchored in pride here was Lavalière wise answer:

"Pierre we live in the United States of America not in the desert somewhere around Siddi-Bel-Abbès. In this country assault and battery are punishable by law. This can contribute to incarceration, even deportation," and he continued: "I'm not going to lose my permanent residency visa over a prick like Arthur!"

Before leaving, Camille had appended a personal note for Arthur on the private room's table. He did it in such a wonderful handwriting: *"The one that smell like a pig, even if he takes a shower would still smell like a pig because it's in his blood. Pardon me your highness and lordship count Arthur Valois Dourville de Mon Cul (of my buttocks), I won't be eating your fucking pastries any longer; just shove them up your ass!"*

After reading the memo, Arthur's gush of haughtiness instantly evaporated. Watching his trembling hands and looking very agitated, I realized that Camille had upset Arthur more than the boss had upset him. For some time after that dreadful event no one working at *Le Cerisier* had heart for anything.

It may be reasonably concluded that by listening to our private conversations, and not being able to talk freely without being spied on, the owner of that high-class restaurant had created an infringement on our human rights. Arthur's behavior had been so rude and absolutely inexcusable. He had wickedly abused his position as a business employer.

In his book- *Disclosing Man to Himself,* Sidney M. Jourard, Ph.D. and a professor of psychology at the University of Florida has this to affirm in regard to free intentional subject: *"Over the years theorists have conceptualized man as a machine; as an organism comparable to rats, pigeons, and monkeys; as a communication system; as a hydraulic system; as a servo-mechanism; as a computer- in short, he has been viewed by psychologists as an analogue of everything but what he is: a person. Man is indeed like all those things, but first of all he is a free, intentional subject."*

My closest and dearest friend Camille who had been on the verge of a nervous breakdown did not fade away from my memory. I often thought of him; that glow of friendship between us was like a powerful fire…

Coincidentally, several weeks later I met Camille Lavalière at Marquesas Way in Marina Del Rey. Since he wasn't expecting anyone to turn up to come and see him it was like some kind of a miracle that we came across each other once more. With a chill wind blowing seaward so many sounds of the port seemed to be setting out with the waves toward the sparkling ocean. Camille, regaining his usual good spirits which had deserted him during the last few days at the restaurant and the enchantment of being here at the marina brought infinite peace to his soul.

After that terrible encounter with Arthur that took its toll on his strength, Camille's smile was so pure. There was such a brightening of his face; so much confidence too with that great zealous throbed of existence. His head was held high and he had a happy gait. It was like sunlight following heavy clouds. My friend sat on a small chair, his legs dangling over the side of the sailboat as a lone dog was eating garbage nearby. He had recovered the equilibrium which for awhile had been set rocking by Arthur. It was now over and done with. Even after he had been treated so badly by the owner of *Le Cerisier* he still believed as Rousseau did 'in the natural goodness of Man.' Along with a sense of exuberance Lavalière cheerfulness was unimpaired as he was aglow with enthusiasm. He was so glad to meet me again. I had the feeling that there was no one else in the world he so much wanted to see.

He was wearing a mock turtleneck, baggy pants that were fluttering about him on the high wind. On his wrist I noticed something like a giant watch, some navigator's chronograph. He kept busy fixing one of his socks, a *Gauloises* cigarette on the corner of his mouth. Right after pocking the thread at the eye of the needle he told me that he was almost ready, creaking of the cordage and the bellying of the sails for a solo earth circumnavigation starting from the docks of the marina. His first great objectives: Bora-Bora and New Caledonia. He already knew that even after a long stretch of time, when he would reach an island there would be empty, unknown sea around with the great vault of sky sprinkled with stars. The only sounds he will hear while basking in the sun, would be the flogging of sails in the wind from his Ericson 27'sloop 1974 model. During heavy storms unable to sleep, he would be counting sheep. Camille would sail the tidal creeks and estuaries. Out to the vast ocean he would be gone for days, weeks, even months with sunrise and sunset sky aflame with red and golden fire, surviving storms, bitter cold nights and also winds from the north. There would be wild, living creatures from the deep, frightening things jumping out of the water, even whales that could accidentally overthrow the vessel.

His boat, baptized *Melody* his first love was lingering there. It just lay like a swan awakening, waiting for the current to take him to sea. I realized that Lavalière had still a young mind encumbered with plans, with so many projects.

As I mentioned to him about the funny comment on paper he had left on the private room's table, he replied: "Yes,

I could not let another day pass by without yielding to the temptation to express myself toward that vicious man. I really did want to get it all off my chest!"

Camille had earned the prerogative of eccentricity through a childhood of submissiveness. Living in a world that his own imagination had created, he had discovered his true nature and the abundance of energy. Now this enthusiastic dreamer, this bold challenger of destiny who had no more than one year of seamanship/sailing school and safety navigator course was ready for the greatest adventure of all: set on beating the sea to thunderous gloom. Camille Lavalière was one of those rare men that took great pleasure in his thoughts. For that reason alone solitude didn't weary him. I already knew that he preferred life in the wilderness to a persecuted existence in the extravagant city. Not knowing the outcome of that enormous saga, he finally bought the boat anchored next to a large two-mast schooner at a very reasonable price after having rented it for the last four years.

And now 'the admiral', after getting familiar with the nautical charts was willing and ready to go, living in solitary contemplation on all the oceans of the planet. I stood there talking endlessly with my friend until his face was lit up by the flush of departing day. The last moments slipped by, irretrievable. Inside the boat there was a note on the panel signed Allan Cunningham:

A wet sheet and a flowing sea,
A wind that follows fast,
And fills the white and rusting sail,
And bends the gallant mast.

For sure he would get his way because his mind was set on it and I was amazed too by noticing such strength of will from his part. Dropping a hand on my shoulder he intimated:

"Pierre, I'm still strong; I'm still healthy and I have a whole future before me, full of sunshine. Yet can I remain that way in ten or even twenty years from now? I'm confident that this is the right time: I'm going to do it."

With a touch of sadness he articulated: "You'll probably never see me again but I won't forget you." Surprisingly he added that he was able to dine on a lump of bread as for now on his greatest appetite was for exploration. For the next few days my friend would be busy outfitting for that long sea-voyage that included a strong hammock. He would await the opportunity to leave as soon the ocean calmed down with the harmonious song of the salt water echoing over the whirled drift. As I wished him good luck, he added with a feeble smile and some bitterness he couldn't conceal:

"There will be no woman on board! That's the most difficult task, nevertheless I can handle it!" and, on a sophistical note, he went on: *"Partir, c'est mourir un peu,* but as long I'm happy I'm not afraid of ending my life a pauper." Surprisingly with still a shaken voice he concluded:

"As for you Pierre, let me tell you one thing: you have been everywhere, seen everything, done everything. Now for so many years you worked for that jerk of a boss and you continue to work for the same jerk, that son of a pig at the same fucking restaurant. The little man doesn't give a damn about you; you know that? You're my friend and as a friend I want you out of trouble. You have to turn your back on that scoundrel and have nothing to do with him. You can easily look for a job at another restaurant that could make better use of your skills. I know you can handle anything. But, on the other hand you must have saved some money. So please do me a favor: get your backpack again and go somewhere, anywhere, to Timbuktu or Rio, I don't care. Just do it: work can wait!"

Lavalière had literally infected me with his ever great aficionado. I was unable to offer a thing to him but my love and prayers for the long journey ahead far on the lonely rugged ocean. After we again memorized each other's face, as a gray northeast wind was blowing, flicking the navigation lights he departed over a good tide...

Nothing was ever heard of him anymore. Our last encounter marked the death of such a warm, honest relationship. I had enjoyed our meeting greatly and it hurt me to see him go. He had been such an agreeable companion. His last words were deeply imprinted in my mind, forever. As I looked at him for the last time, I asked myself the question: how often can I meet such a man and how sad it is that I had to leave him behind with our pleasant memories? Whether somewhere on the ocean or in heaven, his spirit is with God.

Chapter 30

THE CLOUDS HANG low. With the howling wind we were under the frown of a blustering night. This evening at the restaurant it would be very quiet, not only for the inclement weather but because this day marked the beginning of Yom Kippur. Many of *Le Cerisier's* loyal patrons who have become like family members to us were of the Jewish faith.

On one occasion there was a pounding on the front door and soon, the pounding grew more persistent. Surprisingly, a bespectacled, absent-minded looking rabbi wearing a black sable-rim hat, in a suit that seemed to be too small for him, stood at the door of *Le Cerisier*. With a round face like a pumpkin, a protruding Adam's apple and sharp eyes he had a stand out under-jaw. Leaning against the wall, he was peering inside as if looking for someone thinking he was about to enter the synagogue. Stepping forward he asked to be let in.

Realizing his mistake, he first squinted at me suspiciously. However, I probably must have appeared like one of his people for he inquisitively continued to stare at me intensely. And in a sudden flash he greeted me as if I had been an old friend. He first inquired if I was a Jew. I answered him respectfully, saying my name is Pierre Choucart born in Belgium from a Christian family. He did not wait to hear the tail of my sentence. Instead the well-meaning religious man started to extend his blessings along with the *Hamesh Hand* that represented the hand of God for protection against evil. *God knows I needed that exorcism badly.* The friendly rabbi reminded me also not to forget *The Youth Aliyah,* the children of Israel as he quoted to me the scripture in Job 1:21: "Naked I came into this world and naked I shall leave it." I wanted to say 'Amen', but instead I responded rather cheerfully on impulse: "I don't mind dying. I just don't want to be there when it happens." Woody Allen could not have said it any better! As he was about to leave, the rabbi became curious about Arthur as he uttered:

"I have heard that your employer is a good Jew, and you know: there are no better people than the Jews. I sincerely hope one day he would join the Rabbinical Society?"

Yeah! Readers, let me explain here how good a Jew Arthur was. In order to please our Jewish clientele, my employer having such a good flair for business would stretch his short neck like a happy turtle to show his audience with a brilliant gold Star of David hanging on a gold chain and resting over his unbuttoned shirt. As he was imitating a Jewish comedian, he would proudly finger that gold star and gold chain.

Arthur's lawyer, of honorable status in his field was Jacob A. Tannenbaum. He had long white side-whiskers and hunched with lumbago. With that warm Jewish-looking face, Mr. Tannenbaum was a well-known aggressive, skilled and tough attorney from the secluded Bel Air district. He was the man to whom Arthur turned for counsel as a legal adviser. In order to please the lawyer as well as our other Jewish patrons, the owner of the restaurant would talk about *Pesach, matzoth* and emphasize on the merits of Israel's Six Day War. Day after day, the little man would pride himself for the support of Israel and for the understanding of Judaism in general:

"I ALMOST JOINED ISRAEL'S AIR FORCE AS A FIGHTER PILOT," he persuasively concluded.

THE TORMENTOR

On that same Yom Kippur evening, as the moon broke through a cloud, Arthur drove his Nissan pick-up truck for a fill-up at the AM-PM gas station on the street-corner. First, he would quietly take off his Star of David medallion from around his neck and hide it in his jacket's pocket as another figure loomed out of the shadows. His good friend the Hadgi Akbar Ahmed Mahfouz was on duty. With his face turned to Mecca, he just finished his prayer, prior to the ablutions by reciting the Moslemah's day of toil. Arthur approached him quietly and said:

"Salaam Alaikum my friend Ahmed; Allah Kerim-God is merciful" And no sooner had he met Akbar, my employer *ipso facto,* just like 'instant coffee' became not only an instant Palestinian sympathizer but also in using Bob Woodward's sentence in *The Secret Man:* "...a partner in mud slinging against the state of Israel", praising the greatness of Islam and looking out for the Koran's doctrine. The Hadgi would talk about Mohammed, the prophet of Allah driven forth from the holy city of Mecca before finding refuge at Medina. After they both drink a glass of green tea, Akbar requested to be left alone to recollect his sins and reconcile himself with God. This act of devotion from the Hadji burst purely from the natural feelings of his deep religious duty.

* * * *

Because of personnel shortage, Melanie came to join the working force. It was raining hard and she was wet and pallid with her hair all sodden with the first shower of the evening. I, along with Eddy Roy Freedman we were three in the dining room. By this time, because of dark clouds the day was beginning to wane. Again, this was just a plain, nasty inclement weather. The noise of a thunder resounded as the blazing lightning flashed incessantly and it even penetrated through the walls of the building. From the same dark clouds the rain poured again, this time heavily down the narrow windows. All of a sudden the storm increased in violence. Raindrops were pattering on the roof. The leaves from the tree in front of the establishment were wet and sodden. The rain scudded by in forlorn as the wind kept on lashing and lashing nonstop against the façade of *Le Cerisier*. With a sound of far-away rumbling, the sky gorging with water burst over Ventura Boulevard and upon the entire city. The shower of rain was raked by flurries of hail. Before long it poured in buckets as the wind at this point draw near hurricane velocity. On some areas of the large boulevard, the water was up and still rising. There was debris, floating branches, even logs to be seen around. The radio announced that the streets of North Hollywood where I live were also under water.

Miss Valois Dourville de Montrissart didn't really feel like working. Earlier she had had a fight with her father who had requested her to be at the restaurant that night. It was Friday. Arthur didn't want to take any chance in case the business would pick-up.

Around seven o'clock the place was still empty. The prognostics of a bad evening were real. As we listened to the drumming of the rain on the roof that became deeper and faster, outside I heard a noise and rushed to open the door. At the same moment I asked myself the question trying to find out why would anybody want to be out in that kind of weather? Especially in Los Angeles no one would walk in the streets on those kinds of days. There was just a breath of chill air coming in from the boulevard.

First, I looked avidly at the trees and the gray sky until I discovered a cocker spaniel all shivering that was using our plants as a *pissotière*. Lifting his leg in the air, he joyously began to pee. With his nose pointing heavenward he started a long, gloomy howl. Afterward, the poor dog with his body cowering down came slowly towards me, wagging his tail. He sat and moved his front paw as to shake hands. With his tongue hanging, he commenced yapping. As I explained that event to my colleagues, they had a good laugh. It exploded all the way to the kitchen. Abruptly Chef Francis Bevert asked me if the four-legged customer wanted his filet mignon steak 'well done?'

When darkness had set in a bright flash broke in the air. The noise of the thunder resounded and a deluge of rain fell even more heavily. As the night droned on, the three of us sat in the private room.

Sometimes ago, Melanie's friend in Brentwood handed her a book on palmistry. Melanie studied it carefully prior to forecasting our future. Suddenly Eddy and I were obliged to make impressions of our hands on a sheet of smoked paper while Melanie considered the results. I recalled that a line down near my wrist was revealing, according to Arthur's daughter an unbridled and passionate nature. But there was a particular and strange circle on Eddy's hand, meaning (according to Melanie): death by drowning! From palmistry we went into an occult séance since Freedman had enough of that nonsense of 'drowning business.

On the other hand Eddy who still believed that our spirits leave our bodies when we die started screaming. He just felt a ghost was scratching his leg...! At that juncture, in a twinkling of an eye Melanie grabbed a piece of paper and pen, and proposed to play a little game of imitating signatures. I already knew about her skill at forging signatures. She occasionally would counterfeit her father's signature to sign our payroll checks whenever Arthur would be out of town. After she got accustomed to the flourish of my signature, with her feline curiosity she became more and more talkative, even more sociable. She took another piece of blank paper, requiring me one more time to convey my signature on it. Therefore she folded the piece of paper at once, placed it in her jacket pocket. She went to the bathroom before heading home.

Eddy, who had witnessed the scene, became alarmed. He cautioned me later in a whisper that Melanie was smarter than her father; that I should not be a gullible victim of her malicious pranks. He added that she had nourished some poisonous snake in her bosom; that Arthur had also planted the seed of corruption in her. Suddenly, a kind of nagging, unfamiliar mistrust came up in my mind. I really started worrying. Arthur's daughter had become a little devil; a real female Mephistopheles. It was not long before I discovered that my suspicions were well founded.

Next day, Melanie was in the kitchen for a last touch on her cheesecakes. With a lump in my throat I spontaneously inquired what she was really going to do with that piece of paper carrying my signature on it. She had a guilty look, as though she'd been doing something wrong. Staring at me in a way she had never done before, she acted more like an observer at a cattle show. Freeing herself of any feelings, her face lighted up. In a glow, with a shrewish hard uncompromising glance in her eyes, revealing the red and ivory of her mouth she expostulated in defiant triumph:

"Above your signature I wrote that in case of your death, all your financial assets including your apartment in North-Hollywood would belong to me!" She was a best actress than I would have guessed. Now I sense a real reason to fear her. *How was it possible that such a corrupted idea had entered Melanie's brain? But, in a way it was also my fault when I didn't recognize the danger-signal. My heart was chilled by such ungrateful consideration. I was taken by a pang of bitterness at the thought that she could even contemplate a dishonorable thing like this.*

Reflecting about my own family I could not but be aware of certain uneasiness. I began suffering unimaginable anguish. Now I realized how selfish and vicious woman she had become. Melanie's code of morals was more than objectionable. Suddenly, a disquieted feeling deepened in my mind. That vulgar baggage degraded herself to an uncivilized savage. I felt wretchedly ashamed for her. As I related to Eddy that latest statement from Miss Valois Dourville de Montrissart he whispered:

"Pierre, I mentioned to you to be on your guard; this was not an ordinary joke. There is something up her sleeve, more like a diabolical plot," and he added, "That arrogant, dishonest woman already informed her father about you signing that piece of paper and he is very thrilled." Eddy, like an agent of authority with an eye that never sleeps, further continued, "That woman would make you die like 'the death of a dog!'"

* * * *

Tonight at closing time when the last customer had left the restaurant, Melanie, with two girlfriends of hers remained in the private room. They were getting intimate in their little chat. Standing on the other side of the partition I caught a snatch of the conversation that created in me a great deal of concern. Those 'charming ladies' were planning to take down my pants.

Unrelengtingly, as quiet as a mouse after removing my apron I walked to the front door, locked it and headed home. Being totally distrustful of Melanie' schemes I never really expressed any remorse for having refrained to participate in that sort of *divertissement!*

Looking at it from all angles I could think of I had a pretty shrewd idea Melanie was up to something illegal even criminal. I was appalled at the thought of what would happen next. I have been used as a favorite subject for her offensive jokes about physical appearance, calling me a senile limping goat, an escaped lunatic or a stupid bald eagle and worthless blockhead, ready for the old folk's home. She was constantly bursting out into the most opprobrious epithets and threads. She would experience such a great pleasure in tapping, in pounding at the top of my head like a drummer-artist would do on his tambourine. *I guess that the poor woman has not glanced into a mirror lately. Or does she even recognize the person looking back at her: avoirdupois, round and pudgy, fat as lard; 'a pudding-ass woman' with bloated fingers, short legs and swollen cheecks, just as if someone had inflated them. Melanie had lost all her good looks. Like a watermelon, she appeared like a barrel of a female tardy and waddling. Her gluttony had driven her to obesity. Now her breasts were hanging down to her belly. Although her dress was smart, it made her appear portly. Because she was so plum, it seemed that she was bursting through her thighs. However, thanks to her mom, she still had those magnificent eyes that brightened a red-apple face enhanced by a charming narrow mouth. But no thanks to her dad, she's born with a voracious appetite!* Melanie always gnawed at the meat, consuming huge quantities of all sort of things, 'eating a horse' for breakfast like an overfed beast that made the beauty of her womanhood swiftly depart. Instead of being cheerful and lively, Melanie looked like a middle-aged woman and occasionally she suffered from duodenal diarrhea…

* * * *

Many of our friends, even colleagues think of Eddy Freedman as a snob because of his stoic facial expression. Still, I can attest that behind his countenance Freedman was a good hearted, quiet, pleasant man. He was a kindly mannered gentleman knowing many useful trades. Aside from being the unofficial architect of *Le Cerisier* restaurant his exploits were quite impressive in scope. The unruffled sound of Eddy's voice complemented a calm demeanor which reminded me of Tibetan monks whom I met at the Potala. I have not doubted his loyalty and sincerity to me.

On the other hand, Melanie's hatred for Eddy started at a very early age, as earlier as when she was yet a thumb sucking. (Eddy was already around when Arthur's daughter was born.)

Her hatred escalated when he reprimanded her when she was barely seven years old. Until that age, because of so much curly hair, people would compare her to Shirley Temple: no little girl could be sweeter.

At length, Melanie became a skillful accordion player. An Italian musician had instructed her how to play well, while tickling the ivories like a virtuoso. Soon she became so perfect a connoisseur in her musical art. Each time she played, she surpassed herself; she would tremble with an almost unendurable emotion. At the age of ten, Melanie already impressed her parents with her dance steps along with her great dexterity on the accordion. On weekends she would get invited to play at private parties. She had played in San Francisco, Lake Tahoe and San Diego, even in Sacramento for the governor's inauguration.

On one occasion Freedman the long time family friend accompanied Arthur to watch Melanie perform at a Beverly-Hills lawyer's residence. Eddy never really cared for music. However he had a good ear. Contrariwise, from languishing *chansons d'amour* to Philip Soussa to patriotic songs such as *La Marseillaise*, Melanie's deeply rooted passion for music was as great as fine champagne is. In addition, she played waltz, ball musette and polka.

Being an ex-cop, Eddy has not gotten rid of the habit of carrying a little notebook and a pen in his jacket's pocket. On that day, he was ready to check if Arthur's daughter didn't forget any parts anywhere during the performance. While Melanie was playing a difficult rhapsody with a melody that rose to a storm of notes, Eddy started to jot down his comments that occasionally 'the artist' was slightly out of jingle and that some notes were missing. After the mini-concert that was really exquisite, Freedman pointed out to Melanie the areas in her repertoire that had to be corrected.

I had any doubt that that well-meaning man really tried to help her to enliven her musical expertise even more. But Melanie felt criticized and completely betrayed. Suddenly she considered herself as being a spoiled untalented brat; that her burning ambition to be nationally recognized was smoldered.

With her nerves stringing up to the uttermost limit, a tumult had concocted in her mind. Abruptly, in no time, with a broken heart she locked her accordion in a *valise* for good. This was the virtual ending of her artistic career, of her hopes. She won't be running her fingers over the ivory keys anymore. In no time the accordion became like her: out of tune. Suddenly she showed complete indifference to everything outside the boundaries of her narrow world. Even as a kid, Melanie didn't take quite kindly to criticism, as she became instantly traumatized. She thought that Eddy had lambasted her performance. From that day on, there was an even greater divide between them. She never forgave Freedman and always spoke so severely about him.

Not once had she liked Eddy, but now she hated him more and more, looking for some sort of sweet revenge. She had developed a real craving for revenge. Melanie continued to hate Eddy with all her heart and mind to the pit of her stomach as if he had destroyed her artistic career.

Throughout the seasons, they continued fighting tooth and nail. She could not look at him in the eyes and kept on poisoning his life. Relations to one another grew more and more aggressive. As her disgust with Freedman deepened she would refer to him as *l'imbécile*. For a long time they didn't even speak to one another. The dark corner of her heart was silent; as silent as her accordion resting in that suitcase at her parents' house.

* * * *

In the stillness of the morning, the light of the setting moon, clear and cold was still lingering in the western sky. Ultimately I went jogging within La Tuna's canyon mountain domes clothed with forests. On account of the weather I had to wear my gloves, my funny hat on with its earlaps down.

At this early hour Los Angeles took to herself an air of innocence and cheerfulness. That great city was just awakening and I felt like a bee scenting a flower. As the birds were in full chorus, the dew in the grass was still heavy. The Los Angeles River was creeping through broad meadows adorned with scattered oaks where one can hear the tapping of a woodpecker. The woods had a bracing fragrance as the creaking of crickets resounded along with the finches flitting from tree to tree. Such a uniform tranquility surrounded me: this was my best antidote. Alongside the river I could hear a cawing of a flock of crows. A solitary crane was standing there, motionless like a giraffe. Without any smog in the lower atmosphere, the air was pure, brisk, bracing and gratifying. I enjoyed sniffing out the scents of faint breeze. It was a pleasant run, quite like the beat of a metronome. Not too far as the day was brightening imperceptibly, I heard the gentle murmur of a rivulet that escaped from a spring. I drank a little bit of cold water as I inched my way up the ravine.

Aside from the good California weather, with my physical work so many new thoughts came into my head. One of them went to Henry David Thoreau as he suggested: *"Take long walks in stormy weather or through deep snow in the fields and woods, if you would keep your spirits up. Deal with brute nature. Be cold and hungry and weary."* The trail took me past the white stone houses with red tile roofs tucked adjacent to walls of limestone. However, later as I watched the sun flickering under the trees, I still ruminated about that signature I lay down so innocently on that blank piece of paper that Melanie carried home.

Back at my apartment I accumulated a good supply of knowledge. I called a law firm and inquired about a 'living trust' for the better provision of my children. Quite concerned, I kept wondering what other practical jokes Miss Valois Dourville de Montrissart was hiding in her bag of tricks. *What kind of a wild spirit possessed her brain? It is no mistake that Melanie had inherited her father's predisposition for plotting and scheming. I believed she was capable of the most diabolical, noxious harms.*

Chapter 31

A T FOUR O'CLOCK this morning, Marie-Thérèse, Arthur's mother breathed her last. She was over ninety-five years old, dying peacefully with a smile on her face. That kind-hearted, agreeable woman was well prepared to drop the curtain over such a long, prosperous life. She was a pure, saintly woman with no void in her heart and no wrinkle on her forehead; just an extraordinary lady. She had been *le pilier d'acier*- the iron column of a very large, wealthy family that had spread all over Europe. In France, there were relatives of her in Toulouse, Paris, also in the lush fields of Strasbourg.

Before she died, in her mind, Melanie's grandmother already communicated with her late cousin. Arthur heard her murmuring with a lightening sense of relief: "Tonton Bernard, I am coming to join you shortly; please tell dad and mother that next week I will be there to partake on the spiritual feast…" This was a beautiful death; the death of a queen.

I can still recall when, along with my little brother Willy, we took *le train à grande vitesse*-TGV, the counterpart of the Japanese bullet-train to go and visit Marie-Thérèse in her own town of Labège par Castanet, near Toulouse in the south of France. From there, on a clear day you can admire the entire Pyrènées mountain chain. Labège par Castanet possessed the appurtenances of a thriving, prosperous region.

411

Upon our arrival, a perfumed breeze was blowing from the verdant hillside where a stream of water was trickling. We had an immediate vision of the entire area that appeared quite cozy with numerous small farm-houses. However, Granny's residence was the only one standing high, surrounded by a brick wall. The gorgeous home was decorated with geraniums and passion-flowers on the balcony. A frightened dog rushed to the back of the house.

We behold Granny, sitting in a *chaise longue* crocheting wool. She was wearing a green calico flower dress that was fluttering in the wind with slippers adorned with dark-green pompoms. Hanged loosely around her neck, one can notice an Algerian scarf.

Despite the simplicity of her dress, she was still a lady of elegance with much pride in her appearance, in her attire. Her white hair was pulled together with a braid, as she was always prepared for the powerful Mistral weather that can blow everything away in no time. Other seniors around sat on porches, rocking, enjoying the warmth of the day. Furthermore, Granny was a wealthy land-owner. She got respect from everyone.

Along with my brother, after a warm hug from Marie-Thérèse, as her scarf slipped over her shoulders, we moved inside the luxurious house. She did not stop greeting us very cordially, inquiring about our health, about our moral well-being. Realizing that we were very thirsty, Granny brought us a six-pack of beer from the refrigerator. She decided to get a glass of lemonade for herself. Soon we continued conversing in French, our mother's language. She nonetheless spoke pure French with that singing touch from *les gens du Midi*- the people from the South. She had a very refined, vivid way of talking. But I had a strong feeling that she lived a little cut off from the world, alone, so far from Arthur and Melanie, her only loving son and loving granddaughter.

Abruptly, I mentioned about Arthur's apparent achievement with his two restaurants in operation in the U.S., adding that he had maneuvered his way successfully. Gracefully flapping a Chinese fan, she revealed that years ago however her son still had missed the greatest opportunity of his life.

Her story goes that at one time she knew a widowed *châtelaine*- a castle owner near Orleans. The lady-friend felt herself so lonely in that nineteen bedrooms residence that she was willing to sell it to Marie-Thérèse for a price below the cost of a small Beverly Hills home. Granny's idea was to go along with the deal and give the castle to Arthur to innovate it into a giant country-style 'bed and breakfast' inn. As she kept on talking a little loudly, because of the sound of a train rumbling over the viaduct that spanned the precipice of the river, her excitement waxed hotter and hotter in our ears. When the last shriek of wheel against the rail had died, Marie-Thérèse suddenly became sad as she pursued the conversation in a lower tone of voice: "Arthur won't listen! He wanted to go to America. From my viewpoint, America had seemed so remote. It might just as well be the Moon. After he had discovered the movie *Giant* on that large screen, depicting Rock Hudson and James Dean (the instant oil billionaire), this was in my son's blood. He started growing distressed for money," and she went on: "America, America, America, that's all I heard all day long! He even started to dress *à l'Amèricaine!* While watching other U.S. movies, Arthur had grown to admire success, instant success, more than anything else. He wanted so much to become *un nouveau riche* as he was lacking confidence with me, his own mother. Never in Arthur's mind was there any doubt that in America there would be gold by the shovelful to be found in the streets or dollar bills hanging on trees." Bluntly, she repeated: "*Il a manqué une grande opportunité!*-He missed such a great opportunity! Here I was offering my son something concrete: the contingency of a lifetime to build a fabulous wealth in his own country." Furthermore, she informed us by telling that someone else bought the castle. It was an English couple. The castle was transformed almost overnight into a first class hotel-restaurant, later listed in *Le Guide Michelin*. Tables and chairs were added to the patio. They were covered by red and blue umbrellas, facing a one hundred cars parking lot. Soon, many clients showed up. Beside the patio, the inside dining room was equally full. In order to reserve a room for a romantic weekend there was an outstretched waiting list.

While drinking another beer adorned with *Pont l'Evêque* cheese and *petits pains*, Granny told us that lately, for Arthur it wasn't too rosy in California. At one time, the business at *Le Cerisier* was booming, but now it was extremely quiet, as I was well aware of. For a last thought, she then concluded, "As for *La Bagatelle* up in Solvang, it is a *catastrophe*. It's almost uncanny; no customers. It looked like an abandoned first class restaurant. The general distress among employees had grown to unprecedented dimensions; so bad that my son was unable to take care of the employee's payroll. I had to send him a check for the value of twenty-five thousand dollars to assist him as he was growing dreadfully in debt."

Together we went outside in the garden to gasp a last watch at those impressive mountains, a natural border between France and Spain crowned with the principality of Andorra perched on a high plateau. We spent the night in Marie-Thérèse's residence.

In the morning, she walked with us to the bus stop, on our way to Toulouse where we would board the TGV to the Belgian capital via Paris, the City of Lights.

As a tribute to her memory, this was far to have been a marvel of a funeral pomp. It was quite the opposite. Arthur told me that he found a company: *The Nema Society* that specialized in a complete and very cheap cremation. The entire package deal was a little less than four hundred dollars: a real pauper's funeral!

With a tranquil mind, that mere shadow of a man added:

"Pierre, including the flowers and the musical arrangement, this was the best deal in town!" For his closest relative there were no tears shed, no red eyes, no head curved in sorrow as compared to Pompadour, the little dog's demise. Arthur had been much more emotionally involved in mourning the passing of his four-legged friend. It was so disgraceful, so unbecoming. We are talking here about Arthur's mother, his own blood and flesh. Granny was such a warm, goodhearted lady. With native finesse and instinct of elegance she was willing at one time to give her son a castle for free, plus taking care of his financial overseas problems, and buying a house and a new automobile for her granddaughter Melanie. All of a sudden I felt a gathering anguish of pain in the stomach for Arthur's attitude toward his own mother. For a moment I thought I was in a quicksand, ready to disappear from the sight of the owner of that restaurant.

Melanie however was deeply affected; tears were running down her cheeks. Marie-Thérèse was much more than a grandmother for her; she had also been her travelling companion for those luxury cruises, and best friend in life.

* * * *

Aside from the variance of decorations, New Year Eve was *a fortiori*, a replica of Bastille Day event. Again, customers and employees enjoyed frantic dances until the early morning hours. At the stroke of midnight, with the Champagne crackling in the flutes, the restaurant became the center of cacophony. Streamers, firecrackers and colorful hats were flying around...

Six weeks slipped by and we celebrated Saint-Valentine, the lover's attraction and passion-feeling day. Pink hearts, cupid angels and pink balloons were to be on display everywhere in the dining room.

Mr. Joseph Berlowsky, one of Arthur best friend, was the owner of a giant flower shop in downtown Los Angeles. In exchange for a complimentary dinner for him, his wife and son, Mr. Berlowsky brought us along sixty long-stemmed red roses that would be presented to each one of the lady customers. Those expensive flowers, the very best and most gorgeous ones from Joseph's store were delivered at *Le Cerisier* at the precise time that I did the opening for *la mise en place*. At about the same moment, Arthur called me on the kitchen phone, telling me to lay down the roses in the refrigerator after having covered the long stems with several layers of wet paper-towel. And he expostulated:

"Pierre, be very careful; hold them one by one, they are exclusive." Truly, they were absolutely unique. These gorgeous roses elevated on their long stem like flamingo's neck were a delight to the eyes.

As ill-luck would have it, on that cold afternoon, with that particular chill in the air, I did something monstrous, really abominable; the summit of imbecility: the flowers didn't fit in the refrigerator and I decided to cut the long stems in half. With the wet paper wrapped around the remaining graceful stem roses, I lay them down in the same refrigerator on top of a covered container of peeled potato, being unaware that YOU NEVER, NEVER CUT STEMS FROM LONG STEM ROSES!

Later, Melanie arrived at the restaurant. But my attention was ultimately diverted to her. I didn't see her for several weeks. On Fridays and Saturdays, a busboy was helping us in the dining room.

In that late afternoon, as the sun was low but still shining Mademoiselle Valois Dourville de Montrissart revealed to me that she went to Jenny Craig Agency for a weight-watching course that included a tuff regimen of two small bowl of soup a day containing all sorts of vitamins and minerals. Aside from Jenny Craig's wise prescription she also ate one anemic biscuit a day that she dipped in syrup of figs. Along from that strict diet, she rigorously fasted one day a week. The result was absolutely astonishing and her complexion had greatly improved. In her tight-fitting flowery dress, she no longer had a fat bosom. Prior to her meeting with Jenny Craig, she had tried in vain to reduce weight. She starved herself at home for days, only to gain back the vanished pounds within a few hours orgy of double cheeseburgers, fries, ice-cream and sweets she was sharing with some of her beach friends. I stood there flabbergasted. She was breathing heavily. It looked as if her departed elegance and confidence had returned to her with her gracefulness reinstated. Melanie's hair was curling with undulations, waving nicely over her shoulders as her faint *l'Air du Temps* perfume exhaled a penetrating fragrance. Never had she been more charming. With that sensuous look of just having been kissed intensely she probably thought of herself as a child again, as she looked as cute a little Shirley Temple as eyes ever gazed on. Silhouetted against the light, *en grande toilette* with that swing in her hips she laughed good-naturedly in a soft low laugh of content, as she uttered a shriek of joy:

417

"Look Pierrot, I just lost over forty pounds!" As she talked with stillness on her countenance the words came out like music and she appeared less reserved as she held out her hand. I had never seen her being so striking. As I mentioned earlier there was a time she was plump as a partridge with cheeks like big red apples. Now, humming to herself she was startling with *joie de vivre* as she eyed me with irrepressible rapture. That ultimate vision of coquetry which had lain dormant within her manifested itself again and she became lost in a narcissistic self-scrutiny.

Since fine feathers make fine birds she was also clothed as a woman of fashion dressed in the height of elegance with ears pierced, legs waxed and glittering fingernails. In my mind I could have seen her appear in a ballroom and win a first price in a dance contest…

However, it was Melanie who first discovered the evidence of the crime as she went to pick up the bouquet of flowers:

"Oh Jesus Christ, what have you done?" she said. At this point I was still ignorant as to my foolishness. I had been blind and dull-witted to not perceive at first *that you never, never in the world cut the stem of long-stemmed roses*. This particular pedicel has been created that way. With a slap in my face Melanie shouted: "Imbecile, did you realize that you have murdered those gorgeous flowers?"

Unexpectedly Arthur came and joined her daughter. But, as soon as he viewed his beautiful but half-cut stemmed roses he sat down on a booth, his face white as a sheet in a cadaverous pallor, his arms hunging loosely at his sides. He looked like an inert, frozen being, like a sleeper's worn-out soul with a tortured heart. Now the boss was opening and shutting his mouth like a drowsy parrot snapping at flies and

I noticed that the veins on his forehead were swelling. Melanie was holding her father's hand, saying:

"I think dad is about to have a heart attack!"

Surprisingly, Arthur did not storm a vulgar barrage of insults at me as I really thought he would do. He was silent, even abstracted. It was the first time the owner of the restaurant was absolutely speechless. I had the feeling that he had fallen into lethargy.

I hoped in that instant that he could have been able again to whiplash me or to slop a barrel of affronts over my head, for I deserved it. I could have suffered any harsh punishment. Needless to say I had conducted myself as a complete idiot and a most unskillful, maladroit employee. This had been a great appalling mistake. As the owner's face remained impassive I felt like I stood at the edge of a terrifying abyss, ready to jump. I wished I could have disappeared instantly underground to a subterranean passage leading to the desert, or any other faraway place, thus obliterated in my shame…

If Arthur kept quiet, it wasn't the same with Melanie. Like the relief of the guard she decided to take over on the business of pounding on me at every table. After presenting the roses to the ladies she would apologize in a mock sadness before pointing in my direction:

"Sorry, this *dummkopf* over there cut the long stems!" At that precise moment as I decided to approach Joseph Berlowsky's table, the blond curly mustached and pallid hair flower-shop proprietor looked at me with piercing eyes. He was a man of soldiery appearance with that stiff military bearing. Something both intense, even secretive showed up in his expression as my inexplicable behavior almost suffocated me. As the news of my blooper had quickly spread around, the corners of Joseph's mouth faintly twiddled and his fixed gaze glittered in fire. As he eloquently lifted his head, he announced:

"Pierre, I own one of the greatest and fine flower-shop in Los Angeles. I'm in close touch with the great throb of humanity. Flowers always convey something special; they convey love and beauty." and Berlowsky went on,

"By cutting the stems from those long stemmed roses, the very best from my store, you simply have disarranged and almost destroyed my gorgeous flowers. Look at your employer over there: he's pale as a corpse and dying from sadness!"

Arthur, still in a tranquil pervasive silence joined the Berlowsky family at their table to clutch a flute of Champagne. Unexpectedly with great strength, Joseph kept a strong hold of my arm. With an almost royal disdain like an authoritative military peacock, glimpsing simultaneously at the roses and the boss he made a simple yet persuasive suggestion:

"Arthur, you have been deeply persecuted. As for Pierre, the only recourse for that crime is death. Shall we now deservedly strike off his head from the scaffold; hang him on the beam or drown him in boiling water right away as he deserved to be or you want to wait?" In a small cloud of happiness and a faintly quizzical smile the boss knew how to reply. He proposed instead the sharp edge of the guillotine and… without any delay!

There wasn't any doubt in my mind that this may have been the night that I fumbled about in some kind of a thick mist. I must recognize that my foolish behavior had been utterly shocking; just plainly brainless-no other words! At that moment, I clearly remember Dr. John Hoover's wise comment: *"Success and stupidity don't mix. Your boss' stupidity is only half your problem. Your own stupidity can only complete the disaster."*

I really felt so sorry for Arthur. And on that terrible, most appalling day, I LIKED THE MAN.

At the restaurant as I was ready to write down an order a gentleman accompanied by his wife kept gazing at me intensively. On some kind of a machine on wheels, a tube was looped under his nose delivering oxygen to his lungs. On the other hand, I was certain I knew the man from somewhere. Suddenly, he decided to talk:

"Pierre, don't you recognize me?" It was a strong voice. Yet, there was something in the manner of saying my name that didn't make it sound unfamiliar. In a flash I recognized Abraham Strasberg, president of El Bolero in Tarzana.

Given that the name didn't indicate it, El Bolero was a wealthy Jewish private country club that included great men from the Jewish Defense League with access to a golf course and an Olympic-size swimming pool.

At the time I joined Arthur at *Le Cerisier* I was also working in that exclusive resort as 'extra' for banquets, sumptuous Jewish weddings and *bar mitzvah* that usually included a band of several musicians. Quite often I joined the guests in a happy Hava Nagila dance-song routine.

At first I inquired from Mr. Strasberg if Chef Alfred was still working at the club. With a flush of red to his cheeks he quipped:

"You are talking about Alfred von Schlabendurf, our little *SS Haupsturmführer* who openly proclaimed his love for Hitler? Oh yes, even that I'm retired he is still there *en chair et en os*."

On those special *bal masqué* when everyone in the resort would dress with fancy costumes, reminiscent of Marie-Antoinette's wild parties in Versailles, Alfred never miss the occasion to wear a panzer division commander uniform. And, with great pride he would execute the Hitler salute at every table as the clients bestowed him a friendly tap on the butt.

Those same clients would say: "*Bitte Shön Herr Haupsturmführer,* give us another salute and we want to hear those heels smack together!"

As extraordinary, even grotesque as it appeared *le chef de cuisine* and his direct assistants were all Nazi sympathizers working in that well-organized Jewish club. The blue eyed and blond haired Alfred had ironically a bizarre cherubic face. Being a culinary expert with a generous hand, he became not only a servant but also a satirical amusement to those extremely rich Jews: *la crème de la crème* spending their time at the swimming pool, golfing or gawking at the stock-market ticker in the club main's lobby next to the most impressed expresso machine. As long good was their food and wine no one minded about Alfred's views on National Socialism with the ones of his clique in the kitchen. For those wealthy Jews von Schlabendurf was just an enormous joke. In the dining room as well as in the kitchen, Alfred charmed and domineered. However no customer ever dared to set foot in the Nazis' secret temple; their *lagebaracke* as those same Nazis immersed themselves in the preparations for the evening dinner...

In the middle of my conversation with the club's president who cemented our friendship Arthur came along and I made the proper introduction. Earlier, I had told my employer everything about von Schlabendurf and his feelings harnessed like a workhorse with his visions for a new Neo-Nazi German Fatherland. At once the boss asked me to recollect an event that had transpired in von Schlabendurf's kitchen. Yet, Mr. Strasberg was well aware of what I would be talking about. With an encouraging smile he added: "Go ahead Pierre, tell us again about the entire story."

"Well, on April 20, 1976 a gathering of people appeared at El Bolero Country Club as the Grand Rabbi of Los Angeles was also present to request funds to help the state of Israel. Working as a dining room waiter I was well positioned to listen to the rabbi's talk. He was reminiscing of the Six-Day's War and the great sacrifices done by the military. Tears were shed as each Jewish member started writing checks which they placed in white envelopes.

At prayer time I retreated in the kitchen. Alfred, with his three *aide-de-camp* clustered around him was already busy opening a bottle of champagne. Several crystal flutes were aligned on his working table. As he started pouring *le Cordon Rouge*, he articulated:

"Pierre, you arrived just in time. Here is your glass." On this cold day that popped out in a delicate rash of leaves as I innocently (and stupidly) inquired if this was a toast for Israel's success, Alfred didn't understand. He kept staring at me with great astonishment, his jaw twitching:

"*Ach um Gotteswillen,* don't you know that today is Hitler's birthday?"

"Hitler's Birthday?"

"*Natürlich mein camaraden. Das verstecht sich von selbst!*"

Ascertaining the date and the hour I recalled from a TV documentary it was accurate, Adolph Hitler was born at half past six April 20, 1889 at Braunau am Inn, Austria.

With a shocking expression I simply lay down my full glass of Champagne, asked to be excused and went off like a firefighter-truck back to the dining room. In the distance I was able to hear the salute to the former German leader: *Sieg heil, sieg heil, sieg heil.*

Alfred von Schlabendurf never resented any hard feelings toward me for refusing to drink Champagne with him and his crew. He even showed me pictures of his pure bred German shepherd.

At the same time as I suggested to him to read The Rise and Fall of the Third Reich he simply replied: "Forget about the Third Reich. I am now seeking the Fourth Reich!'" Next, I mentioned a comment from Santayana: *The ones who do not remember the past are condemned to relive it!* Over my discourse, Schlabendurf clapped his hands together adding that his new leader knows better, that he is smarter than Hitler!

After this bizarre encounter with Chef Alfred Schlabendurf, I also recalled to him the wisdom of William L. Shiver who was so explicit when he told the world: *"In our age of terrifying lethal gadgets, which supplanted so swiftly the old one, the first aggressive war, if it should come, will be launched by suicidal little madmen pressing an electronic button. Such a war will not last long and none will ever follow it. There will be no conquerors and no conquests, but only the charred bones of the dead on an uninhabited planet."*

Chapter 32

THE DAY DRAGGED by heavy downpour. In the semi-darkness the beating of the rain became stronger by the hour and the trees wept. I promptly arrived at the restaurant. As the crackling noise of the tires was crunching the gravel, I brought the Buick to a stop in its designated parking space.

Wearing a checkered shirt, Arthur was standing in the enclosure of the door with bits of food stuck in his teeth. Eddy Freedman stood just behind him. At once I noticed that the boss was quite drunk. Eddy raised his arm and pointing two fingers at me. I knew the meaning: Arthur already drank two (heavy) bourbon and Coke. Not even realizing that his underwear was caught in the zipper of his pants my employer with frowned brows stared at me like a madman with such an ugly look that reminded me of a snake with bulbous eyes, hissing. With his chin jutted out that complex little man with the point of the middle finger on the bridge of his nose was screaming:

"What a shame to come to work with such a ruined beat-up car. Even a dirty pig won't feel at ease in that lemon. Whenever you got out of that vehicle you obviously smell like a hog!"

Unexpectedly in a volley of wild absurdities Arthur's voice dwindled to a croak. Through his teeth he added: "In the other four-star high-class French restaurants waiters are driving

Porches, Mercedes, Lexus, Jaguars and other ostentatious automobiles for crying outloud!" Barking like a dog, he gave out a sharp sound on the P, M, L, and J, as he was shaking his head like a bird preening itself after drinking. Even that my Buick was not new it was far to be a rickety old gadget and it was still running fine.

Furthermore with the rain still bestowing abundantly my employer ordered me to park my automobile somewhere else as he no longer want to have that 'junk' resting near the restaurant. In a torrent of words Arthur mentioned that if he sees that car again he will piss on it for nobody would give a nickel for that tumble-down antiquity. I gaped sadly into space and swiftly felt a chill creeping down my back. I mentioned to him that I didn't carry any umbrella to walk back several blocks to *Le Cerisier* in a non-stop rainfall that soon turned into a deluge. In perfect indifference, with the same nonchalance as Clark Gable in *Gone with the wind* he yelled through his teeth: "I don't give a damn about the weather, do as I told you! Just take that 'rubbish-thing' away from here!'"

I backed off from Arthur taking short steps toward the Buick before starting the engine. I drove away and found a parking-spot far on the boulevard.

I walked back through the soaking streets. It was cold, it was wet. Afterward, I begin running back toward the restaurant in the heavy rain. The thunder resounded. Soon a deluge of water fell upon the entire City of Angels. The sudden shower even bent the bough of the trees. The ground was rough; the alley nothing but a river of mud and from a nearby kennel I heard a dog barking. At that juncture I tripped over a large stone, flew in the air, before landing on my butt. Shaken to my very bones with hair disheveled I felt the rain blowing without intermission inside my collar. I drifted on my shoulders as the dirt from the grooves in the alley created a puddle of dirty water that made my shoes and socks muddy.

Back in the establishment not only rain but also mud dripped from my clothes, as my shoes were oozing water on the kitchen floor. After I wiped the rain from my face I hanged my damped coat on a hook. My employer, with demented hostility was totally unconcerned. Dysfunctional, with that strange hardness in his face he actually started to laugh, a very nasty laugh. And pointing at his watch he had the guts to say that I was late. *Without any doubt, one can fairly realize how much of a deep grudge that insolent little man carried against me, and how much he blighted my happiness. It was a sobering fact that with me in his most fragrant abuses he conducted himself like a prosecutor, a judge and a jury as well.*

With his constant drunkenness, Arthur looked like a carcinogenic malignancy. I often thought of him as a toxic herbicide weed killer, always searching for someone to vent his rage. I was wondering how intelligent beings could seek to contaminate the entire environment as he did. Again, as a human being, he was no better than a baboon…

For several days after this event Arthur was anywhere to be seen. It was Leon Van Meerstellen who first informed me about the employer's whereabouts. Arthur had packed his things and went off secretly.

Lately, I had a sense that he was extremely concerned about something. Arthur had left for France 'across the pound' with the first available flight for Labège par Castanet via Paris and Toulouse in order to contest his mother Marie-Thérèse latest will.

Granny had left Melanie handsomely provided for. The boss made his move after realizing that with his mother's death, the will no longer was ambulatory. However Marie-Thérèse had stipulated on paper that because of her grand-daughter's kindness for so long all of her remaining wealth went entirely to her. Almost the whole of Granny's fortune was entailed over to the granddaughter. Soon the boss upon taking knowledge of the will felt betrayed. Being the only son he thought that he deserved from his mother most if not the entire riches including an estate in the resort town of Biarritz, with some acreage near Toulouse.

Arthur already had considerable assets of his own in an Andorra and Swiss Bank that had been transferred from a French financial firm. And now apparently, assisted by powerful lawyers he succeeded with the stroke of the pen in having the legal document, that legacy trust codicil and mutated, and to be reverted in his favor. It was awful to look forward to the pleasure of scheming how best to disinherit his own daughter.

Upon his return from Europe when Melanie became aware of the conversion and switch she was shuttling between fear and rage. Standing up suddenly trembling, she retorted:

"I thought everything would be mine... some day! But since you also exchanged testaments with your dear friend Eddy I believe I will be left high and dry and pennyless!" She cried for a long time thinking that this was the most cruel, heartless crime. Tears of outraged virtue were in her eyes and she was overcome with shame. As her anxiety increased she ate without knowing what she ate and drank without tasting anything as she became totally insensible to whatever was going on.

Even though her grandmother already bestowed her with a house and a new Jeep the granddaughter could not contain her pain with 'the great injustice' inflicted by her father. *On the other hand, I had the feeling that she considered the gift of her house and automobile as being a mere pittance for an heiress of the family's fortune. At this point one can realize that both father and daughter happen to be no less than a bunch of vultures going in pursuit of the old lady's wealth!*

After this particular event, Melanie was uninspired to go to work for an entire week. Suddenly it seemed like she was attacked by some sort of a violent disease. With a combination of chest, stomach ailment, and ulcerated sores on her mouth, she stayed home. Her condition grew worse in the days that followed. She was overtaken by a diarrhea and a fever that her own doctor did not undersdand! She suddenly decided to stop eating. No one could get her to ingurgitate any kind of food for several days. After awhile, I resolved to go and inquire whether she was feeling any better.

On my way to her house one of her neighbors explained to me that Melanie has acted so strangely as if she had been in a vacuum; that she didn't even recall the awareness of her own being. First the lady said that she would brood motionless. She added that Miss Valois Dourville de Montrissart had been in a hallucinating fever sinking irrevocably into some sort of quicksand, crying for no apparent reason. She actually saw Melanie dancing half-naked in her own backyard next to the side of the garden overhung with the foliage of trees a coronet of flowers on her head as her two dogs bounded up and down at her side after they had snuffed amongst the dirt and stones. The same neighbor noticed that Melanie after she had been running madly, hitting thorny bushes was rocking on a small wooden horse. She also decided to sit on the dirt at her mini-pond threshing the water with her legs, sending waves everywhere. At that point, Melanie started rooting up the earth, digging and digging dirt the way carnivores do. Furthermore Arthur's daughter fed the dogs with one hand and slapped her own face with the other before beating her breasts like a madwoman. Never before had she led such a bizarre life. It seemed that she was slowly losing her mind.

As soon as Melanie opened the door we first looked into each other's eyes. I could not say that she burst into shouts of joy as there were no sign of elations in her gaze. With cheeks sagging, her hair was carelessly heaped upon her head and she seemed so bored. She had the look of a woman with one foot in the grave. There was in her face an incongruous expression of craving distress. She was not really in the mood for anything. Since the last time I had met her she had really aged; I could scarcely recognize her. Now, with that feeble smile on her lips Melanie did not even care in the least for what she was wearing. All of her clothes and stockings were scattered about. Things were thrown about in disorder on the floor and with the trembling of her shoulders a sense of fear overcame her, paralyzing her movements. Her lips were apart and her eyes half closed as her body was swaying a little. She now appeared to have a convulsion and was frothing at the mouth. Most of her frenzy early enthusiasm seemed to have departed and there was a concerned look on her face. What's more, she started worrying about a blister on her lower lip hoping it wasn't herpes! The late afternoon sun was even repulsive to her, like an inflamed sore in the sky. She had got a number of marks of thorns on her arms and legs and I beheld her heavy, fatigue eyes. Even that she put a speckle of rouge on her cheeks, she still had a lymphatic cadaverous pallor. The thorns had also scratched her face, her forehead and chin. It looked like she might have been drugged. Nothing could rouse her and she started wailing dismally before she threw herself into my arms, weeping bitterly.

Moreover, she seemed to have acquired a disgust of the joyous, fashionable friends at the Malibu Colony which at one time were so enthralling. At present she cared for nothing and for no one. She began mumbling in low whispers: "Only death healed the broken heart."

Yet, at this point I had a feeling that she exaggerated the seriousness of her condition. A lipstick-stained Marlboro lay in the ashtray (this was the very first time I realized that she was an occasional smoker.) As she stuck her tongue out at me she started to laugh. But with rust in her voice that laughter seemed to precede hysteria. She moved slowly like a broken-winged bird and sat stiffly as though unaware of anything.

I decided to prepare a breakfast *sur le pouce* and forced her to ingest small bits of food. I actually spoon-fed her. She could not overcome the disgust which she felt against swallowing any nourishment that included the glass of orange juice that spilled from her trembling hand. She gulped down her food convulsively leaving a great deal of her lunch on the plate.

Before retiring I brushed her hair to make her look like an almost decent woman, and I convinced her to lie down on her bed, covering her warmly. Afterward she hugged my knees and thanked me in a voice that was barely audible. Before long Melanie fell into the deep dead slumber caused by exhaustion. She remained there as motionless as a log.

* * * *

On this bright Sunday of August at the Marina we had the unexpected visit of Helena's sister Clara a head teller at The Bank of The Philippine Islands branch in Los Angeles. While the sunlight had found its way through *une ouverture* in the clouds I noticed that Clara was as gorgeous as Helena but it seemed that she didn't want to look beautiful. It was as though she was punishing herself for being attractive. But even with the somber dress she was wearing, in addition to that bizarre hat covering her shiny black hair, her attitude made her even more appealing.

Together we went to the annual Hindu Festival in Santa Monica. It is a festival where the poor and the rich mixed as in a fruit-salad cocktail. For me this represented a renewal experience of what I anticipated years earlier in Varanasi, India among the poorest of the poor. On the Ganges River's shores and later on in Calcutta, *la poubelle du monde*-the trash can of the world I was introduced to the many phases of the Gitopanisad which is the essence of Vedic knowledge.

With the music of cithara and the incense in the air it was such an extraordinary encounter and I felt rejuvenated. Working at *Le Cerisier* in a contaminated atmosphere under *le joug*-slavery of such a mean employer, I almost forget the pure, untainted aspect of real enjoyment in life. Subsequent to the vegetarian meal, we stopped at a tent where a devotee of Lord Krishna kept on discoursing on the subject of how to be delivered from the nescience of material existence and find a solution to all sufferings. All the gentleness in the world was showing in his eyes.

In a submissive spirit, the devotee quoting from the holy book Bhagavad-gita explained to his listerners that: "Every activity of the human being is to be considered a failure unless other activity inquires about the nature of the absolute. If a living entity says that he is not controlled but that he is free, then he is insane. The living being is controlled in every respect, at least his conditioned life." and he continued, "A person who is not disturbed by the incessant flow of desires that enter like rivers into the ocean, which is ever being filled but is always still can also achieve peace, and not the man who strives to satisfy such desires."

Eventually, the teacher indicated to us that there is a myriad of people walking here alongside the beach with a smile on their face; however, in reality that happiness wasn't there. The smiling boss at the restaurant was the perfect example of this. Once, in front of his subordinates a customer informed Arthur: "You don't fool me! Behind that smirk I can observe an angry, very dissatisfied man!" Our employer knew that that client being a keen judge of character recognized the symptoms rightly attributed to deep anxiety...

Afterward, still at the Hindu Festival, the devotee concluded with the assertion that our food must be prepared with love because love and good ingredients conveyed the perfect marriage: "A happy chef who cooks with love and compassion will create ambrosia, a delight to the palate. On the other hand even with all his experience and his knowledge dictated by the Cordon Blue culinary school an angry chef can only create bad dishes. A restaurant where disharmony is rampant in the kitchen can rapidly result in the loss of some, if not most of its customers."

Next day at *Le Cerisier* I refrained from explaining to Arthur what I had learned at the Hindu Festival. The little man won't understand and I probably would end-up with a slap in the face or worse another long-handed wooden spoon's blow on the head!

* * * *

Melanie, drawn with lack of sleep was still sick. It was plainly visible. She was not herself; her skin was as greenish as a cucumber. Under a nagging depression she was growing thinner and thinner, weaker and weaker each and every day. With constant suffering from insomnia she appeared to be so utterly exhausted that she had almost no strength left to speak. Her incessant coughs had confined her indoors for several days.

Against the doctor's advice, with that long attack of illness that left her so weak she came to *Le Cerisier* with our payroll checks as Arthur was still busy at *The Swedish House of Fine Imports* souvenir shop up the coast in Solvang.

Melanie looked like a risen ghost. With her hair in a mass of disarray she appeared like she had just emerged from the shower.

I also knew that she had been morally wrestling with her father. They constantly quarreled over things that were unimportant.

But there was something else: Jane, the lady with the Bentley; her best friend from the Malibu Colony whose resemblance with the late actress Jane Mansfield was astounding, had been badly hurt. There had been a struggle with a jealous ex-boyfriend. That struggle lasted only a few minutes and the scream which the neighbors heard that night were more than horrible.

The next-door resident, a young man in his late twenties discovered Jane. She was still alive but her cheek lay open in a long gash. Her face had been ripped open from which the blood spurted. The criminal had already fled in his black Mercedes 500, but was later captured by the Highway Patrol near the intersection of the 10 and 405 freeways.

The man who first discovered Jane called nine-one-one. She was carried in an ambulance to Saint John Hospital in Santa Monica.

The weapon had been a sharp kitchen carving knife. The night before, over an earlier scuffle, at least one neighbor heard the former boyfriend screaming: "I'll make you so no man will ever look at you again…!"

All of a sudden Melanie stopped in the middle of the kitchen as she developed strong intestinal pain. Really indisposed she barely reached the toilet in time. She started to throw up like 'Montezuma's revenge' over the kitchen over the bathroom floor. A rather offensive odor of the sour smell of vomit flooded in the entire kitchen. Subsequent to her cursory toilet, I assisted Melanie toward the dining room. She seemed to have an imperceptible pulse and breath that grew fainter by the minute.

Pedro the dishwasher commenced mopping the floor and using white towels to clean the walls. Inadvertently, as Pedro flushed the toilet, a towel fell down and was sucked-in with the flow of water. Almost immediately a serious problem occurred. Everywhere, from the ladies and gentlemen bathrooms to the small basins in the kitchen, water started rising. Water and bits of food soaring out of the toilet bowl had spread all over adding to the disgusting scene.

Melanie, as quiet as a nun was still lying down on a booth in the private room and started to recover. Not only was she ashamed and deeply wounded in her pride, she also felt depressed beyond anything she had ever experienced. She sensed that her situation had been too awful to be endured publicly. Clutching her head with her hands I saw tears of affliction in her intense paleness. She remained crouching in palpitating misery, her agitation intense. Her eyes met mine and with a strange haze she said:

"Pierre, I'm so worn out. I'm tired; dog tired." She was crying frankly, daubing her eyes with the back of her hand. She further uttered:

"Just let me die in your arms. The Lord can take me now!"

As I listened to her I really was afraid she would let herself be caught in the rein of her imagination and seek oblivion. Her pallor was greater than ever and a storm had shaken that poor heart. Just like with the Queen of Sheba in old times there was no longer any spirit in her and her pain really hurt me to the bone.

Chef Bevert decided to wear a pair of rubber boots that he kept in his locker at all times. And along with Pedro and pastry chef Santillas, they swept the water in the direction of the parking lot far away as possible from the dining room's carpet that was already damped on the edges.

Our Dutch friend and neighbor Jules Vertrichten who dropped in earlier came back to our rescue with his rooter machine. In no time the drainpipe was cleared. I was in a hurry to wear my shirt and apron as the knocks on the front door of the restaurant intensified. The 'early birds' were impatiently waiting outside.

Tonight no one had requested the private room, so I urge Melanie to rest a little longer. She still carried that saggy look and she was passing gas as she layed there in a peevish lethargy. Bubbly saliva was dripping from her lips and I could sense the foul smell of her body. Before I went on taking orders, as a nice gesture I held Miss Valois Dourville de Montrissart's hand affectionately. I already knew that kind words from my part were more powerful of all of her medicines. Next, I started to sing that cute song from the old country that I learned with the boy-scouts. That song (which seemed to have only its proper and harmonious meaning in the French language) originated from the Côte d'Ivoire, Africa and it really made you tingle inside the first time you hear it:

> *"Maintenant tu dois faire dodo, ma gentille petite proute.*
> *Plus tard ta mamy t'apportera ton lolo bien chaud, ratata-ta…"*

(You must now sleep my gentle little fart. Later on your mommy will get your hot milk.) I keep watching her in compassionate silence trying to comfort her in her distress. Melanie was now in a state of quietude. As her eyelids fluttered down before she dozed off she softly murmured with a frail laugh of despondency: "Thank you for your kindness Pierrot."

Indeed this was a sad day to remember! As Melanie stood there, she had lost her ethereal graciousness. Even the evening sleepy sun in the sky looked so sad to her.

Chapter 33

F OR QUITE SOME time Chef Francis Bevert immersed himself in the preparation of a sumptuous catering menu for the wedding ceremony of the Hollywood mogul the movie producer and director H.D.W. in the lovely city of Carpinteria, north of Los Angeles.

H.D.W. a good customer at *Le Cerisier* as well moved to Carpinteria recently after having sold his property in Brentwood, adjacent to O.J.'s, the well-known football superstar.

This day was the final day when that great event would take place.

I arrived at the restaurant a little earlier as the sky was still very dark. Arthur and the rest of the crew came along. We had to fill up the caravan of cars and one mini-truck with all the supply of food and beverages, including a pyramid of pots and pans for the sixty-five guests invited for that sumptuous wedding. At this point it looked to me like the amount of equipment was exceeding the need we would have for it.

Arthur and chef Bevert had a meeting in consideration of what would be needed as surplus. Later on, Melanie (who was now in a much better health) and I participated in the discussion as well. The main point that Arthur emphasized was: in case of emergency, where could adequate supply of food be obtained; where was the nearest supermarket or liquor store near H.D.W.'s place can be located? After scrutinizing the map we were on our way. Beatrice Van Meerstellen, Leon's mother joined us too in our task. What's more this would be an assiduous, fulfilled and tough endeavor. All the chairs, tables, plates and Victorian silverware were already in place. For the gay florists this was equally a good day. The producer ordered a ten thousand dollars complete floral centerpiece in addition to extra giant bouquets of flowers in every room.

The perishable food was carefully set in large containers. With the exception of the lobster bisque everything would be cooked on the premises by our own chef de cuisine Francis Bevert. I heard that one admirable feature of the house was a vast kitchen bigger than the one at *Le Cerisier* and equipped with a large *Wolf* stove- a chef's dream.

The menu itself, including an endless list of fine victuals was sumptuous. To start there would be lobster bisque followed by a dish of shrimps prepared *à la Monsieur Escoffier* style. Next, Arthur's greatest specialty: a filet of salmon Montrissart covered with a light *purée de champignons,* baked *en papillote,* inside a pastry shell and served with a Hollandaise sauce. That included two fresh vegetables and *pommes de terre vapeur* marbled. And, to please some guests allergic to fish: tournedos-filet mignon wrapped in bacon and caressed with archduke sauce. For dessert: home-made vanilla ice cream nestled with fried bananas, topped with real hot Belgian chocolate, walnuts and fresh crème Chantilly. Regarding the wine selection, with the appetizers, there would be Chablis Premier Cru. For la piece de resistance: a 1969 Lalande-de-Pomerol. The Veuve Cliquot Champagne was to be served at dessert time, prior to a demitasse of expresso-coffee and brandy.

As we started driving the long road in the direction of Carpinteria, the sun arose with a yellow luster but the wind was upon the increase. Later on, the weather changed. Now, under a flawless sky there was not a cloud in the sky not one wisp of haze.

Past Thousand Oaks we were overwhelmed with admiration. A sweet tranquility, a captivating freshness filled the air as cows were gazing everywhere. Driving very slowly with all the food, bottles, pots and pans, we kept on gazing at the surrounding, at the luxuriance of the flowers. The line of vehicles seemed so solemn almost like a gathering procession for we sensed the significance of this day. Following a long uphill, the road declined gently for a few miles. In the distance, alongside the mighty Pacific near Ventura we discovered a string of little islands. Here the trees clustered to the water's edge. This was still an engirdled, secluded region for the most part unvarnished as yet by tourists or landscape painters. Our way let us sometimes through woods and on other times across open areas.

For awhile Arthur seemed absorbed in the task like a captain of a ship when navigating a vessel through a difficult channel.

As we reached the verge of one of these escarpments more like an out-of-the-way place, the caravansary of vehicles stopped at a clearing. Out there, when the ocean was for awhile out of sight the fresh air and the smell of trees seemed unfamiliar compared to the city' smoked atmosphere. Now the daylight was quite bright in the warm air since the sun was breaking through the clouds. On dry flat rocks lizards were sunbathing without fear.

This time our boss, his head high like a general of an expeditionary force, with his white hair streaming in the wind, a stick under his arm proceeded to inspect everything. He had to be sure that there wasn't any spilling of the bisque, broken dishes or lost items.

439

As soon we had stretched out on the grassy side of the road Arthur strolled away among the trees and simply decided to relieve himself behind a light bush not even being aware that he could have been observed. After he had answered nature's call he spat noisily. Feeling a sense of respite, the so-called well-mannered aristocrat still busy tying-up his belt prior to tucking his shirt back into his pants gave us the 'move on' signal, ahead of cleaning our shoes that were clogged with dirt.

In the distance as we heard the hum of a bee-hive, the convoy went on advancing rhythmically in a long line. We were slowly, but definitely progressing without any setbacks or annoyances. Before long, drizzling rain blurred the sky. Further on we discovered a stream of water that was pouring from the side of the hill, tricking down into the ocean. The small gleaming river was flowing alongside a cemetery, the land of gently resting souls. The countryside was stretching from east to west as far as the eye could reach. The air, cool and refreshing was more ethereal, buoyant and bracing. In a humming concert of myriad of flies the road was stretching ahead to the horizon among ranges of hills lining with an array of big trees heavily foliaged. From the bend in the path, as we slowed down they appeared to bow to us when we passed by.

Near Carpinteria, back in the forest again, we took a dirt side road with ditches on either side which would lead us to the luxurious castle-like residence of H.D.W. The road decreased in size to a sandy track and a trail. First, we headed to an inextricable tangle of vines and leaves. The scenery was rustic, even savage. One can observe some charm in those neglected woods. Through many dark, intricate passages the light was now verging low in the forest. We noticed dense shrubbery, tufted grass and valleys with labyrinths of evergreens. Birds were singing in trills and roulades ecstasy waking up the entire countryside. We beheld an elongated dirt mound. The lawns next to the railed iron fence were immaculate. We curled off into a *chemin de terre* that dwindled to a footpath wide enough to let a donkey and a man through. The road became undulating as we were jolting over the bumps swaying from side to side as we passed the fork to the main entrance. It started to rain. For awhile a clump of trees was masking us from the huge estate. Adding to this the driving rain that was bursting upon us became heavier and heavier blotting us from the view as well. With the smell of poplars flooding the air the caravan of vehicles swept into a solid road meandering and finally leading us to the private domain through a barrier that slid electronically.

At this point our spirits were quite high. The colossal home of H.D.W. surrounded by several vine-clad hills with its French-mansard-roof appeared to us in full splendor. What a view! With the grounds opulently prosperous there was a magic spell of the entire scenery. It seemed to be a religious stillness in the fields. Wide pastures, wooded hills were to be seen in every direction. The building stood, handsome of noble architecture like an old fortified castle, the very image of a *grand seigneur* residence. It dominated the landscape for miles around. So imposing it looked as if it had weathered many storms. For sure that house remembered other happy times long ago past when the only transportations were 'horse-drawn coaches.'

The huge white fortification with large oriel tinted windows, stone balconies and the triumphal arch above the entrance was out of this world. They seemed to rest above two columns with the leaves of the acanthus sculptured on them. The doorway was that large, it would have let in an elephant! The terrace was spaced in an artfully way, ornamented with several statues of marble nymphs. In the glow of the new day, the smell of roses was in the air. Pigeons cooed from a tree near the lawn along with sparrows twittering in the foliage. The rain suddenly stopped. Soon the sun weighted on the awnings as the atmosphere was yet laced with threads of warm from the Pacific.

In the center of the garden elegantly laid out, an ornate fountain splashed languidly into the little pool with so many colorful butterflies shimmering. Part of the tennis court was shielded from the public by a high cemented wall bordering a little house that was appropriated to the servants. The beauty of the estate as well as the landscape that looked like a framed painting was an inspiration. Its architect: the finger of God.

From an aerial view in a small plane, the topographical features of the property and surroundings carpeted with shaved grass must be amazing.

On the terrace, white parasols stood like soldiers. They were embroidered with the letters H.D.W. Outside as we walked to the fountain in the center of the garden we noticed a fully equipped cocktail bar built around a large tree. The branches above the bar were well spread, like the canopy of an umbrella. A little further on, rare birds doing little shrill squeaks were chirping in a gigantic aviary. They assemble themselves at the drinking fountain creating a show of exhibition by flapping their wings. There were many geraniums on display right on the steps of the verandah.

After Arthur had banged the knocker, a dignified looking butler, quite peevish as well opened the door as the hinges squeaked. We waited in order to be introduced to the producer. We first met a young Mulato entertainer who happenned to be the master of ceremonies.

H.D.W., a tall middle-aged man with a short-cut mustache, in a Clark Gable fashion, sturdily built and looking very much like an English Lord came to meet us. His tone of voice was warm, quite polished and polite. After he let us in, the host who had settled himself lavishly started greeting all his friends and relatives who arrived by little groups.

The bar was already in full swing with cocktails *en masse*. The air became alive with chatter, laughter during the enthusiastic meetings of relatives and friends. Next, the host gratified us with a flute of Veuve Cliquot champagne as if we were part of the invited guests.

Balding, with a salt and pepper beard, H.D.W. was very large, like the Titanic. On his wrist I detected a Rolex studded with diamond, brightened by his opal ring. I noticed he had the habit of passing his fingers over the top of his head as though to tousle the hair that was no longer there. Besides, H.D.W's eyes were slightly stretched like those of an Oriental man.

His wife Henriette, a lady of quality was the star that gleamed on him; a pearl among women. With the whitest neck and such a softness of her hands, in addition to firm breasts no angel in heaven could be better looking than her as her prettiness was of an ethereal type. She was a disarming attractive young lady in her late thirties. Strangely enough, as I kept watching the fine line of her profile I noticed that she bore a resemblance in charm to Mary, Queen of Scots from a painting I recently admired at the Paul Getty Museum. I was really struck by the likeness of the portrait.

Slim-waist, in full bloom with long and slender artist-like hands as soft as a chamois skin, with her fine bone structure Henriette would surely be the loveliest representative in a beauty pageant. With big eyes and beautiful red hair she had a vivid mouth in color, in shape with lips the likeness of cherries. With a perfect set of glistening teeth as white as ivory, she had a head Michelangelo would have given to a virgin.

Henriette carried the deepest respect for her husband with the warmest, most tender feelings. They both looked so charming in their light attire, clinging to each other like pigeons on a pent-roof. Never was there a young lady that was better company for him.

H.D.W. and his wife would spend most of the year in that sumptuous estate with the exception of two summer months in a more modest house in Upstate New York. Now that the wedding ceremony was over they both wore casual clothes. The pocket of H.D.W. white shirt was embroidered with the monogram of his coat of arms.

With spacious high ceilings, the rooms were dignified and richly ornamented with the real trappings of aristocracy. The pompous and lavish living room had baroque furnishing. There were carved French cabinets, fat armchairs and a large Chinese rug on the floor embellished with delicate lace-work designs filigree of figures made with gold and silver, and rare engraving in ivory. Chairs made of richly grained wood stood in harmony around a finely decorated Turkish table next to a canopy of green satin edged with silver. In addition I saw a square-back chair, typical of the Sheraton–Heplewhite style along with a wooden chandelier with iron arms and pricked candleholder from the 1800' in Philadelphia. A Steinway grand piano of exclusive beauty stood in the center of the room. This was one of the 'gold teeth' of the mansion. A pianist was playing classical music.

The fireplace incrusted with mosaics on the outside was large enough to roast a large pig. There was another salon that looked more like a boudoir with full of exotic flowers.

From the veranda we discerned a magnificent panorama with a glorious view far away across the land. Right on the chimney-piece and the consoles were strewn the jewel-cases. A ray of sunlight was coming in slanting glory through the window. Nearby on a pedestal stood the marble bust of Frederick the Great, the replica of the one Adolf Hitler had on display everywhere, even in his Berlin's mammoth concrete bunker. In the middle of the living room one can admire a Florentine table covered with mosaic.

A large crucifix fastened to the wall completed the decoration. In the library proper, old and recent books covered all the walls.

Being quite amazed; wild with excitement by the grandeur of the place and the size of the furniture, I suddenly felt myself belonging to another flamboyant society.

All of a sudden, H.D.W. stared at me and with a smile, he articulated: "Pierre, do you like our humble abode?" Still, in an adjacent room one can discern a billiard table and a Mme Recamier couch. On the wall, next to valuable paintings hang an engraving in a golden frame depicting a scene `from the sanctified battle of Kuruksetra, India involving warriors and their horses in a cavalcade. Even the bathroom carried the luxury of regal magnificence. All rooms were lofty with elegance as the extravagance everywhere showing splendidly chiseled objects carved in rare wood seemed at its height.

Moving up two flights on the spiral stairs stood five neatness bedrooms, including the ones for relatives. In the meandering corridor framed photographs of family portraits were adorned along with old paintings.

With a little sunlight still sneaking around the edges of the curtains the maid had just closed down new figures turned up on the terrace. They had come through the woods with their expensive automobiles. Some of those luxury vehicles were chauffeur-driven. Before long the place was thronged with people. H.D.W. appeared like a prince surrounded by his nobility and soon he engaged himself in welcoming those who were newly arrived.

Now, all the guests experienced the first hunger pangs of that time of day. They were on the hungry edge of appetite.

After the unloading of the supply, everyone garrulously ingratiated, started munching on hors d'oeuvres prepared by pantry-chef Santillas. On the festal board we had previously set on display blue point oysters, crayfish, Beluga caviar, goose *foie gras* with truffles. The butler came back, this time with a tray of cocktails that he carried around.

The photographer kept busy snapping pictures of everyone, everywhere, as most of the conversations blended with the lapping of a water-fountain. The priest, quavering with old age was among the guests. With flabby chin and thick lips, he smiled with that old fashioned radiance as he sank back into the armchair of the luxurious green velvet Georgian sofa. He looked a little tired after the rituals. During the wedding ceremony, because of air conditioning problems, the small church had been so hot with the hard sun beating down on the roof slates. The guests looked first at the flower centerpieces before sitting down on their respective seat. On each table one can see a wax candle sparkling on candelabra. Nametags in gold letters were displayed at the edge of the tables along with white roses.

The sumptuous dinner was announced by the sound of pipes as everyone was ready to partake at the feast with great pleasure. Being still ravenously hungry, the aroma of the good food assailed each person in the dining room. They started to eat and drink with so much appearance of satisfaction. There was an inexhaustible supply of food served from a kitchen, larger and better equipped than most of the finest restaurants. In the height of magnificence a Scotchman with red curly hair rather tall stood up. He then gave us that famed Scottish toast from Aberdeen-the silver city:

"Skirl your pipes and beat your drums.
The happiest days are yet to come."

It was an excessively profligate dinner. Nothing was missing. Altogether it was excellent, so were the selection of wines. We served the lobster bisque and poured the exclusive white wine in the crystal glasses as a band composed of four musicians serenaded the guests with great music. The musicians were playing with priestly dignity until one of them belabored his violin with a frenzied wreathing of his body.

I noticed that the bride's grandfather, feeling somewhat tipsy with too much liquor remained dignified. The gentle music continued its wafting through the air. In between the servings of food I couldn't stop admiring all the plants and flowers surrounding us everywhere. It looked like the Garden of Eden. Subsequent to more appetizers the people started to partake of the most exquisite main course. Having first gazed their fill at the well-presented dishes, they proceeded to almost devour them.

While the gravy trickled from their lips amidst the music, the rattling of plates, glasses and the bursts of laughter, our good Chef Bevert as serious a nature, his head reverently bowed came in the dining room to admire the effects of his work. Appreciation from the hosts and guests, all the *beau monde* for what had been accomplished in that kitchen was unanimous. The chef orchestrated the preparations for that sumptuous dinner with such skill and finesse, the way a conductor supervise each member of his orchestra. His achievements were all magnificent; just unparalleled. Delightful odors that had ever set upon the guests filled the air. It was beyond all praise. Bevert so well maneuvered each detail of the most important phases of that extended menu that he received a standing, prolonged ovation.

As the last moments of the clear day lingered, Arthur decided that it was now the right time for us, his dedicated employees to taste some of the food, and we all retrieved to the kitchen. The boss, after washing down another drink looked in my direction, conveying:

"Pierre, don't eat too much, I still have to watch my budget!" This made Beatrice laugh so intensively that she almost choked on a shrimp.

For the grand finale with the green Chartreuse cordial, in addition to the ice cream dessert, we brought in the giant wedding cake so well prepared by Melanie. For her great skill, that adorable young lady also enjoyed special applause as this really highlighted the climax of the wedding. The newlywed first gazed in wonder at the cake and started to cut it. At that moment, I noticed that Arthur's daughter felt utterly intoxicated by the delight of the couple's love toward each other. Afterward, H.D.W. kissed his wife wildly.

Drifting apart from his guests, the head of the household went out for a few minutes as the master of ceremonies stepped forward, requesting silence. He announced a special musical performance composed by H.D.W. himself.

The producer came back. He was holding a shining gold colored saxophone, and joined the people in the band for a great piece of Jazz music of his own. It was absolutely marvelous. H.D.W. with an innocent and calm air that spread over his entire face, received an equally warm and uninterrupted thumps-up as the band begin harping out a waltz.

Soon Arthur was busy counting how many bottles of wine remained sealed. Even as a culinary expert, his ingenuity was nothing short of devilish. He instructed the chef to quickly hide those bottles in the trunk of his car to take them back to the restaurant, even though they were paid for, consequently still owned by the host. *It is good to remember that our employer had fired Leon for the same reason: theft of company inventory!*

H.D.W. had been lavish about everything. A little later Arthur was remunerated by receiving a huge check he was so impatiently waiting for. He stared at it like he just happened to have discovered King Solomon's mines. It took us awhile to wash the dishes, glasses and silverware before packing-up everything in our vehicles.

Outside, the evening was approaching fast, clear and striking as it enveloped in his shadowy veil the stretching fields. We could feel the solemn stillness that had settled down over the entire region. To my city ears, the calmness of the countryside appeared to be so strange.

Inside one of the cars, Beatrice, Leon's mother was so tired that she let her head fall down on my shoulder as we were slowly heading south, back to the City of Angels...

A few days later, Arthur suffered a painful and still undiagnosed ailment.

Chapter 34

ALIKE KIM JONG IL, Arthur, the 5 foot-3 little man, with 'his bouffant hairstyle and elevator shoes', showed a weather-beaten face and his air was heartbroken. He was in no fit mood for merriment. He had real cause to be alarmed.

My employer, deeply embittered seemed to be suffering from a bad night's rest, and looked more preoccupied than usual. In embarrassment Arthur fumbled because of a stabbing pain that has fashioned by accumulated uric acid. That same uric acid had crystallized in his joints, familiarly known as the gout that created in him occasional nervous contortions with the sudden sag in his shoulders. At one point he felt it almost impossible to rise again on his feet as he muttered incoherently to himself. Arthur, not sounding a bit cheerful was broken in body and mind and was now limping with the aid of a cane. His condition seemed quite serious. He also had great difficulty in controlling a nervous jolt of his foot. The attack came earlier during the day and it looked pretty bad. He was absent-minded and winced like a wounded animal. It was such an excruciating pain. Sometimes he had to sit down on a booth in the private room to rub a hand over his toes. Struggling like a martyr to rheumatic gout, Arthur walked slowly and impulsively, so unsteady that he almost toppled over when approaching a table. Furthermore he fouled the evening with curses, thinking that the pain would bring him more deference, even more consideration.

Besides medication, it was urgent that my employer restrained to excessive exposure to hard liquor and from eating red meat. For Arthur, the lover of *steak tartare*- raw meat (gluttony was still his venial sin), this represented a real burden. His heavy alcohol consumption was also part of his social life and inappropriate behavior.

Being forced to be sober, I thought that the boss would take a step in the right direction and stop harassing me. But, as ill luck would have it he was confined to drink cranberry juice that he hated. Being consequently deprived of his favored distilled liquor, and the seemingly joy of drunkenness the owner of the restaurant would find his best aphrodisiac by using his power of being in charge, the power of aggressiveness. At the same time, he became obsessed by the certainty of his eventual near-death.

Sitting alone in the private room, Arthur sadly contemplated his half-filled glass of cranberry juice, when his revelry was interrupted by a knock at the front door. The gay florists dropped by for an early dinner. There were six of them (three couples.) Ultimately, the boss looking at first like a wounded animal, yet still unconquered, appeared to have found his lost enthusiasm as he directed them to a large table. After the greetings, the actor side of him had come on the stage again. With his arm around my shoulders, Arthur announced like a trumpeting herald, with his usual ambiguous giggle:

"My 'dear ladies', (using that feminine idiom) ma petite Pierrette (same feminine vernacular) will now explain to you about the juicy beef on the bone that we have on special today.'"

In complete victory, Arthur in a customary haughty bearing, romping like a circus horse continued his triumph with great theatrical style. However, it turned out to be erotic as well as appallingly vicious and was much too graphic to describe! My pen simply refused to write those obscenities. This came along by exaggeratedly unclean, vulgar gestures. There was a round of applause as the jubilation was completed. It went on, uninterrupted, but it was not over yet. Arthur, in that atmosphere of 'opera comic ' continued his quite stupid discourse:

"Pierrette also brought along 'her' dancing shoes. Before 'she' would explain the menu 'she' will execute a little tap and belly dance for you..." As if nothing had ever happen, my employer went to another group of people in the private room telling them some story that had them all laughing.

After taking the order, with all the blood in my veins rushing to my face as a result of disgrace, I turned away and smiled an irrepressible nervous smile for the situation had been so intolerable. That man, with such malice really lacked the faculty of knowing how far he can go with a particular joke. *Even that it took a while for things to hit me, just like with Roxanne, the naked girl who was dancing for former chef Picharon's birthday, I felt utterly ashamed and humiliated by Arthur's distasteful comments. I was left hanging there a few feet away from my boss who really tried to create in me a manifold of frustrations by insidious means. Ironically, in order to keep the good relationship I had built with my dear customers, I simply had to be contented to endure so much, and being almost as submissive as a slave to his master. So often I wracked my brain as I kept on looking at Arthur in a state of mild hysteria.* One can now understand better the wild imagination, the conscious foolishness of that miserable little man acting in so antisocial a fashion!

But there was more. When I came back in the dining room, everyone's curiosity aroused by Arthur' story was now at its height. Following that barrel of laughs from our patrons, my employer more excited than ever decided to maximize that self-enhancing opportunity that made him appear good, and he continued to talk in a torrent of words from his most exaggerated imagination:

"Earlier in life, Pierre joined the Belgian paratroopers. They accepted him because of his blind loyalty and keenness. He told his commander-officer that he would be ready for any special mission and that if he had to, he would even bail out of a plane without a parachute." (Again the air was full of roaring laughter,) and Arthur went on: "During his training in Belgium, at a place near the Dutch border, Pierre jumped. After he pulled his ripcord lower to land more precisely he still fell into a bed of tulips. And, one day in the wilderness of Africa, just as he hit the ground the wind picked-up his parachute, therefore created a canopy. As he tried to disentangle himself from the cords he was not quick enough in taking evasive action. With the strong wind, this knucklehead went back in the air up to fifteen feet before falling down on his head like a Kamikaze pilot. Pierre told me that this is also known as 'the banana drop.' Following a serious concussion, Choucart spent a week at the Kamina-base military hospital in Katanga province, getting even more emotionally disturbed. Because he hit the ground head first, my little friend here became simpleton. On top of that, while lying on the grass Pierre was bitten by a *tsetse fly* and got infected with the sleeping sickness that made him fall asleep while talking. On several occasions the chaplain came near his hospital-bed to give him the sacrament. As the priest touched his forehead with oil, Pierre thought that the clergyman was his mother-in-law?" Now the hilarity around the table was spreading like wildfire as Arthur's belly quavered joyfully at his own jokes. And from all corners of the dining room, customers were stretching their necks not to loose one word of my employer's recital. All those human faces, red with eating and drinking appeared to me slightly distorted.

Following one of Arthur's comical obtuse, as the entire restaurant broke into frenetic cheering, Eddy acted like a *claquer-* the clapping of hands, inciting customers to applaud. In old-time theatres, the *claquers* were actually paid to perform *la claque.*

Subsequently to explaining the menu, still burning with indignation at the treatment to which I had been subjected I decided to leave the dining room where I remained the subject of conversation and ridicule, and retired to the kitchen. I sat near the phone, staring at the wall. Arthur had boosted himself by inciting the group of gay people on my behalf. The boss had to engage in cognitive stratagems in order to minimize discontentment and boredom. The turmoil and anxiety that Arthur experienced was related to the large disparity of what he was, and what he really wishes to be…

Next morning, in the early hours, I started running in the rain in the Santa Monica Mountains over the rocky and winding path on the slope of the hillock, hoping as the downpour spat in my face that that violent exercise might calm my spirit which had been so profoundly agitated.

* * * *

As we opened the door for our early clientele, the kitchen phone rang. Gustavo Santillas left his pantry and grabbed the handset. A lengthy conversation followed, but Santillas's face darkened with some powerful emotion and he burst into tears. In a somber and grave voice he announced to us that his dear brother Pablo had been killed in a car accident.

In the evening Gustavo's brother had been on his way to *La Marmite* restaurant where he worked as a dishwasher. *La Marmite* was located less than two miles away from *Le Cerisier*. But as ill luck would have it, Pablo, in a state of intoxication hit a sixteen-wheeler truck parked in a street alongside Balboa Park. Next to the driver's seat from his brother's car, several empty bottles of Corona were laying on the carpet-floor.

After ushering Santillas to the private room, Arthur started a dialogue that turned rather sour. First, I understood little of the matter in hand when the pantry-chef raised his voice:

"No way, I can't work for that party on Saturday. *Patron* please try to understand: I have to take care of my little brother's funeral arrangement and bring him back to Mexico. In Nogales, Pablito would be buried with honor and rest in that small cemetery next to our dear mother." and Gustavo went on: "You can fire me if you want, but I must go; that's final!"

As he opened the curtain from the private room, swearing vehemently in a volley of profanity the frustrated boss, in a cold stormy temper swore. He walked up and down the room like a madman, and finally rushed away. Grounding his teeth, the boss banged the kitchen door as he went out. Prior to his departure he had a quick drink of his favorite liquor as he continued to nurture total ignorance of his gout condition that had mounted to his heart.

Arthur was really oblivious of mere graciousness. On the day my brother Willy passed away, my employer didn't show any regard, grief or consideration either. I still remember what that apathetic man told me:

"Well, your brother was always drunk at the first place and often out of work. I don't even know why you have to go to Belgium for the funeral," And he added viciously: "IF HE WAS AS DUMMY AS YOU, FOR SURE IT'S NOT A BIG LOSS!" I was deeply aghast at such an announcement. After those shameful words, my blood pressure went up so fast that my doctor prescribed me *Lisonipril*.

I really cared for my younger brother. Upon hearing about the cancerous ganglion in his throat I made inquiries at UCLA and The Institut Bordet (cancer ward) in Brussels, Belgium and I requested the doctors to coordinate their latest findings on the disease. There was a great deal of energy, of cooperation on each side of the Atlantic among those physicians. However, because of the rapid spreading of the cancer their efforts were of no avail. I still kept the letters from both medical institutions as they provided me with their final results.

Remembering the past, I focused on the happiest times I experienced with Willy, together among the boy-scouts and with our parents. Till the final hour, prior to breathing his last my brother 'lived in the moment.'

After Willy's funeral, while perusing through the personal belongings in his apartment, I found a good deal of religious literature including letters he was exchanging with the chaplain we both knew so well over near forty years past, when we joined the scouts. Given that for several decades I have lived in the United States I had no idea if my brother ever read Monsieur Liebniz's *Discourse on Metaphysics*. But in his correspondence with the priest, he delineated with ample zeal and eloquence on the fact that we cannot, based on our judgments blame God for events in our life. Willy was referring to his own terminal illness.

As for those awful remarks perpetrated by Arthur against my brother's character, over the years I learned in cool detachment to ignore rudeness with smiling ineffable disdain.

* * * *

Again, gout has taken over Arthur's normal body function as he also started to be lame in his knees. The excruciating pain that now throbbed in every part of his body forced him to stay home for the entire weekend. In addition, with old age he had fallen into a state of great weakness.

His partner Eddy Freedman, not wanting to spoil a sunny, blazing ecstatic blue Southern California Sunday decided to invite me to go on a fishing trip. It was a coincidence that Helena, along with two doctors was attending a symposium that weekend at Bayer's Laboratories, the giant German pharmaceutical firm up at UC Berkeley. A fishing expedition that took off from the Malibu Pier was not such a bad idea after all.

The Malibu Morning Fishing Star was an outstanding, newly-varnished boat. With its wood benches all around the deck where fishermen can properly set their fishing rods, it was rather impressive.

As seagulls wheeled aimlessly in the wind, the passengers emerged in three little groups from the shadows of the pier. We boarded the ship along with fifteen other people that included four young ladies, all eager to bring home the biggest catch. Even that we embraced that physical refreshment of marine air, the fishy smell at the harbor was somewhat appalling. The ocean was a low tide, only a few rocks broke the surface.

However, today even that the visibility was clear to the horizon, we didn't experience 'a placid surface of water.' Earlier the raging ocean had kept several boats in harbor when the wash of the surf seemed to embrace the fog. Huge waves were also bursting into a startling of foam against several rocks. As we sailed to the high seas, the weather unexpectedly turned windy and cold. Farther and farther our ship braved the wind that was gathering more strength by the minute.

Eddy, being a veteran at the sport was attired in a fisherman's brown jacket; the one with several pockets on the front and leather padding on the elbows. I, on the other hand donned a simple raincoat. We both shared one fishing rod which Eddy owned.

While my friend concentrated at the surface of the water, after flinging his line, I kept observing a sailor untying some hemp rope. The ocean roughened; the dull groaning grew louder and stronger as it rumbled. Enormous waterspouts broke at the footbridge. The long rolling lines of waves, never ending, never tiring became increasingly frantic. Abruptly a monstrous lurch of the boat literally threw me on the floor as the ship lifted and sagged. This time, I fell against one of the cabin's walls.

Eddy and the other fishermen were holding tightly on the benches and safety cables. As the vessel righted itself before being engulfed starboard under the belly of another wave, we felt a new chain reaction of dizzy motion. Huge waves swayed against the hull as the ship ploughed straight ahead. The boat dipped down, shipping another enormous amount of water, throwing us all forward. The craft shot ahead as if it had been fired out of a canon. And, for a minute I had the strange feeling that the Malibu Morning Fishing Star was going to capsize. The captain gave what help he could in directing the ship's course, but the rocking had seriously disturbed me. An uneasy feeling irritated my stomach and my forehead became moist. I was sick, really sick with *le mal de mer!* As I held the safety cable, I started an unpleasant demonstration. The dizziness spread all around. When the translucent wave subsided I was almost green, yet I anticipated with the suffering of one of the ladies who was quite pregnant.

Sitting at the bow of the ship which moved with a swaying, sweltering motion, the ocean was lashed into great fury. Soon it acquired a dangerous velocity. As I recuperated under a benevolent breeze, I still observed the green, rusty waves that shattered against the heavy shell of the Malibu Morning Star in a whirl of white foam. The rolling waves rose up again. They broke with great power in a deafening sound. One of them, a freakish giant was swaying the ocean in her pursuit. Fortunately, those angry vociferous waves came to a still; only a small lace of foam remained. Suddenly, the heavy winds calmed down as a ray of sunshine warmed us all.

Occasionally, large seals swirled through the surface of the water; their bodies clearly outlined by strange phosphorescence. Now the light breeze drifted down, cooling our faces as we filled our lungs with refreshing clean air. For an instant I had the feeling that we were on an ocean of dreams and I felt strangely contented and totally free. Far out, to the horizon a sailboat looked as if it was hanging in the sky.

My good friend Eddy decided it was time for me to try to catch the big fish as well. With the patience of Job, after he took care of the fishing tackle and the bait, he explained to me the entire procedure: how to choose the bait and how to arch the body slightly before tossing the fishing line and weight far enough into the ocean. Grasping the line firmly in both hands I repeatedly tried the launch, but without any success. Luckily, I made it at a good length from the boat.

However, with what followed, one will acknowledge how clumsy I really was. As I hold the fishing rod, I started pulling, pulling and pulling. Breathing hard and exhausted I screamed with an anticipated smile:

"I JUST CAUGHT A BIG ONE!"

But, here was the culprit: in a blind ignorance I never trawled any fish. My line simply went adrift. It started getting entangled with other people's lines, including one from the other side of the ship that drove under the hull by a large wave.

Soon, those nice people crept slowly across the deck, all of them armed with pointed knives.

An older fisherman took the only initiative for this unfortunate event. Out of his fishing box he snatched an even larger knife and proceeded to cut all the lines. Our colleagues on the boat were extremely furious. As they kept looking at me I felt my teeth chatter with fear. Ashamed of my action, I became almost lifeless like a dead tree-trunk.

Now the situation turned to be extremely unpleasant. One of the men with a mean face, carrying a bottle of Bud Light in his hand was chewing tobacco. After he spit it into the water, he spoke. His voice was hardly more than a hoarse croak. And now, obviously drunk he growled:

"This murderer must pay the penalty for his awful crime. We must hang him and throw his body into the ocean so that sharks could have a banquet!" Under a faint moon, the women showing signs of extreme nervous irritation started to lash out: "Yes, that bastard who thinks he's mighty smart has to go. We like to have him swing high but he also deserved to be tortured before we can throw him into the ocean head first!"

Eddy's indignation was intense as I realized that my fishing had been a wasteful effort. It was not what we had expected; it had been awful. But luckily one of the men hooked a giant catfish over five feet long, weighing at least one hundred and fifty pounds and almost instantaneously the angry mob forgot about my blunder.

Back to port I was so anxious to set foot ashore when the ship came alongside another boat. As we disembarked, with such confusion in my mind, I started walking faster than a boot-camp instructor in the field toward Eddy's car. Eddy Freedman continued to be embarrassed with the situation but at the same time I already had the insight that he anticipated to tell everyone how I had made a fool of myself. I knew as well as I knew the sun will rise next morning that Arthur would be the very first one to learn of our sad fishing trip. Next day at the restaurant, every customer kept on asking me about my endeavor. A lady said:

"Pierre, please tell us about the big fish you caught off the Malibu Coast?" As far as the gas station at the corner of the street, people had talked of nothing else since the news of the fishing expedition became known.

Chapter 35

A GREAT SURPRISE AWAITED me as soon as I arrived at the restaurant. My dear, dear friend Leon Van Meerstellen was back with us after so long an absence. So often I had wished for his return. A feeling of happiness overwhelmed me with that intensity of joy to hear his voice again, and it was warming my heart.

Leon had been re-hired by Arthur. With a joyfull twinkle in his eyes, he was now standing there on his long legs. The boss had warmth preliminary talks with Leon's mother, using his mnemonic skills in remembering the *entende cordiale* from long ago.

The owner of the Swiss restaurant *L'Ours de Berne,* where Leon worked for the last four years bestowed Arthur with excellent recommendation that specify that Van Meerstellen had been a good, honest employee who never touched alcohol. He was now 'on the wagon' for good.

Arthur reconvened his friendship with Leon as mutual respect began to grow again. Leon, for whom my employer had conceived an aversion following the theft long ago, was now gradually getting in his good graces. Strangely enough, considering that he had been fired at the first place in the past, the owner of *Le Cerisier* had developed a sentimental, highly flattering approach toward my friend. Without missing a beat,

Leon started to perform his duties as a conscientious waiter just as if he had never done anything else in his life.

As I clasped him convulsively in my arms, Van Meerstellen with ill-fitting clothes hanging baggily in his tall frame looked old before his time. Bouncing on his long, thin legs again he appeared a little stiff as buckram, like if he had been starched. As his eyes veiled in tears of joy, my nostrils dilated when I scented his perfume which was still lingering throughout the restaurant. His gray hair that had grown almost white was cut after the latest fashion. Even now, Leon was coughing and spitting in a manner with which I was only too familiar. With constant fit of coughing he could not breathe easily, and when he sneezed a short high-pitched uncanny sound could be heard. His lungs were still hissing and whistling. Though he never touched a cigarette in his life he was panting like an asthmatic smoker. From his mother I found out that from early childhood Leon was liable from cold and asthma. And he suffered more from cold in the summer than in winter. In the middle of July Leon would cough and sneeze without interruption. His bad health had been a great drawback to happiness.

Several years had now elapsed since the end of his sad marriage with Wendy. All in all, his face gave hints of a new maturity. Gloomy and weary in a boring existence for those many years of solitude, Leon was still in agony. He was confused as if he had something on his mind at all time. Though he had fought hard to erase back memories he was nonetheless a shadow dissociated from life. After so many years of absence nothing had really changed. Grief and estrangement remained in his heart, and it was strongly visible. As I kept observing him, I realized that the past was linked to the present by an unbroken chain of events. Like an old pendulum that swings backward and forward, even now Leon's life was just swinging backward. He remained a strange and misunderstood man but at the same time as gentle as a lamb.

Since his divorce he never lived contentedly. Ennui and despair were again eating his brains. Concidering that he always worked so hard, he moreover started to hate those gigolos, sons of wealthy parents with their easy and insolent triumphs; their unmerited fortunes and all the enjoyments which life yielded them without pain and…without conscience. They had obtained all those things while they had vainly striven for them.

Yet, never had I noticed so plainly that brilliant light of intellect in his face; that noble stamp of mind. Leon still carried that fantastic, surprising photographic memory. If he read a document twice, he knew it by heart. Aside from enjoying riddles, he was also a dazzling mathematician. Once I used the adding machine, closing a check for a party of twelve people. My friend, peeking from behind my shoulder totalized it correctly in his head as I was barely half way with my own addition with the electronic devise. His intelligence really overshadowed my own.

Furthermore, here is a perfect example of how he always chose his words with such a rare affinity: "We can cultivate the pragmatist knowledge of the justified assumption that you cannot change the course of events." On the subject of the exploration of the universe, this is what Leon articulated from one of his readings: "If not for the church with its critical views regarding the survey of space, we could have been out there centuries ago. Copernicus, Tycho, Kepler and Galileo had put the solar system into perspective. Galileo's book *Sidereus Nuncius* (Messenger of the Star) was a scientific masterpiece. Unfortunately, a veto power of his work was issued from the Vatican." Finally, on the topic of the fantastic world of new technology, my colleague used that famed sentence envisioned by Jules Verne: *"Tout ce qu'un homme est capable d'imaginer, d'autres hommes seront capable de le realiser."* (Whatever a man can imagine, other men would be able to realize it.) Leon had a fertile and creative mind. Still, he would claim that he knew nothing, that he was an ignoramus adding that trying to prove anything is just pure mediocrity.

After a bear hug, Leon and I tightly clutched hands prior to a walk across the crunching gravel of the parking lot. This was such an emotional reunion. Clinging to my arm, his eyes were once more veiling in tears of joy. Now Van Meerstellen was laughing, and before he let himself into reverie he started to sing:

Turlututu chapeau pointu
Ma mère voulait me battre
Turlututu chapeau pointu
Ma mère m'a bien battu.

It's an old story of a mother that kept on beating her son that wore a tricornered hat. As Leon softly tapped the top of my almost baldhead, I ran my hands through his bushy *Zouave* beard and twirled it on my fingers. Now it had grown almost as perfect as a Franciscan brother. At that precise moment, as I continued playing with his beard in a quite puppyish fashion, Leon reminded me so much of the resurrected Jesus as he triumphantly appeared to his apostles. As we continued strolling to the end of the back alley, he tickled me under the chin with such an ease of happiness that made me smile. He now let his head lay against my shoulder. With his upper teeth Leon grabbed some hair from his beard to his mouth, and started to nibble at it. He had so much to tell, a ton of things as in respect to his long absence, for he didn't know where to begin. He spoke in a slow hesitating manner as though it was difficult at that moment for him to collect his thoughts, "I…I…" Leon sought vainly for words. He finally explained to me in some kind of a confessional ease that he didn't anymore enjoy the material advantages of money. He no longer drives that Mac-Pherson struts Camaro car. No would he heard the rattling of wheels on dusty roads when he made the trip from Los Angeles to Las Vegas in less than four hours through a desert trail, or even rode his high velocity 21 speeds *Yamano* bicycle. Still he loved requiems and funeral march.

Regarding his automobile, Leon totally out of luck explained that he had been arrested for DUI in the most unusual way. Being at a party on a Sunday night, and having a little fun among a few relatives and guests, he started consuming several Martini and Belgian beer. Suddenly my friend remembered that he parked his car on the side of the boulevard with a posting sign that indicated:

"No Parking Monday
8.00A.M. to 10.00 A.M
Street Cleaning."

With the feeling that this would have been an all-night celebration, and not willing to take any chances to be in the way during clean-up time, Leon left his friends for a few minutes. Away from that lively party he went inside his Camaro and started the engine. He moved the vehicle to the opposite side of the same boulevard, not even realizing that he was in no condition to drive. But the police was watching.

With those symptoms of uneasiness we usually resented when red and blue lights flashed from a 'black and white' behind us, my friend did not thoroughly comprehend the situation. Why in the world did that cop stop him? He then slowly parked his car at the edge of the curb. Being as nervous as a Greyhound before a dog race, my friend glance an ill-meaning smile at the policeman that met him. Stammering after he meditatively stroked his beard, he said:

"Have I done something wrong officer?" Following the usual request in showing a driver-license with proof of insurance, the man in uniform instructed Van Meerstellen that he did a U-turn over a solid double yellow line. The officer, after commenting that Leon's car was a real beauty, such a fine machine ordered him to step out of his vehicle and 'walk the line' slowly, one foot at a time. But, on the third step my co-worker tumbled down. He fell flat on the asphalt. With a suppressed grimace, after his constitutional rights were given to him, Leon was handcuffed and taken to the Van Nuys Police Station. For his DUI citation, aside from jail-time this was quite a sad and unfortunate event. The cost for the fine, traffic school and attorney's fees amounted to over ten thousand dollars that included a six months suspension of his driver's license. Awhile later Leon had gone berserk in a bar in Mission Hills...

After a pause, Van Meerstellen would tell me everything about the different jobs he worked at during all those years in exile from *Le Cerisier*. I had the feeling that the more Leon talked with that voluble and stentorian voice the more I could feel that he lived with the spirit of embittered resignation. Occasionally he still visited the cemetery. Feeling that he entered a tomb, he fancied that he only saw the faces of the living with the eyes of a dead man...

At one time Leon had been deeply versed in his studies, but his divorce had created severe mental emotional strain. I always had the gloomy perception that Leon had utterly wrecked his career by this unfortunate marriage. Wendy, his beautiful spouse had been allowed to infer that her former husband was a brute. This was just a rumor which I didn't believe at all. Except for his few hobbies Leon had no verve of hedonism remaining. I tried to explain to him that the past is past and that it's all behind him now. Whatever bad experiences, time would close over them. In awhile those bad experiences would all be as if they had never been. But, again and again my friend responded to me with a note of tragedy in his voice that he simply couldn't ignore his ex-wife.

Because of Wendy's attitude, he started to hate politicians and especially religious preachers (always ready to make a quick buck). Churchly hypocrisy had increased drastically to the point that Leon would relieve himself against a church wall! Using words from Hugo's *Les Miserables* regarding the sayings of a French philosopher Leon declared to me "that progress is madness, humanity is a dream; revolution is a crime and the republic, a monster."

Leon was still living a life of reclusion in that moldy stale urine-mouse pee and rotten cabbages building that really resembled a shed that had been converted into a house. It was as gloomy a place as ever I had laid eyes on. Everything had remained just as I remembered it: no more than an old paint- peeling ramshackle residence that could scarcely be called a happy place, with vestiges of a garden in front. The porch had not been swept for months. One side of the house was still shaded by overhanging trees that towered like a giant among all other trees. Again, I accompanied him to his apartment in order to view new race car videos. On that day, the weather had turned unseasonably warm and the air had been muggy. The door of the house itself had an unclean look. I was waving flies away from my face as they were crawling about in unwanted places, everywhere amid a rancid, putrid odor. A lizard was wriggling down the wall.

Van Meerstellen was salving his anti-capitalistic conscience by spending his weekends locked-up in his abode with that all-pervading aroma of cooking. The walls that sweat with moisture and fungi crouched in *dans les fissures*. On one of the walls, was an inscription from The Peace Resource Project:

> *"Only when the last tree has died and the last river has been*
> *poisoned, and the last fish has been caught will we realize that*
> *we cannot eat money."*

And on the other side of the room, one can discover another quote, probably from an existentialist:

> *"Life is a hideous invention of somebody whom*
> *I am unacquainted with"*

The course of the years had not changed the outside of the house too much either. It was an utterly disreputable old tumble-down place with the shingles nearly all off the roof. The street was still narrow, the gutter wide. Even with the *No peddlers and no solicitations* sign affixed on the front door, it was still like a sort of merry-go-round with people going in and out at all times. This was one of the most dishonorable parts of town with slums, cheap bars and prostitutes. Even now, that gas station standing on the corner carried on that pungent mix mephitic foul-smelling air in the street. Across the same street that old shacky brick store was still there.

In Leon's place the two pansies in their earthenware pots stood like security guards on the balcony ramp as a regiment of ants were crossing through. The room seemed smaller than as I remembered, even so everything else was the same; the same *bric-à-brac*, almost like in a refugee camp. The dark and gloomy old dilapidated furniture that he bought at The Salvation Army was now ramshackle and on its last leg. A pair of old worn-shoes along with some underclothing rumpled by countless washing lay on the sofa-bed near a haversack. Only his pajamas lay folded, untouched on that same sofa-bed as if he had slept again with his clothes on. Earlier, Leon had stretched some ropes across the room and had hung clothes inside. As I went about his place a wet garment brushed against my face as I noticed a moth flying out of one of his jacket lying on the desk. Looking outside, on the second floor a man was swinging his legs at the edge of the balcony. Leon offered me some coffee, but I had to remove a bug glued at the bottom of the cup and washed it before I let him pour the beverage. Yet, another fly had settled on an open jar of blueberries' jam next to the sink.

Even though Leon would have no difficulty in finding a lady, a well-born beauty of gentle blood that can love him, wash his clothes and clean his room, he was refraining from the pleasure of the flesh, divesting himself from any sort of sexual activity. For him, the physical aspect of a woman has become an abstraction as he was only seeking the inner beauty.

A client, matchmaker even tried to set-up a meeting with Leon and a Swedish woman. It could not have been a better match since that woman had deep crushes on him. However it was in vain, my friend wasn't interested a bit. Once Leon conveyed me in a serious conversation:

"Pierre, I fancy that in your mind you're always thinking of finding a good female partner for me? Well, just forget it. Love is only another illusion!" He decided to warn young women that he was not interested in their approaches. Out of the blue he gave me that famed Agatha Christie's line reflecting a certain Dame Laura saying that *"Women in love looked their best and men in love looked like depressed sheep."*

Since his divorce, Leon behaved coldly, with cynical eyes towards women. He believed that their voices never had that resonance of true honesty and likeness while speaking to him. He actually discerned them through a distorting glass. For him, even a clean *maison de tolérance*—whore house was totally out of question as he was so much afraid of infectious diseases. The only woman in the world that he really respected aside from Wendy was obviously… his own mother.

As for religion itself it no longer was a subject of conversation. Leon was an agnostic to the bone, sometimes praising Lucifer, the mother of harlots and abominations of the earth. Just to annoy me he would wear a shirt where one could actually read: *"HELL WAS FULL, SO I CAME BACK."* At this point, I believe that the devil had really tormented him. On another occasion, printed on a different shirt he wore, I recognized that sentence from the well-known French writer Jean Genet, a friend of Jean-Paul Sartre:

"I HAVE NO RIGHT TO BE JOYFUL. LAUGHTER DESECRATES MY SUFFERINGS."

On the other hand, Leon would always open his wallet freely to the poor, to the needy when he was even unable to pay for his extravagant overseas phone bills for some car-video clients. In addition he showed great compassion for the wandering vagrants, especially for his friend José Sanchez who was severely underfed-looking and on the bottom-most pit of misery. Sanchez was so destitute that he had nothing with which to clothe himself, except for a few items from the Salvation Army.

Leon would always give a helping hand in order to solace that welter of human suffering, the sight of which is so humiliating to human pride. José was not known to ever have a home as he was without an address. One could always see Sanchez in the street, wearing a pea-green sweater pushing a shopping cart full of a few dirty old clothes and newspapers.

Once, in the heart of winter Leon had found him lying in the gutter. Standing on the street corner with disheveled hair, untrimmed beard, lifeless eyes and worn out shoes, with one that had a loose sole that flip-flapped as he walk and a patched-up jacket, José with some kind of a stupid face held up a cardboard sign with one hand displaying the words: "will work for food." With his other hand he was holding a brown paper bag containing an open can of beer in it.

The pus-stained bandage that wrapped his right hand had always been there since Leon first met him. It still created an odious stench, a real odor of festering boils. Now this has become a permanent running wound. His bad teeth showed that he was not fed properly.

José had a father and mother but none of them loved him. He ran away from home and some strangers clothed him out of charity. In the street he found liberty. He could bathe in sunshine, that's why he hated to live indoors. Even when the hard winter has set in, he would still sleep in the open at night and stood in the rain, shelterless. One of his friends died not too long ago. It was not just from cold, but from hunger as well. About twice a week Sanchez lay in a hammock in a nearby Park. Where he slept the other nights only a few knew.

It was reported that on one occasion he dozed off in a tree with the branches bending, along with the harsh raucous call of roosting crow that cawed drowsily. José fell, tearing down some of the branches and nearly broke his neck as a frightened cat leaped from under a bush. On other occasions he would lay on the wet ground without anything under him but old newspapers or cardboards. One day he had been smacked on the head with a baseball-bat by a gang's member. For several days the unfortunate homeless walked around with a battered face.

José ate what people gave him: a ham sandwich here, a doughnut there. He would stay without a morsel of bread for a day or two. Once he devoured half a banana found on the dump. And occasionally Leon would provide him with fresh fruits or a Coke, never beer or hard liquor. Van Meerstellen has tried very hard to help José to observe decent standards of behavior, but without success.

The homeless friend often acted strangely; he had a particular way of staring at people. On one occasion Melanie came to visit Leon and, with a good heart bestowed José her own hamburger she just purchased at McDonald. The poor fellow didn't eat anything since the day before. In a strange occurrence that ungracious man, lean and cadaverous with famine, in a cruel, idiotic manner simply snatched the sandwich from her hands and threw it at her face requesting a dollar-bill instead! In his case cruelty arose from greater misery. At times José would stand motionless for several hours, gazing at some dew in an open field a block away from a gas station, and nibbling fresh grass. This open field was something of a sanctuary for him. He would stay there quietly, listening to the birds in a nearby tree, or he will sing filthy songs. Gangs with guns were to be seen around and José would hide under a bush. He stayed there till it started to get dark as he was still terrified to come to the open. Surprisingly when awakened sober he would speak in good school-educated accent. Except for people like Leon, nobody loved him and nobody will cry when he would depart this earth…

To my astonishment, aside from religion doctrines that he hated, every so often, upon meditation Leon's thoughts wavered as he was claiming to be a skeptical God seeker, more like 'The Force' of the universe. Nonetheless, he was more inclined to look the other way when he once uttered:

"Pierre, let's consider the position of atheists toward death." Next, he read to me an excerpt from H.P. Lovencraft: In Defense of Dragon: *"It is easy to remove the mind from harping on the lost illusion of immortality. The disciplined intellect fears nothing*

and craves no sugar-plum at the day's end, but is content to accept life and
serve society as best it may… There is nothing better than oblivion, since
in oblivion there is no wish unfulfilled. We had it before we were born, yet
did not complain. Shall we then whine because we know it will return…?"

I was still wondering why that brilliant university man
would endure life working as a waiter. He had such a clever
head on his shoulders. With his great knowledge, especially
in the field of accounting he could have reached the height in
prosperity, with so many other gratifications. Up to this day I
have not understood his obsequiousness; his servile attitude
to a paranoiac and idiot boss. Now, Leon would look up at
Arthur with the stricken eyes of a German shepherd, waiting
to be told to spring into a river. With all his great intellectual
faculties, why in the world would Van Meerstellen live in a
quiet desperation and continue to obey even flatter the man?
This really boggles the mind.

Presently the pleased Arthur looked at him as the prodigal
son; the sad son who was lost in the wilderness who finally
came to honor 'his savior.' Now, the boss was ready to 'kill the
fatted calf' for Leon. I had the perception that there had been
some evil influence watching over Van Meerstellen. He was
caught in the web of a 'spider-boss.' Leon didn't come back
just as the extravagant son but as the favored son, favored even
over daughter Melanie as well.

In front of customers, my employer would take my co-
worker into his arms, holding him close. He would proclaim:
"This is the kind of a son I would have liked to have. I should
never refuse anything which he condescended." Leon would
let the little man, that peasant-stock barely literate to become
his Master-Potter who can decide how to shape him. Whenever
Arthur would ask me a question regarding a particular item,
if I didn't reply at once he would unkindly add with both
eyebrows raised:

"I should have known better not to ask that question to an ignoramus! Leon knows everything, I taught him well and I will get the proper response from him!"

Little by little, to my astonishment Van Meerstellen appeared to enjoy his position as the man who has all the answers to satisfy Arthur and who would be there to resolve any problems the little man would come up with. After the houseflies Leon became the employer's favored pet, his minister plenipotentiary and special representative. My friend profoundly admired his master Arthur to the point of imitated even execrated him. He was completely subdued, even endowed under the little finger of a frail despot. The well-trained puppy would constantly watch the boss's face, standing by to leap at his overseer's command, ready to lift his front paw and sticking on him like *une mouche à caca,* in a lowly obeisance. This reminded me of a donkey harnessed to a shaft trudging round and round the pivot of a mill. In Leon's mind there no longer were any vestiges of freedom and personal dignity left as he showed rigid, undeviating submission.

And so suddenly Leon changed his attitude by giving himself great airs. He gained that same authority entrusted to him by the owner of *Le Cerisier.* But that excessive rein grew more and more intolerable.

In seeking additional control he was moved by envy of the power which had so far dominated him. Van Meerstellen who acquired such strength and prestige tried to purge my mind to win me over completely too. I stood really stupefied over this. My friend started to pick on me in order to boost his new awarded authority in the eyes of the chef and everyone else in the kitchen. He set himself up as a ruler without any regard to our friendship, just to be in charge of everything. Leon, the new co-*imperador,* the imperial majesty and great cerebrum followed the boss everywhere, even to his house to get his payroll-check in advance. Now Arthur allowed Leon to speak in a way he would not have tolerated from any other employee. My colleague and myrmidon spoke of Arthur as being a great, if not the greatest hero in the field of culinary expertise.

Knowing that 'the obedient soldier', 'the soldier on the march' received *carte blanche* from the owner of the restaurant, Leon longing for the power, started to act like a cruel despot himself. Now, my dear colleague thought he was a superior being who also stood over the masses and he became a strange person. Leon had a thorough knowledge of his new position. He continued to exert it effectually as to produce deep tyranny. He shrewdly conveyed to me that he was at the helm of the boat, in full control.

Eddy himself was unable to understand Van Meerstellen's new demeanor, adding that Leon has a real stress disorder; that he better contact a psychologist in no time!

Leon continued to play a peculiar game with me. Just like a spider that lets the fly flutter for awhile, Van Meerstellen, with a self-satisfied smile that crept across his face would act in a friendly manner until he would pound at me like a savage. He really became felonious and psychopathic. As I tried to speak to him he would stick out his tongue. And in order to amuse the customers Leon would tell them in a very non-brotherly fashion that I was 'severely brain-damaged.' Carrying that burning desire to feel eminently on top of the scale, he kept insulting me by all means, using me as one would a door-mat.

One evening Leon opened the bathroom door. He observed me as I was peering at my face into the mirror, and he articulated seigneurially like a Grand Vizir: "If you keep on glancing at yourself too long in that mirror, you'll behold a chimpanzee!" Again, with a hint of authority and ungentle mood, in front of clients he would announce in a distorting expression and with a mirth that was chiseled by a strange rattle:

"Pierre has been with us for years, and now he is suffering the stigmata of old age with no mind left. He is also quite deaf and becoming more senile each day." On another occasion he conveyed: "Pierrot is helpless, demented and confused, a real klutz almost ready to be institutionalized!" and, just for a last laugh, here is what Leon broadcasted in front of French speaking clients:

"*Pierre a une araignée dans le plafond; il est aussi pratiquement aveugle et sourd-muet!*" (Pierre must have a spider crawling in his head; in addition he is almost half blind and deaf!)

In my dreams, I beheld a throne erected for his majesty king Leon, a laurel wreath in his hair. The desire to have the power has turned him into a sort of a devil too. *Dear Leon, it looked like you know your lesson, for you have learned it well from Arthur, your mentor! Let me give you a quote from G.K. Chesterton that you can share with that boss you admire so much: "There is a great man who makes every man feels small. But the real great man is the man who makes every man feels great."*

* * * *

All of a sudden, to my great surprise, things have changed drastically and Leon became more amiable. Almost every day Melanie would call Leon at the restaurant and carry on long conversations. They spoken their own undisclosed language the way children do. This reminded me of the lyrics from a song: *Inventing lovers on the phone!* Like the hum of insects, they were 'cackling' about the weather or some minor problems. In the beginning, their conversation was really nothing but noise.

They could as well have talk to cows chewing mournfully at the grass in the meadows.

Once more Melanie gained so much weight, as she kept stuffing herself like a daylaborer. I observed her as she was eating an entire French baguette that she dipped in some extra pepper sauce the chef had intentionally prepared for her. At lunchtime she would enjoy nibbling at those large and wonderful sandwiches with a potage du jour at *The Soup Factory*. From her tremendous appetite Melanie who had grown into a prematurely old and sour woman was constantly indisposed by indigestion. She had eaten so much and now she breathed heavily. I noticed that her blouse clung to strong breasts as her derrière moved with litheness.

But earlier, with her unimaginable fatness and sores under her arpits, Leon's heart was pure of the faintest feeling for her save that of respect and gratitude. In response to the warmer tone of Melanie, my friend boasted only an unconcerned voice. Later, as he started cheering her heart things have changed. Both were non-ambitious and non-fulfilled.

But for Melanie my coworker was so God-like in her eyes that she was driven towards him by every heave of her pulse. Leon saw how keenly her sharp, loving little fanatical eyes were fixed upon him. She was simply burning at the touch of his hand. I had observed in their blushes a certain growing intimacy. They made such a pretty picture together as they seemed to harmonize most perfectly. At all events, for Leon the very superficial resemblance of Melanie with Wendy, his former wife was in itself sufficiently startling to cause a slight quiver in his heart. He also felt those eyes sounding him to the innermost depths of his being. In his own eyes, she became his well-informed French woman with many merits. Leon, with quite uninhibited mind had finally set out in pursuit of an ideal love, and he had found it. Like a shipwrecked navy man catching sight of an island he now felt a flicker of a new life awakening.

Melanie's phone-calls were actually a clever way to manipulate Leon. She was attracted to him like a fly is drawn to light, spreading herself over him like the night over the planet. Every time she met Leon, her heart throbbed so violently that she had to sit down as her face blushed fitfully. Her hips were swaying gently as her legs quivered. Her thoughts were melting into delight. The music of love was in the air as she broke into a gentle laugh. Soon they would leave messages of love-*billet-doux* on each other's e-mail. Mademoiselle Valois Dourville de Montrissart was inundated with an angelic joy.

Late in the evening Leon would enter Melanie's garden as Romeo did Juliet's. During the night he had experienced excited dreams from which he awaked sweating, also quite embarrassed.

For her, Leon was the handsomest creature in the universe. She would stand before him like a hypnotized animal. She continued worshipping Van Meerstellen the way a religious person worships a saint. With her shining face she was beautiful enough to inspire Leon with a passion, as he just forgot his earlier promise never to fall in love again. First he had no desire to look at anybody's daughter, but now things have changed.

As time marched on Leon finally realized that women can be kind, loving human beings. He doubted whether Melanie had ever felt for another man more than a gentle esteem? That extreme happiness of their youth flickered again in his memory and, in that clarity of vision Leon knew without any doubt that this love was complete and honest. For the first time their two hearts found words in which to express their feelings.

In the beginning Leon made furtive visits at her house. It was true that during those visits he piqued himself on rendering Melanie all the duties of respectful gratitude. Later, in the rambling multitude of his emotions, Leon first kissed her little hand. Her hand trembled and he saw that Melanie's lips were trembling too. With tenderness beyond description he passed his arm about her waist. Next he knelt down in front of the young lady and openly declared his love to her. One evening he left her though not till he had stolen a cursory kiss. Now they both agreed never to sleep without dreaming of each other. A few days later as Leon watch the swing of her body, the trembling vibration of her breasts, he felt arising within himself the waves of desire.

At first, before that testimony I hardly noticed the little hints which were resorted to in order to bring them together, but soon enough everything became clear to me. Previously Melanie was seeking ephemeral paramour lovers such as the Fire Battalion Chief, but with Leon it was much more than just physical love. During their youth she had been a goddess to him and she was still a goddess now.

I still remember that on their first kiss in the dining room, Melanie's eyes vaguely rested upon the Austrian dessert marble table as though she was nearly unconscious of what he did. It was just like fine music. They nearly always adored playing as if they were still little kids, picking up snails crawling around the tree in front of *Le Cerisier*. They often went back to Calabasas Park stretching themselves out upon the bank, among the daisies in order to live again the legend of their infancy; the poetry of their teenage years when they first knew happiness by carving their names into the bark. This had been the framework of their reveries. Leon, joyful as a bridegroom on the eve of his nuptials, with his arms trembling with the desire to seize her, would run after her. They were experiencing such a violent access of delight.

Ironically, each Sunday they would drive up the coast enjoying milking cows in an Oxnard farm. Sometimes Melanie would let her left cheek resting against the herbivore's flank. She stayed in that position long enough until some kind of a smile came over on the cow's face. They loved to hear the sound of milk fizzing into the pail (after awhile they knew cows by their names.) They also ate marshmallow on a stick. Melanie felt so beautiful to him, so exciting. In that striking delineation of Juliet from Shakespeare he would gracefully recite those three lines:

"My bounty is as boundless as the sea,
My love as deep; the more I give to thee,
The more I have, for both are infinite."

At other time, as the shadows deepened under the tree they walked together on the wet sands in Laguna Beach. They simply stood there to hear the run of the waves. On rainy days they would smell the earth and laugh happily under a large umbrella. They were always planning where to go next or what they would do on special occasions, such as Christmas.

Since Van Meerstellen had divorced his wife, Melanie's parents no longer doubted that Leon discovered happiness with their daughter. Arthur never saw her looked so well; it was as if she was the most fortunate creature in the world. Leon was the most eligible match for her. The Valois Dourville de Montrissart's and Van Meerstellen's watched their children grow together with affectionate attention. They were destined for each other from infancy.

Because of the close relationship of Melanie with Leon Arthur changed for the best. He now made her daughter an amiable, lovable lady to prepare her for the high assignment in life for which she was destined, omitting nothing which could improve her.

In no time Melanie started loosing weight and once more she became beautiful. Both their parents boasted joyfully over those young adults's intimacy as they already undertake to express their feelings that a wedding in a near future appeared a certainty. Year after year, since her daughter infancy Angeline and Arthur had dwelt on the project of this alliance with unalterable fervor.

On other occasions, aside from those happy recollections, I had the perception that Van Meerstellen was renouncing his identity to experience the delight of obedience, poverty and chastity. Although he excelled academically he was still facing social ostracism.

I still remember that, prior to his changed attitude to life while working alone in the dining room, a client inquisitively posed me this simple question: "Tell me Pierre, what Leon really hided under his beard? I am unable to read him. I don't know why, but as I look into his eyes, I can see sorrow and death!"

However Van Meerstellen had another good side. He loved his mother dearly but didn't care for his stepfather.

Marc Van Meerstellen, the former colonialist from the ex-Belgian Congo had vast acquisitions; immense social prestige in the Katanga province. He left Africa prior to the revolution. All of his lands were seized during the military occupation. Under the state of Emergency Act he had asked help from the Belgian government which refused it following the great turmoil. While the destiny of the Congo region was being decided by Mr. Patrice Lumumba, an ex-African sergeant, also owner of a lemonade company who eventually became Prime Minister Marc managed to fill up his pockets with gold.

Along with some heartless mercenaries he also hid a few small diamonds from rich Katanga mines which he had stowed away in the lining of his safari boots. He was now living in Long Beach on the lap of luxury with his new Asian wife in the business of importing dainty, exquisite Belgian horses. But, my old-time friend had ignored the son and former spouse almost entirely. He was a Christian too just like Leon's real father, but he withdrew a little from the Church and from the world. Until Leon's divorce Marc had helped him financially in his studies. Now he considered Leon as the black sheep of the family. He had also a daughter who lives with her husband in Bakersfield.

Years ago, Marc Van Meerstellen and I worked in *La Rotonde,* an executive dining room on the 52nd floor of a high-rise building located in downtown Los Angeles. I was a captain wearing a fancy tuxedo, he was a waiter. During the late 80's when I last met Marc in person I had enjoyed practicing my Swahili that I learned with the paratroopers. Surprisingly he quipped that Leon was up to no good; that he had wasted his life. He continued by saying that at one time a bright future was open to Leon. Now he had annihilated that future by quitting school thus cutting short a brilliant career.

However, there were strong positive qualities about Leon which for themselves would have set him somewhat apart from other people. Every time the caring son received his payroll check, a portion of it would be handed in the cripple fingers of his poor mother. His reverence for his mother had gradually become a sort of religion that withdrew into the depths of his soul.

Beatrice Van Meerstellen, the most affectionate lady in the world lived on a small Social Security allowance. Leon would help her by paying part of the rent. But for so long, Beatrice had been an unhappy mother who saw that her son was taken by anxiety. She noticed that her child had greatly, unexpectedly changed. But she knew what it was to be a mother. The sensibility of her maternal heart toward Leon was stronger than ever. Mrs. Van Meerstellen's eyesight was very poor. At least two doctors said she would eventually go blind. Because of serious back pain and intolerable headaches she became obsessed by the certainty of her approaching death.

At home, Leon also took good care of his fuzzy aging cat that he loved with so much passion. Once I caressed the quiet feline who arched itself and started purring loudly. Most of the time, his pet-friend kept crouching in the doorway. He had developed a case of toxoplasmosis; an intestinal parasite that sometimes developed with older cats. Leon repeatedly said he trusted his pet better than any human being.

If my co-worker was often unpredictable, on the other hand with our patrons he was a perfect gentleman. He greeted the customers with that touch of compassion in a cool, but pleasant manner. He would describe the menu the way a poet would do about nature, always chivalric even while pouring out the wine. Through it all he remained professional. As Leon was pulling out the rosy flesh from a lobster's shell right at the table there were relentless demands from our clients. He had a way to make them happy. Things ever ran smoothly, that really added to the pleasure of eating. Van Meerstellen was such a great connoisseur of wines that some customers would seek his suggestion for the right bottle to please their palate. He really enlightened our clients by acting so respectfully. My friend was the perfect butler. Well versed in at least three languages he could have worked in the greatest estates of the land.

Aside from his changeable attitude, especially with me; his more than florid flatteries toward Arthur, Leon was after all a fine, but complicated human being. I've always spoken in the highest terms of Van Meerstellen's qualifications.

Last month (forgetting all of his picking on me), as my birthday was rolling around he bestowed me a miniature bronze bust of Napoleon Bonaparte he brought back from his last trip to the French capital. We were still a good team, and with his field of craftiness, in spite of everything, it was a real pleasure to work with him.

Chapter 36

JANUARY 17, 1994, 4:31 A.M, as the night was slipping away, I was jolted from my sleep, overthrown from my bunk bed and rolled on the floor carpet like a dead fish. I first thought it was a bomb that nearly tore the side of my apartment. I felt a nasty shock, more like a violent movement of the earth. It was a tremor with a heavy rumble of the ground; almost as if a heavily laden train was crossing a bridge made of steel.

Suddenly my place of residence in North-Hollywood started to sink from one side: the upright piano slid in my direction. It was a long chuckling sound as the floor kept rising and falling.

In order to avoid being crushed by the piano I quickly opened the front door and headed instantaneously toward the balcony. All I could hear was a jumble of blaring squeaks. The ground kept on rising up, trembling, rocking under my feet. The roof broke free at the edges as the entire building shook on its foundations. In the shock, in the surprise of it all I stood still for a few seconds and could hear the beating of my heart. Along with creakings, groanings, clatter of breaking glass, cracks in the floor and falling debris was to be observed everywhere. The water that had been in the swimming pool went overboard. It was surging all around, in the yard. In

486

the apartment across from my own, the sound of water was hurrying past the doorway. An oscillation of all lights within the building occurred as a loud creaking with groaning, great uproar was going on. I was utterly bewildered by that roar. The rasping grew louder, and I became quite conscious that the entire structure upon which I stood was moving. Several of my neighbors had already stepped outside. They were on their knees, holding hands in silent prayer. In the next building, other people were uttering loud cries.

Another jolt created an ominous rumble as the walls heaved and then the ground righted itself. Unmindful that I stood there, *en déshabillé-* in my underwears, with a light jacket over my shoulders I hurried to joined my neighbors in holding hands.

At this point I realized how petty and insignificant all my former fears had been when it seemed that I have been clinging on a floating wreck with the howl of Arthur, the triumphant demon!

The crowd was growing with people from the other side of the building who were still in their pajamas and nightgowns. Everything became dysfunctional. The electricity was shut off, yet luckily someone had a portable radio with high frequency: we just experienced a six-point-seven earthquake centered in Northridge.

Still, another aftershock caused the rolling and pitching of floors and streets. It seemed that the ground had given way abruptly beneath our feet. A leathery-faced man was going to fall over the balcony ramp. I grabbed him by his right leg. With some help I pulled him back on the cement ground that started to get loose. Several splits appeared, it was horrible to watch.

As the sun was hidden by smoke by so much dust, the cars in the streets were powdered with that same dust. It seemed that the earth was rising and falling off its orbit! One more shock was felt. It was like a sickening rollercoaster ride with a shuddering of awesome proportions. There was a frightening sound; a deafening roaring thud again like the rumbling of a volcano, impossible to point out where it came from since it was incessantly everywhere and nowhere. I noticed gaping fissures on the staircase and across the street. On a surrounding house a slate roof gave way as if there had been an explosion. Great piles of wreck were building up on all sides. Soon I discovered a titanic mass of stones among a jumble of debris. Everybody was shivering; there were salvos of coughing in the air. Someone shouted: "This is hell on earth!" Some people acting strangely were crouched on rooftops. Now the rain was slashing and tearing at them like wolves' teeth. They had been drained of their houses by the compelling magnet of the disaster. Screaming voices all played to the tune of panic. I saw a two-story building that tilted over significantly.

The phone was still working. I tried to reach Arthur, then Leon. Both lines were out of work. Finally I was able to contact Melanie. She told me that the floor of her house had caved-in as dust fell from the broken roof. She confirmed to me that the roof from the Northridge fashion-center came crashing down along with other buildings such as the Northridge Hospital Medical Center. All the neonatal cases were taken by 'medivac' helicopters to the Saddleback Memorial Hospital in Laguna Hills.

The radio announced that the Kaiser Permanente Hospital was already declared total loss; that an overpass on the Golden State Freeway collapsed. Surprisingly, within a second fault the city of Santa Monica got her part of misery. Another overpass went down on a commuting route near La Cienega Boulevard and Fairfax Avenue. Entire neighborhoods were shattered. In Northridge, at the epicenter of the quake several trains derailed along the tracks. Melanie got news that the preliminary report specified that seventy-two people already died and there were over twenty thousand homeless. One of her friend who slept just below a large aquarium was taken to the hospital urgently. The aquarium literally exploded as it fell at the edge of the bed. Fishes and pieces of glass were flying in the air. The friend needed over fifteen stitches on the face alone, resulting from the cuts.

The quake lasted ten seconds; nevertheless the brutish strength changed the life of millions forever. The first interpretation of the main culprit was a seventy-mile fracture in the earth's crust. The Office of Emergency Management for the County of Los Angeles mentioned that: "the earthquake occurred on a previously—unknown blind thrust fault under the mountains north of Porter Ranch and produced the strongest ground motions ever instrumentally recorded in an urban setting in North America. Scientists later measured that it had raised the elevation of Oat Mountain, north of the city by about twenty inches."

Desolation in addition to mourning was all over. As the beating of my heart settled down, with some stars gleaming coldly I waited and waited until sunrise. Holding firm against the railing I went down the stairs toward street-level. Afterward, I opened the garage-gate with the crank, went in my car and drove to *Le Cerisier*. Not too far from my residence a narrow thread of smoke drifted from the cooling ruins. A mini-mart attached to a gas station was almost totally flat. The lobby of the North Star Hotel on Victory Boulevard resembled a mountain of debris.

In the streets I watched the faces of two men in a heated argument over a collision of their vehicles. They didn't know this was an act of God. Minutes later, when realizing that Mother Nature was the culprit they would forget their differences. That was as far as the argument went.

The Red Cross showed itself at every turn by rescuing those still alive under the ruins of the hospital. Its personnel kept on sending lots of food such as sterilized milk, bread, soups and other supplies, this along with clothes and blankets. There were great, heartbreaking stories: a woman with her baby was rescued alive after so many hours underground, in total darkness. Again, the frightful destruction of property extended itself all the way even further than the city of Santa Monica where several bricks condominiums with at least one hotel were partially destroyed. Thousands of destitute, some seriously wounded were directed to emergency centers. Along with the Red Cross, other agencies, firefighters from the entire great Los Angeles County (though some from other cities, and other states as well) were in hand, working like heroes to save more people still trapped under piles of dust and stones.

In Sherman Oaks, I checked out the restaurant. To my surprise, beside the huge mess in the kitchen, with pots, pans on the floor among some broken dishes, the dining room was safe. Several weeks ago Leon had the terrific idea to install wires in front of the open wine cellar protecting all of the very expensive vintage wines that were actually on display.

A few days after the earthquake, the city household inspectors had declared Arthur's residence unsafe. A red tag was affixed on the dilapidated property. The doors were shut and padlocked. My employer then found a house for rent in Tarzana, with option to buy.

At that time the Salvation Army alone had already fed thousands of people. The property damages would total billions of dollars. Destruction to wood-frame apartment houses was widespread in the San Fernando Valley to the Pacific shore, especially for the lower-level parking garages.

The power of the earthquake had lifted many of the structures off from their foundations…

Finally my employer's file for the insurance claim came to a close. Rather than to have the check sent to his new residence, the boss invited the insurance adjuster and his wife for a dinner at *Le Cerisier.*

While having their coffee and dessert, the adjuster handed Arthur a manila envelope. When Arthur glanced over the document he felt a sort of paralysis creeping over his fingers.

As he was anticipating an asinine reaction from the owner of the restaurant who just openned the envelope with the check inside, Leon grabbed my arm signaling for both of us to better watch a ludicrous episode about to unfold.

Arthur kept on staring and staring at the check. His eyes started to glitter with such an excited interest as his hands began to tremble. When he had at last got it straight our employer crossed himself. A sparkle of pleasure was mounting up, and he leaped in the air like a puppet. Indescribably blithesome, the little man planted a big kiss on the adjuster's cheek. The man was obviously repulsed by that surprise reaction. In contrast Leon and I were amused at watching this grown man acting so gratified as a child with his newfound toy. We simply could not take our eyes away from him. A towering wave of merriment was in the air as Arthur waved that precious paper with an intense and fixed smile.

Following the clinking of glasses he took a gulp of wine. His throat became contracted in a joyful sensation and he uttered a warm chuckle. Our employer was chewing his food rapidly like a rabbit, bursting out laughing with each bite.

As soon the insurance-man and his wife had left, Arthur paced the dining room relishing the moment. Unexpetedly he glanced at the painting of the Madonna and Child hanging on the wall, feeling good in his skin. Again as he did before in a sign of humiliation he prostrated in front of the icon and crossed himself, saying: *"Misereatur tui omnipotens Deus…,"* some of the few Latin words he remembered from church, without knowing the meaning of them.

While it may look like Arthur was rewarded for Nature's wrath, for other people life wasn't that rosy anymore. Thousands were still living in their building makeshift shelters or slept in their cars. Their homes were destroyed or heavily damaged,and it was too risky to get back in. Tent cities were built everywhere in the 'Valley' area. Many of those unfortunate people didn't carry any earthquake insurance. They were all anxiously waiting for federal assistance from FEMA-Federal Emergency Management Agency.

We never knew the total amount of Arthur's check. He never told us anything. But on the other hand, he did something absolutely illegal that would give him lots of problems later on. Instead to use those funds as intended for; that was to fix or rebuild his unsafe house he simply bought the new residence that he previously rented.

In the months that followed, the neighbors from that 'red tag' dwelling that was crumbling and abandoned started complaining as this became a foul-smelling pest-house. The entire residence had a despondent air of neglect and desertion. The garden that was once cultivated was now left to ruin. That one time beautiful place was so dilapidated, it could break someone's heart. With all the dirt that has been accumulated the driveway seemed to have vanished. It was impossible to shut the gates, the rust having soldered them to their hinges. The shutters were falling off and part of the roof was caving in. There was a general air of nostalgic decay as the moss already covered the stone figures of a silent fountain. Grass also grew on each side of the gravel walks. Rust was everywhere with wild shrub growing-up to two feet high, as wild branches crawled over the yard's wall.

Stinking mud at the bottom of the dried-up swimming pool emitted offensive odors that made bees, crickets and butterflies drowsy while strange animals were also running wild at night. The smell of that sump of damp and rotting leaves would poison all sorts of beasts. Earlier, some of the water from the pool went overboard. In its course it had swept inward to the walking path that was still marsh. The chorus of crickets; the croaking of frogs were equally unbearable. Even the birds fluttered with a proprietary air. At other times, an eerie stillness continued to hang over the place. The entire house was falling dreadfully into decay. Some of the doors were likewise off the hinges as the vermin was creeping out. Furthermore, *les escargots* took possession of the garden. An old bicycle that was corroding stood next to the fence that was falling to pieces.

Everything that had been left in a very bad state as the desolation in that swampy hole had tested the nerves of the neighborhood once more. Local residents started writing letters couched in freezing and chocking terms. Those letters would be delivered to city hall. People were complaining that because of Arthur's negligence the house was naturally bound to deteriorate. Their own properties already had devalued for this was a prime site. With the sudden boom of real estate, the land in that particular area had acquired real value. At one time, Arthur talked over plans to tear down the house. There were only talks, nothing ever happened.

As for Melanie, she was allowed to return and live in her own home. However, the building was out of its foundations. She likewise received a considerable amount of money from the insurance in order to pay for the restoration. That money went straight to her bank account; no repairs were ever made.

Now, with those broken foundations, every time it rained she had to pump water out from the dining room, the kitchen and the garage. The daughter even sued the insurance company for wrecked furniture, mirrors and other inside damages. However the lawsuit was unsuccessful. With all the hours of attorney's fees, she had spent thousands of dollars in vain.

* * * *

Long ago I received a present from a dear uncle stricken with lung-cancer, and living in Belgium. It was an exceptionally gorgeous Oriental vase lacquered by a soft blue glaze. It was an object of great value. At the bottom, *un sceau*, or special seal familiar to expert antique dealers was visible.

California being an earthquake state I decided to place that precious vase, still wrapped in a closet of my apartment. As a collector item I believe it was safer locked-up than on display on top of a piece of furniture.

Several months after the Northridge earthquake, with my vase still intact, Adele, a cousin and her grandson from the old country came to The Golden State for a month's vacation. They stayed with me all the time and I took them everywhere, from San Francisco to San Diego, Las Vegas and the Grand Canyon.

But, on the last day of their holiday in California something very unfortunate happened. For no particular reason I decided to open the drawer where I kept so many souvenirs and to my surprise the little vase wasn't there any longer! As my cousin and grandson were enjoying a swim in the heated-pool the urge came to me to empty my cousin's large suitcase but it was only an enticement and I didn't do a thing. Feeling compassion for the young boy, not wanting to ruin his vacation (unwise of me), I didn't mention a word about the missing vase. I took them to LAX for a safe return with Air France to Belgium via Paris. There had been warning signs earlier as Adele kept on opening and shutting drawers, constantly turning things upside down but I didn't pay too much attention to it.

Considering that my action possessed some merit, that shadow left my thoughts for awhile but the thought came back, stronger than ever: *"What a stupid, utter fool I had been, with that virtue of clemency, just to protect the good image of the family and to retain the charming memories?"*

At the restaurant, Arthur noticed my concern and quipped:

"Well *mon petit* Pierre what's happening with you?" So I explained the entire situation to him. And he was quick to respond: "Yeah, that's you all right, playing the Good Samaritan, the enlightened protector of poor souls but acting like a moron as well. Your cousin is just a corrupted woman. You gratified her, the grandson with your hospitality; this is what you got in return!" And, in order to calm me down, after throwing his arms around me with a bear hug, for the very first time we shared a bottle of *Clos du Bois* fine Chardonnay.

* * * *

Throughout all those years there were a few occasions when Arthur would show compassion but he was still most disagreeable. What infuriated me the most was the way that that boss of mine was using me in his jokes to trash his imbecility at our customers. Given that his stories were just pure fantasy of the mind, those same customers would consider me as a no-brain.

One day, Arthur would elaborate to our customers with great detail that his béarnaise sauce was made with new-laid eggs from caged-free chickens: "I personally went with Pierre to that Oxnard farm to meet my feathered friends and grab those beautiful brown eggs for the restaurant."

Of course we never have been there in the first place! Those "beautiful brown eggs" were rather white as snow. They came from across the street at the 99 Cents Store! From the same store the boss would get white asparagus dipped in water in a jar. For our clientele, again, it was quite a different story. With flights of eloquence he conveyed:

"This morning petit Pierre went to LAX to pick-up fresh white asparagus from a Brussels Air flight which has just arrived directly from Belgium! They would be served tonight as one of our great house specialty: *asperges à la Flamande,* asparagus topped with warm chopped hard-boiled eggs and melted butter." My only response to those fantasy narratives so well elaborated by that little man was a simple shaking of the head. By denying all this, I would have made the boss very upset as people would have realized how a big liar that indeed he really was…

After tasting so many dishes from *La Nouvelle Cuisine,* along with his drinking of hard liquor to wine and champagne, Arthur was putting on weight quite fast. He decided on a strong regimen of a mixture of lemon juice, cayenne pepper and honey all blended together: one glass in the morning, another one in the late afternoon. With incredible willpower my employer didn't take any kind of solid food for a period of two weeks. He kept on that routine course of therapy without missing a day. The result was incredible. Arthur had lost thirty pounds over fifteen days! With great excitement, several of our heavy patrons decided to follow his example on that marvelous treatment.

Nevertheless, soon enough the boss went back to his drinking; to his copious meals. I even saw him ravenously devoring steak tartare-raw meat. Furthermore, it seemed that it was too hard for him to simply refuse a complimentary glass of champagne or fine wine offered to him by our regular customers. Within a month or so, just like magic, Arthur's enormous belly did a reappearing act. So far, so good for that fine regimen!

Chapter 37

UPON MY ARRIVAL at *Le Cerisier* a fight erupted between Melanie and Arthur. Melanie had a strangely unhappy twisted face. There were discolored pouches of skin beneath her eyes. She was thin and a little pale, looking as if she hadn't slept for a week. She came in the kitchen, appearing intensely depressed. It was as though the whole world had conspired against her. The whimsical affection toward her father appeared to have gone. All of a sudden those exciting things in life have stopped happening; only boredom remained.

Arthur's wife, Angeline had been taken urgently to the hospital because of high fever and palpitations. Apparently, Melanie took care of everything while Arthur was more preoccupied with the business at the restaurant. It's a fact that every day, after work the daughter would spend several hours at the convalescent home, playing bingo with her mother and other patients. Arthur would drop by at his convenience.

Now, there were bitter exchanges of words. With tears of outrage, Melanie became voluble. She started yelling like the whistle of a fast train, almost like a sociopath with that reptilian glitter, as her hands clenched involuntary into fits.

Sitting in the private room, wearing a yellow *Lacoste* shirt and navy shorts, Eddy Freedman quietly drank his cold martini before nibbling his trout almandine from off the backbone. With crickets peeping behind the cupboard, as Eddy mopped up the last trace of his butter-lemon sauce, he all of a sudden was taken with a sort of silent amusement. His lips became pursed in such a way as to let me realize he was whistling a tune. Looking still benignantly pleased, in a squirt of laughter Freedman, after rubbing his eyes wearily revealed to me in a near whisper:

"Pierre, it looks like the rats are fighting again!" During those conflicting times Eddy always adopted a middle course. With a calm indifference he showed a position of neutrality, but deep inside I already knew that he took the side of Arthur. It seemed that the current infighting embarrassment with his mentor was ironically a great source of pleasure for Freedman for I have never seen him in better spirits. Since by no means I intruded or pry into the affairs between father and daughter I decided to keep company with my friend Eddy.

Augean stable, dysfunctional and acting like an errant knight, Melanie, with a look of extraordinary distress in the face, eyed Arthur sharply. They were acting like two hungry wolves engaged on biting each other's tails. Shaking her head ever so strongly, she threw her hands in the air telling her dad who just forked a piece of herring into his mouth:

"I just hate the sight of you. I know that you don't love my mother, that you have the insolence to treat her so badly. You spend all of your time with Eddy like he was your twin brother and you keep forgetting your spouse. Last time we visited mother, as I was trying to control her weight you were already half-drunk and you started flirting with young nurses!" she went on, "I believe you were never in love and never will be. You have already broken your wife's heart. She is so miserable with you. You never thought of the grief in which she must be plummeting. You'll be driving her into an early grave!"

This was true. More than once Angeline thought of going away from her husband during his absence at the house. But she feared that this, instead of benefiting him, might be the means of hampering and humiliating him yet more if it should become known. Once she explained: "I think of my husband more kindly when I'm away from him." But there was still in her heart that sort of hope that he would change, some hope she could not entirely extinguish...

This time, from the door-window between the kitchen and the dining room I watched the muscles trembling in Arthur's throat. After a moment of tense silence, he expostulated:

"You have no right to talk to me like that; just tell me what you driving at?" asked her father. Step by step, through the stages of the quarrel things went out of control. In an even louder voice, heavier than I had ever heard before Melanie broke from rage into tears. They stared at each other for another long strained instant. Bursting out of indignity, her eyes were filling as she was about to speak. With her jaw quivering and a sterned mouth with severe eyes it was as if the screaming of the wind blew the words from her mouth: "Aside from visiting mother each and every day I also baked different flavored cheesecake for the restaurant. I bought all the ingredients out of my own pocket. After you sell them to your customers, you take all the profit to yourself!" Her cup of humiliation was full to the brim. Melanie was offended. She became furiously angry as her father was gazing away, avoiding her inquisitive eye. His silence was like an icy gulf. Now, red faced with her hair utterly disheveled and foaming at the mouth, her voice rose again to its highest pitch. She concluded in a deluge of tears:

"You owe me five thousand dollars! Did you hear me Papa? Five thousand dollars! I've kept all the receipts for the last two years."

Rubbing his hand over his chin, pale-face and tense, Arthur asked: "What on earth are you talking about?" Sniffing at him like a she-wolf, in the labyrinth of her sorrows she heard herself breathing hard. After catching her breath, veins in her forehead bulged as the flush of her cheeks almost turned purple. The response rushed from her lips as she went on:

"What am I talking about…What am I talking about? Simply that you're not my father, you are somebody else. You act like a zombie, wandering with no direction in life because you don't know what you live for. Furthermore, you claim to be a good Christian by going to church twice a year during Easter and Christmas. You pray only under great stress or for financial reasons; for me this is pure hypocrisy. With that stingy attitude and lack of charity you insult God!"

The boss was completely stunned and lost for words. His eyes were rolling up at the ceiling in dismay, and he stared at her with his mouth hanging open. She was right; I really commiserated with her grief as she suffered deep humiliation.

At this point, Melanie had no time to frame another sentence. There was a hard look on her face as if she hated him. Apathetic as always, with a solemn displeased frown, Arthur left his daughter by herself in the kitchen.

He sent her a shooting glance over his left shoulder and crept away to the private room like a lame fox as he stumbled awkwardly against the bread table. Wounded pride had exasperated his wrath. At that precise moment, not only did Melanie hate her dad with a peculiarly feminine virulence, he hated her as well.

Exhausted and broken by so much emotional strain she finally left the premises. Nursing the yet un-cooled embers of his anger Arthur waited, wrung and bitter until he knew Melanie was no longer there. The boss felt that his daughter had mortally offended him.

With blood mounted to his head he was fuming so much that he asked Eddy to fix his usual drink- bourbon and Coke. This time the gaze of his expressive eyes was quite uncomfortable, so Eddy bestowed his friend with a double shot. He drank it down at a gulp. (Sometimes I had the feeling he would burst with all that liquor inside him.) As Arthur felt genuinely scandalized, the strong cocktail brought him renewed confidence. Once more, glancing inquisitively aside out of the door-window which commanded a view of the kitchen he continued assuring himself that his daughter had in effect walked away and be out of sight. Subsequent to a breach of silence, while jerking his thumb over his shoulder, my employer not wanting to be the loser in that altercation ended the incident with a voice vibrating in a subterranean chuckle:

"Well, that little pest is gone! What a shameless bitch to address me in such terms! How dare she spoke to me in that tone of voice? I warned her to keep her tongue behind her teeth! She give me the creeps, my Gosh, such a filthy mouth, and what a sour-face. Even that she's still young, she acted like an old bag. The Boot Camp, that's what she need... That stupid goose ought to have been whipped as a child!"

Then, I became really surprised at the liberty he gave his tongue as he continued: "What the hell that little squalling brat thinks she is? Talking to me that way as if I was a piece of dirt, and still pestering me for money on top of that as if I was made of money? Although I had a million dollars she won't get a penny from me. The sooner she leaves my sight for good, the better. Years ago, that vicious child should never have left that convent... *Merde de merde de non d'un chien,* what an impertinent girl that keep on intermeddling with my business! She already forgot all of my sacrifices in raising her! I know her friends have influenced her; they will eat her like vermin, especially that boyish-looking one with that Joan of

Arc haircut who really acted like a slut. It's the same friend who played with unholy toys and who believed in the Satanist pentagram. In the old country, that daughter of mine would be branded as *l'enfant terrible*!"

At that particular time I had the feeling that he could have strangled his own daughter. Once Arthur had eased up on his yelling he decided again that he needed another bourbon and Coke...double shot that he drank in short sucking gulps! On the other hand, he didn't realize yet that he had been the one who had unearthed that nasty scandal!

One thing I knew for sure: the tension between them had really been palpable. A great gulf had been created between father and daughter. Now they would fight tooth and nail. They would hate each other more than ever as they almost became real enemies. The family's quarrels which followed this event were very sharp, as my employer continued to rule her. The entire bumpy conversation ended icily, it had been 'like salt in a sore!'

From that day on they kept moving backwards and forwards, from strong arguments to reconciliation; from reconciliation to strong arguments. Even if they argued for as long as a decade, they would never see eye to eye. Much later, a little peace was only maintained between them with the greatest difficulty. This could have been a fine and quiet afternoon but Irony is a subtle teacher. Nevertheless, rapidly matters of infinitely greater concern for Arthur occurred.

On that same day, less than an hour later as a crowning misfortune, that feverish activity the boss just had experienced was interrupted. It was replaced by the arrival of Mr. Yan Wong. And suddenly all the little wrinkles came scampering into his face like sandpaper.

Mr. Wong the broad-shouldered butcher, his skin shrunk up with furrow and with a three days' growth of

black whiskers came in, ferocious and raging. A stifled growl
which sounded like distant thunder came out of his mouth. He
started giggling as if his neck was scared of the weight of his
head. He was crossbreed, almost as dark as a desert Bedouin;
a mixture of some kind of mythical slant-eyed oriental and
fuzzy head Malay that represented a collision of cultures.
His *visage*, showing gold-filled front teeth expressed a real
threat as his cheekbones protruded sharply. His hair was long,
tangled and greasy. With his harsh weather-beaten face and
muscled like a tiger he had at least twice Arthur's strength. He
reminded me of one of those old-time dragons that blew fire
from their mouth. Monumental, with tremendous strength
in his shoulders and arms he was able to crack a walnut with
his fist. His flattened nose was not genetic: it was sculpted
through years of boxing in the rings. Still one can observe in
his gait the manners of a prizefighter. However, for a man so
well build he had a curious little *derrière*.

After he had been ruminating all that time, the giant of
a man like *une armoire à glace*, so imposing, went on Arthur's
throat. With narrow piercing eyes all sunken, he announced
that he had a bone to pick-up with him that his reason for
being here was that he wanted an important matter to be
settled.

In that strong broken, unpolished British accent he
addressed himself to the owner of the restaurant point blank.
The butcher further demanded that from this day on no meat
would be delivered to the restaurant until he collected some
funds. Yan talked with a sort of a whispering voice, but with
deep anguish. Every brawn of his face was now stretching
tight. The middleman, pointing a menacing forefinger made
it clear to the owner that he helped him build a fourteen
thousand dollars credit line. (The unfortunate man didn't
realize that opening a credit line to Arthur was like lending

seed to a canary. The canary will only pay you back with a song.) Shrugging his shoulders nervously the butcher was now sweating. His eyes were angry and cold. Those harsh words produced on Arthur a particular effect. Moving his neck like a bird it looked as if he had just received a bucket of iced cold water on his head. And Mr. Yan Wong continued:

"Arthur, I trusted you. But I just ran the numbers and a reckoning of the account: I have made everything as easy as possible to help you and you haven't paid me for the last three deliveries." He said this with emphasis and conviction. Finding it harder to keep his voice under control, he went on:

"I feel that you have outrageously abused my generosity." The storm grew exceedingly high as Mr. Wong mopped his face with his handkerchief. The gaze of his expressive eyes prolonged Arthur's uncongenial attitude. In getting the upper hand, the butcher's expression changed radically. His voice shook a little, but he was still in full command:

"Now, in plain English: since you have refused to honor the terms of our agreement, if you don't hand me a thousand dollar check within twenty-four hours I would be forced to go to court. I won't rule out to secure a lien on your business; and that's final. I'm not going to wait until pigs fly. Just remember the consequences: your bad debts would tarnish your good name forever! With a lien against *Le Cerisier* you can be utterly ruined! But if you want a fight, so be it!"

Deciding that a form of constraint was required, the butcher revealing one of those unexpected turns of temper tried to make Arthur more at ease. In a more amicable tone, with a gentle sense of courtesy, after he laid his hand masterfully on my employer's shoulder he added with carefully chosen words: "My friend, this is not *la mer à boire;* I'm not requesting you to donate one of your kidneys for Christ' sake!"

Arthur swallowed all this with mounting nervousness. He longed to speak but the words died on his lips; he could think of nothing to say. Our big talker of a boss had become a silent man, totally voiceless. For awhile, my employer stood in an agony of indecision before finally making an agreement with the butcher.

Mr. Wong was not alone in having problems with Arthur. Most of our creditors were pressing him to be paid. As soon as the butcher left, the 'tormented emperor', pulling a long face and looking more like a frightened rabbit became hysterical again. *This surely required another round of bourbon and Coke, followed by another one just in order to control his nerves.* In such a frenzied moment, Leon and I feared that the boss would be very obnoxious tonight during dining hours. He had been drinking non-stop like *un Polonais*- a Polish man.

As we heard the chimes of the nearby church at exactly five o'clock, Arthur who had now changed his libation habits to *Stella Artois,* a Belgian beer, became absolutely and totally drunk. A sickening smell of ethanol was on his breath. An hour later, staggering on his feet, my employer forced himself on a group of customers sitting on the corner booth. He was so tipsy that he could not speak plainly any more. As the boss poured more wine in their wine glasses (including his), the bottle slipped from his fingers and fell, rolling on the carpet floor.

After having replaced the wine Arthur started talking heavily like the sound of a trumpet from the height of a mountain to his uninterested audience. With his marvelous gift as a whimsical storyteller he then revealed in paraphrases a strange story which I never heard him tell before. Again, being quite familiar with Arthur's lies this was such an incoherent fable, like a rope of sand.

During his time in the *French Marine Marchande*, his boat was anchored in the port of Luanda in the African-Portuguese colony of Angola which I also visited at one time with my paratrooper unit. At a local village Arthur had been invited to a birthday barbecue party. Like a hungry tiger he devoured ample pieces of meat cooked in a hot *pili-pili* sauce which he chased down with a gallon of *Simba*, the national brand of beer of The Democratic Republic of Congo. Following a small talk with the birthday celebrant who happened to be the chief of that little community, Arthur asked what particular cut of meat he had just digested and from what type of animal was it, adding that it was really delicious. The chief had a big laugh as he proudly revealed to his satisfied guest that the *pièce de résistance*, that fine meat was none other than a Bantu prisoner from an enemy tribe who was captured a day earlier! And he added:

"For hours the man had been thoroughly cooked in the *marmite*." Then the chief concluded: "My men flattened the captive Bantu; they tenderized him with the addition of fresh *mvumba-mvumba* (salted herbs found mainly in the savana), for good flavor!"

With that disgustingly distasteful tale from our employer our gourmet patrons showing a face of mock horror seemed not to remember coming in at *Le Cerisier* with a hearty appetite for an epicurean dinner. Subsequently to that great make-believe account the boss stammered a few more words, more like a cacophony of sounds. As his head fell noisily on the table, seconds later he was asleep. His friend, the compassionate Eddy decided it was time to take Arthur home… at once.

Chapter 38

O N THIS SULTRY moonless evening, the thermometer still indicated ninety degrees. In Burbank, at 2.00 PM the temperature had reached over one hundred degrees. Unfortunately, less then a week ago Arthur had been twice overtaken by misfortune. But this time, when I arrived at the restaurant, the boss stood there. He seemed quite alarmed at what had occurred. He craned his neck in front of the parking lot with a piece of lettuce stuck to his chin. After he took off his glasses and polished them with a white handkerchief, he stepped back inside the establishment. Arthur appeared to be like a painter from his easel that surveyed his work as a whole; except that horror was all over his face. Gazed, with parted lips Arthur was pointing his nose to the sky. Unable to restrain a certain sense of bitterness he started howling full-throated as his hair was raising, cresting on the neck. He really looked sour, and sick too.

As usual I greeted him but as he still took a glance of agony at the heaven he appeared too self-absorbed to even notice my presence. Arthur was obviously deep in thought. I had an uneasy feeling that something more than usual was going on. Even now that I was standing next to him, my employer continued to be unconscious of me, so unnerved was he at the sight: here, there, everywhere, a mountain of debris of trees and branches had been dumped in our parking lot that became a dirty field of wood, twigs of dead leaves and ragweed. This could also create the perfect environment in which crabgrass can grow, not forgetting that the splintering of wood could be rotting in the heavy rain, creating a pungent, highly oppressive odor. Like a stinking slum, rats and wood-lice would live in perfect harmony.

Arthur always spied on persons walking in the parking lot but this had been a late night or very early morning operation. Now Arthur seemed to have encountered an unsurpassed difficulty. Stunned by the situation, showing even more anxiety that deepened in his eyes he kept navigating around, his voice thick in his throat. Wandering like a lost soul he flew into a storming rage as he began cursing and kicking the woodpile every which way akin a lunatic. As he furiously muttered between his teeth he started drawing in his breath from the other side of the debris close to the wall alongside the alley. For a moment my employer was off balance as he could not withstand the emotion. And, on top of this a pigeon made a dropping on his shoulder...and it was quite voluminous!

Things looked so bad that Arthur felt as if at any moment the ceiling of the restaurant would cave in. With shoulders quivered he began to pace down long strides in the alley, abstractly like a caged animal, swearing, getting out of temper. Arthur tried to think but his thoughts wandered. He was at a loss as what to do next. He stood still looking on the ground like a dog in search of food.

With that fool smell of dampness, fungus and crawling insects (the woodpile was already swarming with them), the flies started to come in. We had to spray heavily with bug bombs. The situation was utterly chaotic as ravens were already circling over the debris. A couple of squirrels sat on top of the branches and jabbered at Arthur in a friendly manner. This unfuriated the boss even more since he was far to be in a state of cheerfulness. He started punching at nothing but the air. For a moment he stood there like a scarecrow.

Leon arrived. With his eyes fixed on that pile of wood he began coughing to clear his throat. He broke into a violent non-stop sneezing attack as the dust was searing his lungs. It was a drawn-out and wheezy cough, like an early attack of hay fever. He was sneezing with such a blast that was accompanied with a deep roar. Every time he tried to talk, more coughing fits interrupted him. Later on, after a break Leon blew his nose noisily and was able to gain a steady control of his breathing.

Now, like the wash from a ship a track of mud was all around the kitchen-floor that just happened to be mopped.

Tree-trimmers were given some extra money from homeowners in order to pay the fee at the dumping site. Instead of driving to the landfill site, those small time business people were able to manage a lucrative still dishonest operation: they disposed their load at *Le Cerisier's* back alley into the parking lot and pocketed their extra *dinero*. A neighbor who heard the noise of the dropping indicated to us that it sounded like a giant coal bucket falling down a cellar stairs. On those earlier morning hours, the same neighbor came to the window just in time to hear those three Spanish words from the driver: *"Muy bien amigo."*

As Arthur perceived all those branches in a way a ship captain would gaze at splintered wreck from a sinking vessel, he kept on staring and staring again at the parking lot with feverish fear, being at a loss as to what to do next. Our employer had to pay the city compensation for the cleaning, and it wasn't cheap! With the heat all this wood could turn into a pest-ridden oven as we had to wait at least two or three days for one of the city mammoth trucks to pick-up that trash.

Following that stormy event Arthur started wandering aimlessly from table to table before retiring to rest in the private room. It proved a long hot summer and the sun was pouring down the worst heat of the season with great intensity. The solar disk vibrating and insistent was drinking the moisture of the soil and the sap from plants. That day Los Angeles was sweltering in a heat wave. The air so fresh in the spring was now stagnant, with searing pastures.

Suddenly, disappointment crossed him everywhere with even more sorrow awaiting him. It was one of those days on which nothing seems to go quite right. Trouble and more trouble were brewing fast as a gloomy tumult of events was now in the forecast. My employer was struck with yet additional calamity as even deeper bad luck had followed him. That difficulty came upon him which he had never the least reason to expect.

Just like leaves on the approaching storm Arthur's mind was trembling with anxiety. At about the same time that the restaurant was to open for business, because of the height of the summer heat wave, a complete blackout occurred. Most of the employees in the nearby business establishments started to converge onto the sidewalk. I decided to join the crowd outside. Other business-owners became horrified as to the consequences of that dreadful event. This had become a neighborhood affair for the entire block, all the way to the gas-station at the corner of the boulevard. Soon, generators from city trucks illuminated the now tranquil Ventura Boulevard.

Back in the restaurant my employer who sat in the private room rose to his feet and began pacing about. Nodding his head vigorously he ordered me to inquire about the length of time necessary in order to restore power.

Once outside again, the foreman announced to me that the repairs would take at least six to seven hours or even much

511

more until the situation can be definitely clarified. This was depending on how damaged the main underground element was.

Arthur, after first worrying about our supply of fresh fish and meat in the glass-refrigerator and the freezer glanced at the reservation book: tonight every single table was reserved. With fluttering eyelids and shallow breathing, he knocked the book with his sweaty palms, and articulated: "Anyway, I am not going to close the place! We surely can expect a full house with an even complete second sitting."

The owner of the restaurant with a cat's stubbornness then rushed to his truck and went to a local hardware store. He came back as fast as a hummingbird with five giant gas-lamps, two for the kitchen and three for the dining room. Now, without any air-conditioning in the dining room, nor any ventilation system working in the kitchen the temperature kept on rising and rising. It became insufferable especially with the addition of extreme warmth from the gas-lamps. With the relentless beating heat it seemed like a scorching African desert. At the same time I took off my apron and rolled up my sleeves above my elbows.

Chef Francis Bevert was already white like sheet with sweat running down his face. At one point we conveyed him outside the establishment, as the temperature was becoming more intense by the minute.

Melanie, wearing a white shirt clicked the latch of the back door and entered the restaurant like 'a big bang.' She was being informed of the sad situation as soon as she arrived.

At once she told her father in an explosive mood and with such an air of gravity that it would be impossible to stay in business without any power. She added:

"The whole thing is hopeless; you should know it!" This was Arthur's bellowed reply: "Listen kiddy, we don't have any shortage of gas, hey," and he continued: "Outside, on the sidewalk, I recognized Mr. Sven Jorgensen, wearing a white suit and silver string ties. This man is a billionaire from Santa Ynez Valley. He owns one of the sprawling ranches in California. He was also the best client from the restaurant in Solvang. I can't possibly refuse him to have dinner with us *non d'un chien*!" Melanie's disappointment was serious. She felt so humiliated by her father's brainless attitude. Twitching her shoulders and hands, in an unrelenting disapproval tone of voice and increasingly sour expression, she lashed an avalanche of words:

"Papa, you're acting just like an old crybaby! I don't care if the governor of California was waiting in front of *Le Cerisier*. This is the most awful hot day of the month. With over a hundred degree heat in the dining room and the oppressive heat in the kitchen, you still expect us to serve food? It's the goddamn most stupid decision I ever heard! In that unventilated kitchen, who can breathe for less than a couple of hours and still live?" she went on, and on as anger flamed between them: "The chef is sick; he's choking and coughing and almost at the death's door. Owing to the heat, like a pit of hell everything in the kitchen is melting and I felt like scurrying insects are already crawling all over my skin," and she concluded: "I thought Pierre was an idiot. Surely, by every criterion I believe that you are the one ready for 'the funny farm', because you got screws loose. I can't believe how grossly deficient you are. You need medical attention because you behave like a real thickheaded and foolish employer! I am hurt and outraged beyond all measure...!'"

With rather a puzzling air Arthur wasn't quite sure yet if he was going to stay open or close the restaurant for the night. Over a long, profound thought it still took him awhile to come into the realization that as the result of this unforeseen development we simply couldn't operate normally. Arthur had the look of a deeply injured man; the seconds were dragging so slowly. As he brought down a torrent of vituperation reluctantly, in a tone of inexpressible bitterness the boss finally decided to send everybody home before closing the door of our little abode. This time, *le patron* had been thoroughly outmaneuvered by his own daughter. I could hardly bear the sight of his depressing face: he had a sad puppy-eyes look. Arthur would certainly never forget that event. It had been the worst evening of his life with no business while the reservation book was full with the names of some of our best customers.

The night was as sultry as the day. At the slightest effort I was drenched with sweat. There was no coolness after dark and I barely fell asleep later around the early morning hours.

* * * *

In a surprising way, Arthur introduced me to one of his old acquaintance: Zizina, the Egyptian lady.

The mean-looking Zizina Pavliz wore a black dress and her wrists were clanking with a bizarre cluster of costume jewelry. With that strong smell of *Shalimar* perfume she had a pink ribbon in her long hair that had knotted itself in several braids with the addition of a black hat. She was boasting of such a pronounced adornment. With a face like a horse, appearing like a withered flower and a perpetually croaky voice and sharp tongue she was the daughter of the personal physician of a former African King. She had strange protruding ears and a lumpy nose. With her toothless gums that emanated a strong smell of Listerine she ate only soup, mashed potato and pudding. Her wrinkled face scourged by time and trouble had almost a grotesque, pathetic appearance as her lips were still voluptuously full but quite vulgar. She became a drunkard from mere chagrin. For reason unknown to me terror appeared to lurk right in the corner of her eye as there was an extreme forbidding of her features.

In the early sixties, Zizina made a living in Los Angeles by marrying so many French, mostly restaurant owners staying in the U.S. illegally. For the moderate sum of four hundred dollars a minister would perform that circus marriage resulting in the issuance of a green card for the groom. The 'Egyptian princess' would stay married for a little while before seeking a new 'prince' for exactly the same fees. It was widely believed that she married over fifteen unscrupulous gentlemen, four of them being homosexuals. I only knew Mrs. Pavliz by sight as indeed most of the French restaurateurs did.

Edouard Pillon, my previous employer at *La Fourchette d'Or* in Beverly Hills also an ex-Zizina husband died of aids in 1992. He was only thirty-seven years old. Arthur knew Edouard quite well since he occasionally went to *La Fourchette d'Or* accompanied by Eddy and O.R. a famed New York comedian and actor. O.R. often appeared on the Johnny Carson's 'Late Show' wearing those extravagant, gigantic sunglasses that always shielded his eyes and accentuated his nose.

Eventually Zizina's little commerce came to an end when immigration authorities paid her a visit in the middle of the night. This happened on the second month of one of her fictitious and convenient wedlock. There were no traces anywhere to be seen around, suggesting that a man had ever lived within those quarters. Furthermore, aside from her 'stool pigeon' marriages, she told fortunes. Zizina, well versed in astrology was equally involved in black magic, telekinetic and voodoo spells dealing with necromancy. Mrs. Pavliz was proficient in the art of casting spells as well as driving away evil spirits. On one occasion she told Arthur that she used the pin-sticking process and *mau-mauing*. If she disliked a person deep enough she would in her salaciousness make that person suffer by sticking a pin in a look-alike doll of him or her. She believed she was able to cast a spell over someone that would drive him or her insane. She also claimed that at one time she threatened an old man who insulted her to send birds against him that would peck out his eyes. So many people are still afraid of her as she always gave the bad look, the evil eye. What's more Zizina asserted that she knew how to cure wounds as well as how to inflict them. She would amaze Arthur by her anecdotes of the direful omens and foreshadowing sights.

Now in her old age, being a veritable sorceress with her dark mystic face, strange protruding ears sunken breasts and voluminous white hair she had lost part of that exclusive charm. She also suffered severe fit of coughing, and oftentimes her lungs rattled with each breath. Zizina's behavior was so odd and she became quite ga-ga.

Lately, the restaurant was quieter than usual and there were fewer guests. As the business at *Le Cerisier* was lingering, waning in strength, Arthur who believed in ghosts and haunted houses called upon his fairy godmother Zizina to perform an act of purification of the entire restaurant.

That purification involved a weird ritual done in order to chase away wicked spirits responsible for business slowdown. And soon, an extraordinary scene took place. After Zizina started reading from a piece of paper that seemed to emanate from some occult control she lay down her fetish on the marble service table and tell Arthur with a serious, almost grim expression:

"I can feel that unruly, whispering spirits are floating all around here and I have to replace them by friendly ghosts!" While blushing and lifting her long-lashed eyelids she added that from under a table she could hear Satan's diabolical laughter. "I have to wrestle with the Devil and I'm going to win!" The boss long suspected the grotesque superstition that evil spirits occasionally showed up at *Le Cerisier,* creating a curse that necessitated some form of exorcism. As demented as she might appear, Arthur did not doubt that Zizina was Mary Magdalene resurrected.

Prior to the purification itself, in order to invigorating the good spirits the Egyptian woman who furthermore proclaimed to be a true Rosicrucian, decided to wear a white nightgown that almost reached down to her ankles, and a black hat with a black feather planted on it. She also carried a cane that she clutched with unsteady shaky fingers.

First, she made the sign of the cross on the front windows and doors and started mumbling prayers. Next Ms. Pavliz requested Arthur to wear a white chasuble that she brought along and flanked by a quadrate cross suspended on a string. I was to follow the boss in some sort of a *chemise de nuit*, night gown before clapping him on the left shoulder every time she pronounced in an almost inaudible voice, the mystic words: *khakha misritia pustus abrani.* This really looked like a macabre dance of death!

Adding to that primitive ritual, with a lighted candle in the hand and a sacred song on her lips Zizina continued her weird mysterious wording. Referring to bible scriptures she explained that, "The day of Shad-dai is a day of distress and of anguish, a day of darkness and of gloominess, a day of clouds and of thick gloom!" and she continued: "As for someone coming in this place and taking sides with Satan, there will be a rotting away of one's flesh. While one is standing upon one's feet, one's very eyes will rot away in their sockets, and one's very tongue will rot away in one's mouth!" "Amen" said Arthur as he kept gawking at the ceiling. I noticed that my employer felt strangely exalted as though he was partner in performing that quite unfamiliar religious act. Furthermore Zizina proceeded to bless every table in the dining room, the front door and also the kitchen oven and all the refrigerators.

Suddenly, in that oft-described demoniac unearthly shriek Zizina was seized by an attack of panic. She fell to the floor with dreadfully distorted arms and legs as her little black hat had slipped on the side of her head. In that position, the weird lady openly called upon demons to leave the restaurant at once. With the accompaniment of incantations she finally would announce that the spell had been lifted.

After awhile, with *bienséance* weaving reverently forward, a beaming Arthur handed the Egyptian woman the one hundred and fifty dollars check as promised, for the purification. The boss kissed her. As she left, tossing her little handbag in the air, she conveyed:

"Tata dear, call me anytime you feel like. By the way I can guaranty you that tomorrow you will have a full house." I thought for a moment that she was leaving the restaurant on a fiery broomstick like a witch-she really was...

On the succeeding evening as it was drawing towards 6.00 PM, Arthur was waiting with great excitement, hoping the miracle predicted by his fairy godmother Zizina would finally resurrect his business. Just as my employer stepped out to breathe some fresh air a crow flew low over his head and he thought this was a good omen. With a protracted pause he squeezed my hand repeatedly and explained to me about his dream from last night: "Pierre, I heard the hymn of angels in perpetual adoration."

However it was far to be what the boss had expected, and he started to look utterly disappointed. There no longer was any hymn of angels: the reservation book for that day was still empty. In desperation Arthur leaned against the wall. He murmured incoherent supplications for a long while till he suddenly started up reciting the mantra: *Khakha misritia pustus abrani*. But it didn't seem to help either; his luck so far had been quite bad.

As the evening wore along, eight o'clock chimed at the first Presbyterian Church a block away. In the dining room sat a solitary person, silently brooding: It was Mr. Peter Longfeld from DARPA: Defense Advanced Research Projects Agency, the only client to come and taste a dish from our *nouvelle cuisine* menu. Some of his best friends actually worked at the Jet Propulsion Laboratory in Pasadena. But, strangely enough, almost immediately Mr. Longfeld had company standing on watch next to his bowl of onion soup with a side of shredded cheese. It was a rat; a quite large rat that seemed to have 'parachuted' itself from the attic. With great disgust, having lost his appetite the gentleman simply cancelled his order of the 'crrrrrrissspy duck' prepared with cherries.

Arthur realized too late that the evil seed which was cast upon Zizina' soul may have produced a terrible harvest. All her prayers, all her incantations have been of no avail. So far so good as regard to the purification?

For quite some time I could not help thinking again of that wild, bizarre ritual; for the way the Egyptian princess Zizina Pavliz, that real wicked tart had so well manipulated the poor Arthur!

Chapter 39

Brussels, Belgium 8:00 A.M.

AS SOON AS I emerged from the Delta aircraft I headed down the steps. At the Zaventem Terminal Building, following the inspection of disembarkation card and passport I directed myself to the exit-door under a soft, calm rain. When I left the Brussels International Airport on that cold September morning, with the land grey and the sky steel, the frosty air felt good on my face. I also scented the fresh cut grass from the lawn in front of the building.

Subsequently of another year of harassment, insults, hurts- you name it, I believe I was entitled for that four weeks holiday.

Now, far away from *Le Cerisier* restaurant and Arthur I went to meet my ailing mother at the Côte d'Azur residence in Jette. From there I walked to *rue Des Chalutiers* to encounter my cousin Adele.

It was so exciting to walk around the capital again and renew acquaintance with so many familiar places of interest. For me, in the Belgian capital every spot everywhere was so poignant with memory; so much good souvenirs and so many historical aspects. I could have been taken blindfold wherever in the many narrow streets of the city for I knew almost every stone. Here still stood my former house in that cul-de-sac area. There was my old school completely restored and sumptuously resting at the edge of *le parc de la forêt*. This was also where I studied dramatic art. To see buildings which have weathered storms for at least seven centuries, to hear the clack of sabots-wooden shoes upon the cobblestones and watch a show of 'lights and sounds' at *La Grande Place,* I was unable to find the proper words to express my feelings. Every place whispered its most secret share of memories. However I hardly recognized other areas where everything has changed, such as the Bank of America standing next, well above *la Cathedrale Sainte Gudule.*

Ultimately I visited a *château* and several fourteenth and fifteenth centuries-old churches. I listened to the morning hymn, the chanting and Bach music from those giant pipes. One of my nephew still do the weekend pilgrimage to an old abbey near the city of Bouillon, reminiscent of the crusader Godefroid de Bouillon, king of the delivered city of Jerusalem.

As in many other European capitals, everybody seemed to be absorbed in the new world technology: the 'robot century', the century of disco, of rap music. In the Belgian metropolis where *Bruxelles chantait sous une pluie fine et ruisselante-*as Brussels kept on singing under the rain in great harmony, so many little cafés to taste fine Belgian beer has vanished. They have been replaced by non-alcohol *salons de thé* where Muslim foreigners from North Africa and Turkey would discuss the latest political events before prayers at the local mosque.

My dear cousin Adele was the little thief that stole my vase; an exclusive, well-valued work of art while visiting me with her grandson in California. She had become an expert in opening drawers and I don't know what else.

I already knew that she had well concealed the *bibelot-*trinket before I arrived, and was afraid and uncomfortable for I would discover its hiding place. I felt neither joy nor excitement, only embarrassment with a sense of sadness at being at her side. I fancied that I couldn't trust her any longer.

Following a violent debate where she obviously had denied again everything about the theft, I left. She probably thought that there was no harm to grab a little souvenir from a close relative since it would remain within the family scope. However, from that day on I've considered her a mere *sans gêne*, senseless kleptomania bandit.

After a short trip to Sluis, Holland with my mother and her long-time friend Hubert (who took care of her after the fatal car accident that killed my father), I took on a new direction. I called on Claudine Rotenberg, MD who lives on a farm-house with her three children on the outskirts of Waterloo.

Waterloo was the site of Napoleon's final battle and defeat as he was fighting all the armies of Europe. During my youth I often visited that famed city. I was so impressed by Napoleon Bonaparte, that little man from Corsica that later became the emperor of the French.

According to Victor Hugo "The last battle was only a clash of sabers and an enigma as obscure for those who gained it as for him who lost it. It was a price won by Europe and paid by France." Some historians from that period had even predicted that in case of Napoleon's victory at Waterloo, his next move would have been toward the North American continent…

Claudine, a dear friend of the Valois Dourville de Montrissart's family was quick to request from me some fresh information about Arthur and daughter Melanie. The lady-doctor also visited the Golden State several years ago and we recalled so many good souvenirs. After holding my hand, she asked: "Tell me Pierre, is Arthur still picking on you?"

Eventually I made a foolish decision. This was an obstinacy that could have taken me all the way to the *taiga*, that vast unlimited pine forest stretching throughout Siberia to a remote Gulag labor camp!

I boarded a *Europabus* in downtown Brussels bound for St-Petersburg, Russia via Germany, Poland, The Baltic States: Lithuania, Latvia and Estonia. Earlier I had obtained my Russian visa in Los Angeles.

At the Russian Federation Documentation Center in Westwood, employees would rather suggest the term 'invitation', a notably polished way to avoid the word 'visa.' And that respectful invitation wasn't that cheap! Unfortunately I found out much later that if you don't speak Russian, you don't travel that sprawling country alone. You must join a tour group, along with an interpreter.

Subsequently to that long ride, when leaving Tallinn, Estonia toward the Russian border, the bus pitched and tossed on an uneven road that was still under construction. It felt like I was on a sailboat during a hurricane. Although the *Europabus* was rolling from side to side, to that point I was still in a wonderful mood. The night, clear and beautiful enveloped in its shadowy veil the wide-stretching fields bordering a forest of thick pine-tree. Earlier in Riga, Latvia while waiting for the bus to refuel, I saw streaks and patches of snow that still lay on the roof of the bus-depot. But soon the sky was blue; the sun had warmed out the frost from nearby mountains.

I disembarked in the center of St-Petersburg as the sun kept on rising.

In that great city nobody, but nobody spoke a word of English. No English signs were posted anywhere near.

In the distance, I observed the giant arch design of a McDonald franchise. Being hungry and in order to eat I had to point out with the finger some items on the menu for a quick lunch *sur le pouce*. After exchanging a few more dollars for Russian rubbles I went to a local store that looked almost empty and bought a postcard showing The Hermitage Museum. Afterward, I boasted the card to every person in the street. A kind automobilist finally understood my request. Kindly, he drove me all the way to The Peterhof, the brain center of St-Petersburg.

I spent two admirable days visiting the summer palace and, in the lower gardens, the three summer pavilions: *L'Hermitage, Marly and Mon Plaisir.*

The architect Le Blond, upon request of the Czar Peter the Great created Peterhof, a 'Versailles by the sea' where water soars high in the air, splashing over beautiful statues. In the Palais itself, just like in Versailles there was *la sale des pas-perdus*-the room of lost paths or Great Hall. Next day, not too far from Nevsky Boulevard near the canals modeled after the ones from Amsterdam, I boarded the midnight express train for the Russian capital…

As I woke up in the early morning clear frosty hours, I watched the forests, dark, dense and impenetrable, towering dark forests for hundreds and hundreds of miles. Looking more deeply at the endless *taiga,* I remembered a passage from Pasternak's book *Doctor Zhivago:* "…A sleepy, oily sun blinking in the forest, sleepy pines blinking their needles like eyelashes, oily puddles glistening at noon. The countryside yawns, stretches, turns over, and goes back to sleep."

With titillating *Ballaleika* music in the background the fascinating domes of the giant Moscow Central Station irradiated in full splendor. There were so many rails, some that run right across Siberia. What captivated me the most was that colossal railroad map affixed on the wall showing Trans-Siberian trains scheduled to Alma-Ata, Irkutsk and Vladivostok.

The problem I encountered in St-Petersburg manifested itself again in Moscow. This time I acquired *une carte postale* viewing the Red Square with the onion domes of St-Basil Cathedral facing the Kremlin and the Lenin Mausoleum.

With tremendous luck, in the late afternoon an exchange-student from Mongolia, tapping my shoulder expressed himself in broken English by saying: "You follow me!"

Riding the most extraordinary metro in the world with crystal chandeliers, marble floors and unique paintings we arrived at Red Square in no time. The sky was gold and crimson. It was a soft blending of colors, a harmony of colors. Considering so much bribery even among police officers I was surprised that my new-found friend refused the tip I was offering him for his kindness.

Near the Lenin Mausoleum I finally found an Australian professor of languages from the Patrice Lumumba University. After a little chat, Mr. Brand suggested to me not to try to get any information from the police, as he conveyed:

"Pierre, I live here long enough to know for sure not to trust the so-called law and order officers. They are rotten to the core. It's really an organization of thieves, of professional blackmailers. Mr. Putin himself is planning to replace them all, mainly to stop the harassment against tourists."

Until recently Moscow had the reputation of being dull and old-fashioned whereas St-Petersburg looking more to the U.S. and the European Community felt comparatively quite modern and more educated. That same metropolis has always occupied a position of intellectual headship where so many writers had their works published. I remember that women in St. Petersburg were extremely beautiful, very up-to-date with the latest style from Rome, Paris or New York. Some ladies with their blouses clunging to strong breasts and their derrière moving with such agility at every step, walked with high-heels that made their gait a little tense. At that same Mc. Donald near the Peterhof center that I visited twice young women working behind the counter looked more like mannequins…

Later after a few days spent in the Russian capital (mostly around Red Square, the Kremlin and Gorky Park), upon the return-trip by train to Tallinn, Estonia new confrontations occurred right at the border.

Sharing my compartment with an Estonian couple that by miracle spoke good English our conversation was cut short by the arrival of the military border security. We had to stand up and handed our passports. One of the soldiers, his shirt gapping at the neck, with his lower lip that almost fell on his lap inspected my travel-document. Shaking his head from left to right, after blinding me with his flashlight he simply said: *Niet.* He pocketed my passport and disappeared. At this point, my Estonian friends articulated but one word: TROUBLE…!

Twenty minutes later the same soldier heaved into view again, accompanied by another inspector and a lady wearing gold star-spangled epaulets on her shoulders, with a colorful badge on her sleeve.

The high cheek boned, baby blue eyed superior officer carried a sort of a machine: it was a scanner. She began to scan each and every pages of my passport. At that precise moment, I recalled Leon's wise warning when he had suggested to me to update my old European Community Passport for a new one carrying the latest technology that included a memory chip. Unfortunately I had disregarded his counsel thinking everything would be fine. Now, it looked as if the commander didn't understand that I actually dared to walk on Russian soil with an old Belgian document that carried a Russian visa… issued in California?

On top of this my translator said that the head of 'border operations' requested me to tell her how much money I had remaining:

"Around three hundred dollars," I uttered. All of them kept staring at me with open-mouths, really astonished; probably thinking how in the world was I able to carry so much currency, an entire month's salary for an average Russian citizen?

On this turn of event there was no doubt in my mind that I would be sent to a remote place in Siberia as a spy and have my money confiscated when to my astonishment, *la commandante* gazing at me like a mother behold her child affixed the exit stamp in my passport. Looking at her, straight in the eyes, I expressed my joy with just one Russian word, the only one I learned: "*Spasiba.*"-Thank you. My response in their language was welcome with a hearty laugh. Following the security clearance I was on my way back to Tallinn. This was the end of my life's short Russian experience.

Talking about Russia, in 1839 the Marquis de Custine gave this information: "Whenever you are unhappy... go to Russia. Anyone who has come to understand that country well will find himself content to live anywhere else." and in a broadcast dated October 1, 1939 Sir Winston Churchill concluded: "Russia is a riddle wrapped in a mystery inside an enigma."

Upon my return to Estonia I had but one thought: *"For once Arthur had been right in his assessment when he made it clear to me that Russia got rid of communism, but communism fanaticism was still in the mind of countless Russians. Perestroika and the collapse of the Soviet Union, the evil empire to use Reagan's maxim didn't affect so many Russian citizens who cannot cope with real freedom and democracy."*

Back in Los Angeles, at *Le Cerisier* my employer fabricated a new, fantastic and unbelievable story about my Russian experience that would be heard at every table for weeks to come. With grandiloquence and aroused with a certain emotion in his voice, Arthur announced:

"Pierre went to Russia and was almost sent to a labor camp in Siberia as a spy. However later on at the Kremlin Putin personally invited him for a cup of tea before giving the Russian leader a copy of his previous book!"

The truth is that that meeting never occurred. This was another fantasy of Arthur's wild imagination. Nevertheless, upon my return to California I sent a copy of the book to President Vladimir Putin with a 'certified translation letter' from the Russian Federation Documentation Center.

Of all the countries I visited on all continents on the face of the earth, Russia (probably because of too much bureaucracy and of language barrier) didn't mean much to me except a sense of hysteria. It is a different country with different problems. On the other hand when I first migrated to the U.S., I found the Americans so very lovable; so very friendly. It was and it's still the land of crushing hospitality with open-faced, pleasant people. No wonder those same faces hardly wrinkled!

* * * *

Today, as I arrived at the restaurant after the sun had long gone out of sight behind a block of houses, a surprise awaited me. Mr. S. Joulson, a former Belgian minister *de La Défense Nationale,*(now an old man), accompanied by general Van Reymenant, two senators from the Brabant and Limbourg provinces decided to pay us a visit.

Mr. Joulson was a man of intellectual refinement. Back in the 60's the former defense minister decided after the image of the Peace Corps to have some of the military stationed in the former Belgian Congo (now the democratic republic of Congo) to join the Tosalisana, associated with Humanitas-*entraide entre peuples*. Tosalina Na Lingomba was seeking volunteers to go and teach in remote Congolese villages. The minister's difficulties to achieve his goal, his insipient impulse were well borne for God saw that it was good. The responsive spirit from the government *Place Royale,* in Brussels was extraordinary and stentorian. The funds for school material followed with no delay.

I had been blessed indeed to have first met the defense-minister at the Kamina base in Katanga province when I was just a nineteen year old paratrooper. Even now after all those years, in the minds of *les anciens*-the old soldiers the slogan 'the children of Joulson' is still alive…

The reservation for those guests of distinction was made earlier by the Consul General of Belgium in Los Angeles. The diplomat, aware that *Le Cerisier* was one of the best French restaurants in Southern California had requested for his outstanding visitors a simple, but typical Belgium dish: *beefsteak-frites, salade and Stella Artois.* And for the occasion Arthur arranged a special table with a large bouquet of fresh-cut roses resting in a crystal *Saint Lambert's* vase.

When the V. I. P. entourage arrived at *Le Cerisier* in a black limo, Leon and I prided ourselves in meeting such high-ranking people from our mother country. Immediately, Arthur joined them at their table for another libation.

Right in the middle of the dinner Melanie emerged at the restaurant through the kitchen door, almost totally drunk, and disheveled. (Forewarned earlier by Eddy, Arthur and Melanie had a horrible fight that morning.)

She first directed herself to *les officiels* and stared at her father; her mouth an ugly grimace. As her lip lifted slightly there was an expression in her face which I didn't recognize. After showing the finger she articulated: "Son of a bitch, who do you think you are? You're just a coward; a good for nothing employer. I just hate you!"

Standing there with a fast beating pulse, her very action pierced my heart. It almost made me cry. I felt inclined after sealing my eyes and ears to sink into the ground. With all his problems, his good, his bad working seasons at the restaurant Arthur survived the wear and tear of seventy-plus years, but what had just happened had been too much to handle. In the entire abode, there was a clamor of knives and forks as every customer stopped eating for awhile. One curious client with some kind of dazed intensity snooped about as to who that young lady was, insulting the owner of the restaurant with such graphic obscene gesture. I dodged his question and shrugged my shoulders for the loud badmouth woman was my employer's daughter.

I knew Arthur to be a tough old bird, but this time he was profoundly affected. With cheeks so hot, his salt and pepper eyebrows arching upward I watched his alarming metamorphosis with stupor. Sweating in shame, with the corners of his mouth trembling in he attempted not to cry. He left the location abruptly after apologizing to his notably distinctive clients. The sharp pain, the weight of humiliation inflicted on him, that unfathomable aggravation carried on by his own flesh and blood daughter almost caused Arthur to have a cardiac arrest. His depression had been so severe that he could have hidden himself in a coffin.

* * * *

On this cold evening, Jack and Jill came to eat at *Le Cerisier*.

Jack who studied marine engeneering was a professional decorator, also a water-fountains creator who owned a large nursery where he collected numerous tropical plants. He already had contracts with several large amusement parks all over California, including the one claiming to be 'The Happiest Place on Earth.' Jack was a good but exceedingly sensitive man, somewhat ponderous in manner and appearance; just a person of respect.

His wife Jill, a Bel Air criminal lawyer always dressed casual. They owned a well-restored Duisenberg car they were so proud of.

Upon their arrival, in order to direct them to their table, I simply said: "This way Jack and Jill." and the husband tally up:

"...went up the hill
to fetch a pail of water;
Jack fell down and broke his crown,
and Jill came tumbling after."

Subsequent to this warm introduction, Jack and Jill (who never used their last name for a reservation) ordered a fine bottle of 1972 Gevrey Chambertin. Looking at me after a fancy chuckle over a joke, Jill beckoned me to get a glass for myself in order to taste that delicate fruit of the vine. This was a delight especially for the fact that Arthur wasn't around that day. He for sure would have again snapped up the glass of wine from my fingers. This was an exceptionally good wine that was so generously offered to me.

Knowing very well about Arthur's rule for me not to enjoy any wine or champagne offered by our patrons, Jack, holding my hand decided to talk. There was warmth in his voice when he pronounced:

"Pierre, you should wake up. A man with your character should not waste his life, working under the joug of an idiot and arrogant boss!"

On one particular occasion, after the owner of the restaurant told a couple that I was mentally handicapped, Jack came to my defense saying:

"Arthur, I strongly objected the way you treat Pierre. He is the best, honest and reliable employee you ever hired. He's also a good, well-adjusted human being and I'm damn really tired to hear your BS!"

Chapter 40

ANGELINE'S CONDITION IMPROVED. She went back from the hospital to the convalescent home and Arthur decided on buying a specially built van for the handicapped. This way, his wife won't have to rise up from the car seat to her wheelchair.

Later on I heard of a little *escarmouche*, a skirmish between Melanie and Eddy. I went to find out what the argument was all about. Melanie rattled that last Sunday exceptionally she went out with her parents and Eddy to that renowned Chinese restaurant *Wong Kwai*, located in Brentwood. This was for Angeline's birthday and this time it was Eddy Roy Freedman's turn to take care of the bill. I found out that with vehemence Eddy had displayed his opposition with the approval of Arthur. Since Freedman had performed some work in the house, my employer declared in a domineering voice that it was perfectly right that his friend would be a guest in compensation for a job well done. Eddy had just installed a new air-conditioning unit at the owner's residence.

Melanie wasn't pleased. She was consumed with grief, clearly calling Eddy *un pique-assiette-* a sponge person and a beatnik. She added that Freedman was living on the Valois Dourville de Montrissart's like an old fungus. I believed that what irritated the somehow laconic Eddy the most is that being a sane, healthy man he continually had to fight the emotionally, so-called conditioned superiority of Arthur's daughter. That neurotic disturbance and conflicting boldness created by the daughter's deep-rooted feelings, as she continued to strive after power was unbearable. Oftentimes Freedman felt like 'a dog in a manger.' Having the loving qualities of tenderness and gentility he would have to subordinate himself to the idiosyncrasy of Melanie's broodings.

My co-worker lost both his parents. Now he was left with one unfeeling relative. Eddy's brother, a former top executive from Chrysler hardly talked to him, so did his sister living in a sumptuous hacienda-type mansion south of Reno, Nevada.

Freedman's only true friend was none other than Arthur. Although their characters were extremely different in every ways they had a sincere communal sentiment that binds them together. It was actually Eddy who designed and built *Le Cerisier*. His technical craftsmanship, his brilliant mind that created a fine eating resort from a dilapidated, very old building reflected his utter ingenuity. He so much wanted to be accepted by every member of the Valois Dourville de Montrissart's family. Yet, because of Melanie's bearings this never happened.

Every time I talked to Eddy, he warned me in regard to the owner's daughter, tricky, unethical conduct and evil-intentioned achievements. He kept mentioning to me about Melanie's acrid, also great skill to imitate signatures. Freedman was right. His wisdom was fully acknowledged when Melanie changed for the worst as she became the cynosure of some future event.

* * * *

Without any forewarning Chef Francis Bevert decided to leave *Le Cerisier*. Months ago the chef had secretly contacted Air France. He had submitted an application for a position as executive chef to supervise the preparation of meals for the French National Airline. His résumé had been scrupulously examined. After a prerequisite formal course on approved airline topic that was short and formal, he finally landed the job. The new task was gratified with excellent salary and fringe benefits such as free overseas travels…

Gustavo Santillas was now elevated to his new position of *Chef de cuisine*. At the same time of Bevert's departure, Melanie flew to the old continent for a two-week vacation to join her relatives in Toulouse, France.

Now that Santillas savored the fruits of his new rank, Arthur had to hire someone to take care of the pantry. Awhile later Gustavo had a serious argument with the boss as regard to his own very special preparations. But as time went on Arthur saw no reason not to leave more serious decisions entirely to the man's discretion.

A new assistant joined our team. Yolanda Lapin, a young lady from San José, Costa Rica was very petite with neat waist, good upstanding bosom and still infantile in manners. She also had small feet, slender hands with a shadow of a smile on her lips. With honest gray eyes, a little nose very *retroussé,* and a joyful character she would be perfect for the job.

Lapin had been married at sixteen for *les convenances* to her cousin Signor Don Ricardo. A good deal older than herself, Don Ricardo bestowed her with a good social position in her own country. Nevertheless love wasn't in the air and there had been darkness in her soul. The walls of that extravagant hacienda in Central America were like of a prison-cell. Now, with her cherub face, she looked quite refreshed; happy as anyone can be.

Surprisingly, Arthur warned Yolanda not to pay too much attention to me because in his own words: I was quite irrational and a little mentally disturbed!

* * * *

Jules Vertrichten, a Dutchman was our neighbor from across the street. He owned a muffler-shop and also specialized in repairing high luxury antique automobiles.

Tall and copper skinned, his weather-stained face showed the complexion of an old parchment. With an unusual short proboscis, blotches on his forehead he had strange yellowish eyes, the loving eyes of a Spaniel. He was very gentle with people, with animals as well.

Jules wasn't fat, just full-bodied. Even that he was already of an advanced age he had a sexy moodiness of manners irresistible to women. Rheumatism that had crept into his bones did not keep him from his favorite past time which was fishing. Jules still carried his fishing with a burning passion that old age had not quenched. With that peasant complexion, he constantly laughed at everything. He was one of the best men on earth who got most of his education from the silent teaching of adversity. In a way, Jules reminds me of a picture I had once seen of Father Damien among lepers from Molokai in the Hawaian Chain. I had liked Jules' single-minded ingenuousness from the first moment I met him. An expression of gentleness always flitted across his face. His hair was of a burning crimson and his cheeks were covered with several days' growth. He was wearing a handkerchief knotted round his neck. Recurrently, a cigarillo was clipped between his lips. Jules had the rasping intake of a chain-smoker and because of salt water his very hairy hands the size of a shovel were raw and puffy. With a pleasant voice, the Dutchman with Herculean strength was quite humorous. Definitively in the sport of bodybuilding, he would run to do anything for us. He also loved poker-games and played 'the shirt off his back'.

Jules possessed a large boat anchored near the Fisherman's Village in San Pedro. Occasionally, providing the fishing was exceptional he would bring us some Sea Bass, Dorado or Yellow Tail.

Once, Vertrichten arrived at *Le Cerisier*. He was wearing a coat that hanged from his neck to his ankles over a turtleneck, tight designer jeans and combat boots adorning his mammoth feet.

On that day, like a real *loup de mer*-a wolf from the sea he displayed a giant Bonito with a shining golden head he had caught twelve miles off the Ventura Coast. We were all present in the kitchen when he dropped that colossal marvel of a fish on the chef's table.

While we stood there quite surprised by the size of the Bonito, Jules surveyed us, good humored and with affectionate glances.

The moment Vertrichten left the restaurant he wished us *bon appétit!* We were unable to do justice to his kindness.

With a look of surprise, mingled with curiosity and watering mouth, I raised a cautious finger and openly expressed my own feelings:

"Goody, we will have a feast!" said I. But as ill luck would have it, Arthur, in an explosive burst of laughter and a tinge of malice turned in my direction. He gaped at me as if I was a three-legged turkey. The boss roared a furious 'NO' that brought stares of astonishment from everyone. Looking at me once more out a long stream of breath he added:

"Holy Mother of God; *es-tu tombé sur la tête?*- Did you fall on your head? Over my dead body you'll eat this! How can you even suggest such a stupid thing?" and, after rolling his eyes for a second Arthur went on: "Let me tell you: touch that Bonito and you're a dead duck! Chef Santillas will skin this fish from head down to tail." Becoming obstinate as a mule the boss summed-up: "Out of this beauty just like Christ as he miraculously multiply his one fish to feed so many people Santillas will cut at least twenty-five to thirty filets for our customers. It would be prepared *à la Véronique* style, with grapes."

I had not the ready wit to retaliate, but the clearheaded Leon Van Meerstellen, always *à l'avant-garde*-ahead as regard with the articles of law and the facts regarding health regulations explained clearly to the owner that the Bonito fish is not to be served to our clients. It did not have the seal of approval from the Health Department. He was raising in a quite objective way the question of simple honesty. I continually admire Leon for his integrity, his fountain of morals. For him the law must be respected to the letter. Our employer perpetrated a serious infraction of the legal rules and there should be no way to play 'hide and seek' with the authorities. But, a shortcut through official bureaucratic procedure was his specialty.

Occasionally Arthur would also buy meat, apparently just 'stolen goods' coming out of a truck carrying no address or firm name after the driver had not been able to sell it to someone else. Arthur's penchant for skirting around decrees, even within the flexible limits of regulations admonished that we had better conspire with his scheme. The boss never considered it dishonorable to transgress and violate the law.

Furthermore, he instructed us to explain, with an off-the-rack answer, should our customers inquire as to the origins of such a delectable fish:

"Our distributors are from San Pedro Harbor. They only deliver the inspected fresh catch of the day for *Le Cerisier.*" It was with a great deal of uneasiness that we had to obey the orders of *le petit Napoleon*...

Again, Valois Dourville de Montrissart's proclivity to bypass the boundaries of law did not surprise me at all. He had his own idiosyncrasy, his own code of ethics. So often, our employer kept on recalling to us the unfortunate experience of Mr. John Lamardi, an engineer and a loyal client from *Le Cerisier* who was clubfooted from birth.

John broke his left shoulder after falling with enough force off an unlit stone stairway which led down to the parking lot of a famed San Francisco restaurant. Since Mr. Lamardi sued the owner of the eatery for half a million dollars and won with twice as much money, (for the jury sympathized with him), our pot-bellied boss feared that a similar event might occur in our establishment. He then instructed us that in case of injury to one of our patrons, we should not in any circumstances call an ambulance. Instead we should comfort 'the victim' inside the restaurant. We should offer a dessert or an after-dinner drink on the house before directing him/her out of the abode, to the sidewalk. Arthur would decline any responsibility for any sort of accident. In his cold, well-calculated ingenious mind, his band-aid remedy was his solution to avoid lawsuits. He added in an apathetic, and so an uncompassionate way that it would be embarrassing to him for the consequences; for all the paperwork involved.

Chapter 41

WHAT I AM about to narrate may seem so extraordinary as well as incredible. I needed a good deal of boldness to begin this chapter because I elaborate on a subject of deep concern, not only for Americans in general but for all people of the world as well.

This day was a day when the sky seemed enormous. One cloud, as large as a city was cruising near the sun, whilst several other clouds appeared to be anchored far to the horizon and quite lazy to move…

Melanie just got back from Europe. The date: September 11, 2001. Following her Trans Atlantic flight, because of being late she missed her connecting plane for Los Angeles which was the doomed Flight 11 with American Airlines that crashed in one of the towers of the World Trade Center. Surprisingly Melanie was still able to reach the West Coast and the City of Angels. There had been a last minute cancellation of one of the passengers with another airline, and she got her transfer. She made it safe.

Considering the tragic events involving the Twin Towers, the Pentagon and the plane crash in a Pennsylvania field that became such a sad tragedy on a worldwide scale the sky became silent; only birds were flying.

Just as I arrived at the restaurant her father and all her best friends surrounded Melanie. A murmur of sympathy arose from everyone. Earlier, Arthur had informed me of her arrival. I slipped quietly in the midst of the gathering. With crimson fingernail polish, Melanie was wearing a coquettish, simple blue crêpe dress and her hair brushed the tip of her shoulders.

As saddening as things were for thousands, her face had an expression of innocence. With the uncertain air of one trying to remember a dream, pondering the veil of memory and blur of nostalgia her eyes were still carrying the shock of it. After that terrorist act, her mental tension had increased drastically. She did not know the place in month, week, season or year. With a smear of lipstick she was pretty as a porcelain statue, and scintillated like a bright star. Nevertheless the poor thing had aged a little; she was also frightfully pale. At times in a violent agitation her right arm was trembling, as her body shivered. It was difficult for her to repress her emotions. She was now looking absently at her fingernails with that uncertain air of one trying to remember a dream.

As soon as Melanie caught sight of me she got hold of her green-scented handkerchief and started weeping sulkily as though we would never see each other again. Holding her hand that I awkwardly patted she continued to burst into a hysterical fit of tears that shined like diamonds. She was tense and I still felt the tremor of her body. Having penetrated the depth of the earth, she was more beautiful than she had ever been. As I detected that gentle perfume, her lips parted graciously.

At that precise moment at *Le Cerisier* I sensed a communion of hearts, a warm feeling of protectiveness, of tenderness. Arthur wiped his face which was covered by drops of sweat. His eyelids had stiffened; they were unsurprisingly trembling.

For the first time I kept forgetting all the baseness, mental turmoil, hate, and indignities that the pen cannot write down. Now, with food for reflection I realized how closely we were bound together; that I was part of the Valois Dourville de Montrissart's family. In a show of emotion I fought my own tears as long as I could but then they also break out from me, pouring down my cheeks.

For several days Melanie didn't report for work. The boss told me that occasionally she was still flushed and delirious just at the thought that she had escaped a horrible death. Arthur's daughter was afraid to go to bed in the dark because she had nightmares. In her dreams came all the alien screech of voices as her bedroom carried the smell of dead bodies; the smell of burned flesh. She imagined creepy images of brimstone flames around her; that her head was torn off, that she died and was buried. In the same dream Melanie came back to ground zero, staring at the fire and searching for her head; searching everywhere for it. In that repulsive hallucination she noticed that her body was still engulfed with flames created with devilish, poisonous zeal by terrorist cruelty. She had the vision of burning shadows crowding round. There was also a pattering that came straight towards her with the sniffing of nostrils from the dead. She saw one of the terrorist that took over the plane, prior to hitting the towers as the flames crackled and licked the air. He had a big head with the horns of a bull, eyes of great beasts of prey. He kept pushing her in the fire with a long stick and thrown dead rats at her. She felt her very bones melting inside and would wake up horrified with gnashing of teeth. Each night, the terror reappeared in all its intensity.

Later on, as relief flooded her body, the world became picturesque again, and Melanie surrendered herself to Divine mercy. The daughter finally discovered her God who gave power to his fine creatures. The one true God who governs according to His will. *God moves in mysterious ways. Though His reasons may be hidden, they have never been unjust because He bestowed man free will to build or destroy. War, terrorism and general world insecurity are the results of our own miscalculations, of our wrong judgments.* Now and then, Melanie's experience might be a direct insight from The Higher Source.

Arthur's friend, Claude Lemarchand also an acquaintance from the French couturier Yves Saint-Laurent was the proud owner of the nightclub *Les Parapluies de Cherbourg* located in Santa Monica.

Several months ago Mr. Lemarchand flew to that South Pacific paradise of Tahiti on a two week vacation. On the last day, before leaving Papeete, Claude cancelled the flight back to Los Angeles with a Honolulu connection.

There were no apparent reasons for his change of mind. He wasn't late at the airport as was the case with Melanie but he experienced a strange perception, more like a premonition. Lemarchand didn't feel good about that particular flight.

However everything went fine with the first plane. Yet, the connecting aircraft in Honolulu bound for Los Angeles crashed three hundred miles off the shores of Oahu. There were no survivors: over two hundred people died.

Just as with Claude Lemarchand, Arthur had the firm conviction that his beloved daughter had also been saved by divine intervention.

Synchronicity is a word invented by Carl Jung. It means a direct contact, almost an ultimatum from God. This had been the case with Lamarchand.

Telepathy can also be a sign that goes well beyond our five senses. In that same line of thinking, twin brothers or twin sisters always carry a special affinity to each other, even if they live in a different environment.

This was the case of Bill and Peter Delvallier, a set of twins I knew very well, also clients at *Le Cerisier*. They always came at the restaurant, accompanied by their spouses before sharing a bottle of wine with Arthur.

One morning Bill, a resident from Woodland Hills called upon his brother in Manhatten, New York, over there on a business trip. They found out that the night before, at exactly seven P.M. in their time zone each of them in those particular locations dined at a steak-house. They both started with a shrimp cocktail followed by a pepper steak medium-rare. For dessert: a plain cheese-cake with a *café-filtre* as an increment. Outside the establishment, at about the same time zone, they both lighted a full flavored Marlboro cigarette!

* * * *

Tonight, Los Angeles was in a clamor of downpour. At the restaurant, we met three new faces: Phil and Kathy Williams and Tony Crushin who would become some of our best friends.

Phil was a well-brushed gentleman always dressed in the latest fashions. Feeling good in his skin he was a competent business attorney, also a partner in one of the most flourishing law-firm in Brentwood. As a successful lawyer, men, women respected, feared and envied him. He then decided to join Tony in a large Sino-American venture.

Tony being endowed by nature with a romantic imagination was associated with a Chinese enterprise in Xian Economic Development Zone that specialized in making furniture. From Shanghai a shipping company would bring all the fittings to the port of San Pedro, ready to provide fine hotels and resorts of the best equipment all over the U.S. Mainland.

Tony Crushin, with a keen intelligence and vigorous will, still in the flower of youth was exceptionally good to me. He didn't look at all like a wealthy businessman. Still, quite effeminate he had been raised by fine parents who believed in tangible discipline and by keeping him on the straight, narrow path of honesty, of punctuality. His long flaxen hair was as smooth as a baby's; it was fixed as a ponytail that came down on his neck. He had a calm face that looked like that in a painting of ascetic monks depicted in some old monasteries lost in time. One can observe transparence in Tony's eyes bright like those of a young girl. There was such a great serenity of the mouth; a softness in his mellow voice with any shrewdness in it. He was that kind of human being that always musingly murmured a poetic thought. This reminded me of the wonderful words of Dr. Alexis Carrel in: Man, the Unknown, *"When we encounter the rare individual whose conduct is inspired by a moral ideal, we cannot help noticing his aspect. Moral beauty is an exceptional and striking phenomenon- one never forgets it. This form of beauty is far more impressive than the beauty of nature. It gives to those who possess its divine gifts a strange and inexplicable power. It increases the strength of the intellect. Much more than science, art and religious rites, moral beauty is the basis of civilization."*

Occasionally Crushin was accompanied by a girlfriend.

Kathy wearing a pink ribbon in her hair was a beautiful lady, a pale brunette slight and graceful with such a great knowledge of international politics. As Phil's spouse she was the one with the gift of speech. Her loveliness was indeed quite unique. Aside from being strict in the management of her household she also graduated in psychology *summa cum laude* from USC. With lapidary dignity, from that same famed university she also had developed such elegance to master the language arts. She had a real refined woman's mind, not just clever but amusing as well.

Kathy wore a dark-blue cocktail dress that looked suited rather for a fashionable gathering in Paris or London than for in a Sherman Oaks restaurant. The odor of musk perfume trailed her as she walked about. With her perfect neck she could look as lovely in shabby clothes as well. The pose of her head was like that of the Greek Venus. As she walked you can easily imagine she had descended from a pedestal. I literally devoured her with my eyes as I felt an intoxication of pleasure just to look at her. In the midst of customers in so many different shapes I fancied that I was seeing an angelic swallow among wild animals. She had a lovely controlled, clear voice; a sincere voice intense in feeling, so pure it looked as if it didn't belong to earth. Moreover she was part of a chorale at St. Sebastian church in Pasadena. As a soloist, she went to Rome with a chorus and sang for Pope John-Paul II at St-Pieter's. Once Kathy sang in the restaurant and my soul was uplifted by her extraordinary vibrant voice.

For Phil his wife was the object of worshipping admiration; the object that inspired his thoughts. Never in his life had he met a woman he wanted more. He really loved Kathy far above anyone else in the world not just for her beauty but for her masterpiece of education as well. The female Papal Nuncio with that nightingale's voice enjoyed talking to me. She had such a warm smile; that kind of smile that went straight to the heart. Eventually it didn't take her long to notice the way Arthur was treating me.

Those *joyeux lurons*-happy campers took the pleasant habit to come and dine at *Le Cerisier* at least twice a week bringing with them the finest wines from the market. Some of those wines were actually so rare that they became almost collector items.

Once, at the dusk of sunset our friends came back with a bottle of Romanée-Conti 1958, a 1964 Chambole Musigny, also a Château d'Yquem Sauternes as a dessert wine. Those three bottles were worth well over fifteen hundred dollars. In a bemused gaze feasting his eye, the boss observed the display of those exceptional vintage wines. Then as fast as a bull in the arena he dashed off and sat with them. Once more he focused on the bottles while telling all of his unbelievable stories lacking so much of common sense. At the same time as Kathy with her Dior sunglasses resting on her forehead called upon me to taste the Romanée-Conti, Arthur in a treacherous and cruel manner said:

"No way that this dummy is going to drink that wine. I won't even let him sniff it!" Then Arthur looking into my eyes conveyed in a lower tone of voice: "What's happened with you! Ain't you got any sense? Don't you ever take it into your head that you cannot drink with our clients? That doesn't seem like a whole lot to ask heh?" and he added: "Things are really getting out of hands with you!"

Quite often a woman sees more clearly than a man does. Kathy always considered that education is the same for men and woman but it will be in the female heart by excellence, as love and devotion bound by a code of loyalty are absolutely primordial. The truth is: women are generally remarkable for the tenacity of their ideas of the *juste cause*, of their noble sentiments. Inconstancy of heart is the special characteristic of man. But Kathy was that type of woman always impelled to come to the defense of a man who lives under the control of another man. She happened to be a lady of exceptional bravery that speak her mind and won't turn her back on such irrational behavior. At all times I was exposed to so much misery. The main issue was for Arthur to render me unhappy by all means.

The flow of female eloquence by Kathy was accompanied with arguments that she expressed with such tone and action in order to stop the boss to hurt my feelings. Abruptly the young lady threw her napkin on the table. In a restless movement of her knee she stood up. With her face that put on it's almost stage of sculptural severity the color upon her cheeks spread over her face and neck. The curves of that gracious mouth now expressed a sourness scorn. She was furious, really furious. This statement from my employer had exasperated her beyond measure. With the delicate outlines of the nose, her anxious air imparted something strangely enchanting to her.

Finding it hard to keep her voice under control she mentioned that first of all this was their own wine adding that if I won't be allowed to taste it they would simply leave the premises for good. Looking deadly serious she went on talking zealously with a vibrating voice and great firmness:

"Arthur, you're such a smarty-pants! Now I'm giving it to you straight: I'm tired that you keep on badmouthing Pierre. Not to mention all the other forms of outrage, of oppression. You are continually pissed off at him all the time using him like some malleable clay! I don't want to hear any more of such humiliations."

In her indignity toward Arthur, Kathy gazed at me with as good a grace as she could. I had the feeling that she honored me with a condescending smile. At this point I looked intently in her face. She was a woman of courage and those remarks gave expression to her deepest sentiments.

The boss said nothing. This time he didn't even utter a syllable. He pushed back his chair and appeared to give it a moment's thought. It seemed that he just got an unexpected cold shower over his neck. At the same instant a sweat broke out on his forehead. Now my unfortunate employer resembled a withered leaf that whirled around in the breeze. He declined from his sitting position as if he was going to crawl on the carpet-floor before rising up like a floating balloon pouring with sweat, a tremor shooting down his arm. Arthur's face was still stiffening into amused disapproval, but with that burning look in Kathy's eyes it took an anxious understanding. As he sat down again he had a grotesque, pathetic appearance with an air of displeasure. Shifting nervously in his seat he then leaned further forward in his chair with his hands gripping the edge of the table, Arthur felt suddenly full of indulgent care.

Next with trembling fingers he handed me the glass of that superb fruit of the vine. In an ironic smile but with still reluctance in his face and shrugging his shoulders sadly he finally decided to talk. He conveyed in a conciliatory voice with his mouth wide open like the hippopotamus:

"Here, petit Pierre, drink it but very slowly. Sniff it delicately first. It has such a delicate bouquet; the very best there is!"

Arthur thought that he was one of those self-assured individuals who are brilliant even despotic as long no one opposed them. But in the case with Kathy the distress in my employer's face became almost despair. This cured me instantly as a rare peace descended upon my soul and I could not help smiling. This incident was noticed by several *habitués* in the dining room. As they were gawking they likewise approvingly smile. Kathy had behaved with perfect chivalry.

Upon leaving the restaurant, the three of them gratified me with a bear hug. From that day on Kathy took me under her wing. Then she came back forward slowly, her eyes on me. In a last burst of passion she pressed my head against her breast and touched my face with her fingers. At that precise moment even that she was a married woman I felt from her that light element of flirtation, more like an overture to intimacy and I almost kissed those too appealing lips of hers. But I behaved, realizing that after all she had a loving husband.

Later on my love for Kathy, that pleasant sensation that aroused in me had transformed more on a platonic level. In a female emotional way Kathy had shown great concern by giving me cheerfulness. Now I regarded her as my natural protector. I can compare Kathy's moral beauty to what John Lord in *Beacon Light of History* indicated about Madame de la Fayette as she complemented Madame de Sévigné for her attractiveness and intelligence, *"Your varying expression so brightens and adorns your beauty, that there is nothing so brilliant as yourself: every word you utter adds to the brightness of your eyes; and while it is said that language impresses only to the ear, it is quite certain that yours enchants the vision."*

Then as we nearly stood on the sidewalk I listened to Tony Crushin's deep breathing at my shoulder. I heard him saying that same sentence I so far have heard repeatedly:

"Pierre, you are 'a gold mine.' Look at you, around the world you went; you jump from airplanes. You also run over twenty Marathons,'"and he added, "That little man of a boss should realize what a great asset you are in this place. He should be thankful to have you, a good, sincere employee!" Coming from Tony those remarks made me glow in some sort of holy pride. I never thought that such a few words contained so much joy. In a way my good friend had renewed in me that unbounded confidence…

On the other hand whenever Kathy came back, oftentimes alone as her husband was busy preparing court papers, Leon would eloquently bluster: "Pierrot here is your Mother Superior; go ahead you can flang yourself into her arms!"

* * * *

On this bright day Arthur divulged to me what he thought was a little secret which I already heard from discreet hints dropped by his late mother as she let the cat out of the bag: Leon Van Meerstellen's real father was a semi-neurotic man of Polish extraction under the name of Lech Boliartsky.

Originally from Wadowice, Lech Boliartsky became a brilliant businessman who also managed offices in Belgium and Germany. He actually was a personal friend of the Wojtyla family. Among Mr. Boliartsky's not-too-long distant progenitors there had been an Archbishop and a Jesuit Priest. His other claim to distinction was that he also knew quite well the former Polish Prime Minister who was related to his grandmother side. On weekends Lech would entertain priests and bishops with wine, coffee and pastries.

As destiny would have it, Karol Jozef Wojtyla would become the Holy Father bearing the name of John Paul II, Bishop of Rome, Vicar of Christ and successor of St. Peter. Being a real athletic sort of man Boliartsky used to jump in the flooded, cold Skawa River where Karol took his daring morning swim. However, Leon's father religious nature and fellowship with holy people never rubbed off on my friend. Beatrice, Leon's mother was sad that her only son had not taken a university degree she was expecting for. Earlier, he had left his academic training owing to his failed marriage. Beatrice fondly reminisced her son's celebrations of the sacraments in childhood…baptism, confirmation and first communion. Leon went to a Jesuit school; he knew the creed and the catechism well. He took the communion wafer, the body of Christ and even served as an altar boy. In addition he used to spend Sunday's singing at the choir.

Considering her first husband's faith within the Catholic Church; his apparent acquaintance with his friend from the Holy See's higher hierarchy, and his affinity with so many zealous people, Beatrice would have given her life for her son. She had made plans for him to prepare himself for the seminary, thus becoming a good priest with that strong suit of biblical faith. She would have loved to have her only son dressed in an ecclesiastical robe. As a priest Leon would have been free from the temptations of this world. He would have been married only to the church instead of a 'Jewish Princess!'

Likewise this happened at the time Melanie felt the *soi-disant* irrepressible secret desire to enter the convent. However destiny took a different path for both of them. They both lost faith. Just like an athlete on the jump-board Leon bounced into a bad marriage and started to live in a madhouse. The mother was outspoken in her opinion that if her son would only have kept his faith in God he would have been able to deal with life's uncertainties. But Leon was unable to adopt that profession for his calling wasn't there. She humbly concluded: "My son continually rejected help from God, the Higher Source! However he could at least have taken His guidance. I don't want Leon to die without the last rites; I want him to be at peace with God."

I wondered too how Leon so feebly capitulated to the faith and even shunned it. How ironic he chose to become a self-proclaimed agnostic?

Scientists have found that animals that had a particular damaged brain lost their appetite to the point that they might starve to death even with ample food around. Being surrounded by ample heavenly food from that religious family, was Van Meerstellen starving spiritually? On the other hand, even with that seed of doubt that was implanted in his brain, my friend still cultivated loving-kindness, justice and modesty.

* * * *

Coming home from work last night, I noticed instantly that the light from the answering machine was blinking but decided on unwinding first with a glass of Towny Port on the terrace listening at some dogs yapping excitedly. My day has been pretty quiet until I hit that play button 'for one message waiting' and heard a most unsettling communication from Saint-Benedict Hospital near the Sunset strip in Hollywood. I recognized Dr. Diego Menneti's voice almost immediately. I sensed urgency for my primary physician had dispensed me with the usual 'how are you' with his singing Italian accent as he did previously. He had been my regular doctor for over twenty-five years of good health. And now this: he announced that my PSA had been drastically elevated up to 6.5 points. This was quite a drastic situation. With a touch of sadness I scrunched myself together. Hence, Dr. Menneti directed me to consult as soon as possible with Dr. Abraham F. Williamson, a world-renowned urologist, also from Saint Benedict...

With the cool morning wind the palm-trees with their iridescent leaves appeared like ballet dancers in front of the hospital entrance. The parterre of flowers was now in full bloom. As I listened to the splash of a nearby fountain I thought I had never discovered a garden so florid. It was carpeted with narcissis, violets and daffodils. You can even sit on the wood benches on the terrace overlooking a colorful Indian church and meditate. Even the few birds sitting on high wires were laughing. Happiness was in the air. The impeccable cleanliness, the whiteness of the building imparted a sense of peace in me.

Sitting patiently in the doctor's office I envisioned my new doctor to be of the old school with disheveled silver hair and squinting eyes beneath thick glasses. My imaginings were proven wrong as soon as the door opened with Dr. Williamson calling out my name.

Tall, with a full head of light brown hair I thought he was extremely young to have already achieved such fame in this field of medicine and to hold the responsible position as the head of the urology department. A warm handshake assured my confidence in my new physician as he explained to me the variances of prostate cancer, from mild cases to the last stages that are no longer operational. I had to undergo biopsy first.

A week later I received sad results: the cancer had already so far progressed. Only a surgical removal of the prostate gland-a prostatectomy could save me. At this point even radiation was out of question because of extreme glandular enlargement. I was all shaken-up by the news yet I went along with the doctor's wise suggestion. Everything went fine. After another examination with stethoscopes and the results of anesthesiology and the successful surgery Dr. Williamson prescribed me thirty days of complete rest...

I came back to work at *Le Cerisier*, stoop shouldered but well refreshed after that forced vacation. As I still wore pampers for protection against incontinence hell broke loose and once more I sank into the abyss for this was the worst situation of all.

It was plain that Arthur had been nursing a bottle of Canadian Club Whiskey. Giggling hysterically the language he used was most objectionable. He then slapped me in the face and like a madman added in a hoarse whisper: "Pierre you are so pale I just want to learn for myself if you were still alive!"

In the dining room even after the operation I realized that I remained little more than a plaything brought out to amuse the customers; it was a disgrace. In his wild imagination that tiny man who despised every bone in his body told everyone that I went for a sex change operation, that I was also wearing pampers! Those were the most disheartening words someone could imagine to hear. It was all very tasteless and extremely embarrassing. As I felt more and more uncomfortable, some clients were laughing like happy idiots, staring at me so foolishsly. But on the other hand I had not the ready wit to retaliate. Mustering my courage, I smiled. However I swallowed it hard as I felt like going to pieces mentally.

Fortunately regarding my incontinence, as luck would have it that evening, Dr. Rabinadrah Singh Patel, who happened to dine with his wife, and not knowing how far the boss intended to continue in that line of discussion, railed at me for my pain. The good doctor then decided to rescue me from that emotional impasse. Although Dr. Patel was a little in the wind with that second bottle of Kendall-Jackson Zinfandel, he was still in command of his tongue. Hunched in his chair, after throwing his serviette on the table, he felt a sudden anger at Arthur's stupidity, and he started bursting upon him so impetuously.

Wagging a finger at the boss, with stiff politeness the Indian physician spoke in the most severe, injured tone of voice. Doctor Patel said Arthur was talking nonsense; that the joke was in extremely bad taste. He added that, even as a friend of the house he deeply resented his little rat's attitude; that he was a goddamn stinker, a mean son-of-a-bitch, also a real pain in the *derrière*. The doctor conveyed with unclouded frankness that my employer no longer was amusing, that my physical condition following that major surgery was not a matter for laughs and ridicule.

Looking now at my employer with great concern, with a noise that resounded in his chest as in the vault of a basilica, he was flushing red. Arthur tried to interrupted but the doctor in his quite severe lecture silenced him. As he pulled my employer at his sleeve he continued talking:

"Arthur, you're a fool. Once more I beg you to hold your tongue! You don't know what you're saying! But, in your distorted imagination, trying to talk to you is like trying to put socks on a millipede. You keep on behaving in such unbecoming ways; you really ought to be ashamed of yourself! I believe that aboriginal savages from Australia acted with more decency than you do. Those people still carry certain ethical, moral rules. You have become like the beasts of the forest. Your place should be in a zoo! Pierre is a good man and you are just a screwball; a vile brute. You always have to say a lot. It's only figment of your own fancy as you keep on beefing up silly stories. For all the nonsense I have heard from you, this is the worst of it!"

Hence Dr. Patel breathed deeply to regain his calm. He was a cultivated scholar and decent, good-natured man of the old school. He had spoken so intensely showing wonderful tact quite charmingly, that Arthur sank down.

He bounced on his chair, his shoulders shrugging forward twisting and staring at the ceiling as silent as the grave. The boss's bad, awful language had been seriously contested. Shifting his eyes every which way, in a desultory manner he finally withheld his storm of profanity as he kept his lips firmly shut. For a few seconds the air was tense as a worried look appeared over Arthur's brow, with eyes distressed. With shaking fits he was roaring like an insane man.

The admonition from Dr. Rabinadrah Singh Patel was welcomed with cheers. A roar of hurrahs came from every table as a sigh of relief cleared the tension in the entire dining room. It was followed by a soft purr of contentment. The doctor had pronounced those words with fire, emotion and a great deal of dignity. The respect, the applause were prolonged well after he had ceased to speak. On that day, the good and thoughtful physician had liberated me from an unspeakable humiliation. "Thanks for defending me Doctor Patel."

* * * *

We all know quite well the story of Robin Hood. According to the old adage over the centuries, its poetical account has been translated in so many languages. Yet Arthur was far to be *un Robin des Bois*. Instead of stealing from the rich to give to the poor, my ungrateful employer took from the poor to give to the rich (meaning himself.)

I cannot emphasize this better than with the following example: a few days ago Jules Vertrichten, our Dutch friend from the muffler shop across the street kindly installed a new muffler on my employer's Nissan Truck. Arthur was using his vehicle to carry fruits and vegetables from the downtown Farmer's Market. Vertrichten did the job absolutely free of charges. Aside from this benevolence, in the course of years, our Dutchman had been so good by giving us fresh fish from his fishing-trips alongside the California coast that Arthur invited him and his wife for a champagne-dinner on the house.

They came in at the restaurant on a quiet Monday evening. I was the one that took care of all their needs.

Jules wore casual clothes and for the occasion he had a clean shave. His burning crimson hair was tinged with gray at the temples giving him a quite elegant look.

His wife, with eyes that never stop smiling, was graceful, with a kind face. She was dressed in a well-designed garment with her hair that was gathering at the nape of her neck. They both were gentle, well mannered, and respected in the community.

The Dutchman noticed as I already did that they were the only customers or more explicitly the only guests in the establishment. Earlier, on that cold day Arthur being in a surprisingly good mood instructed me:

"Pierre, let them decide: anything they want from the menu. Put down a bottle of Cordon Rouge on ice in the silver bucket. The champagne must be on display on their table upon their arrival at the restaurant. For the main course, offer them a bottle of Pomerol from our reserve!" *With our special customers, Arthur was inclined to adopt a moral and sentimental attitude. He would honor, also preach 'virtue' and would weep openly when one of those patrons had lost a dear one over a long illness or accident. Taken generally, our employer was of mild disposition toward them, showing honesty and politeness. As for us, his faithfull employees, it was a different, sad, ungrateful story.*

I did my very best to please the couple in any way possible. When the flutes were almost empty, I poured more champagne. I even helped the lady to extract the escargots from their shells.

After decanting and pouring the fine, quite expensive wine in their crystal glasses, I presented the Chateaubriand at the table and cut it in equal portions before adding a dash of archduke sauce. This was a real delight to the eye as they partook at the banquet with great pleasure. At dessert-time I flamed the crème brûlée that was served with a *demitasse*.

The dinner was accentuated with a profuse washing-down of delicate pear cognac. Subsequent to the lofty feast, Jules was so pleased that he started to sing a Nursery rhyme entitled *Black Sheep*, dated 1744. It was brilliant, sincere and harmonious as well:

Baa, baa, black sheep, have you any wool?
Yes sir, yes sir, three bags full;
One for the master, and one for the dame,
And one for the little boy who lives in the lane.

Surprisingly, at the close of their meal as I proceeded to accompany our friends to the front door, I first noticed that Vertrichten had laid down a large one hundred dollar bill on the table next to the empty bottle of the outstanding wine. I just couldn't believe my eyes. With this engaging disposition he had been a man of noble character; a real gentleman to the true sense of the word. My heart was beating so fast. I was really overjoyed, knowing that there are still good and considerate people as the Vertricthens, that I could say nothing but a warm thank you. Without getting my *pourboire*-tip yet I stood at the door and smiled as I watched them cross the street since their house was adjacent to the workshop.

Back inside the restaurant, I noticed that Arthur was tightening his belt as he came out from the bathroom. His zipper was still open (as he often forgot that detail.)

Now as I already mentioned earlier, one will understand better about the devilish mind of that little man who in one hand can so well please some customers but at the same time will betray his honest employees: Right in front of my eyes, before I had no time to grab 'my only; my extraordinary large tip of the day', my employer seized the one hundred dollar bill. Stretching his neck, he had snatched the money with the same strength of the claw of a large bird and clutched it tight. In an irrational way with his face positively fiendish and chin that jutted out like a wild animal, he said in that cool, unspeakable disdain: "There is no way you can accept this! I'm giving Jules back his money."

But one wrong always entails another. Rushing out the door in a rabbit-run my employer was unaware that I watched him from the sidewalk. Then it flashed upon me that he never crossed the street the way the Dutchman and his wife did. Hastening around the bloc of buildings leading to the alley, Arthur came back from the other end like the furrow gallop of a cavalry, totally breathless. He then seized my hand with such strength and put his arm about my shoulder reassuring me that he had acted properly.

With such baseness in that statement, the liar who had covered himself with shame was now happy like a dog with a bone. The disgust within me came when with his eyebrows arching upward and under lip drooping he had the audacity to shamefully utter with even more intensity:

"Pierre please believe me, I did the right thing. I offered the dinner and it was unfair for you to accept any money from Vertrichten."

Granted that a minimum provision should be made, Arthur reckoned in a different tone of voice as he chuckled gurglingly like a baby in a cradle: "Your fifteen per cent tips would be added to your paycheck. I'm also giving you for free a slice of the *paté maison!*"

Strangely enough, the owner of the restaurant seemed to be very pleased. He was cheering up the way a boy-scout feels after a good action. I kept quiet during a moment for the lie had been too obvious. Now with that unwinking mind Arthur was breathing an affinity for evil.

Knowing that the liar and thief had pocketed the money without any scruples and any sense of the fundamental decencies it was as if I had been turned into stone. I felt myself burning with a hot flush over my face. By God it was awful! All this was so humiliating; so hard to endure. How could that little man have done something so improper? What perversity, what degradation, what manipulation; it was such a repulsive ploy! There were no words for my disdain.

Because of him I was in a state of disgust with myself. The boss wasn't just a poor liar; he was a clumsy, immoral liar. At the present time impelled to the verge of the abyss I was falling faster and faster. My only (extraordinary, even unthinkable) tip of the day had been stolen by a robber and a traitor.

It looked like as up to now I had never known him sufficiently. I did not foresee this. I always have showed a gentle subservience, a gentle humbleness toward Arthur. However he was still full of stormy passions that he had rouse for his own evil ends. How sordid everything had been! The boss had an even more sinister personality than I thought. I felt humiliated to the core and all my joy was gone.

After the mental agony of having been so shamefully betrayed I could find no comfort for such disreputable action. All of a sudden I resembled a child who sees the castle he had been dreaming about vanish away as he awakened from sleep, unable to calm his distress. I always had the feeling that stealing money from his employees was against his nature. I never had been treated like this before- as if I did not exist. I stood there, bitterly trying to find out why this rapacious event had ever occurred in such a crouching merciless way. Arthur's heart had been made of ice. Now my employer had become a stranger to me.

For Arthur money and gold have a peculiar smell. He not only loves money; he worshipped money the way a crow loves its eggs. It has been said that the love of money is the root of all evil; a slogan so well appropriated for that little man. Materialism was so deep in Arthur's veins. This is what William James has to say on the subject of materialism and the eternal moral order: *"Materialism means simply the denial that the moral order is eternal and the cutting off of ultimate hopes…"* However, my employer believed that in getting a great amount of money by any means possible, he might succeed in forgetting the emptiness of his heart.

The Vertrichtens were my dear clients that night and I would have appreciated their kindheartedness. This would have been my most pleasant remuneration ever.

Arthur was already gone. I left the restaurant a while later and locked the door with my latch key. As I strutted away, the moon was rising slowly out of a bed of clouds as I heard the voice of the wind.

Devoured by restlessness, I became so tired working in a place where happiness was inconceivable. For me, honesty meant something real; something deep. For all human beings in general the ultimate cause of their being is integrity, nobleness and righteousness with grace and love.

As a teenage at the time I started earning a little money, meaning 'doing good things for mankind', my parents were so proud of me, for we were honest. My father was also a hardworking man. What happened to *amour propre*-self esteem? Arthur had wounded my dignity as I had been cruelly demeaned. This had been a treacherous, delusive plan, an embittering disloyalty harbored by an employer without conscience. Now, my dreams of reconciliation with that man had turned into nightmares. I already knew it would be agonizing to come back to work.

Incidently, next day, on my way to *Le Cerisier* I almost bumped against Jules Vertrichten who just got back from the lumber store with his wife. Even that I didn't collect my reward that was so awfully stolen by Arthur I respectfully thanked him once more for his generous tribute on my behalf.

Jules then shrugged his shoulders and quipped in a delighted, engulfing smile: "MY FRIEND, YOU DESERVED EVERY PENNY OF IT: THE SERVICE WAS OUTSTANDING, ABSOLUTELY IMPECCABLE IN ITS CHARM; IN ITS PRESENTATION, AND WE DO LOVE YOU!"

Chapter 42

A NGELINE VALOIS DOURVILLE de Montrissart was again transported urgently from her convalescent home to the ER at the Good Apostle Hospital in Burbank. This time her condition had worsened. After suffering from spells of palpitation she had been seized in the night with sickness and pain. A stroke had paralyzed almost every part of her body.

Upon hearing of the situation I set aside all my scheduled errands for the day and hastened to the hospital's ICU, fearing the worst.

As I entered the barely lit suite I readily noticed Angeline lying down solemnly in her bed. With only a small lampshade illuminating her face revealing the ivory of her mouth, I became aware of her sculptural loveliness; her striking resemblance to the noble ladies portrayed in the paintings of Raphael... *I can't seem to describe my feelings seeing this real dame, a lady of high rank of unequalled virtues and charity with evenness of temper, now lost in a universe that she didn't recognize. Earlier in the European scene she had experienced a glowing, exhilarating social life. Is she maybe reminissing of the day back to the green valley of her birth when she waltzed in opulent ballrooms, with lovely clothes among cabinet ministers, ambassadors and all other most distinguished figures in society, the aristocratic way that she was brought up- brushing elbows with prominent, illustrious people...?*

Like someone awakened from a dream my fleeting reflections were abruptly interrupted upon noticing Angeline's eyes slowly lit up. She just woke from a deep sleep. Upon recognizing my presence she cast that sincere, delighted smile I was so familiar with. Inspite of her frailness she managed to hold my hand with such maternal affection. A light floating haze of blush shadowed her cheeks and now her eyes were filled with tears as she was far to be at the high mark of cheerfulness.

Angeline wasn't happy with Arthur. This kind woman was suffering, shedding tears in secret. However, it was true that she loved him and was devoted to him. There was no suffering she would not have resigned herself to, no sacrifices she would not make were it for him. *Could it be that upon meeting me again, the punching bag of her husband's mockery all these years; the same husband that was making everybody laughed at me? Making the whole city laugh its head of me, now standing next to her in consolation, she became cognizant of the vanity of Arthur's pride and mediocrity? Maybe she remembered that all his life, Arthur had never treated her kindly, never even paid any attention to her?* I still wonder if she finally discovered him as a grimacing personage who took on the noble name from her shrouded knightly ancestry; that dignified name; that sublimation of all the Valois Dourville de Montrissart lineaments. Arthur lacked one major quality in carrying such a name: he never, never was and never acted like an aristocrat. For him, to be called Valois Dourville de Montrissart was just a snobbish way to make himself feel important, even respected. Yet, without respect to others, the boss bypassed the stringent primal awareness that is of what noblesse is all about. By now Arthur probably realized that he had been a stranger to his wife.

After awhile, Angeline was lacking energy once more. She lost consciousness and fell deeply into reverie. Her health was failing, as her spirits were quite low. With her husband's attitude to life, there had been such humiliations; such cruel sufferings, a constant torment to her. For Angeline all had ended in disgrace. Now, I sincerely believe she wasn't sad at leaving this life. It seemed that she perceive the approaches of death with bravery as the tender emotions of her youth had fallen into an abyss.

A few days later the situation with Mrs. Valois Dourville de Montrissart didn't improve. Atrial fibrillation defined in Merriam-Webster's is "very rapid irregular contractions of the muscle fibers of the heart that resulted in the lack of synchronism between her heartbeat and pulse."

The doctor called upon Arthur. In order to save his wife, *a fortiori* a heart operation had to be executed at once. Unfortunately fate was to decide otherwise. A few months earlier, Angeline signed a very important document that is termed DNR- Do Not Resuscitate. This was an official paper respecting her last wishes that precisely specified no defibrillation or extensive surgery whatsoever, also no sustained life by other artificial means in the event her condition worsened.

However she did not seem able to make a proper recovery. She already had stopped to take all of her medication for the last six weeks and was temporarily connected on a respirator.

I came back to see Angeline as Arthur tried to take the dying words from her mouth. In a very quiet voice he announced:

"Pierre is here my dear, and he brought you a nice plant." Nevertheless, the physician was waiting for Arthur and Melanie's instructions.

They both agreed to respect Angeline's last intent. With a heavy heart they resolved to adhere to the arrangement. Once more after all the sufferings a certain feeling of peace, of well being took possession of her. She had dreamed as she was aging with a dignified face for the rerouting of all uniqueness of the family's heredity.

Two days later the breathing machine along with the tubes she had running everywhere were disconnected. She then started to sink deeper and deeper into peaceful painlessness until still tranquility with no thought of waking up as she was riding to an unknown world; a better world still, into a timeless eternity…

Melanie called me at once saying that her mother had just joined Granny. She added that she died, a blissful smile frozen on her face. *I will never see her in this world again.* Those few words were my only thoughts on that moment of sorrow. Again, a sense of immense loss filled my heart. I cried like a little boy. I really loved Angeline, my mentor who couldn't bear the sight of cruelty. She had been the most honest creature that ever lived. So often she would protect me against Arthur's vile assaults. Angeline was like *ma petite maman d'Amérique,* all-knowing, all-caring: a real second mother to me. Never more will I enjoy that smile, those attractive hands upon my shoulder and her great understanding.

As for Arthur, her death hardly caused a ripple. I met him later on; his face was undisturbed. He stood there with eyes that did not weep…

* * * *

Occasionally at work I would encounter French clients but as many French restaurant owners can testify Parisians are a pain in the *derrière* for most of the time those *bons vivants*-happy campers were very demanding. A few of them exhibiting that typical Parisian pomposity and haughty manners would consider their servers as no less than slaves. Some even gave me the notion that they were living in another century.

Actually the French Revolution was Paris itself for the capital imposed its will on the less resolute provincial towns and hurled defiance at the whole might of counter-revolutionary Europe.

On several occasions I have been insulted by snobbish Parisians. Those so-called men of intellect acting as if they were all educated at *La Sorbonne,* claiming to be the charm of poets thought that the rest of France, if not Europe has become a mere servile suburb to the French capital.

This is one of their favored sayings: "One lives only in Paris; elsewhere one vegetates." It is a fact that there is an arrogant supremacy assumed by Paris over all other French cities. Parisians who speak as if they are going to vomit their words still regarded the provincials as second-class citizens with little or no education. Those so-called 'high society' people with unbridled egotism consider themselves superior to everything because they abased everything to themselves. Parisians always undertake to live and think for everyone else. It looked as if French citizens from other cities were waiting for those impertinent people from the capital to decide whether or not they will laugh or weep. Those same people really believe that they are the best of God's creatures, spending their evenings at the *Opéra Comique* and drinking Champagne at *Les Champs Elysées.* With supreme cynicism they still imagine that breathing Paris preserves the soul and that the French capital is the ceiling of human race.

For most of them the French Empire was really the counterpart of the Roman Empire and Napoleon Bonaparte is still the incarnation of their country, also the great conqueror of Europe. Bonaparte thought that God speaks French and that He would give him the final victory. However, this great emperor never saw 'the writings on the wall.' Waterloo had been the dramatic response to his arrogant attitude. Just as during the time of Louis XIV- *le Roi Soleil*- the Sun King: a real Parisian must look pale and not precisely in good health. Red cheeks denoted mere serfs working on a farm.

There is a story of a *bourgeois-gentilhomme* dying of tuberculosis in a baroness' arms. The baroness simply said: "He was a great intellectual, look: not a speck of red on his face!" Nonetheless, some Parisians keenly aware of their glorious past believe in 'sanguinary cures.' Just like in Molière's *Le Malade Imaginaire,* a few doctors from the French capital still indulged their patients in purgatives and bleeding, with the greatest promptness. For them, bleeding is the best remedy for colic, increased fever or severe smallpox.

I would like to point out that Arthur still practice bleeding therapy along with his friend Eddy. However, in the eighteenth century, even with 'sanguinary cures', Montesquieu deplored the fact that so many people were cut off in the flower of their youth.

The inhabitants from the French capital also believe that they are the only ones to be worthy enough to be buried at the famed *Père Lachaise* cemetery. People from other prefectures would mingle in amongst the Parisian *élite*. Those same folks by moving in the midst of such fashion and elegance could thus efface some provincialisms of toilet or of language.

The artificial atmosphere of high Parisian civilization destroys in women the sentiment and the taste for duty. They leave them nothing, but the feeling and the perception for pleasure. The French capital is a place where so many people have nothing to do but to play and amuse themselves.

I have met some of those Parisians, who after experiencing the beautiful weather on the warm Santa Monica Beach would claim that the Paris' gray climate was still the most pleasant of all. In reality Paris is not an easy city to make one comfortable permanently. At the turn of the twentieth century, a famed French Academician knew this quite well when he proclaimed in a speech that "Paris is the most delicious of places to visit.

As long as you're a tourist in the City of Lights, 'April in Paris' is wonderful; just sublime. But on the other hand it's also the worst of places to live in permanently and the only pity about Paris is that it has inhabitants. They are careless and appear to live and die without reflecting much of what they are doing. Paris steals their time, their minds and souls; it devours them. Parisians are pagans, because the pleasures of the senses, of the mind alone interest them.'"

At the time of Louis XV, as one would questioned an inhabitant from Metz or Aix-en- Provence about decisions regarding politics or other matter, the answer was always the same: "We are provincial folks: we must wait to see what Paris does." They dare not make a move. In fact they dare not even express an opinion until Paris has spoken.

As a teenager I often visited Paris, just a few hours away by train from the Belgian capital. On one occasion I accompanied my old friend Charles Romelaer to the large French metropolis. Charles was an artist-painter from Antwerp, also an expert in chalk drawings.

Along with Romelaer in his two cylinder Citroen car we made it all the way in front of *Notre Dame* where, under the stone eyes of the gargoyles my friend started drawing a multi-colored chalk-picture of the Madonna and Child right on the sidewalk. At the same time, with the tune of my guitar, I started to sing Edith Piaf's greatest success: *Non, je ne regrette rien.*

People, mostly tourists started to throw coins in a small cigar wooden box that we brought along. Later in the afternoon, just then as Charles finished his masterpiece to the pleasure of so many photographers, we collected enough money for a dinner at the Montmartre's *Café de la Paix*.

One evening, four citizens from the City of Lights, all of them dressed in the late fashion came for a gourmet-dinner at *Le Cerisier*.

As I was going to take their order, one of them kept on reading *Le Figaro* while his tall brown hair and blue eyed friend was holding me by the arm saying: "*Garçon*, what part of France are you from?" As I informed him that I was from Belgium he looked at me as if I had contacted some kind of contagious disease. Then he started belittling Belgians:

"Oh, *Quel dommage*, I am so sorry to hear this! It is a serious illness but don't worry, a cure might be discovered soon." This had created lots of roaring laughter among them and other patrons in the establishment as well.

Arthur, with his elephant ears ever *à l'avant- garde* of all events ran silently to the table like a hare. Faking that slang Parisian dialect very poorly, (his attempt to disguise his Toulousian accent with so many provincialisms was quite amusing) he started yelling in a sinister intent:

"You probably found out that this *dumb-dumb* is from Belgium? What he didn't tell you is that his mother is Flemish!"

The Frenchman who was holding me by the arm earlier clasped and squeezed my hand even more tightly in a way that there could be no escape from his hold. Looking haggard in a peculiarly abstracted voice he said: "*Mon Dieu, ça c'est autre chose, quelle catastrophe, c'est un véritable éboulement! Vraiment, est-ce que c'est possible?*"-What a catastrophe! Is it possible; can it really be that bad?"

For sure, impolite behavior is really their specialty. The chief occupation of the Parisians is: talking nonsense. Still, with so much inconsistency, you will find them in high positions in the government or in courts of law. Parisians almost always complain of everything, with loud bursts of laughter. Back home from a trip, those people breathed Paris; they have it in their soul. Again, they really believe that Paris is the ceiling of the world and that they are 'the high social breeding.' The French capital with its *can-can* and other sovereign gaiety tried to impose upon the world its ideal of human civilization, side by side with its buffoonery.

* * * *

On this day there were so many thoughts in my mind that I hardly knew where to begin. I went over them as I was training in the Santa Monica Mountains for next week Long Beach Marathon.

Well, let me start with Arthur, as he related yesterday at the restaurant on a specific event when daughter Melanie bestir herself in the land 'Down Under.' Sitting at a table with some wealthy clients from Bel Air, Arthur had been very pleased to explain to them that during her stay in Australia with the firefighters, Melanie got acquainted with one of the richest land-owner from the country. This was Arthur's moment of excitement as he announced that Mr. Frank McCassey, a sturdily built Irishman that made his fortune in the multitudinous businesses of import-export had decided to meet Melanie, and showed her his Western-Australian desert estate.

In that sprawling land, one evening, after meal as the waning moon did rise directly from behind the bushes revealing a vast desert area, McCassey, in a strong Australian accent instructed 'Melanaie' to cup her hand around her ear to sense the whistle of the desert wind. Looking around as far as the eye can see, Arthur's daughter compared the place to Texas. And in a stream of eloquence, the courteous McCassey retorted blusteringly:

"Melanaie, I love Texans being so proud of the size of their state. Last year I met the billionaire, oil magnate René

Barney Salasky III in his castle-home in San Antonio. We had the greatest B.B.Q. you can imagine. Nothing was missing, from the pig *en broche* to steaks, even Polish sausages Salasky brought back from his native Poland." and Frank continued:

"I arrived in San Antonio at the precise moment that René's private jet landed in the small airport on his return-flight from Manila, Philippines. René and some other Polish friends were invited in the Philippines for the birthday of the first lady. That's the woman, you know with the collection of two thousand pair of shoes!" In getting a little closer to Melanie, McCassey went on:

"Now my dear, I'm not bragging, but between us I have to tell you that my estate with all the land alongside the Nullarbor Desert from Nurina to Ooldea, and as far as the outskirts of Port Augusta, surpass Texas in size!"

The customers at *Le Cerisier* were utterly impressed with the story; the providential encounter of Melanie with the Australian tycoon. As for Arthur, insofar as I could tell, those clients's enthusiasm was music to his ear. Now, after a polite good-bye to his willing listeners, the boss looking a little arrogant with happiness decided to sway like a ballerina to the private room to enjoy his favored drink. My employer had found his reward in his gratified vanity.

* * * *

As a youngster, Jean-Michel Bertrand had been one of my classmates and a travel-companion as we hitchhiked throughout Europe from Belgium to Switzerland, Italy, Monaco, Germany and all of France.

With his glistening black hair, white teeth, piercing eyes and definite superabundance of strength, Bertrand reminded me of Masséna, a general of the French Empire. Jean-Michel's father was *procureur du roi*-the king's public prosecutor and a judge of the highest court in Belgium. As a magistrate and *homme d'esprit* he was also a fine writer, but he thought he wasn't good enough to have his work published.

Bertrand and I did keep in touch throughout those long years. So he finally decided to come to meet me in the Golden State. Later on I took him to *Le Cerisier* and introduced him to Arthur. Together, we celebrated his arrival over a bottle of Cabernet Sauvignon.

My loquacious employer didn't lose a second telling Jean-Michel all about his fantastic exploits as a test-pilot with the French Air Force; his game of tennis with a Danish prince or toasting champagne with the Shah of Iran...! It didn't take long for Bertrand to realize those stories were just 'hot air', simply a fancy of the mind!

Now, as a psychologist my friend related to me of Arthur's conflicts of feelings and impulses: "Your employer's vision of the world can be described as a synthesis of painful contradictions from his childhood. In his unconscious mind that associated guilt feelings and anxieties, he keeps on unfolding his dreams of fantasy that become reality for him." and he concluded, "There is a strong possibility that his genetic inheritance was controlling his behavior; his delusional personality."

Aside from jogging together around the Sepulveda Dam I took Bertrand to Las Vegas, San Francisco, Universal Studios and Disneyland, the usual tour of the west...

Back at the airport on the last day of his vacation, as I bade him farewell, Jean-Michel started to laugh till he almost choked. These were his last words: "Pierre, I'm still pondering over Arthur. Even now, I wonder if he is for real! It looked as if he was not quite sure which planet he had just landed on. That man is the biggest joke I ever encountered."

Chapter 43

O N THIS LATE afternoon, I really felt indignant and ashamed of Arthur's attitude. It was like a blast of wind on a quivering candle. Unable to stomach this, I was almost ready to faint as my blood beat in my temples.

The boss told me with such profound baseness that he just made the same funeral arrangement for Angeline as the one done for his own mother, that is to say: the cheap three hundred and ninety-five dollars deal cremation from the *Nema Society*. And, with a face like hard marble he bragged:

"You know Pierre, with this kind of transaction, it's like I just hit two birds with one stone. Now both ashes from Granny and Angeline WHOM I REALLY LOVED would rest in their urns on top of my buffet."

Our loyal customers at the restaurant, Angeline's friends as well were informed of her funeral through e-mail. Some of them, who are now couples in their middle age have come to know Angeline since their youthful dating days. Many others who have become successful business people have been delighted by the variety of hors d'oeuvres that she had created. A few actors, television personalities who have spent winding down at *Le Cerisier* during their struggling days have listened to her encouragement, to her optimism.

So on that day, most of the *nouveau-riche* came to say goodbye to a 'friendly stranger' who has once touched or even have become part of their lives.

* * * *

Saint John of the cross is a gothic revival style built into the steep side of the hill. It was an aged solemn church with light radiating through stained glass. The wonder of its grandeur, of its peacefulness took my breath away. Its venerable front was adorned with all sorts of serene handy works such as marbles and sculptures. It suggested great beauty that really appealed to the imagination. A wood bench leaned against the side of a tree with a spring gurgling nearby. Facing a grandiose flight of steps, one can observe the full length of the church riding splendidly on its high podium.

There was utter stillness, utter calm all round, as a few pigeons descended from the church roof to alighted on the parking lot. With the sun slanting westward it stood there like a hidden treasure surrounded by luxuriant vegetation. On the right side, the religious building rounded off the lush promontory overlooking some humble house-the home of the clergy. A colorful parterre of azaleas greeted the churchgoers about to attend a somber ceremony.

A cursory vision of the interior reveals several stonework angels that decorated the baptistery. In addition, there was a carved wooden pulpit next to the altar that housed a triptych portraying Mary and Child, also first century martyrs. Noticeably, next to public rituals and Calendar Rites there were fourteen niches along the walls depicting in sculptured figures of the events of Christ's suffering on the cross. As I looked with amazement at the stone structure of the altar, and the impressive tabernacle, that lovely church appeared to have a spiritual life of its own.

Quietly, over the heavy smell of incense that filled the air I sat down on a wooden pew, waiting for the church to fill up. It had been a hot day and people were not dressed too becomingly for the circumstance. The stained glass windows representing the Lamb of God and some saints flooded the house of prayer. They seemed to console me with a light of divine essence that created a peaceful effect. Whiffs of incense, scent of candle wax clung to the walls, and started to emanate. Again that truly rendered the place with an almost heavenly feeling.

Well over one hundred friends crowded the church to bid farewell to Angeline Valois Dourville de Montrissart. Several well-known actors, a few singers, comedians, other restaurant owners along with a state senator, as well as most of our dear *clientèle* were also present.

In the scarcely breathing silence Arthur and Melanie solemnly, but with such a somber mood and long faces drained their feet, dawdling through the center aisle. The boss, his mouth thin with bitter line was unconsciously assuming the various facial movements. He showed a face perfectly devoid of all sincere expression. Arthur was impassive, quite unperturbed like a cold white mask that I knew so well. He never had had the sense of having found haven in a warmer nature than his own. His late wife Angeline had sacrificed her entire life for him. Aside from her illness she had been subjected to so many indignities which finally killed her.

Arthur was wearing a neat black suit with black tie; the daughter, a black dress. Her light hair was a contrast to her dark gown. Hanging around her neck, on a gold chain one can observe that precious sapphire as big as a pigeon's egg that she inherited from Angeline. Melanie had never been more beautiful. Her deep mourning embellished her languishing, regal grace. It made her pale complexion yet better; it heightened the brilliancy of her look. She was all shaking as she carried her mother's ashes in its urn, toward the altar. Unsurprisingly an unfathomable abyss had settled in her heart. Now she had to adjust her life without her mother. At the requiem mass she was in a flood of tears with a dreadful feeling of loneliness.

Father Corcoran, very canonical in his cassock and white chasuble ascended the pulpit. In addition, he wore the humeral veil that signified hope, penance and mourning. He was a stodgy, pompous man with an ascetic-looking face, dogmatic and positive as priests are apt to be. Nevertheless, he appeared to be a man of God, of clean character.

His delivery was quite emotional. At one point his voice was reaching some heavenly height. It was a well-conducted ceremonial. The clergyman, with some ecclesiastical pride, very respectably praised Angeline, the noble woman from France. A dame of title, bearing a historic name, who had undergone such painful experience during her stroke. He also commented her as a lady of the world who was able to express herself in six different languages, who traveled all the continents; who dine with royalties and renowned celebrities. The priest added that Angeline was a great loss to everyone, in fact to all good people. She had been a wife without equal, faithful and devoted, a woman without reproach, full of solicitude for her daughter, her family, her name. But she could also speak plainly to an offender whoever it might be, though never spitefully.

When the good pastor commended Angeline, there was a convulsive smile that twitched Melanie's lips. Angeline's charisma had attracted a great number of friends, who had never met her but who had been drawn to her; who had now come to meet her for the ultimate time.

Then, Father Corcoran concluded that Mrs. Valois Dourville de Montrissart was going home to a better place: from a tent on planet earth to a fantastic mansion in heaven for eternity. The priest finally revealed that: "This angel of enlightenment would awake to life immortal, where sickness and death would be no more."

Before the lamentation, *le chant du cygne*- death song, Gounod's Ave Maria, when the music took on practically heavenly purity, Father Corcoran, in his *audi alteram partem* retorted in a peremptory manner that we were all on a waiting list to enjoy that sublime, that exquisite spiritual life; a life of extraordinary bliss.

Again, in the same manner as when his mother passed away, Arthur's prevailing mood seemed to be one of tension rather than sorrow. My employer did not shed a tear for the silver-haired woman who was his wife. Just as in the beginning of her illness, Arthur still remained indifferent. He was sitting abstractedly, immobile with a vacant eye. It seemed that his mind was elsewhere. Even that he wore a band of black crepe on his sleeve as a sign of mourning, the boss looked so little affected. He had listened to the sermon quite absently.

As I sat next to Eddy, I felt ashamed and embarrassed for Arthur; for his attitude. He actually had been more absorbed with a fly that had landed on the shoulder of a person sitting in front of him.

Leon posed with his mother in the front row. They kneeled in the pew.

With her face sunk in her hands, her head bowed as a nun in deep prayer, Beatrice Van Meerstellen was deeply affected with sorrows. For Beatrice, beside her son, no one in the world mattered except Mrs. Valois Dourville de Montrissart.

She was Angeline's best friend, since Leon was but just a little boy playing games of hide-and-seek with little Melanie in Calabasas Park...

After the death mass, the service and prayers I stood outside the church once more to watch the mountains. They were illuminated by the shadowed afternoon sunlight. Unexpectedly, near a clump of firmly rooted bushes opposite to the rectory, partly hidden by the falling countryside, I chanced upon a peacock with his iridescent tail outspread next to a solitary heron that stood there, with his neck erected in its own peculiar style. On that moment, I remember Angeline's beautiful neck, so proudly exalted. A dame with so much compassion that always happily overlooked the business at *Le Cerisier* with such a lovely nature. She had been generous and tender, with an outstanding intelligence.

Everyone was invited at the restaurant for a giant catering of hot and cold appetizers. Arthur was eating with as much appetite as though nothing had happened. For the occasion, classic music filled the air. Angeline so loved those great composers from a glorious past. She was especially fond of Schubert and Debussy.

In the middle of the brunch, as small grilled filet of salmon in a mild lemon-butter sauce came in addition to all the delicacies, lights started flickering. Thence, an inebriated Arthur 'half-seas-over' more than anybody else, with his shirt damp with perspiration and shaking with each throb of his heart rushed in the middle of the dining room toward the light. Just as a baby in a cradle, this time showing a little emotion, he lifted his hands towards the ceiling. With wildfire in his blood, in a trembling voice, he mumbled that Angeline was talking to him; that the flickering of lights meant that she is now in her astral body; that she has arrived à bon port, up to heaven. Arthur, bright and sharp like a bird added:

"Everybody, please enjoy the food for she is watching us!" All around, low laughter mingled with soft weeping.

Of course my employer never realized that under the watchful pale moon, people from the DWP were working on the electric line down the street, thus creating some shortages of power!

* * * *

The narrative which follows can appear to the reader as extreme. It also point out the real identity and character of Arthur, the self-proclaimed aristocrat of an illustrious family: The Valois Dourville de Montrissart's.

After his wife's funeral, Arthur decided to close the restaurant for a few days. Then an idea had formulated up in my mind to call upon my friend Steve Decarpantel in Mesa, Arizona to fly his Cessna four-seated cabin monoplane to Van Nuys Airport for a trip to Death Valley.

Steve, in complying with FAA regulations had just obtained his pilot-license a few months ago. Altogether, along with Arthur, Eddy and I we were planning that outing with the understanding that all expenses would be divided up equally.

On several occasions I had visited Steve in his Mesa resort. Decarpantel who stood an imposing six feet three with the nature of an aristocrat was an *aficionado*-sports fan, also one of those rare human beings who never seemed to grow old. Even now his eyes were strangely clear, his hair as soft as that of a teenager, and with fine skin he was still handsome. There was a sense of stoicism about him that continued to fascinate me.

Before the takeoff, the superstitious Arthur had blessed the aircraft with holy water that he carried in a bottle of Evian.

The flight itself was outstanding. Steve had been well-prepared. He manipulated flight instruments with great dexterity. From Van Nuys Airport, we reached that desert area at constant optimum speed, ever increasing with gravitational pull in a low altitude without any trouble.

The heat in Death Valley resembled a furnace, while the surrounding lands reminded us of the lunar surface with only rocks and cracks in the soil, like around an extinct volcano. However, according to the information sheet from AAA-travel, "so many animals live there, all of them mostly nocturnal. The temperature in Death Valley can easily reach 120 degrees-baking hot, thus making it one of the hottest spots on the planet. It is actually the lowest place in the North American continent. Geologists would have it that during the Ice Period the entire area was an immense lake. The water eventually evaporated, leaving layers of mud with salt deposits. No human beings have inhabited the Valley for thousands of years." In a way, it seemed that we were going back into the womb of time.

We enjoyed a great stay at 'Coyote Desert Hotel' where we were entertained by a group of French musicians, also tourists. One of them, Jean Belon, on a previous trip even walked in the heat of summer across Death Valley. With a good supply of food and water, he also carried a giant umbrella.

Subsequent to a long promenade on Main Street, the only hefty artery in town, we directed ourselves to the hotel-disco. Along with an assortment of snacks and antipasto, we drank margueritas, Corona beer and Long Island ice-tea, till late at night. This really was a pleasurable experience...

The return-flight to the City of Angels had been a quite dramatic experience that might have cost us our lives; some event I will never forget for as long as I live!

"I'm going to check everything, including the tire-pressure," said Steve. Oh yes, he made sure the inspection was perfect on all details with the exception of the gas gauge that indicated an almost empty tank. (He actually started the entire journey with less than a full tank.) This gaffe could have been the result of too much consumption of beer, of hard liquor the night before at the disco. This digression made him forgetful of the most important assessment for a pilot.

Once up in the air again, after a little while Steve Decarpantel realized the blunder. His eyes rested on us for a moment. He started to perspire heavily and became quite disturbed. Some kind of a confused, dazzling flush came over his face. In spite of himself his mouth was shivering in a curious frown as the embers of disillusion nerved themselves under his teeth. His whole behavior and countenance altered at once.

At that juncture the engine began to rattle. With fear in his voice, Steve informed us that we won't make it to Los Angeles, and it was even too late to turn around, back to the desert city.

Arthur with hatred that sprang up in his heart, his face all red and turgid was unable to hold himself any longer. As he became restless as an eel, with sweat running down his flabby cheeks, he decided to the peak of hysteria to humiliate me for the ultimate time. Gazing malevolently, with his chin pointed in my direction he forlornly opened his mouth, thrusting out his tongue first like a frightened child who jump in the swimming-pool for the first time. Next, Arthur shouted in multi languages fashion as it was his practice: "Pierre you are a nincompoop bastard, *un trou-de-bal* and a *dummkoph*." After tweaking my ears, he pulled my hair a bit and gave me such a look as could not have been matched by the Devil himself. Arthur continued:

"You're *malade dans la tête*- not quite right in the head and totally irresponsible! With your stupid, good-for-nothing plan to fly us to Death Valley, we are now going to crash in the desert among scorpions and rattlesnakes. My God: what a horrible death!" Then, still talking to me *bec à bec* in a tone of hasty displeasure he expostulated: "You never want to see further than your nose. Because of you and your dull Brussels-sprout brain I'll never be around to celebrate my next birthday!" and, in that state of 'in extremis', deliberately annoying, with tears in his eyes he concluded without even realizing that he used Rousseau's last words: "Now I'm to see the sun for the last time!"

I also noticed that my employer had wet his pants. Then the exertion became too much for Arthur: his wrists felt swelled up and shuddering. His eyes also appeared blood-flushed. He kept listening helplessly to the jangling of the engine with the tension that continued breaking up in his belly. He was becoming totally unmanageable, almost delirious as he was jerking his head like a reptile. Suddenly, as that certain terror took possession of him even harder, he went down on his knees as he was holding firm with his hands on the edge of his seat. Between his fingers hang a rosary, given to him by his late spouse. He then began to pray in his native French language: *"Je vous salue Marie, pleine de grâces..."* and *"Notre Père qui êtes aux cieux..."*

However, those well-thought-of words seemed to be mere sounds coming out of the mouth of a very frighten human being. It was just a singular prayer made by tradition; by unadorned custom. At this time, Arthur with the smell of a sweating horse was weeping bitterly. Next he looked around, still in anguish, and his thinking shifted entirely. In his wild imagination he now had to creep up to a warm being and bury himself in welcoming arms. Just like a little kid, I heard him saying in a low tone of voice, with eyes vacant in expression: "I want my mommy...I want my mommy!" In his mind, it seems that his little hands were still clutching at his mother's breast to suck her milk.

As usual, Eddy Freedman with his hair plummeting wobbly over his ears kept quiet, very quiet. He even appeared to be totally indifferent of what had occurred. In quest to foreseeing all the possibilities he took the 'I don't give a damn' attitude. Life for him was just an *intermezzo*. Abruptly, his malevolent face became strangely illuminated with tranquil peace as he sat motionless with unconcerned eyes. Afterward, Arthur's partner decided to talk in a downright horrendous way in a manner so disturbing that made us shivering to the bone. In his quite inappropriate remark he made the picture rather revolting: "As you well know, there are no parachutes on board- Well, to all of us I wish *bon voyage*...to the threshold of eternity!" Looking at him, to summarize in a single sentence, I had the feeling his thoughts resemble that of Socrates in Plato's *Apology:* "Death may be the greatest of all human blessings."

At that point as the reserve supply of gas had been exhausted, the propeller almost came to a sudden stop. We no longer heard the clattering; it was replaced by the wind that was roaring against the fuselage. With this undeniable reality, as we decelerated to minimum power the stabilizer that provided longitudinal stability (related to the angle between the chord of the wings and that of the stabilizers) became virtually non-functional.

I was utterly afraid too, even petrified, not precisely in a state of cheerfulness. For sure this was no day at the beach! After a short silence, in bitter recurrence of the situation I sunk deep in an abyss of thought trying to concoct the idea that everything would be fine. But at the same moment, the words of the writer Alan Seeger permeated in my mind with full force: "On the eve of the battle of Somme July 3, 1916,

Mr. Seeger created the following eerie poem-*I have a rendezvous with death:"*

> I have a rendezvous with Death
> At some disputed barricade,
> When spring comes back with rusting shade,
> And apple-blossoms fill the air.
> I have a rendezvous with death
> At midnight in some flaming town
> When spring trips north again this year
> And I to my pledge word and true
> I shall not fail that rendezvous.

Alan Seeger was mortally wounded the next day on July 4, 1916.

But I already knew that in case of my death I would be surrounded by loving faces, faces of my relatives, of my closest friends. Afterward, being in a kind of mystic state that appeared to me more like a revelation, something happened. As the devils were raging outside the aircraft, in my mind, over a burst of religious fervor and in a sort of communion, I experienced a transfiguration. Soon, with peace in my heart, I swiftly perceived my entire family, with Helena at *Cena Domini.* They were all dressed in brilliant white robes, as bright as steel blades amidst other people adorned in the same fashion. Furthermore I saw my grandchildren Louis, Georges and Samantha. My granddaughter Samantha was wearing a garland of plumeria scented flowers around her beautiful white swan neck. With gentle Hayden music in the background, I discerned the vision of a new world with all the wonder that would be. With that *divina particula aurea,* it was almost as if I had touched the face of God. Thereafter I felt a ray of sunshine that inundated my face as my eyes opened even more and more on that new, wonderful universe; a universe of intrinsic beauty where love and peace irradiated…

Still, in the back of my mind I carried some kind of confidence that our pilot would find a way out from our distress. The future was now in his hands. As in an excruciating dream, we waited dangling.

I wanted to recall here that during the time of the independence of the ex Belgium-Congo (now the Democratic Republic of Congo), I did an operational jump with Steve Decarpantel from a C-119 military plane, along with sixty other paratroopers over N'djili airport in Kinshasa. Beforehand to an ambush that killed our captain (disemboweled and tear in pieces by Bantu rebels carrying machetes), my friend, also a sergeant-chef took all responsibilities to direct our campaign successfully. In the confusion, without any commands from a high-ranking officer, it was each man for himself though Decarpantel decided to take charge and did an unusual great job. Steve was even decorated by lieutenant-general Jan Van Rompelmeert.

My expectations of Decarpantel's decision proved to be accurate. As good luck would have it, after considerable thought he came to the conclusion that he had to try to land somewhere, anywhere. And with the ultimate wave of caution, Steve's hands worked precisely with sound experience. So suddenly, we began to glide, down, down, down, the longest slither ever. As we started the precipitous descent for a final plunge into the abyss, every moment threatened to be our last. I suddenly felt like an eagle with wounded symmetrical wings too weak to lift himsef straight who kept on falling, falling, falling to terminal velocity. For a few seconds, but long dragging seconds we had the feeling to be severed from the world. Everything that had been before was simply an illusion, an illusion now gone like a fly caught in a light breeze. Our lives were hanging but by a hair, as we could still sink in the ground the way a stone throw from a bridge sinks into the river. The sun was there in the sky, too sturdy to look at, and the ground below so serene, but still distant; so distant! This was the greatest suspense of our lives as we completed our descent over rocks and potholes.

With almost surpassing any human strength, Decarpantel, after scrutinizing the entire area made a forced landing on an abandoned strip near Baker. Zigzagging awhile with the rattling of the wheels, we all bounced on our seats several times until finally the Cessna came into a full stop in a great cloud of dust. The sun bloomed through the aircraft's windows, still flooding in. Eventually we all breathed a sigh of relief. With our hearts finally at rest, our blood ran quicker in our veins as we were all stimulated. There was a recrudescence of life, the incursion of a warmer blood. Focusing on the site, stillness and calmness was all around the discarded strip. The place was so quiet, seemingly beyond the touch of time. The excitement of life deep inside us was a revelation. There was sheer and electrifying joy in the air. Unexpectedly I came to think it a very astounding occurrence that the sun will continue to shine for all of us.

At that precise moment, this little barren region of California with its simmering climate, with the sand in the air that burned and irritated our throats seemed to us as the most beautiful, the most serene place on the entire planet: just a gorgeous spot in the midst of a sterile, burning desert. Even the cacti as well as other plants that grow in that scorching soil carried certain attractiveness. Unconsciously, on that instant, I couldn't stop recalling a particular sentence from Jack London in *The Call of The wild*: "There is an ecstasy that marks the summit of life, and beyond which life cannot rise. And such is the paradox of living; the ecstasy comes when one is most alive…"

An uncontrolled ripple of laughter came down from Arthur's throat. It was such a bliss bordering on delirium as he realized we were still alive, that he wasn't dreaming. He was elated as he had ever been in his life, and I looked in astonishment at his sudden transformation. Arthur threw his arms in the air as he was beyond himself, with eyes that seemed to dance in its sockets. He continued raising his arms to Heaven with such solemn gratefulness; his entire body was now trembling with joy. My boss was in a state of wild ecstatic happiness. After he had reached the uttermost limits of despair in an abnormal motor excitement I saw tears in his eyes, but this time those tears sprang from utter contentment.

In a transport of enthusiasm, hopping from delight like a fish in a pound, he looked at me. Once more with shedding tears of joy he started to do a little pirouette while clapping his hands. Combing his fingers through my hair, and uttering a groan of ultimate peace he uttered in a whoop of giggle:

"Well mon petit Pierrot, we made it! Oh yes, we made it; we made it! This is a glorious day…the best day of my life!"

Abruptly, in a surprised move, with an avalanche of words as a wave of color came back on his cheeks, his hand kept holding on mine very tightly. Aroused with pleasure, altogether with a gentle sense of well being, Arthur, with that touch of a schoolgirl intimacy pinched my cheek first. He then planted a big wet kiss on my forehead. Next he tickled my right ear as his lost cheerfulness had reemerged. For awhile Arthur continued with his elation. There were more hugging, more kissing *en veux-tu, en voilà*. The link between my employer and me was indefinable. It was totally unreal, still very firm. That little boss of mine whose heart had never known what it was to love; the same man who once articulated that: "my brain was smaller than that of a mosquito butt" moved swiftly like a swallow on the wind in a mood of sheer humility. Again, in intense moments such as this as his look was full of compassion; full of tenderness, I LIKED THE MAN. For awhile I also felt myself in in some kind of weightless state.

As Steve's heart throbbed with emotion he felt a strong compulsion to burst into tears. His eyes were also glowing with an excitement he couldn't suppress. The odd strained look on his face had passed away. Now he appeared to be like the aperture in the wall beyond which the sunshine radiated on an outside, magnificent world. *A chaque saint, sa chandelle-* honor to whom honor is due. If not for his hasty decision, we could have been dwindling into oblivion to 'kingdom-come.'

Looking at Steve's face, correspondingly I recalled a bible scripture: *"There were giants in the earth in those days; and also after that, when the Sons of God came in unto the daughters of men, and they bear children unto them, the same became mighty men which were of old, men of renown."* My friend; my former comrade-in-arms was a giant too, but not a wicked giant, just a kind gentleman with a good heart and with tremendous good spirit. Steve had shown us an incredible courage with singular dexterity. He had acted like an angel, and that angel had just saved our lives.

The only one with a still expressionless face, with a somewhat sinister, perceptibly taunting smile was Eddy who sluggishly awakened. Unfortunately that good man did not ascribe any crucial meaning to his life.

Everything was happening so suddenly. But soon another miracle came about: on the bosom of the desert, at a distance of less than half a mile away, a dark object was moving rapidly in our direction. It was a four-wheel vehicle, and before long it came to a complete stop.

An old, still fair good-looking farmer wearing a Texas-style hat, a worn-out leather jacket that included a 'Vietnam War sign' embroidered over his right pocket and a marijuana plant design on the left decided to help us out. The man that lived in an isolated small ranch nearby already knew about our forced-landing. He brought us two jerry-can of kerozene in his '50's Chevrolet truck. That kind human being didn't even charge us a penny extra for his gratifying service...

From here we pursued our journey across the sandy waste. Unexpectedly the weather had becoming cloudy and we made it back to Van Nuys in a veil of rain, safe and in somewhat good spirit. Later on, after we had landed on the airstrip next to a twin-engined Beechcraft, we moved on to the Captain's Quarter airport café where we all clutched a flute of Cordon Rouge Champagne for that very successful day. After all, this had been a fine, but dreadful occurrence...

Through it all, everything came on as before and I went back to work. But I constantly thought of such precious recollection as this unpredictable flight to Death Valley.

At *Le Cerisier* restaurant, Arthur with his shoulder jerking up at every step was so uncommonly proud. An impulse of excited vanity took possession of him. He announced to our customers that as a former Air Force Commander he was the one responsible to rescue us from an eventual plane crash by instructing our pilot to proceed for an emergency touchdown!

Again and again, with that statement that sounded like a trumpet-call my employer needed flattery to survive, independently of those colossal lies. (As a reminder, the real truth is that Arthur had just been an assistant cook-a *cuistot* at the French AFB in Tours, France; he had never set foot inside a military jet and never even saw combat.)

Upon hearing this elaborated, well-fabricated story, Eddy Freedman who was quietly sipping his apple-martini in the private room became hilarious; totally out of control. Along with giggles and chuckles it was a contagious, irresistible hoot. Eddy clapped his hands together so violently in girlish excitement to a point that I also found myself infected by that epidemic laugh carrying such enthusiasm.

And now that I had encountered a real brush with death I live life to the fullest. I enjoy the delicate warm smile of Helena, and simple things such as birds singing around the channel at the marina on Fiji Way, before they soared sky-high from under a few clouds.

* * * *

This morning at the crack of dawn, in the coolness of a light breeze, as I ran alongside the Los Angeles River I kept thinking about yesterday's slightly embarrassing event at Saint-Benedict Hospital where I found myself under interrogation by *Nurse Ratchet*. She was intent on gathering answers to quite personal questions on a survey for the urology team. Without batting an eyelash, with her stethoscope around her neck, she blurted out:

"Mr. Choucart, do you still have a good sexual life? Do you have a normal erection?" My face must have turned red and blushed with some sort of humiliation for I heard my soft voice retorted *"sure Nurse Ratchet."* As soon as she finished jotting down my answer she fired another question:

"Mr. Choucart, did you have any difficulty during intercourse?" Keeping up a straight face, *Nurse Ratchet* went on and on with more questions until finally: "On a scale of one to ten; ten being most satisfied, how do you rate your sexual function now?" I must commend her, a charming, slender nurse with fallen hair, shining eyes and wet lips for indeed she did a good job…

I continued jogging up to the sight of the hill. Abruptly, upon reaching the top, like Rocky Balboa, struggling to catch my breath, I shouted out my final answer to *Nurse Ratchet:* TEN! Though it was a very exhausting run, I managed to whip up a smile as I wiped out a little white foam from the corner of my mouth.

I was planning to give out the 'erotic' episode at Saint-Benedict with Eddy for a good laugh. Surely, he would be amused again for he had experienced the identical treatment with *Nurse Ratchet* in the same hospital. Following painful impediments of urination, Eddy had also been diagnosed with prostate cancer earlier but he had opted for intensive radiation and implantation of radioactive seeds instead of surgery.

On second thought, even though Eddy was generally an accomplished charming fellow the fear that my story would reach Arthur's ear was real. I already knew beforehand what my employer would say. Knowing the little man quite well he would again weave an entirely different scenario, adding unimaginable details in which I would end up being a eunuch. And undoubtedly his convoluted version would be again trumpeted like a recital on every table at the restaurant.

* * * *

On this day, with a ray of the sunset hidden in the west, the group of Parisians came back for an early dinner. Subsequently to explaining *les specialitées du jour,* one of them with a boil on his left temple touched my elbow with his spatula hand. Before I had time to present the wine-list at their table he first glanced sideway at other customers and articulated:

"*Garçon,* you know that no civilized man would have dinner without wine. What do you suggest?"

But suddenly Arthur who stood behind me at all times came forward saying in that same fake Parisian jargon: "I will take care of your wine. Back in the old country I was a *sommelier.* I was the one that recommended a special vintage wine to the Prince of Wales during his visit in France." and, looking at me, he went on: "That Flemish Brussels' cabbage animal here doesn't know a thing about good or exceptional wine!"

Chapter 44

ANNO DEI, 2002. On the second day of February, late in the night Melanie woke me up with a phone call and she frantically narrated the tragic fire that gutted the beauty salon adjacent to the restaurant. She had been informed of the fire by our neighbor the Dutchman Jules Vertricten who had been working late in restoring a model T Ford.

We all were aware that the store-owner, Salim Demetru originally from Sofia, Bulgaria would often snooze in one of those high leather chairs after a hard day's work.

That evening with a lighted cigarette in his mouth, he suddenly fell asleep. Rapidly that speck of a torch dropped to the floor and ignited flammable items lying nearby. Fortunately, a cab driver who was cruising by noticed smoke rising out from the store and immediately dialed emergency–911. It was not long before fire trucks arrived.

The flames had flared up very quickly with a column of smoke that coiled straight upward. The smoke already turned black, rising in whirls. The fire fed itself on the dry tufts that grew around the tree on the sidewalk. With one gigantic leaping flame, the roof became ablaze.

Cautiously, the firefighters dragged Demetru away from the store. He had been in his underwear, partly covered with a blanket, and heavy with sleep. Next to the leather chair an empty bottle of Johnny Walker was found. Demetru had been drinking too and was slightly burned on his right leg and right arm. He was thankful to have been saved, but ultimately sorry that he was arrested for negligence. As Salim was being carried on to the ambulance, he found enough strength to sing that famed Beatles' song:

> *Michelle ma belle, sont des mots*
> *qui vont très bien ensemble,*
> *très bien ensemble…*

The fire had raged. The firefighters thought the foaming flames were lapping up the sides of the building; that it had spread to the restaurant. One of the men hammered and smashed *Le Cerisier's* front door with an axe so forcefully that the wood groaned before shattering to pieces. The door lifted completely off its hinges had burst and triturated from its bolts. It was an old, but outstanding solid door made of oak that was lined with iron designs just like the ones made for castles or manors, to be discovered in most parts of Europe. The blows made the entire establishment tremble. This had been a strong, muscular door that for many years had rotated quietly on well-oiled hinges. Three other firefighters had joined in with hoses and had flooded the place. Within seconds *Le Cerisier* had been soaked; the booths, the carpet, the rest of the furniture, including the kitchen.

Standing outside the restaurant, Melanie overcome with a sense of loss had cried out: "What a disaster; our little abode has suffered a hurricane!" She continued by telling me that in her anger and haste she had argued with the battalion chief as to why the establishment had been hosed down when apparently the fire had stopped in its tracts, sparing the dining room and the kitchen. *This was no time to dispute with people trying to save our place of business from nothingness, my dear Melanie. But of course, this was so typical of you: force your unreasonableness onto a decision that was obviously wise at that moment.* After making it known to me that she was the little heroine in that catastrophe, Arthur's daughter hang up the phone.

I didn't get much sleep that night. However I was up earlier in a hurry to visit *Le Cerisier,* apprehensive of what I would discover. After all, in spite of having to live on with a despicable boss, I've grown accustomed to working unfailingly for so many years in such a beautiful place...

At the restaurant I was overtaken by the smell of smoke and the disarray from last night's fire as the establishment was still very hot.

I heard voices echoing in the distance. As I approached I realized those voices were talking excitedly. At times the conversation was no more than a murmur and hum. I first peeped through the dining room door that was left half open to let the smoke out. Through the fumes from the door ajar a long crack of light was showing upon the center of the room.

As I expected, without wasting any time, Arthur, Melanie (with her face still saddened by anxiety), Leon and the chef were already there standing in the dining room in session with the insurance team amid a rustle of stationery sheets of paper, memorandum scraps that lay on a table covered with a checkered tablecloth. I watched their faces to see what was happening. The group was consulting in undertones.

I kept observing the boss with his spectacles slightly out of balance and his chin in his hand as he gazed intensively with his nose buried in the insurance files. His attention was drawn to that mountain of papers, shifting one folder after another as he avidly studied each detail. A secretary kept busy scurrying notes across the pages.

Arthur was dressed in a three-piece grey tight-fitting suit as if he would be going to get his picture taken. He talked so fast with much gesturing. He was pirouetting like an orchestra's conductor so absorbed in that brisk of hearty conversation. Over cold beers and limonades, the talk went on. In the course of it Arthur decided to present himself as the man of the hour. Within the many arguments, everything seemed to be drifting just in his direction for he laughed blissfully. The boss really thought that he was the cynosure of that stage as he was acting as an intermediary between the adjuster and the insurance people. Everyone was listening to him without a murmur, with their heads still bent and eyes looking down at insurance's papers; at scattered documents. After a short break, they continued the discussion with renewed vigor and excitement. I couldn't stop but break out into a laugh. The scene so reminded me of a sight when I discovered Varanasi, India: sacred cows were roaming the streets. As soon as they were dropping dung, flies almost immediately zeroed in on for the feast.

Unbelievably, Arthur apathetic as he was assured us in a friendly smile that our wages would be covered by his business interruption insurance policy while the place was undergoing restoration.

Once the group had cleared all the remaining folders and notes from the table, they finally left the restaurant. I spent the rest of the day with Leon to place all the non-refrigerated items in retort pouch packages. Meats and fishes were already placed in air tight- plastic bags in the freezer.

* * * *

As regard to the fire-damaged, it was estimated unanimously by the insurance people that *Le Cerisier* would be closed for several weeks. The booths were all wet. They were already impregnated by the smell of smoke, along with the curtains, the carpet, table-clothes and our entire reserve of linen.

It would have been rather awkward for me to go on staying here for so long, doing nothing. So, after a few days spent at the marina watching the soft lapping of the waves from the channel against the rocks, it was just the right time for me to drive and aim along to snow-drifted Monterey- pine trees enjoying in a gust of wind, a row of ice-capped mountain in Big Bear.

Only a few wispy clouds were idling around in the clear sky. I braced the keen fresh air of the mountain; the balsamic odor of the trees before visiting my grandchildren further north in Fresno...

The entire Willorteen family had just moved to Fresno from San Clemente because my son-in-law's company had been re-located. Along the road, I felt strange. For inexplicable reason this was all *déjà vu*. I felt akin to the site: the way clouds mass up in the sky in the evening, as they were streaking to the west. At times they would descend and embrace the earth. The sight of the verdant, well watered prairie was all too familiar even that I never visited this region before.

In the distance I saw lofty buildings with their roofs that seemed to touch the sky. They are mostly related to the massive California administration and are to be seen all around. This is a remarkable city a little remote; it is also a city where life offers little diversities. The streets were very clean. It feels as though they had just been sprinkled. But at dusk the entire area became utterly silent; no special activities whatsoever.

An unnatural calm descended over the region as the low, late winter-sun shone.

Surrounded by gently rounded hills, the smoke was billowing from the chimney of the Willorteen elegant residence. The garden behind the house, with plenty of fruit trees, roses and daffodils raised in tuffs was as gracious.

It was such a great atmosphere for a warm reunion. As the sparrows were twittering shrilly in the foliage of the chestnut trees some of the neighbors of those enchanting dwelling-places that I met on the promenade of scrubby palms even greeted this unfamiliar face on the whole with respectful curiosity.

For me, after the life-inferno with that ruthless employer at the restaurant, a man (if I can call him by that name), that treated me so badly, no less than a beast in the wild who has humiliated me to the bone, this became a day of rare tranquility. As the last rays of the sun still shone, being with my relatives was like a flow of inexhaustible refreshment. In front of the house, statues of the most exquisite workmanship were on display.

Inside the residence the living room had been expensively furnished in modern style along with tapestry representing pastoral scenes. The entire property was bright, thriving and well kept. Then I heard little footsteps approaching.

My grandchildren Georges and Samantha were hopping in the air like wild deer, spreading their personalities warmly through the room. With eyes bright with happiness they gave me *à bras ouverts*-with open arms such a great welcome, as they literally devoured me with kisses.

Toddling down the stairs in her black calico house-dress, my daughter Dedette was throwing her arms aloft with the jerky motion of a marionette, as happy as a bee in the bosom of a flower. With the clapping of her hands, she sank upon me with something very much like an ecstatic cry of joy. Half spun about on her toes, after rubbing her eyes, she was screening a vivacious face. *Ravissante* in a feline motion, her long-lashed eyes dancing with an irresistible zest for life were lapsing into a smile, as her luxuriant hair was reflecting in the sunshine every tone of gold and brown. The prettiness of her youth was in main part her mother's gift.

I still remember her as a little girl with her school uniform from *Les Soeurs de Marie*-The Sisters of Mary. I also recalled her fear before an appendix operation. During lightning, before the storm she was afraid to go to bed in the dark because she saw certain brimstone flames around her.

Now, with fresh skin, beautiful teeth and still large innocent eyes, her feminine charms so well enhanced, reminded me of those dames walking elegantly on the Champs Elysées with that innate talent for recognizing good wines and perfumes. Unlike her older sister Corinne in Spokane, Washington, Dedette, glitteringly bright was an excellent artist-painter, always endeavoring to amuse. She always spoke in high-flown elocutionary method. As a vivid memory of her own childhood, she never separated herself from Pistachou, her teddy-bear that was a gift from a dear uncle when she was barely two years old. Since Pistachou was now totally hairless, Dedette who still sleeps with her favored toy had decided to give him *la grande toilette*. She had spread pink lipstick on his nose, and, along with earrings, a green shawl lay most becomingly around his neck with the addition of green bootees.

Aside from writing successful children's books she also has several paintings on display in a Sacramento Gallery, even at the public library.

Upstairs, from their two-storey dwelling, stood Dedette's drawing-room heavily charged with the perfume of narcissus,

and a lamp with an openwork brass shade. With a book of
Omar Khayamm lying on the table, along with a few Japanese
prints, there was a caricature of Alexander the Great on the
wall. This was her secret room with her hidden treasure that
she so much cherished; where she was always seeking, with
a touch of Hanna-Barbera style, to make the most of her
possibilities. She knew as Henri Miller puts it in *Tropic of
Cancer*, that "An artist is always alone-if he is an artist... the
artist needs loneliness." Dedette was a professional illustrator,
though calm and detached with the air of one performing
trivialities to kill time. Aside from her work of arts, or pruning
the roses, she kept strict account of all her husband's affairs.

Prior to their return to Southern California, (along with
their little dog Hercules that was not much bigger than a rat),
my daughter and her husband had been working for several
years, their fingers to the bone in a religious farm upstate
New York.

At one time Medusa, the mini python who was Georges'
pet snake, almost swallowed Hercules, thinking he was some
kind of a rabbit!

My beautiful room with its own kitchenette opened on a
terrace divided with a bamboo partition. What's more, with a
wavering of flapping wings there was a small aviary that was
filled with birds of all sorts.

Tonight, I noticed in the sky a fragment of a moon, but
with the heavy clouds the moon sunk, and now the night grew
as dark as a grotto. I was thoroughly tired and I fell asleep at
once...

In the early morning, before I got another turn on the
pillow, as if moved by a sudden impulse, the children would
swing the door wide open and awaken me in amusement. With
that disorder of sheets and blankets they would be scurrying in
their night clothes teasing me before dancing across the room.

However, in the middle of the night I had experienced a horrific dream; a dream that woke me up in cold sweat, leaving my night shirt quite damp. It was definitely more like of a premonition for events to come.

Incidentally the room where I slept was also my grandson's room. Next to the terrarium where Medusa, the mini python was able to slither sinuously among the leaves there was also a *bonbonnière* filled with so many candies.

But in my nightmare, Medusa became a colossal eighteen feet snake with the head of a man. And the head of that man was none other than Arthur's. Just like a tiny mouse, my heart began to beat so fast. I felt hypnotized, exhausted with terror by the power of the half animal, half man's eyes and the touch of its long sinuous body. With his forked reptilian tongue flopping out of his mouth and his breath yelping through his teeth he then started to crawl into my bed, winding up my right leg, twisting it over. At that juncture, the serpent with my employer's bulbous crossed eyes started hissing into my ear. All of a sudden with his sharp fangs, after he salivated heavily the partly human/partly evil beast bit into my cranium and then sucked my brain emerging from it. He kept on drawing off that substance from my head until he felt well nourished.

In the morning the sunlight was streaming into the room; it carried a gentle breeze and pleasant warmth. But the horrendous, distorted dream was still real, almost tangible. In my sleep I had kept on twitching and tossing restlessly on the pillows. Nevertheless as I focused on at the terrarium with Medusa' shining little head erected in my direction I felt in communion with him. Unexpectedly, I had the feeling that he tried to talk to me. Even that the curtains were still partly drawn, daylight filtered round the edges.

Through some kind of a hunch, with bright spots dancing before my eyes, Medusa welcomed the new day, adding telepathically that I shouldn't worry about a thing. From the window I saw that the weather was fine. The sunshine was glancing off the roofs of the other houses across the street as a little bird was cooing among the trees.

Dedette's husband, Stephan Willorteen with the figure of a Greek athlete is a tall fellow with very black hair parted down the center, set on his head squarely. At other times, with his hair cut quite short he looked like a famed Hungarian violinist. He was a man with several trades to his credit.

Over his Levis jeans he wore a strong leather belt with a silver buckle incongruously chic, matching his Yves St. Laurent designer shirt.

With his eye as accurate as a carpenter's level he was an excellent, skillful golf player, very strict about sportsmanship, keeping fit at all times. He had recently been appointed to the lucrative post of 'executive' with Calitrony-Cement Industries, a branch of the giant Tarpillar Corporation. Stephan, a well-meaning, thoughtful man, always endeavoring to amuse had a big heart with intense love for humanity and great concern for the unfortunates. What he liked best in the world was his wife. How very lovable her face was to him. Whenever Dedette came back from a shopping spree, he would tilt his head like a sculptor about to begin a work of art. On the other hand, her husband was her hero; her champion. Even that he was so much involved in the multifarious details of his new position with Calitrony he would always find time for a kind word for her.

Stephan was one of those rare human beings seeking some form of perfection in the midst of what he believed to be a wicked, ungovernable sinful world. He wasn't just content to enjoy the mystery of his existence; of the existence of his family. He had to explore it, explain it and solve the conundrum of the universe *ad majorem Dei gloriam* through faith, love and charity. He was strictly against the pomp, the vanity of this distressing humanity.

In the late hours, with an enthusiasm he could hardly restrain, after he patted me on the shoulder, Willorteen would take me into the garden as the dusk deepened into night. There were always many stars, even shooting stars but often veiled in a slight mist. Tonight the big trees were motionless. They seemed still, for the dusk hid the yellow blotches on their leaves. Their outlines were still rounded against the sky. We winded our way in the semi-darkness as the long weariness night was approaching.

Once Stephan offered a job as 'a flagman' for the firm's heavy traffic cement-vehicles to a homeless that slept in the street and who was eating a side of bacon he found on the dump. Furthermore, Willorteen provided a cheap room for the indigent at a friend's house. My son-in-law was equally a man of integrity. In the same manner as Mr. Kim the Korean Health Department inspector that refused a largesse gift known as 'palm greasing' from Arthur, Stephan with the adamant strength of his personality had never either given or taken a bribe. Like the reliable inspector who, in good cause had decided to close *Le* Cerisier restaurant for the weekend (upon finding six cockroaches in the private room), Willorteen, a proficient human, being of dissimilar character had correspondingly climbed the ladder of decency.

Nevertheless he took each opportunity to entertain his children, laughing noisily at everything. At the county-fair during week-ends the children would ride a pony, jerking the reins aimlessly, playing at the merry-go-round as their daddy fulfilled his youth's dream of being Robin Hood at the archery. With a gentle nature and highly respected in the community there was not one mean bone in his body.

In addition, aside from his grafting, at times he alluded wonderingly to his literary taste. Stephan loves funny riddles. What's more he enjoyed the strange slapstick of such a man as Richard Armor, virtuoso of light verse:

Nothing attracts the mustard from wieners
As much as the slacks just back from the cleaners

Being a strong, hard muscled-man, Stephan's golfing would keep him away from the hulks of inertia and tradition. His partner on the course was none other than Monsieur Putoise who owned the finest funeral parlor in Fresno.

Monsieur Jean-Gaston Putoise de la Sauvinière, a French aristocrat hopelessly snobbish with a biggish well-sculpted nose, prognathous jaw, pink as a suckling pig had a face molded by materialism and he smelled like an old man. He had enormous shoulders with a curious pigeon breast.

With his squalid hat perched sideways on his head, a *Fleur-de-Lys* emblem embroidered on his jacket-pocket and suede gloves over his hands, his appearance was such as to strike the attention of the most casual observer. He often used the crude language of a jackass voiced macaw. Ironically he was moreover a deep cynical unbeliever- a depraved dissenter from established religious dogma. He had cold eyes without any sign of human emotion in them; eyes that never changed their look even if murder happened. Aside from his successful business he always appeared tired and beat up!

Lately, Stephan resented Jean-Gaston continued presence on the course (his dislike of Putoise had been instinctive in unmeasured terms from the beginning), but after work, on those late hours of the day there was no one else to score with. Before the game the mortician always enjoyed drinking at least two glasses of gin-tonic. So often the gin was still humming in his head. That partner, a groveling soul that overlay values with gross; senseless details, believed in the motto of Lao-Tzu, a sixth century B.C. philosopher: *"Life on its way returns into a mist, its quickness is its quietness again,"* and he would added, *"When a man dies, it's as if he's never been…"*

The fourteen holes course was behind the concierge's house. At one time, on a verdant summer's late afternoon, Putoise, the careless maladroit player putted a golf ball that struck the concierge's wife on the stomach.

Now, in a majestic composure the springing motion in Stephan's legs was increasing rapidly. However before hitting the ball, Putoise always gave way to a coughing fit, before spitting on the fresh cut grass.

But, on a particular day owing to the recent rain the ground was still soft. Over a light breeze, the Frenchman chewed slowly his upper lip raised, and he spat out a pulpy mouthful that looked like a glob of green sputum. The spit landed straight on one of Stephan's new patent-full grain *Innolux* leather golf shoes.

Instead of apologizing for his action, Putoise really aggravated the situation. In the same manner as 'count' Arthur Valois Dourville de Montrissart, my bossy employer, Putoise de la Sauvinière, over a blasphemous utterance like the ring master in a circus laughed the cracked laugh of an elderly man. With foam spewing at his mouth his face changed to bestial grossness. *I have no recollection of the language in which Stephan expressed himself. But the incident itself is still vivid in my mind. I have put down the story in substance, if not literally.*

Of course this incident infuriated my son-in-law. With a haggard look in the eye he retorted a sharp cry like that of a rabbit when the fox has him by the neck; so mad that a force from within impelled him to tossed his lollypop into a waste-basket. As he has descended into the valley of humiliation,

Stephan winced as if he had been struck. Pacing backward and forward like a caged tigerI believe at that point that he felt a frantic impulse to raise his arm and strike Putoise across the face...

One might already be aware of the fact that for me this would have been an ordinary event, almost a normal day for a creature like Arthur (at the image of Jean-Gaston Putoise de la Sauvinière) to spit on my shoe or in my hair, but not for Stephan Willorteen.

After having cleaned his shoe from that spatter, his body gave a convulsive twitch. He became haggard and restless as he had fallen into one of his odd silence. Shamed and so much degraded he continued cursing Jean-Gaston mentally as he was filled with hot, blind rage. With outraged eyes and sweat pouring off his face, Stephan had been really pissed.

Subsequent to wiping the perspiration from his forehead, he withdrew from Putoise unto granite silence, with his eyes set and stony.

It is seldom that any man breaks out in this way through emotion. Abruptly, I hazarded the opinion that Stephan had been really shocked by the attitude of his golf-associate. Being myself for so long at the service of a man such as Arthur, I really anticipated with Stephan's uneasiness.

Bon gré, mal gré, Monsieur Putoise was simply an arrogant, irritable mad dog that ought to be committed to a clean institution. Stephan stumbling wildly cut across the field toward the main road leading to his house.

As the flamboyant colors of the California sunset flaunted their splendors across the crimson-gold sky had faded into pink, with the disk of the sun cut with so many shades of surrounding trees, a lone jackal yapped once somewhere far of the golf course.

Later, Dedette fluffed up *une omelette aux fines herbes* for Stephan's supper but that whirlpool of anger was nonetheless with him. Jabbing into the meal with his fork and feeling lonely as Prometheus on his rock, his wife was wondering if he won't croak of indigestion. He was talking in a toneless, unnatural voice as though his tongue was unaccustomed to words. This was his inclination when lost in thought. However, after awhile Stephan always found reassurance with the thought that he had a wonderful wife at his side to comfort him. Even that there was still in his eyes a shadow of a frown with a sign of bitterness on his lips, she would brush his hair away from his forehead with a slow, gentle gesture before giving him a big hug.

Although Stephan was always quick to forgive and forget, it was difficult for him to have completely ignored the action of that vile, empty jacket person as Monsieur Jean-Gaston Putoise de la Sauvinière. As a lurid fool, with quite objectionable code of morals that man had degraded himself to uncivilized behavior...

Aside from his job, his golfing, his other gym elaborate apparatus or chopping wood, Stephan would go with his family to bivouac at the Kern River. With the humming concert of myriad of flies, through intricate defiles over irregular, rock-stream paths, he would take the habit to break into a trot like one swell looking horse- clop...clop...clop... With his face gleaming in the rising sun and the springing motion in his legs increasing, his family would follow with a prim strut, swinging out their legs with each step. His wife and children would puff a little bit to keep up with his rapid stride. While their spirits rose higher with full of zest for life, they would hopp across a little wooden bridge to the other side and back again where the reflected sun glared up from the river under the bridge. They would watch the stream that roared and plunged with aimless passion as it rushed with frightening speed under some sort of a cliff. Clouds would start drifting very slowly and gloomily out across the river that had smoldered in the late afternoon sun. The rain would wash the handrail away, leaving the bare plank only which lay a few inches above the speeding current that raised and gyrated under them. The children would be stopping here and there to pluck a flower. At all times Willorteen tried to catch a big fish. Next, he would request the chef at the hotel to cook it for their dinner...

A few days later, Helena came to join me by train from Los Angeles' Union Station. At once we started planning our next trip to Vancouver B.C and the ferry connection to Alaska.

Before the farewell to that lovely, very artistic family over *un bon vin du pays*-a good wine, Helena graciously started cooking breaded veal chops done slowly, simmering in butter. Like hot food *à la carte,* they came out a golden brown enough to make your mouth water. And for dessert: *chausson aux pommes*-apple turnover.

Surprisingly Samantha gave us a solo ballet performance of Tchaikovsky's Nutcracker-*pas de deux.* She danced as lightly as a feather all around the living room. It looked as if she had wings and was soaring delightfully to heaven like a bird. Georges's magic fingers were stringing along on his red violin. All purity and candor were blended in this blissful, gracious exhibition as it captured our hearts.

Prior to those harmonious balletic grace-swan steps and instrumental execution, Georges and I went to the Fresno State Park for a two mile run. It was a crisp, refreshing day. The sky was still clear as the last rays of the setting sun fell on the wide open space. We started way over at the far left corner of the park. By the end of the sprint we were neck and neck for a few seconds, but it wasn't long before I was puffing and blowing. Soon it was all over. My little grandson, in a most exceptional and ultimate kick had beaten this Legacy Los Angeles Marathon Runner; that Boston Marathon Candidate by no less than twenty-five feet..!

After I left the Buick in the driveway of the house we boarded a Greyhound bus. Along with Helena we first stopped in Seattle, Washington, then to Spokane for another family reunion. A blanket of snow already covered the city that was clean and glittering. Here the air was more ethereal, buoyant and bracing. The area proved a great surprise to us, as compared to the Golden State.

Corinne and her husband Johnny had decided to settle down in Spokane, next to Johnny's parents: the Coldys who were the most simple-mannered people alive, real fine human beings.

My elder daughter and son-in-law live in an elegant, cozy townhouse in a subdivision amid a honey-comb of houses surrounded by hedges and walls that rose gently alongside a graceful park. It was so wide a view that when the bright, hard sunlight wandered across the land, it picked out one line of roofs at a time. They didn't live too far from an old army warehouse, next to a cemetery. On the spacious terrace of their apartment that suggested a certain amount of taste, some birds showed a proprietary air as though the place had been built exclusively for them with the fragrance of grass and trees. Here, one can find tranquility in undiminished fullness.

The slim, wise-eyed exotic Corinne dressed in the best from *Mademoiselle* (notably well-outfitted, but still with simplicity of style) was wearing a star-sapphire on her middle finger that she bought in an irresistible caprice at *De Beers* store in Rio. It had a glorious gleam that flickered in my eye. I never saw anything so lovely. Its price had been beyond her purse but she had dreamed so long for it. Just like her sister Dedette she was still blooming, like a wild flower her skin looking unsullied, clear as a peach. Giving glances similar to the glances of a woman behind a veil she was all soft curves, yet tall too. It was like music to see her walking in her fancy tipped shoes. Her eyes, now looking at us seemed to turn to some exquisite rapture. Corinne would spent hours in trying hats, some of Dedette's hats (she had a great variety of them), or dresses as she kept peering at herself in a tall, narrowed mirror. One of the hats with a yellow feather on it came down over her head, covering her forehead and part of her eyes.

Corinne also knew how to give a room an intimate feeling; a feeling that gives you the sensation that delightful people had just left it. Because of church affiliation there was in her a kind of *je ne sais quoi*, physical prudishness which she fought hard not to betray. Well-versed in four languages, including a fastidious Indian dialect 'Guarani', Corinne along with Johnny have spent thirteen years as Christian missionaries in the *galleries-forestières*-deep rain forests, piranhas's infested rivers of Paraguay and Bolivia. Over there, so many leeches sucked their blood, brushing cobwebs from their faces, lashed knee-deep by the brink of impassable bodies of water among the most primitive people on earth. Oftentimes floods and rains would wash away bridges and roads. They had to learn how to avoid literal starvation. The fear of death had been more than real, but even under those harsh conditions they never lost that taste for serenity.

Now Corinne, with a curious reverence for literature had decided to immerse herself in the readings of early Victorian novelists such as the 'figures of strong outline and gnarled feature' of the Brontë sisters's roaring successful writings. Music, paintings, books were all the reason of the joy of her soul and of her pride. Occasionally her face was flushed with sleep as her eyelids hung heavy over their pupils. With her readings, her mind was more incarnated than at any other time when the spiritual beauty inclines to the corporal. This had made a profound, sturdy influence over her mind. It had molded in her manners of discretion, humility, *savoir-faire* and *savoir-vivre*. Corinne's interest in the Brontë family virtually had reached the level of a cult as she loved their unrestrained styles and mystifying, almost divine works.

Aside from her readings or paintings, she was equally an accomplished photographer. She had eyes gifted with keen vision. In order to catch the grandeur, the magnificent splendid spread of colors over the ocean when the sun was setting gloriously, Corinne would take ten, fifteen, even twenty pictures of sunset within seconds of interval to each other until the astral disk disappeared on the horizon. On a mountain area near the Canadian border my daughter took several snapshots of myself and her husband standing in the snow. She won a prize at the Cannes World Exhibition of amateur photographer and even took a picture of the president of France.

Her apartment was well equipped with *le dernier cri* divans and couches from IKEA fine furniture among a profusion of flowers. On the modern kitchen table, a small cabinet was built in to hold silverware. It was a pleasure to watch Helena in such admiration over the entire scene. Alike her younger brother Phil in Apple Valley, Corinne also surprisingly stuffed my mouth with marshmallows. Besides this whim from early years my daughter always enjoyed tongue-in-cheek a little. With her eyelids drooping down, she articulated:

"Dad, you write as if you were *le fou de Dieu!* You are virtually irrational; quite unpredictable, living your fantasies like a rebel. But I also can feel the substance in which the pulse of life is beating in its artistic form," and she continued: "You're an unruly poet, although with a profound, sweet and pure philosophy." Personally I often recalled Flaubert's thoughts: *"Our hearts must be sensitive in order to feel the passions of others..."* Writing is also a matter of hard and painstaking concentration.

As a snowstorm took on intensity, Johnny Coldy muffled up in a dark overcoat with mock astrakhan collar, hair disheveled and arms swinging appeared to us like a symphonic orchestra conductor. He had been running as fast as his legs could carry him in that snow screeching angrily at each step, from the city-bus into the icy flakes and swirling winds that were whistling through the streets. As he arrived, we heard the crunch of snow on the front door. The spinning sleet swept from the sky and it seemed to cover the earth with a white blanket. So many banks of snow presented such a picturesque contrast to that of Los Angeles. In the streets, because of the hard winter climate I saw many people with rugged weather-beaten faces, but still healthy.

Inside the house, Johnny still with wet flakes on his face was shivering from the cold, his teeth chattering. Taking off his coat he then scraped off the remaining snow from his *bottines*-high shoes and clacked his heels like a *haupsturmführer*-German officer.

Alike Stephan he gave me a bear hug too before cupping his hands against the warmth of the fireplace, as the snowflakes outside restlessly whirled on the ground. Corinne had just built up the fire. It was dancing. As the little flames leaped up with the crackling of the fragrance of burning wood, the shadow of Johnny who stood close up to it seemed to dominate the entire room. He sat down next to the draught of hot air coming out from the fireplace. The roar in the chimney was quite agreeable. Feeling the warmth to his back and shoulders, he daintily unlaced his boots; let fall one boot, then the other thus showing his violet socks like those of a cardinal, and let his legs dangle to be comfortable.

Amid the toasts, the popping of corks we enjoyed the calm of our first day in that northern state. Outside, as the storm grew in fierceness, the snow fell thicker and thicker, heavier than the night before. The street appeared almost deserted, save for a few very dirty dogs. They went across the main artery to a narrow building on their way to a square, facing the Opera House.

Johnny, aside from his partly Russian nobility lineage was a hodgepodge of nationalities: Spanish, Greek and Rumanian. He was a tall man as well, that practiced radical humility and was naturally somewhat shy. But so often, shy people achieved great things in life (so was one of my officers with the paratroopers in the ex-Belgian Congo who gave his life trying to save an injured soldier, after their helicopter was shot-down over Lake Tanganyika.) If you had a good look at Johnny's eyes, you forget his shyness. This was the keynote of his gentle, humorous nature. He would hit the butterfly trail as he devoted himself to butterflies and better class insects. However, Johnny almost always reminded me of Patton when that famed general said in the French language to his subaltern officers: *"L'audace, toujours l'audace!"* Now, when Johnny Coldy reared back his shoulders, there was no stoop in them; you could easily picture him standing at the helm of a ship. So often, Corinne with a negligent hand on her hip felt so proud of him. On the other hand Johnny sometimes amused himself by observing her in some household occupations or by playing the harp. Corinne's husband learned how to leap from the board of that Olympic swimming pool, of that trampoline of bashfulness to *terra firma,* in one of the most remote area of the globe.

Without any *summa cum laude,* other advanced degrees or honors from *la grande école,* as a good proficient preacher and Ciceronian orator, with an excellent command of the Spanish language and distinctive charm, Johnny became an important figure throughout the South American continent. In spite of much physical sufferings caused by so many mosquito bites and other bloodsucking insects, his unique unquestioned religious authority has attracted people from everywhere. As for Johnny's religious activities, I personally assisted to one of his discourse near the world's largest hydro-electric plant at Itaipu Dam, sitting on Iguasu Falls. On the parking-lot of that small community, I saw crowds that came from all the surrounding countries. There were numerous cars with Peruvian, Uruguayan, Argentinean and Brazilian license-plates. I've heard that over one hundred people also arrived in the region on mules. Others walked barefoot in excess of twenty miles through mud, hostile jungles, across rivers, across swamps. They had pressed bravely on, regardless of heat, rains and snakes just to hear Johnny. There was even a parachutist from Colombia who jumped on the site from a hot-air balloon. With a bible tied-up behind his shoulder-straps, he almost landed on top of a grazing cow.

Now, back home, in addition to his work as a minister, Johnny was also a drummer in a jazz band at *The Whip*- night club in downtown Spokane. The rhythm of the jazz band from afar was like a heart thumping. It was hotter than a summer night. Movie-stars, senators, even the governor of the state of Washington enjoyed an evening at *The Whip*...

In the middle of the rattling of plates and glasses, the bursts of laughter and the music, Johnny, after polishing his glasses looked at me good-humoredly. Then, breathing on my cheek he inquired in a Socratic method whether Arthur; that short 'Air Force Commander-yellow test pilot' and cheap theatrical clown was still in charge of *Le Cerisier* restaurant?

Johnny Coldy, gasping, choking and sputtering over a malaria crisis would ran screaming to the clothes's closet, dragging a short-sleeves safari-jacket and tropical knee breeches from his garment-bag, thinking he was still somewhere out in the Amazon. Then, *aussitôt dit, aussitôt fait*-soon after that, he got himself a baby-gun and went hunting squirrels who were wagging their scruffy tails, uttering squeaks as startled ravens leapt back.

At one time, on a warm summer night, during one of those breaking points as a last act on a set stage Corinne found her husband laying on a narrow bench alongside the park with his hair tousled and his shoes unlaced, blinking his sleepy eyes at nothing, deaf even to the barking of a dog, even wondering when the daffodils would flower. At that juncture after he lifted his head to the moon with only the drumming of the woodpecker on the beech tree that disturbed the serenity, Johnny went on sucking the bones of a little fish, spitting the remains on the ground. He seemed to be straining for oxygen. Then, oblivious to the surrounding he would close his mouth just to avoid swallowing a fly.

Upon my return from Africa I was suffering from stomach amoebic-rhizopod protozoans, but my companion-in arms with identical symptoms of malaria as Coldy- caused by anopheline mosquitoes became uncontrollable. He almost bit an Irish terrier's ear after the animal had pissed on his leg that it mistook for a tree...

Subsequently to what they had experienced in the wilderness of South America, Corinne with an unweaving good humor and patience was more intent on watching her husband's moods or predispositions than her own.

Nevertheless, from his religious superiors in the Missionary Society Headquarter in New York, Johnny obtained an award. He then recalled the exalting speech William Faulkner made upon receiving the Nobel Prize for literature: *"I feel this award was not made to me as a man, but to my work-a life's work in agony and sweat of the human spirit, not for glory and least of all, not for profit."*

Next day the wind had veered round to the north, but by the late morning hours the weather was fine. Now that the sun was up, it glitters on every bit of snow; such a wonderful spectacular scene.

In the late afternoon we went to Johnny's parents' cozy, but well furnished mobile home. To our surprise this turned out to be some kind of a costume party, the same kind of costume party I had experienced at *Le Cerisier* restaurant during Alloween. Brad the head of the household looked so comfortable in his guise of an Arabian Sultan. My son-in-law's sister and husband joined us. Under the glamorous Brazilian music from giant speakers, Isabelle, Johnny's mother with that sultry charm of the south, wearing a white bib-apron and sheer black stockings prepared us quite delicious tacos and strawberry-margaritas. *La gourmandise* was shining on everyone's face. When Isabelle noticed the way we devoured her tacos, she shed a sequence of happy tears before cooking more and more of them.

Then Brad covered my head with a Bonaparte-style *chapeau,* and Helena with an Iranian chador. Ultimately, in the lurid light like a vaudevillian romp Corinne and Johnny gratified us with a great *merengue* dance, absolutely outstanding. Johnny wore a big black Gaucho hat with castanets between his fingers, and Corinne (being quite herself by this time, with all the passion of an emotion too long bottled), a perfectly stunning coral-color negligee reminiscent of the Brazilian carnival. Alike Egyptian frescoes there was also charcoal around her eyes. They were dancing, writhing with such charm and extreme enthusiasm. Surprisingly Johnny's sister, furtive and provocative marched on upon stalk legs in tight stockings her rosy lips curved toward a smile. Her head was covered with a mysterious green turban and green lace veil. She joined us in the twirl as we all sang the Copacabana theme song so well immortalized by Barry Manilow:

> Her name was Lola, she was a showgirl
> With yellow feathers in her hair
> And a dress cut down to there
> At the Copa, Co, Copacabana; Copacabana
> Music and passion were always the fashion
> At the Copa, they fell in love…"

Chapter 45

THE FESTIVITIES, LAUGHTERS and songs went on and on. That night, feeling somewhat tipsy over too much Corona and margaritas we all 'hit the sack' quite late. Within a week or so after we jerkily threw a thick jacket over our shoulders we were saddened to leave the family. Johnny gave us a few cream puffs with whipped-cream filling for the road. Helena was so delighted to go and discover Canada as it was her first extended trip on the North-American continent.

This morning it was pouring cats and dogs but all the snow had been washed away. Once more, we boarded the Greyhound Bus for a new adventure…

The sky-scrapers of the *citée balnéaire*-city by the ocean, of Vancouver B.C. where the grace, the beauty prevailed everywhere impressed us greatly. Imposing cement structures were lining like striking sentinel over the opalescent water of the Pacific, under a silver sky. Each structure was built with solidity, with opulence. The main street as a whole had a character and an air of achievement. Canada, at one time was an extremely individualistic country whose inhabitants were faintly conscious of their nationality. Now, it's one of the best lands in the world, warm and enchanting. In British Columbia as well as Ontario or the Northwest Territories there is still some inkling toward the old British Empire. The tradition is there. Ancestors fought to keep Canada British for a very long time. Sentimental people from the East would talk of the romance of the ones from the West. Now, those pioneers can watch with startled eyes the wonderful fruits of the seed they sowed.

As the day was fading imperceptibly into night upon the wings of the hours a ferryboat in a small lurch took Helena and I like an enchanted dream all the way to Skagway via Ketchikan, Sitka and Juneau. The radiance of the moon was not quite gleaming; it was veiled in a drape of light clouds. Other ships were making their way toward the horizon on the vast Pacific, for some exotic regions.

Earlier with the benefit of her expert knowledge, Corinne twisting herself happily in her seat as we stood heartily on her side had pointed out to us *sur-le-champ*, over an open map of Alaska, the areas of interests in such immense a region; 'a big land with a big heart' wrote a kind scholar.

As we navigated steadily under a dying moon we first stopped in Ketchikan the canned salmon capital of North America if not the world. Situated about ninety miles north of Prince Rupert the Ketchikan cannery operate non-stop on a twenty-four hour shift. It was founded in 1885 along with the large Ketchikan Pulp Mill Company. This is where tons of fish are cleaned, cut and cooked before being canned to be distributed the world over. The captain explained to us that over ten cruise-ships a day anchored in that Alaskan southern-most city.

Then the ferry went up north to Sitka, alongside the Pacific Ocean on Baranof Island. We hugged the coast until we reached Sitka.

In that notoriously picturesque remote city along with a group of British tourists and the tour guide we visited a glacier next to Mount Edgecumbe, an old extinct volcano surrounded by vast fields, peaks of eternal snow and heaven-aspiring cliffs. Numerous crystals appeared like brilliant gems. In some other areas one can discover masterpieces of sculpture along with stalactites in the most fantastic shapes. On the right side of the glacier, a fake door of ice caressed with the iridescent sparkle of sunlight reminded us of a cathedral entrance. It was so good to be away in such wilderness for awhile. The guide informed us that at one time a man slipped in a crevasse from an adjacent glacier. Three years later, some glacier climbers discovered the body of that unfortunate person in a cavern that had bridged long ago at the foot of the ice-mountain. The poor soul, frozen looked as if he had just died a few hours ago.

In Sitka, the Russian Heritage lingered everywhere. The Russians arrived here with their priests and bishops in 1741. They stayed in the region for about a century, until the Alaska purchasing by the United States.

On our way to Skagway, we invariably enjoyed a peaceful feeling in that northern region stretching to the horizon where, in an enchanted splendor, among carpets of snow that muffled the countryside we watched at night those tracts of heaven: the Aurora Borealis with a view across the moonlit freezing high valleys. The place was still silent of the latest technology, even businesses. For miles and miles there was hardly a sign that humanity existed on that part of the world. There were only rocks with endless woods of scrubby pines. A few other areas burned by fire appeared stricken by calamity; it was just bare and lonely. We kept on observing those northern lights in a sky embroidered with so many stars twinkling frostily to 'the Grand Nord.' Here, we experienced the effects upon mental stamina of cold, of isolation, and feeling the freezing air in our lungs. With the snow gleaming in the moonlight, the stars were constantly in motion writhed by currents as though being moved by an extra-terrestrial force. The extreme low temperature was creeping up from the ocean, as the wind coming in from the North Pole was like a stab to the lungs. Helena felt like a child again. Suddenly she started to sing a melodious tune with such great enthusiasm:

Twinkle, twinkle, little star
How I wonder what you are!
Up above the world so high,
Like a diamond in the sky.

The sky, the air was different too from those we knew in Southern California. It was such a new, delightful world.

Once more, steering at the canal at the stern of the boat lingering till the last moment before we stepped ashore a little further, I couldn't stop to listen to nearby passenger's conversations since they talked so loudly. Those chats were nothing but ill-timed jokes so much reminiscent of Arthur' stupid, nit-wit arrogance: "I'm now CEO of French Cookies, Inc." Or: "My nephew knows the President of the United States quite well. He sang for his birthday in D.C. and they had tea together…!"

With the pale light of the early sun we disembarked on the final destination. Soon, we went strolling, gamboling here, there through some blustery roads with the snow crunching under our feet. Next we explored the sleepy 'old word town.'

Skagway situated at the head of Lynn Canal is also the site of the Klondike Gold Rush. The heavens were so calm, so serene. The air with the smell of sweet forest was fresh and invigorating. With snowflakes flapping against the face, the cold was piercing us to the bone. Even through the harsh exposure to the elements, with the silence of the forests we felt good; very good. Helena was muffled from head to foot in a thick jacket, two shawls, and looking as rigit as a log. Soon the fringe of my hair was tipped with frost. A gush of youth's sensation flowed into my heart as I leaped over in the snow in my own heavy coat, like a child. Again, it felt so gratified inhaling the pure air, being so far away from the restaurant in Sherman Oaks and that grumpy boss of mine clothed in the skin of a wild beast. We often quenched our thirst downstream where the waterway became a brook. What a perfumed and clean water it was, nothing in Los Angeles tasted like this!

Earlier at *Le Cerisier* restaurant, the warm-hearted Eddy Freedman gave me the address of his cousin Darrow in Skagway. Along with his wife Nicole, they owned a fine, successful souvenir-shop. Her French was so perfect. I believed she could be a good tutor with some American family.

Their house made mostly of wood stood in the heart of the virgin forests of Alaska. The back entrance of the residence was at a top of a flight of steps. Outside, a riding horse was tethered to a tree. Nicole was the one that took care of the souvenir-shop located in downtown Skagway.

Darrow with rather ugly clothes, the clothes of a tuff hunter was a grey-mustached man with a slight stoop. With a face that looked like a Greek statue no man had ever grown grey more beautifully. I felt an instant liking for him. The prompt vigor of all his movements, with the clopping of his army boots was that of a much younger person, without any personal vanity. Darrow's favored sport was still fox-hunting in the snow.

While his wife prepared us lunch the far-away good looking cousin took Helena and I down to the cellar. There, in the center of the cold room a dead deer was hanging from the ceiling by a strong hook. The air was still full of the smell of the animal. Helena became horrified. With hysterical agitation she kept saying over and over: "Poor Bambi; oh, poor Bambi!" With tears in her eyes she turned her face away as she lost her footing and almost stumbled. Now, with eyes closed she was afraid to look once more at the dead animal.

With perfect amiability and gentle patience Darrow tried desperately to explain to her that this place in its wild environment wasn't Los Angeles or New York or any major city in the continental U.S. where you can drive to a super-market, get your meat well wrapped under cellophane with a price-tag on it. At the same moment there was a deafening roar of a shotgun flickering in the nearby forest and Darrow added: "Here we have to hunt for our food, store up food, water and wood. We have a serious problem of alimentation; consequently, we simply cannot change our way of living. You also have to understand that in this particular location there are few restaurants and for sure none like the four star: *Le Cerisier* in Sherman Oaks. Also, no movie-theatres or immense buildings like in so many large communities containing all things that any person could conceivably want."

Helena drew a long breath as she did not experience that kind of consolation yet. As Nicole cooked our lunch, we struck down into the woods for awhile. Of course, I never told her (and she never figured it out) that, that fine piece of meat so well aromatized over a light pepper-sauce with boiled cabbage we ate for lunch was none other than the deer's thigh.

Helena on her high horse again began to talk with a recovered gaiety. We spent a quiet, peaceful night in their warm abode as the wind was blowing hard against the shutters.

Subsequent to hugging and kissing our new-found friends, we departed in good spirits. Earlier, Darrow had mentioned to us that he would eventually sell the house since they were planning to move to New Zealand (Nicole's birthplace.) He added that if we were interested in the purchase of the property, the price-tag would be very reasonable...less than the value of a new Lexus!

From Skagway we decided to take the bus to the Canadian side. Once inside the vehicle, with snow everywhere, in a raucous noise, the engine started. The weather changed drastically and we shivered from the bitter cold. It seemed to become one of those arctic windstorms that seals dreaded because the water lies like glass under a hurricane too wind-beaten to even winch up a wave. In no time the entire sea would be frozen with the fish imprisoned under ice as ships can be marooned.

On to White Horse, Yukon, with a foot of snow that was covering the ground, the bus, with its ice-frosted windows careened to avoid a moose crossing the highway. A little further a tree snapped in several pieces barred the way. The wind was blowing, driving clouds of snow on the hissing winding road. It was so hard just to walk during a stopover. It was cold as death, in a country were the days are brief and nights so long!

In the Yukon capital, as we still shivered from the bitter cold, there was something in the untidiness of those grimy houses, of the disorder of the backyards. Only a few of them carried some kind of dignity that ran a thrill of nostalgia through us.

Abruptly, I expressed my surprise upon discerning who I thought were Japanese tourists. They were to be observed everywhere, in the plaza, in bars and restaurants. First I heard like a murmur of chats coming from one of the eating places. But, as I listened closely to their strange, unusual conversations quite unlike the Japanese language, I realized that we were dealing with Inuit Eskimos.

Chapter 46

I T HAD BEEN ten consecutive weeks already since I was out of work, following the fire at the restaurant. That long trip to Washington State and Alaska did me more good than all of the migraine medications I swallowed everytime Arthur would harass me. I went back to work completely rejuvenated.

Today, however as the long afternoon dragged, to use FDR's powerful words it was also 'MY DAY OF INFAMY' from my employer. It seemed as if a cement block had fallen on my head...

As a pleasant habit, I joined Helena on Fiji Way in Marina Del Rey's enjoyable surroundings. Fiji Way and its marina denoting the nearness of the ocean combed with sail boats and luxury ships such as *the Serengeti* owned by the Johnny Carson estate was but a stone's throw away from the Catalina Island Express Flyer boat that lay moored with her bow alongside the jetty. For local pleasure seekers, there were also barges called water-taxi that would take you from Fiji Way to Mother's Beach.

From our water-taxi that chugged away toward the center of the channel, we lazily watched the seals playing their games, deflecting and curving harmoniously on the surface of the water that appeared like a mirror of brightness. Aside from the quintessential yachting vista, the exclusive waterfront residences at the height of luxury were pointing out exceptional architecture. The tall windows expressed an air of pretension. Surely people over there live a tranquil, abundant life. Those extravagant balconies facing so many fishing boats rocking at their buoys created that unique atmosphere, typical of elegant California living. All around we felt a quiet sense of well being. The current of the channel where the water left a frothy scum became swift. As we kept on watching young couples kayaking with quick hard strokes, their Mae West inflatable life jackets on, my beeper (as an obsolete technology) suddenly blasted noisily; it even awakened an old man resting on the bench: It was Arthur's number.

Back on dry land, I picked-up his message from a local public phone. The boss harangued eloquently in a paternalistic delightful tone of voice for me to show up at the restaurant next day at precisely ten o'clock A.M. His announcement appeared like a charmer's music to a snake. With *Le Cerisier*, not being re-opened yet, in the back of my mind this call was but for one purpose: it would have to be related to the business interruption insurance settlement. I didn't know at this point that the excitement of the morning would turn to apathy!

At the restaurant, in a clatter of tongues again I met Arthur and Leon with the insurance people. All of them were speaking in the slyness of whispers. The chef who came earlier already left. Van Meerstellen didn't stay there too long either; standing for an instant under the lintel of the doorway, singing a snatch of a song, my colleague ran out, happily with a big smile on his face. He unobtrusively stuffed a white envelope in his jacket's pocket. Only three people working full-time were supposed to have received that insurance protection plan: the chef, Leon and I. After the conversation was allayed, Leon and the group had dispersed.

Thereupon the boss urged me to accompany him to the lumber store to get a piece of wood to cover a crack in the dining room's wall. He went inside the store alone, dropping the reservation book right on my lap. I waited that Arthur was inside the shop. Under the weight of a feverish desire, out of sheer curiosity I opened the book. Then I leafed through its pages and discovered with great delight a white sealed envelope addressed to me. For a long time, I was holding it in my hand feeling the heavy pulse of my heart, but I resisted the impulse. With the thought in my mind that Arthur would have been happy bestowing that envelope to me himself, I slipped the document back between the pages before closing the register, convincing myself not to retrieve it. I believed this was the proper way to proceed; that it was right to do what my conscience told me to do. Nevertheless, for a moment, I was unable to shake off the desire within me to look at the envelope once more. But, as the union secretary explained to me later on it would have been disrespectful of me to have simply picked-up any sort of document without the boss's permission. In a manner of habit I never dared to take so great a liberty as to attempt to grab anything on my own before asking for it first. I believed that if I couldn't be kept straight by this nothing could straighten me. This was and still is my nature. Unfortunately it had also been my Achilles's heel too. How wrong I was, especially with Arthur this had been a capital error. It seemed that I already have forgotten the incident on that quiet night at the restaurant with my Dutch friend Jules Vertrichten and his generous one hundred dollar tip that Arthur so nonchalantly, so ungraciously had stolen from me! After all those years, it looked as if I didn't know him enough!

Back at the restaurant, realizing that the envelope was still in the reservation book my employer instead to handle it to me seized the opportunity to leave the dinning room. In a flashing instant he literally glided out of the room. Arthur nonchalantly was off like *un coup de vent*, faster than the charge of the Light Brigade. He simply vanished from view. In a quick change of heart, appearing like a raging animal bouncing in the air, he had crept out to the back door together with the reservation book and the sealed envelope in it. I was able to hear his steps for some time but I stood there, motionless. Well, just like the maxim said: "the opportunity makes the thief." Arthur went in his truck and within seconds he was completely out of sight. This had been an ill-judged implementation of a former well-judged, honest intent. Now I felt a shiver down my spine. Arthur was in such a hurry that he had knocked his side against the knob of the door that slammed shut after him.

In a glint of intuition my worst thoughts were confirmed. The truth at length flashed upon me: it was clear; it was evident that Arthur was up to another dark deed. By this time I could read his mind like a book. The picture of what had happened became vivid; it was plain as the prominent proboscis on his face. I definitely realized now that I had walked into a pitfall. I felt like a rat caught in a trap ready to bite at anybody approaching me. My mood of high expectancy had turned to despondency. Now I understood quite well that my trust in him had been wild folly. At that precise moment I remembered the wise words of Plutarch: *"He is a fool who lets slip a bird in the hand for a bird in the bush."* I had allowed myself to be robbed stupidly.

My mind became a battleground of contradictory emotions, any longer knowing what was right or what was wrong. I was left alone with a fit of violent anger, shaking to my very bones thinking how dull I had been. I felt a mournful sinking at the heart. Any vestige of sanity seemed to have been swept away from my mind. Suffering a broad variety of shames, of embarrassments I wept bitterly with more weakness than a young boy did, as I felt that the whole world had abandoned me. It was useless my remaining there any longer, but stagnate.

So, after locking the establishment's front door, I drove back to my one-room-and-kitchenette apartment in North-Hollywood. As I kept on driving, I felt more confused, more disgusted. Once at home, afflicted with sorrows I started pacing restlessly, kicking the walls, agonizing over what I should do. I thought that I would wait till morning to reach the owner of the restaurant. Yet, after pulling off my shoes, I sat on the bed my feet dangling over the carpet. Still overpowered by some abominable anguish I changed my mind and called my employer right away. I first apologized to rouse him from his sleep at such an uncivilized hour. In answering my question about that white envelope issued with my name on it he replied in an explosive burst of a horrible, obscene dry chuckle cold as the frost:

"What envelope? What insurance money? Pierre, you must have been dreaming! I haven't the slightest idea of what you're talking about. You know as well as I do that it takes months if not years for the insurance company to come up with any settlement!" The tone of that discussion had really impinged on my mind. At that precise moment I knew that Arthur's scheme was running upon one single train of thought: how well to swindle me with that insurance money! Now I could do nothing about it.

By his action he was now criminally liable. On that instant it was as though the world had turned evil and I became so confused. Panting for breath after hanging up the handset I stood there for a long time in silence, watching the raindrops running in the embrasure of the windowpane. I hardly drink hard liquor but this time, trying to steady the tumultuous beating of my heart, I got a shot of whiskey to calm my nerves. In a righteous indignation this looked like a cutting-edge- *un bistoury* stick in my stomach. I was lost like a sailor adrift on a raft following a shipwreck, tumbling into a dark hole. That miserable meanness nutshell of a man tried to mutilate my mind by retrenching my pride and my honor. I could have endured almost anything. However, what Arthur did to me had been too awful. It was an embittering betrayal from an uncaring boss. To have worked for *Le Cerisier*, doing the best to please our clientele for all those years, and abruptly live with the feeling to be nothing was really too much to bear. While I buried my face in my hands I again listened drearily to the beat of the rain upon the pane when a fly droned against the window. On that dreadful moment I felt I needed some air.

With the low hum of traffic the wind had gathered more strength. I decided for a walk through the soaking streets to think things over before going to bed. At that precise moment, my thoughts went to Jonathan Swift when he articulated: *"...I cannot but concluded the bulk of your natives to be the most pernicious race of little odious vermin that nature ever suffered to crawl upon the surface of the earth."* With my face hidden in the darkness, I saw a raw of luminous dots roaring low overhead through the night sky like a well ordered constellation. I knew that a plane; some kind of a private jet was just about to land in Burbank Airport. The streets were empty; there were no people to be seen anywhere near. In the distance a dog barked; I also heard the throttled cry of an owl. They were somewhat happy but I was miserable and my heart was beating so fast. Aside from his baseness, I honestly never thought the boss could have done this to me because in my mind, in God's green earth this sort of dishonest occurrence couldn't happen, not even imagining that in fact such wickedness existed. At school, back in Belgium I was taught what was right; what was honest. I once read that: right is justice and truth. It is the property of right to remain eternally beautiful, also pure. Once more, I realized that my employer was not only a tyrant, but a sneaky thief as well. I had always been truthful with the Valois Dourville de Montrissart's family. In the past Melanie who had forgotten a great deal of *la langue de Molière* had constantly relied on me in order to correct a letter or an important document in French, that was bound for relatives in the old country.

Considering the amount of insurance money involved, no less than four thousand dollars, Arthur had incriminated himself in a grand theft. My employer had broken his word when he promised me to take care of the payroll through his business interruption insurance. This strained me more than I knew. Now the restaurant appeared so inhospitable; it became 'an enemy country' and 'a house of hell!'

As I walked back to my place, I had mixed thoughts but nonetheless my mind was seldom able to concentrate itself upon things I would have to do. Even at this late hour my apartment seemed to be the meanest place in the neighborhood. Like a horse in a mill I began in an aimless manner to pace the room again, round and round, unable to do anything; unable yet to think clearly. My employer appeared to have been a smart, calculating expert who had brilliantly succeeded in such an intentional vulgar scheme. I also behaved like an ignorant baboon. All I could feel was a miserable failure which had followed on all I had done the night before. I could not shake the foregone conclusion that disappointment will come again. I have to recognize that when I did not detect evil the moment it appeared, was a lack of true wisdom from my part. I started to pray, but my prayers didn't resound in my heart. The minutes, the hours crept anxiously. It was late when I went to bed. Shutting off the light, I first sat on a chair sinking in a thought which I could not grasp. That night I woke up in panic bathing in cold sweat as fatigue was deadening my body.

In the light of morning my anxieties did not vanish. Toweling off vigorously after a quick shower I dressed in frantic haste, forgetting to eat and drink. Totally distracted after still brooding over last days's event I did something stupid. In my carelessness, I brushed my teeth with hydrocortisone, anti-itch cream instead of toothpaste. Subsequently I began rinsing my mouth with water thoroughly over and over again. Looking at my face in the mirror I didn't like the sight of it.

I jumped in my car and drove back to *Le Cerisier*, bracing myself to face a serious problem; ready to confront that liar. I was still yawning as a sign that excessive exhaustion had overtaken me. The light rain continued to fall above the city and I was shivering in the cold air. It took me ages with my automobile to get out of the line squirmed by the congestion of vehicles, with my nostrils assailed by the fumes. Next I stopped at the Vanowen street crossroad where the traffic jam was almost on monumental proportions. I narrowly escaped a collision, when a car swerved from one side to the other. The hissing of a freight train was grounding its weight upon the wet rails; I could hear the clank of buffers as the convoy almost slowed down to a stop. Buses were roaring. I noticed their sloshing wheels alongside my vehicle. A little further, next to a sign 'Men Working' the mud was whispering on the wheels. I also had to veer off to avoid a dog. Young female students, carrying their backpacks over their raincoats walked slowly; they were holding hands, laughing loudly on the way to their campus. However I was thinking of other things; my thoughts were far away from the romantic scenery.

In Sherman Oaks, at the end of a short walk from my parked-car, the nearer I got to the restaurant the more agitated

I became. I shivered faintly as I was prepared for the worst. My mouth was so dry that I had to take a swallow of water from a bottle I carried in the car. A dog was growling over a bone; however I could smell a rat a mile away. I first gazed across at the houses behind the walls alongside the alley partly covered by a green umbrella of leaves. I went on like a fast shadow on that path, still empty at this hour. I paused for awhile next to a tree, undecided; just guessing what I was up to. For the first time in so many years I smoked a cigarette to calm down my nerves.

As I reached *Le Cerisier* in a recurrence of a shower of rain, I could not think without a certain tremor just like a premonition of the things that were going to happen. I knew what the message would be, I knew this as sure that I was of tomorrow's sunrise.

No sooner had I got inside the establishment, the air felt stagnant. I heard the dull boisterous of a loud conversation. For a moment the room became absolutely still. As expected, the simian Arthur's brow clouded at my sight before turning his head from wall to wall with sweat on his face. With his glasses down to the tip of his nose he laughed a quiet brief chuckle as he hitched up his pants and tautened up his necktie. His eyes met mine quickly then he looked away, as that disgusted smile wrinkled his tight-pressed lips with that almost perpetual grin. That crooked, ironic laugh could have melted the snow on top of Mount Kilimanjaro. Now that I had felt the weight of his gaze I could hear the chanting of evil; it was all over the place. I inched my way closer to my employer. After mustering another smile he looked down at his shoes. His chin was stretching with the look of a restless horse. For a few seconds all was silent. Save the voice of the grandfather's clock, the silence was unnerving. Suddenly Arthur's voice came out of his throat differently, just like the high-pitched yapping of a little dog. In such a calculated plan, in that same hoarse uneven voice he reiterated what he had said the night before on the phone, abrogating the fact that there never had been an envelope under my name tacked away in the reservation book. As I listened lethargically at the mumbling of his still cotton-dry mouth, a hint of malice came in his eyes. I started arguing but my knees were trembling; I felt some kind of jackhammering in my left leg. I was sick at heart as I felt down in the bottomless pit of humiliation. It was like being hit in the stomach with a slegdgehammer. Such a gross vulgarity showed in my employer's acquisitive face as his mouth cracked once more into some kind of a smile. Now he was eating a snack. He had pain to get the morsels of food down, so he made a violent effort to swallow; to unlock his throat with a noisy, nervous hiccup and sudden squeals. Catatonic, it looked as if he was ready to choke in his lie. I was so devastated; it was as though the whole world had turned evil!

In my peripheral vision my attention riveted toward Leon Van Meerstellen who happened to be there as well to start working for the re-opening of the restaurant. He was leaning next to one of the front booths and kept staring at me, stony-faced from the corner of his eye. Leon stood there, surreptitiously, in an unadulterated concentration as rigid as a cigar-store Indian or a decrepit old mummy. I felt baffled, also deluded with his profound awkward silence because he was able to breathe the thundercloud of trouble in the air. His quietness was burdensome, it felt like the grave. Leon never said a word. He just stood there with his hands on his thighs.

I thought my dear colleague would have behaved in a more gentlemanlike manner. I even had the feeling that, for a brief moment he was on the point of speaking; of revealing the truth, but he kept silent, as silent as an empty church. Nothing in Leon's face changed that I could see. How unexpected were the strikes of destiny! His stillness was awful; his indifference enraged me beyond measure. Leon was my friend. He had been rewarded with the insurance settlement money and surely, instead of nodding noncommittally he could have stood up and saved the day for me.

Later on Van Meerstellen, surprisingly kept on lying, giving me irrelevant information by way of answer, telling me that he only received a loan, denying that he ever got any compensation in regard of the fire. I couldn't forget the fury that at first possessed me. At this point, I thought to let myself in the care of a physician, specialist in nervous ailments. *Yet, on second thought, even though I had been disrespectfully overlooked and placed on the backburner, I understood Leon. My co-worker had been re-hired. He was in no position to contradict Arthur who bestowed him back his old job. A favor for a favor, that's all there was. My friend just took what he considered 'le juste milieu.' And right now, trying to speak to him about some influence he has on Arthur was rather like trying to walk on a tight rope over a precipice.* I then made a point not to criticize Van Meerstellen's behavior any longer. However he became increasingly withdrawn. My 'blood brother' who I still so admired and respected was absentminded when talking to me. Leon was still sticking with Arthur like paper on the wall with his yes-sir attitude, feeling quite important too. In the midst of my discouragement came a really dreadful episode. Abruptly, I realized at once that there was a conspiracy.

As I questioned the chef, he first stared straight ahead with the bland smile of an idiot as if he was afraid to look at me. Next, he simply turned his back away declaring in a helpless manner with some kind of hideous grimace, in a way I did not like:

"Why don't you talk to the *patron*; this isn't my problem!" With his strange behavior he seemed very nervous. He found nothing else to say. It was so obvious that Santillas tried to escape this conversation. At this point, my suspicions were at once aroused. I had the feeling that, aside from the insurance settlement, Arthur had bought his silence by bribing him off with a gift of some sort. Because of Leon as well as chef Santillas demeanor, my descent into the valley of unjustness and humiliation became a free-fall with no immediate rescue at the horizon. Again I became quite sick mentally; I hardly knew on that moment how to continue to do my job properly.

All of a sudden I realized that in the condition I stood, writhing in agony by Arthur's dragon teeth, consequent, even replete execution would be necessary. My resolution of this matter had to be acted upon at once. There was solid ground for it…

* * * *

After the fire incident, Eddy had graciously decided to refurbish the entire dining room. Because of heavy water damage, most of the pictures, all the books on bookshelves had to be replaced, and the red curtains from the front windows washed thoroughly. Eddy also supervised the workers as they placed the new burgundy-carpet on the floor. The booths that were impregnated by heavy smoke were brought back to us by truck from a dry-cleaner expert's factory in Downey. The entire restaurant, now shining clean, smelled as if it had just been scrubbed.

Of course, for our customers it was Arthur who took all the credit for Eddy's hard work. I heard the boss telling the clients: "I am the one who did all the redecorating, and believe me it wasn't easy!" Again, the same yarn was rehashed at every table. The quiet Eddy, in a simple dignified manner didn't contradict Arthur; he was just smiling deprecatingly and hummed absently to himself. But I noticed the corners of his mouth had a certain curve of anguish.

Chapter 47

IT BECAME SO hard for me to percept why Arthur had treated me so monstrously. From that moment things happened in a startling crescendo.

In the drizzling rain that blurred the sky and the wind dashing angrily in a shrill scream, I lost no time and headed straight to the Labor Board.

An officer who was assigned to me listened intently about the case. He made a phone call to the Employment Development Department (EDD) and instructed me to go there without any delay; an agent would help me. *This could be the start of a maze of going around in circles of government agencies. I can now imagine standing in those dreadful lines for hours, tangled in official red tape to get a resolution for my problem?*

But much to my delight, once in the EDD building I was given immediate attention. The irony of it all was that I no longer was eligible to receive unemployment benefits because of the ten weeks delay in filing for claims. Feeling dejected I was ready to leave that cold building when an old lady who also heard my statement from her desk waived for me to stay. Her round face was partly concealed by fallen hair and with glasses so thick that her sight must have decayed by stages. Her insightful advice to my predicament deceived her bleak appearance. She revealed that I had a prerogative to appeal at the Office of Appeals in Altadena. It was just the answer that I had hoped for. I felt rejuvenated and in high spirit! In sheer kindness the lady also had impelled me to write to the judge prior to our meeting. As I left the EDD office with its looming walls, the streets were already embroiled by the shades of nightfall. However I waited a few more days until the judge at The Office of Appeals was ready for my claim.

* * * *

Tall with a full head of grayish hair Judge Arnold H. Wilkinson was a venerable kind man with a face of great sagacity that reflected a tranquil radiance that easily allayed my anxiety. He was the administrative height. The judge had an air of neatness with a sweet and commanding look. Rather than remaining seated in his own black leather recliner the unassuming magistrate decided to position himself next to me as though we've known each other for some time.

Except for the recording device that was 'listening' to our conversation, the session felt more like a friendly chat that lasted well over two hours. As my attention was caught on the tape-recorder the judge recalled the previous letter I wrote to him. Now he wanted me to make a verbal statement of the facts. I explained everything with clarity and accuracy. It took him some time before he found it possible to make any response. With his hands clenching and unclenching he became mostly concerned by my employer's misrepresentations, also with the fact that I could have been a victim of a fraud and forgery scheme. The lawman inquired if I was aware of someone skillful enough to imitate my signature. Judge Wilkinson became *toute Oreille*. He was intently thinking when I mentioned Melanie's game on imitating signatures. In a well-crafted speech, slowly and gravely he articulated:

"Pierre (the magistrate kindly called me by my first name) in regard to that insurance for those ten weeks we are not talking here about little change. I've already studied your case with serious attention. Considering the vastness of the sum, if forgery was committed by Arthur's daughter, there is also lieu to excogitated grand theft. As an EDD Judge I would be unable to pass judgment. Still in my book if the proof can be established there would be a unanimous verdict of guilt."

After spreading his arms wide and weighing the drawback evidence the judge added with unusual confidence: "For everything you said it seemed to me that Melanie can be a dead pigeon and I definitely will assist you the best I can. Bear in mind that I serve justice and I will help you to see that justice be done." Melanie didn't realize it yet but she had set herself out on a course that might lead to her own destruction.

The decision concerning the overdue unemployment benefits would be forwarded to me within a week. His warm handshake reassured me in a serene wave of satisfaction that a flicker of hope was in the air; that I would be justified. I had the feeling that the best was yet to come. In my heart a radiance of hope even amounted to cheerfulness as a great sense of relief had flooded in me.

As I stepped out of the courtroom and walked to my car, my mind was beleaguered of Arthur, of his daughter's devious plot. At that moment I knew that an irrefutable evidence of forgery with a capital 'F' became apparent. Aside from money matters my stomach was still in knots. I naively thought (even with the harassment) that after countless years of servitude and devoted work at *Le Cerisier* I no longer would be just an employee but rather part of the Valois Dourville de Montrissart's family. *It was incomprehensible and inexpressibly sad why Melanie, financially endowed by her grandmother's wealth and most recently by an earthquake insurance indemnity would maliciously cheat me of a measly compensation that for her would look like a skinny chicken in her purse. I couldn't understand how that woman who can be so gentle was capable of such a theft! Like plants growing in dark rain forests, something demoniacal had grown in her. Can she realize that she could languish in prison for years over this before facing deportation?*

That night at the restaurant Melanie was at first tongue-tied. She started to laugh, yet the laugh rang strangely as her face appeared convulsed. She was in a curious nervous state. There was something with her mouth whose corners kept on changing from comedy to gloominess. Tapping her teeth with a fingernail she could not contain her transparent curiosity about the outcome of my meeting with the judge for she has adamantly formulated her own conclusion earlier by saying:

"There is no way that the matter would see the light of day in court."

As Melanie, unaccountably embarrassed gave me a look of absolute hard abhorrence I could almost imagine her derisive grin; I could hear her roar playfully in a witchy voice and a face cracked with a grimace: "I told you so!" any minute now.

Then she formulated a practical and quite threatening joke on the phone. With the help of a co-worker at the law-firm where she worked during the day Melanie had attempted purposely for me to drop the case. Her co-worker actually impersonated an immigration officer telling me that I would be facing serious problems if I don't discontinue my investigation. This happened to be a practical and very sad April fool's joke with the intention to scare me. But now everything became crystal clear. As I communicated to her the possibility of grand theft her usual smug self became agitated. She was nervously plaiting her fringe scarf and shuddered at that thought. Suddenly her lovely face became almost grim as she had lapsed into the silence of despair. Right before my sight the know-it-all and mighty Melanie slowly metamorphosed, feeling her bones melting. In a few scarcely audible words her voice weakened and sounded nervous. Then, Melanie regaining her power of speech threw her hands in the air and fiendishly retorted in a hoarsely voice that my insurance check might have been lost in the mail! That was obviously an appalling lie; just a thoughtless remark. Arthur's daughter was playing a game, however I knew she was all stirred up underneath. At this point I had not the smallest doubt of all her contrivance. In her contorted face I noticed something strange as her round belly shook with a giggle. I realized now that I had caught her in a predicament. Yet at the same time I had incurred her wrath. An alarm clock was now ringing in my mind and it crushed my heart.

In a flash, I recalled Eddy's warnings that Melanie was tricky. Working in a law firm has acquainted her with the perfidious stratagems of some prosecuting attorneys. Knowing her previous manner of retaliation with criminal intents, also her owning a gun I anticipated the worse for my life. Like her father she was evil to the core and I wished at this point that for that vicious activity I could weld her to the wall in a dark dungeon.

Within that nest of robbers, lost in the middle of some total upheaval, the paranoia that set in impelled me to give an account of the theft to the nearest police station to seek protection. At that precise moment I knew I must do what I should have done much earlier. I then prepared a full one page report of the sad event.

At the *commissariat* a sergeant affixed a 'visitor' label on my pocket-jacket before directing me to the office of fraud and forgery where I showed my letter of introduction to a detective. Before leaving, over a warm conversation the detective cautioned me:

"Mr. Choucart, you have to be conscious of the irony: some drastic events must happen in order for us to intervene. We cannot just act under presumption," and the detective added something I was already aware of: "As for the fraud and forgery, in your particular case since you don't have any material evidence yet this matter should be referred to the District Attorney. But at the same time be careful: An accusation without any proof, or any physical evidence carry little weight!"

* * * *

"The mind which sometimes presumes to believe that there is no such thing as a miracle is itself a miracle." -Scott Peck.

Oh yes, God can work miracles. In less than a week later as a sign of good omen fresh reassuring news arrived through the mail. I was now feasting my eyes on the letter from Judge Arnold H. Wilkinson.

Ensuing 'good cause' he had reversed the prior EDD statement. I became eligible for benefits under code section 1153 (b). Even that I was coming down with the flu I beamed out in a cloud of happiness. As my face felt a little hot, I kept on shouting 'Yippee.' A heavy weight appeared to have been just removed from my heart. With an exclamation of delight; of intoxication I leaped in the air enjoying my great victory. In the glory of this conquest, heady with pleasure and immensely satisfied I had only but one thought: how wonderful the judge, my proviso had been in his decision. I saw how clearly he had thought out the whole matter; everything had been in my favor. This man of law in an act of kindness and consideration just put me right with my mind; with the world. To my life's end I swear, this kind human being would have a spot in the deepest shrine of my memory. My heart was lighter than it had been for weeks especially as I pinpointed out that an Appeal Judge usually never reversed an EDD decision; this was almost unheard-of.

Suddenly as I took a fresh look at myself, once more I was uplifted with a tranquil sense of well-being. As I felt like walking on air, an overwhelming *joie de vivre* came over me. I wanted to embrace everybody in the streets. It was as if I had being pulled from below feeling like a flying fish leaping out of the ocean.

Comfortably seated in the armchair in my living room, once more I took a good look at the Judge's letter. I kept on reading, re-reading it over and over again. The last part of the document was the most satisfying: *"Good cause includes the claimant's employer warning, instructing or coercing the claimant to prevent the prompt filing of such claim (California Code of Regulations, Title 20, section 1536-10. b). The evidence established good cause to backdate the claimant's claim to the date of June 12, 2... based the evidence which established that the claimant failed to apply for unemployment insurance benefits earlier was due to misrepresentations made by his employer. Although the employer promised the claimant that he would be returning to work at a moment's notice, the delay ended up to covered the span of several months. Further, the employer misled the claimant in that he promised continuing salary, through insurance coverage, which never materialized. The claimant reasonably relied upon his employer's representation to his own personal detriment. Based on the evidence, it is found that good cause exists to backdate the claim.*

Decision: The Department notice of determination is reversed. The claimant is eligible for benefits under code section 1153 (b.)"

As I tried to suppress my emotions my eyes were filled with tears but there were tears of delight. For me this had been the best evening on earth. That night after stretching out, a deep sleep fell upon me. I slept peacefully. Next morning, with my spirits revived high, and just like the birds I started to sing:

Alouette, gentille alouette, alouette, je te plumerai.
Je te plumerai la tête, je te plumerai la tête
et le bec, et le bec, alouette, alouette, ahhhhh…

Now, given that I was awarded only minimum wages Arthur and Melanie weren't pleased with my achievement. I noticed that this victory I had gained from a decent, compassionate judge made Melanie clenched her hands until the nails almost pressed into the skin of her palms. She looked at me with that still strange smile. She seemed to have melted away like a snow-flake in the water. And now she had become a bitter, sarcastic woman.

Arthur, thinking probably that 'this dumb-bell' was not so dullard after all, changed attitude. Even the timbre of his voice was different and there was an expression of concern on his face. He eyed me in that bashful, somewhat confused way. I even had the feeling that he was crushed by the weight of his guilty conscience. Soon, involuntarily the boss showed me an undeniable respect. Arthur's unusual politeness reflected fear for what he had conspired. In my mind there no longer was any doubt that the entire insurance theft was the work of at least two criminals. Especially for the forgery Arthur had been in bed with Melanie, she was his accessory. But the fetus of the crime had really been engendered by my employer. On several occasions I watched them speaking low in a conspirator's whisper. They were like 'a hissing nest of a tangle of snakes.'

However, suddenly things changed in my life. The anxiety was not completely lifted; the old chill came over me once more. All those past events returned in my mind in full force. I felt again that same sensation of shame and humiliation. After those lies and all the conspiracy I became dog-tired from the strain of the day's work mostly by pretending to feel good when I didn't. The succeeding weeks my discomfort turned into inflamed bitterness, and I was overtaken by a serious dilemma. This was no longer related to the financial aspect but for the fact that after all that time I had been treated no less than a rotten street dog. The urge for vindictiveness became so tighten that I felt myself crouching in misery.

With my sudden explosive temper Leon Van Meerstellen didn't even recognize me. Little things started to upset me and I became a paranoid lunatic, sliding into a pit of hellish torture. My depression spread itself to everyone at *Le Cerisier,* especially with Leon my closest friend. With ferocious obstinacy I grew irritated and I howled like a lion. I was angry most intensively with the world. Just like critics in literature who discern nothing but faults because they sometimes shut their eyes to beauties I suddenly breathed evil everywhere. Deep in thought, gasping hard and exhausted I find that I had nothing left to write about. Because of my anxieties the books I so much enjoyed reading failed to interest me. Even my guitar became out of tune just like me. However in my mind it was time for me to decide on whatever measures were to be taken. I knew that justice, the way I conceived it had still to be done as I really had to go to the bottom of this. In order to think properly just like some people kept silent about their joys, for awhile I was silent about my grief.

* * * *

One bright morning in a tranquil pervasive silence with the solitude of my anxious, troubled heart I wore my sport shoes and flannel shirt. And in a ray of sunlight I went jogging a comfortable gait in a cloud of dust whirling from the path on the rough sand, rocks and leaf-covered trail of La Tuna Canyon's mountains in Sun Valley. I had hoped that that violent exercise might calm my spirit which never had been more deeply agitated. The sun and the waning moon hung high in the sky as I kept admiring the magnificence of the surroundings. The region was filled with the smell of fresh earth as I abruptly felt elation in my athletic endeavor. Later with my shirt soaked through I stumbled over a root. I then laughed like a child and kept on jogging until I dropped with fatigue. Down, alongside the parapet of the shivering Los Angeles River flatland among squirrels crawling along from branch to branch as sweat salted my eyes I stopped and rested under the shade of a big tree. After the recent heavy rain discernable from afar through the branches I watched the gleam of the rippling waves of the river.

With a light caress of the desert-born Santa-Ana winds across the face and the blue of the late morning sky, my heart was still throbbing violently. Once more my thoughts tortured me cruelly as this was the strongest internal conflict I had ever felt...

And so suddenly in solemn stillness I decided to breathe gently. Finally, shaking all distressing thoughts from my mind I reached a modicum of frantic serenity. Listening to my inner voice of truth and right I did what I had not done for a long time: I went down on my knees and began to pray.

By some strange miracle all my sadness, all my trembling hence vanished. It was as though a heavy burden had been lifted from my back. I felt that I was myself again as a great calm enveloped me.

Then I fully realized that it would not have been wise for me to follow through on the fraud and forgery investigation. Regaining my good spirits that had deserted me for so long I became deeply touched with Pastor Rick Warren's thoughts, from his book: *"Resentment always hurt you more than it does the person you resent. While your offender has probably forgotten the offense and gone on with life, you continue to stew in your pain, perpetuating the past."* However, strange remnants of a forgotten period awaked from time to time and reflowed into the consciousness. Unless someone went through a lobotomy operation, memory cannot be lost but it can be submerged under useless and bothersome details.

As the woods and trees born the same testimony I continued my run. In the freedom of motion my feet were like wings and unexpectedly my fatigue turned into pleasure. Looking over the mountains as far as the eye could reach, I only saw love; an immense reserve of love everywhere that inundated my heart. On that day on I discovered compassion in realizing that a happy disposition always finds materials for enjoyment.

Considering once more that Judge Wilkinson had been so good to me and that a man/woman has no business to be depressed because of disappointment I dropped any further investigations regarding insurance matters and I became much of a peaceful man, starting a renewed phase of my life. For awhile I had felt so unhappy just for wanting revenge. In my head there had been foolish nonsense. Now I decided that it was over, done with, finished and I didn't resent Arthur and Melanie any longer for what they have done to me. This employee's burning fever of 'getting even' was gone. In my mind I kept on repeating "What's this future going to be except what I make it!"

From day to day life ran its normal course. I immersed myself totally in daily labor not thinking about this matter anymore. I kept working at *Le Cerisier* with uncomplaining acceptance of whatever might befall on me, with that slim hope that eventually the boss would show *un beau geste*- a change of heart to compensate me for the minimum pay I collected from the EDD. That never happened. With some assumed coolness, Arthur was still unmoved by any feeling of remorse…

Chapter 48

TWO YEARS AFTER the fire incident the wealthy stockbroker, owner of the building decided to close the restaurant for good. It was now being transformed into a real estate broker office and consequently my job became phased out of existence. On their last visit at *Le Cerisier*, my friends Tony Crushin and the Williams, our wine connoisseurs awarded me both with a goodbye-card. As it was written with the pen of an angel, here was Tony's:

"Pierre, you are one of the most unique human being I ever met. Thank you for just being you. I'm so proud to know you and I'm thankful for all these years we have known each other. Love you"

Phil and Kathy Williams awarded me with the following:

"Pierre, thank you for all of your good
humor and warmth. We are at your disposal
at any time should you wish to call upon us
regarding any matter whatsoever."

Tony with his oversees enterprise kindly reminded me that as soon I'm ready to accompany him to China he would take care of everything, including the airline fare. Likewise his friends Phil and Kathy, Tony moreover assured me of his readiness on all occasions to render me any service that might be in his power. I also noticed that Kathy was quite pregnant. It's not that she became less attractive but I had the feeling that she had neglected herself as if her looks were no longer under her command. Her strong feelings were now destined for the future of that child-to-be. Phil on the other hand looked as if he was even more caring for his lovely wife.

On closing day in our little abode we went through a period of disturbances and anxieties: for 'the Last Supper' the restaurant was crowded to full capacity. On that special occasion the place was crammed with people; most of them long time well-known customers. Every single table had been taken over not for two but for three sittings until the early morning hours. The 'early birds' arrived at 5.00 PM. A French flag at half-mast that stood on the roof next to *Le Cerisier* neon sign was billowing in the wind, next to blue, white and red balloons.

For Arthur Valois Dourville de Montrissart that evening was a personal evening of national mourning. Thirty-two years spanned of successful business on the same location had been a great achievement. But the greatest moments at *Le Cerisier* were over and Arthur knew it. Just like a professional matador in the arena, my employer had flashes of the old greatness when he used to kiss the ladies's hands with such gaiety. The owner had compared his restaurant like a ship going forward to prosperity to the 'New World.' *Le Cerisier* had been 'the finest vessel in all of France.' "And I was and I'm still the captain of that ship," he added. But now, Arthur's star seemed waning.

Then at last, the solemn moment arrived. *Aux grands maux, les grands remèdes-* Great remedies for great evils: Arthur, wearing a white coat with a *fleur-de-lys* embroidered on the front (just like Monsieur Putoise on the golf course did) decided to walk between tables with a drum suspended from his shoulder by a belt. He then started rolling the batons with the spirit of the French Revolution. In his acceptance of the death of the restaurant the boss showed by this action the grandeur of the last moment. On this eleventh hour he appeared to be like a commodore, watching his ship sink with his wealth gone. I already knew that the owner of the restaurant would be leaving Los Angeles for good. This second larger U.S. city is the place where people strive to succeed. It had been Arthur's beehive for so many years as a gathering area where he so proudly had introduced *la nouvelle cuisine*.

Reminescent of Arthur's late wife Angeline, old-time customers now retired came back for that very last meal with some sort of intimacy. Again, this had been the place where they had proposed to their girlfriends. A place where in a surprised gesture they had dropped their engagement rings in the hollow-stemmed flutes filled with *Dom Perignon*. Eventually this was leading some couples to the institution of matrimony. A few of those patrons, now happy divorcees had found new mates.

Arthur looking heavy-lidded and drowsy, and with a trace of sadness in his voice started frothing. To my surprise his nuisance that he had tagged on me for so long was over. My employer finally rewarded me with warm words: *"YOU ALL KNOW WHAT I THINK OF PIERRE. I ALWAYS THOUGHT HIM TO BE A FINE WAITER AND A GOOD HUMAN BEING. HE HAD BEEN SUCH A GREAT INSPIRATION TO ME AND TO THE ENTIRE VALOIS DOURVILLE de MONTRISSART'S FAMILY. I CERTAINLY WILL MISS MY PIERROT A LOT!"*

* * * *

For the last thirty-two years Mrs. Shirley Beaton was my employer's accountant and private counselor at *Le Cerisier* restaurant.

Shirley was and still is a good-looking lady of high birth, petite with smiling eyes and extreme gentleness. It looked as if love radiated from her. She took care of payroll matters as well as of Arthur's taxes. Earlier Arthur had been quite erratic in balancing most of his accounts. Owing to her exceptional skills I likewise decided to let her take care of my own tax returns. During all that time Shirley provided Arthur with continuing sound informations; an arsenal of informations for my employer constantly feared for his money matters, for his expenses and his revenues. However the owner of the restaurant had a peculiar way to financially rewarded Shirley for her services: once a month he would invite Mrs. Beaton, her husband Guillaume and other members of the family for dinner at *Le Cerisier.* Arthur thus would deduct the price of the amount of food consumed as payment for the same services.

Nevertheless Shirley's bills were never paid in full. A remnant of credit would continuously be left on the side as that line of credit kept on growing and growing. Arthur would reward her with warm titles such as 'Royal Highness' or 'Cleopatra', the Egyptian Queen. So fond was his regard for Shirley that he would fall on his knees kissing her gracious hands for all she had done for him.

One afternoon my employer was carrying a stack of papers under his arm. As I asked him about some explanation regarding a late reservation in the reservation-book he would retort: "Pierre don't bother me, just ask Leon. I've an important appointment with Shirley: I cannot wait."

At lunchtime, Shirley and Arthur would walk out of the accountant office, watching the birds singing their choruses under the blushing morning sky. They were on their way to

Denny's coffee-shop for a quick meal. Oftentimes Mr. Beaton would join them after closing a real estate transaction. On Valentine Day Arthur even brought roses to Mrs. Beaton, and occasionally along with Guillaume they went for a promenade, watching some horse-back riders galloping on the equestrian line alongside Riverside Drive. At other times when Shirley just finished working on the payroll they would go to Balboa Lake with some crumbs from the restaurant to feed the ducks as Arthur also carried on a thermos of hot chocolate…

Several months after the closing of *Le Cerisier* I met Shirley for I had an appointment regarding my tax preparations.

The office was large with fine porcelain on the shelves and a heterogeneous collection of dolls from all continents. They were displayed everywhere. Mrs. Beaton sat on a reclined leather-chair behind her cedar-scented mahogany desk that she tapped with the tip of her pen. Just then as she finished collecting everything she needed for tax purposes, I asked her about Arthur; if she had seen him lately? Clapping her hands together, a shadow came over her face and there were tears in her eyes:

"Pierrot, the closing of *Le Cerisier* was also the nemesis of our relationship. Just like Judas Arthur betrayed me as he indignantly even refused to meet me or to answer my telephone-calls." Raising her hand delicately she continued, "That little man owes me over seven thousand dollars! Now with a laudable degree of cruel finesse he is using all the tricks in his arsenal to evade paying me."

At *fortiori* I explained to Shirley about my own past dilemma, that Arthur never bestowed me my check that he collected from the business interruption insurance after the damages caused by the fire next door from the restaurant. Mrs. Beaton was quick to answer:

"I'm not surprised at all!" and on a different tone of voice she conveyed:

"I know that when Melanie was young she had her part of suffering as her father annoyed her so often. And each time Melanie screamed" Then Shirley added: "You know what Pierre? Sooner or later people pay for their bad deeds!"

As I stood up on my way out, that wonderful lady bestowed me a bear hug with two kisses on the cheeks. Then, with a kind face she concluded our meeting by saying: "Take good care of yourself Pierrot."

* * * *

"There is nothing that so much seduces reason from vigilance as the thought of passing life with an amiable woman."
- Samuel Johnson.

After having spent some time with my mother in Belgium, once back I met Leon again in a street on Van Nuys that was darker and more solemn than a cathedral-aisle. He was waiting for Melanie. They had remained together in unbroken intimacy.

Leon was no longer seeking refuge in a monastery, detaching himself from worldly concerns. At that time they already greeted each other daily from the twilight of the morning till the pink of dawn. A change in his demeanor became evident. The solitude which he had so long endured no longer existed. Leon was out of his sheltered existence. He now felt manhood with the need for mastery. Van Meerstellen was actually working in a German restaurant with a new spirit that incited him to a fresh, feverish activity.

Coincidentally at another time I came across with both of them as Leon just finished his eight hours shift at the same establishment. The natural warmth that Melanie kept so well hidden for so long was glowing in her eyes. For both of them life had a new direction; a new meaning.

Presently for Leon who was wearing a clean white shirt, women had gained some charm, even moral beauty. No longer were their intellect disdained. There was a strange tenderness in Van Meerstellen's voice as he took a resolution that even surprised him. He openly declared to me that there is no beauty among women like the honest beauty whose seat is in the soul. And, full of warmth he would exclaim: "Women are beautiful and they are the source of all delightfulness."

I remember that we walked together for awhile and she was whispering words of love to him. Then she gently shook her head while blushing. Now, Leon revealed his mother's nature; her natural affection.

We stopped near a tree and rested for awhile eating apples Melanie carried in her bag. Holding hands with anticipation of still greater happiness to come, altogether we started humming the theme of a love song quite popular all over France:

"En revenant de la belle fontaine,
en revenant de la belle fontaine,
j'ai rencontré trois jeunes capitaines..."

At that time, following a number of kissing sounds, the true fulfillment of their lives appeared like sweet music as they seemed to live in a golden web of happiness. Now Wendy, Leon's former wife was definitely in the past since he was in love with another woman.

In those *couturier* clothes Melanie was more shining than ever. I also became aware that her hefty belly was quite round with early pregnancy, unless that bit of extra weight was simply a beer belly (of course I didn't ask.) Since Leon had shaved his beard, he had put on a little flesh and appeared more attractive as his face glowed into a radiant smile. Without his beard he had lost some dignity. With his hair combed smooth, he now looked more like a schoolboy but every woman's eye was upon him as well. Suddenly, he seemed to have been blessed with a second spring of youth. However he was still using that certain strong, quite erotic Algerian aftershave. His mild brown eyes at one time so vague and distant were actually glowing. His face, on which I was so accustomed to see a haunting bewilderment, was now calm, even composed. His cheerfulness was real. It no longer was based on cynicism.

Now, with unhappiness that lay behind her, Melanie was *rayonnante d'amour*. She also thought Leon to be the most elegant man on earth. She felt like a cherub leaning on an angel's shoulder. Her affection for Leon was now the breath and life of her entire being. Leon was her refuge and her stronghold. They were like two canaries tired of flying, which had perched on a telephone pole.

Perhaps she would be able to help him believe again in some reason in the universe thus put him in good terms with God. It seemed that he had almost come up out of the sea of doubt. If Leon still believed in nothing spiritual yet he had faith in the virtues of the heart, of goodness in the world. On the other hand my friend doesn't anymore kick, shake his fist nor piss on church walls! By this time even that he could not see, touch nor taste faith he learned how to give substance to a thing not seen. Meditation was next on Leon's agenda. Through meditation he found the potential energy that able him to reach throughout the universe for fulfilment.

Then, amazingly almost like a miracle Van Meerstellen had been lingering near Our Savior's Church where he could hear the evening service. He would stand there with a small prayer-book in his pocket-jacket as if he was a member of 'the little flock.' Leon's vocabulary also changed. He would use sentences such as: in the name of God or by all the saints in Heaven…Quite surprisingly too, it has been reported that in a transport of affection he kissed a bishop's hand, before bending low with one knee on the floor. He did this with so much fervor and humility. The Belgian Monsignor Armand Devries, a man of superior intellect was a dear acquaintance of Leon's mother. Then, my former colleague also became friend with a scholarly Jesuit as he followed the writings of l'Abbé Pierre, the humble French revisionist priest…

Melanie, I still remember that in the old days you said lovely things to me and it was one of my most vivid memories. You even considered me as your elder brother. I recalled the wonderful trip to the snow country at Big Bear, high above the city of San Bernardino. You were muffled in a thick shawl as we swung and swerved down the slopes like sleds. The sun was gleaming on the snow. Afterward you fell down on your butt. You started rolling down the hill like "une boule de neige", a snowball, when a large crow followed you in the descent. Melanie dear, did you remember that you were sinking into the snow? I rescued you as you were all shivering with cold and you had a sore bottom? Your pulse was so high, yet life was wonderful, even exciting. You had the heart of a child. I rubbed your head and, at that precise moment you told me about your love for Leon. For the very first time I realized that you were capable of deep affection. You have also occupied too great a place in my life for me to just forget about you. The very last thing I want is for you to be happy and to stay happy. So, go ahead, sing a song…and rejoice.

Yes I, Pierre Choucart had my fill of emotions on the grand scale. In the beginning, after the closing of the restaurant I was taken by that half-conscious agony of breaking a mental habit (in the same manner as some Christians enchained with their churches, resentful to quit their congregation even after a sexual scandal had occurred.) My mind fluttered irascibly to escape from that mental habit. I succeeded for awhile to overcome this dilemma but still it came back to me. It took me some time for my intellect to rest like my body. Subsequent to mental readjustment I started to collect my thoughts. But with the year drawing to a close, after I have suffered physical injury and mental humiliation life flowed pleasantly. And now like a fish in a pond a great sense of happiness had set my heart pounding. At the present I'm happier than I have ever been in my life. And just like Polycrates I became even a little frightened at my own happiness-I no longer know the meaning of anguish, burden and inertia as joy absorbs all other feelings. I also sleep and eat better than I have ever done before. It was important for me to seek in God the answer to my life's enigma; the justification for my strange and most misunderstood feelings toward Arthur. Now that I am in the twilight of my years I take much better care of myself, appreciating life more passionately, having learned from my personal adventures and experiences. I have now developed a sense of eternity since leaving this world has become more of a reality. Old age is a time to cultivate wisdom, since you are not taking anything along on the day of departure...

I kept enjoying my retirement at Helena's cozy and romantic condo at the Marina that mellowed each day to a morning light with a new radiance in such a great climate. With that new freedom I began to wear my hair rather long. Helena was just the sweetest little thing from that unique, beautiful beach area. The bedroom had a stunning view across the channel. Just to breathe the fresh salty air that is wafting from the ocean with the sound of water breaking on the shore give me an unparalleled joy each time I set foot outside. My relationship with Helena was not based on the old-fashioned kind of love but just a pure love with unwavering confidence in each other. I bought a bicycle carrying a basket affixed in the front handle-bar and wait for Helena to hand me the grocery list. I also helped her for the cooking as we became self-sufficient, meaning less dining out in expensive restaurants. This was equally part of my daily routine. On week-ends I usually took Helena to dance at the Fisherman's Village where different bands entertained people with rumbas, sambas, fox-trot, or jazz. It's always an extraordinary experience to swing in the open air where we could hear the ocean from where we stood among the clapping wings and cooings of the seagulls. After awhile we learned how to dance like a wave of the sea. Furthermore, every Thursday we landed at Chase Park for a free concert facing the very end of the channel. At the Marina, in such an environment it was pleasant to write, especially in the early morning summer. I realized now that for many years I have been living very much by routine. But you always have to seek happiness. Daphne du Maurier expressed it so well when he said: *"Happiness is not a possession to be prized; it is a quality of thought, a state of mind."* Now I always woke up with the smell of fresh brewed coffee. This was the part I loved best in the whole day. Gazing back at the water dotted with sailboats under the bright sun, the city of Marina Del Rey glittered white and rose from the shore like a beautiful virgin. At night one could see the lighted red buoys flickered on the surface of the water to give safe passage to yachts and sailboats. During one of those night walk, I caught myself smiling; smiling at Arthur, Melanie, Eddy and all the people that I worked with at *Le Cerisier*; of my own accomplishments, my occasional agonies and laughters throughout those years spent in that Sherman Oaks restaurant. Within those agonies and laughters I had put my mind to work as hard as I could, doing the work that was set for me to do. Now I also took a bath of serenity.

I became intoxicated with books, especially old books from *fin de siècle* with musty smell, cracked leather bindings and yellowed pages. Pages worn from being handled, browsing in bookshops or stay at home and write with the background of Gregorian music played on the stereo. At the same time, I stopped reading magazines; they seemed to me like left over meals with pieces that incongruously lay in so many places. Reading the hidden graces of good old books was still my first love and such an exciting way of spending the hours. I furthermore would bath in the Jacuzzi, the swimming pool or went for long runs as a fresh leisurely wind was blowing over the channel. Seals were bobbing their heads up and down in the water. In the distance there often was a shrill toot of one boat's siren and a deeper groan of another's. Next, in pristine simplicity, amidst black-crowned herons and seals I realized that as long you are in good health, active in sport and in excellent spirit old age is far to be a downward slope. Edward Carpenter in 'The Lake Of Beauty' is talking here of the beauty of the world: *"Let your mind be quiet, realizing the beauty of the world and the immense, the boundless treasures that it holds in store…And love himself shall come and bend over, and catch his own likeness to you."*

* * * *

Sipping a Blanc de Blanc white wine before tasting the mossy rocks flavor of various *fruit de mer* with legs dangling over the water from the channel, my brand new cell phone broke the silence with that military theme from John Philip Sousa. It was Melanie: her father had been taken urgently to The Good Apostle Hospital. He had a violent grand mal-like seizure and had suffered a heart attack. Arthur must undergo a quadruple bypass surgery.

Feeling an intensity of fear of something terrible impending, mixed with the joy of meeting him again I quickly dressed. Then I made my way down the staircase through the corridor into the courtyard. I bumped against Helena who just got back from her window-shopping spree. In an attempt to calm myself I unraveled to her the situation with my friend and former employer. Afterward, out of breath, I supported myself with one hand on the car-porch pole, forgetting that my automobile was at the dealer's garage for repairs. I had no other choice than to content myself by getting on the Culver City bus connecting with the MTA-Metro bus to the rapid transit speeding train. I continued to walk to the first vehicle with greater haste and only heard the hollow sound of my own beating heart. With a clank of buffers, the railroad cars slowed down to a stop in North-Hollywood where I caught another public transportation to the hospital. This, with the waiting between buses and the train represented almost a two hour drive from the Marina…

At The Good Apostle Hospital I was directed to the nurses' station where I was informed that Mr. Valois Dourville de Montrissart was on the third floor, room 312. Everywhere, the patients were blessed with harmonious Haydn music.

As he was lying in bed in the half-lighted room, the unshaven Arthur was gazing vaguely in some kind of a dream into space pondering if whether or not he already had reached the Heavens. When my former employer saw me, he smiled but it was a weak smile and his voice, a whisper as I experienced painful emotions that emanated from him. A lump rose in my throat and that lump was big enough to choke a pig. Never in the world had I expected a change like this. Arthur appeared older. With that real unpleasant sensation I was taken by great compassion. Almost immediately a grim of happiness came to

his lips. A little saliva was frothing from his mouth as Melanie
kept on sponging his forehead.

However, aside from this sad untying, considering that
I had forgiven and forgot about the business interruption
insurance matter I noticed a quick, strong conspiratorial
glance that she exchanged with her father. Melanie was such a
good actress. There was contempt by the way they were rolling
eyes at each other; by that unusual look interchanged between
father and daughter as she lifted one corner of her mouth in
a smile. It seemed as if between them a corrupted grin had
developed with a sort of common understanding; both of
them looked guilty as hell. They might as well have spoken
aloud. I understood clearly that in this sorrowful moment
they also celebrated their victory for they had successfully
cheated me over money matter. Their plan had been hastily
conceived. Melanie especially with that great skill to forge
signatures had played her part to perfection. There was on
her face a grimace of ill-concealed satisfaction. A smart but
quite ugly performance had been fulfilled in the gloomy
atmosphere of that hospital room. This was just as old wounds
that break out afresh in the body when under the influence
of a disease. Yet, for me it was now over and done with; the
past is past. Aside from my observations I no longer hold any
grudge against them. When one talked of the past it must be
without bitterness. Likewise in life we cannot live without
contemplating forgiveness; forgiveness to our bosses even to
our former enemies.

Above the hospital bed, hanging on the wall was a
religious picture of a consolatory Madonna and Child painted
in celestial purity. At that precise moment Arthur's eyes were
fixated on a wooden cross; our 'Crucified Savior' being on
a stand strewning nicely with chrysanthemum. Around the
bed, Melanie and two of her best friends lowered their heads

in silent prayer. With hands clasped in each other tears were running down their eyes. One of the daughter's acquaintances was dressed in black with a long rosary dangling from her belt. She started clutching it between her fingers. Upon Arthur's request (he definitely wanted to be on the safe side with the Lord), the priest was already there in full canonical and liturgical vestments. With a cheerful nod of the head the clergyman blessed the boss with the last rites...*ego te absolvo a peccatis tuis* and the consecrated oils. At that juncture he declared to Arthur that his entry into eternal life would be such a wonderful elevating sight. This was an eloquent sermon. With infinite joy that that vision portended, my former employer perfectly composed already ascertained himself flapping his wings over a cloud. He not only contemplated death yet he now accepted it bravely. The priest along with Melanie and her friends closing their eyes like ostriches started to sing in eerie unison the *Hosanna in Excelsis*. Abruptly the room appeared to have been taken at first hand by divine mysticism. To our surprise at the same time that we were praying the Lord's Prayer the bells from a nearby church began to toll. They kept on pealing and pealing merrily. After the clergyman heard my employer's confession he gave him *l'extrême onction-* the last rites.

Now in a canonical Christian lamentation, Arthur's distorted face shone with delirious joy. The terror of death had been with him along with the dread of the hereafter until he saw the priest ready to recomfort him. Looking at this world he was expected to leave, his dying words came slowly from his mouth as we heard him struggle in a faint whisper: "Jesus is holding my hand and I can see the angels." After the Athanasian creeds and the sacred ceremonial, as good brethren we all genuflected for the holy blessings...

However the operation had been successful and the boss recuperated in no time. Now Arthur realized he was still alive on planet earth and that it was not time yet for the more desirable life on the other side: HEAVEN CAN WAIT!

* * * *

I once encountered many blind alleys. I felt like I was stranded on the dark-side of the moon knowing I was up against something I didn't know how to cope with. I have lived on humiliations, on insults. I swallowed the affronts but all along I continued to cultivate love. While I often disregarded the harsh treatment under Arthur's rule I had done my duty to the best of my abilities and I have always pleased all my customers. The adversities, losses and disappointments mean nothing now because I believe in the goodness in everyone also in brotherly love and gentleness. Earlier in life I experienced with the paratroopers the upper limit of human self-empowerment. Surely this helped me with that unbroken spirit of faith, that proclamation of dignity to be able to stand on the hill. Feelings became something to discover rather than to suppress. I also developed a little humility in my life. Next, I overlooked the boss uncontrolled mind. I even learned how to love that man who was seeking so much pleasure at the misfortune of others; a man who seat people down in order to feel important! I continually envisioned Arthur as my tormentor but still behind the mask exist a totally different man. First of all, my employer has to extricate himself from the turmoil of 'hard liquor' and make a fearless moral inventory of his way of life. Afterward he would be able to leap over on the trampoline of joy, of honesty. Humility is high virtue and pride is correspondingly a severe sin. Yes my friend: you can change for the best and the outlook seemed as fine as possible. Perhaps your musical genius will resurface? I sincerely trust that your life might be pound-up in the arts…"

What happened to Eddy was anyone's guess. He probably went back to sultry Palm Spring for awhile; relaxing in his time-sharing villa as he would rather lives in that desert paradise than anywhere else. Now Freedman feels good in his skin for he had renewed his old friendship with Melanie.

After his Mexican divorce and the loss of his house in Puebla subsequent to a nervous breakdown Gustavo Santillas retired in his uncle estate.

Melanie moved with Leon to Denver, Colorado where they got married prior to buy an old fixer-upper farm. Melanie never lost contact with her friends from the Malibu-Colony.

As for yours truly life has become bliss. This *recueil* is the crowning achievement of my existence. Now that I am jingling my purse of memory I can feel the coin of joy; the squandering precious coin of life.

Author's Note

Countless British and American authors from the past inspired me with their thinking in building-up a manuscript page after page that took me several years to come to fruition. In the light of such powers of passion, of composition from 'the hands of masters' I have found the novels from the nineteen and early twentieth century the most pleasurable, the most excitingly imaginative. From the reading of those books dating as far as the Napoleonic and Victorian periods where landlords kept serfs under strict bondage my train of ideas as related to Arthur Valois Dourville de Montrissart became a framework that led me to the birth of *The Tormentor.* I always kept in mind that in order to please others I must please myself first. All my writings are based on actual events. I have established the truth on the basis of irrefutable personal documentation though purposely altered somewhat to avoid too close identification. The author has also been careful enough not to omit any facts that could have come to his knowledge. Moreover on numerous occasions as a francophone by birth I have used French set-words or phrases. I believed this was proper in order to flourish the book. One will find *The Tormentor* to be hilarious as well as dramatic with so many irrational scenes. What's more it is a book which arouses people's passions and around which controversy still rages. Readers can realize the major part of the entire book is to point out that Pierre Choucart who had suffered such a great shame can nonetheless love Arthur, a man he ought to have hated; a man who had taken him for brainless even retarded. Yet, even when most depressed, Choucart recurrently prayed; not for himself but for his employer. Correspondingly he survived mostly with that strong discipline, demanding total submission that he inherited from his paratrooper unit but most of all from the love he had shown toward his employer, *Ce Pauvre Diable Arthur*- That Poor Devil Arthur. Just like the sayings of the Russian writer Andreï Makine: *"Among so much humiliations, his dream had been an antidote, and the notes-a refuge."* Love remains the comforter of humanity; the soul of all living beings. In most human interaction, be it in the working environment, at schools, even in governments there will always be that one person; that villain who lives an empty life where nothing gives real pleasure except for harassment. A gorgeous sunset won't be attractive to a disheartened person. But by the power of love the same disheartened person can achieve contemplation and feel goodness and wisdom. Fiction usually pretends to conform to reality; however my book doesn't fantasize to conform to facts since it is reality. My personages even under fictitious names are not characters of my mind; of my creation.

The French author Gustave Flaubert wrote a series of letters to his mistress, the poetess Louise Collet. The content of those missives represented the reflection of my own sentiments-the fact that being a writer is sometimes a comfort. Here are some excerpts of Flaubert's thoughts: *"Our hearts must be sensitive in order to feel the passions of others...I lead a harsh life, stripped of all external pleasures. I sometimes have bitter moments which make me almost scream with rage...when you feel as if your brain is coming apart like a bundle of dirty laundry..."*and unexpectedly Monsieur Flaubert came into the realization of how much joy he found in his writings: *"...I was experiencing the most exquisite pleasure from the emotion of my idea, from the words that I expressed it and from the satisfaction of having found the words...I have caught a glimpse of just such a spiritual state, superior to life, for which fame would be nothing and even happiness futile."*

About The Author

Born in Belgium Jacques A. Meyer displayed his rapidly developing spirit of adventure early in life. He enlisted in his country's paratroops unit at the age of nineteen and found himself in the middle of Africa: the Democratic Republic of Congo (formerly the Belgian Congo). At the close of that country's turmoil the author decided to immigrate to Canada and on to the United States which has become his own country. He worked as a freelance writer and as a *journaliste de passage* in war-torn Cambodia. Being a Los Angeles Legacy Marathon runner Jacques is also a world traveller and a great lover of nature. He is the author of *Terre Mon Amie*-A Journey Around The World On A Low Budget and *Embrace the World*. Meyer lives in Los Angeles.

e-mail: jacques262@yahoo.ca

Printed in the United States
By Bookmasters